ECONOMIC GROWTH IN THE FUTURE

Edison Electric Institute Committee on Economic Growth, Pricing and Energy Use

Chairman
Jack K. Horton, *Chairman of the Board and Chief Executive Officer*
Southern California Edison Company

T. L. Austin, Jr., *Chairman of the Board*
Texas Utilities Company

Herbert B. Cohn, *Vice-Chairman*
American Electric Power Company

Gordon R. Corey, *Vice-Chairman*
Commonwealth Edison Company

Don C. Frisbee, *Chairman of the Board*
Pacific Power & Light Company

Marshall McDonald, *President*
Florida Power and Light Company

William C. Tallman, *President*
Public Service Company of New Hampshire

Committee Staff

Executive Director
Dr. William F. Thompson, *Economist*
Philadelphia Electric Company

Assistant to the Committee Chairman
Dr. Kenneth D. Wilson, *Executive Assistant*
Southern California Edison Company

ECONOMIC GROWTH IN THE FUTURE

The Growth Debate in National and Global Perspective

EDISON ELECTRIC INSTITUTE

McGraw-Hill Book Company

New York St. Louis San Francisco Auckland Bogotá
Düsseldorf Johannesburg London Madrid
Mexico Montreal New Delhi Panama
Paris São Paulo Singapore
Sydney Tokyo Toronto

Library of Congress Cataloging in Publication Data

Edison Electric Institute. Committee on Economic
    Growth, Pricing and Energy Use.
    Economic growth in the future.

    Bibliography: p.
    Includes index.
    1. Electric utilities—United States. 2. United
States—Economic policy—1971-   3. United States—
Economic conditions—1971-   —Mathematical models.
I. Title.
HD9685.U5E3   1976   330.9′73′0925   76-20644
ISBN 0-07-018967-6

Contributors

In the conduct of this study, assistance was obtained from a number of eminent authorities and researchers who participated as consultants and advisors. Certain sections of the report are predominantly the work of one or two consultants. Other sections represent the combined efforts of a larger number of consultants as well as the staff. All material was reviewed by several consultants and advisors representing different points of view. The broad spectrum of views represented within the consulting group makes it almost certain that some consultants will not agree with certain of the conclusions of this report.

Consultants

Frank Alessio, Ph.D., Electric Power Research Institute
Prakash Apte, Columbia University
Kenneth Boulding, University of Colorado
Herman Daly, Ph.D., Louisiana State University
John Dosher and colleagues, Pace Company, Houston, Texas
Helmut Frank, Ph.D., University of Arizona
Luther Gerlach, Ph.D., University of Minnesota
De Verle Harris, Ph.D., University of Arizona
Edward Hudson, Ph.D., Data Resources, Inc.
Barry Hughes, Ph.D., Case Western Reserve University
Craig Johnson, Ph.D., Columbia University
Dale Jorgensen, Ph.D., Harvard University and Data Resources, Inc.
John McKetta, Ph.D., University of Texas
Mihajlo Mesarovic, Ph.D., Case Western Reserve University
Ezra Mishan, Ph.D., London School of Economics
William Nordhaus, Ph.D., Yale University
Peter Passell, Ph.D., Columbia University
Charles F. Phillips, Jr., Ph.D., Washington and Lee University
Milton Searl, Electric Power Research Institute
Robert Taussig, Ph.D., Columbia University
Robert Theobald, Editor, Futures Conditional

Advisors

In addition to the consultants listed above, several individuals and organizations served as advisors to the study by contributing material or reviewing and commenting on the study design and on drafts of specific sections.
Carl E. Bagge, President, National Coal Association
Dick Donovan, Head of Research Services, National Association of Electric Companies
F. Donald Hart, President, American Gas Association
Frank N. Ikard, President, American Petroleum Institute
Reginald Jones, Chairman of the Board, General Electric Company
Carl Madden, Chief Economist, U. S. Chamber of Commerce
Philip N. Ross, Manager, Power Systems Planning, Westinghouse Electric Corp.
Sam H. Schurr, Director, Energy Systems, Environment and Conservation,
Electric Power Research Institute
John W. Simpson, Director, Westinghouse Electric Corporation
Irwin Stelzer, President, National Economic Research Associates, Inc.
Ian Wilson, Staff Associate, Business Environmental Research and Forecasting,
General Electric Company

Industry Contributions

A number of knowledgeable people within the electric utility industry contributed both information and advice throughout the conduct of the study.

Edison Electric Institute is the principal association of America's investor-owned electric utility companies. Organized in 1933 and incorporated in 1970, EEI provides a principal forum where electric utility people exchange information on developments in their business. Its officers act as spokesmen on subjects of national interest.

Since 1933, EEI has been a strong, continuous stimulant to the art of making electricity. A basic objective is the "advancement in the public service of the art of producing, transmitting, and distributing electricity and the promotion of scientific research in such field." EEI ascertains factual information, data and statistics relating to the electric industry, and makes them available to member companies and the public.

Preface

This report is the product of an eighteen-month study initiated and sponsored by the Edison Electric Institute (EEI), principal association of the nation's investor-owned electric utility companies. The project was conducted under the direction of a special EEI Policy Committee on Economic Growth, Pricing and Energy Use. The Committee was made up of senior executives from seven EEI member companies. The staff was drawn from member companies and EEI personnel. Much of the work of the project was done by consultants who are experts in their respective fields and who represent widely varying points of view. The broad spectrum of views represented within the consulting group makes it almost certain that some consultants will not agree with certain of the conclusions of this report. Responsibility for the accuracy of the report, of course, lies with the Committee and its staff.

Reference is made in the report to "industry conclusions and recommendations." The industry referred to in these cases is the membership of EEI which does not include publicly owned electric utility systems or the manufacturers of electric equipment. It should be recognized that among EEI member companies themselves, there exist differing opinions on the broad public policy questions addressed in this report. Although it would be impossible to have unanimity of opinion on such matters among a group as diverse as the EEI membership, the industry position has been approved by the Board of Directors of the Edison Electric Institute.

Contents

EXECUTIVE SUMMARY

Highlights

This summary of a study of the future of economic growth in the United States represents the culmination of 18 months of intensive research and analysis by expert consultants drawn from diverse technical backgrounds.

The study was conducted by the Edison Electric Institute, the principal national association of investor-owned electric utility companies, both as an input to the national policy debate concerning growth and as a guide to future planning by the electric utility industry.

The project was undertaken in recognition of the fact that, while economic growth has traditionally been regarded as a fundamental social value and policy goal, it is now being challenged by some critics who view it as the cause of many current problems and who believe it may lead to an eventual global collapse.

Some 20 consultants and a number of business and research organizations contributed to the project. A variety of analytical methods were employed, including the use of a computer model to simulate the operation of the United States economy under policies designed to produce "high growth," "low growth," and "moderate growth." The result is a set of three scenarios of the future under different growth conditions. The scenarios are augmented by judgmental forecasts by authorities in specialized fields.

The study produced a number of conclusions and recommendations. The highlights of these are as follows:

- Potential limiting factors can be managed so that desirable forms of economic growth can be sustained by the United States for the foreseeable future. Under policies which provide a balance of economic and environmental needs, continued growth at moderate rates is both feasible and desirable. Under such policies an average growth rate for real GNP of 3.5 to 3.7 percent per year could be expected over the next 25 years. Even under policies intended to curtail growth and achieve a "steady state" as rapidly as possible, the

transition would take 10 to 15 years, and the resulting annual increase in real GNP over the next 25 years would average about 2.3 percent.

- Continuing economic growth will improve the "quality of life" as well as the standard of living. Growth is necessary to: aid in maintaining employment; improve the conditions of the poor; finance cleaning up the environment; and maintain a favorable position in international relations, particularly with regard to trade, balance of payments, and defense.

- An attempt to halt growth arbitrarily would require authoritarian measures with a commensurate loss of individual freedom.

- United States economic growth over the next 25 years is likely to be constrained more by shortages of capital than by shortages of energy or raw materials. Revisions in public policy are needed to encourage capital formation and private investment in productive facilities. Government deficits are a primary cause of inflation and serve to preempt capital funds needed for investment in productive facilities.

- Improvement in environmental quality can be made consistent with economic growth through the use of environmental controls supplemented by economic incentives. Environmental standards should be based on cost-benefit analyses. Once established, environmental regulations should be stabilized and not subjected to frequent revisions.

- With the birth rate in the United States currently below the replacement rate, there is no cause for concern about population exceeding the capacity of the nation to accommodate everyone. Even if birth rates shift back slightly above the replacement rate, the nation's agricultural capacity would be more than adequate.

- Energy demand will grow at a slower rate than GNP. Under conditions of moderate economic growth and increasing environmental investment, energy growth can be expected to average 2.8 to 3.0 percent per year over the next 25 years.

1

- Oil and natural gas cannot provide the basis for long-term economic growth. To achieve energy independence it will be necessary to make a basic shift from oil and natural gas to coal and nuclear fuels.

- Electric energy consumption would increase at an average rate of 5.3 to 5.8 percent per year under policies assumed for a moderate-growth scenario. Use of electric energy will grow as a result of the shift from oil and gas to coal and nuclear fuels. As is also the case of total energy consumption, electric energy growth rates will vary significantly over time and from region to region.

- An "ultimate solution" to the energy problem, in the form of essentially limitless supplies, is technologically within our grasp. It includes increasing use of coal and nuclear breeder reactors over the intermediate term, supplemented by solar and fusion power over the longer range future.

- An ultimate solution in regard to supplies of non-energy mineral resources requires deep-sea mining and the ability to mine "average rock" for its varied but low-grade mineral contents. These solutions are not yet technologically feasible. Recycling possibilities lessen, but do not eliminate, the concern about this situation. Thus, mineral exploration, mining, and refining warrant increased R & D effort now to avoid or minimize later problems.

- The Energy Resources Council should be continued and strengthened to give it authority and responsibility for United States energy policy.

- Primary reliance should be placed on a combination of free-market prices and improving technology to make available increasing quantities of basic natural resources and discourage wasteful uses.

- Oil and gas wellhead prices should be deregulated as rapidly as possible without causing major disruptions in the domestic economy such as resulted from the abrupt oil price increases in 1973-74.

- Agricultural output should be maximized so that food can be sold in world markets to meet the needs of developing nations and to help overcome the United States balance-of-payments problems arising from the importing of oil and other raw materials.

- The study also contains a number of conclusions and recommendations relative to the electric utility industry. To accomplish the shift to coal and nuclear fuels, electric utilities will have to increase their construction activities. Unless steps are taken to increase the present level of internally generated funds, almost two-thirds of the capital needed to fund this construction must be raised in the nation's competitive capital markets. In the next 15 years the industry will need approximately $500 billion from the capital markets. One hundred billion or more of this will have to come through newly issued common stock. These amounts can be raised only if the industry is financially healthy. An average return on common equity of 15 percent or more will be needed to demonstrate financial health, even if the rate of inflation subsides to the 4 or 5 percent per year range. Higher returns will be needed by some companies, depending on individual corporate financial circumstances. Continued high inflation will also require higher returns on equity.

Recommended changes in regulatory policy which will promote financial health include: (1) use of forward test years; (2) allowing tariff changes to become effective without suspension, subject to later refund; (3) increasing book depreciation rates and normalizing tax deferrals; and (4) inclusion of construction work in progress in the rate base as construction proceeds. The primary objectives in electric rate structure design should be to approximate as closely as feasible the cost to serve each customer, and to provide sufficient revenues to cover all necessary costs of doing business including adequate return on investment.

Background and Approach of the Study

Growth as a Public Policy Issue

Economic growth, in the form of expanding population and material production and consumption, has long been a fundamental social value and a public policy goal in the United States. At present, however, growth is being viewed by some critics as the underlying cause of many of the nation's environmental and social problems, and as leading eventually to a global collapse. In order to avoid this, the critics have argued the necessity of moving toward a "no-growth" or "steady-state" economy. This would mean maintaining population at a constant level, limiting the production and consumption of material goods, and minimizing the use of physical resources.

The opponents of growth reflect a variety of perspectives. They include: academicians and scientists using theoretical approaches and global forecasting models; environmentalists seeking to halt ecological encroachment; and citizens who see the costs of growth and increased urbanization as outweighing the benefits.

Despite the diversity of their motives, this articulate minority has become a "zero-growth movement," which is having significant impacts on policy decisions regarding development. At the national level, the outcome of the growth debate has the most profound implications for the future of the United States and the rest of the world. At the local and regional levels, the net result of individual actions to halt development could constitute a *de facto* national policy of limited growth.

The Electric Utility Industry and the Growth Issue

To date, arguments have usually been couched in terms of a choice between growth or no growth, while in reality the possible range of proposals for public policy action is much broader. Approached positively, the question of growth does not represent a choice between "good" and "bad" alternatives, but rather an opportunity to explore a variety of courses to a more desirable future. The need to orient the growth debate toward positive alternatives led the electric utility industry to undertake this study.

In addition, electric utility companies have been thrust into the center of the growth debate by a combination of circumstances. The rate of growth of electricity usage makes the industry a conspicuous element of economic growth. Present means of producing electricity have environmental impacts and consume limited resources. Also, the physical facilities required for generating and distributing electricity are highly visible.

There are other motivating factors stemming from the unique characteristics of the electric utility business. Electric utilities are regulated monopolies which operate in accordance with public service franchises. They are obligated to serve all of the power requirements in their service territories. This presents a dilemma when facilities to meet public service needs are opposed by groups which claim to act in the public interest. To meet service needs, utilities must plan far into the future, and anticipation of economic growth patterns is essential for such planning.

Finally, it is the industry's social responsibility to recommend and support public policy actions on the part of appropriate governmental authorities, although it is not the role of the industry to make final determinations about such policies.

Approach and Objectives of the Study

This study employs a broad, public policy perspective and a systems approach. It goes beyond purely economic issues to consider the processes of change in our society and our capacity to adapt to new conditions. The objective is to arrive at conclusions which provide a basis for policy recommendations.

An effort was made to identify, illuminate and analyze all of the major issues. A variety of analytical methods were employed. A computer model was used to simulate the operation of the United States economy under conditions of "high growth," "low growth," and "moderate growth." The result is three scenarios of the future under different growth patterns. In addition, several judgmental forecasts were prepared by experts in such fields as energy supply and material resources. In all, more than 20 consultants were used with widely varying technical backgrounds. (A list of consultants, many of whom are not associated with the electric utility industry, appears at the beginning of this book.)

The study required 18 months. The objective of balance in presentation guided the preparation of the final report, and this is reflected in the inclusion of separate statements of the pro-growth and no-growth views. Neither of these represents the industry view which is presented in the form of conclusions on specific issues.

Prototype of chart depicting three alternative growth scenarios—high growth, moderate growth and low growth. Actual projections for key areas of growth are presented in "The Analysis" beginning on page 12.

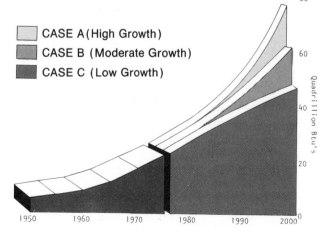

CASE A (High Growth)
CASE B (Moderate Growth)
CASE C (Low Growth)

The Pro-Growth View

At least half of the increase in western per capita output is due to improvements in technology, and there is no compelling reason to believe that technology cannot continue to outpace population increase and resource scarcity in the future in order to allow economic growth which is compatible with a clean environment.

Population growth cannot be sustained indefinitely, however, and economic growth based solely on this factor may represent no improvement in human well-being. Only economic growth stemming from increases in per capita consumption should be counted in measuring improvement in the quality of life of the average citizen.

There are four primary arguments in favor of such continued economic growth: 1) economic thought and experience tend to discount the Malthusian vision of inevitable scarcity; 2) growth means a better standard of living; 3) growth is a more realistic alternative than a mandatory redistribution of income for reducing poverty; and 4) growth provides jobs needed by a still-expanding population.

The argument that a scarcity of natural resources must inevitably bring growth to a halt overlooks the practical incentives of a free market and the potential for technical advance. Higher prices provide incentives for producers to substitute cheaper (more plentiful) resources or to recycle processed materials. Rising prices also tend to reduce overall demand. Scarcity makes it profitable to develop and invest in resource-expanding technology. Further improvements in agricultural technology, for example, should reduce the factor of food scarcity as a long-term constraint to economic growth.

Anti-growth arguments based on the capacity of the earth to absorb waste heat from energy use contemplate events so far in the future as to be inconsequential for policy making today. Advancing technology includes new methods of dealing with pollution and enhancing the environment. The cost of correcting environmental pollution can best be met with continued economic growth. Further, growth improves the "quality of life" in the form of living space for privacy, adequate food, leisure time available from work, education, income for comfortable retirement, and high-quality medical care.

In the United States and on a global scale, economic growth is a more realistic alternative for reducing poverty than the redistribution of income. Increased demand for raw materials will give producing nations an advantageous bargaining position and lead to increased wealth on the part of many developing countries. Within the United States, continued economic growth will provide the means by which millions of disadvantaged citizens may improve their lives.

Given an expanding population, growth will provide necessary employment. Also, historic experience indicates that as countries develop economically, their rates of population growth decline. There is evidence that in most cases gains in per capita income from economic growth are not wiped out by population growth.

Attempting to stop growth in place of stopping its side effects is a fallacious approach to the problems of growth. There are specific policy decisions outstanding which deserve attention. On the environment, for example, there is the issue of short- and medium-term trade-offs between maintaining output and minimizing its deleterious effects. It will be necessary to accept certain environmental costs if output and economic stability are to be assured. The most pressing issue for natural resource policy is whether it is necessary or advantageous to achieve greater self-sufficiency in energy resources—and if so, how to go about it.

4

The No-Growth View

Problems of growth and the economy must be approached as a whole because they are interrelated and simultaneous. They involve environmental quality, food supply, energy use, and technological adaptation.

The unprecedented population growth of the last century has been accompanied by an even greater rate of increase in the production of material goods. Even though the United States birth rate has declined below the replacement level, the population will grow by about 90 million before it levels off at about 290 million around the year 2030. At the world level, even a birth control breakthrough will not keep the total population, currently 3.9 billion, from surpassing 6 billion in the year 2000.

Raw materials converted to commodities are eventually discarded in the form of waste. Waste cannot then be converted back into raw materials except by expending energy, and energy inevitably ends up as waste heat which cannot be recycled.

While the economy grows, the environment maintains a constant size. The resulting interference with the ecosystem inhibits its ability to perform life-support functions. Therefore, more economic growth can only lead to even greater depletion, pollution, and interference with the ecosystem.

The factor of food supply presents an example of the limits to growth. The necessity to feed a growing population at an increasing level of per capita consumption has made agriculture dependent on a continuous subsidy of nonrenewable fossil fuels, chemicals, and mineral fertilizers. More food can be produced, but only with increasingly damaging ecological effects. Energy use presents similar problems.

We must accept natural limits to the scope of economic activity and shift from "technological adaptation" to "ecological adaptation." No growth and a "steady state" offer the only viable means to this end.

The steady-state view is based on: 1) thermodynamic laws concerning the conservation of matter and energy; 2) the biological process of the continual flow of sunlight; and 3) moral precepts of "sufficiency," "stewardship," and "holism." As resource scarcity becomes increasingly general, substitution ceases to be a sufficient answer. The amounts of energy needed for processing low-grade ores and recycling would have to come from nuclear fission power until fusion arrives, and many believe the environmental costs are too high. There are finite limits to the environment's capacity to absorb wastes, and there is an ultimate pollution limit in the form of waste heat. Man's impact on the environment is growing at around five percent annually, doubling every 14 years. There must be a shift away from an economy dedicated to increasingly limited physical growth to an economy that views moral growth as a substitute.

The transition effort should build upon the institutions of private property and the price system. A system of auctioning depletion quota rights to preserve resources, a system of transferable birth licenses to control population, and the creation of "amenity areas" devoted to human and aesthetic values are suggested.

Economic growth is leading to a breakdown of modern society reflected in strikes, terrorism, alienation, and apathy. Unless steps are taken to control growth, declining human well-being will be experienced in such forms as ecological disruption, genetic calamity, epidemics, nuclear catastrophe, crime and violence, and political unrest. Growth has not erased, and will not erase, poverty and inequality. Technological growth can only be expected to worsen the situation by eroding personal liberties.

The Electric Utility Industry's Conclusions and View of the Future of Growth

The pro-growth and no-growth views are two ends of a continuum of thought on the growth question. A review of the growth debate indicates that the two views are based on different assumptions about the nature of man, the concept of resources, the role of economic growth and technology, and the adaptability to change of our socioeconomic system. The debate raises a variety of issues which are organized under four primary questions. These questions and their conclusions in respect to the United States are:

1. Is Continued Economic Growth Sustainable?

It is concluded that the potential limiting factors of natural resource scarcities, population growth, food production, land availability, pollution, psychological and organizational limits, and the entropy law, can be managed in ways which will allow desirable forms of moderate economic growth to be sustained for the foreseeable future. There appears to be enough time to allow ultimate limits to growth to be approached gradually, so that adjustments can be made on an evolutionary rather than revolutionary basis. The adjustment mechanisms of advancing technology, the price system, public policy and regulation, and social change provide effective means for dealing with the problems. It is probable that unforeseen evolutionary changes in technology and society will alter life so substantially that ultimate "limits" will be perceived very differently in the future.

Natural resource availability need not present a constraint to growth. Advancing technology and the price system will work to moderate the depletion of resources and extend the timing of ultimate limits far into the future. Shortages and rising costs will, however, bring major changes in the patterns of resource use and significantly alter the future direc-

tions of growth. Recycling will become essential as a supplement to the use of raw materials.

With the birth rate in the United States currently below the replacement rate, there is no cause for concern about population exceeding the capacity of the nation to accommodate everyone. Even if birth rates shift back to slightly above the replacement rate, the nation's agricultural capacity would be more than adequate.

Neither food production nor land availability appear to make continued economic growth unsustainable. While food shortages can be expected to cause periodic disruptions in the developing nations, food production in America can be expanded to keep pace with population and economic growth for the foreseeable future. The utility of land can be expanded by technology, making the timing of an absolute limit remote.

As for the problem of pollution, the costs of corrective measures can be expected to have a significant dampening effect on growth, but it is reasonable to expect that the problems will yield to current and future control technology and new economic incentives.

On the question of psychological and organizational limits to growth, it is concluded that there are no inherent limits to man's capacity to adapt and cope with complexity. Given the will to do so, man can devise ever-more-intricate organization forms and make them work. It is a matter of social choice whether this will be done.

Existing mechanisms of adjustment are far from perfect, and there is no assurance that dislocations can be avoided—but there are solid grounds for belief that advancing technology, the price system, public policy and regulation, and social change all provide effective means for dealing with the problems of growth.

2. Is Continued Economic Growth Desirable?

It is concluded that patterns of growth can be pursued that are desirable on the basis of improving the "quality of life" and providing equitable and mutually advantageous relations with other nations.

The question of whether continued growth is adversely affecting the "quality of life" should be decided on the basis of specific effects and consequences rather than as an overall moral judgment on the value of growth. On this basis, particular types of growth could be selectively encouraged or curtailed. In respect to the contention that continued growth is undesirable because it is based on exploitation of other countries and leads to dependence on foreign resources, it is concluded that the use of other countries' resources is mutually beneficial whenever prices are determined in accord with principles of free international trade, and that countries exporting raw materials are in a position to gain a larger share of trade, wealth, and influence.

3. Is Continued Economic Growth Necessary?

It is concluded that continued growth is necessary to: aid in maintaining employment; improve the conditions of the poor; finance cleaning up the environment; and maintain a favorable position in international relations, especially with regard to trade, balance of payments, and defense.

4. Is Zero Economic Growth a Workable Alternative?

It is concluded that a transition to a zero-growth condition would present major political and administrative problems which could only be overcome by the imposition of strong institutional authority, with a commensurate loss of individual freedom which would be unacceptable to the American people.

This conclusion in no way denies the validity of the concerns raised by zero-growth advocates. However, the changes advocated by proponents of no growth, if they become necessary, would best be achieved gradually via the democratic process and the mechanism of market choice.

Having considered the specific questions and issues, it is concluded that the significance of the growth debate does not lie in any real choice to be made between "maximum growth" and "no growth." Some form of economic growth will continue, and its composition will be different from the past. A "new concept of economic growth" is evolving as the economy adjusts to the constraints and problems which gave rise to the growth controversy. Indeed, these factors already are resulting in slower rates of growth. In the United States and some other advanced countries there is increasing reluctance to commit energies and potentials single-mindedly to growth. The transformation of the economy is observable in trends toward expansion of the service and information sectors over production. One reason for the decline in the growth ethic may simply be what economists refer to as the theory of "marginal utility." As one obtains more of any commodity, its use and value to him declines. As major sectors of our society have become more affluent in terms of material goods, the growth objective has become less pressing.

The full implications of the present change process are difficult to foresee. A hopeful view is that current trends point to a natural evolution toward a form of economic expansion that could be described as "clean growth," "quality growth," or "optimal growth."

Patterns of growth depend as much on cultural attitudes as on economic factors. Neither the present pro-growth view nor the no-growth view is descriptive of or adequate to our times.

It is generally agreed that GNP and national income accounts do not, and are not intended to, reflect broad social progress. More broadly based measures are needed to augment and complement present indexes in charting society's advance. Such measures would provide a basis for building a new sense of national purpose.

It is imperative that the processes of policy consideration and decision making remain open and democratic. Decisions on economic growth must always be subordinate to the maintenance of a free society which maximizes individual choice.

Recommendations

The work of this project provides the basis for a number of recommendations on broad public policy. These recommendations are advanced as considerations and suggestions. The intention is to set forth guidelines and objectives rather than to advocate specific actions and programs. The emphasis is on the long-term (15-25 years and more) future and the problems which pose potential constraints to economic growth.

A Suggested Approach to Problem Solving

A comprehensive and coordinated approach to problem solving is required to develop public policies dealing with the problems of growth. Such an approach should consist of three elements which would proceed simultaneously. The *first element* is problem identification and description. This would involve an orderly sequence of steps: 1) defining the boundaries of specific problem conditions; 2) identifying available alternatives; and 3) developing action plans for problem resolution. Included in this first element would be the tasks of deciding on priorities and methods for achieving generally agreed upon goals. Problem identification also raises more fundamental questions concerning what kind of society the United States should be in respect to reliance on the market system vs. governmental control, and what benefits the economy should provide and for whom. At this level of problem solving, growth and the economy are viewed as means, and the questions must be resolved through the less ordered but still effective workings of the political process.

The *second element* may be termed goal setting. This effort would be directed at formulating medium- and long-range achievable objectives. Goals provide a basis for action and a standard against which to measure results. It is recommended that the following general goals be used as a framework for more specific objectives; 1) preserve freedom of choice; 2) minimize sharp fluctuations in prices and employment; 3) maximize opportunities and market choices for the individual; 4) balance the requirements for a clean physical environment and a healthy economy; 5) maintain production levels which will provide improvements in the standard of living and the quality of life; 6) assure national security; and 7) pursue rates of economic growth which will allow the accomplishment of the other general goals, now and for future generations.

The *third element* is problem resolution. Here the emphasis would be on direct attacks on specific problems. An incremental step-by-step approach is recommended which recognizes the need for conferral and mutual adjustments among all interested parties.

Economic Growth

Based on the findings of this study, it would be unnecessary and unwise to attempt arbitrarily to limit economic growth in the United States during the remainder of this century. It is also clear that "growth for growth's sake" is an obsolete objective. The directions of growth should be guided by the conclusions ·drawn on the specific issues as summarized in this Executive Summary under "The Electric Utility Industry's Conclusions and View of the Future of Growth," and in the main report.

The analysis completed for this study suggests that an average growth rate (real GNP) of 3.5 to 3.7 percent per year could be sustained over the next 25 years under policies which seek a balance between economic and environmental priorities. Such a growth rate can be recommended as a public policy target. This quantitative recommendation, and those of this type in the other sections, are meant to designate the center of a desirable and achievable range. As planning targets, they could, of course, be adjusted to changing circumstances.

It is suggested that the following set of policy objectives would allow the recommended growth rate to be achieved and promote the balancing of economic and environmental needs.

a. Continue the development of natural resources within guidelines which minimize environmental damage and give consideration to costs and benefits.

b. Account for the social and environmental costs that can be identified for all industries.

c. Encourage improvements in technology.

d. Rely on a freely functioning price system to provide adequate supplies of resources and allocate them among competing uses in an optimum manner.

e. Devote additional capital, in gradually increasing amounts over the remainder of the 1970s and early 1980s, to the objectives of improving the environment and economizing on the use of raw materials. This investment should be concentrated where net benefits can be shown to be high.

Resources—Energy

An average energy growth rate of 2.8 to 3.0 percent can be expected through the year 2000 if the overall economic growth rate of 3.5 to 3.7 percent is realized. Rates of energy growth in this range are compatible with a vigorous, carefully balanced plan to achieve greater energy independence.

Arbitrary restrictions on energy consumption should be avoided as unnecessary and unwise. Moderate energy growth will be required to sustain economic growth as well as for processing and recycling materials and for environmental protection activities. Energy policy should be directed at assuring a reliable source of supply and reducing growth of demand by eliminating waste. In addition, energy policy must give consideration to national safety and welfare (both economic and military in nature). These considerations warrant government intervention in the free-market process in limited areas or in case of emergencies.

To reduce United States dependence on foreign oil, it is recommended that national objectives be established to: 1) increase domestic energy supplies so that imports are reduced to about 10 percent of total energy consumption by the latter half of the 1980s; 2) develop fuel storage capacities sufficient to offset a six-month embargo; and 3) prepare a plan for curtailing oil use during the same period.

Careful consideration should be given to choosing the proper balance between investment in such "defensive" facilities as storage and standby production facilities—which are expensive and nonproductive in normal circumstances—and investment in developing new domestic sources of long-term supply such as nuclear breeder technology.

To achieve greater energy independence, it will be necessary to make a basic shift from oil and natural gas to coal and nuclear fuels. Development of facilities to liquefy and gasify coal will complement this shift by enlarging the areas of consumption to be served by coal. Ultimately, oil and gas consumption will be limited by market pressures to those uses where coal and nuclear power are not feasible substitutes, such as for petrochemical raw materials.

In the crucially important area of energy research and development, it is recommended that as much research as possible, particularly short-term applied research, be conducted under private auspices; and that government research and development concentrate on longer-range ventures such as the nuclear breeder, solar energy, and nuclear fusion development.

It is recommended that oil and gas wellhead prices be deregulated as rapidly as possible without causing major disruptions to the domestic economy, such as were caused by the abrupt increases in oil prices in 1973-74. Deregulation would allow the price allocation process to work more efficiently.

The second main thrust of energy policy, in addition to assuring a reliable supply, must be toward conservation and the elimination of waste. Conservation efforts should include a joint effort by industry and government to provide consumers with information on which to make energy-efficient choices. If allowed to function efficiently, the price mechanism can be relied upon as the primary means for promoting wise use and discouraging wasteful use of energy. Government policies should be concentrated on facilitating the free functioning of this price mechanism and only in the case of an emergency should direct government control actions be applied to reduce consumption.

Large amounts of energy are used for transportation and space heating. In an emergency, significant immediate reductions in energy consumption could be achieved in these areas without adversely affecting the economy in a major way.

Continuation and strict enforcement of the 55-mph speed limit should be only an initial action in the transportation area. Actions to encourage improvements in mileage characteristics of automobiles should be high on the list of transportation priorities, e.g., smaller and lighter cars and more efficient engines. Careful analyses of safety and pollution control devices on automobiles are needed to balance costs against the various benefits. In addition, it is recommended that government encourage the development of mass transit and other energy-efficient transportation techniques including those that do not use scarce oil and gas. Regulation of freight rates and freight movements should also be made more flexible and thus more energy-efficient.

Localities should be encouraged to strengthen those aspects of building codes which are energy related. Federal assistance should be made available to local agencies which determine building codes. It is important to assure that the technical basis for code changes is adequate and that the changes have met cost-benefit criteria. Changes that add significantly to first costs of residential construction should be examined with particular care to avoid pricing more low- and moderate-income purchasers out of the housing market.

Efforts to assure energy supplies and promote conservation must be carefully coordinated. The diverse government agencies whose actions impact on energy supply and demand must be monitored and focused toward consistent and compatible national goals. The parochial interests of individual agencies must be subordinated to and coordinated with the overall national goals of: continued economic growth, wise energy use, environmental improvement, greater energy independence, and enhancement of the overall quality of life. For these reasons it is recommended that the Energy Resources Council be continued and strengthened to give it authority and responsibility for carrying out United States energy policy.

Resources—Materials

Continued moderate economic growth will require continued growth in consumption of materials. However, the rate of growth of consumption of non-energy mineral resources will be slower than the rate of growth of GNP. This is because the services component of GNP is growing faster than the production component and because efficiency of metals utilization is improving. It can be expected that the increase of consumption of the five major metals (iron, aluminum, copper, zinc, and lead) will average 2.8 percent per year, in conjunction with a 3.5 to 3.7 percent per year growth in real GNP. Increases in recycling of metals could reduce the growth rate of newly mined metal somewhat below the 2.8 percent figure.

Such a growth in consumption is well within the resource capacity of the United States, as supplemented by reasonable levels of imports. In a few strategic metals such as manganese, chromium and nickel, the United States must depend almost entirely on imports from a relatively few countries. In most other cases, however, United States import policies reflect the existence of large, low-cost mineral deposits dispersed among a number of countries including the United States.

It is recommended that primary reliance be placed in the combination of rising prices and improving technology to make increasing quantities of materials available. These factors will also cause the percentages of recycled metal to increase. The development of stable, balanced, and consistent government policies is as crucial as technological progress in determining the future of the United States minerals industry. Without stability, private investment cannot be expected either in research and development or in new full-scale mining operations.

The establishment of government policies is particularly important as a prerequisite to undersea mining. Here, international agreements are lacking, and government policy intentions and assurances are needed to back up private initiative.

It is recommended that the United States develop contingency plans to counter the threat of an import embargo of any of the important minerals—however remote such a threat may seem now. The plans should include stockpiling, recycling, plans for emergency consumption cutbacks and a search for substitution possibilities.

The ultimate solution to such artificial shortages must be improved international cooperation through a world organization with some degree of power to enforce agreements. The establishment of such an organization should be of prime importance as an objective in all international trade negotiations.

Population

With the fertility rate currently below the replacement level, there is no basis for concern about the ability of the United States to accomodate its population. It is unnecessary to adopt any measures to control population size.

In regard to population distribution, the historic movement from rural to urban areas has slackened, and no measures to limit further concentrations are necessary. It remains important, however, to encourage efforts to rejuvenate central cities so that middle- and upper-income families will be induced to return. Efforts by the private sector to participate in this rejuvenation should be facilitated. Rising energy costs, especially in the area of transportation, may provide an impetus to city renewal efforts.

Agriculture

Agricultural output should be maximized so that food can be sold in world markets to meet the needs of developing nations and to help overcome the United States balance-of-payments problems arising from the importing of oil and other raw materials. Farm subsidies, acreage allotments, and incentives to limit output are inconsistent with current national objectives and should be discontinued. Research should concentrate on developing high-yield strains and fertilizers and pesticides which do not have undue effects on ecological balances. Additional research should be aimed at expanding arable land and maximizing the usage of renewable fertilizers.

Environment

Continuing improvements in environmental quality can be consistent with economic growth. Capital diversion from "productive" facilities to pollution control devices will tend to slow growth somewhat. The degree of slowdown need not be major, however, if the costs and benefits of proposed environmental standards are carefully balanced and the status of technological developments properly assessed. Environmental quality standards will have to be enforced by regulation supplemented by financial incentives. Over the long term, tax credits for pollution control expenditures and pollution taxes or fees could be considered.

Environmental quality regulations should be subject to cost-benefit analysis. Once adopted on this basis, standards should not be subject to frequent changes. Uncertainty in this area inhibits the development of new energy supplies. Environmental aspects of nuclear power are of particular importance. A concerted effort on the part of the government and industry is needed to resolve remaining questions in the public's mind about nuclear power safety and safeguards.

Finance

Federal deficit spending is a critical problem which contributes to inflation and to nearly all of the nation's other financial problems. It appears likely that United States economic growth over the next 25 years will be constrained more by shortages of capital than by shortages of energy or raw materials. Therefore, revisions in public policy will be needed to encourage capital formation and private investment in productive facilities. A variety of devices such as investment guarantees, tax credits, capital allocation rules and government loans are being suggested. While such devices may be used to remedy emergency situations, more basic actions should be taken to reduce disincentives to capital investment and encourage pricing policies in regulated industries which will provide an adequate return on investment and attract the required new capital.

Financial Integrity of the Electric Utility Industry

The electric utility industry is the most capital-intensive industry in the United States. As the United States shifts from oil and gas to coal and nuclear power, the electric utility industry will be required to process more and more of the nation's raw energy sources into forms useful to the ultimate consumer. Construction of the facilities needed to process these raw energy sources will not be feasible unless the industry is financially healthy and able to raise large amounts of capital funds in the competitive capital markets.

The single most important requirement for a financially healthy industry is the opportunity to earn revenues without delay which cover all costs including the costs of invested capital. A measure of

the degree to which this requirement is met should be the industry's ability to attract new capital at competitive rates and without diluting the capital of previous investors.

It is recommended that active national-state-industry cooperation be aimed at promptly revising regulatory methods and policies to provide utilities with the opportunity to earn adequate revenues. At current costs of debt and with the current debt structures of electric utility companies, the capital markets reflect the need for a return on common equity of 15 percent or more on a national average. The primary need for such a return is to enable utility companies to compete for capital in the capital market.

Utilities must be able to sell new common stock shares at a price at least equivalent to book value if they are to obtain new equity funds without diluting the equity of existing shareholders. Earnings on common equity must be sufficient to restore to common stock yields a significant premium over bond yields. In the last ten years utility bond yields have risen from about 4 percent to over 9 percent, while earnings on the book value of common stocks have remained static in the 11 to 12 percent range, or they have declined. Thus the margin (between 4 percent and 11 percent) which existed a decade ago, and which made it attractive for common stock buyers to assume the additional risk of common stocks, has been obliterated. This has resulted in stock prices substantially below book value. Given the need to sell ever-larger amounts of common stock, this amounts to a steady erosion of old stockholders' equity and it will eventually make the sale of additional common stock essentially impossible.

It is also necessary to have a return on common equity which will achieve an interest-coverage ratio adequate to permit efficient marketing of new long-term debt. To permit such marketing, coverage ratios must be well above the legal minimum for interest coverage. (Terms of the mortgage frequently require that before-tax earnings available for interest and other fixed charges be at least twice the interest charges on all outstanding debt issues and on the newly proposed issue; i.e., that the interest coverage ratio be at least 2.0.)

For most utility companies these requirements can be met in the current and prospective financial environment only by returns on common equity of 15 percent or more. In contrast, allowed earnings under present regulations are often in the 12 percent range (some are higher and some lower) while realized earnings for the industry as a whole were below 11 percent in 1974. This major discrepancy between realized and required earnings is the reason that

11

some utility companies today are in extreme financial difficulty and unable to raise the capital needed to finance essential new facilities.

Several regulatory and tax policy changes are recommended to enable electric utility companies to achieve an adequate return and improve their current critical financial conditions. These include: 1) permitting the use of forward test years; 2) allowing tariff changes to become effective without suspension, but possibly subject to refund within three to six months when so ordered by the regulatory commission upon completion of hearings; 3) expanding the scope of automatic adjustment clauses beyond fuel; 4) expediting regulatory proceedings by eliminating duplication of basic statistical information examined adequately at earlier hearings and substituting simple update information instead; 5) increasing allowable book depreciation rates by decreasing estimated useful lives for most classes of property; 6) normalizing tax deferrals; and 7) including a portion of the cost of construction work in progress in the rate base as construction proceeds.

It is also recommended that the investment tax credit rate be increased and that the percentage of income tax against which it can be credited be increased. Lastly, equity investment should be encouraged by allowing the tax-free reinvestment of dividends in new issue stock or by making the dividends on common stock and new preferred stock tax free to the recipient.

International Relations

While the primary emphasis in this study was on the United States, it was clearly impossible to examine the nation's future for the next 25 years and more without considering international relations. Therefore, the report includes an evaluation of the prospects for long-term world growth and examines some of the potential interactions between the United States and the rest of the world.

The Changing Priorities of Growth

It is the conclusion of this report that some form of economic growth will continue and that "a new concept of growth" is called for. An attempt is made to describe the nature of this concept through such terms as "clean growth," "quality growth," "optimal growth," and the idea of "betterment." None of these terms really captures the sense of continuous change and multiplicity of forces being experienced. Indeed, it may be inappropriate to try to characterize a new concept of growth in one term or phrase. Such terms tend to suggest a finality which does not exist in a world which is constantly changing and evolving.

The Analysis

Where We Stand Now

How the problems of growth are approached is related to an assessment of where we stand today and how we arrived at this stage of development. The current status of the factors determining economic growth is presented in the report in the form of a statistical profile and without evaluative conclusions. The factors covered are: population, employment, productivity, standard of living, material resources, environmental policy, the economic system, government policies, social and political conditions, and social change.

United States Economic Growth and Energy Use

An analysis was conducted to determine the effects of different policies on economic growth over the long-term (25 years) future. The econometric model developed by Data Resources, Inc. was used along with other forecasting methods to generate three scenarios. These describe the future under a high-growth objective; a low-growth objective; and a moderate-growth objective. For the high-growth scenario it was assumed that the public policy climate would remain positive for growth. A continuation of historic conditions and trends was assumed in which there were no serious social or physical resource constraints on growth. For the low-growth scenario a national policy objective of achieving a steady-state society was assumed. Accordingly, there are increasingly rigid constraints imposed in the model on use of energy and materials and on resource availability. A continuing low birth rate was assumed. Other constraints include increases in the use of capital for environmental programs and a decline in the productivity of capital. The moderate-growth scenario assumes conditions which represent an intermediate position between the two extremes. Conclusions from the three scenarios are compared for each of the categories of: population and agriculture, economic growth, personal consumption, non-energy minerals, energy demand, and energy supply.

Population and Agriculture. Population trends for the three scenarios are shown in Chart ES·1. If the fertility rate rebounds to 2.5 (the average of the 1960s), as is assumed in the high-growth case (Case A), the United States population by 2020 would be around 350 million. This is within the "carrying capacity" of the nation. A fertility rate of 2.5 causes population to increase indefinitely, however, and if maintained would result in a national population of

Chart ES•1
UNITED STATES POPULATION

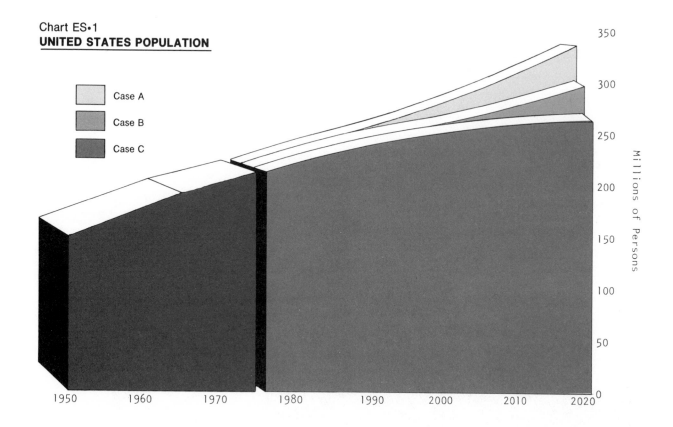

over 2 billion people (or about 10 times the current level) by the year 2200. A variety of natural and social pressures might be expected to alter fertility rates long before such population levels are reached.

In fact, in 1972 and 1973 the fertility rate in the United States slipped below the replacement level of 2.1, assumed for the moderate-growth case (Case B), and approached 1.8, the rate used for the low-growth case (Case C). Under moderate growth, population will rise to about 330 million and then stabilize. With low growth, it will peak at 270 million and then begin to decline.

The United States now produces sufficient foods to sustain a population of 350 million at adequate levels of nutrition. Increases in productivity and in acreage have the potential to accommodate the population growth under high growth and still continue to increase agricultural exports, at least through the next 50 years. Under the more likely moderate growth of population, there will be additional potential to increase exports.

Economic Growth. Chart ES•2 presents three different patterns of economic growth. In the high-growth (Case A) scenario, GNP rises at 4.2 percent per year. This is only slightly below the 4.3 percent rate which occurred between 1961 and 1972. In a future under moderate-growth conditions, average

GNP growth would be 3.5 to 3.7 percent per year. When the constraints assumed for the low-growth (Case C) scenario are combined with low population growth, the resulting forecast is an average annual increase in GNP of about 2.3 percent. The moderate-growth case is considered the most likely path of economic growth.

Personal Consumption. Physical output per capita varies significantly for the three scenarios. In terms of real personal consumption per capita, high growth will provide an increase from about $2,700 per year in 1975 to almost $6,000 in the year 2000 (in constant 1958 dollars). In the moderate-growth scenario, personal consumption will rise to nearly $5,800. Under low growth the figure will be only $4,112. Similar relationships can be seen from the trends in real GNP per capita shown in Chart ES•3.

Non-Energy Minerals. Growth in minerals consumption is a prerequisite for continued economic growth. However, as the United States moves from an industrial to a post-industrial society, metals consumption will rise less rapidly than real GNP. In the high-growth scenario, consumption of the 5 major metals is forecast to rise at 3.2 percent per year over the 1970 to 2000 period. This compares with the real GNP growth rate of about 4.2 percent for high growth. Rates of growth of mineral consumption are

13

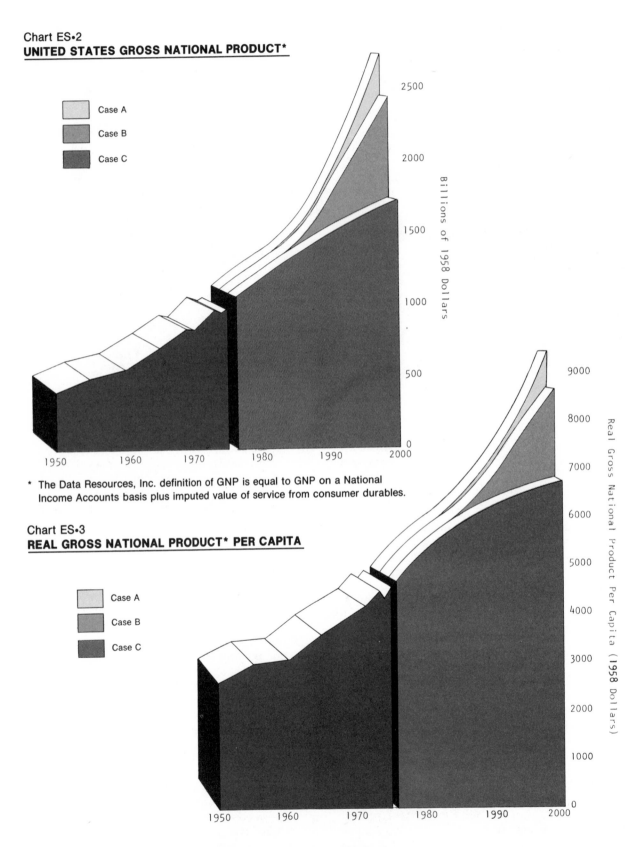

Chart ES•2
UNITED STATES GROSS NATIONAL PRODUCT*

Case A
Case B
Case C

Billions of 1958 Dollars

2500

2000

1500

1000

500

0

1950   1960   1970   1980   1990   2000

* The Data Resources, Inc. definition of GNP is equal to GNP on a National
Income Accounts basis plus imputed value of service from consumer durables.

Chart ES•3
REAL GROSS NATIONAL PRODUCT* PER CAPITA

Case A
Case B
Case C

Real Gross National Product Per Capita (1958 Dollars)

9000

8000

7000

6000

5000

4000

3000

2000

1000

0

1950   1960   1970   1980   1990   2000

* The Data Resources, Inc. definition of GNP is equal to GNP on a National
Income Accounts basis plus imputed value of service from consumer durables.

correspondingly lower for the other two scenarios. The average is 2.8 percent per year for moderate-growth Case B, and 1.6 percent for low-growth Case C. Similar relationships are evident in the per capita consumption of metals shown in Chart ES•4.

Energy Demand. As in the case of minerals, energy demand will continue to grow at a slower pace than real GNP. Under moderate economic growth (Case B), energy growth over the next 25 years averages 2.8 to 3.0 percent per year in contrast to 3.7 percent for real GNP. Chart ES•5 compares the energy-growth patterns of the three scenarios. Growth in consumption of electric energy will be much faster than for energy as a whole. This too will represent a continuation of past relationships. In the moderate-growth-policy climate assumed for Case B, electric energy demand would grow at an average rate of 5.3 to 5.8 percent over the 25-year period. Even under low-growth conditions, electric energy demand

would grow an average 3.7 percent per year. The conversion from oil and gas to coal and nuclear fuels works to maintain higher rates of electric energy growth. Chart ES•6 depicts energy consumption for electricity for the three scenarios. Consumption of energy sources for production of electricity will constitute between 45 and 55 percent of all energy consumption in the year 2000 as against about 27 percent in 1975.

Energy Supply. The consumption pattern of various fuels will shift gradually over the forecast period from dominance of oil and natural gas toward increasing use of coal and nuclear power. At present, coal, hydropower, and nuclear fuel provide only 23 percent of the nation's energy. Oil and natural gas provide the remainder. As indicated in Chart ES•7, the share of coal, hydro and nuclear is expected to approach 33 percent by 1985 and over 50 percent by the end of this century. Within that time period, the

Chart ES•4
UNITED STATES PER CAPITA CONSUMPTION OF FIVE MAJOR METALS*

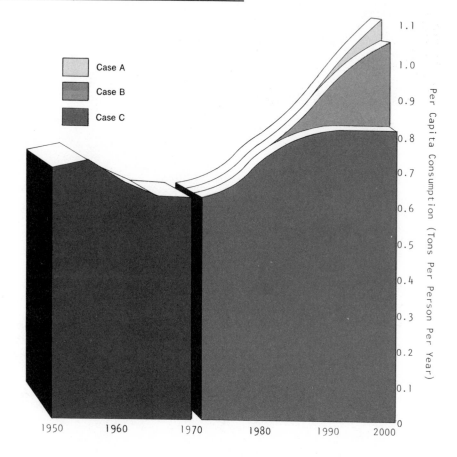

* Iron, aluminum, copper, lead, and zinc.

15

Chart ES•5
UNITED STATES ENERGY CONSUMPTION

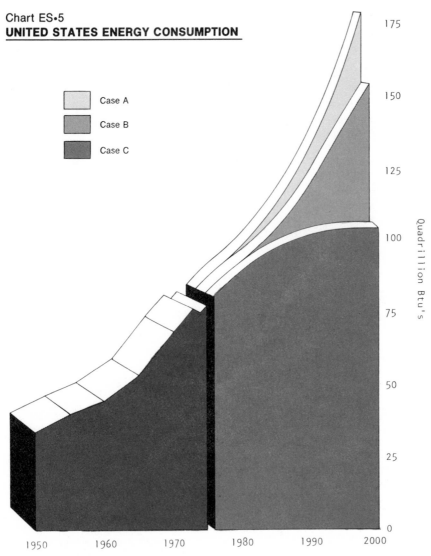

Case A
Case B
Case C

Quadrillion Btu's

175

150

125

100

75

50

25

0

1950   1960   1970   1980   1990   2000

Chart ES•6
**UNITED STATES ENERGY CONSUMPTION FOR
THE GENERATION OF ELECTRICITY**

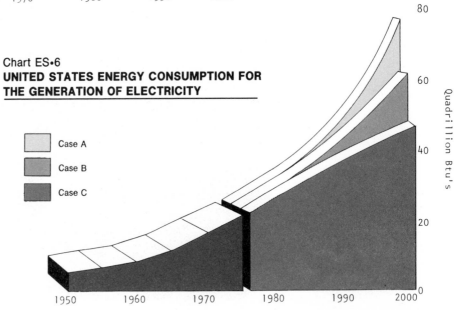

Case A
Case B
Case C

Quadrillion Btu's

80

60

40

20

0

1950   1960   1970   1980   1990   2000

potentials for sources such as geothermal, tides, winds, and trash are small, although geothermal power may be significant on a local basis in the western United States. Solar and fusion power are not likely to make major contributions until well into the 21st century.

Under the conditions assumed for the moderate-growth case, there can be adequate energy supplies. Case A assumptions of few environmental restrictions and no importing problems lead to a forecast of plentiful supplies. However, even the sharply reduced demands under low-growth conditions are unlikely to be met fully under the restraints which are assumed for Case C. Rationing and other legal restrictions on energy use would be necessary to close the supply-demand gap.

Energy imports under moderate growth are projected to remain essentially constant at about 18 percent of total demand until 1980. After that they will gradually decrease to about 12 percent in 1985

and to 10 percent by the end of the century. A 10 to 12 percent level of imports is judged to provide a reasonable balance between risks of interruption of the imported energy and costs of providing a higher level of domestic supplies. Under the environmental restrictions assumed for Case C, domestic supplies would be so limited that the percentage of imports would remain high throughout the period. The low-growth scenario shows imports rising to 24 percent of total consumption in 1980, staying at that level through 1985 and then dropping to 18 percent by the year 2000.

World Economic Growth

An analysis of the future of world economic growth was done using the Case Western Reserve University Multi-Level World Model. This analysis considered population, agriculture and food supplies,

Chart ES-7
UNITED STATES ENERGY SUPPLY PATTERNS FOR CASES A, B, AND C

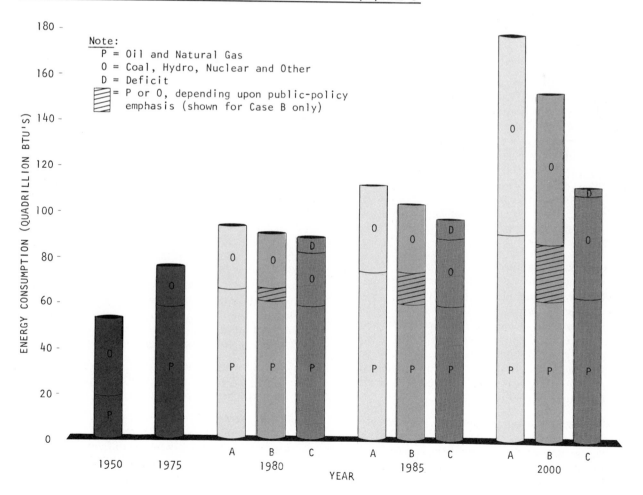

energy and non-energy resources, general economic growth in regard to the gap between developed and developing countries, and population and quality of life.

At current growth rates and with no major changes in the level of birth control effort, the world population will nearly double by the end of this century, and will multiply nearly 20 times by the end of the next century. It is unlikely that such a large population can be adequately provided for, and starvation deaths on a large scale in the underdeveloped regions are a real prospect. Vigorous population control efforts can reduce the burden considerably. Even a delayed and modest effort would yield significant results. To date, however, population control programs in various countries have met with varied success.

Food supplies present a potential constraint on world economic growth. The effect of food shortages is direct and absolute. In many parts of the world today, producing food occupies almost all the working time of large fractions of the population.

There is hope for expanding the area under cultivation and for multiple cropping—except for the regions of Southeast Asia, China, and Western Europe. The major limitation on increasing food supplies in this manner is availability of water.

Four scenarios are presented which illustrate the nature and magnitude of the problems involved. It appears that the constraints presented by food and agriculture can be overcome by increased effort and technology, but it will require more international cooperation than has existed up to now. Annual investment aid needed from advanced nations to Southeast Asia, to cite one area as an example, would be in the order of $7 billion, providing population is controlled. This amount would be required to help that region achieve self-sufficiency over a period of 50 years.

Reasonable assumptions about growth in energy consumption yield a demand projection for the year 2000 between two and four times the world's present energy use. Constraints will emerge clearly in the case of fossil fuels which cannot alone form the basis of long-term economic growth. Wise use of energy must be given a high priority particularly in advanced countries. Besides eliminating inefficiencies, changes in lifestyles may be required to save significant amounts of energy.

Shortages of major metals and minerals are not likely to emerge as a threat to continued world economic growth within the next 50 years. The historical pattern of development in advanced countries extended to 2025 suggests that their economies will be nearly 5 times as big as in 1975 and per capita income will reach $22,000 in 1975 dollars. In contrast, the poorer regions will grow slowly and will be starting from a much lower base.

The gap between the developed and developing worlds could be reduced through aid. A policy of early substantial aid would speed attainment of self-sufficiency on the part of the underdeveloped regions. The costs of aid are considerable. An early-action scenario predicts a total aid contribution from the developed world of about $2.5 trillion over 50 years—expressed in 1958 dollars. This is about 2½ times the current United States GNP.

Electric Power Pricing and Financing

Pricing

The growth issue and the conclusions and findings of this report have a variety of implications for the electric utility industry. Many of these have to do with pricing practices. Some opponents of growth suggest that utility rates should be changed to discourage energy consumption or to achieve certain social objectives. In addressing these questions the report reviews past, current, and proposed pricing practices and evaluates the major criticisms now being raised.

Pricing practices in the electric utility industry are complex for a variety of reasons: 1) the industry is fragmented into a large number of companies; 2) policies of different state regulatory commissions vary; 3) companies serve different types of customers under different circumstances which impose different cost burdens; 4) the industry is highly capital intensive and payments for the use of capital are a substantial part of total costs; and 5) electricity storage is impractical in large quantities so that a kilowatt-hour sold at a peak-load period has a far different cost from one sold at another time.

The following principles and practices related to the pricing of electricity appear best suited to meet the needs of society in the future.

- *Cost to Serve.* The primary goal in fixing rates should be to approximate the cost to serve as closely as is feasible, while maintaining a reasonable balance with metering and billing costs, and public understanding. In some cases, efforts to improve load factor may warrant certain deviations from cost to serve.

- *Revenue Requirements.* The utility's total rate structure should produce sufficient revenues to cover all necessary expenses of doing business, including a rate of return on all investment to compensate present owners fairly and attract additional capital at reasonable costs. Both customer and investor interests are served over the long run by a financially healthy industry.

- *Regulatory Response.* Regulatory lag should be reduced so that it does not prevent the efficiently managed utility company from earning the authorized return. Measures to accomplish this include: use of forward test years; expanding the scope of automatic adjustment clauses; and allowing tariff changes to become effective without suspension, subject to possible refund.

- *Long-Run Incremental Costs.* Attention should be given to long-run incremental costs in designing rates. Long-run incremental costs refer to the costs of additional production, and include all categories of costs.

- *Customer Classifications.* Customers with similar service requirements, market demands, and load characteristics should be grouped together as a class and charged a specific schedule of rates which reflects the costs to serve that class. Rates should move toward equalizing rates of return from all classes.

- *Rate Blocks.* Block structuring of energy and demand charges for large customers should be continued only to the extent that such blocks are justified by cost considerations such as load factors, coincidence factors, and customer costs. In addition, rate blocking for residential customers should continue as long as it remains the best practical means for approximating costs to serve. It should be noted that rate blocking does not preclude flattening of rates where cost considerations so suggest.

- *Peak-Period Pricing.* Rate structures should move toward more accurate reflection of differences in the costs of serving on-peak and off-peak customers.

- *Social Costs.* The judicious incorporation of measurable social costs into the pricing of all goods and services throughout the economy would be beneficial. Incorporation of these costs into only one sector of an industry or one sector of the economy may severely distort resource allocations.

- *Inverted Rates.* A proper regard for the distribution of customer costs, capacity costs, and energy costs has in the past produced a rate structure in which the price paid per unit of energy declined with increasing use. In today's environment, high fuel costs have at least temporarily made energy costs a higher fraction of total costs than was true in the past. This tends to justify a more nearly "flat" rate, but not an inverted rate. The idea of inverted rates is wholly inconsistent with the principle of basing rates on costs to serve.

- *Accomplishing Social Goals.* Using energy pricing to reallocate income among various groups would be both improper and impractical. If such reallocation is judged by the electorate to be desirable, it is best carried out by the public systems of taxation and governmental assistance.

- *Research Efforts.* In-depth studies are needed to examine the technological and economic feasibility of time-of-day metering and associated on-peak/off-peak pricing to all customer classes. Similar efforts are needed to determine price elasticities and cross-elasticities of users' demands for energy. Empirical studies should also be aimed at determining the impact on rates of true long-run incremental cost pricing, and assessing the shifts in resource allocation if other parts of the energy industry do not simultaneously revise their pricing structures.

Financing

The electric utility industry faces major problems in financing its future growth. This report concentrates on the longer-range financing problems of the next 15 to 20 years, although some discussion of the current financing situation is also provided.

The major conclusions of the analysis include the following:

a. Over the period to 1990, construction expenditures will grow at an average rate of about 10 percent per year in current-dollar terms as the industry responds to the requirements of the "moderate growth scenario" indicated in Case B. (Under the moderate-growth policies assumed for Case B, growth in kilowatt-hour consumption would range from 5.3 to 5.8 percent per year.) Current-dollar forecasts assume that inflation will subside over the next few years to the 4 to 5 percent per year range.

b. Limited financing ability over the near term will require compensatingly higher expenditures in later years, probably in the 1980 to 1985 period.

c. Under conditions of "moderate" economic growth, total current-dollar requirements for capital from 1974 to 1990 inclusive will approximate $750 billion. Unless steps are taken to increase the present level of internally generated funds, i.e., those from retained earnings, depreciation, and tax deferrals, nearly two-thirds of these capital requirements will have to come from external sources.

d. This will require raising from $400 to $450 billion in the competitive capital market; over $100 billion of this will have to be newly issued common stock.

e. If the nation is entering a period of long-term capital scarcity, marketing such huge quantities of new debt, preferred stock, and common stock will be impossible unless the industry can exhibit favorable and consistent earning trends.

f. If inflation rates subside to the 4 to 5 percent per year range and government deficits can be constrained, capital will be more readily available. Under these circumstances it is estimated that an average industry figure of 15 percent for return on common equity will be adequate to attract the funds required. Higher rates of return may be necessary for some companies, depending on individual corporate financial circumstances. Higher rates for industry averages will be needed if inflation remains in the 7 to 10 percent range.

g. The electric utility industry will consume some 9 percent of the total investment funds generated in the United States over the next 15 or 16 years and will continue to account for about 25 percent of the funds raised for nongovernmental uses in the competitive capital markets.

h. "High" and "low" conditions of economic growth would require about $820 billion and $480 billion, respectively, of capital over the period of 1974 to 1990, in contrast with the $750 billion estimated for "moderate" growth.

CHAPTER 1

Introduction

A. Growth as a Public Policy Issue

The idea of "growth" is one of the most fundamental social values held by our society. It has been both an implicit national purpose and an explicit public policy from the birth of the country up to the present time. Until recently the appropriateness of growth as an economic objective and a social value was not seriously questioned. Now, however, the growth ethic is being challenged.

Economic growth, in the form of expanding population and material production and consumption, is now being viewed by some critics as the underlying cause of many of the nation's environmental and social ills. These critics see continued growth as adding to the present problems and leading, finally, to a global collapse.

To avoid a breakdown and improve the "quality of life" it is argued that a condition of "no growth" or "steady state" is necessary in which population would be stabilized, the production and consumption of material goods would be limited, and the use of physical resources would be minimized.

The opponents of growth reflect a variety of perspectives and interests. They include: 1) academicians and scientists using theoretical approaches and global forecasting models; 2) environmentalists seeking to halt the further encroachment of development on nature; and 3) citizens who see the costs of growth and increased urbanization in their communities as outweighing the benefits. In the first category the most prominent example is the work of the Club of Rome conducted at Massachusetts Institute of Technology (M.I.T.) and published in the book, *The Limits to Growth.*[1] An example of concerted action on the part of environmentalists to create a mechanism for controlling development was the passage in California in 1972 of an initiative measure which created a number of commissions to regulate development on the California coast. In the third category, several cities have adopted measures aimed at limiting population or controlling development within their boundaries. There are also numerous examples of citizen actions opposing specific projects or developments in their own areas.

Despite the diversity of their motives and the fact that they appear to represent only a minority of the population, these opponents of growth represent what might be termed a "zero growth movement." It is not a movement in the sense of a well-organized group dedicated to a specific goal, but the accumulated activities of these groups have begun to have significant impacts on policy decisions and the course of the nation's development. At the national level the academic and philosphical discussion of the growth question has become a major intellectual debate. It is part of a general reappraisal of the national purpose, and as such, it has the most profound implications for the future of the United States and the rest of the world. At the local level, opponents of specific developments frequently use the no-growth arguments from the intellectual debate to advance their causes, although they may not really believe in no growth as an overall policy. Nevertheless, the net result of individual actions to halt development at the regional and local levels could become a de facto national policy of limited growth.

The growth debate has not as yet produced clearly defined public policy alternatives. At the local level the issue is usually limited to opposition to a specific project. The academic discussion tends to be theoretical and abstract. In both cases, however, the arguments are usually developed in terms of a choice between growth or no growth. This is, of course, simplistic. Approached positively, the question of growth does not represent an either/or choice between good alternatives and bad. Rather, it represents an opportunity to explore a variety of courses to a more desirable future. The need to reorient the growth debate toward positive alternatives is one factor which led the electric utility industry to undertake a study of the growth question.

B. The Electric Utility Industry and the Growth Issue

In conducting a study of economic growth, the electric utility industry is venturing beyond its traditional sphere of interests and expertise. The industry is, of course, directly concerned with energy growth which is one component of economic growth. The questions about continued economic growth, however, involve a much broader range of economic and social issues. There are several considerations which led the industry to undertake a study of economic growth.

The first factor is obvious. Electric utility companies have been thrust into the center of the growth debate by a combination of circumstances. The rapid rate of growth of electricity consumption makes the industry a conspicuous element of economic growth. Present means of producing electricity have environmental impacts and consume limited resources. Also, the physical facilities required for generating and distributing electricity are highly visible.

Another more positive reason for addressing the broad issue of growth is that the industry has command of a large volume of information about growth patterns and the relationships between energy and the economy. Also, energy is a key factor in determining whether economic growth can be sustained. These information resources, combined with the industry's financial and internal research capabilities, provide the potential for a constructive contribution to the growth debate. In addition to having the capability, it is part of the industry's social responsibility to recommend and support public policy actions on the part of appropriate governmental authorities, although it is not the role of industry to make final determinations about such policies.

There are other considerations which are fundamental to this effort on the part of the industry to contribute to the discussion of growth policy. These considerations stem from the unique characteristics of the electric utility business and its relationships with the communities it serves and its role in the total economy. Electric utilities are natural monopolies and as such are regulated. They operate in accordance with public service franchises under which they are obligated to serve all of the power requirements in their service territories. Whether or not to make the investment needed to meet expected electricity demand is not now considered to be a matter of choice. The utility is required to do everything possible to assure reliable service, and this requirement is paramount in management decision making.

The obligaton to serve can present an electric utility company with a dilemma when facilities to meet public service needs are opposed by segments of the public who claim to act in the public interest. The regulatory framework surrounding a utility's actions makes it more vulnerable than other segments of industry to actions directed at slowing or halting growth.

In addition, because of the scale of facilities required to provide electric power service and the time required for design, review, and completion, the industry must plan new projects farther out in time than most other industries. It must also make large financial and plant construction commitments with very long lead times. These requirements make the forecasting of economic growth patterns and their related energy demand levels a matter of strategic concern.

Lastly, and of vital importance, is the fact that electric utility companies provide an essential public service. Their product is unique, and their location is permanently fixed. These factors make power companies an integral part of their local communities and the national economy. Indeed, the industry's future and the future of the local and national economies are completely intertwined and inseparable.

These are the reasons leading the industry to seek answers to the questions about economic growth and the future. They represent a combination of industry interests and responsibilities. The industry and the society both need a better understanding of the range of possible choices if they are to resolve the basic problems associated with growth.

C. Approach and Objectives of the Study

A study of economic growth and the future requires a broad public policy perspective and a systems approach. The society and the economy must be viewed as an interdependent system. To deal adequately with the growth issue requires going beyond the purely economic issues to consider more fundamental questions about the processes of change in the society and its capacity to adapt to new conditions. The approach of this study has been to probe such basic questions and arrive at conclusions which would provide a basis for public policy recommendations.

Questions about the sustainability and desirability of economic growth present major analytical challenges. The task requires the identification and weighing of many trade offs. The scope of such a study must be wide, and this creates problems. These problems and any resulting weaknesses in the analysis must be accepted, however, because the question of whether and how the national economy should continue to grow cannot be dealt with from a narrow perspective.

While it is impossible to explore every question associated with growth and the future, an attempt

22

has been made to recognize and illuminate all of the major issues. This is a major objective in itself, even without attempting to resolve all of the peripheral questions thus raised. On the basic issues, the goal was to arrive at conclusions that are definitive and useful in policy deliberations.

The most difficult questions concerning growth have to do with conditions in the future, a subject about which there can be no certainty. No one can guarantee that a growth-induced catastrophe will be avoided or that measures to inhibit growth will not produce equally disastrous results. However, the possibility and probability of such an occurrence and the feasibility of more desirable alternatives can be systematically analyzed to provide a basis for plans and choices made today.

One of the objectives guiding the preparation of the report was balance in presentation. Many aspects of the growth issue involve matters of judgment and preference. There are strongly divergent opinions on many of the questions. An effort has been made to give balanced consideration to the different views. The project employed a diverse group of consultants not identified with the electric utility industry. Several different research methods were used. As a result, the report is a combination of qualitative discussion and quantitative analysis. It is hoped that this overall approach results in a report which creates its own credibility.

D. Organization of the Report

The objectives stated above are reflected in the organization of the report. Following this introductory Chapter 1, the body of the report is organized in three parts. Part I is devoted to a qualitative discussion of the growth issue. Chapter 2 is a statement of the pro-growth view. The no-growth view is then presented in Chapter 3. These statements are followed in Chapter 4 with a discussion of industry views and conclusions.

The pro-growth and no-growth position statements are considered reasonably complete and representative of their respective positions. Both sections are intended to provide contributions to the intellectual and policy debates.

Part II contains a more quantitative analysis. A foundation for this analysis is provided in Chapter 5 in the form of a statistical profile of "where we stand now." A detailed description of the future of growth in the United States is then set forth in Chapter 6.

This analysis is in the form of three scenarios for the long-term, 25-year future of the United States. The scenarios present: 1) a future under high growth; 2) a future under low growth; and 3) a future under moderate growth.

The quantitative analysis is continued in Chapter 7 with a discussion of world economic growth.

Part II is concluded in Chapter 8 with a set of findings and recommendations which flow from the analytical effort.

Part III deals with the implications of the growth issue and the findings of this study for the electric utility industry. The first Section (Chapter 9) is on electric power pricing. The critical matter of financing is covered in Chapter 10.

Several appendices are included containing back-up material for different sections of the report.

E. Purpose and Uses of the Report

This report is intended for use in public policy discussions dealing with growth and the future. Electric utility companies will find the report useful in relating their activities to the growth issue as it unfolds in their areas. The report represents a substantial and constructive contribution to the public discussion of whether and how the nation and local areas should grow.

An attempt has been made in this report to maintain a positive, public interest, and action-oriented approach. It is hoped that such an approach will elicit responsible and constructive responses from the advocates of the different positions.

What is needed is a broader, more explicit, and more enlightened discussion of national goals and purposes. Without such a dialogue and a resulting commitment to some general course of public policy action, the nation can only drift into an uncertain future. Such a process of non-decision and default would necessarily diminish the nation's potential. The alternative is to foster and sustain a sense of national direction. This will require some resolution of the basic questions surrounding the future of economic growth. This report is intended as a step toward that goal.

FOOTNOTES

1. Meadows, Donella H. et al. *The Limits to Growth.* New York: Universe Books, 1972.

PART I

The Future of Growth:
The Different Views

THE issue of the future of growth has many dimensions: social, political, and philosophical as well as economic. This multi-dimensional quality has made the debate complex and frustrating. These problems are dealt with in this part of the report in the following way. First, the pro-growth view is presented in Chapter 2. This is followed in Chapter 3 by the opposing no-growth view. Neither of these statements represent the views of the electric utility industry. Indeed, these statements represent two ends of a continuum of current thought on the growth question. As position statements they reflect biases in their choices and interpretations of data and theory.

By stating the two conflicting views as faithfully as possible and juxtaposing them in this way, it is possible in Chapter 4 to assess the strengths and weaknesses of each and to develop a set of industry conclusions. These conclusions are then formulated as a statement of the industry view of the future of economic growth.

CHAPTER 2

The Pro-Growth View

A. Summary Statement of the View

The viability of continuous growth has been a subject of concern and debate among economists since the Industrial Revolution. Skeptics have doubted the feasibility of a continual rise in living standards. Is it possible to continue the growth of both population and per capita consumption on a planet with a finite resource base? Research and experience in recent years have negated these doubts by clarifying the nature and sources of economic growth. It is now possible to make informed and optimistic estimates about the future of growth.

Western economic growth has been largely driven by technological advances. At least half of the rise in measured per capita output is due to improvements in technology. Technical change has been so powerful a force that it has completely offset the law of diminishing returns as it applies to land and the increased scarcity of resources. Although it is impossible to say with certainty that this trend will continue indefinitely, there is no compelling reason to believe that technology cannot continue to outpace population increase and resource scarcity in the future.

Besides the question of the *viability* of continuous economic growth there is the issue of the *desirability* of continuing growth. Some critics argue that society has reached a level of affluence where additional consumption adds little or nothing to the level of well-being. Affluence has led to some controversial expenditure patterns, such as large, low mileage automobiles, high cholesterol diets, and suburban sprawl. However, a close look at the consumption patterns of even the most advanced societies indicates that increased income is predominantly spent on better housing and medical care, more education, leisure and goods which enhance the quality of life, and other less controversial items. Future growth of per capita consumption is essential for continuing improvement in the quality of life of the average citizen.

While growth of per capita consumption (properly measured) is a legitimate goal of economic policy, the question of population growth is more debatable.

Population growth cannot be sustained indefinitely, and economic growth based solely on population growth may represent no improvement in human well-being. Only economic growth stemming from increases in average per capita consumption should be counted in measuring the benefits of growth.

Perhaps the most critical point in the growth debate is the issue of whether it is economic growth itself or the side effects of growth which are undesirable. Critics of growth argue that the side effects of growth are highly dangerous—they point to air pollution and resource exhaustion. Some side effects are undesirable—but these can and should be separated from growth itself. Automobiles can be built which are relatively pollution free; electricity can be produced with minimal harm to the environment; and scarce resources can be recycled or substitutes can be used. The United States is currently in the process of making these kinds of adjustments. The choices involved in separating the undesirable side effects from growth and in choosing among different qualitative paths will provide major policy issues for many years to come.

It has been argued that the only alternative to the increasing problems of growth is to halt growth completely and move to a "steady state." This represents a questionable and risky objective, and it is becoming increasingly clear that the goal of "clean economic growth" is a feasible and preferable alternative. Clean growth can provide the resources both to improve the living standards of poorer citizens and to advance the environmental cleanup. Neither of these objectives could be realized under a no-growth condition.

B. The Beliefs and Arguments Supporting the Pro-Growth View

1. The Benefits of Continued Economic Growth

The predominantly pro-growth view held by the economics profession and the negative reactions of most economists to calls for zero growth may be attributed in part to strong historical lessons. These have to do with the crucial role of technological change, the inherent instability of demand in well-developed economies, and actual experience in the face of previous pessimistic analyses of factors expected to limit growth. With this in mind it is useful to begin this review of the benefits of growth with a brief summary of the evolution of economic thought and experience concerning growth.

a. Economic Thought and Historic Experience

The processes of growth have interested economists since the eighteenth century. Adam Smith and Thomas Malthus described an expanding economy in which enterprise and thrift might raise living standards through growth. However, it was concluded that, ultimately, rigid biological limits would dominate the process and impose limits. Prosperity would lead to population growth and population growth would force the use of increasingly unfertile land. It was theorized that ultimately the only true equilibrium in per capita income level would be at the level of subsistence; living standards must fall to the point where population is stabilized through malnutrition or social conflict.

David Ricardo expanded on this dismal theory by describing the effects on income distribution. Since there is a limit to land, population growth was believed to result in a diminishing wage rate. This implies more than the Malthusian equilibrium at subsistence. As labor becomes more plentiful, land becomes increasingly scarce and land rents go up. As Malthus would predict, the world in general would slowly drift toward starvation. Only individuals lucky enough to own land would earn increasingly large incomes.

The dismal theories of Smith, Malthus, and Ricardo faded in the late nineteenth century, not because their arguments were refuted, but because they were found by experience to have little validity in terms of predictive power. Real wages in Victorian England and the rest of the industrializing world continued to rise rather than fall. The Malthusian vision receded, not because population leveled off, but because the supply of arable land open to settlement outside Europe was so large. Even more significant from the view of the mid-twentieth century, the development of ever more efficient techniques promised to bury Malthusian determinism permanently. Malthus' limit depended on the inability of production to keep pace with population indefinitely. However, it was found that technological change could nullify the prospect of diminishing returns—for example, by making it possible for crop yields to grow as rapidly as the labor force. In effect, the "limit" was deferred indefinitely.

The limited applicability of diminishing returns to modern growth patterns was confirmed by Edward Denison's research on the sources of growth in the United States and Western Europe.[1] Using data from 1950 to 1962, Denison disaggregated the sources of growth in output per employed person. Twenty-seven percent of the total growth was attributed to the accumulation of capital in such forms as buildings and machines to complement labor services. Thirteen percent of growth was due to more efficient allocation of the factors of production —largely the movement of inefficient labor from farms to cities and a reduction in the number of small shops. Another 16 percent could be attributed to economies of scale in production.

What is striking about the Denison analysis is the enormous role of technological change (34 percent) and education (22 percent) in improving labor productivity, while the net contribution of land and natural resources was actually negative (-1 percent). The contribution of technological change may be even greater, since the 22 percent associated with education is based on very generous assumptions.

An even more powerful factor in economic history which lessened interest in the problem of limits to growth has been the more pressing problem of economic stagnation and unemployment. During the decade of world depression, and after, the question of limits seemed superfluous; empty factories and coal mines and masses of unemployed labor hardly suggested a crisis of overconsumption. The problem was one of demand—how might it be possible to find buyers for the goods produced at current capacity?

Alvin Hansen suggested in 1941 that the demand shortfall in the 1930's was not a random historical accident.[2] Within the private sector, aggregate demand reflected individual investment and consumption decisions; for capacity to be fully employed, investment must balance what individuals fail to consume out of total available resources. In poor countries, most people have no choice but to spend virtually all their incomes. However, as economic growth raises per capita income, the amount of savings could be expected to increase more than proportionately. This is a predictable result of families being able to afford the luxuries of planning for emergencies, the education of children, retirement, major consumer durable purchases, etc. The private desire to save can become a permanent drag on growth, with every increase in capacity taking the economy further from full resource utilization. Only government intervention—as suggested by John Maynard Keynes could save a wealthy economy from economic stagnation in the long run.[3]

Hansen foresaw an increasing need for government stimulation of the economy to maintain full employment. During the same period, Roy Harrod and Evsey Domar described an unstable, full employment equilibrium in which savings must release exactly the right amount of resources to allow capital growth to match growth of the labor force.[4] Let savings fall short of the appropriate rate, and the economy would explode into a disastrous inflationary boom. Let savings be too great, and the economy would spiral down into depression, again with no self-corrective mechanism. The essence of the message was that private enterprise economies are inherently unstable, the primary source of the instability being the independent behavior of savers/investors.

No one really believes in the knife edge, boom-or-bust instability inherent in the Harrod-Domar models, but the point is that the focus of concern is far from that of Ricardo and Malthus. The strength of the post-Depression emphasis on demand rather than supply problems can be further illustrated by more recent concerns about automation. Automation became a widely acclaimed phenomenon associated with growth in the early 1960's. As many as two million jobs, it was suggested, might be eliminated each year by the substitution of machines for labor. Proposed solutions ranged from discouraging technological change to retraining the unemployed as computer programmers and electronics repairmen.

The facts or the logic of the automation scare are not at issue here; the whole "problem" died quietly in the full employment years of the mid-sixties. What is of interest is how the issue of adjustment to changing labor skill requirements was phrased in terms of how to cope with unemployment. The perceived threat was too much capacity rather than too little. There is no question raised by this condition about the sustainability of growth.

In summary, economic thought and experience have been away from the Ricardo/Malthus vision. They have tended to confirm the desirability and feasibility of continued economic growth.

b. Growth and the Quality of Life

A second set of positive arguments dealing with the benefits of continued economic growth is related to the "quality of life." The current challenges to growth have tended to prompt more defensive replies to criticisms than positive enumerations of the benefits of growth. This is partly because economic growth is an established phenomenon, one whose worth to society was unquestioned until the past few years. Also, of course, some of the newly emphasized problems associated with growth deserve atten-

tion. Overall, however, the virtues of growth may go unexpressed simply because they are almost embarrassingly obvious.

Growth means a better standard of living. This means more goods and services to go around; more food, clothing, shelter, and medical care to make life possible; and more leisure, entertainment, luxury, art, and personal mobility to help increase the quality of life. For the two-thirds of the world living near or below subsistence, the case for growth needs no further amplification. The continuation of poverty in underdeveloped countries and in parts of the United States is a matter of deep moral and political concern.

Nor is it necessary to dwell long on the virtues of increased incomes for the more affluent living in the prosperous nations. For most, survival is not an issue—the struggle to make ends meet revolves around choosing between a multiplicity of alternatives. This does not mean that increased prosperity is not worth having. While one might question the consumption of what some may consider frivolous gadgetry, most of the benefits associated with affluence are worthy objectives. The quality of life would surely be said to be improved by growth in living space for privacy, adequate food, available respite from work so that leisure itself could be enjoyed, education and cultural experiences, income for comfortable retirement, and high quality medical care. Other things being equal, increased incomes would certainly be of value for most people, most of the time.

The critics of growth assert, however, that other things aren't equal, that one must subtract the disamenities associated with growth to calculate the balance. Some of these disamenities can't be measured precisely. For example, Ezra Mishan has written: "Our eyes are ever on the future and our calendars marked for weeks and months ahead. . . This greed for the rewards of the future. . . hastens us through our brief lives. . .and cheats us of all spaciousness of time."[5]

The intangible quality of this complaint raises many more questions than it answers: Does Mishan believe that people in less industrialized, economically stagnant cultures are happier? If we were to opt for reduced growth would Americans somehow become less future-oriented and more content with their lot? Would a proper accounting of national income statistics show the supposed gains from economic growth to be nonexistent? William Nordhaus and James Tobin have tested this argument by the device of recalculating measured national income to account for disamenities of modern life.[6] This was done by subtracting from income, government services (such as police and defense) which in less complicated times were largely unnecessary, and also by netting out the social costs of pollution. Urban crowding, crime and insecurity can be considered social costs of growth—hence the need to subtract a portion of income gains associated with urbanization. Nordhaus and Tobin used the wage differential between rural and urban areas as a measure of the disamenity.

After all of these recalculations and others on the same order, they found that what might be termed "clean" or "real" per capita income rose 42 percent between 1929 and 1965. This is as contrasted with the conventional 88 percent growth in per capita net national income. In other words, the benefits of growth in national income far outweigh the disamenities of modern life. All things considered, growth has resulted in improvement in the quality of life.

c. Growth and Income Redistribution

A third positive argument for growth relates to the choice between growth and redistribution of income to overcome poverty.

Poverty remains a nagging problem in the developed countries of the world. It is a problem which can be approached by continued growth or a redistribution of income. Continued economic growth is by far the more realistic alternative. The political history of the last few decades in the United States suggests how difficult it is to achieve even modest redistribution. In 1947 the bottom 20 percent of families received 5.1 percent of national income while in 1972 they received 5.4 percent (before taxes). The share of the richest 20 percent declined only slightly—from 43.3 percent to 41.4 percent—during the same period.[7] Although it is technically possible to use taxation and expenditure programs to redistribute income, it does not appear from past experience that the political process is very effective in doing so.

While there is no discernible national trend toward redistribution, in the long run the incomes of unskilled workers have kept pace with the economy. Even allowing for inflation, the average income of the bottom tenth of the population grew by 55 percent between 1950 and 1971.[8]

Analogous arguments apply with even greater force in the case of the less developed countries. The amount of income that would be needed to make a dent in the problem is staggering. Yet there is simply no evidence that the rich nations are willing to make any major sacrifices. Economic development aid is shrinking rather than growing; plans to use the

creation of international financial liquidity instruments (SDR's) through the International Monetary Fund as a form of painless bilateral aid have been fought bitterly by Western Europe.

The approach of using economic growth as a solution to world poverty has been attacked by critics who argue that growth and domestic income inequality are linked together. It is claimed that in order to raise the growth rate in a fully employed economy, economic capacity must be diverted from consumption to capital goods. Since rich people consume a smaller proportion of income than poor people, transferring income from poor to rich reduces total consumption and frees resources to increase capital investment. In practice this can be accomplished by taxing consumption rather than income, and by subsidizing investment activities. Thus, growth is said to produce inequality in the distribution of income.

Despite the seeming plausibility of this theory, a systematic analysis of actual experience with distribution and growth shows that growth has been linked to increasing equality rather than inequality.[9] Simon Kuznets has explained the link in socioeconomic terms. Development is associated with the rise of the middle class, which is generally recruited from the low end of the income distribution. Another empirical study has found a pattern of widening inequality early in the development process and then narrowing inequality as development progresses.[10] This would be the expected result: the temporary sacrifice of a part of current consumption for the sake of greater future benefit. The alternative is improvidence and impoverishment. Investment leads to the capacity for greater consumption.

d. Growth and Full Employment

The fourth positive argument for continued economic growth has to do with the goal of maintaining full employment. Economic growth in the form of high levels of demand for capital goods spreads through the economy by means of the so-called multiplier effect. It increases demand for consumer goods, and thereby provides jobs in every sector of the economy. Hence, a major reason for economic growth is to maintain high employment, particularly if population continues to grow.

Although growth may not be absolutely necessary to maintain full employment, the link between the two is strong. The issue is a particularly important one, since the people who suffer most from unemployment are the people who can least afford it. One study based on 1960 statistics suggests that a one percent increase in unemployment reduces the average income of the very poor by ten percent, while reducing the income of the middle class by only $\frac{1}{50}$th of one percent.[11] Unemployment patterns have probably changed somewhat since then, but there seems to be no question that the poor bear more than their share of the burden.

In summary, there are strong positive arguments in favor of economic growth related to economic theory and experience, the quality of life, growth vs. income redistribution, and the desirability of maintaining employment.

2. Responses to the Arguments Against Economic Growth

Serious criticism of economic growth as a social goal is a relatively recent phenomenon, though some of the current arguments can be traced back more than a century. One thread of criticism (identified with Ezra Mishan) attacks the goal of growth itself. It is claimed that the purported benefits of growth are illusory, that "progress" has not made people happier. Another thread of criticism links the growth issue to conflicts between nations for markets and resources and with the asserted exploitation of less developed countries.[12]

But by far the greatest source of criticism of economic growth has come from the environmental movement. Here the attack takes two directions. First, that the process of growth has unpleasant, cumulative side effects, i.e., pollution, the destruction of wilderness, congestion, and that these outweigh the benefits. Second, that growth is not sustainable due to the finite capacity of the planet, and an unplanned approach to these natural limits of economic activity will cause hardship or disaster.

The first of these two themes is expressed by the editors of *The Ecologist Magazine*[13] and Barry Commoner.[14] The second theme is epitomized by the M.I.T./Club of Rome report titled, *The Limits to Growth.*[15]

a. The M.I.T./Club of Rome Report

The *Limits to Growth* report, prepared by M.I.T., deserves special attention as a major work in the zero growth challenge. The *Limits* work was based on a simulation model in the form of a series of mathematical relationships intended to represent the behavioral and technical relationships determining world economic output and population. In the world model, the system consists of the aggregate relationships between population, industrial production, agricultural output, exhaustible natural resources, capital goods and pollutants. Taken as individual equations, the structure of the model is rather

straightforward, following what appears to be common sense if not proven fact. (The relationships are not drawn from empirical studies.)

When the model is set into motion with data representing estimates for each of the parameters, the results are dramatic. Industrial output and food output per capita are forecast to rise for several more decades, then abruptly collapse in the first half of the next century. Industrial output per capita reaches pre-World War I levels by the last quarter of the 21st century. The critical variable determining this abrupt turnabout (approximately fifty years in the future) is the diminishing supply of natural resources. Population continues to rise for about one hundred years, then succumbs to the negative pressure from reduced food and consumer goods supplies.

Even more disturbing than this so-called "standard" world model scenario is the model's insensitivity to more optimistic choices of parameter values. A doubling of the hypothetical natural resource base—on the assumption that the initial estimates were conservative—changes the immediate cause of collapse, but little else. If pollution per unit of output is cut to one-fourth its 1970 levels, and optimistic assumptions are made about the size of the raw materials base, the world economy still reaches a per capita consumption level which is unsustainable within a century. Assumptions permitting the doubling of food production per acre or the introduction of birth control also create similar dismal results. A final "superoptimistic" simulation, cutting unit pollution by three-fourths, doubling land yields, disseminating birth control information and recycling three-fourths of natural resources generates delays in the collapse mode, but not indefinitely.

The validity of all of these conclusions depends upon the adequacy of the world model to capture fundamental economic relationships and the accuracy of the parameter estimates chosen. *The model has been found to be faulty on both counts.* The more serious criticisms of the model and its conclusions can be enumerated as follows:

• The model treats the world economy as a whole, aggregating developed and underdeveloped countries. However, experiments which divide the world into just two sectors, developed and underdeveloped, alter the model's outputs a good deal in a positive direction.[16]

Perhaps a more serious question raised by the original experiments is the validity of the implicit assumption that today's underdeveloped economies are simply young versions of the developed economies.

• Multiple runs under different assumptions suggested that the basic collapse mode was not sensitive to a wide range of alternative conditions. The "optimistic" model runs merely showed a delayed catastrophe.[17] Subsequent work with the model contradicts these findings. If the natural resource, pollution, and production subsystems are redesigned to allow for modest but continuous exponential improvement in technology, rather than once-and-for-all improvements, *the existence of a limit depends upon the expected rates of technological change.* An experiment assuming a 2 percent annual rate of natural resource discovery, a 2 percent annual reduction in resources required to grow a unit of food, and a 2 percent annual reduction in resources required to reduce pollution per unit of output found no limit to output or population growth.[18] In another simulation exercise, Nordhaus imposed a hypothetical 2.5 percent rate of technological change and found that per capita consumption will achieve a steady-state equilibrium for rates of population increase below 2 percent per year.[19]

• A much praised feature of the world model is its network of feedbacks, i.e., adaptive processes by which the simulated economy adjusts to sectoral shortages by shifting resources. T. W. Oerlemans et al add similar feedbacks in which capital allocated to resource extraction increases as natural resources are depleted.[20] If modest rates of technological change are also added, collapse can be avoided entirely.

• Much of the plausibility of the world model rests on its capacity to track the actual experience of the past seventy years. Running the model "backwards" into the nineteenth century—an idea which violates no conditions of the model—has yielded very poor results.[21] What the model would predict within twenty years diverges sharply from actual events.

• An even more serious problem arises if one begins the simulation at a point in time other than 1900.[22] From an initial point of 1850 (using actual 1850 data for initial values for the variables), the world economy collapses by 1970.

The only conclusion to be drawn is that the world model does not capture the basic relationships determining economic output and population. It must be considered a faulty instrument for estimating the future of economic growth.

b. Growth and the Environment

In general, but not in all cases, increasing levels of economic activity have been accompanied by increases in the generation of pollutants. The composition of pollution has changed dramatically; but overall, there appears to have been a trend toward increases in ecologically threatening effluent production.

The attack on growth based on the dangers of pollution consists of two separable arguments. First, that growth generates environmental side effects which, although they may not cause mass destruction, are more harmful to society than the benefits associated with the additional economic output. Second, that growth strains major ecological systems and thus threatens the survivability of life. The first issue involves what economists refer to as negative economic externalities, costs which are not accounted for in the market and prices. The question is whether pollution can be reduced to acceptable levels without interfering with economic growth.

Technology is available to permit cutting pollution per unit of output to nearly zero for most processes. However, the costs increase dramatically as the zero pollution level is approached. Also, pollution cannot be eliminated for all processes at the same time; the waste products of pollution control systems must go somewhere. On the other hand, the total cost of reducing pollution to reasonable levels is generally not a large percentage of income for the regions affected. Investment in equipment needed to cut United States water pollution by 87 percent has been estimated to cost $60 billion, less than 5 percent of one year's national income.[23] The clean-up of London's air pollution (80 percent reduction) has an annual per capita cost of 36 cents.[24]

It is obviously not necessary to curtail growth in order to control pollution. How much the job will cost will depend upon how efficiently the task is organized and what standards and priorities are established. One approach to this task will be a general strategy of internalizing the external costs of pollution. (For a general discussion of this approach see Charles Schultze et al, the 1973 Budget.)[25] Along these lines it has been suggested that taxes on unit pollutant output be based on an estimate of the damage done by the pollution. This would be an alternative to regulating effluent discharges directly, or setting a minimum standard of antipollution technology. Taxes would provide incentives for reducing damaging discharges at the least possible cost. As long as the tax rates approximated the real social costs involved, the system would generate a level of pollution close to social optimality. Variations on this basic approach would be needed for different forms of pollution. Some pollutants may be so dangerous, or their effects so difficult to measure that direct regulation would be preferable.

In summary, environmental pollution can be controlled, and the costs involved need not be a constraint on continued economic growth.

The second argument about growth and the environment concerns the possibility of an environmental disaster. Opinion is divided on whether there is a threat of global ecological disturbances and whether this possibility is linked to economic growth. This issue was the subject of an M.I.T. conference held in 1970.[26] The conference staff papers do not predict any catastrophic ecological changes, although the predictions are heavily qualified by recommendations for continuing inquiry and a large admitted degree of uncertainty.

The uncertain nature of world ecological threats makes it difficult to evaluate the impacts of continued growth. However, technical innovation can be applied to potential ecological contamination. Economic incentives can also be provided to encourage ecologically neutral or desirable innovation.

In summary, the evidence does not support a conclusion that continued economic growth must lead to an environmental disaster.

c. Growth and Natural Resources

Critics of growth have pointed out that economic growth involves increasing rates of use of finite natural resources. Since such resources are nonrenewable, these rates of extraction cannot be sustained indefinitely. These critics argue that resource scarcity represents a real barrier to growth, one that must be faced in the near future—a century or two at most.

The concept of natural resource reserves is ambiguous unless placed in the setting of a market and

an applicable level of technical knowledge. Consider three different definitions:

Known global reserves—an estimate of proven stocks which would be profitable to extract and sell under existing technology and prices.

Ultimately recoverable reserves—.01 percent (1/10,000) of the estimated mineral content of the earth's crust to a depth of one kilometer.

Crustal abundance—the estimated mineral content of the earth's crust.

In Table 2•1, the three measures are shown as ratios to current annual consumption rates for selected minerals. Which definition is a relevant measure of scarcity depends upon the future pattern of extraction costs and market prices for resources, which in turn depend upon the rate of progress in extraction technology and the capacity of the world economy to substitute other factors of production for primary raw materials.

Adjustment to scarcity is accomplished as a resource becomes scarce and as that fact is reflected in its price. Higher prices provide incentives for producers to substitute cheaper (more plentiful) resources—plastics replace metals, etc.; or to recycle processed materials—scrap aluminum is used to produce more aluminum. Higher prices also tend to reduce overall demand.

Scarcity makes it profitable to invent and invest in resource-saving technology. One example of a case where this has occurred is solid-state circuitry which requires less operating energy and cuts the need for conductive metals in electronic equipment.

Estimates of aggregate production functions from 1900 to 1950, made by William Nordhaus and James

Table 2•1
SELECTED RESOURCE RESERVES—THREE MEASURES
(Years Remaining at Current Annual Rates of Consumption)

Mineral	Known Reserves	Ultimately Recoverable Reserves	Crustal Abundance
Aluminum	23 Years	68,000 Years	38,500,000,000 Years
Copper	45	340	242,000,000
Gold	9	102	57,000,000
Lead	10	162	85,000,000
Iron	117	2,657	1,815,000,000
Zinc	21	618	409,000,000
Molybdenum	65	630	422,000,000
Phosphorus	481	1,601	870,000,000

Sources: U.S. Geological Survey; Statistical Abstract of the United States.

Tobin, suggest that in fact it is relatively easy to substitute capital or labor for natural resources and that resource-saving technology has advanced quite rapidly. According to Denison, the increasing cost of obtaining natural resources reduced the United States growth rate during 1920-1957 by only 0.05 percent per year and resource scarcity would provide even less drag for the twenty years thereafter.

One alternative approach to the question of the constraint on growth imposed by resource scarcity is the concept of "efficient allocation over time." This approach involves analysis of what the "optimal" rate of resource use should be. From the limited perspective of economics, the optimal rate of use of a depletable resource is the rate at which the present value of future income will be maximized. The calculation is analogous to that of a business firm which must choose between investment opportunities which yield different profit profiles. Is $1000 two years from today worth more or less than $2000 earned six years from today? The answer depends upon the interest rate at which the business values the use of its capital over time.

For an economy, using more of a limited resource today to generate productive capacity means (other things equal), there will be less of the resource in the future. However, the optimal rate of exploitation is the one which balances the potential productivity of the resource in use with the future value of the resource to society. Thus, one might mourn the depleted mountains of rich iron ore in Minnesota, but society is probably better off with the iron in steel structures today than if the iron were still in the ground.

In an economy where markets are competitive and where there are no significant external effects (like pollution), the market will determine the efficient rate of recovery of resources. Consider a mine operator who has the choice of selling an extra ton of copper this year and earning a return (interest) on the receipts or waiting until next year. Unless copper prices are expected to go up by at least the return rate, it makes sense to sell now. From society's viewpoint the decision should also rest on the same criteria. Interest rates reflect as well the potential productivity of copper out of the ground. If copper prices are not rising at a rate at least equal to the interest rate, it is in society's interest that the copper be used now rather than later.

By this reasoning, a test of whether nonrenewable resources are being used too rapidly is whether the price of the resource has gone up more rapidly (in purchasing power terms) than interest rates. Harold Barnett and Chandler Morse conclude that most resource prices have remained constant in real terms during the last few decades.[27] This would suggest that exploitation rates up to 1963 had been too slow rather than too fast. Changes in the price patterns of resources in the last decade may have changed the conclusions of this analysis. (This section is a greatly simplified discussion of allocation over time. For a more complete treatment see Henderson and Quandt, *Microeconomic Theory.*)[28]

Efficient allocation of energy resources is a central concern under the general issue of how to deal with resource scarcity. The availability of nonrecyclable energy is potentially a more relevent resource constraint in the long term than the existence of recyclable materials. The constraint becomes more sharply delineated by the fact that the most likely way of stabilizing consumption of virgin raw materials is to substitute energy inputs through recycling. Exponential economic growth without exponential energy consumption is theoretically possible, but not likely. Fossil and fission fuel reserves are large, as indicated by Table 2·2. They are in fact so large that one might argue that the constraint they place on growth is irrelevant. It is probable that much greater energy reserves from new generation methods will be available within a century. The two most promising are probably controlled nuclear fusion and solar energy. Including the breeder reactor and fusion power, there is enough to sustain 1000 times the current use level for thousands of years. It has been suggested that the new energy technologies will

Table 2·2

UNITED STATES FOSSIL AND FISSION FUEL RESERVES AND RESOURCES (Quintillion Btu's) *

	Currently* Useful Reserves	Ultimately* Recoverable Resources
Natural Gas	0.3	6.5
Crude Oil	0.3	16.5
Shale Oil	—	150.0
Coal	9.0	65.0
Uranium (Light Water)	0.3	22.0
Uranium (Breeder)	—	200,000.0
Total	9.9	200,260.0
Current Annual Consumption	.075	
Years at Current Consumption	132.	27 Million

*Quintillion = 10^{18} or 1,000,000,000,000,000,000 Btu's.

Sources: Fossil Fuels: United States Geological Survey
Uranium: AEC

merely shift the limit imposed by energy from one of supply to one of heat disposal. This constraint is discussed later in connection with ultimate limits considered under the heading of "Growth and the Entropy Argument."

A test of the efficiency of energy resource allocation over time has been made by Nordhaus.[29] Nordhaus investigates a pattern of utilization in which conventional energy sources—fossil fuels and current fission technology—will eventually be replaced by nonconventional sources such as breeder reactors, fusion, or solar power. He then projects fuel demand and the approximate cost of recovering these fuels and calculates, through mathematical programming techniques, the optimal path for consuming the finite stock over the period. The calculation also generates a path of prices which would balance the supply and demand at the appropriate consumption levels.

Nordhaus concludes that petroleum prices (pre-Middle East War) are above the efficient price and that the United States domestic natural gas price is below the efficient price. In other words, current petroleum consumption is below the efficient rate. Although the calculation itself is quite complex, the underlying logic is simple. It is efficient to exploit cheap energy sources first, but at current inflated petroleum prices, investments in expensive substitutes—synthetic shale and coal liquefaction—will take place before they reflect the scarcity of cheap oil.

The question of food scarcity is the last issue to be discussed in this section on growth and natural resources.

Food is not an exhaustible natural resource, but many of the arguments applied to natural resources are applicable or analogous. Land is an input in the production of food, and it is argued that food supplies are naturally constrained by the quantity of arable land. Critics of growth argue that the law of diminishing returns will apply and that the quantity of labor, capital, and fertilizer necessary to increase food production will rise sharply. Moreover, it is said that the ability to substitute other factors for land in food production is complicated by serious environmental problems—insecticide and fertilizer runoffs, the lowering of the water table through irrigation, etc.

The validity of the criticism turns on assumptions about the future of technological change in agriculture. The substitution of other factors for land has, to date, not substantially raised the relative cost of agricultural products. Land yields have matched demand requirements in developing countries for the

past 80 years.[30] It seems reasonable to expect further major improvements in agricultural technology.

Substituting capital (irrigation, fertilizer, machines) for land may face diminishing returns, but technological change may reduce dependence on capital intensive cultivation methods. Notable progress has been made in biological pest control, hydrocarbon-based synthetic foods, and direct nitrogen fixing. Intensive cultivation need not ruin the soil, as shown in Holland, which has been farmed with increasing intensity for many centuries.

On balance, there is no strong case for pessimism about food scarcity as a long-term constraint to economic growth. There may, however, be problems of distribution and serious shortfalls in the near term.

d. Growth and the Entropy Argument

The second law of thermodynamics, or the entropy law, has been applied to economic activity.[31]

Entropy refers to the characteristic of physical systems of evolving inevitably from high organization and energy potential to inertness and low energy. This concept has no meaning when applied to the economic system, however, unless some far off time horizon is posed such as the next few thousand years. Such a time period is of little relevance to policy planning today.

Considering "ultimate" constraints on growth, the rate of energy consumption may have the most relevance. Even if we achieve the technical ability to generate virtually unlimited energy through nuclear fusion, the amount generated will be "ultimately" limited by the capacity of the earth to absorb waste heat.

The relevance of this theoretical constraint, however, is not evident. Man-made heat-producing activities currently amount to only $\frac{1}{15,000}$th of the heat absorbed by the earth from the sun.[32] Several hundred times this level, plus all the solar energy we could harness would not impinge on the ultimate limit. Energy consumption of this magnitude is far in the future, even allowing for exponential growth. If and when we do reach such global levels, the constraint will be real. But this is hardly relevant for global policy decisions now, and one suspects may not pose a problem in the future. Where waste heat absorption is a real problem in some urban areas it may serve as a constraint to that area's growth.

e. Growth and Concerns Related to International Relations

Postwar economic growth has been accompanied

ECONOMIC GROWTH IN THE FUTURE

by increasing interdependence between national economies. This phenomenon has prompted criticism of growth from widely diverging political perspectives on the grounds that: (a) growth increases United States dependence on foreigners and thereby diminishes our national security and flexibility in foreign relations; and (b) growth is being sustained through the exploitation of the raw materials of the third world.

Dependence on other nations is a fact of modern economic life and is not necessarily disadvantageous. The value of raw materials imported by the United States nearly doubled between 1950 and 1969; mineral imports rose by 231 percent in current dollars.[33] Table 2•3 shows how this compares with GNP and exports. In the past few years the United States has become a net importer of petroleum, and imports from the Middle East may constitute approximately half of United States source of crude during the next decade. The primary sources of dozens of raw materials—notably asbestos, beryl, chromite, cobalt, manganese, mercury, nickel, platinum, tin—will be other countries. It is reasonable to infer that the demand for foreign reserves will grow with United States GNP.

There is no question that economic growth has led to short-run dependence—contrast the impact of the loss of Middle Eastern oil in 1956 with the loss in 1973. The cheapest source of many materials is overseas and, consequently, private corporations have chosen to exploit those reserves first. A policy of maintaining large stockpiles of vital resources and increasing production of domestic resources to reduce short-term dependence may be indicated. However, it is not clear what role economic growth will play in changing that dependence. The technological sophistication and increasing potential capacity to substitute for scarce resources that accompany growth lead in the direction of reduced dependence. One might argue from the oil boycott experience the need to: (a) subsidize the development of higher cost

Table 2•3
GNP VALUES AND EXPORTS IN 1950 and 1969

	1950	1969	Percent Increase
GNP (Billions of Current Dollars)	284.8	930.3	226%
Exports (Billions of Current Dollars)	13.8	55.5	303
Imports (Billions of Current Dollars)	12.0	53.6	347

Source: Economic Report of the President, 1974, pp. 249-251, 259.

domestic sources of materials; and (b) reduce the rate of growth in demand for foreign resources through taxes or tariffs. This is a matter of dispute, however, and in any case, it does not follow that the rate of energy flows should be stabilized.

Exploitation of underdeveloped countries as an argument against economic growth does not stand up under today's conditions. Exports are essential to many developing countries. Few foreign governments are compliant to the interests of consuming nations, and increased demand for raw materials can be expected to decrease the ability of the advanced countries to exploit primary producers.

f. Economic Growth and Population Growth

Critics of economic growth argue that: (a) economic growth is pointless, since population will automatically restore a subsistence per capita income equilibrium; or (b) economic growth actually triggers population changes that reduce income in the long run.

The fact is, there is no verified theory of population change. However, the cautious consensus among demographic specialists leads to quite different conclusions about the impact of economic growth on population growth. One theory of demographic transition is based on historic experience and applies to developing countries today.[34] The theory sets forth population patterns to be expected in three stages of development. In stage one, birth rates and death rates are high and population is in Malthusian equilibrium. In stage two, relatively limited economic development provides the opportunity to lower mortality rates dramatically. Transportation improves, reducing the probability of mass starvation from regional harvest failures. Simple public health measures such as insecticide spraying, vaccination against major diseases and some control over the disposition of sewage further reduce premature deaths. Since birth rates are not simultaneously cut, rapid population growth ensues. In stage three, increasing urbanization, cultural changes, and the dissemination of birth control technology lead to a fall in the birth rate, often to a level (or below the level) necessary for zero population growth.

Whatever the underlying causes may be (see Gary Becker for one theory[35]) the general pattern described in the above theory appears to be consistent with actual experience. Table 2•4 shows average annual birth, death, and net population growth rates for developed and developing countries. Birth rates have fallen in every decade since 1900 in the developed nations group, while net population growth has fluctuated from 1.3 percent to 0.3 percent. For

36

Table 2•4

AVERAGE ANNUAL BIRTH, DEATH AND NET POPULATION GROWTH RATES FOR DEVELOPED AND DEVELOPING COUNTRIES
(Percent)

Decade	Developed Regions			Less Developed Regions		
	Birth Rate	Death Rate	Net Population Growth	Birth Rate	Death Rate	Net Population Growth
1900-1910	3.4	2.1	1.3	4.1	3.4	0.7
1910-1920	2.6	2.3	0.3	4.0	3.7	0.3
1920-1930	2.8	1.6	1.2	4.1	3.1	1.0
1930-1940	2.2	1.4	0.8	4.1	2.9	1.2
1940-1950	2.0	1.5	0.5	4.0	2.8	1.2
1950-1960	2.3	1.0	1.3	4.1	2.1	2.0
1960-1970	1.9	0.9	1.0	4.1	1.7	2.4

Source   "The World Population Situation in 1970" Population Studies, No. 48, United Nations.

developing countries, presumably in stage two, birth rates have remained high while death rates have fallen steadily. Evidence from the United States census suggests that fertility in the United States, the highest recorded in any Western country at the beginning of the nineteenth century, fell to one-half the peak by 1900. Hence, for developing countries in stage two, continued economic growth may actually result in reduced rates of population growth when the third stage of economic development is reached.

Thus, experience has shown that gains in per capita income from economic growth are not wiped out by population growth.

3. The Growth Issue in Perspective

There are certain aspects of the debate on economic growth which require special comment by way of conclusion. The first of these concerns the problems created by conflicts between various scientific disciplines.

The failure to reconcile methodology is frustrating the need for real problem solving in the growth question. A certain amount of the debate has dealt only with minor intellectual differences. Often, arguments pro and con do not match up and analysis is impossible. This is partly because arguments about growth straddle traditional disciplines. Economists have discounted ecological arguments while natural scientists have ignored the framework economics provides for dealing with resource allocation under scarcity. Economists have had little difficulty in discrediting the M.I.T./Club of Rome model and

have mistakenly concluded that they have settled the basic controversy. The fact is, much remains to be settled, and the polarization of experts along ideological lines can only make the task more difficult.

Stopping growth as opposed to dealing with the side effects of growth is an inappropriate focus for the growth debate. Much of the growth debate has focused on the relative importance of the disamenities of growth instead of on means for severing the connection between growth and its disamenities. Thus, experts argue whether the benefits of high electric power consumption are worth the environmental damage. This may be explained partly as political pessimism, a belief that institutions can't be reformed—if we want electricity we must accept the consequences. Yet, if one were truly pessimistic about institutional change, it would not be worthwhile contemplating institutional controls on growth. A society unwilling to curb industrial effluents would not be likely to alter industrial production in any major way.

There are several *policy decisions outstanding* on how to deal with the problems which have been discussed above given the constraints imposed by politics and nature. On the environment, there is the issue of short- and medium-term trade-offs between maintaining output and minimizing its effects. While pollution control technology is advancing and being applied, it will be necessary to accept certain environmental costs, if output and economic stability are to be assured.

There are several approaches to reducing pollution

to "efficient" levels. One, overall standards could be set and pollution outputs regulated. Two, effluent taxes could be employed to internalize environmental costs. Three, subsidy incentives could be offered to cut pollution.

The central issues for natural resource policy are whether it is necessary or advantageous to become self-sufficient (or at least more self-sufficient) in energy resources and how to go about it. Is self-sufficiency required for national independence, or would large buffer stocks be sufficient? If self-sufficiency is necessary, should we tax energy consumption, ration energy, guarantee incentives to raise fuel production with subsidies, and/or subsidize research in alternatives to fossil fuels?

Dealing with irreducible uncertainties is a difficult but real aspect of the growth problem. Research on the environment and the economy can provide some of the information needed to make choices about growth. But clearly much vital information is now and may always be lacking. For example, we cannot predict with certainty when (if ever) fusion power will become practical, or how successful we will be in designing ecologically benevolent industrial and agricultural methods. We will probably never know with certainty what environmental crises lurk a few decades ahead.

Of course, this kind of uncertainty is not a new dilemma for mankind. If technical change had ceased in 1850, society would have faced prospects as disruptive to expectations as if it were to cease in 1980. We are dependent upon things we cannot predict with precision—this has always been the case in the past and can be expected to be so in the future.

Decision making under uncertainty demands conservatism. In the case of growth, however, it is unclear where conservatism lies. The costs of no growth could be higher than the costs of continued growth.

If institutional authority is imposed to limit growth, the consequences would entail high risks. Political considerations place real constraints on the feasibility of income redistribution or control. If such measures were attempted, they might produce a marked increase in international unrest. In short, measures to achieve a steady, no-growth condition would require a higher level of social and economic controls which would infringe on the maintenance of individual freedoms.

The discussion of these additional aspects of the growth issue may help to put in perspective the difficulties involved and the need for considered and constructive policy actions.

C. A Pro-Growth View of the "Energy Crisis"

In the pro-growth view, the "energy crisis" of 1973-1974 and the ongoing problem of energy supplies reflect problems which are to be expected in advanced economies. The reasons behind the energy crisis are far removed from any real scarcity of enery resources. The problems stem from conscious policies followed in the United States and abroad. These policies had the effect of creating a short-run configuration of forces which made a significant price rise necessary to assure supplies.

One set of policies leading to the energy crisis was the environmental legislation of the late sixties. As a result of the Underground Mine Safety Act of 1969, the Clean Air Acts of 1967 and 1970, and the standards set by the various regulatory bodies, it became more expensive to extract, refine, and process the different energy products. Against this background, the combination of vast resource discoveries and lack of similar legislation abroad made the economic advantage turn sharply toward imported petroleum. As a result of these events and other policies related to imports and nuclear conversion, the domestic production of coal, natural gas, and petroleum leveled off during the early 1970s. This led to a dramatic increase of imports consisting mainly of petroleum. The sharp increases in United States demand for foreign petroleum set the stage for the most dramatic and visible impetus for the energy crisis—the embargo of the United States by Arab producers.

These structural changes in the energy producing sectors would have led to a sharp realignment of relative prices had price controls not been in effect. The price of natural gas has been controlled since 1954, while other energy prices have been subject to sporadic controls since August 1971. On the one hand, price controls prevented the very sharp movements which undoubtedly would have occurred in the winter of 1973-1974; on the other hand, price controls were responsible for the "shortages" of natural gas and petroleum products which were the cause of considerable concern.

The events of the last few years leave the United States in a very exposed position until a definite energy policy is established. Given the long lead times necessary to discover new reserves, to build more efficient machines and factories, to open new mines, and to build new refineries, it may be at least a decade before the United States economy can adapt fully to the energy crisis. During this period, the economy will be subject to strains in capacity and perhaps in its balance of payments.

The long-run outlook for energy is one of the most

important questions facing the country today. Although there can be no certainty, there is a good possibility that the goals of moderate-cost energy and a clean environment can be made compatible over the long haul.

The long-run allocation of energy resources and how energy requirements could be met in the long run are beginning to be analyzed. William Nordhaus has developed a model which accounts for the costs and availability of alternative energy sources both now and in the future.[29] The analysis suggests optimism on two grounds. First, a careful calculation of resources indicates that they are truly vast, even ignoring nuclear resources. If nuclear resources are added, the resource base for energy is virtually infinite. The second source of optimism is the price path implicit in the efficient utilization of resources. The prices of energy products are scheduled to rise, but with a more rational energy policy, the rate of increase could be relatively moderate over the long term. Indeed, the actual prices for 1974 exceed the efficiency prices calculated for the early part of the twenty-first century.

Other recent quantitative studies of the energy market are in rough agreement with the basic proposition that the energy crisis is more a reflection of short-run disturbances than longer-run shortages. If energy is used as a test case for the central propositions of the anti-growth argument, it is hard to see why growth must stop because of resource limitations. Quite the opposite, economic growth is necessary to increase extractive and processing capacity, to develop new, more efficient technologies, and to develop fuels and processes which are more consistent with the stringent environmental standards being set for the nation.

FOOTNOTES

1. Denison, Edward F. *Why Growth Rates Differ.* Washington, D.C.: Brookings Institution, 1967.

2. Hansen, Alvin. *Full Recovery or Stagnation.* New York: W.W. Norton, 1938.

3. Keynes, John Maynard. *The General Theory of Employment, Interest and Money.* New York: Harcourt, Brace, and World, Inc., 1964.

4. Harrod, Roy. *Towards a Dynamic Economics.* New York: Macmillan, Inc., 1948.

5. Mishan, Ezra. *The Costs of Economic Growth.* Baltimore: Penguin, 1967.

6. Nordhaus, William and Tobin, James. "Is Growth Obsolete?" In *Economic Growth.* National Bureau of Economic Research. New York: Columbia University Press, 1972.

7. United States Government. *Economic Report of the President.* Washington, D.C.: Government Printing Office, 1974.

8. Passell, Peter and Ross, Leonard. *The Retreat from Riches.* New York: The Viking Press, 1973.

9. Kuznets, Simon. *Modern Economic Growth Rate Structure and Spread.* New Haven: Yale University Press, 1966.

10. Oshima, Harry. "The International Comparison of Size Distribution of Family Incomes with Specific Reference to Asia." *Review of Economics and Statistics* (November, 1962).

11. Passell and Ross, as cited above, p. 127.

12. Julien, Claude, *America's Empire.* New York: Pantheon, 1972.

13. "A Blueprint for Survival," *The Ecologist,* Vol. 2, No. 2 (January, 1972).

14. Commoner, Barry. *The Closing Circle.* New York: Alfred A. Knopf, 1971.

15. Meadows, Donella H. et al. *The Limits to Growth.* New York: Universe Books, 1972.

16. Cole, H. S. D. et al (eds.). *Models of Doom: A Critique of the Limits to Growth.* New York: Universe Books, 1973, pp. 119-121:

17. Meadows, as cited above, Chapter V.

18. Cole, as cited above, p. 118.

19. Nordhaus, William. "World Dynamics: Measurement Without Data." *The Economic Journal,* Vol. 83 #332, Dec. 1973, pp. 1156-1183.

20. Oerlemans, T. W. et al. "World Dynamics." *Nature* (August, 1972), p. 251.

21. Cole, as cited above, p. 113.

22. Cole, as cited above, Chapter 9.

23. Gutmanis, Ivars. *The Generation and Cost of Controlling Air, Water and Solid Waste Pollution: 1970-2000.* Washington, D.C.: Brookings Institution, 1972.

24. Beckerman, Wilfred. "Economic Development and the Environment: A False Dilemma." *International Conciliation* (January, 1972).

25. Schultze, Charles et al. *Setting National Priorities, the 1973 Budget.* Washington, D.C.: Brookings Institution, 1972.

26. Matthews, William and Wilson, Carroll L. (eds.). *Man's Impact on the Global Environment.* Cambridge: The M.I.T. Press, 1970.

27. Barnett, Harold and Morse, Chandler. *Scarcity and Growth.* Baltimore: The Johns Hopkins Press, 1963.

28. Henderson, James M. and Quandt, Richard E. *Microeconomic Theory.* New York: McGraw-Hill Book Company, 1971.

29. Nordhaus, William. *The Allocation of Energy Resources.* Washington, D.C.: Brookings Institution, 1973.

30. Hayami, T. and Ruttan, V. *Agricultural Development.* Baltimore: The Johns Hopkins Press, 1971.

31. Georgescu-Roegen, Nicholas. *The Entropy Law and the Economic Process.* Cambridge, Massachusetts: Harvard University Press, 1971.

32. Ayres, R. U. and Kneese, A. V. "Economic and Ecological Effects of a Stationary Economy." *Annual Review of Ecology and Systematics* (1971).

33. International Monetary Fund. *International Financial Statistics.* Washington, D.C.: International Monetary Fund, 1971.

34. Chamberlain, Neil. *Beyond Malthus, Population and Power.* New York: Basic Books, Inc. 1970.

35. Becker, Gary. "An Economic Analysis of Fertility." In *Demographic and Economic Change in Developed Countries.* National Bureau of Economic Research. New Jersey: Princeton University Press, 1970.

CHAPTER 3

The No-Growth View

A. Summary Statement of the View

Major crises are being caused by the approach of dealing with today's problems by dividing them up into pieces and parceling them out to specialists. Although each specialty has something of importance to say, it is very doubtful that the sum of all these specialized inputs will ever add up to a coherent solution. This is because today's problems are not independent and sequential; they are highly interrelated and simultaneous. They must be approached as a whole, even if it means foregoing full knowledge of all the parts.

Economics is the discipline that has least justification for taking a narrow view. Therefore, it is appropriate to start with a few remarks on "the economy." These are followed by discussions of environmental quality, food, energy, and technological adaptation which are interrelated subtopics. These summaries represent statements of the growth problem. They are followed by a description of the no-growth or "steady-state" alternative.

The economy consists of people and physical goods. For the last century or more the most salient characteristic of the economy has been its enormous quantitative growth. Population has grown at rates vastly in excess of any previously known in history. This unprecedented population growth has been accompanied by, and in part made possible by, an even greater rate of increase in the production of material goods. World population has grown at around 2 percent, doubling every 35 years, and world consumption is growing at about 4 percent, doubling every 17 or 18 years.

Production and consumption are not really the right words to describe this process. In reality, man neither produces nor destroys matter and energy; he only transforms them from one state to another. Man transforms raw materials into commodities and commodities into some form of waste material. In order to maintain ever larger populations of both people and goods, the volume of raw materials transformed into commodities and ultimately into waste has increased greatly. In the United States in 1972 about 43,000 pounds of basic nonfood raw materials *per person* were used to produce com-modities, and will eventually end up as waste.

Waste cannot be converted back into raw materials except by expending energy that must inevitably end up as waste heat which cannot be recycled. Nature can recycle some wastes, but it takes time, and care must be taken to avoid overloading natural systems. Recycling is limited by the process of degradation of material and energy, or the second law of thermodynamics. Matter can only be recycled at something less than 100 percent efficiency, and energy is unrecyclable.

The economy has grown because man made it grow. Procreating is a more popular activity than dying, and man has been more vigorous in reducing death rates than in controlling birth rates. Even though the United States has reached a replacement birth rate, the population will continue to grow because a large proportion of the population (because of the baby boom of the 1940s) is now moving into the high fertility age brackets. It will be fifty years before these people enter the high mortality age brackets. The population will grow by about eighty million before it levels off at about 290 million around 2030—if replacement fertility is maintained.

At the world level, even a birth control breakthrough will not keep the present 4 billion people from surpassing 6 billion in the year 2000. Even though many, but not all, governments have decided that further population growth is not desirable, they are likely to have it for at least the remainder of the century, especially in the developing countries.

Although many have begun to question whether further population growth is desirable, only a small number are questioning the possibility or desirability of further economic growth. Among nations, the system which grows fastest is still considered the best. One appeal of growth is that it is the basis of national power and an alternative to sharing. It offers the prospect of more for all with sacrifice by none—a prospect that is likely to prove illusory.

The growth-dominated mode of managing the economy has serious implications for environmental quality, food and energy supplies, and the possibilities for adaptation.

The environment has remained constant in its quantitative dimensions while the economy has been rapidly growing. The size of the environment has not and cannot increase. More people transforming more raw materials into commodities results in higher rates of depletion. The transforming of more commodities into waste means higher rates of pollution. It is necessary then to devote more effort and resources to defending ourselves from the unwanted side effects of growth. We must be careful not to count such defensive or regrettable expenditures as "growth," and should cease treating the consumption of geological capital as current income.

The growth-induced increase in depletion and pollution have direct adverse effects on the environment, but they have indirect and longer term effects that are worse. The indirect effects are the interference with natural ecosystems which may inhibit their ability to perform their life support functions. For example, the most important of these is photosynthesis. This can be interfered with by changing the acidity of the soil that supports plant life, a change which in some areas has resulted from acid rains induced by air pollution caused by burning fossil fuels. In addition, the heat balance and temperature gradients of the earth can be changed by air pollution and by intensive local uses of energy, with unpredictable effects on climate, rainfall, and agriculture. Deforestation results in the loss of water purification, and in the loss of flood and erosion control, as well as the loss of wildlife habitat and timber.

As the economy grows, man's impacts on the environment increase. The impacts are usually of a random, unforeseen nature, and therefore are likely to be harmful. Unfortunately, the typical reaction to this heightened perception of scarcity is to call for still more economic growth—leading too often to still more depletion, pollution, and further interferences with the ecosystem. This process can be illustrated specifically with reference to food and energy.

Food is the source of energy required to run human bodies and is closely related to the more general energy questions. World per capita food production has remained remarkably constant for the past twenty years, actually declining slightly from 1969 to 1970. The world's hungry are still just as hungry as 20 years ago. Food prices, especially for protein, have been rising dramatically. In 1969 the total catch of world fisheries of 63 million metric tons represented a 2 percent decline from the previous year. This occurred in spite of increased efforts, and indicates that the oceans are being overfished. Over-exploitation and coastal pollution are reducing the productivity of the seas.

Food, unlike coal or petroleum, is a renewable resource; it is a means of capturing the continual flow of solar energy. But the necessity to feed a large and growing population at an increasing level of per capita consumption has made agriculture dependent on a continuous subsidy of nonrenewable fossil fuels, chemicals, and mineral fertilizers. For each calorie of food produced in the United States, about 1.5 calories of fossil fuels are consumed by agriculture and related activities. As Howard Odum says, industrial man no longer eats food made from solar energy; he now eats food made partly of oil.[1] As fossil fuels become scarcer and more expensive, agriculture will have to rely more on solar energy and human labor. It may be that more cropland will be devoted to sugarcane in order to make alcohol to mix with gasoline for fuel. This is the reverse of the process of turning petroleum into food that was attracting attention a few years ago. Agriculture may have to start maximizing productivity (especially of protein) per ton of fertilizer or per BTU of fossil fuel input, and worry less about productivity per acre or per man.

The drive to increase agricultural productivity leads to the replacement of low yield species by newly developed high yield species, which results in greater homogeneity of crops, i.e., in a reduction in the diversity of the genetic stock and consequently to a greater vulnerability to future pests and diseases. This requires even more protection by pesticides. More inputs of fertilizer, and fresh water irrigation are required by "green revolutions" with resulting problems of water pollution and shortages.

As suggested by agriculture expert Lester Brown, the question is not can we produce more food, but what are the ecological consequences of doing so?

Energy presents the same questions. It is not, "Can we produce more energy?" but, "What are the ecological consequences of doing so?" and, "Are the benefits worth the extra costs?" and, "What source of energy will best serve man's total needs?" Unfortunately, these questions are not only unanswered, but remain largely unasked. Only the very shortsighted question, "How can we most quickly convert fission power from military to civilian uses?" has been asked. Fission has received top priority in governmental R&D with fusion second and solar energy third. Solar energy is by far the superior source in that it is nondepletable and nonpolluting. Everything in the biosphere is preadapted to solar energy by millions of years of evolution. By contrast, nothing is adapted to plutonium, which did not even exist until very recently, and which is probably the most toxic and dangerous of all substances.

By stabilizing energy consumption now, and making careful use of petroleum and coal, there would be time to develop solar energy technology and perhaps even fusion. If the fossil fuel capital is wasted, it will not be possible to construct either a solar or a nuclear based economy.

Growth of the economy within a finite physical environment is eventually bound to result in a food crisis and in an energy crisis, and in increasing problems of depletion and pollution. Within the context of continuous overall growth these problems are fundamentally insoluble, although technological stop-gaps and palliatives are possible.

Technological adaptation has been the dominant reaction to the problems of growth, aided by the information and incentives provided by market prices. What is needed, however, is a shift in emphasis toward *ecological adaptation*. That is, there must be an acceptance of natural limits to the size and scope of economic activity. Concentration should be on moral growth and qualitative improvement within those limits, rather than on the quantitative expansion of physical goods. The human adaptation needed is primarily a change of heart, followed by conversion to an economy that does not depend on continuous growth.

In conclusion on the nature of the problem, Arnold Toynbee has summed up the situation very well:

"More and more people are coming to realize that the growth of material wealth which the British industrial revolution set going, and which the modern British-made ideology has presented as being mankind's proper paramount objective, cannot in truth be the wave of the future. Nature is going to compel posterity to revert to a stable state on the material plane and to turn to the realm of the spirit for satisfying man's hunger for infinity."

No growth and the "steady state" represent an alternative to the problems under discussion. These concepts do not imply an end to all progress or a static freeze. According to Webster's first definition, "growth" includes the concept of maturity at which point physical accumulation gives way to a steady state. Thus, "steady state" is a more descriptive term than "zero growth," although both imply the cessation of gross physical accumulation.

The *"steady-state economy"* is a *physical* concept. It is characterized by constant stocks of people and physical wealth maintained at some chosen, desirable level by a low rate of throughput. Throughput

flow begins with depletion (followed by production and consumption) and ends with an equal amount of waste effluent or pollution. Throughput is the maintenance cost of the stock. As such, it should be minimized for any given stock size, subject to some limits stemming from the legitimate need for novelty. The lower the throughput, the longer-lived is the stock of wealth. Conceivably, commodities could last too long, though that hardly seems to be an immediate danger.

The psychic dimension of wealth, i.e., its want-satisfying capacity, may forever increase due to increasing knowledge and technical improvement. But the physical dimensions are limited. It is obvious that in a finite world nothing physical can grow forever. Yet, current policy seems to be to try to increase physical production indefinitely.

Any technical improvement that increases the life of a depreciating physical stock without diminishing the service it yields (e.g., an engine that gets more miles per gallon) is a clear gain. It means that the throughput flow required to maintain a given stock of gasoline in the tank is less for each amount of miles travelled.

Stocks and their associated maintenance throughputs are limited by space, by the mass of the earth, by heat release, and far more stringently by the intricate web of ecological relationships which too large a throughput will destroy. Moral and social limits, though less definable, are likely to be even more stringent. For example, the social problem of safeguarding plutonium from immoral uses and consequences is more likely to limit breeder reactor usage than is the physical constraint of thermal pollution. The steady state will be socially desirable long before it becomes an immediate physical necessity.

Economists disregard physical dimensions and concentrate their attention on value. There is no really satisfactory measure of true value, since "utility" or "psychic income" simply cannot be measured. Value is conventionally measured in terms of money. Money serves as a kind of substitute for both "value" and "commodities in general." Money, as a unit of account, has no physical dimension. The concrete reality being measured is too often reduced to identity with the abstract unit of measure. But in fact, wealth has a physical dimension. Even knowledge requires physical organisms with brains, calories to run the brain, and light for the transmission of information. Knowledge can increase the ability of the stock to satisfy wants, perhaps without limit, but the physical stock that satisfies wants, and the throughput that maintains the stock are both subject to limits. Efficiency in the steady state consists in maximizing the degree to which the stock can satisfy wants, and minimizing the throughput necessary to maintain the stock.

This role of money fetishism in supporting a growth ideology has been noted by Lewis Mumford:

"Now, the desire for money, Thomas Aquinas pointed out, knows no limits, whereas all natural wealth, represented in the concrete form of food, clothing, furniture, houses, gardens, fields, has definite limits of production and consumption, fixed by the nature of the commodity and the organic needs and capacities of the user. The idea that there should be no limits on any human function is absurd: all life exists within very narrow limits of temperature, air, water, food; and the notion that money alone, or power to command the services of other men, should be free of such definite limits is an aberration of the mind."[2]

Once attained, a steady state at some level of population and wealth, would not be forever frozen. As values and technology evolve, different levels might be both possible and desirable. But the growth (or decline) required to get to the new level is a temporary adjustment process, not a norm. The momentum of growth in population and capital now governs technological and moral development. In the steady state, technological and moral evolution would be independent rather than dictated by growth. They would precede and direct growth rather than be formed by default by the pressures of growth. Growth (positive or negative) would always be seen as a temporary passage from one steady state to another.

B. Assumptions and Values Underlying the Zero-Growth or "Steady-State View"

The steady-state view is based on physical, biological, and moral first principles. The *physical first principles* are the *laws of thermodynamics,* of which Albert Einstein said:

"A theory is more impressive the greater the simplicity of its premises is, the more different kinds of things it relates and the more extended is its area of applicability. Therefore, the deep impression which classical thermodynamics made upon me. It is the only physical theory of universal content concerning which I am convinced that, within the framework of the applicability of its basic concepts, it will never be overthrown."[3]

From the first law (conservation of matter-energy) it is obvious that we do not produce or consume anything, we merely rearrange it. From the second law (increasing entropy) it is clear that our rearrangement implies a continual reduction in potential for further use within the system as a whole. (Entropy is a lack of useful energy.)

Entropy applies to materials as well as energy. For materials it means that order turns to disorder, the concentrated tends to be dispersed, the structured becomes unstructured. For energy, entropy means that usable energy is always diminishing, and useless (low temperature) energy is always increasing. The distinction between useful and useless energy is an economic distinction. The entire subject of thermodynamics originated with an economic problem, the maximum efficiency of heat engines, so the relevance of entropy to economics should come as no surprise.

Entropic constraints are not abstractions far off in the future. The effect of the entropy law is as immediate and concrete as the facts that you can't burn the same tank of gasoline twice, that organisms cannot live in a medium of their own waste products, and that efficiencies cannot reach, much less exceed 100 percent. The low entropy of highly organized stocks of wealth and human bodies must be maintained by the continual importation of low entropy inputs from the environment and the continual exportation of high entropy outputs back to the environment. The entropic flow (the throughput) beginning with depletion and ending with pollution is the necessary *cost* of maintaining the stocks of commodities and people. Too large a throughput can disrupt the biosphere and impair its capacity to assimilate wastes. The world's sources of useful (low entropy) matter and energy become depleted, while the sinks for waste (high entropy) matter and energy become polluted.

The second or *biological first principle* is the continual input of new low entropy in the form of sunlight. This makes it possible to maintain and increase the order and complexity of the earth via photosynthesis and life processes. Solar energy only arrives at a fixed rate and the entire biosphere has, over millions of years of evolution, adapted itself to living off this fixed income of solar energy. In the last two centuries (a mere instant in the history of the biosphere) man has ceased to live within the annual solar budget and has become addicted to living off the capital of terrestrial stocks of low entropy (fossil fuels, minerals). Terrestrial stocks of fossil fuels represent a minute fraction of the energy available from the sun, but unlike the sun these stocks can be used at a rate of man's own choosing.

Several big problems emerge from the addiction to

living off capital stocks. First, our terrestrial capital will clearly become more and more scarce, and finally be used up. Substitution will extend the life of all resources, but will not "create new resources."

Second, since man is the only species living beyond the solar budget, the human species will be thrown out of balance with the rest of the biosphere, which, because of evolution over eons has become ever more elaborately adapted to the fixed solar flow. It is only natural that this unique expansionary behavior should cause repercussions and feedbacks from the rest of the system in the unhappy form of pollution and breakdown of local life support systems. It is surprising that these breakdowns have not occurred more than they have. The ecosystem evidently has considerable slack, redundancy, and resilience. But the slack is being used up in one dimension after another. No one doubts that man has the capacity to destroy the biosphere, whether directly by war, or indirectly through the growing commercialization of chemical and radioactive poisons.

The upshot of these considerations is that man must move toward an economy more dependent on solar energy. Terrestrial capital should be used, but more and more in ways to capture solar energy. To burn up fossil capital in trivial and unnecessary consumption (such as transporting nonnutritional foods in plastic throw-away containers in trucks travelling across paved-over farmland) is folly.

No one advocates an immediate or even a long run return to a berry-picking economy; our current population size and life styles make that impossible. But we can try to stabilize rates of throughput of energy and basic materials, and direct technology toward solar energy and renewable resources.

The physical and biological first principles (i.e., first and second laws of thermodynamics, and the evolutionary adaptation of the biosphere to solar energy) point toward the eventual necessity of a stabilized economy. Ignoring the first and second laws results in excessive depletion and pollution, which in turn provokes ecological disruption.

There are also some *moral first principles* indicating the desirability of a steady state. Nearly all traditional religions teach man to conform his soul to reality by knowledge, self-discipline, and restraint on the multiplication of desires, as well as on the lengths to which one will go to satisfy a desire. The increasing dominance of "man" over nature is really the increasing dominance of some men over other men with knowledge of nature serving as the instrument of domination. This may not be intentional or always a bad thing, but it should be recognized for what it is. There is a limit beyond which the extra

costs of surrendering control over one's environs and activities to the experts becomes greater than the extra benefits. For the advocates of growth there is no such thing as "enough," even on the material plane.

The first moral first principle is the traditional attitude that there is such a thing as *material sufficiency,* and beyond that admittedly vague and historically changing amount, the goal of life becomes wisdom, enjoyment, cultivation of the mind and soul, and of community.

A second moral first principle is a *sense of stewardship* for all of Creation, and an extension of brotherhood to future generations and to subhuman life. Clearly the first demands on brotherhood are those of presently existing human beings who do not enjoy material sufficiency. The answer to this failure of brotherhood is not simply more growth, but is mainly to be found in more sharing and more population control.

This suggests another moral first principle—the virtue of *humility.* Much of the drive to convert the ecosphere into a technosphere comes from the technological ambition of quite ordinary men who think that the scientific method has given them godlike powers.

A final moral principle is *holism,* the attitude that recognizes that the whole is greater than the sum of its parts, that reductionist analysis never tells the whole story, and that the abstractions necessary to make mechanistic models always do violence to reality. Growth models built on reductionist principles are dangerous guides.

In sum, the moral first principles are: the concepts of sufficiency, stewardship, humility, and holism. In social science today appeals to moral solutions and a change in values are considered as an admission of intellectual defeat. The quest is for technical solutions, not straight-forward moral solutions. Power-yielding techniques have been assiduously sought for, while the cultivation of right purposes has been neglected.

If one accepts these biophysical and moral first principles, it will be hard for him to reject the ideal of a steady-state economy.

C. Brief Description of Methods and Techniques

The method employed in the no-growth position is deduction from first principles. The position also employs quantitative analytical techniques such as the computer simulation model of *The Limits to*

Growth type. This is an application of the systems dynamics methodology.   But, it is important to remember that the steady-state view does not stand or fall with systems dynamics.

Systems dynamics is basically a technique for converting tacit mental images of how the world works into explicit written statements.   The causal relationships are taken from accepted theories or mental models and expressed in the language of feedback loops.   Positive feedback loops are self-reinforcing: larger population, more births, still larger population, yet more births, etc.   Negative feedback loops are self-limiting: larger population, more deaths, smaller population, fewer deaths, larger population, etc.   The relative strength of these two feedback loops determines the actual growth of population. Similar loops are postulated for capital stock—an investment loop that generates positive feedback, a depreciation loop that generates negative feedback.   Then interrelationships between the two basic populations (people and industrial capital) are postulated to operate through pollution, agricultural capital, cultivated land, etc.

The critical point is in indentifying among an infinity of possible causal chains, the most crucial and dominant ones, and to determine whether each relationship is immediate or delayed, and if delayed by how much. Once assumptions have been made about the actual shape and time lag of each relationship, then with the aid of a computer simulation the net general effect on the whole system of some particular change can be traced out to a degree that would be impossible for the human mind alone.

Sometimes the results are surprising or "counter-intuitive"—but that depends on whose intuition is being talked about.   Many people find the conclusions of The Limits to Growth to be intuitively obvious.   But people whose mental model include growth as a norm, no doubt regard the conclusions as "counterintuitive."

D. Arguments Against Continued Growth

1. Depletion Limits

Resource scarcity represents the traditional Malthusian concern.   The authors of The Limits to Growth calculated exponential reserve indices for basic resources.   The index is the number of years presently known reserves would last if the present percentage growth in annual usage were maintained. Of the nineteen minerals considered, only one had an exponential reserve index of over one hundred years (coal). Gold had an exponential index of nine years, copper and lead were 21 years, silver 13 years, tin 15 years, zinc 18 years, and petroleum 20 years. The indices were recalculated using five times the known reserves, with the result that the number of years left increases, but by much less than a factor of five—e.g., the lifetime of copper reserves increased from 20 to 48 years, and petroleum from 20 to 50 years. The authors conclude that, "Given present resource consumption rates and the projected increases in these rates, the great majority of currently important nonrenewable resources will be extremely costly 100 years from now."

No doubt substitution will be helpful in minimizing the burden of emerging general scarcity, but it offers no certain solution. The problem is not just to cope with the exhaustion of one or two resources, but to find ways of doing without more copper, lead, gold, silver, tin, zinc, tungsten, and mercury, all within a period of 30 years. This will require more than just substitution.   Also, substitution of, say aluminum for copper, aside from reducing efficiency in most uses, will cause aluminum to be consumed more rapidly than the present rates on which the reserve indices were based.   Some metals have unique properties for which no substitutes are available. Some metals are like vitamins—only small amounts are needed, but they are essential. Some people suppose that plastics can be substituted for metal, but plastics are made of petroleum, and that too is in short supply, as is timber.   Other critical resources with no easy substitutes are helium (low temperature work) and potassium (fertilizers).

Another proposal is to substitute energy for materials by greater recycling and by mining low grade ores all the way down to average rock. The quantities of energy needed for this would have to come from nuclear power.   Many people believe the environmental as well as economic costs of nuclear power are too high.

The upshot is that if resource scarcity is increasingly general, then substitution ceases to be a sufficient answer. This point is elaborated later in a discussion of absolute and relative scarcity.

2. Pollution Limits

Pollution is related to depletion as the outflow from a tank is related to the inflow. Depletion occurs at the input end of the throughput pipeline, and pollution at the output end. As there are finite limits to stocks, so there are finite capacities to waste disposal sinks. The ultimate pollution limit is waste heat. It cannot be gotten rid of by recycling, as can materials pollution. In fact, recycling materials must inevitably increase thermal pollution, and indeed all energy use, not just wasted energy, eventually ends up as low temperature heat. Even supporters of growth, such as William Nordhaus, are careful to note this limit. Nordhaus, speaking of energy consumption, has indicated that "a five hundred fold increase (160 years at a 4 percent annual growth rate) would be environmentally unacceptable."[4] Others suspect that a less than five hundred fold increase will be unacceptable, for reasons of ecological disruption discussed below. Alvin Weinberg has noted that we may have to adjust the world's energy policies to take account of the global heat limit within as little as 30 to 50 years.[5]

3. Environmental Disruption

The potential of man's activities for provoking environmental disruption can be crudely assessed by comparing man-induced material and energy flows with relevant natural counterparts. Man's global energy conversion is about twenty times as great as the energy conversion that takes place through feeding human bodies—assuming that everyone consumed the standard diet suggested by the U.N. Food and Agriculture Organization. In density of energy per unit of continental area, human energy conversion is now about two-fifths as great as net photosynthesis, and is roughly equal to the natural outward flux of geothermal heat from the earth's interior.[6] Perhaps more significant than size is the uneven distribution of man's energy conversion. Ninety-four percent of it is in the Northern Hemisphere and 75 percent is in perhaps 0.3 percent of the earth's land area.[7]

Natural seepage of oil to the oceans is around 0.1 million metric tons per year, while the "seepage" caused by man's activities is around 2.2 million metric tons. The flows of sulphur to the atmosphere induced by man are about equal to the natural flows. Likewise for mercury flows to the environment. Artificial fixation of nitrogen from the atmosphere for fertilizers exceeds the amount fixed naturally, and also exceeds the natural rate of denitrification. The run-off of excess nitrogen causes eutrophication of streams and lakes.

These and many other impacts are summarized in very rough estimates in the *Study of Critical Environmental Problems* (SCEP) done at M.I.T. The SCEP study estimated that man's impact on the environment is growing at around 5 percent annually, doubling every 14 years. Of course this figure is merely a guess, but that the impact is growing can hardly be doubted. Some impacts may be beneficial (CO_2 promotes plant growth), but there is good reason to expect that the net effect will be overwhelmingly harmful. Any interference of a random nature with a complex system, or for purposes extraneous to that system, has a high probability of being harmful and disruptive, for the same reason that a random mutation is usually harmful to an organism. Even a change which at first glance might appear neutral, such as a change in rainfall patterns, will in fact be very disruptive since agriculture, towns, water supplies, etc. have all been structured around and adapted to past patterns of rainfall. The potential for disruption in the future, however, may even be greater than that suggested by SCEP's 5 percent growth of impact estimate. Nuclear power will introduce a quantum leap in potential for adverse environmental impact.

4. Social Disruption

The potential for social disruption is increased by economic growth because increasing specialization means increasing interdependence and thus greater vulnerability to the breakdown of a single part. Strikes, terrorism, alienation and apathy are becoming more prevalent in modern society. This theme will be elaborated in a subsequent discussion of technological advance.

5. The Question of Timing

It makes a substantial difference whether the limits of current growth trends are ten years, a hundred years, or ten thousand years in the future. A prediction that it is going to rain sometime is not very useful; it would be much better to know when. Yet absence of evidence that it will definitely rain this week should not be considered evidence that it will not rain. To put it another way, a man who jumps out of an airplane does not need an altimeter in order to know that he had better take along a parachute. The problem with the present economic system is not a matter of its altitude (although that is something of a problem), but that there is no parachute. Its institutions are designed for the free fall of economic growth. The system does not know how to be stable. Too much depends on growth, and that dependence should be reduced.

In the arguments above it was assumed that the limits are not known to be ten thousand years in the future, and that they may be fairly close. The timing of the various limits was discussed under the four categories: depletion, pollution, ecological disruption, and social disruption. The goal must be to avoid these limits by learning to recognize and institutionalize a true economic limit that balances all the marginal benefits with all the marginal costs of growth, and stops when they are equal.

In sum, the reasonable conclusion to be drawn from this survey of limits is that caution and restraint should take precedence over rapid growth. No one can *prove* that we will hit limit x in year t, limit y in year $t+1$, etc. If this were possible there would be no debate. But there are enough suggestive numbers to lead to a presumption, if not an airtight conclusion, against growth-as-usual, even in the middle run of 10 to 50 years. As the time period is lengthened, the case against growth becomes stronger. The timing uncertainties qualify only the arguments for the impossibility of growth—the arguments for its undesirability are unaffected by these considerations.

E. Arguments for Zero Growth or a "Steady-State"

This section will deal with the concepts of scarcity and wants and how they relate to a steady state. Efficiency and technical progress in the steady state will be discussed along with the problems of transition. Lastly, the aspects of growth that are causing a decline in human well-being are enumerated.

1. Scarcity and Wants

Scarcity and wants are probably the two most fundamental ideas in economic thought. Each concept has an absolute and a relative aspect, and the failure to distinguish adequately these aspects and their changing importance, or rather the tendency to treat each concept in terms of one of the aspects alone, has produced much confusion.

Relative scarcity refers to the scarcity of a particular resource relative to another resource, or relative to a different (lower) quality of the same resource. The solution to relative scarcity is substitution.

Absolute scarcity refers to the scarcity of resources in general. Absolute scarcity increases as growth in population and per capita consumption push man ever closer to the carrying capacity of the biosphere. The concept presupposes that all economical substitutions among resources will be made. While such substitutions will certainly mitigate the burden of absolute scarcity, they will not eliminate it. Even if a growing burden is always carried in the most efficient manner, if it keeps growing, it will eventually become too heavy to carry at all. The total of all resources is finite, and the price system and technology cannot overcome the law of conservation of matter-energy, the entropy law, and the laws of ecological interdependence.

Economists have noted the distinction between relative and absolute scarcity and have concluded that absolute scarcity is not very relevant.[8] The denial of absolute scarcity is still evidenced by reading the papers in the section, "Natural Resources as a Constraint on Economic Growth," *American Economic Review,* Papers and Proceedings, May, 1973.

Considering *relative and absolute wants* or needs, the following definitions were advanced by Keynes:

"Now it is true that the needs of human beings may seem to be insatiable. But they fall into two classes—those needs which are absolute in the sense that we feel them whatever the situation of our fellow human beings may be, and those which are relative in the sense that we feel them only if their satisfaction lifts us above, makes us feel superior to, our fellows. Needs of the second class, those which satisfy the desire for superiority, may indeed be insatiable: for the higher the general level, the higher still are they. But this is not so true of the absolute needs. A point may soon be reached, much sooner perhaps than we are all of us aware of, when these needs are satisfied in the sense that we prefer to devote our further energies to noneconomic purposes."[9]

The important point is that only relative wants are insatiable. Modern economic theory treats wants in general as insatiable. The economic doctrines of the relativity of scarcity and the absoluteness of wants has led to a blind commitment to continuous growth. If there is no absolute scarcity to limit the *possibility* of growth, and no relative wants to limit the *desirability* of growth, then "growth forever and the more the better" is the logical consequence.

Despite the prevailing economic doctrine, there is such a thing as absolute scarcity, and there is such a thing as relative wants. Nature does impose an absolute general scarcity in the form of the laws of conservation of matter and energy, the entropy law, and the finitude of the earth. Low entropy is the common denominator of all useful things (resources) and is scarce in an absolute sense.[10] The stock of terrestrial low entropy (mineral deposits, fossil fuels) is limited in total amount, while the flow of solar low entropy is limited in its rate of arrival. These facts in the face of growing population and growing per capita consumption, guarantee the existence and increasing importance of absolute scarcity.

It may be objected that this form of absolute scarcity is irrelevant because low entropy is superabundant relative to man's needs. But man's needs include running the entire biosphere, for an extended period of time. As economic growth lowers entropy (increases the order, reduces the randomness) of the human sector of the biosphere, it raises the entropy (reduces the order, increases the randomness) of the nonhuman sector. But in increasing the entropy of the nonhuman part of the biosphere man interferes with its ability to function. The fact that such interferences are now much more noticeable than in the past indicates that more attention must be given to absolute scarcity. The price system handles relative scarcity fairly well but is much less effective in slowing the increase of absolute scarcity.

The exclusive focus on relative scarcity leads economists to the approach of "internalizing externalities" via pollution taxes as the sufficient cure for environmental problems. Internalization, however, acts only on relative prices. Growth in population and per capita consumption lead to increasing absolute scarcity resulting in more and more "external costs." To internalize these external costs is a good fine-tuning policy for increasing resource allocation efficiency, but it does not stop the increase in absolute scarcity resulting from continuing population growth and growth in per capita consumption.

The existence of *relative wants* is obvious and has been recognized by such economists as Thorstein Veblen, John Maynard Keynes, and John Kenneth Galbraith. Ezra Mishan has recently made the point in this way:

"In an affluent society, people's satisfactions, as Thorstein Veblen observed, depend not only on the innate or perceived utility of the goods they buy but also on the status value of such goods. Thus, to a person in a high consumption society, it is not only his absolute income that counts but also his relative income, his position in the structure of incomes. In its extreme form—and as affluence rises we draw closer to it—only relative income matters. A man would then prefer a 5 percent reduction in his own income accompanied by a 10 percent reduction in the incomes of others to a 25 percent increase in both his income and income of others.

The more this attitude prevails—and the ethos of our society actively promotes it—the more futile is the objective of economic growth for society as a whole. For it is obvious that over time everyone cannot become relatively better off."[11]

It is argued that an economics that treats all scarcity as relative (partial) and all relative wants as though they were absolute, leads to an unreasonable and dangerous obsession with growth. The recognition of absolute scarcity and relative wants (which become increasingly dominant at the margin as growth continues) would lead to the alternative of a steady-state economy.

2. The Transition to a Steady-State

There must be a shift from an economy dedicated to physical growth to an economy that views moral growth as a substitute for increasingly limited physical growth. What kinds of institutions are required to bring about the transition to a steady-state economy, and permit its continuance once attained?

The key characteristic of a transition plan must be that it builds on existing institutions and can be approached from existing initial conditions, rather than requiring an impossible "clean slate." The plan to be suggested builds on the existing basic institutions of private property and the price system, and is to that extent fundamentally conservative. It demands an extension of these institutions to areas previously not included: mainly to the control of throughput by limiting aggregate depletion of basic resources via a *system of auctioning depletion quota rights,* and secondarily to the control of population growth by a *system of transferable birth licenses.* Such a major extension of the market to such vital areas would be intolerable unless the problem of inequality is remedied by the institution of minimum income and maximum income and wealth limits. Some such limitation is implicit in most justifications of private property, and is desirable on independent ethical grounds.

The advantage derived from relying on the price system for allocation of the limited aggregates is that it permits decentralized decision making and allows the maximum degree of micro or individual freedom and variability that is consistent with the aggregate limits imposed by non-market considerations of ecological balance and conservationist ethics. The imposed aggregate quotas are variable from year to year and would permit any degree of gradualism desired in making the transition. This is especially important because the timing of the transition in the present state of knowledge is highly uncertain. The higher prices resulting from the quota auction would also provide price inducements to resource-saving technology and to conservation, as well as an additional source of government revenue.

Turning to the institutional mechanisms whereby per capita income may be stabilized over the future, the difficulties at present are political and ideological. Once a consensus has been reached within a society that further economic growth is undesirable, either because it is liable to incur unacceptable risks or because, on balance, it looks to be subversive of the good life toward which people aspire, the necessary means pose no more than a transitional problem. Such problems are comparable with, though probably less difficult than, those experienced by the British government during World War II.

49

It might seem at first that the task could be considerably simplified if, over time, an ideal allocation of resources were to require—in the absence of all commercial efforts to persuade us to consume more goods and newer goods—that all the gains in productivity be taken out in increased leisure. But although the resulting constant-physical-product growth is ecologically easier to maintain over time than the conventional increasing-physical-product growth, it does, by definition, depend upon a continually "advancing" technology which is the crux of concern. This applies to an increasing "real" income in which services are gradually substituted for products. For, contrary to popular belief, the tendency for services to grow as a proportion of rising GNP is unlikely to result in less use of natural resources. The services that come to mind; recreation, entertainment, communications, travel, higher education, research and medicine; require prolific amounts of capital equipment and therefore also, in a growing economy, encourage technological innovation.

In contrast, the steady-state economy presumes opposition to technological change on broad ecological and humanistic grounds. In effect, exceptions to the rule are to be allowed only where the arguments and the evidence speak strongly for the introduction of a specific innovation, or for supporting a particular branch of research, on urgent humanitarian grounds. "Soft," intermediate, decentralized and solar dependent technologies would be preferred over the current "advanced" technologies that are more and more based on depletable or dangerous and centralizing energy sources. A relevent decision-making body should be staffed with distinguished citizens who can call on expert advice in order to appraise the spectrum of likely consequences. This body should be answerable directly to a democratic assembly. The market would, then, continue to work subject to additional constraints which would include: (1) the specification of each general type of product and of each type of machinery to be produced in the economy (any firm, however, could enter the market and compete for orders); (2) no technical research would be undertaken by any private body without approval; and (3) no commercial advertising would be undertaken, although private consumer services entrusted with the task of providing impartial information would be permitted and the government itself could undertake campaigns to persuade the public to economize in the use of materials and energy.

Among the advantages of operating an economy within these constraints are: (a) that instead of some sixty or a hundred or so brands and models of a good, choosing among which confuses and exhausts the consumer, there would be only about a half dozen models or types of a good which would be

different in ways that were clear and significant; and (b) that changes in specification, if any, would be made only at infrequent intervals and only when there were clear and substantial advantages in doing so. Under such a dispensation, the demand for materials and energy, instead of rising continuously over time as is currently expected would sink to a lower level above which it would not rise but for population increase.

The composition of goods could change over time according to changes in taste, and according to the structure of industry. Prices would respond over short and long periods to reflect market forces. Although some firms would grow, either because the demand for some of the products they produce grew or because they could produce at lower cost (even though using the specified industrial process), the growth of capital per head over time would be restrained by the slow pace of aggregate demand and also by a requirement that there be no dividend-retention by the firm. All additional capital for expansion would be raised from sources outside the firm. Any excess aggregate saving at "full employment" would be offset by excess government expenditures. One of the main tasks of government under such a dispensation would be that of humanizing the physical environment, a task which, considering the dilapidated and dehumanized condition of practically all large urban and suburban areas today, would absorb resources on a vast scale for many years.

Within such a social context, encouragement would be given to local governments to experiment in the setting up of a variety of "amenity areas," initially free from all motorized noise, within which the more environmentally sensitive citizens could take up residence. As experience with such areas grew over time, a market in environmental amenities would come into being through choices expressed by people in their movements.

The suggestions for a system of auctioning depletion quota rights, a system of transferable birth licenses, and the creation of "amenity areas," might be viewed by some as somewhat radical approaches to achieving a transition to a steady-state economy. It should be pointed out that the transition could also be approached through the more conventional means of changes in public attitudes leading to a new consensus, public education campaigns, etc.

3. Declining Human Well-Being Under Growth

To conclude the arguments for zero growth there will be a discussion of aspects of economic growth which are causing a decline in well-being. This begins with an enumeration of technological effects which have the potential of threatening human survival. These include:

1. The threat of *ecological disruption* resulting from larger scale and more drastic interference in the biosphere.

2. The threat of *genetical calamity* arising from increased radiation and from thousands of new chemicals coming on the market each year about whose long-term effects singly or in combination we know very little.

3. The increased danger of *epidemics* or pandemics, owing to increased travel opportunities.

4. The threat to human survival arising from the growth of *more resistant pests* and new strains of supermicrobes in response to the widespread use of anti-biotics and more powerful drugs.

5. The danger of a *nuclear catastrophe* or of annihilation of a critical portion of humanity by more horrible means as a growing number of smaller countries, often headed by fanatics, come to possess the secrets of thermo-nuclear destruction and biochemical warfare.

6. The danger that the postwar trend toward increasing *crime, violence,* and *blackmail* (including threats to nuclear facilities) will plunge society into an anarchy from which it might be saved only by the most repressive government.

7. A related danger that because of large-scale complex systems such as found in sewage disposal, oil refining, water purification, and electricity generation, and the availability of small weapons technology, the survival of populations in urban areas is becoming highly vulnerable to *sabotage.*

8. The threat of *internecine warfare*, especially within the poorer countries, arising from the continued frustation of expectations of material betterment and aggravated by the growth of tourism, communications and mass media.

9. The *conflicts and unrest* within and between countries that has begun to arise from the expanding scale of (illegal) immigration from the poorer to the richer countries of the world.

In the case of genetic or ecological risk, it might be that the probability of large scale irrevocable dam-age is slight for any single chemical compound. But, as the numbers placed on the market mount rapidly, the probability of any one or combination of such compounds producing some catastrophe within a given time span can grow to become a virtual certainty.

The significance of the risks and the fact they can only increase is not fully appreciated. First, even if society pushes on, hoping to be able to detect and arrest dangerous development in time, the mere awareness of the increasing hazards produces a level of anxiety that acts to reduce welfare. Secondly, technological growth can be expected to erode the area of personal liberty and increase the power of bureaucracies. This expansion of government activity since the war is attributable only in part to the increasing cost of security, internal and external, although such increasing cost is itself a product of technological developments. Some part also is attributable to the growth of welfare service. More significant, however, is that a large part of the growth of government bureaucracy results from the kind of economic growth we are experiencing.

Economists have failed to make the connection between continuing economic growth and declining personal liberty simply because they habitually think in terms of growth of an abstract "real" income, and not in terms of the particular kinds of technology that are the main force behind economic growth. Thus, to choose from the post-war examples that come to mind, the rapid growth in automobilization, in air travel, in television, in communication, in new and more dangerous industrial processes, has been accompanied by an expansion of government regulation and administration. The environmental pollution, of which we have become increasingly aware over the last twenty years—whether from new industrial processes or new gadgetry—has elicited legislation giving the state increased powers of control of private business and private citizens, presumably for their own protection. Year by year new agencies are set up by Federal and State governments with authority to set standards, to regulate, and to investigate.

The developments to be expected over the next thirty years or so—the expected continuation of traffic congestion on land, sea, and air, in lakes and in rivers, the increasing power of noise and nuisance-creation in the hands of individuals, the improvement of "bugging" devices, the "break-throughs" in genetic engineering, the danger of new chemicals, the power of new small weapons, the scientific progress in indentifying, tracing, and incapacitating people —will result in a public demand for yet more state control and more police powers.

Other technical developments in information processing—in microcircuits, in storage and retrieval systems that enable detailed dossiers of millions of people to be kept by large firms and Federal agencies, are hardly to be welcomed even by the most pro-growth economist. Yet they are almost certainly unavoidable. As Jacques Ellul remarks in the *Technological Society,*[12] if a thing is technologically feasible it will sooner or later be used irrespective of the human consequences.

Furthermore, as societies become increasingly urbanized and so increasingly vulnerable to sabotage and terrorism, thanks to the weapons and facilities provided by technology, the public will be all the more willing and eager to cede increasing powers to governments of over-all surveillance, and of search and arrest on suspicion. The technologically-induced hazards listed above, act to accelerate the decline of privacy and personal liberty. In its draft environmental impact statement on plutonium recycling the AEC called for a federal police force and legislation that would permit personnel background checks that would infringe on current privacy rights. Safeguarding plutonium will require restrictions on civil liberties of a kind not previously experienced in peacetime.

Finally, the claim is made that economic growth increases communication and understanding between people. This is the reverse of the truth. The growing interdependence of an advanced economy is the result of increased specialization of task. Although the economic system can justly be described as interdependent, for each individual it has become a system in which he finds himself increasingly dependent for the goods and services that sustain him on the efforts of others. But not directly, as when neighbors would come to help with the harvest or to make up a hunting party—only indirectly, via the increasing range of depersonalized services and goods available to him as a consumer.

The rapid growth of travel and communications over the past 50 years is a mechanical phenomenon. People are increasingly crowded into metropolitan areas, spend more time in their automobiles, travel more often with hopes of taking in more in less time, and spend more time gazing at their television screens seeing what is happening at the other end of the world at the time it is happening. Technically speaking, these activities are impressive. However, if it is sympathetic communication, the direct interchange of thought and feeling, that is to be our touchstone, then the twentieth century spread of transport and communication has had an adverse effect on this. Television, for instance, quite apart from the effect of its programs on character-formation, enables families to sit together, or apart,

for hours incommunicado. Where once people's enjoyments depended largely on informal contact and hospitality, on participating in games and conversation, voices are now muted in deference to the media.

The promotion of labor-saving innovations itself poses a threat to human fulfillment inasmuch as such products are designed to reduce the direct dependence of people on other people, and to refer them instead to some ingenious machine. Personal contacts have diminished with the spread of supermarkets, cafeterias, vending machines, and of course with the universal ownership of TVs, transistors, and autos. They will continue to diminish with the trend toward computerization in offices and increased automation in the factory and home, with the trend toward patient-monitoring and computer diagnoses in hospitals, with the trend toward closed circuit television instruction, teaching machines and automated libraries.

Indeed, if one takes the view that the bonds of trust and affection can grow only slowly, and that long association and familiarity with friends, neighbors, and localities, are among the most potent sources of gratification for ordinary men and women, then the sort of technology that is developing, perhaps unavoidably, cannot but lead to frustration in this vital regard. For not only, as just indicated, does it act to sever direct contact between people, the technology that is evolving is such as to transform the physical environment into one of perpetual motion, with every neighborhood degenerating into a place of transit that results from and produces a compulsive mobility in society at large, giving us time only for the brief encounters necessary to maintain functional friendships and for grasping at "instant pleasures."

Again, to conceive of economic growth simply as an engine that produces a broadening stream of consumption goods is to evade the really critical problem: What kind of a society is economic growth likely to produce?

Currently accepted indicators of social welfare offer no vindication of growth. Divorce, suicide, homicide, alcoholism, drug-taking, crimes of violence (especially among the young), plus the incidence of blackmail, terrorism, and obscenity have been growing steadily over the last two decades. Are they connected, and if so in what ways: with television ownership, with motorization and increased mobility, with the unending spread and build-up of urban areas, with the stresses produced by exposure to increasing noise, to media-dependence, or to the rapidity of change?

These are just some of the questions that haunt the minds of those who observe the advance of growth with misgivings.

F. A Critique of Pro-Growth Arguments

Several arguments advanced for growth and the reasons they are unacceptable can be summarized as follows:

1. There is a Manifest Human Desire for Economic Growth

It is argued that growth and progress are universally desired. Public opinion polls could be used to find out if the public *believes* that further economic growth will promote their well-being. Such surveys could not discover, however, whether economic growth can *in fact* be counted on to promote their well-being, and this is the pertinent question. Thus, it is the current system of beliefs that is being questioned. And the view that the consequences of continued economic growth will be detrimental to social welfare is a judgment that currently may be in conflict with the beliefs of the majority of people.

2. There is No Alternative to Continued Economic Growth

The argument that economic growth should not be condemned unless a clear and feasible alternative policy is presented, is not acceptable. If a current practice is believed to be harmful, there is reason to press the inquiry even though no alternative practices are known to exist. Granted the absence of alternatives, a distinction has to be made between a proposal to abandon an existing practice or policy, and a proposal to criticize and assess the effects of the existing practice or policy. Thus, it is unreasonable to charge that effective criticism of economic growth is invalid just because there does not happen to be a feasible alternative.

Nor is such criticism academic. Alternative policies will begin to evolve only when people have begun to think about the desirability of swerving off the growth course. There are no insuperable technical difficulties in making the transition over time to a more-or-less steady-state economy.

3. Economic and Technological Growth has the Potential for Doing Good

It is argued that science and technology are neutral—"It all depends upon how man uses it." This

way of thinking about the future is not very helpful. "Man" in this context is associated with the qualities of a god. But the applications of science are in the hands of men—men who have emerged from history, organized into nation states, ideologically aligned, and perpetually in conflict. In a society of imperfect beings and imperfect institutions, science cannot safeguard against misuse of its discoveries.

Thus, the potential of science for good is not the issue. What is pertinent is the actual application of science today and the likely applications tomorrow. Conjecture about the impacts of science on man in the future requires an appreciation of the existing power and reach of modern science and some idea of probable scientific developments over the foreseeable future. From this, we can speculate about the consequences on human lives, bearing in mind the moral limitations of men and the pressures exerted on them by modern political and economic institutions.

4. Growth Promotes Economic Welfare

The benefits of growth are said to include helping the poor and ailing, promoting high culture, and expanding higher education. If it is a question of maintaining the growth momentum in order to help the "have-nots" in the underdeveloped two-thirds of the world, several questions must be raised. First, to what extent did economic growth in the West, and the spread of its industry, technology, and medicine, to the lesser developed parts of the world, contribute to the over-swollen populations and to the pollution and poverty there? Secondly, how important is the aid given to poor countries by the West? The United States, the chief donor, gives sums that total less than one half of one percent of the United States GNP. Charity on this microscopic scale can hardly provide ethical justification for the continued pursuit of economic growth by the West. Thirdly, there is no clear warrant for the belief that continued economic growth in the West will on balance be advantageous to the poor countries. It can be argued that aid or trade or both render these countries less stable, less self-sufficient, less self-reliant, and more vulnerable. For one thing, continuing innovation in the West can be expected to produce yet more substitutes for the raw materials that make up so large a proportion of the exports of less developed countries. For another, the simple manufactured goods of the less developed countries are expendable for the West and are subjected to a battery of trade restrictions in order to protect Western industries.

If instead, it is a question of helping the poor in the industrialized countries or of promoting the arts, or of expanding adult education there, it seems sensible to ask about the sums envisaged. Will $100 billion suffice? That figure is about three years' growth of GNP at current rates. To be really extravagant, we might manage to justify another five years' growth or so for all such worthy purposes, but hardly more.

But even this is to concede more than is necessary. For with its manifest abundance of "demerit" goods that are produced in Western economies today—with so much produced that is trivial, inane, regrettable, if not inimical—we already have more than enough resources for the production of those "merit" goods which loom so large in pro-growth propaganda.

5. There are Real Constraints on System Change

It is argued that institutional resistance to major change makes zero growth unfeasible. The propriety of gauging the likelihood of future developments in the light of existing attitudes and institutions has already been discussed. It is unlikely that Americans today or in the near future would agree to a transfer of, say, some $30 billion or $50 billion annually to the less fortunate citizenry. Although such sums would surely suffice to remove all poverty in the United States, they amount to less than 3 to 5 percent of current GNP. From this growth men are apt to conclude that a little more can be done for the poor only by continuing to do a great deal more for the affluent majority. If, however, the pursuit of economic growth over the years has been maintained only by the priority given by individuals to self-seeking, and if that self-seeking is aggravated by the discontent that is generated by the system itself, then such "institutional constraints" are among the more shameful products of economic growth.

6. Stopping Growth Would be Painful

Growth advocates frequently refer to the hardships that arise when the economy does not grow during some period of time. In each of the short-lived periods of stagnation of the American economy, for instance, there has been an appreciable rise in the number of unemployed, a decline in the share of labor income (except during the more prolonged depression of the 1930's), particular hardships among the poorest segments of the population, a frustration of people's expectations, and increased conflict among the working classes. These features are not pertinent to the issue, however, because they are particular to a growth-bound economy in which a period of no growth or slow growth is the result of market failure or inadequacy of monetary and fiscal policy, and therefore necessarily entails unemploy-

ment which is the cause of hardship and frustration.

Those concerned primarily with slowing growth to increase the quality of life have never proposed creating unemployment in the existing growth economy as a means of realizing a steady-state economy. Rather their objective is to persuade the public to abandon the pursuit of economic growth in favor of a steady-state economy within which there are to be institutions for maintaining high employment levels. Once the ethics of a no-growth economy are accepted, and the competitive striving for more is a thing of the past, it will be easier to agree upon measures for: 1) removing the poverty that still lingers in Western countries, 2) redirecting expenditures away from mindless extravagance and waste, and 3) bringing about a more equal distribution of income.

7. Life in the Past Was Unpleasant and Difficult

It is argued that economic growth has brought improvements over life in the past. Contrary to expectations, however, growth in wealth over the last few decades does not appear to have been accompanied by any general refinement of taste, manners, or sensibility. If anything, there has been a steady abandonment of traditional checks to vulgarity and obscenity. Eighteenth-century believers in progress would be astounded at the technological capabilities of today, and they would be dismayed at the use that has been made of them. How on earth, they might ask, can we justify the sheer ugliness and sprawl of our large cities, their endless clamor, fume, litter, dirt, tawdiness and desolation. These are the most pressing of tangible externalities with which economists appear quite unable to cope.

The historical comparisons made by defenders of growth are unfair. The growth advocates select the bleaker periods of the past, the "dark satanic mills" and other grim features of the "Industrial Revolution." Moreover, they tend to accent those aspects of life which, just because of rising affluence and indiscriminate consumerism, have assumed disproportionate importance—hygiene, longevity, youthfulness, mobility, instant entertainment, self-indulgence, effort-avoidance. Inadvertently, they fall to recognize the features that were common to all pre-industrial ages, the large number of holidays and holy days, the lack of clear distinction between working and living, and a less constrained sense of space and time. Omitted also are the influence on men's well-being of a more settled way of life, a keener joy in nature and easy access to the countryside.

There were, admittedly, many dark periods in the past, as also in the very recent past, but there were also sunny periods and, in some areas of the world, high points of civilization. It would be parochial to conclude that today life is happier for the bulk of mankind than at any time in recorded history.

Nevertheless, the more relevent question to be asked is whether, in consequence of continuing economic growth, life is becoming more wholesome, more decent, and more enjoyable, for ordinary people in the affluent society. Judgment should be based on the interpretation of events over the last 30 to 50 years and on likely developments in the foreseeable future. And in this connection it should be apparent that the considerations that signify are for the most part nonquantifiable—such concepts as "Measure of Economic Welfare" as developed by Nordhaus and Tobin notwithstanding.[13]

The concept of *economic welfare* as something distinguishable from and addable to social welfare is not tenable. If economic developments could be separated from social and political ones, one might reasonably speak of an economic contribution to social welfare. But the range of repercussions, tangible and intangible, that flow from the economic events of the last 50 years makes it virtually impossible to separate out such a contribution.

Lastly, the Nordhaus and Tobin estimate of the value of increasing leisure can be seriously misleading. It is true that compared with prewar norms, official working hours have declined, though not spectacularly. But if what matters for welfare is free time, unpre-empted time, the picture can look altogether different. It is not merely that executives, professionals, managers, and academics all work harder today than in the past. The rapidity of technological change, and the threat of obsolescence cast a shadow over the "leisure hours" of the workers. Add to this development the thesis so amusingly presented by Stafan Linder's *The Harried Leisure Class* which depicts Americans as amassing fashionable gadgets and "leisure" or "recreational" goods in such profusion that they are driving themselves frantic trying to find the time to enjoy everything and have little or no time left over for goods maintenance, thus encouraging the throw-away habit.[14]

8. Growth is Needed for Military Defense

It is argued that unless the world as a whole, or at least the great powers, are agreed on moving at the same time off the growth path, no one power would dare to do so alone for fear of falling behind in the "arms race." The war potential of a great power, it is commonly believed, depends upon its economic strength and its rate of growth. The assumption is

that there is a pervasive technological inter-dependence which is characterized by the term "spin-off." From such an assumption it would follow that if a country wishes to keep abreast of aero-technology it should promote civil aviation.

A belief that a country should act in this way may have been appropriate in earlier times when the contemporary technology was relatively primitive, and innovation was an incidental by-product of the spread of enterprise and the extent of the market. Today, in contrast, innovation is increasingly a product of highly organized scientific research. Any notion that the encouragement of, say, civil aviation is necessary in the interests of air defense is a myth. In the United States, for example, resources devoted to research in aircraft technology could be maintained, indeed expanded, while simultaneously withdrawing resources currently expanded in operating commercial airlines and manufacturing commercial airliners.

In general terms, a policy based on the premise that promotion of economic growth in general provides a necessary condition for satisfactory progress in any one or more priority sectors cannot be defended today. It is in fact the antithesis of economic efficiency. If there was a desire to improve conventional war technology it would be ill-advised to subsidize the production of air-pistols or fireworks, or promote automobile use, or give economic privileges to oil companies or manufacturers of textile machinery. It is far less expensive to direct scientific research toward the specific ends in view.

G. How Those Holding the No-Growth View Perceive the "Energy Crisis"

The "energy crisis" does not represent a confirmation of the no-growth view. It is more the result of short run oligopoly economics and Middle East politics than a crisis in physical supplies. The *real* energy crisis is the resulting press to increase energy supplies at any cost, while taking only the mildest measures to restrict demand. Especially dangerous, in the opinion of some, is the rush to nuclear power with its many unresolved technical and social problems. The "energy crisis" has also pressured people into accepting lower emission standards on air pollution, more strip mining, more pipelines and superports.

If the "energy crisis" forces the society to look more toward solar energy and renewable resources, and to scale down our demands to fit the natural flows of the biota, it will have had a very salutary effect. Unfortunately, the reaction so far is in the opposite direction. Project Independence is an example.

One important development is the work of the Ford Foundation's Energy Policy Project. In its report, *A Time to Choose,* the project offers a zero energy growth scenario as one of three feasible alternative energy futures for the United States.[15] The other two scenarios they consider are "historical growth" (a continuation of past growth trends until the year 2000, with no consideration of what things will be like after that), and a "technical fix" scenario (which cuts the historical growth rate in half by use of more efficient technologies, and minimal changes in life styles). The zero energy growth scenario assumes growth at a decreasing rate, leveling off to zero in the year 2000. It requires both technical change and significant, though nonrevolutionary changes in life styles. The technical fix scenario is a logical first step toward zero energy growth and should be supported.

FOOTNOTES

1. Odum, Howard, T., *Environment, Power, and Society,* New York: John Wiley & Sons, 1971.

2. Mumford, Lewis, *Technics and Human Development: The Myth of the Machine.* New York: Harcourt Brace Jovanovich, Inc., 1971, p. 276.

3. Schlipp, P. A. (ed.), *Albert Einstein: Philosopher-Scientist.* New York: Harper & Row, 1959, p. 33.

4. Nordhaus, William D., "Resources as a Constraint on Growth," *The American Economic Review,* May, 1974, pp. 22-26.

5. Weinberg, Alvin M., "Global Effects of Man's Production of Energy," *Science,* October 18, 1974, p. 205.

6. Lovins, Amory B., "World Energy Strategies," *Bulletin of the Atomic Scientists*, May, 1974, pp. 14-32.

7. Lovins, as cited above.

8. Barnett, Harold J. and Morse, Chandler, *Scarcity and Growth.* Baltimore: Johns Hopkins Press, 1963.

9. Keynes, J. M., "Economic Possibilities for our Grandchildren," *Essays in Persuasion.* New York: Norton, 1963 (originally published in 1931).

10. Georgescu-Roegen, Nicholas, *The Entropy Law and the Economic Process.* Cambridge, Mass.: Harvard University Press, 1971.

11. Mishan, E. J., "Growth and Antigrowth, What are the Issues?" *Challenge,* May-June, 1973, p. 30.

12. Ellul, Jacques, *The Technological Society.* Alfred Knopf.

13. Nordhaus, William and Tobin, James, "Is Growth Obsolete?" In *Economic Growth.* National Bureau of Economic Research. New York: Columbia University Press, 1972.

14. Linder, Stafan, *The Harried Leisure Class.* New York: Columbia University Press, 1970.

15. Ford Foundation, *A Time to Choose: America's Energy Future,* Ballinger Press, 1974.

CHAPTER 4

The Electric Utility Industry's View of the Issues and the Future of Growth

A. Introductory Comments

The preceding sections have detailed two opposing views of economic growth. The two positions were presented in separate statements so that both could be reported as directly and completely as possible. By setting forth the two positions side by side it is easier to see the differences between their approaches and to begin to analyze their strengths and weaknesses.

The statements of the pro-growth and no-growth views represent two ends of a continuum. While both statements are considered representative, many advocates of the two positions could be expected to hold a variety of views lying between the two extremes.

In this section separate issues are set forth in a systematic way and conclusions are stated for each. Preceding this analysis, assumptions underlying the pro-growth and no-growth views are discussed.

The analysis and conclusions in this section are general and qualitative. They are intended to provide a framework for the detailed and quantitative analysis which follows in Part II. The discussion of some conclusions is extended beyond the issues typically considered in the growth debate. These "corollary discussions" involve policy questions of public interest and of concern to the electric utility industry. They are intended as positive contributions to the growth debate in the form of commentaries on real and important policy questions.

This section of the report concludes with a summary statement of the electric utility industry's view of the future of growth. The conclusions in this section are expanded in Part II with specific recommendations for public policy action.

B. Assumptions Underlying the Views of Growth

When the opposing views of growth are compared, it is clear that they are derived from conflicting value judgments and assumptions about reality. The dis-

agreements go far deeper than arguments about the validity of quantitative data or the importance of different factors affecting the economy. The arguments originate in divergent perspectives or "images" of the world. These varied "world views" are made up of different sets of assumptions about: 1) man and how he relates to the universe; 2) the nature of resources; 3) the role of economic growth and technology; and 4) the stability of the socioeconomic system and mechanisms for change.

It is, of course, difficult to identify and state implicit assumptions. To make distinctions clear it is necessary to generalize and overstate. However, an appreciation of underlying assumptions is one way of looking at and trying to understand and analyze the two views.

1. Pro-Growth Assumptions

The nature of man and his place in the universe are very special in the pro-growth view. It is assumed that man's unique capabilities give him the power and the right to employ nature for his own purposes. Man is adaptable and can be extended beyond natural limitations as demonstrated by the creation of machines and electronic devices which extend human capabilities almost without limit.

Man's knowledge and capabilities are assumed to make him supreme over nature and able to achieve what he wants. Man has a desire to better his condition, and his wants expand to the limits of available supplies. In attempting to improve his condition, man acts rationally and in accordance with his self-interest. The freedom and right to do this are important elements in man's social system.

Resources in the pro-growth view are assumed to expand to meet demand. Resources and economic goods are considered a function of demand and as such are relative. There is no absolute scarcity, and market forces work to slow consumption where relative scarcities develop. It is assumed that economic transactions can be mutually beneficial and do not represent win-lose situations.

Economic growth and technology are assumed to represent positive progress. Economic growth tends to increase the standard of living for everyone. The human condition is improving over time and would begin to decline without growth. It is assumed that the problems associated with growth are not inevitable results of growth but occur because of malfunctions in the economic system which can be corrected without halting growth. Technology can and will advance to solve the problems.

In respect to *the stability of the socioeconomic system and its mechanisms for change,* the pro-growth view assumes that stability is provided by automatic adjustment mechanisms which operate to maintain equilibrium over the long term. It would be more difficult to maintain stability in a no-growth condition than in a growth condition. Problems can be analyzed in terms of their separate parts by assuming a condition of "all other things being equal." Risk and uncertainty can be minimized through increased understanding of constituent parts of the problem. System parts interact automatically in ways which work to achieve the overall public good and to promote system survival.

2. No-Growth Assumptions

Man is seen as one part of the natural world in the no-growth view. He may employ nature to his benefit, but his activities and powers must be in harmony with nature. It is assumed that there are absolute limits in nature which man cannot alter or overcome. In disregarding these limits man is destroying the natural systems required for his survival. The complex, mechanical systems man has created are considered destructive of the human spirit.

It is assumed that human wants are not inherently insatiable. They can be influenced by artificial and relative factors such as advertising and social norms. In making choices, man frequently acts with imperfect knowledge. He does not always act rationally.

Concerning *resources,* it is assumed that there is a finite stock of nonrenewable resources which when used up cannot be replaced. Distribution of these finite resources represents a zero-sum or win-lose situation in which one party's gain must be at another's expense. It is assumed that the world has a tendency to consume the stock of resources at an increasing rate. Therefore, a lower standard of living will eventually result, even if consumption rates are stabilized.

Economic growth and technology are assumed to be the primary forces responsible for pollution, resource depletion, and unequal distribution of wealth. Further economic growth will reduce the quality of life. Technology is having dehumanizing effects. Continued growth is not essential to continued economic well-being. It is assumed that some form of deliberate material and population equilibrium is achievable.

Stability of the socioeconomic system and its mechanisms for change are considered inadequate in the no-growth view. Advancing technology and the growth objective make the world system inherently unstable. The more complex the economic system becomes, the more vulnerable it is to a failure of one part. Automatic mechanisms which might work to slow consumption either respond too slowly or are neutralized by other factors, many of which are constantly changing. Delays in the feedback process permit the system to operate in an "overshoot mode" which will result in disaster. It is assumed that the only way to avoid a collapse is to intervene with the use of institutional authority.

3. Comment on the Assumptions

As indicated earlier, these brief statements of assumptions underlying two complex positions, are, of necessity, generalizations and focused on extremes. Also, the method of examining underlying assumptions is only one approach to understanding social phenomena. However, this examination of the two different world views does suggest the bases for the two positions and the need for some middle view which will lead to new policy conclusions.

C. Statements of the Issues and General Conclusions

Fundamental to arriving at conclusions on the complex questions of economic growth is the development of clear statements of the issues. The first step in doing this is to define the terms "economic growth" and "zero economic growth."

"Economic growth" is defined as the increase in total production of goods and services in both the public and private sectors, plus population growth. Goods and services need not be traded in the market to represent growth. The commitment of resources to public goods and services also represents a form of economic output or growth.

"Zero economic growth" means an end to any increase in production or population. Although there could be changes in the composition of output, nothing could be gained without giving up something of equal value. As a practical matter, most advocates of zero economic growth are concerned with *limiting* increases in production and population rather than attempting an immediate and absolute halt to growth.

The "steady state" is a physical concept, implying the maintenance of constant stocks of people and physical wealth with a low rate of production and consumption or "throughput." Nonpolluting and nonresource depleting economic activity could continue to grow in a "steady state."

Specific issues on growth can be grouped under four primary questions:

1. *Is continued economic growth sustainable?*
2. *Is continued economic growth desirable?*
3. *Is continued economic growth necessary?*
4. *Is zero economic growth a workable alternative?*

The first question concerns, primarily, the matter of physical limits. The answers depend mostly on quantitative analysis although data and scientific judgment on some limiting factors are incomplete or conflicting.

The second primary question about the desirability of growth involves judgments about whether the costs outweigh the benefits. Question three on the necessity of growth relates to the functions performed by economic growth and the consequences should growth be halted. The last question deals with the viability of the suggested no-growth or "steady-state" alternatives.

1. Is Continued Economic Growth Sustainable?

There are eight specific issues under this primary question. Each will be stated followed by discussion and conclusions.

Issue 1-1. *Do natural resources scarcities make continued economic growth unsustainable?*

• The No-Growth View

The no-growth view looks at resources in strictly physical terms from an engineering perspective. Viewed in this way, it is clear that exponential physical growth cannot be sustained with a fixed or finite inventory of resources. The production of material goods cannot be expanded indefinitely.

• The Pro-Growth View

The pro-growth perspective views resources in relative terms from the perspective of economics.

The availability of a resource is a function of its inventory, its utility, and its technological accessibility. Several factors work to override resource "scarcity." In particular, technical progress has more than kept pace with resource depletion. It is reasonable to expect that the productivity of resources (i.e., the functions performed per measure of materials used) will continue to increase. The pro-growth view argues that technology will continue to widen the opportunities for substituting plentiful materials for scarce ones and for recycling.

• The Industry View

In the industry view the most important consideration as to whether resources will force limits to growth lies in the distinctions between renewable and nonrenewable resources and recyclable and nonrecyclable resources. Because the bulk of conventional energy resources such as fossil and nuclear fuels are nonrenewable and nonrecyclable they appear to have the greatest potential for limiting economic growth. Although reserves of nonrenewable energy forms are very large, expected use rates could still exhaust them within the foreseeable future.

There are two factors which moderate the effective limits presented by the finite nature of natural resources. One is the advance of knowledge of reserves. As Kenneth Boulding has pointed out, "known" natural resources have been found at a faster rate than they have been used for at least 200 years.[1] When this factor is taken into consideration, the finite nature of natural resources is significant only in an ultimate sense and in the far distant future.

The second factor is the potential for substitution. For energy this means conversion from nonrenewable fossil fuels to alternative forms of energy. Given the growing incentive to develop virtually limitless forms of nuclear power and solar energy, it seems reasonable to expect that these alternative energy sources and others could provide a continuous supply of energy needed to sustain economic growth over the long term.

For materials, substitutions are possible from scarce to more abundant minerals, and refined materials can be recycled. Both alternatives will require the use of more energy. Only through the application of energy can the process of "material entropy" (the diffusing of the concentrated) be overcome. The entropy arguments are discussed under Issue 1-7.

Both moderating factors—the discovery of new reserves and substitution—depend on the continuing advance of knowledge and technology. The timeliness of needed advances is critical. While technological advance seems a reasonable expectation, it

INDUSTRY VIEW

will probably require greater investment. As a result, the relative costs of energy and other resources can be expected to rise.

• Conclusion

It is concluded that natural resource availability could, but need not present a constraint to continued economic growth. Factors moderating the physical dimensions of resources can be expected to extend the timing of "ultimate" limits far into the future. At the same time, however, shortages and rising costs of relatively scarce resources will bring major changes in the patterns of resource use and will significantly alter the future directions of growth. It is also concluded that greater recycling of materials will become essential as a supplement to the use of raw materials.

Issue 1-2. *How do population growth patterns affect the sustainability of economic growth?*

• The No-Growth View

The no-growth advocates view population growth as a primary source of the problems associated with growth. Population growth on a finite planet cannot be sustained indefinitely, and the longer it continues the more strain it places on the earth's life support capacity. Ultimately, these strains will lead to an inability to provide resources to all.

• The Pro-Growth View

The pro-growth position accepts the reality of the absolute space limit on population but argues that birth rates tend to decline in response to a drop in infant death rates and other factors. Population growth remains a positive factor in sustaining gross economic growth. The decline of birth rates in the advanced nations is already showing up as a factor reducing economic growth rates. It is theoretically possible for economic growth to continue with a stable or even a declining population. The growth in production could be absorbed by rising per capita consumption. However, a decline in population results in a reduced work force which limits growth of output unless compensated for by increases in productivity.

• The Industry View

The maximum sustainable global population—one in which birth and death rates are equal—depends on a given degree of knowledge and technology. This has been described by Wilkinson as a technological niche.[2] Current birth rates in the United States indicate that public policy actions are not necessary to control population. The dynamics set in motion by past birth rates will cause population growth to continue for about 75 years. This factor will continue to promote some form of economic growth for that long. Population growth poses a much more severe problem for developing countries than for the United States.

If the fertility rates were to decline to the replacement rate over the next fifteen years, the ultimate population in a typical developing country such as Mexico would level off at 2.5 times its present level. This pattern would hold true for about two thirds of the world's population.[3] However, such an assumption would be very optimistic, given present patterns. Apart from the practicalities, the consequences of trying to achieve zero population growth in a short period of time by use of institutional authority would be very serious. The result would be accordion-like changes in age distributions over the years.[4] Such fluctuations in age distributions would create social dislocations and would also result in considerable waste in capital and labor in particular functions such as education. Different rates of population growth in different countries may cause strains in the world system. It appears now that in 50-100 years, currently advanced and dominant countries will have a much lower percentage of the world's population than they have now.

• Conclusion

It is concluded that population will eventually have to stabilize. However, with the birth rate currently below the replacement rate in the United States, there is no cause for concern about population exceeding the capacity of the nation to accommodate everyone. Even if birth rates shift back slightly above the replacement rate, the nation's agricultural capacity would be more than adequate. In the less developed countries where large numbers of people live on the edge of starvation, there is an immediate need to reduce population growth.

Issue 1-3. *Are there limits to food production which make continued economic growth unsustainable?*

• The No-Growth View

In the no-growth view, food production is already beginning to be outrun by population and economic growth. Further growth can only result in rising death rates due to malnutrition or actual starvation.

• The Pro-Growth View

Pro-growth advocates view current food shortages as more of a distribution problem than a long-term global supply problem. They point to the fact that agricultural technology has more than kept up with population growth.

• *The Industry View*

The relative cost of food can be expected to go up worldwide. This will have a general dampening effect on economic growth because it will reduce the amount of income available for more discretionary consumption and investment. Increased prices of food will affect the poor countries most severely. Inflation caused by food prices may also cause stress in the international monetary system.

To maximize potential food production, increased effort will have to be given to land conservation and erosion prevention. In the underdeveloped world, institutional changes, technical know-how, and increased investment are needed to increase production. Thus, the constraint that food shortages represent for continued economic growth can be moderated by technology, conservation, and new incentives and investment.

• *Conclusion*

It is concluded that food production in the United States can be expanded by technology to keep pace with population and economic growth over the long term. In the developing nations regrettably, food shortages and starvation may cause periodic disruptions and possibly violence which will work as constraints on economic growth.

Issue 1-4. *Does land availability represent a constraint on the substainability of economic growth?*

• *The No-Growth View*

In both the no-growth and the pro-growth views, land is usually included as a natural resource. No-growth advocates see land as one of the absolute quantities which, along with population and physical resources, present firm limits to growth.

• *The Pro-Growth View*

The pro-growth position sees the utility of land as being expandable by technology. In this view, the absolute limit presented by the earth's total land area is so remote it is not relevant to current public policy choices.

• *The Industry View*

The analysis of land as a constraint on economic growth is parallel to that for food. That is, the

productivity of land can be expanded by technology, conservation, and new incentives and investment. The ultimate limit presented by the finite nature of the earth's surface does not represent a constraint on economic growth which requires policy consideration today. Problems are, however, being created by the inadequacy of present processes of deciding on the appropriate use of land.

• *Conclusion*

It is concluded that land availability, as in the related case of food, could be a constraint on economic growth but that the utility of land can be expanded by technology which makes the timing of the absolute limit extremely remote. New policies and processes for determining the uses of land are needed as pressures on land use increase.

• *Corollary Comment*

There is an aspect of the question of land availability which has not normally been part of the growth debate and which warrants further comment. This has to do with the trend toward the separation of property ownership rights from property use rights and the implications this trend has for the efficient use of land.

It was decided relatively early by society that rights to land should be limited and that societal interests required that land use be restricted. This has in recent years been accomplished through zoning which was ruled constitutional in the United States in 1926. Such controls obviously affect the efficiency of land utilization. More recently, it has been argued that because of zoning regulations and other public acts, much of the increase in land values cannot reasonably be said to belong to the owner of the land but belongs instead to the society. Rights to ownership in land are being steadily cut back. Some states, Vermont for example, have unilaterally removed from the owner the right to many forms of activity.

One of the major sources of limitations on owner decisions about his land has been the recent requirement for environmental impact statements which are designed to prevent damage to the environment through lack of forethought. This concept has validity in principle, but there is growing frustration with the way in which the requirement is being met in practice. At one extreme the impact report is used by environmentalists against the owner of the land as part of a tactic of delay and obstruction. Unfortunately, real issues frequently do not get considered during this process. At the other extreme there may be no real opposition to the proposed use and the impact statement may be merely a matter of going

INDUSTRY VIEW

through the motions. Again in this case, potential issues receive only superficial consideration.

The problem with this mechanism is that it is cast essentially in a win-lose adversary frame. This does not provide a balanced cost-benefit analysis to determine the most efficient use of the land. More effective decision making might be possible under an arbitration model where both sides agree that they will accept the judgment of an independent and objective analyst and arbitrator. Considering the problem of availability of land, it is essential that land use decisions be made expeditiously. An approach which stresses objectivity and efficiency and meeting the interests of both sides in a timely manner is essential for land-use control in the future.

Issue 1-5. *Does the problem of pollution make continued growth unsustainable?*

• *The No-Growth View*

In the no-growth view economic growth must inevitably result in increased pollution. This is considered unavoidable because of the laws of conservation of matter and energy. The mass of raw materials used in production and consumption is conserved and ultimately must be returned to the environment as some form of waste. Since the carrying capacity of the earth's environment is finite, pollution presents an absolute limit to economic growth.

• *The Pro-Growth View*

The pro-growth position views pollution as resulting from the failure of the market system to account properly for common property resources such as air. Pollution can be controlled by creating a market in which the capacity of the environment to absorb pollution is treated as a scarce resource. When the costs of pollution are accounted for, economic incentives will work to limit pollution to acceptable levels. The pro-growth position assumes that pollution control technology either exists or could be developed to limit known contaminants.

• *The Industry View*

Although the pollution problem is in the realm of the physical sciences and therefore presumably subject to quantification, it is difficult to find an overall assessment of current environmental conditions and prospects. Recently applied technologies are affecting the amounts and types of pollution released, and refinements in data collection and analysis are making formerly collected data obsolete. Despite these difficulties, the Council on Environmental Quality reported in its 1972 and 1973 reports that air quality was improving.[5] While no such generalization was made about water quality, an EPA study of 22 river basins reported in the 1973 annual report indicates that bacteria and oxygen demand, the pollutant indicators receiving the most widespread attention, showed general improvements in the preceding five years.[6] Among the difficulties in evaluation cited in the 1973 EPA report on clean air, is the problem of projections being developed on the basis of existing technology with no allowance for innovation.[7]

Advancing technology and increasing investment could allow pollution reductions while output and population continue to grow. Means of correcting many current ecological threats are known, and investment in pollution control technology and equipment has been rising rapidly. The timing of the required advances is, of course, critical and the costs can be expected to go higher. Cost/benefit studies could provide the basis for economic incentives to channel growth toward less pollution-intensive technologies and into the production and consumption of recyclable materials instead of disposable ones.

The only form of pollution which presently appears uncontrollable and which, therefore, might represent an ultimate limit to economic growth is the amount of waste heat from the use of resources (fossil fuels) which can be assimilated by the earth's absorption capacity. There are conflicting views on the effects of waste heat on the world climate. More research is required to determine the climatological effects of all types of pollution.

• *Conclusion*

It is concluded that pollution problems may inhibit but need not present absolute limits to economic growth. Pollution problems can be made to yield to current or future pollution control technology and new economic incentives. The costs of such corrective measures, however, can be expected to have significant dampening effects on growth.

To say that pollution need not present a limit on continued economic growth is not to minimize the seriousness of the global pollution problem nor to say that the task of protecting the environment will be simple. The difficulties in dealing with these problems are discussed under Issue 1-8, which concerns the adequacy of current adjustment mechanisms.

Issue 1-6. *Does the increasing complexity of society present psychological and organizational limits to the sustainability of economic growth?*

• *The No-Growth View*

In the no-growth view there are social and psychological limits to man's capacity to adapt to the increased complexity of society. Advanced economic and political systems are already producing a variety of social problems. There is a level of complexity beyond which present forms of organization will break down. Small-scale organization is more desirable and more sustainable than large-scale organization.

• The Pro-Growth View

In the pro-growth view it is assumed that man's capacity to develop and adapt has only begun to be realized and that he can continue to evolve social structures necessary to sustain a complex society. It is argued that as economic growth provides an endless progression of ever more refined goods and services, life becomes richer with possibilities of human fulfillment and expression.

• The Industry View

There is considerable comment in the fields of psychology and medicine about a "general social malaise." This might be described as being characterized by vague feelings of apprehension and uncertainty about the purpose and meaning of work and life. It is difficult to determine how widespread these nebulous feelings are in the population. However, it is safe to say that they are having negative effects on economic productivity and human satisfaction.

As organizations and economic arrangements become more complex, they become more vulnerable to being disrupted by failures of constituent parts. It has been suggested that this necessitates the intentional creation of redundant and overlapping systems.

• Conclusion

It is concluded that there are no absolute limits to man's capacity to adapt and cope with complexity. Given the will to do so, man can devise ever more intricate organization forms and make them work. It is a matter of social choice whether this will be done.

Issue 1-7. *Does the entropy law apply to economics to make continued economic growth unsustainable?*

• The No-Growth View

In the no-growth view the entropy law—the physical law describing the inevitable process by which organized matter and usable energy are degraded and made unorganized and unusable—can be applied to the economic process. Low entropy, i.e., ordered matter containing high energy potential, is scarce in an absolute sense. The stock of useful or low entropy materials and fuels is limited, as is the

flow of low entropy solar energy. Growth of population and consumption must eventually begin to exhaust stocks and produce absolute scarcities.

• The Pro-Growth View

The pro-growth view discounts any constraints imposed by the entropy concept because of the long time horizon involved. A time period of the next few thousand years is not significant to policy planning today.

• The Industry View

The application of the physical law of entropy to economics appears to represent a *choice* of a theory which has negative implications over alternative theories with more optimistic orientations. The ultimate constraining effects of global entropy would only be realized in the far distant future and only if they are not overcome by the counter process of evolution. As a pessimistic theoretical view, the entropy concept can be compared with the scientific notion that conscious life is a passing accident. The two ideas provide an extremely pessimistic view of life in a deteriorating universe as has been expressed by Norbert Wiener:

> "To those of us who are aware of the extremely limited range of physical conditions under which the chemical reactions necessary to life as we know it can take place, it is a foregone conclusion that the lucky accident which permits the continuation of life in any form on earth, even without restricting life to something like human life, is bound to come to a complete and disastrous end."[8]

More optimistic alternative theories are available in the biological and system sciences. In the biological sciences the idea of *evolution* suggests the process of change and progress and the prospect of a better future. Systems theory includes the concept of *negentropy* or the power of information to increase order. These notions are merged in the thought of Teilhard de Chardin whose optimistic theories suggest that as the world evolves from one stage to the next, the quality of everything improves, the structure of all elements of nature becomes more complex, and nature itself becomes more organized and unified.[9] The evolution toward increasing complexity is ascent toward more intricate mechanisms, greater organization, and further improvements in the quality of concentration. These notions represent a "law of complexity" operating in human and natural systems. They amount to a "law of negentrophy" which is contradictory to the conclusions suggested by the application of the entropy law to economics.

• *Conclusion*

It is concluded that the entropy concept can only be applied to economics and the growth debate in a theoretical sense, and that it presents no practical limit which would dictate current policy. Ultimate entropic constraints will be felt far in the future. There is no certainty that man will evolve in positive, survival-promoting directions, but neither does the entropy law dictate an inevitable economic collapse.

Considering the range of alternative theories, it is concluded that it would be better to attack the specific problems associated with growth directly rather than attempt to stop economic growth across-the-board. The future of growth will be determined by numerous factors interacting in ways which are imponderable. The idea of halting growth represents a dangerous hit-or-miss approach to problem solving.

Considering this industry conclusion on the basic matter of how to proceed, it is necessary to review more completely mechanisms of adjustment and problem solving. The adequacy of these mechanisms will be discussed as a separate and final issue under the question of the sustainability of growth.

Issue 1-8. *Are existing mechanisms of adjustment adequate to deal with the problems associated with growth?*

The preceding discussions made reference in several places to mechanisms for dealing with the problems associated with economic growth. These mechanisms are: advancing technology, the price system, public policy and regulation, and social change. Each will be discussed separately.

• *Discussion*

Technological advance is given heavy weight in the industry's conclusions. This view is based on historical experience and the nature of the problems associated with sustaining growth. Many of these are technical problems. For example, the problem of resource depletion can be made manageable by converting to new energy sources and greatly increasing the recycling of materials. Similarly, the problem of pollution is susceptible to investment in pollution abatement research and equipment.

The question is whether it is reasonable to expect that technology will continue to advance as needed in the future. Although there can be no absolute assurance of continuing technical advance, there is no reason to expect a slowdown. Significant technological advances can be expected in energy conversion, materials recycling, and pollution control.

This is not to suggest that technology can be applied as a one-time solution to environmental problems. Continued economic growth implies an ongoing process of problem creation and technological amelioration. Technologies directed at production efficiency, resource conservation, and pollution abatement are not always benign and can themselves have undesirable effects. Care must be taken to assure that the process of generating solutions remains a human process and that it does not work to foreclose more options than it opens. Institutional mechanisms such as the recently created Office of Technology Assessment under the Congress can work to meet these concerns. The problem of unforeseen side effects is a matter requiring continuing attention.

It should also be noted that technology does not necessarily advance at a steady rate; it may take place in disjointed quantum jumps. Thus, technical capabilities are not instantaneously available whenever needed. In addition, new technology can be resisted by institutions supported by existing technology. Lastly, it should be expected that the advance of technology will be achieved at increasingly higher costs.

In light of all of these caveats about technology as an adjustment mechanism, it might be useful to contemplate what would happen if technological progress were to cease. In addressing this issue, the economist Fremont Felix has suggested that when a society stops advancing technologically, its economy takes on the characteristics of a natural system.[10] It continues to grow toward some maximum size, but grows at an ever declining rate. The growth rate of a sunflower, for example, slows as it responds to the limitations of its soil, water, and lighting conditions, as well as to the circulatory limitations of its own increasing size. In a similar fashion, the growth rate of an economy that has ended technological progress tends very gradually to decrease with age, as the economy responds to the technological limitations of its resource base. Thus, there is minimal long-term danger that the economy will collapse should the advance of technology falter. Whenever a slowing of technological progress occurs, the limitations of the resource supply serve to restrain the economy from what would then be an excess of growth. Energy might be one of the first resource supply constraints felt in this way. In short, the economy could be expected to adjust to a slowing of technical progress without suffering a collapse.

The price system, along with economic incentives and disincentives, was a second mechanism discussed for dealing with the problems associated with growth. It applies to the problems of resource depletion and pollution.

The depletion of a resource is marked by higher costs and lower yields. As costs increase, returns on capital investment diminish. The law of diminishing returns then results in a gradual decline in investment until market prices rise to match the increasing costs. Thus, the price system often works as an adjustment mechanism to rechannel growth in sustainable directions.

How well the price system works to avoid resource shortages depends on two factors. One is the elasticity of substitution—i.e., the extent to which a relative increase in the price of a resource turns users to substitutes. The second factor is timeliness or whether prices will reflect future shortages as well as current shortages.

Prices of raw materials tend to reflect future shortages in the short term. For example, commodity prices in 1974 rose sharply in response to perceived shortages. For the most part, however, the price system has difficulty in accurately reflecting scarcities in the long-term future. No one can foresee all future events, especially atypical weather patterns and political actions such as embargos. This weakness may cause a somewhat disjointed pattern of reactions between shortages and prices.

Another factor impinging on the working of the price system is government policies and regulations which have grown up to affect the use of resources and prevent the price mechanism from operating freely. Such political interventions in the economy greatly reduce the effectiveness of the price system as an adjustment mechanism for dealing with the problem of resource depletion.

The price system can also serve as an adjustment mechanism for dealing with the problem of pollution. What is required is the extension of the price system to cover what has traditionally been treated as free or nonmarket goods. This is known in economics as "internalizing externalities."

One approach is to tax the use of the environment. Another approach would be to sell a limited number of polluting rights with the amounts being compatible with the carrying capacity of the environmental resource to be used (such as a river). If such rights were specified and distributed by competitive bidding, they could be traded freely in the market.

A fuller application of the price system to environmental goods could set up greater positive motivations to limit pollution. It would also provide a range of choices. The polluter could pollute and pay, stop production, invest in pollution control equipment, shift to a non-polluting production process, or change to a new product or location. The freedom to optimize promotes equity and efficiency.

The adequacy of the price system to function as an adjustment mechanism for controlling pollution depends on whether means can be found to assign costs accurately to the maintenance of environmental benefits. This is difficult because the benefits of pollution control are in areas where the market system does not normally operate to establish prices. As a result, subjective judgments must be made, and this creates problems. The economists' approach to pollution control of internalizing externalities is valid in principle but difficult in practice.

Public policy and regulation is a third adjustment mechanism to be discussed. It is clear from the discussion of the mechanisms of advancing technology and the price system, that it is impossible to place full reliance in either or both in dealing with all the problems of growth. For this reason intervention by public policy and regulation is needed as an additional mechanism of adjustment. When the price system does not respond fast enough to maintain an adequate supply of a given resource, government authority can be used to increase production and encourage conservation. If necessary for a short period, it can be used to regulate consumption. In the case of environmental protection, regulation in the form of environmental quality standards is needed in the absence of economic incentives.

Many other specific examples of regulatory measures could be given. The point is that well-conceived and administered government policies and programs are necessary back ups to technology and the price system. They are needed to foster the development and utilization of new energy and antipollution technologies, promote the enlightened use of land and raw material resources, and, if necessary, check excessive growth in population. One factor to be considered in the development of regulations is the need for some stability in the standards set. Attempts to meet standards which are constantly changing are inefficient and costly.

The more government control to be exercised, the greater the need for public oversight. This suggests the need for greater public access to information and improved mechanisms for policy review.

Related to these requirements is the fact that existing measures of national performance in the form of economic indicators are inadequate. The system of national accounts is too narrow a perspective for developing effective public policy and regulatory strategies for dealing with the problems of growth.

Considerable effort has been given to developing a set of social indicators (measures of social well-being) to augment the existing economic indicators. Difficult problems remain to be resolved, but a broad system of social indicators could provide the basis for a direct attack on the problems of growth.

Social change is a fourth mechanism of adjustment for dealing with the problems of growth. This mechanism includes changes in values and social behavior. There is considerable discussion today about the degree and permanence of social change taking place. One view is that the rate and kinds of changes amount to a "cultural revolution" which will permanently transform lifestyles and the whole social order.[11]

Social change need not be of this magnitude to impact on economic and resource consumption patterns. Relatively minor value shifts are reflected in the demand for goods and services and consequently in their prices. The emergence and spread of an environmental and conservation ethic has had, and can be expected to continue having, major effects on antipollution efforts and resource use patterns. Thus, social change can serve as possibly the most effective long-term mechanism of change for dealing with the problems of growth.

• Conclusions

To conclude on the issue of the adequacy of mechanisms for dealing with the problems of growth, *it is believed that advancing technology and the price system, augmented by public policy and regulation, provide the means for effective direct attacks on the problems associated with economic growth. In addition, social change may work to reduce the problems by easing demand pressures and in other ways not yet anticipated.*

On the overall question of whether continued economic growth is "sustainable," *it is concluded that in the United States all of the potential limiting factors of natural resources, population, food, land, pollution, complexity, and entropy can be managed in ways which will allow desirable forms of economic growth to be sustained for the foreseeable future.* While there are ultimate limits to physical growth, these can be adjusted to over time. It is probable that unforeseen evolutionary changes in technology and society will change life so substantially that these "limits" will be perceived very differently in the future. The question of timing is critical to the reality of limits to growth, and there appears to be enough time to allow limits to be approached gradually.

The form and composition of economic growth will change through the workings of the adjustment mechanisms of advancing technology, the price system, the intervention of public policy and regulation, and social change. The changing composition of growth is discussed in Part II of the report.

2. Is Continued Economic Growth Desirable?

The second primary question raised in the growth debate concerns the desirability of continued growth. This question raises two specific issues.

Issue 2-1. *Has growth ceased to be desirable because it is having adverse effects on the "quality of life"?*

• The No-Growth View

The no-growth view sees the costs of continued growth as outweighing the benefits. Moreover, the costs are not limited to the physical and environmental problems discussed in the preceding section. They include dissatisfaction with the social and psychological aspects of life. There is a feeling that continued growth is having an adverse effect on the human "quality of life." This general concern is supported by the argument that economic statistics do not reflect changes in satisfaction.

• The Pro-Growth View

In the pro-growth view there is no reason why rising levels of consumption must be accompanied by a declining quality of life. The benefits of growth clearly outweigh the costs. The quantitative aspect of this question has been analyzed. It was found that a comprehensive measure of economic welfare has increased over the last few decades, even after subtracting for the disamenities of modern life.[12]

• The Industry View

An assessment of the "quality of life" involves subjective value judgments. How these judgments are made depends on the prevailing ethic of the society and the general moral tone of the time. In a free society, such judgments should be made by each individual for himself.

To provide a basis for deciding on the "desirability" of continued growth, it is more useful to attempt to measure the utility or disutility of specific consequences of economic output than to attempt to pass moral judgment on the value of growth in general. The outputs of goods and services are certainly one form of input to social utility or "satisfaction." There is a possibility of getting more satisfaction out of less goods, but this does not mean that more goods would have less utility. "More from less" would only be a part of a larger process by which total utility is increased.

The issue of the impact of technology on satisfaction is an example of this point. Until recently, the impact of technology was generally assumed to be favorable. Now, some have begun to stress the dangers of further technological innovation. This has led to a conclusion that technology should be halted in order to foreclose the possibility of its adverse impacts. The potential of science and technology for good or evil should not be the issue. What is of concern are their actual effects. It is not useful to critique the fallacies and problems found in science or its potential for decreasing or increasing satisfaction. What is needed is consideration of the likely results of technological advances. There is no reason that technology must have a dehumanizing effect. Knowledge can have a humanizing or dehumanizing effect depending on how it is applied. "Happiness" is not derived from economic conditions or technology. The general degree of "satisfaction with life" is more dependent on the currents of moral and philosophical thought which underlie the society and give meaning to life.

• *Conclusion*

It is concluded that the degree of "satisfaction with life" is not determined one way or the other by economic growth and technology. The "quality of life" must be determined on a relative basis by weighing specific alternative conditions and effects rather than on the basis of a blanket moral judgment. On this selective basis, particular types of growth could be encouraged or deterred.

Issue 2-2. *Is continued growth undesirable because it is based on exploitation of other countries?*

• *The No-Growth View*

As a subsidiary argument against growth it is sometimes claimed that growth of the developed countries is based on exploitation of less powerful countries. This issue also involves the related consideration of the desirability of United States dependence on foreign resources.

• *The Pro-Growth View*

In the pro-growth view the exchange of capital and goods for raw materials is assumed to be mutually beneficial and not a case of exploitation. Indeed, there is now a concern that the advantage has moved to the raw material-rich countries and that it will be costly, and possibly dangerous, to depend on foreign sources for critical raw materials.

• *The Industry View*

The wealth of a nation is in the combination of its people and its productive capacity. The developing countries need the capital of developed nations such as the United States to buy industrial products to build productive capacity for their people to use, more than they need their own raw materials in the ground.

Countries which export raw materials to the United States and other advanced nations are in a position to win increasingly favorable trade arrangements. The underdeveloped nations can be expected to gain a larger share of trade, wealth, and political influence.

In regard to United States dependence on imports, only about 7 percent of the total GNP is based on imports. In European countries as much as 50 percent of GNP is imported and exported. The geographical scope and diverse productive structure of the United States economy makes it relatively self-sufficient. The United States is, however, largely dependent on imports for some key materials. Stockpiling of these critical materials in amounts which would sustain the economy through a period of embargo, such as the Arab oil embargo of 1973, would provide some cushion against such a development.

Moderate dependence on some foreign resources is desirable because the trade of capital for resources creates markets for United States export goods. Also, the use of foreign resources is often much more efficient than use of the substitute domestic supplies.

Considering the benefits of raw materials exportation for developing countries and the shift of relative advantage in their favor in such trade matters, the persistence of feelings of exploitation presents a puzzle and a source of continuing problems. More serious attention should be given to determining why so many people who are benefiting in an objective way by their relationships with the United States and other importing nations feel such a sense of "subjective exploitation."

• *Conclusions*

It is concluded that the use of other countries' resources is not exploitative and that moderate dependence on some foreign resources is desirable.

On the overall question of whether continued economic growth is "desirable," *it is concluded that some patterns of growth continue to be desirable in improving the "quality of life" and providing equitable relations with other countries.*

3. Is Continued Economic Growth Necessary?

The third primary question in the growth debate concerns the functions of economic growth and the consequences if they were not fulfilled. These functions are reviewed as four separate issues.

Issue 3-1. *Is continued economic growth necessary in order to maintain employment?*

• *The No-Growth View*

The no-growth position asserts that, under the present organization of industrial society, the only way government can prevent unemployment is by continually stimulating economic growth. It is assumed that in a no-growth society manpower requirements, employment, and income could be maintained at adequate levels by measures such as reducing the number of hours worked and increasing leisure time.

• *The Pro-Growth View*

In the pro-growth view the generation of employment is a primary function of economic growth. The levels of unemployment expected to result from any significant economic slowdown would be unacceptable.

• *The Industry View*

There are a number of devices which might be used to maintain employment without economic growth. These include monetary and fiscal policies and a shift to more labor-intensive processes.

A decline in private investment could partially be offset by increases in household purchases or government purchases of services. Such adjustments would entail some economic dislocations, but they would not be insurmountable. While it would be theoretically possible to maintain employment under a no-growth condition, the measures required imply a major restructuring of present economic arrangements.

• *Conclusion*

It is concluded that a cessation or slowdown of economic growth would increase the difficulty of maintaining employment. Employment could be maintained without economic growth, but not without large-scale public policy changes. Current patterns of employment should and will change as the composition of economic growth changes.

• *Corollary Discussion*

The necessity of maintaining employment raises a question which warrants further comment. It has to do with the appropriate patterns of substitution between capital and labor, given changing economic conditions and the continuing problem of inflation. It has traditionally been assumed that it is appropriate, where economically advantageous, to replace labor with capital. This has served the objective of increasing worker productivity and promoting growth. As fewer and fewer workers are required to produce the material goods needed by the society, it may be necessary to reconsider the advisability of a continued drive toward capital intensity. Some moderation of this objective appears appropriate as employment patterns find some middle ground between the traditional industrial era idea of everybody holding a "job" and the post-industrial notion of widespread "leisure." Work will continue to be a social and psychological necessity, but it may need to be structured differently than in the past. The emphasis on jobs as the only source of income and as a predominant human activity may be tempered by other forms of action such as community participation, continuing education, and other activities now considered leisure-time pursuits.

Issue 3-2. *Is continued economic growth necessary to overcome poverty and improve conditions for the poor?*

• *The No-Growth View*

In the no-growth view economic growth has failed to solve the problem of inequality in the distribution of income. Growth works against measures needed to correct social and economic imbalances.

• *The Pro-Growth View*

Pro-growth advocates feel that disparities in the distribution of income are compensated for by growth which makes it possible for everyone to have more each year. Also, large-scale redistribution of income is considered politically infeasible. Therefore, growth is the only way poverty can be reduced.

• *The Industry View*

After a prolonged period of economic growth, poverty remains a national concern. There is no assurance that these relative differences will necessarily be alleviated by more growth, although with growth there has been a slight narrowing of the differences. At the same time, there is no basis on which to expect that a move toward zero growth would improve the prospects for a redistribution of income. To the contrary, increased competition for income might work to the disadvantage of the poor.

There are several potential approaches to achieving greater social equality under a condition of continued growth. The following examples have been pointed out by Daniel Moynihan: greater equalization of incomes; distribution of a greater proportion of goods and services outside the market system, as in health and medical care, recreation, retirement benefits, schooling, transportation, and housing; or limiting what the rich can do with their money.[13]

It is essential to recognize the difference between the developing and developed countries in regard to growth and the problem of poverty. In the poor countries continued economic growth is a necessity to avoid famine. A no-growth policy in these areas would be tantamount to condemning large numbers of human beings to death. Growth in the poor areas of the world is an absolute necessity, at least until present rates of population increase can be brought under control.

• *Conclusion*

It is concluded that continued economic growth will not necessarily end poverty or correct the unequal distribution of income. Growth, however, has and will continue to improve the absolute conditions of the poor as compared to what could be expected if growth were stopped. The cessation of growth could lead to conflict between the rich and the poor countries and also between the haves and have-nots in the United States.

Issue 3-3. *Is economic growth necessary to finance cleaning up of the environment?*

• *The No-Growth View*

The no-growth position does not appear to address the argument that growth provides funds needed to finance cleaning up the environment.

• *The Pro-Growth View*

The pro-growth view sees the environmental clean up as requiring substantial investment which, together with the capital needed to renew production capacity and increase output, is straining the financial capacity of the economy.

• *The Industry View*

Continued research and development will be required to discover how to deal with the environmental imbalances created during the years when ecological interconnections were less apparent. Continued large investments in environmental clean-up facilities will also be required. Investment in such research, development, and facilities could be continued under a condition of slowed growth. However, it would seem more likely that if growth were to slow down, the effects would be felt first in the form of cutbacks in those activities with less immediate and less direct payoffs. Research, development and investment in pollution control technology is in this category.

• *Conclusion*

It is concluded that economic growth provides investment capital and advanced technology needed for restoring the environment. Funds for environmental research could be provided under a condition of slowed growth, but at greater relative cost.

Issue 3-4. *Is continued economic growth necessary in order to maintain a favorable position in relation to other countries in regard to the balance of payments and maintenance of national defense?*

• *The No-Growth View*

No-growth advocates argue that the balance of payments problem is based on fallacious premises. It is believed that the expenditures needed for national defense could be supported under a no-growth condition.

• *The Pro-Growth View*

In the pro-growth view international competition is another problem suggesting the need for growth. Growth is necessary in order to maintain a positive balance of payments and to support national defense.

• *The Industry View*

The area of international competition and balance of payments is one of the most complex in economics. It involves international comparisons of productivity for which there are no good means of measurement. One approach is to compare rates of productivity increase. This must then be balanced against rates of inflation to determine any competitive advantage. Countries which are able to increase productivity and control inflation will have an advantage over those which do not.

It seems clear that a unilateral decision by any country to stop economic growth without consideration of its international effects would be a disastrous failure. As long as present worldwide policies are continued, no one country can reject the growth objective completely. Any shift away from growth would have to take place internationally over an extended period.

A reduction of growth in the United States would not necessarily bring a drop in world production. Over time, it would result in the transfer of production activities from the United States to other countries. Balance of payments deficits would have a weakening effect on the dollar and the national economy.

The nation's national defense capacity rests on the economy's production potential. A component of

INDUSTRY VIEW

production capacity could be allocated to defense whether the economy was in a growth or "steady-state" mode. However, unless other military powers also adopted a "steady-state" mode, it would require ever increasing proportions of total United States output to maintain a comparable defense posture. In either a growth or no-growth situation, defense expenditures represent a drag on economic welfare.

• *Conclusion*

It is concluded that continued economic growth is helpful in maintaining a favorable position relative to other competing nations in the field of international trade. Economic growth also increases the production capacity for national defense, but sufficient capacity could possibly be maintained without additional growth.

On the overall primary question of the "necessity" of continued growth, *it is concluded that the objective of maintaining employment would be met more easily if growth continues than through the measures that would be required to provide employment under conditions of slow growth. Also, continued economic growth is helpful in improving the absolute conditions of the poor, financing cleaning up the environment, and maintaining a favorable position in relations with other countries.*

4. Is Zero Economic Growth a Workable Alternative?

The final primary question concerns the viability of no growth or a "steady state." There are many specific issues associated with the question of the practical feasibility of zero-economic growth, but they cannot be separated as distinctly as the questions about continued growth. Therefore, this section consists of a discussion of the primary question itself. There is a review of concrete proposals for achieving zero growth. Then attention is directed at questions related to the control of technology, the redistribution of income, the transition to a no-growth condition, and the implications associated with the use of institutional authority to limit growth.

Proposals for achieving zero growth tend to be stated in general terms. There are, however, six proposals for specific actions which will be discussed.

Three fiscal measures are proposed in "A Blueprint for Survival":[14] 1) a raw materials tax which increases with the scarcity of the raw material in question, and is designed to enable reserves to last over an arbitrary period of time, 2) an amortization tax based on the estimated life of the product (for example, 100 percent for products designed to last one year and zero for those designed to last 100 years

or more), and 3) a power tax that would penalize power-intensive processes.

A raw materials tax would be feasible to the degree that the availability of different raw materials could be determined. Since reserves and resources are a function of knowledge which is constantly changing, it would be difficult to administer such a tax. It would also create distortions in world markets unless it was administered uniformly by all countries. An amortization tax and a tax on power-intensive processes would present similar problems of calculation and administration. Presumably, power-intensive pollution control processes would be excluded.

The fourth proposal is a quota auction program suggested by Daly to limit the use of resources.[15] Quotas would be set on new depletion of each basic resource during a given time. The right to deplete to the amount of each quota could be auctioned off by the government at the beginning of each time period.

Such a program would create a market within a market. Given adequate administrative machinery, it could probably be made to work. It would, however, be subject to manipulation and abuses.

Daly also advocates a system of transferable birth licenses to control aggregate births. This idea involves one of the most sensitive and hazardous of political issues. Administration would require an enforcement capability that would be faced with difficult moral choices.

Both proposals for birth licenses and a resource quota auction system are theoretically feasible, but they present formidable political and administrative problems.

The sixth proposal, by Mishan, is to establish amenity rights comparable to property rights.[16] It would require the designation of special amenity areas. This could present legal problems in regard to existing property rights. The related administrative problems could probably be managed, however. Amenity areas could be created as experiments at the local level on a voluntary basis. Such areas could be expanded or reduced in response to the choices of people in the areas affected. It is clear that the maintenance of environmental amenities would be at the cost of a variety of restrictions and regulations on living and economic patterns.

It is concluded that all of the proposed actions for achieving zero growth are theoretically feasible, but that they would be very difficult to make work unless the public was convinced they were essential in order to avert a major crisis and/or an authoritarian rule was imposed.

Control of technology. Overt action to halt technological advance is sometimes suggested as part of a zero-growth strategy. However, this would be inconsistent with conservation and environmental objectives. It would reduce the potential for substitution of lower for higher grade resources required to maintain the constant flow of resources in a "steady state." It would also foreclose improvements in technological control of pollution needed to avoid overburdening natural absorption capacities. In order to sustain zero-economic growth it would be necessary to achieve even more advanced technology and scientific understanding. It should be noted that some zero-growth advocates agree that a "steady state" would require an advancing technology.

It is concluded that a lack of technical progress would be incompatible with a viable "steady state." This conclusion has implications for the growth of investment and capital stock. If technical advance is to be maintained, it probably will require some growth in investment and capital stocks for research and development.

Redistribution of income would be a major problem associated with a zero-growth condition. In theory, the issue of redistribution of income is separable from the question of economic growth. A society with zero-growth rates could conceivably range from a state of considerable equality to one of gross inequality. However, it seems unlikely that the majority of lower income people would accept the lesser chance for a higher standard of living implied by a zero-growth condition. Even recognizing that no single individual would be frozen at his present level of material goods, zero growth would reduce the probability of "getting ahead." Regardless of the individual's position in society, he has always been able to hope that he will have it better next year than he had it last year.

Economic growth generates hope, not so much by raising the minimum level of the poorest, but by providing opportunities for poor individuals to rise into more affluent groups. "Since the end of World War II, the number of individuals in professional and technical occupations has increased at over three-times the growth rate of the labor force as a whole."[17] As growth began to slow, the hope for material improvement would be greatly reduced, and the symptoms of a class struggle could be expected to become manifest. This process has been observable in Great Britain recently as labor unions have periodically brought the economy to a virtual standstill in attempts to get a larger share of national income.

The expectation of growth has also been the basis on which capital is continuously invested and reinvested in industry. Without the prospect of growth,

capital flow into industry would begin to slow. In a zero growth economy net investment would be zero, but this would not mean the absence of a capital market. Under such conditions capital savings could begin flowing into relatively unproductive investments such as real estate. Savings could also slow.

It must be concluded that zero-economic growth could only be achieved within a framework of a political-economic system in which income was distributed more equally than it is at the present time.

Considering the possibility of income redistribution, it is useful to note what the historical experience has been. First, income distribution within industrialized societies is remarkably constant from country to country. Japan is one exception where there is a more nearly equal distribution. Income distributions in developed countries have remained fairly stable during times of peace.[18] Low-growth societies in history have not had equal income distributions. The historical experience with income redistribution does not mean that some relative redistributions would not be politically feasible in the future. It does suggest, however, that the probability of major change in this area is low.

The larger question associated with feasibility of redistribution of income is as it applies to developed versus underdeveloped nations. Pressure for equalization has already been observed in the form of confrontations between developed and underdeveloped countries. It can be assumed that the capacity and inclination of the United States to share with other countries would diminish under a steady-state condition.

It is concluded that zero growth would have to be accompanied by a relative redistribution of income within the United States and that the likelihood of this is low. At the international level, it is more likely that equalization could be achieved by raising the level of poorer countries than by lowering the level of the richer ones.

Managing a transition from growth to no growth presents major questions about the workability of zero growth. Some advocates of zero growth contend that it is enough to challenge people to think about the directions in which growth is taking us. It is asserted that only when people have recognized the need for new directions and values will it be possible to get them to consider possible strategies. This approach may have some validity, but it also has the risk of creating uncertainty and undermining the human spirit. It can have a demoralizing effect.

A more direct attempt to address the problems of adjusting to a zero-growth system has been made by

Donella and Dennis Meadows, authors of *The Limits to Growth* report.

"One glaring problem confronts mankind. If it should choose to conceive of man as a humble part of the biosphere, there is essentially no body of knowledge from which to design a new institution and values consistent with that concept of man. Two hundred years of growth have left biases and blind spots throughout the physical and social sciences. There is today no economic theory of a technological-based society in which there are essentially zero interest rates, no net accumulation to society's productive capital, and in which the principal concern is equality rather than growth. There is no equilibrium sociology which is concerned with the social aspects of a stable population, whose age composition is skewed toward the elderly. There is no equilibrium political science in which we might look for clues to the ways democratic choice could be exercised when short-term material gain is ruled out as the basis for political success. There is no equilibrium technology that places high emphasis on the recycling of all matter, on the use of the sun's pollution-free energy, and on the minimization of both matter and energy flows. There is no psychology for the steady state which might provide man with a new self-image and with feasible aspirations in a system where material output is constant and in balance with the globe's finite limits."[19]

This expression about the problems of managing a transition from growth to no growth by two of the principal advocates of zero growth is a particularly significant commentary about the workability of zero growth. However, there are still other factors to be considered.

From an economy management perspective, internal adjustments are more easily performed under conditions of growth than in a "steady state." In a growing system mistakes can be easily corrected, e.g., if too much resources are committed to one sector this can be corrected by holding back for a while until the rest of the system catches up. In a no-growth system any increase in one part would have to be accompanied by a decline in another, and this is much more difficult to manage.

An attempt to achieve a steady-state global economy would require the development of advanced international agreements in the fields of trade, macroeconomics, and environmental control, all of which are intimately interrelated. Acceptance on the part of both rich and poor countries of a set of standards in these areas does not seem to be forthcoming in the near future. It is unrealistic to expect any revolutionary developments in these areas. The only realistic expectation is for marginal changes resulting from incremental policy shifts.

It is concluded that the transition to a no-growth condition presents problems which are beyond the state-of-the-arts of economy management and democratic decision making; and, therefore, zero growth is not a workable alternative under the present United States political system and the world economic system.

The use of institutional authority would be required for a transition to zero growth. A "steady state" is a condition that would have to be imposed if it was to be accomplished in a short period of time.

As suggested above, a zero-growth condition would greatly intensify the forces under the headings of class struggle, racial conflict, and trade union disputes. It seems doubtful that these forces could be contained within a zero-growth society or that such a zero-growth condition could even be achieved without some form of authoritarian rule. The use of institutional authority to bring about zero growth would represent an infringement upon *individual freedom.* Speaking of the "crisis of industrialized nations," Dennis Gabor, the physicist, has said:

"What we have to lose, what is at stake, is the most precious thing our civilization has given us, in addition to material satisfaction—an unusual degree of freedom. No other civilization before us allowed so much individual freedom. This freedom is now in very, very considerable danger."[20]

The movement toward centralized authority that would be necessary to control growth would reduce the responsiveness of the economic and political systems to change. Centralization would constrict the flow of information and narrow the pool of talent available to develop adaptive responses to problems. The solution of the problems associated with growth lies in the decentralization of power so that those who have the knowledge and confidence to use it can work to solve the problems. This is the approach being increasingly advanced in management theory and practice.

An authoritarian rule might theoretically work more effectively *if* the leader were fully aware of all the questions and problems which face him. Unfortunately, this is not and cannot be the case under the conditions of complexity which make up the problems of growth. The other fallacy in the turn to institutional authority lies in the famous quotation from Lord Acton that power tends to corrupt, and "absolute power corrupts absolutely."

It has been suggested that one result of a zero economic growth condition would be a greater sense of community. This is an extremely optimistic view of human behavior under scarcity, as illustrated by the experience with the gasoline shortage of 1973-1974.

It is concluded that a zero-growth condition would be workable only if it were enforced by strong institutional authority which infringed heavily on individual freedom. In the absence of such authoritarian rule, zero growth could be expected to be attended by considerable human suffering resulting from conflicts within and between the world's nations.

On the overall question of the workability of zero economic growth, *it is concluded that a transition to a zero-growth condition presents major political and administrative problems which could only be overcome by the imposition of institutional authority with a commensurate loss of individual freedom and that this is not an acceptable nor workable alternative.*

This conclusion in no way denies the validity of many of the concerns raised by zero-growth advocates. However, the critics tend to project a sense of hopelessness, a feeling of being backed up against the wall. In place of broadening the search for solutions, this intensifies efforts to gain one's own share of the shrinking resources.

The cautions of the no-growth position are not useful unless they are accompanied by suggestions of hope and feasible alternatives. The forecast of a doomsday future can easily become a self-fulfilling prophecy. If they are to take place, the changes leading to the profound transition from growth to no growth would best be achieved in an incremental and evolutionary fashion. It is believed the process would require education over generations.

D. Statement of the Electric Utility Industry's View of the Future of Growth

Before describing the industry's view of the future of growth, two general conclusions can be drawn about the current status of the growth controversy. First, there are two different types or levels of opposition to economic growth. At one level there is the intellectual debate about the continuation or termination of economic growth in general. This debate is in theoretical terms and it involves only a relatively small number of intellectuals and researchers. The concepts and arguments associated with the no-growth position in this debate are, however, being broadly communicated and used.

A second level of opposition springs up against specific developments and projects. Many people oppose growth in one form or another in their own communities. This opposition is based on practical, self-interest considerations at the moment. The ideas and rhetoric of no growth are used by those involved in the pursuit of these limited objectives. For the most part, however, such people are *not* opposed to growth in general and would not subscribe to the assumptions underlying the no-growth view. Nevertheless, opposition to a variety of individual projects works to inhibit overall growth.

The different levels of opposition and the diversity of motives associated with antigrowth advocates make it difficult to define a no-growth position and assess the degree of support it has among the public at large.

The second conclusion has to do with the requirement for planning and control inherent in the no-growth position as it is associated with the ecology movement. Some who advocate no growth for environmental reasons speak of restoring natural balances and living in harmony with nature. At the same time, they call for planning, intervention, and control. To be truly "with nature" instead of "over nature" would mean letting evolutionary forces follow their course. Interventions to limit growth would be inconsistent with this approach. They would represent greater human control over nature, not less. These conclusions about the no-growth challenge serve as a background for the following statement of the electric utility industry's view of the future of growth.

The significance of the growth debate does not lie in any real choice to be made between "maximum growth" and "zero growth." Some form of economic growth will continue, and its composition will be different than in the past. A new concept of "economic growth" is evolving as the economy adjusts to the constraints and problems raised in the growth debate. Indeed, all of the factors which have been discussed are resulting in slower rates of growth. The transformation of the economy is observable in trends toward expansion of the service and information sectors relative to the production sector. In the production sector itself, resource supplies and pollution controls will result in major increases in the recycling of materials. Environmental constraints will also require expansion of technology and investment in pollution avoidance and control efforts.

We have not yet perceived the full implications of the present change process. The real questions involve how to adjust to what is already happening. A hopeful view is that current directions point to a natural evolution toward a form of economic expansion that could be described as "clean growth," "quality growth," or "optimal growth." The notion of "betterment," that is, growth in good, is also useful.

The economy, in fact, no longer reflects a "maximum growth" objective. In the United States and some other advanced countries there is a growing unwillingness to commit energies and potentials singlemindedly to growth. Economic controls and environmental priorities have been superimposed on production and consumption objectives. It can be expected that traditional measures will show a slowing of growth as adjustments are made to internalize externalities and shifts are made in sources of energy supply.

Patterns of growth depend as much on cultural attitudes as on economic factors. Neither the present pro-growth view nor the no-growth view is descriptive of or adequate to our times. One reason for the decline in the growth ethic may simply be what economists refer to as the theory of "marginal utility." As one obtains more of any commodity, its use and value to him declines. As our society has become more affluent in terms of material goods, the objective of maximizing growth has become less pressing.

If there is to be an orderly transition to a sustainable society and a form of economic expansion that might be described as "quality growth," it may be necessary to pursue an opposite course for the short term than for the long term. In the short term, while fossil fuels are available, it may be necessary to promote rapid growth in knowledge and capital goods in order to develop the technology for a high level, sustainable society. Such a sustainable society might require a pattern of reduced growth over the long term.

As economic objectives are balanced by other measures of cultural progress, it will be necessary to augment and complement present economic indicators, such as GNP, with other more broadly based indicators and measures. It is generally agreed that GNP and national income accounts do not, and are not intended to, reflect broad social progress. New measures would provide a basis for building a new sense of national purpose—a new vision of the next 200 years.

Finally, the process of policy consideration and decision making must remain open and democratic. Decisions on economic growth are subordinate to the imperatives of sustaining a free society which maximizes individual choice.

FOOTNOTES

1. Boulding, Kenneth. "The Wolf of Rome." *Business and Society Review*, No. 2, Summer, 1972, pp. 106-109.

2. Wilkinson, Richard G. *Poverty and Progress: An Ecological Perspective on Economic Development.* New York: Praeger, 1973.

3. Revelle, R., ed. *Rapid Population Growth.* Baltimore: Johns Hopkins University Press, 1971.

4. Ryder, Norman B. "Two Cheers for ZPG." *Daedalus,* Fall, 1973, pp.45-62.

5. Council on Environmental Quality. *Environmental Quality* (The Third Annual Report of the Council on Environmental Quality). Washington, D. C.: United States Government Printing Office, August, 1972; and (The Fourth Annual Report of the Council on Environmental Quality) September, 1973.

6. Environmental Protection Agency. *The Economics of Clean Water* (Annual Report of the Administrator of the EPA to the Congress of the United States). Washington, D. C.: United States Government Printing Office, 1973.

7. Environmental Protection Agency, *The Cost of Clean Air* (Annual Report of the Administrator of the EPA to the Congress of the United States). Washington, D. C.: United States Government Printing Office, 1973.

8. Wiener, Norbert. *The Human Use of Human Beings.* New York: Avon Books, 1967, p. 57. (Originally published, 1950.)

9. de Chardin, Teilhard. *The Phenomenon of Man.* New York: Harper & Row, 1959.

10. Felix, Fremont. *World Markets of Tomorrow.* New York: Harper & Row, 1972.

11. Keniston, Kenneth. "A Second Look at the Uncommitted." *Social Policy,* Vol. 2, No. 2, July-August 1971, pp. 6-19.

12. Nordhaus, William and Tobin, James. "Is Growth Obsolete?" In *Economic Growth.* National Bureau of Economic Research. New York: Columbia University Press; 1972.

13. Moynihan, Daniel P. "Counsellor's Statement." In *Toward Balanced Growth: Quantity with Quality.* National Goals Research Staff. Washington, D. C.: United States Government Printing Office, 1970, p. 12.

14. "A Blueprint for Survival." *The Ecologist,* Vol. 2, No. 2, January, 1972, pp. 1-44.

15. Daly, Herman E., ed. *Toward a Steady-State Economy.* San Francisco: W. H. Freeman and Company, 1973.

16. Mishan, E. J. *Technology and Growth.* New York: Praeger, 1970.

17. Brooks, Harvey. "The Technology of Zero Growth." *Daedalus,* Fall, 1973, p. 144.

18. Brooks, as above, pp. 144-145.

19. Meadows, Donella H. and Meadows, Dennis L. "A Summary of *The Limits to Growth*—Its Critics and Its Challenge." Unpublished mimeographed paper presented at Yale University, September, 1972, p. 18.

20. Gabor, Dennis. *Thoughts on the Future,* MR-179, A Speech Delivered at UCLA on October 20, 1972, Institute of Government and Public Affairs, UCLA, 1972, p. 58.

PART II

An Analysis of Alternative Growth Patterns and Recommendations

---

I N PART I of this report the opposing views of economic growth were presented followed by a statement of the industry's conclusions on specific issues. In this Part II a far more exhaustive analysis is undertaken leading to much more definitive conclusions and recommendations.

Chapter 5 begins with a detailed summary of "where we stand now." An assessment of current status is considered the first step in problem analysis for public policy formulation.

Chapter 6 is a detailed quantitative analysis of alternative futures of economic growth. Its focus is primarily on the United States economy. This chapter is presented in the form of three scenarios which describe the future under: 1) a high-growth objective, 2) a zero-growth objective, and 3) a mid or moderate-growth objective. Special attention is given in these scenarios to the relationships between economic growth and energy supply and demand. The role of electric energy is highlighted.

Chapter 7 presents an analysis of certain factors determining the future of *world* economic growth. While the main focus of the overall study is the question of continued growth in the United States economy, the report would not be complete without a quantitative analysis of potential global constraints on growth.

Part II is concluded in Chapter 8 with a set of overall conclusions and recommendations on the future of United States and world economic growth. The recommendations are offered for public policy consideration.

CHAPTER 5

Where We Stand Now

A. Introduction

How we approach the problems and potentials of the future of growth depends a great deal on an assessment of where we stand today and how we arrived here. This section of the report focuses on the factors determining economic growth and presents a summary description of their present status. The description is in the form of a statistical profile. The factors covered are: population, employment, productivity, standard of living, material resources, the economic system, government policies, environmental policy, social and political conditions, and social change. In each case an attempt is made to describe where we stand now without drawing evaluative conclusions.

B. People-Related Factors

The best place to begin a description of where we stand now is with the people-related factors of population, employment, productivity, and the standard of living.

1. Population

Population is a major factor in economic growth. In mid-1974 the United States population numbered 211 million. This is about 6 percent of the earth's people. Today almost three quarters of the United States population lives in urban areas of 2,500 or more. About 70 percent live in cities of 50,000 or more and their surrounding areas. Population density in the United States is such that 68 percent of the people live on 12 percent of the land (Table 5•1 and Chart 5•1).

The trend of urbanization was strong during the decade of the 1960's. In 1960, 38 percent of the population lived in 23 large metropolitan areas of one million or more. By 1970 the Census revealed that 29 such areas accounted for 44 percent of the population. For the year 2000, projections indicate that 85 percent of the population will live in cities of 50,000 or more and almost two thirds of the population will be concentrated in metropolitan areas of

over a million people. These areas will be predominantly along the seaboards and the Great Lakes.

It should be noted that a recent Bureau of the Census report (*Population Profile of the United*

Table 5•1
POPULATION DISTRIBUTION* (APRIL, 1974)

Area	Population (Millions)	Population (Percent)	Land Area Occupied (Percent)	Land Area Occupied (Persons per square mile)
Metropolitan Areas Central Cities....	61.8	29.7	0.5	4,462
Outside Central Cities............	80.4	38.6	11.5	203
Non-Metropolitan Areas..................	65.9	31.7	88.0	20
Total	208.1	100.0	100.0	59

* Excludes Armed Forces and residents in institutions.

Source: United States Bureau of the Census.

Chart 5•1
1973 POPULATION DISTRIBUTION

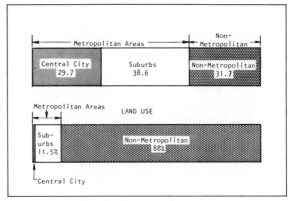

Source: United States Bureau of the Census

77

States, 1974; Bureau of the Census, March 1975) showed a net decline in central city residents and that a 1974 Department of Agriculture report showed a slowing and possibly an actual reversal of the rural to urban population movement. In some areas, including California, farm populations began to rise.

During 1974, the net increase in population was 1.59 million, a trifle greater than in 1973 but hardly more than half of the average annual increase during the latter part of the 1950's. In 1974 the total fertility rate reached a new low of 1.86. This fertility rate is the average number of births per woman over her lifetime. The replacement rate necessary to maintain a constant population over the long run is about 2.1. Total fertility rates have been in a long downward slide throughout most of the nation's history, moving from about 7 in the early 1800's to the current level. If the total fertility rate were to stabilize at 1.8, a peak population of about 270 million would be reached about 2025 after which it would begin to decrease.

Today, 45 percent of the population is 25 years old or younger (Chart 5•2). Over the next 50 years, if the nation approaches a stabilized population, the median age will gradually rise from its current level of about 28 to just over 40. If, however, fertility rates reverse (as they did after the depression following 1929), the population 50 years from now will be significantly larger and somewhat younger. An extra

Chart 5•2
POPULATION OF THE UNITED STATES, BY AGE AND SEX: JULY 1, 1974

(INCLUDES ARMED FORCES OVERSEAS)

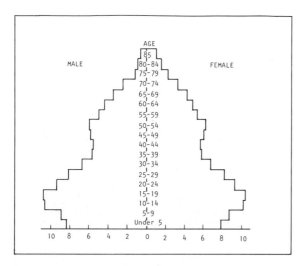

Source: United States Bureau of the Census, *Current Population Reports.*

Chart 5•3
ACTUAL AND PROJECTED POPULATION: 1900-2020

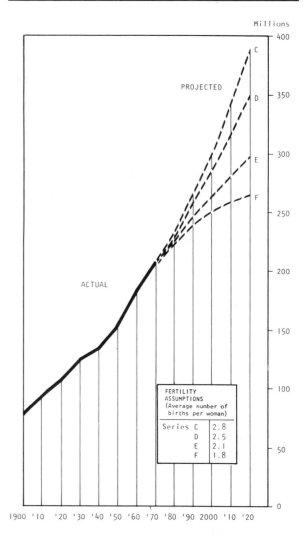

Source: Executive Office of the President. Office of Management and Budget, *Social Indicators, 1973.*

child per woman (total fertility rate of 2.8), for example, would boost the population to almost 400 million by 2025 (Chart 5•3).

Another factor which has increased population is the lengthening of the average life span. Life expectancy in the United States rose sharply from 34 years in 1800 to 68 years in 1950. Half of that increase came during the 19th century and the other half after 1900. Since 1950 the rate of increase has slowed and the expected life span now is about 71 years. Women have consistently lived longer than men. In 1920 it was 2-3 years longer. Now, it is close to 8 years longer. The widening gap in life span has been sufficient to overcome the continued higher birth rates for boys (1,050 boys for each 1,000 girls). The population has shifted from about 48 percent female in 1910 to 51 percent female in the census year 1970. Women will probably continue to outnumber men.

In summary, estimates of future population trends rest on assumptions about fertility, mortality, and immigration. Census surveys conducted in 1971-74 revealed that young wives aged 18 to 24 expected to bear fewer children than those in that age group surveyed in the past. The data suggested a 2.1 birthrate which would yield zero population growth over the long run, assuming mortality and immigration rates remain relatively unchanged.[1] On this basis the population in the year 2020 is projected to be about 300 million.

2. Employment

Employment is the second people-related factor for discussion in assessing where we stand now. Between 1950 and 1974 employment rose from 59 million to 85.9 million, a 45 percent increase. Only a little over 1 million of the additional 27 million jobs were in goods-related industries; i.e., agriculture, mining, manufacturing, and construction. The rest

were in service related industries. This continuing trend is indicated in a comparison of the distribution of occupations of employed persons 1950-1970 (Chart 5•4).

Increases in agricultural productivity since 1950 have made it possible to increase output by 50 percent, while at the same time farm employment has been cut in half and harvested acres reduced from 336 to 284 million. The trend in decreasing agricultural employment and population relocation to jobs in the cities has prevailed through the nation's history. At the time of the American Revolution about 80 percent of total employment was in agriculture. By the beginning of the 20th century the figure was down to 40 percent, and in 1974 it was 3.5 percent.

Many observers see the inevitability of a similar but slower trend toward decline in the manufacturing, mining, and construction areas. Taken together, employment in these industries peaked just after World War I at about 35 percent of all employed persons. In 1974, it was down to 31 percent. Mechanization and improved productivity have been important factors in the change.

Professional and technical employment has grown at a rate three times that of the average. These are

Chart 5•4
OCCUPATIONS OF EMPLOYED PERSONS

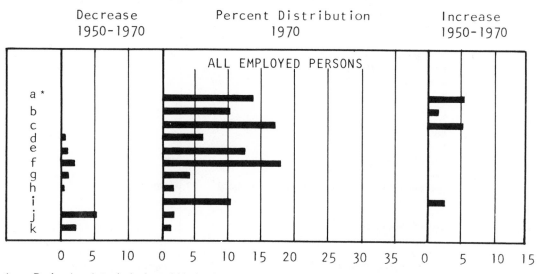

* a—Professional, technical, and kindred workers
  b—Managers, officials, and proprietors
  c—Clerical and kindred workers
  d—Sales workers
  e—Craftsmen and foremen
  f—Operatives

g—Nonfarm laborers
h—Private household workers
i—Service workers, except private household
j—Farmers and farm managers
k—Farm laborers and foremen

Source: *Social Indicators, 1973.* Executive Office of the President: Office of Management and Budget.

jobs that normally require some college education. In 1950 there were about 4.5 million such jobs; by 1960 the number had risen to 7.5 million, and it is now about 12 million. This trend too is likely to continue.

Female employment has risen from 17.3 million in 1950 to more than 33 million in 1974. Women have, in fact, accounted for better than 60 percent of the increase in total employment since 1950. Much of this increase has taken place in the expanding service sector. Although the influx of women into the work force has been supported by changes in attitudes toward the female worker, the distribution of women workers through occupation groups remains much the same. Only within the past few years has there been any indication that women were beginning to break out of the traditional "female-job" mold. However, the movement of women into non-traditional occupations is expected to accelerate, along with continued growth in the numbers of women employed outside the household (Chart 5·5).

To summarize, the following trends in employ-ment patterns are expected to continue for a number of years: (1) gradual decrease in manufacturing jobs, (2) increases in service jobs, (3) increases in technical and professional employment, (4) increases in women in the labor force, and (5) broader distribution of women throughout all job classifications.

3. Productivity

The United States has experienced economic growth (i.e., growth in material output) at rates much faster than can be attributed to the growth in the inputs of either labor (i.e., man-hours) or capital (deflated cost of plant and equipment). The difference is improved productivity; that is, improved efficiency with which labor and capital inputs are used. High productivity has been a major factor in making possible a high standard of living and in enabling the United States to compete successfully in international trade with countries having much lower wage scales.

The most common productivity measures are

Chart 5·5
OCCUPATIONS BY SEX

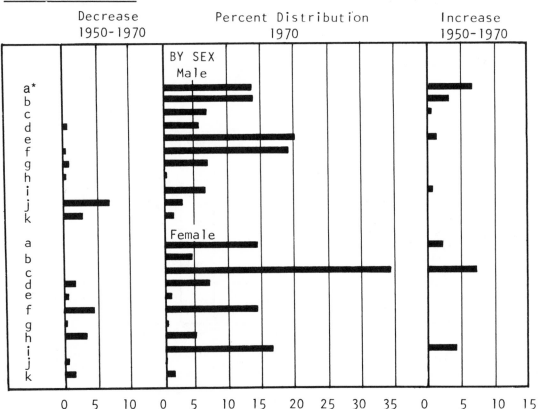

Source: *Social Indicators, 1973.* Executive Office of the President: Office of Management and Budget.
* See Chart 5·4 for key

presented as ratios of physical output per unit of labor (e.g., man-hours). Although this concept is easily measured and easily understood, it ignores the contributions of the other factors of production; capital and land. Measures of productivity which do include these other factors have been developed in recent years. A short description of some of this work is presented in Appendix F.

A table from Appendix F is repeated here to show the relative contributions to economic growth in the United States between 1961 and 1972 of: (a) increases in the quantity of labor and capital inputs and; (b) increases in the efficiency with which the inputs were used and combined (Table 5·2).

Table 5·2
SOURCES OF UNITED STATES ECONOMIC GROWTH: 1961-1972*
(Percent per Year)

Increases in Quantity	Contributions to Growth
Capital Stock	1.04%
Labor Man-hours	0.95
Increases in Efficiency	
Capital Productivity	0.44
Labor Productivity	0.50
Total Factor Productivity (Combination)	1.35
Total Economic Growth	4.28%

* See Appendix F.

A study of long term economic growth shows that the rate of productivity growth in the United States has been increasing over the long term, when measured in the conventional terms of output per man-hour.[2] From 1800 to 1850 the annual rate of increase was close to ½ of 1 percent per year; from 1850 to 1900 it was perhaps 1.2 to 1.3 percent per year, and from 1900 to 1950 it was well over 2 percent per year. An examination of the post-World War II record suggests the current normal potential rate of improvement is in the range from 2.6 to 3.0 percent per year.

To the extent that labor, capital goods, and land are being allocated in increasing amounts to efforts that are non-productive in a market sense (e.g., eliminating industrial pollutants), the productivity improvement potential of the nation is reduced. For example, in 1974 about 10 percent of total expenditures for new plant and equipment were for items to control air or water pollution and improve

occupational health and safety. In some industries, such as steel, nonferrous metals and paper, the percentage of new capital dollars going to such activities approaches 20 to 25 percent.[3]

For essentially all of its almost 100 year history, the electric power industry has maintained one of the most rapid rates of increase of labor productivity of any industry in the nation. Over the decade from 1960 to 1970 this rate averaged close to 6.5 percent per year. Since 1970, however, the rate has hovered in the neighborhood of 3.0 to 4.5 percent. This is low in comparison to historic figures for the electric power industry but still significantly higher than for the nation's overall private economy, which averaged about 2 percent per year during this same period.

4. The Standard of Living

The standard of living is the fourth people-related factor for discussion. It is defined as the aggregate of goods and services, including health and education available to the individual. Money income is a useful measure since it includes wages, rents, and insurance benefits. In our highly urbanized society, nonmonetary income, for example, food associated with farm life, is not significant for most people. Less quantifiable factors, such as environment, which influence the companion concept—"Quality of Life"—are discussed later.

Money income in 1974 before taxes for the average United States household was about $13,000. Although inflation has exaggerated the apparent progress, real family income has expanded steadily as total GNP has grown and total goods and services have increased. On a constant dollar basis (corrected to remove inflationary effects) there has been almost a 60 percent increase in family income in the United States since 1950. Since the average household has decreased significantly in numbers of persons during this period, the increase in constant dollar income per capita has risen even more rapidly than for households—in fact, by almost 75 percent. As a result, a greater portion of income is now spent on goods or services once considered luxuries.

The persistent rising trend in real income has shifted significant numbers of Americans out of the classification of low-income or poor. Using the Bureau of Census definition of low income, which depends on family size, place of residence, and inflationary trends, the numbers of persons in the low-income population declined steadily from 22 percent of the total population in 1959 to 12 percent at present (Table 5·3).

Improved money income for the average family

Table 5·3
PERSONS BELOW THE LOW-INCOME LEVEL: 1959-1974

Year	Number (millions)			Percent of—		
	All Persons	Persons in families	Unrelated individuals	All Persons	Persons in families	Unrelated individuals
1959........................	39.5	34.6	4.9	22.4	20.8	46.1
1960........................	39.9	34.9	4.9	22.2	20.7	45.2
1961........................	39.6	34.5	5.1	21.9	20.3	45.9
1962........................	38.6	33.6	5.0	21.0	19.4	45.4
1963........................	36.4	31.5	4.9	19.5	17.9	44.2
1964........................	36.1	30.9	5.1	19.0	17.4	42.7
1965........................	33.2	28.4	4.8	17.3	15.8	39.8
1966........................	30.4	25.6	4.8	15.7	14.2	38.9
1966[1].....................	28.5	23.8	4.7	14.7	13.1	38.3
1967........................	27.8	22.8	5.0	14.2	12.5	38.1
1968........................	25.4	20.7	4.7	12.8	11.3	34.0
1969........................	24.3	19.4	4.9	12.2	10.5	33.6
1970........................	25.5	20.5	5.0	12.6	11.0	32.7
1970[1].....................	25.4	20.3	5.1	12.6	10.9	32.9
1971[2].....................	25.6	20.4	5.2	12.5	10.8	31.6
1972........................	24.5	19.6	4.9	11.9	10.3	29.0
1973........................	23.0	18.3	4.7	11.1	9.7	25.6
1974........................	24.3	19.4	4.8	11.6	10.2	25.5

[1] Beginning with the 1967 survey, data based on revised methodology for processing income data.

[2] Based on 1970 census population controls; not strictly comparable to data for earlier years.

Source: *Current Population Reports,* Bureau of the Census, Series P-60, Nos. 81, 86, 94, 99.

reflects primarily the overall expansion of the economy rather than any major changes in income distribution. Over the last 35 to 40 years income distribution has changed only slightly, with much of the shift occurring in the 1930's and early 1940's. Since World War II the most significant change has been in the decreasing share going to the top 5 percent of United States families (Table 5·4 and Chart 5·6).

A significant change at the bottom of the income distribution in the last few years has been the growing importance of non-monetary income. In the fiscal year 1973, for example, federal government payments in kind were valued at $17.6 billion.[4] This included such items as medicaid, food stamps and rent supplements. If it is assumed that 75 percent of the value of these payments in kind was received by the under-$5,000 group of families and unrelated individuals (roughly the bottom 20 percent), it would have the effect of raising their average equivalent income by some 50 percent; i.e. from about $3,100 to about $4,600 per year.

Health and education services are indicators of a society's resource allocation philosophy, and they influence the elusive factor "quality of life". Major advances have been made in both these areas since World War II. Among these are the increases in longevity referred to earlier.

As noted, United States life expectancy doubled over the 150 years prior to 1950, and rose from 68 years in 1950 to 71 years in 1970. Other indicators of improving health care in the United States are: (1) an increase in spending for health care from 3.5

Table 5·4
FAMILY INCOME SHARES

	Percent of Aggregate Money Income of Families	
	1950	1974
Lowest 20 Percent	4.5%	5.4%
Second 20 Percent............	12.0	12.0
Third 20 Percent	17.4	17.6
Fourth 20 Percent	23.5	24.1
Highest 20 Percent............	42.6	41.0
Highest 5 Percent..............	17.0	15.3

Source: *United States Statistical Abstract, 1973; Money Income and Poverty Status of Families and Persons in the United States 1974 (Advance Report),* Census Series P-60, No. 99 (Table 4).

percent of gross national product in 1950 to more than 7 percent at present; (2) a growth in employment in medical and health service occupations from 1.5 million in 1960 to 3.95 million in 1974; and (3) a more than doubling of the number of beds available in nursing homes from 547 thousand in 1963 to 1.2 million in 1971.

Finally, improvement in infant and maternal death rates should be mentioned.[5] Infant deaths have been reduced from 29 per 1,000 live births in 1950 to 19 in 1971, and maternal deaths from 83 per 100,000 live births in 1950 to 20 in 1971 (Chart 5·7).

With respect to *education*, one direct measure of accomplishment is the percentage of the young adult population with some attendance at college. In 1950 only 18 percent of the men aged 30 to 34 years and

Chart 5·6
DISTRIBUTION OF INCOME

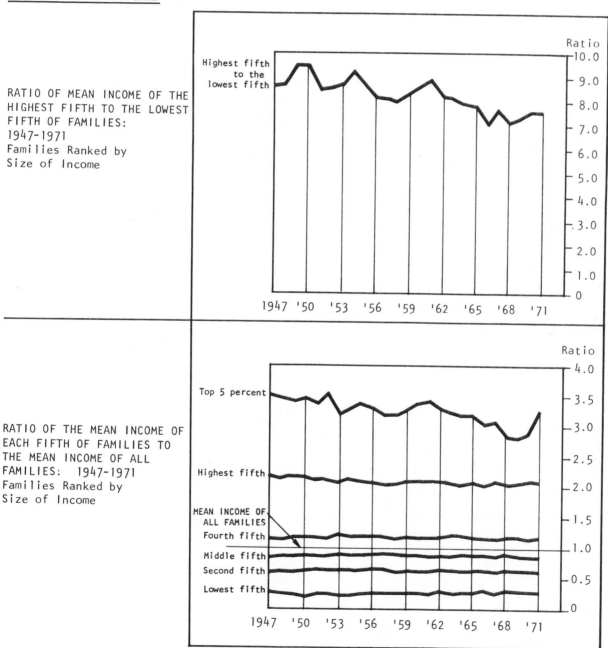

RATIO OF MEAN INCOME OF THE HIGHEST FIFTH TO THE LOWEST FIFTH OF FAMILIES: 1947-1971
Families Ranked by Size of Income

RATIO OF THE MEAN INCOME OF EACH FIFTH OF FAMILIES TO THE MEAN INCOME OF ALL FAMILIES: 1947-1971
Families Ranked by Size of Income

Source: Executive Office of the President: Office of Management and Budget, *Social Indicators, 1973.*

83

Chart 5•7
UNITED STATES INFANT MORTALITY RATE

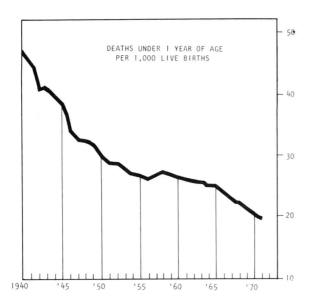

DEATHS UNDER 1 YEAR OF AGE
PER 1,000 LIVE BIRTHS

Source: Executive Office of the President: Office of Management and Budget, *Social Indicators, 1973.*

now tilled, there is another available for optional use. Substantial portions of grain production are not consumed domestically, but contribute importantly to commodity exports and so play a favorable role in the balance of trade. High United States agricultural yields result from a combination of superior applied technology, climate and other geographic factors, and an economic and political institutional framework supportive of maximizing agricultural productivity.

Food consumption habits have changed, reflecting increases in personal income. Beef consumption per

Chart 5•8.
ENROLLMENT IN INSTITUTIONS OF HIGHER EDUCATION: 1957-1971
By Level and Degree-Credit Status

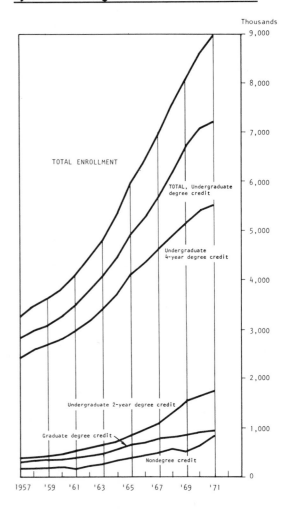

Source: *Social Indicators, 1973* Executive Office of the President; Office of Management and Budget.

only 14 percent of women in the same age group had attended college. By 1970 attendance by this age group had grown to 33 percent of the men and 23 percent of the women (Chart 5•8). During this same period the number of persons enrolled in schools and colleges rose from 31.3 million to 58.8 million, for an 88 percent increase during a time when the school age population (ages 5 through 24) grew by 64 percent.

The percent of gross national product contributed by the education sector grew from 3.4 percent in 1950 to 8.0 percent in 1972.

In summary, this review of the people-related factors influencing growth indicates that the trends in the United States are toward longer life, fewer working hours and higher pay, more education, and wider leeway in choices of careers and lifestyles.

C. Material Resources

The discussion of where we stand now with material resources includes consideration of food, minerals, and energy.

1. Food

The number of acres harvested to meet United States food needs has declined sharply since 1930 despite the constant rise in population. For each acre

capita rose from 55 pounds in 1940 to 115 pounds in 1972. The present per capita consumption of grain in the United States is almost one ton. Only about 150 pounds of this are consumed directly in grain foods.

Grain consumed, directly or indirectly, continues to accelerate as per capita income rises, and to date, no nation has reached a per capita grain demand plateau. Many industrial countries enjoying rising incomes are increasing their demand for meat but cannot supply their grain needs domestically. Spreading droughts in areas of Asia and Africa have added to this problem. As a result, Canada and the United States have become the source of almost all food exports with concomitant reductions in grain reserves. In responding to world demand, the United States is supporting food production research and increasing the planting of cropland.

Even though some less developed areas have benefited greatly from the high yield crops of the "Green Revolution," the technologies so productive in North America have not found widespread application. This has been due to a number of complex reasons not readily resolved such as insufficient capital, water, fertilizer, and energy. Cultural beliefs and other training difficulties have also slowed application of the new technologies.

There has been a steady decrease in fish catch since 1970. This and the depletion of grazing land places greater pressure on other food sources.

Attempts are being made to develop new technologies to increase efficiencies in production of grains, and to increase their protein content and their conversion to meat.

In conclusion, food production capacities are under increasing pressure to meet rising world demand. In the United States the agricultural sector meets domestic needs with no real difficulty and is an important contributor to exports.

2. Minerals

In discussing natural resources, a distinction is made between *resources* and *reserves*. *Reserves* are known, identified deposits from which minerals can be extracted profitably with existing technology and under present economic conditions. *Resources* include reserves and other mineral deposits that may eventually become available—including known deposits that are not economically or technologically recoverable at present, or those deposits that may be inferred to exist but which have not yet been discovered.

With about 6 percent of the world's population, the United States generates about 35 to 40 percent of the world's gross product. In the process, the United States consumes about 20 percent of the world's total production of major metallic ores and 19 percent of its major nonmetallic ores. (Consumption is here

Chart 5•9
YEARS OF SUPPLY FROM DOMESTIC RESERVES AT CURRENT RATES OF CONSUMPTION

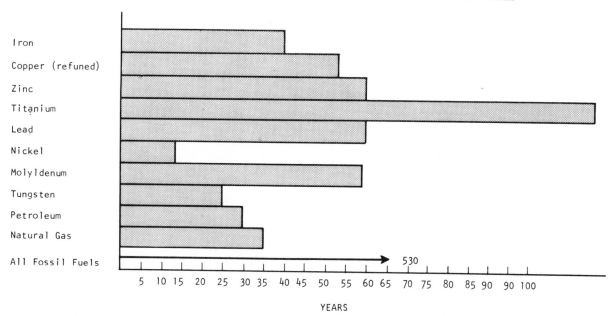

Source: United States Department of the Interior, Bureau of Mines: "Projection of the Year," *Minerals Handbook,* 1970.

defined as production plus imports. It does not reflect exports.) Imports constitute about 38 percent of United States consumption of metallic, and 21 percent of consumption of nonmetallic ores.

In general, with the exception of Europe, the continental United States has been more intensively explored than the rest of the World. Therefore, it is not unlikely that the bulk of new discoveries will be abroad, and that, as United States consumption continues to rise, dependence on imports will increase. If this prospect is combined with a continuation of the rapid growth in consumption of mineral resources by the rest of the world, competition among nations for increasingly scarce resources will intensify. The long term availability of mineral resources on a worldwide basis is considered in more detail later. Expected supplies from domestic resources as estimated by the Bureau of Mines in 1970 are shown in Chart 5•9.

Reserves shown are tonnages available from ores already discovered, and economically recoverable at current prices and technology. With improved technology, significantly larger quantities assumed to be present as resources would be available at the higher level of technology and/or prices.

3. Energy

Since the end of the second World War, there has been a dramatic shift in the type of resources used in energy production from solid fuels to liquid and gaseous fuels (Table No. 5•5).

Table 5•5
ENERGY CONSUMPTION

Resource	1947 market share	1974 market share
Coal	48%	18.3%
Natural Gas	14	30.1
Oil	34	46.0
Hydro Power	4	4.2
Nuclear	0	1.4

Source: United States Bureau of Mines.

The changes in general fuel mix have resulted from a variety of factors including: price, convenience, cleanliness, availability, and changes in technology. Increased availability (at least in the earlier years of the period), cleanliness, and low price were the factors which made natural gas the most rapidly growing source of energy. With oil, expansion of the use of the automobile and the airplane, as well as availability and convenience were

the major spurs to rapid growth. Coal lost ground to oil and gas because of relative inconvenience in handling, and polluting products generated during combustion. Hydro power has been limited by a lack of suitable new sites.

The energy industry has not always found it possible to forecast the magnitude and timing of shifts in market share with the accuracy desirable in an industry with very long lead times. However, where imbalances in supply and demand *have* been foreseen (e.g. the natural gas shortage), public policy has not always been responsive.

In the electricity generation segment of the energy market, over the 5-year period after 1967, there was a rapid shift from coal to oil due to: (1) the imposition of restrictions on sulfur emissions, and (2) the need to substitute easily available combustion turbines for delayed nuclear units. For about 15 years prior to 1967, oil constituted about 8 percent (on a BTU basis) of the fuel used in electricity generation. This percentage grew to about 19 percent in 1974. In terms of barrels of oil, the shift required an increase in consumption of about 350 million barrels per year (or almost 960 thousand barrels per day). This single shift in consumption patterns is equivalent to nearly half of the early 1974 shortage of liquid petroleum products (Table 5•6).

Table 5•6
GENERATION BY FUEL—TOTAL ELECTRIC UTILITY INDUSTRY
(Percent of Total Kilowatthours by Thermal Generation)

	1974*
Coal	53.1%
Fuel Oil	19.2
Gas	20.5
Nuclear	7.2
	100.0%

*Preliminary

Source: Federal Power Commission.

Recently enunciated government policy aims to achieve energy self-sufficiency well before the end of this century. This will require resolutions of the current mismatch between resource availability and resource use. This mismatch is illustrated by the data presented in Chart 5•10.

Energy consumption in the United States as well as elsewhere rises with growth of GNP. (A more detailed examination of the nature of this relationship is provided in Chapters 6 and 7.) For the most part from 1950 to 1974, energy consumption in the

United States grew at an average rate of 3.5 percent per year, while real GNP grew at a slightly higher rate of 3.7 percent per year.

The percent of total energy consumed by each of the user sectors has not varied much since 1950. Transportation has remained much the same, shifts having taken place between the households/commercial and industrial sectors. However, the *type of fuel* used within a consuming sector has shown dramatic changes (Table No. 5•7 and Chart 5•11).

In 1950 coal contributed over 35 percent of fuel used in households and the commercial sector. By 1972, this had dropped to about 2 percent while the percentage of natural gas doubled and electricity tripled. Coal was almost eliminated for transportation uses during this period, dropping from almost 20 percent in 1950 to less than one percent in 1972. Similarly, industrial consumption of coal fell from over 46 percent to less than 20 percent.

For the transportation sector, the shift from coal was to petroleum as diesel transport expanded and trucking took more of the freight market. For the households and commercial sector as well as the industrial sector, petroleum retained its percent of the total energy consumed, while coal gave way to electricity and natural gas.

Projected energy use distrubution patterns are discussed in more detail in Chapter 6. Projections indicate the relative importance of coal and nuclear power which are expected to increase while oil and gas will decrease. Major emphasis in coal technology today is toward eliminating or reducing sulfur related problems and developing processes of liquefaction or gasification of coal.

Chart 5•10
UNITED STATES RESOURCES AND USAGE OF FOSSIL FUELS

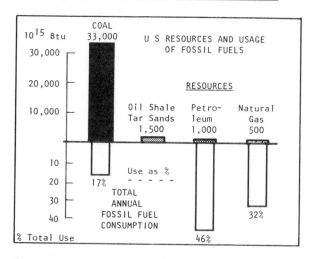

Source: *Public Utilities Fortnightly*, June 6, 1974, p. 43.

Table 5•7
AMOUNTS OF ENERGY CONSUMED 1950-1974 BY SECTOR

Sector	Coal (Trillion Btu)	Coal (Per-cent)	Petroleum (Trillion Btu)	Petroleum (Per-cent)	Natural Gas (Trillion Btu)	Natural Gas (Per-cent)	Purchased Electricity* (Trillion Btu)	Purchased Electricity* (Per-cent)	Total (Trillion Btu)	Total (Percent by Sector)
Household & Commercial										
1950.............	2,913	35.8	3,038	37.3	1,642	20.2	546	6.7	8,139	27
1974 (p)......	291	1.7	6,390	36.5	7,116	40.7	3,687	21.1	17,484	29
Industrial										
1950.............	5,957	46.3	2,641	20.5	3,727	28.9	559	4.3	12,884	44
1974 (p)......	4,208	17.7	5,826	24.4	11,129	46.7	2,665	11.2	23,828	40
Transportation										
1950.............	1,701	19.7	6,785	78.5	130	1.5	24	0.3	8,640	29
1974 (p)......	2	—	17,608	96.3	664	3.6	16	0.1	18,290	31

p = preliminary

* At 3413 Btu per kilowatthour purchased. Raw energy consumed to generate this electricity has decreased gradually from a heat rate of about 14,000 Btu per kilowatthour in 1950 to about 10,500 in 1974.

Source: Division of Fossil Fuels, Bureau of Mines, United States Department of the Interior.

Chart 5•11
ENERGY CONSUMED BY SECTOR, 1950-1974

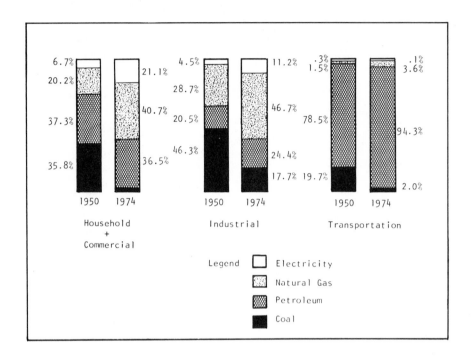

Source: Division of Fossil Fuels, Bureau of Mines, United States Department of the Interior.

4. Electricity

Electric utilities are not final consumers of energy but are processors who change energy from one form to another to be sold to ultimate consumers. Characteristics of electricity have led it to grow in use at a rate nearly twice that of energy as a whole. In 1950, gross energy consumed for electrical generation was less than 15 percent of the United States total. By 1973 over 26 percent of total energy consumption went to electrical generation as the industrial and household and commercial sectors of the economy increased their demand for electricity as a percent of their total energy demand (Chart 5•12). Electricity production is projected to require inputs of from 40 to 50 percent of gross United States energy use by the year 2000, according to some forecasters; e.g., the Bureau of Mines of the United States Interior Department (Table 5•8). More detailed forecasts of electricity and total energy consumption in the United States to the year 2000 are provided in Chapter 6.

Table 5•8
ENERGY INPUTS FOR ELECTRICAL GENERATION 1950-2000*
Percent of Total United States Gross Consumption

Year	% United States Total Gross Energy Consumption
1950	14.7
1955	16.6
1960	18.5
1965	20.8
1972	25.6
1975	27.9
1980	31.2
1985	34.6
2000	41.9

* Projections 1975-2000, United States Energy Through the Year 2000, Dept. of the Interior.
Source: Division of Fossil Fuels, Bureau of Mines, United States Department of the Interior.

Chart 5•12
TOTAL UNITED STATES GROSS ENERGY INPUTS BY SECTOR

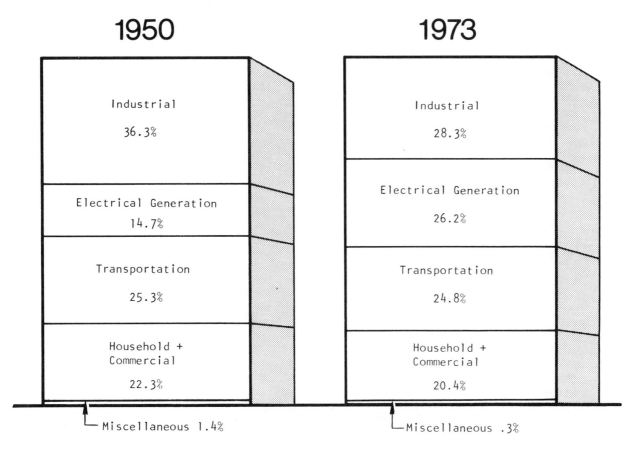

1950

Industrial	36.3%
Electrical Generation	14.7%
Transportation	25.3%
Household + Commercial	22.3%

Miscellaneous 1.4%

1973

Industrial	28.3%
Electrical Generation	26.2%
Transportation	24.8%
Household + Commercial	20.4%

Miscellaneous .3%

Source: Division of Fossil Fuels, Bureau of Mines, United States Department of the Interior.

5. Summary Statement on Resources

A rising standard of living means rising per capita resource consumption. As life continues to improve around the world, there will be increasing competition for the world's resources. Although world and United States resources still appear to be large, the potential for dislocations, such as occurred in oil in late 1973, appears to be growing. Food and minerals, as well as energy, could be affected. As the United States becomes more dependent on imports, its vulnerability to such dislocations is increased.

D. Environmental Quality

It is difficult to make general summary comments on where we stand now with respect to environmental quality. Recently applied technologies are affecting the amounts of pollution released, and refinements in data collection and analysis are making formerly collected data obsolete. Every sector of the economy generates potential pollutants. Some are identified at the point of production (e.g., mine tailings) others at the point of consumption (e.g., municipal waste). Present concern and effort are centered on air and water quality, with lesser attention to noise and visual pollution. Another very important and closely related effort is to improve occupational health and safety.

Probably the best overall assessments of environmental quality are those in the Environmental Protection Agency's annual reports to the Congress made in compliance with the amended Clean Air Act and the Federal Water Pollution Control Act.[6] The environment includes so many diverse aspects that any single overall expression of quality is of limited value. Even within the specific areas of air and water pollution, generalizations are difficult to derive. Despite these difficulties, the Council on Environmental Quality was able to report in its 1972 and 1973 reports that air quality is improving. While no such generalization could be made about water quality, an EPA study of 22 river basins commented on in the 1973 annual report indicates that oxygen demand by bacteria, the pollutant receiving the most widespread attention, showed general improvements in the preceding five years.

Among the difficulties in evaluation cited in the 1973 report on clean air was the problem of projections being developed on the basis of existing technology with no allowance for innovation. In addition, problems are created as standards are constantly being reviewed and changes are being incorporated. In the 1973 Annual Report titled *The Economics of Clean Water,* the EPA declared that: "The quality of the nation's waters can be discussed in only approximate and qualitative terms, since no set of truly representative water quality monitoring stations exist."

Difficulties also are caused by the lack of reliable scientific information on the consequences of various concentrations of pollutants in the environment. A similar lack of information hampers efforts to assess the costs of achieving different degrees of environmental cleanliness. Consequently, there have some times been sincere but misguided efforts to achieve or at least approach 100 percent removal of pollutants without adequate concern for either the direct costs or the indirect consequences of 100 percent clean up.

In the environmental quality field, considerable attention has been given to fossil fuel combustion for energy, wastes generated by agricultural and industrial production, and the disposal of municipal wastes. These will be discussed separately.

1. Fossil Fuel Combustion for Energy

In a highly industrialized and mechanized society, combustion of fossil fuels to provide the energy necessary for increasing transportation and production of goods and services, has been accompanied by substantial air pollution. Principal problems lie in the areas of noxious gases and particulates.

While there is some environmental contamination at mines and in refineries where fuels are prepared for consumers, most problems arise during product use. Particular consuming sectors yield more of one kind of air pollutant than others as detailed in Table 5•9.

The transportation sector, for instance, is primarily responsible for carbon monoxide and hydrocarbon emissions. Industrial processes and stationary combustion contribute most of the sulfur oxides and particulates. Here pollution control technology in the

Table 5•9
ESTIMATED NATIONWIDE EMISSIONS, UNITED STATES, 1968 (Millions of short tons)

Source	Carbon Mon-oxide	Par-ticu-lates	Sulfur Oxides	Hydro-Carbons	Nitro-gen Oxides
Transportation	63.8	1.2	0.8	16.6	8.1
Stationary Combustion	1.9	8.9	24.4	0.7	10.0
Industrial Processes	9.7	7.5	7.3	4.6	0.2
Solid Waste Disposal	7.8	1.1	0.1	1.6	0.6
Miscellaneous	16.9	9.6	0.6	8.5	1.7
Total.......	100.1	28.3	33.2	32.0	20.6

Source: Sterling Brubaker, *To Live on Earth,* 1972, p. 22

form of stack gas scrubbers and electrostatic precipitators is being developed to control pollutants associated with coal combustion. In the case of nuclear generation, thermal emissions and the disposal of radioactive wastes are central problems.

2. Agricultural Production

Wastes disposal becomes a problem where animal or crop residues are unusually concentrated, as in feedlots or processing operations. Livestock produce about a billion tons of manure each year and another billion tons are added in the form of slaugherhouse waste and carcasses. Food, fiber and other industries processing organic materials often dispose waste into rivers and streams, thus creating biochemical imbalances in these waters. An entirely different set of pollution problems related to food production arises from the use of agricultural chemicals—fertilizers and pesticides.

Fertilizer use in the United States has approximately doubled in tonnage over the past 20 years.[7] The nutrient content of fertilizer (nitrogen, phosphate, and potash) has more than tripled over the same period. The experience in countries like the Netherlands, where the average application rate is 10 times that in the United States, suggests that despite intensified use in the United States fertilizer pollution problems can be solved.

There is much less assurance about environmental tolerance for chemicals used to eliminate weeds and insects. Such chemicals have recently been increasing in use at a rate of 15 percent per year. Insecticides and fungicides are said to cause the most severe environmental problems. The rapid development of a wide variety of formulations, based on several hundred different chemicals, and the consequent difficulty of determining the environmental consequences of each of them constitute a major impediment to quantifying pollution impacts.

3. Industrial Production

Industrial production creates by-product wastes at the various stages of production, and at the point of use in the consumer household. Recycling is practiced to a degree but is impeded by physical problems and cost considerations. Table 5·10 presents an estimate of the fractions of major metals consumption in the United States that come from recycled materials. Relatively little nonmetal materials are recycled, with the exception of a few substances such as paper.

Table 5·10
**RECYCLING RATES: 1967-68
(Millions Tons)**

Material	Total Consumption	Total Recycled	Recycling as Percent of Consumption
Iron and steel......	105.900	33.100	31.2%
Aluminum...........	4.009	.733	18.3
Copper	2.913	1.447	49.7
Lead	1.261	.625	49.6
Zinc	1.592	.201	12.6

Source: *Salvage Markets for Materials in Solid Wastes* United States Environmental Protection Agency, 1972.

Products such as detergents, lubricants, and pesticides are almost impossible to recycle because they are broken down and dispersed in use. The chemical industries generate residuals which are potentially the most damaging. Their effects on the environment are still poorly understood. Synthetic organic chemicals—plastics—often are not biodegradable and thus may be particularly troublesome in larger volumes, even though most of them are chemically inert. Production of such chemicals rose 125 percent between 1960 and 1968, and further rapid increases in coming years seem certain. These products generally represent the highest-value uses for petroleum, and so may be expected to grow in use even in the face of oil and gas shortages.

Mining and metallurgical industries produce large volumes of residuals ranging from slag and air-borne particulates to mining and processing acids.

4. Households

Households wastes, consisting primarily of garbage and sewage, average 5 pounds per person (4 pounds of garbage and less than 1 pound of sewage). Roughly 80 percent of garbage and household trash is combustible, with paper products constituting a major fraction of the combustible material. Promising techniques are being developed for disposal by combustion with some net energy output, although paper recycling may sharply limit the potential for trash as an energy source. Research may also lead to other economic uses of solid waste.

The principal environmental effect of organic matter in sewage is the demand on the dissolved oxygen in the receiving bodies of water. This problem is solvable by relatively simple sewage treatment facilities. However, the estimate for providing such facilities nationwide where they do not exist is $115 billion.

Chemicals from household detergents and other cleaning compounds entering the sewage stream constitute a more difficult treatment problem.

To summarize, positive progress is being made in improving the quality of the environment and in controlling further pollution. However, man-made pollution continues to impact the natural environment in a variety of ways which are not well understood. The maintenance and improvement of environmental quality will require major continuing efforts and investment.

E. The American Economic System

The United States economic system is often characterized as a mixed economy in the sense that it basically is a "free enterprise" system on which there have been superimposed government and other institutional restraints. The term "free enterprise" is used to describe a system based on: (a) individual initiative; (b) private property, including private ownership of the means of production; and (c) free competition in the buying and selling of goods and services, including the services of both labor and capital.

The basic elements of present United States economic and political institutions were brought from Europe by the first colonists. However, as the institutions developed in this country, they were greatly influenced by the individualism and self-reliance of the American settler and pioneer.

As the country matured, however, more and more constraints were judged to be necessary. As with all social institutions adaptable enough to survive for some two hundred years, the current economic system is a heterogenous mixture of theoretical considerations, pragmatic reactions to changing circumstances, and historical accidents.

Despite this heterogeneity, it is possible to distinguish two major economic concepts from which much of the present system derives. These concepts were developed about 150 years apart by two English economists. Adam Smith described the concept of free enterprise at the time of the American Revolution.[8] John Maynard Keynes articulated the rationale for government intervention during the years between the two World Wars.[9]

1. Free Enterprise

Adam Smith's idea of a "laissez faire" economy included: (1) free trade, (2) no attempt by the government to fix prices or regulate the quantity or quality of goods, (3) freedom for the individual to enter any occupation he might choose and to do so in any location he desired, (4) determination of wages by unfettered bargaining between employee and employer, and (5) strict limitations on the functions of government to include only: (a) defense and maintenance of domestic tranquility, (b) dispensing of justice, and (c) establishment and maintenance of those public works which could not be made commercially profitable. All of these except the principle of free trade received a welcome reception in the new nation.

The strength of Adam Smith's exposition lay largely in his convincing description of the "invisible hand", which proposed that the best interests of society as a whole are achieved automatically if each individual in the society is allowed freedom to act in his own selfish economic interests. The proposition, of course, must be qualified by some basic rules of conduct enforced by government. The Smith concept, however, was to minimize such government interference.

A condition of complete laissez faire never developed in the United States or elsewhere. Today we live in a "mixed economy" where both private and public institutions exercise control of the economy. Nevertheless, today a vast amount of economic activity proceeds with little or no direct government intervention. Thousands of products and a variety of services are marketed by millions of people largely of their own volition and without any centralized governmental plan.

The price system, competition, and the profit motive are at the heart of the "mixed economy", just as if it were a private enterprise, laissez faire system.

The price system and competition continue to function in influencing consumer choices and investment decisions.

The bare outlines of a price-based competitive system are perhaps best described by paraphrasing and quoting selectively from Paul Samuelson's classic textbook, *Economics*.[10]

"All commodities and services, including labor, have prices. Everyone receives money for what he sells and gives money for what he buys.

If more is wanted of any goods—say, shoes —a flood of new orders will be given for it. This will cause its price to rise and more to be produced.

Similarly, if more becomes available of a commodity such as tea than people want to buy at the last-quoted market price, its price will be marked down by competition. At the lower price people will drink more tea, and producers will no longer produce quite so much. Thus, equilibrium of supply and demand will be restored.

What is true of the markets for consumers' goods is also true of markets for factors of production such as labor, land and capital inputs. If welders rather than glass blowers are needed, job opportunities will be more favorable in the welding field. The price of welders, their hourly wage, will tend to rise, while that of glass blowers will tend to fall. Other things being equal, this will cause a shift into the desired occupation. Likewise, an acre of land will go into sugar cultivation if sugar producers bid the most for its use. In the same way, machine-tool production will be determined by supply and demand.

In other words, we have a vast system of trial and error, of successive approximation to an equilibrium system of prices and production. The matching of supply and demand, and of prices and costs is instrumental in solving the three basic problems of any economic system; i.e., (1) *what* things are to be produced, (2) *how* they are to be produced, and (3) *for whom* they are to be produced.

1. *What* things will be produced is determined by the votes of consumers—not every two years at the polls, but every day in their decisions to purchase this item and not that. Of course, the money that they pay into business cash registers ultimately provides the payrolls,

rents, and dividends that consumers receive in weekly income. Thus the circle is a complete one.

2. *How* things are produced is determined by the competition of different producers. The method that is cheapest at any time, because of both physical efficiency and cost efficiency, will displace a more costly method. The only way for producers to meet price competition and maximize profits is to keep costs at a minimum by adopting the most efficient method. The price is society's signaling device. Like a master who gives carrots and kicks to coax his donkey forward, the pricing system deals out profits and losses to get *What, How,* and *For Whom* decided.

3. *For Whom* things are produced is determined by supply and demand in the markets for productive services: by wage rates, land rents, interest rates, and profits, all of which go to make up everybody's income—relative to everyone else and relative to the whole. Of course, the character of the resulting distribution of income is highly dependent upon the initial distribution of property ownership and on acquired or inherited abilities."

Of course, the above description ignores a number of major imperfections. Sometimes "competitors" do not compete. Sometimes a dominant company in a given industry possesses such market power that it can produce more or less what it wishes and price it more or less at a level to maximize its profits. Sometimes advertising is misleading. Sometimes quality of items produced is shoddy and unsatisfactory. Sometimes government intervention discourages rather than enhances competition. Sometimes government rules have undesirable side effects not anticipated by legislators. In many of these cases the consumer will normally be capable of achieving corrective action by refusing to purchase the articles involved. In other instances government action is called for to effect a solution or to correct an earlier, misdirected government "solution."

2. Government Intervention

One apparently serious shortcoming of a private enterprise, laissez faire system was described by John Maynard Keynes. Keynes concentrated on the possibility that a private enterprise economy could achieve equilibrium for long periods of time at a condition of high unemployment just as readily as it could at full employment.

Keynes emphasized that each person's, and thus a society's total, income is used either for consumption or savings. These savings are then turned into investment which supports further production and, thus, further employment and further consumption. However, saving and investment are separate activities performed largely by separate segments of the economy: saving is primarily by individuals and investment primarily by business. In a "mature" economy, Keynes visualized that a lack of potentially profitable investment opportunities could result in an excess of savings, even with very low interest rates to encourage investment and discourage saving. This could happen if there were an inordinately large accumulation of capital assets which would produce goods at a more rapid rate than they could be consumed.

In such a situation, restricted investment would limit the new employment opportunities and a high-unemployment equilibrium could be reached from which it would be difficult for either labor or business to escape unaided. Government was seen as the obvious and, in fact, the only source of such aid.

The cure was to be effected by increasing investment, but the medicine was to be given primarily to consumers in the form of inducements to increase their demand. Government spending in excess of its tax revenues (fiscal policy) was the source of these inducements. The increased demand would stimulate new investment. Additionally the government, through its control of the money supply, could assure that low interest rates and readily available funds (monetary policy) provided a supplementary encouragement to investment. The increased investment would boost employment, and in time a new equilibrium with higher employment and higher consumption would be attained. As unemployment disappeared and inflation became the equal and opposite danger, it too could be controlled by applying the same basic remedies; i.e., fiscal and monetary policy actions, but in reverse.

Many of Keynes' ideas were incorporated in the national policies of the "New Deal" during the 1930's, and in the policies of subsequent administrations after the end of World War II. The responsibilities assigned to the Federal Government by the Employment Act of 1946 were of definite Keynesian origin and put government intervention in the economy on a generally accepted basis. The breadth and depth of this intervention has increased steadily ever since. The section to follow on "Government Policies," discusses the impacts of government on the economy.

3. Inflation

One of the most serious economic problems in the American economic system today is the accelerating inflation experienced over the last decade. A number of recent developments which have been translated into increasingly severe inflationary conditions are: food shortages, energy price surges, the effects of environmental protection costs, the coincidence of high-level economic activity in all the developed countries, the devaluation of the dollar, and the government deficits of the Vietnam war years. In contrast, however, a number of potentially deflationary occurrences such as the recessions of 1967 and 1970, and the collapse of the full-size car market in the United States in 1974, have had only minor impacts on prices. Only in the case of basic commodities (e.g. lumber) does the system still seem to remain sensitive to deflationary pressures.

The United States has not had a long history of continued inflation. Until recently the pattern has been alternating inflationary and deflationary cycles. As noted by Gabriel Hauge, the wholesale prices on average in the United States were no higher in 1945 than in 1875.[11] Thus, it appears that a number of rigidities have developed which make the United States economy inflation-prone and deflation-resistant. Two such rigidities which have contributed to this rather strong inflationary bias are: industry marketing practices which maintain or increase prices in the face of reductions in demand, and labor bargaining practices which react similarly in the face of falling demand for labor. Another primary source of inflationary bias which has been built into the economy since World War II is the unbalanced way in which Keynesian economics has been applied. Since 1946 and the passage of the Employment Act of that year, domestic public policy has been directed almost single-mindedly toward achieving national employment objectives. The performance of the economy has been judged primarily by the number of jobs it produces. With this bias, fiscal and monetary actions concentrated on maximizing economic growth and full employment despite an almost continuous string of government deficits in good years and bad. In fact, the Federal Government has managed to create surpluses, aggregating about $20 billion, in only 7 of the last 28 years while running deficits totaling $179 billion in the other 21 years.

This tendency of government to generate deficits results from attempts to satisfy claims from various sectors of society which in the aggregate are excessive. Politicians are sensitive to such claims, and understandably so, since nearly all of them are legitimate attempts to solve real needs. Unfortunately, the economy has a maximum potential output. Inflation is caused when the aggregate claims on output exceed that maximum potential, and when these claims are "monetized" by government deficits

and the money-creating capability of the banking system and the Federal Reserve Bank.

F. Government Policies

Government policies and activities are major factors in the assessment of where we stand now. Purchases of goods and services by the government sector (federal, state, local) in pursuit of government policies, as well as transfer payments which influence the purchasing power of designated groups, have major effects on economic growth. Expenditures for services provided by government are shown in Table 5•11.

The most striking changes have occurred in the upward shifts in the fields of education, health, welfare, and public assistance. By 1973, expenditures on health, welfare, etc. were some 8.6 times as large as they were in 1955, while spending on education was about 6.4 times as large. In contrast, spending on national defense, veterans' benefits, space, and international relations had only doubled. In 1955 government expenditures constituted about 24.5 percent of the total GNP of $398 billion. By 1973 government total expenditures had grown to 32 percent of a GNP of $1,295 billion. These increases are a continuation of a long upward trend which began with government expenditures of

Table 5•11
FEDERAL, STATE & LOCAL GOVERNMENT EXPENDITURES
(Billions of Dollars)

	Function	1955*	1973
1.	National defense, veterans benefits, space, international affairs..	$46.5	$99.3
2.	General government, interest paid, civilian services (e.g. postal service)	12.9	74.4
3.	Health, welfare, public assistance, old age and retirement	14.6	125.8
4.	Highways, housing, communications, natural resources, agriculture	11.7	39.0
5.	Education	11.6	74.5
	Total	$97.3	$413.0

* 1955 was used as the base year to avoid distortions created by military expenditures in Korea during 1952. Care has been taken to avoid double counting in the case of grants-in-aid from the federal to the other levels of government.

Source: United States Government Statistics, National Income Accounts and July 1974 issue of *Survey of Current Business*

some 10 percent of the GNP just before the depression of the 1930's.

The growth of government is part of a continuing shift in the United States economy to services such as health, education and recreation, as opposed to consumer goods. Government at one level or another is seen as the only practicable channel for delivery of many such services. For this reason the continued growth of government seems assured.

It must be noted that private industry provides many of the goods and services used by government to perform its varied functions. In other areas such as public old age benefits and welfare payments, the government acts as a transfer agent from the taxpayer to the recipient.

The growth of government is reflected in public employment. Today one of every six workers in the work force is a civilian government employee. During the period 1952 to 1973, total civilian employment rose by about 35 percent while nonmilitary total government employment more than doubled, rising from 6.6 million to 14.1 million. Most of this increase was at the state and local level. Federal employment only rose from 2.4 million to 2.7 million from 1952 to 1973 while the state and local figure jumped from 4.2 million to 11.3 million.

Public education, with more than 5.9 million full-time employees, is the largest single source of government employment and represents a major portion of local tax expenditures. Some 4 million are employed in elementary and secondary education at the local level. The rest are in public higher education, primarily at the state level. Employment in public education has risen at a 5.7 percent annual rate over the last twenty years. The greatest growth was in the 1957 to 1968 period in response to the postwar baby boom and the impact of the National Defense Education Act of 1958 which encouraged more students to go to college and stay longer. From 1957 to 1972 the number of PhD degrees awarded annually rose from less than 7,000 to about 30,000.

In recent years the factors causing the public education boom have weakened and they are projected to weaken further. The postwar baby crop has largely moved out of school and into the labor force. Federal expenditures seem to have reached a plateau, although research and development grants related to energy and the environment may provide a new source of higher education dollars during the coming decade. Overall public employment is distributed in the categories as shown in Table 5·12.

In conclusion, many factors have contributed to the growing importance of the public sector in the economy. The growth of social needs and the

Table 5·12
GOVERNMENT CIVILIAN EMPLOYMENT: 1973 (Thousands)

Year and Function	Total	Federal[1]	State	Local
Total 1973	14,139	2,786	3,013	8,339
National defense and international relations	1,053	1,053	(X)	(X)
Postal service	692	692	(X)	(X)
Education	5,922	21	1,280	4,621
Teachers	3,214	(X)	391	2,823
Highways	604	5	287	312
Health and hospitals	1,375	221	553	601
Police protection	616	35	66	515
Fire protection	299	(X)	(X)	299
Sanitation and sewerage	206	(X)	(X)	206
Parks and recreation	191	(X)	(X)	191
Natural resources	413	225	158	30
Financial administration	381	112	103	167
All other	2,387	422	567	1,398

(X) Not applicable
1 Includes Federal civilian employees outside United States

Source: United States Bureau of the Census, *Public Employment, Annual*

increasing cost of providing public services such as education, law enforcement, recreation, and welfare suggest that the importance of government in the economy will continue to expand.

G. Social and Political Conditions

Social and political conditions are, of course, significant determinants of economic growth. This section presents an assessment of where we stand now in these areas based on the perspective provided by certain social indicators and public attitudes.

1. Social Indicators

The following fields are used to provide statistical measures of social well-being: public safety, education, housing, leisure and recreation, and exercise of franchise. (With the exception of exercise of franchise, data for this summary have been drawn from: *Social Indicators 1973*, Executive Office of the President, Office of Management and Budget, Washington, D.C., 1973.)

Public Safety: Violent crime began to rise sharply in the 1960's, climbing from less than 200 per 100,000 population, to almost 400 in 1972. During the same period crimes involving property rose from some 1,000 per 100,000 population to over 2,400. In 1972 over 40 percent of the population over 18 years of age was afraid to walk alone at night. (Source: American Institute of Public Opinion, Princeton, N.J.) The crime rate in cities of over 250,000 population was twice that of cities between 100,000 and 250,000.

Education: In addition to the earlier discussion of education, it may be noted that the high school graduation rate has risen from below 50 percent in 1946 to almost 80 percent in 1972. Over 60 percent of those 18 to 24 years old have achieved a high school education. Undergraduate enrollment in schools of higher and continuing education grew from less than 10 percent of the 18 to 24 year olds in 1940 to about 24 percent in 1972. It peaked in 1968.

Housing: Families living in substandard housing units dropped from about 50 percent in 1940 to about 7 percent in 1970. There are more than twice as many black families in substandard housing as all other races. In 1971, 80 percent of all persons were satisfied with their neighborhoods, but less than 50 percent were completely satisfied.

Leisure and Recreation: Better than 95 percent of United States households have television, and the average daily viewing time is almost 6½ hours per household. As income rises, there is greater participation in sports and physical leisure activities. However, most United States leisure time is spent in sedentary activities.[12]

Exercise of Franchise: The percentage of persons of voting age in the United States who exercised their vote in presidential elections declined from 63.1 percent in 1960 to 55.7 percent in 1972. This decline was experienced despite the extension of the voting right to 18, 19, and 20 year olds in 1972.[13]

2. Public Attitudes

Public attitude surveys show a continuing decline of confidence in institutional leadership—i.e., educators, politicians, scientists, and businessmen. On a scale of "believability", the business leader often seems to rank well below other leaders and opinion setters.[14]

In a 1973 Harris Survey it was reported that, with the exception of the press and television news, all other institutions measured, including medicine, organized religion, the Supreme Court, the Congress, major companies, and the military, had suffered losses in public confidence. Among the public, principal concerns are with inflation and the economy, and integrity in government (Table 5•13).

While the confidence in government is declining, there is a belief that government at all levels can be made to work well. There is little if any evidence that the American people seek to change basic standards of society. Rather they seek to expand the citizen's role and increase communication with leadership (Table 5•14).

With regard to confidence in business leadership, Louis Harris has concluded that:

"The people do not ask that corporate institutions be abolished, but they are demanding broader and better performance, or they will opt for different leadership. Surprisingly, this comes not from the low income and least privileged segment of society but rather from the traditionally privileged, the better educated young and people of higher income. And this group is saying that unless things change there will be mounting demands for a change of leadership at the helm of business. The main question they will be asking themselves is: To what extent are businessmen using all the power available to them to make the United States establishment really work?"[15]

H. Social Change

An effort to present a profile of "Where We Stand Now" must include a discussion of the general

Table 5•13
ISSUES OF CONCERN

	Percent* 1973	1972	Change
Economy/inflation	72	57	+ 15
Integrity in Government	43	5	+38
Crime	17	16	+ 1
Drugs	14	19	− 5
Welfare reform	13	15	− 2
Pollution/ecology	11	13	− 2
Taxes	11	40	−29
Energy shortage	10	—	+ 10
Education	9	7	+ 2
Alienation/social breakdown	8	1	+ 7
Race/discrimination	7	21	−14
Older People	7	10	− 3
War in Indochina	4	29	−25
Health care	3	5	− 2
Housing	2	3	− 1

Source: United States Government Printing Office, *Confidence and Concern: Citizens View American Government—A Survey of Public Attitudes,* Washington, D.C. December 1973.

* Percent of respondents expressing concern

96

Table 5.14

PUBLIC ATTITUDE TOWARD INSTITUTIONAL SYSTEMS SUMMER, 1974

(Percent)*

	Political system	System of justice	System of business and industry	System of organized labor
a. Basically sound and essentially good	8%	9%	16%	11%
b. Basically sound but needs *some* improvement	42	41	46	41
c. Not too sound, needs *many* improvements	28	31	22	25
d. Basically *unsound*, needs fundamental overhauling	19	14	9	14
Don't know	3	4	7	9

Source: *Roper Reports Public Opinion Survey,* July 1974.

* Percent of respondents expressing various views.

phenomenon of social change and the subject of changing social values. In this section the process of social change is described and the major forces shaping social values are noted. The concept of social values is discussed, and directions in changing values are outlined. Lastly, speculations are advanced as to the depth and permanency of changes in social values.

1. The Process of Social Change

Social change has been defined as the "process by which alteration occurs in the structure and function of a social system."[16] Examples of social change could range from a national revolution to a new manufacturing technique, a new form of local governance, the practice of birth control methods by a family, or shifts in buying patterns in the marketplace.

Social change occurs at the level of the individual or the level of the social system. Change takes place as the individual adopts or rejects an innovation or a new way of doing something. The process in which an innovation becomes generally accepted is called diffusion, modernization, learning or socialization. Change at the social system level has been most typically called *development,* and involves the general introduction of new ideas which alter production methods and/or social organization. Changes at both levels are closely interrelated.

The process of social change frequently takes the form of a *movement.* Some examples of contempo-

rary movements are Black Power, ecology, consumerism, and the Jesus Revolution.

Social change usually follows an evolutionary course. The process has been defined in a very positive way by Julian Huxley as "a self-maintaining, self-transforming, and self-transcending process, directional in time, and therefore, irreversible, which in its course generates ever fresh novelty, greater variety, more complex organization, higher levels of awareness, and increasingly conscious mental activity."[17]

2. Major Forces Shaping Social Values

There are several major historic, economic, and social forces which have shaped social values in America in the past and which remain dominant influences today. The impacts of these forces and the reactions against them are the source of "changing social values." These forces are: industrialization, urbanization, the growth of science and technology, social leveling, organization and specialization, and affluence.

a. Industrialization and the Emergence of a Post-Industrial Society

The term, "The Industrial Revolution," describes the transformation which occurred between the middle 1700's and the middle 1800's in which agricultural activities were replaced by materials manufacturing activities as the dominant factor in the economy. During this time, hand labor was replaced

97

by machinery and wind and water were replaced by the steam engine. The factory and the factory town became the dominant social institutions. The main human role was unskilled "blue-collar" workers organized under an elaborate division of labor.

While the trend toward industrialization is continuing, new forces are working to produce a transformation to what has been termed a post-industrial society. It is a ". . . shift to industries based not only on new and different technologies but also on different science, different logic, and different perception. They are also different in their manual workers."[18] The social transformation represented by the post-industrial society may be as profound as that which occurred in the industrial revolution.

b. Urbanization

The long-range trend toward urbanization—people moving from rural areas to urban areas—is closely associated with industrialization. Urbanization was constant through the end of the 1960's. The process prompted one noted demographer to comment that: "The human species is moving rapidly in the direction of an almost exclusively urban existence."[19]

Very recent population surveys seem to indicate that the long standing movement from rural to urban areas is slowing or may even have been reversed. If so, this would represent a historic development. Even if a reverse flow is underway, however, it will take some time to overcome the dominant trend of urbanization.

c. Growth of Science, Knowledge, and Technology

Science, knowledge, and technology are following a trend of exponential growth. Time intervals between the discovery of major natural forces are constantly shrinking. The number of scientists has been doubling every fifteen years. Most of the scientists that have ever lived are alive today. Similarly, the number of scientific journals has been growing at an exponential rate. Science and technological development are accepted as national enterprises and are heavily supported by federal funds.

The growth of science and technology impacts on society in many ways. It requires a more highly educated work force; educational standards for employment must rise; investment in education increases; and power and authority shift toward those who are more highly educated.

Two major components of the growth trend in science, knowledge, and technology are automation of production and automation of information. Invention of the electronic digital computer was a major factor in making automation possible. Computers have also provided a major stimulus to the growth of science and knowledge.

d. Social Leveling

Another force shaping social values is "democratization" or "social leveling." Many areas, such as politics and the professions, have undergone this process. The process is continuing in other areas. For example, the entrance of blacks into the mainstream of American life is a major step in this trend. David Riesman has described the democratization of taste as being manifested in the widespread knowledge about the use of wines, books, music, and the arts. According to Riesman and others, the "leisure class" has been constantly growing.[20]

These trends represent the realization of the democratic belief in egalitarianism, the principle "all men are created equal." The inequalities that once separated social classes, age groups, sexes, and races, are continually disappearing. One example is the determination of women's groups to establish equality of the sexes. Another example is the shift in the legal definition of adulthood from 21 years to 18 years.

One significant aspect of the continuing trend of egalitarianism is the emergence of a "meritocracy." Leaders in all fields are being chosen by ability rather than through inheritance or economic power. This social trend is necessary in a highly technical society in which operations and organizations are so complex that they must be led by those most qualified. Hence, leaders are being selected for their abilities. This social trend has contributed to the rapid rise in education.

e. Organization and Specialization

One of the most powerful forces affecting social change today is the dual trend toward organization and specialization. The economist John Galbraith stated in 1971 that "The decisive power in modern industrial society is exercised not by capital but by organization, not by the capitalist but by the industrial bureaucrat."[21] The evolution to an "organizational society" stemming from The Industrial Revolution has also been described by others.[22] The success of the space program has been attributed to extraordinary organization rather than to the genius of individuals.

Large-scale organization has evolved in the form of bureaucracy, characterized by a hierarchy of authority, a system of rules, and impersonality. This organizational form is a major factor in the shaping of social change today. The division of labor involved in large-scale organization has promoted the trend toward specialization. As the volume of information pertaining to each field of specialization has increased, the specialists have more narrowly limited their areas of expertise.

The trend toward specialization has stimulated a parallel trend toward professionalization. The experts who comprise a profession have a sense of group identity, highly specialized training, and a system of internal communication and administration, including a body of ethics and standards of performance.

f. Affluence

One of the most widely discussed socio-economic forces is affluence. Affluence has been described as real income per person consisting of real consumption plus real saving per person where real consumption includes use of free goods as well as priced goods.[23] In the United States, average real income per person has roughly doubled every 50 years for two centuries and is forecast to rise even faster in the next 100 years.[24]

The continuation of poverty in the midst of affluence must also be noted. This discrepancy is being overcome, however. In 1960 the United States Bureau of Census classified 40 million people, or more than one out of every five, as living below the poverty level. In 1974, there were 24 million, or 12 percent of the population, classified as officially poor with one third of all blacks classified below the poverty level.[25] The disparity has led economist James Tobin to conclude that "The degree of inequality of income between rich and poor in this country is out of proportion with what is needed for the efficient progressive functioning of the capitalistic system."[26]

Thus, the trends of increasing affluence and slowly declining poverty are not fully told in statistics. The disparity between rich and poor continues to cause major social problems which are exacerbated by mass media advertising which feeds rising expectations.

3. The Concept of Social Values

The phenomenon of changing social values is frequently referred to in general terms but the meaning of the concept is seldom made clear. Values are expressed in human choices and behavior or lifestyles. Thus, a value is more an action or a process of valuation, than a describable quantity or quality.[27]

The concept of values also refers to a belief system—that is, views about fundamental matters of truth, justice, love, and beauty, etc. Beliefs and feelings on such subjects are interrelated in what is called a *value system*. A value system tends to be held consistently in a society. At the same time, however, there may be an infinite variation in the priorities and scale of values of different individuals. Values may be held consciously or unconsciously. The value system determines attitudes and reactions to events. The values held unconsciously, at the emotional level, can produce strong reactions in individuals and societies.

Values of individuals and societies are observable in choices and behavior associated with: 1) the use of time and other resources; 2) the order in which things are given up; and 3) the types of risks taken. Values are also manifest in the kinds of symbols, goals, and leaders which are prevalent.

Another perspective on social values is the notion that people tend to place a low value on things which they can take for granted because they are prevalent or abundant. This idea has been applied to explain the dynamics of value shifts between generations where the younger generation tends to reject or place a low value on those things valued by the older generation which had to strive to achieve them.

Values are based on the instrumental qualities of the thing or behavior valued; that is, what works or what serves to meet some need. Doubts about whether some arrangement or process is working well can lead to a questioning of the value. The growth issue illustrates this point. The question has been raised whether traditionally functional activities are indeed functional. Does growth "work"? Is it "valuable"?

4. Directions in Changing Social Values

The major economic and social forces described and the reactions against them are producing changes in social values. These changes are in several directions as discerned by different social observers.[28] They can be described under the headings of humanistic values, pragmatic values, utilitarian values, and sensate values. Underlying these higher values are the basic human values stemming from the physical needs for survival. These include food, shelter, etc.

a. Humanistic Values

Humanistic values are reflected in man's growing interest in himself and his environment. This value orientation is expressed in the concern for "quality of life." Another manifestation is interest in community participation. Humanistic values are in general contrary to materialistic values. Attitudes toward freedom provide an indication of humanistic values. In 1974, ". . . five of the nation's top public opinion analysts (reported) there is growing respect for the rights of others and the right to be different, a realization that when one group's freedom is attacked, the freedom of all groups is threatened."[29] Humanistic values are frequently expressed through institutionalized social responsibilities in programs like social security and other forms of social insurance supported by society.

b. Pragmatic and Utilitarian Values

Historically, pragmatism has been and continues to be a strong social value in the United States. This value is concerned with methods of solving problems. Intellectual pursuits are valued according to this criterion. Utilitarianism is a companion value to pragmatism. The utilitarian value framework views social institutions, such as laws and other instruments of society, in terms of their utility.

c. Materialistic Values

Materialistic, or sensate, values are those associated with gratification of the senses. These values are contrasted with values based on spiritual needs or abstract ideas.

> "The sensate form of culture and society is based upon the ultimate principle that true reality and value are sensory and that beyond the reality which we can see, hear, smell, touch and taste there is no other reality and no real values."[30]

Sensory values were traditionally concerned most with wealth, health, consumption, sensual pleasures, physical comfort, power, and personal recognition. The concern for material goods as a value characterizing modern society has been referred to by art historian Kenneth Clark as "Heroic Materialism."[31]

The long-term trend toward materialistic values is in the process of being fundamentally altered by a resurgence of humanistic values. This is illustrated by the resurgence of interest in religion and mysticism which represents a new search for or belief in supersensory reality. It remains to be seen whether the longer term materialistic trend or the new emergent humanistic trend will prevail as the overall direction of social values in this area.

d. Empiricist Values

Empiricism as a value is related to sensate values. It is concerned with sense experience as a source of knowledge. Empiricism provides the basis for science. It is fundamental to the belief that man can control and manipulate the physical world.

e. Concluding Comment on Directions in Changing Social Values

The longer term trends and the newer directions in changing social values illustrate the dual nature of man. He is both physical and spiritual. These two aspects are mutually exclusive and produce values which coexist in a state of dynamic tension. At different times one or the other may tend to predominate. The current direction appears to be toward a resurgence of the spiritual to a level at least equal to the material. This suggests the merging of the "two cultures" of science and the humanities.

5. Speculations About the Depth and Permanence of Changes in Social Values and the Underlying Factors Prompting the Changes

One view of the current changes in social values is that they are symptomatic of a society in the midst of a profound and even revolutionary transformation. The terms post-industrial revolution, "cultural revolution," and "transitional era" have been used to describe the depth of the changes. These descriptions suggest an expectation that changing social values will permanently alter lifestyles and the whole social order.

The new "post-industrial society" is characterized by several factors which are stated in capsule form here to provide a clear definition of what is meant by the term.

(1) The conversion from a production to a *service-based economy.*

(2) Changes in production technology by which *automated and computerized means of production and administration* are transforming the conditions of production and management, and substantially *eliminating the struggle for material existence.*

(3) Changes in composition of the labor force to highly trained and specialized workers constituting a *technical elite.*

(4) *Changes in social values* stimulated by new science and technology, electronic media, and/or moral and cultural regeneration amounting to a *cultural revolution.*

Whether or not these changes in sum or in part constitute a "revolution" is a matter of discussion and debate. One theory is that advancing science and technology represent the truly revolutionary forces.[32] In this view, the reactions against science and technology in the form of the youth rebellion and social turmoil of the 1960's marked a normal process of social adjustment to a period of technical and economic transition. In this theory the "counter culture" represents a counter revolution against the rapid changes caused by technology. The counter revolution will pass and the mainstream of the technical revolution will prevail.

A second theory is that new values, new consciousness, and new lifestyles constitute the true revolution. This view is set forth by Charles Reich in *The Greening of America*.[33] In this view, science and technology are ultimately counter-revolutionary and thus will not prevail.

The dichotomy presented in these two theories is simplistic because both forces can be expected to continue simultaneously. However, the two theories do indicate the depth of current changes in values and the social order. What is involved in these changes is man's view of the world and how he fits into it. Until relatively recently, this view was derived from concepts of Newtonian physics and Aristotelian logic. These concepts and even their underlying laws have been challenged and displaced in the physical sciences by Einstein's theory of *relativity*, Bohr's concept of *complimentarity* and Heisenberg's theory of *indeterminacy*. Such basic changes in what is thought to constitute reality in the physical world have been translated and transferred via philosophical thought, art, and literature to the social context and ultimately find expression as new values.

The new concepts raise doubts for some about traditional values, and they create ambiguity. During this period the old and new value systems or world views are competing for general acceptance. The debate about economic growth is one manifestation of the dynamics of changing social values.

FOOTNOTES

1. *Social Indicators 1973*, Executive Office of the President, Office of Management and Budget, Washington, D.C. p. 246 and *Population Profile of the United States*, 1974, Bureau of the Census, p. 3.

2. S. H. Slichter, *Economic Growth in the United States, It's History, Problems and Prospects*, Louisiana State Univ. Press, 1961.

3. McGraw-Hill Survey of Pollution Control Expenditures, May 1974.

4. *Economic Report of the President 1974*, p. 168.

5. While statistically in this category the United States is below other advanced countries, some discrepancies may be due to statistical definition. The United States defines "live birth" as a "pulsing umbilical cord" even if the infant does not survive birth, while a number of other developed countries define "live birth" as survival after varying periods following birth.

6. *The Cost of Clean Air*, Annual Report of the Administrator of the EPA to the Congress of the United States, October 1973, in compliance with Public Law 91-604, the Clean Air Act, as amended, and *The Economics of Clean Water*, 1973, Annual Report of the Administrator of the EPA to the Congress of the United States in compliance with Section 26(a) Federal Water Pollution Control Act.

7. *United States Statistical Abstract*, 1973, p. 593.

8. A. Smith, *The Wealth of Nations*, 1776.

9. J. M. Keynes, *The General Theory of Employment, Interest & Money*, 1936.

10. Paul Samuelson, *Economics*, McGraw-Hill, New York, 1964, pp. 39, 40.

11. Gabriel Hauge, "Our Curable Case of Inflation," *The Conference Board Record*, October 1974.

12. John P. Robinson and Philip E. Converse, *"66 Basic Tables of Time-Budget Data for the United States"* as reported in *Social Indicators 1973*.

13. *United States Statistical Abstract*, 1973, p. 380.

14. Third Roper Reports Public Opinion Survey, Item F-11, January, 1974.

15. Chamber of Commerce of the United States, Washington Report, November 26, 1973, p. 3.

16. Everett M. Rogers and Floyd Shoemaker, *Communication of Innovations: A Cross-Cultural Approach*, 2nd ed. New York: The Free Press, 1971, p. 7.

17. Julian Huxley, "Evolution, Cultural and Biological," *Yearbook of Anthropology*, 1955.

18. Peter Drucker, *The Age of Discontinuity*, New York: Harper and Row, 1968, p. 12.

19. Kingsley Davis, "The Origin and Growth of Urbanization in the World," *Readings in Urban Geography*, Harold M. Mayer and Clyde F. Kohn (eds.), Chicago: The University of Chicago Press, 1967, p. 64.

20. David Riesman, *Individualism Reconsidered*, Glenco, Illinois: The Free Press, 1954.

21. John Kenneth Galbraith, *The New Industrial State*, Boston: Houghton Mifflin, 2nd Edition, 1971, p. xix.

22. Robert Presthus, *The Organizational Society*, New York: Vintage Books, 1965 edition.

23. Barnham P. Beckwith, *The Next 500 Years: Scientific Predictions of Major Social Trends*, New York: Exposition Press, 1967, p. 89.

24. Beckwith, p. 90.

25. *Money Income & Poverty Status of Families and Persons in the United States:* 1974 (Advance Report) Census Series P. 60 No. 99, July 1975.

26. Quoted in the *Los Angeles Times*, July 19, 1972.

27. This concept of values as a process of valuation is developed more completely by Kenneth E. Boulding in, "The Formation of Values as a Process in Human Learning," a paper in *Transportation and Community Values*, Report of a Conference held at Warrenton, Virginia, March 2-5, 1969, Highway Research Board, National Academy of Sciences, Washington, D.C., 1969.

28. Pitirim A. Sorokin, *The Basic Trends of Our Times*, New Haven: College and University Press, 1964; Herman Kahn and Anthony J. Wiener, *The Year 2000: A Framework for Speculation on the Next Thirty-Three Years*, New York: Macmillan, 1967; Herman Kahn and B. Bruce-Briggs,

Things to Come: Thinking About the Seventies and Eighties, New York: Macmillan, 1972.

29. Quoted in the *Los Angeles Times,* February 24, 1974.

30. Pitirim A. Sorokin, *The Basic Trends of Our Times,* New Haven: College and University Press, 1964.

31. Kenneth Clark, *Civilization,* New York: Harper and Row, 1969, Chapter 13, "Heroic Materialism."

32. Kenneth Keniston, "A Second Look at the Uncommitted," *Social Policy 2:2 (July/August, 1971) pp. 6-19.*

33. Reich, Charles, *The Greening of America,* Bantam, 1971.

CHAPTER 6

United States Economic Growth and Energy Use

A. Introduction

The primary purposes of this chapter are: to investigate the range of feasible growth alternatives available to the United States over the long-term future; to assess the opportunities and risks associated with each alternative; and to identify the path which appears to maximize opportunities and minimize risks.

The approach to this analysis is comparable to that followed in Part I where the pro-growth and no-growth arguments were presented separately and then compared. The approach for this analytical effort is to develop three different scenarios for the future of growth. Each scenario is examined quantitatively and in detail, and in one scenario a major variant to the basic assumptions is also examined.

The development of such scenarios is a way of examining the practical consequences of policy actions intended to promote or inhibit growth. In other words, the scenarios are attempts to foresee what might happen over the next generation or two under different growth philosophies.

A variety of quantitative modeling techniques, as well as other less formal forecasting methods, are employed to produce and analyze the scenarios.

1. Development of the Scenarios

The three basic scenarios developed for this analysis encompass a broad range of possible future patterns of economic and energy growth. At one end of this range is an historic growth scenario which assumes a future governed by continued efforts to promote, if not to maximize, economic growth. It represents a continuation of conditions in the 1950's and 1960's during which there were no serious social or physical resource constraints on growth, and the population was growing at rates between 1.0 and 1.5 percent per year.

At the other extreme of this range, a low-growth scenario examines a future dominated by a concerted

national effort to move rapidly toward a steady-state society. In the low-growth environment, increasingly rigid constraints are assumed to be placed on many aspects of economic activity as well as on the consumption of depletable resources. In this environment, population trends would receive close scrutiny and every attempt would be made to prevent the total fertility rate from rising above its current level which is about 1.8 children per woman over her entire child-bearing years.

These two scenarios are attempts to represent the extremes of the *practical* range of United States economic growth possibilities over the next 25 years. The *theoretical* range might be somewhat larger; e.g., higher growth rates could be achieved by an all-out mobilization of the nation such as might be achieved under wartime conditions. Under all but disaster-induced conditions, however, the high and low growth alternatives are meant to approximate practical maximum and minimum growth alternatives for the nation.

Between the historic and the low-growth scenarios is a third case which reflects a number of developing economic and social forces tending to dampen earlier growth expectations. It is an attempt to depict an intermediate view which in many respects may be the most realistic of the three. The actual pattern of growth which will evolve in future years depends on technological, public policy, and resource developments which cannot be anticipated completely today.

2. Scope of the Forecasts

A number of different aspects of the growth phenomenon are included in the scenarios:

(1) Population,
(2) Agriculture,
(3) Growth of Income and Consumption,
(4) Minerals Demand and Supply,
(5) Energy Demand and Supply,

(6) Conservation and Environment,
(7) Pricing Policies,
(8) Capital Requirements, and
(9) Relations with the Rest of the World.

The objectives of the scenario analysis are to determine how these 9 aspects of growth interact to form the quantitative outlines of a future economy.

The time horizon of the forecasts is primarily the 25 years ending with the year 2000. However, the general prospects for the United States as it enters the 21st century are also evaluated.

A modern industrial society consists of a number of complex interdependent sectors. An event which affects one sector is felt throughout all the others by way of these interdependencies—or couplings. In examining the future of economic growth, therefore, it is necessary to consider as many of these sectors and their couplings as possible. It is a dangerous and artificial abstraction to concentrate on only one segment—such as energy—as if it could be uncoupled from all the rest.

By examining the broad variety of sectors enumerated above, this study has attempted to avoid the very real dangers of sub-optimization, i.e., of solving one problem in one part of a complex system only at the cost of ignoring or aggravating other equally important problems elsewhere in the system.

3. Forecasting Methods

The three scenarios are primarily based on the use of an econometric model. However, a variety of forecasting techniques was employed in developing the detailed implications of each scenario. These techniques included simple trend analysis, general technological forecasts, and combinations of trend analyses and judgmental forecasts.

Some of the major forecasting tools which were used are summarized below. More complete descriptions of these tools are provided in Appendices A, B, C, and D.

a. General Economic Conditions

A long term macro-econometric model prepared by Data Resources Inc. (DRI) was used as the primary tool for forecasting United States general economic conditions.[1] The DRI model also provided the means of simulating the impacts of environmental investment and conservation behavior. In reviewing the output from this model in the remainder of Chapter 6, it is important to remember that there are differences in the definition of GNP between the DRI

model and the National Income Account statistics. (See footnotes to Table 6.5).

b. Agriculture

An econometric model of the world food situation, developed at Case Western Reserve University, was used to determine prospects for United States agriculture and its relations with the rest of the world.

c. Output by Industry

An interindustry (input-output) model, also prepared by DRI, was used to examine output by industry and by sector (e.g., agriculture, manufacturing, households, etc.). This interindustry model is designed to forecast energy demands and energy supplies.

d. Energy Demand by Consuming Sector

Judgmental forecasts of energy demand by consuming sector, (e.g., transportation, residential) were prepared by the Edison Electric Institute (EEI) staff, giving consideration to a wide variety of other forecasts.

e. Energy Supply by Source

Judgmental forecasts of energy supply by source (e.g., oil, coal, nuclear) were prepared under the direction of the staff of the Electric Power Research Institute (EPRI) by a consultant. The forecasts were based on examination of the resource situation, the technology, and the environmental problems associated with each of the energy sources.

f. Energy Conversion

To complement the efforts described in the preceding two areas, detailed output was examined from a number of runs of the Pace Co. energy model. This model consists of a series of judgmental estimates of demand and supply linked together by a computer-based linear program. The program models the energy conversion industry and is formulated so as to minimize total energy costs for society, given the supply and demand constraints. The energy conversion industry is so defined as to include all industrial activities involved in transforming raw energy resources into the forms required by the final consumer; e.g., petroleum refining, electricity generation and distribution, etc.

g. Minerals Supply and Demand

Separate judgmental forecasts were made of the supply-demand situations for each of the major non-energy minerals. Consumption of each mineral was keyed to the DRI economic projections, using quantitative information on past trends in mineral consumption coupled with informed judgments as to reserve adequacy, costs of recovery, and technological change.

h. Capital Requirements

A detailed financial planning model, designed for electric utility company long-range planning, was adapted to forecast overall industry financial requirements. This model was developed by the Philadelphia Electric Company. The model: (1) transformed electric energy demand forecasts into kilowatt capacity requirements, (2) estimated earnings requirements, and (3) produced forecasts of external financing needs of the industry. Output from the DRI, EPRI and Pace forecasts was fed into this electric utility industry financial model. The financial results of this modeling effort are included in general terms in the scenario descriptions which follow. The detailed results of the financial modeling appear in Part III of this report.

i. Limitations of Forecasting Models

At best, mathematical models are only very approximate reflections of reality. However, they do provide a structured and internally consistent framework for evaluation, and in that sense they can be of great assistance in developing alternative views of the future. The models used in the study are among the best currently available. They have all been tested for calculational accuracy and internal consistency and have been subjected to certain ex-ante and ex-post tests of forecasting accuracy.[2]

It must be emphasized that the prime purpose of forecasting is to improve the quality of current decisions by exploring *possibilities* for the future, rather than to predict accurately what specific future *will* occur.

An additional discussion of the limitations of forecasting models is provided in Appendix A. In view of these recognized limitations, attempts were made to obtain two separate and largely independent forecasts of both energy demand and energy supply. Future energy demands were based primarily on the DRI inter-industry model but a separate estimate was obtained from the EEI judgmental forecasts by consuming sector as described above under "Output

by Industry" and "Energy Demand by Consuming Sector." Future energy supplies were based on the EPRI judgmental forecast but were supplemented by estimates from the DRI inter-industry model. Energy demand and supply estimates from the Pace Co. model were examined and compared with the DRI, EEI and EPRI efforts.

B. Summary of Conclusions

Major conclusions from the scenario analyses will be summarized under the categories of: (a) population and agriculture, (b) economic growth, (c) personal consumption, (d) non-energy minerals, (e) energy demand, and (f) energy supply. These factors will be compared and contrasted for each scenario (Case A—high growth, Case C—low growth, and Case B—intermediate growth). Finally the prospects for the nation in the years after 2000 are considered, with emphasis on the intermediate growth alternative.

The summary concentrates on real Gross National Product since it is the best available and most widely accepted measure of the nation's overall growth. Real personal consumption per capita and real family income distributions are emphasized since they are good measures of the absolute and relative economic welfare of average citizens. Minerals and energy receive concentrated attention both as basic ingredients of economic growth and as nonrenewable resources, which have been of great concern in recent years.

Unfortunately, there is no single measure of the quality of life which can be forecast to provide a counterpart to the economic measures discussed in the summary. However, when economic growth is balanced with a concern for the total environment, the quality of life can be expected to rise with increasing economic welfare. As discussed in Chapter 4, the adjustment mechanisms of technology, the price system, government regulations, and social change can promote types of growth which enhance both economic welfare and quality of life.

1. Population and Agriculture

Neither increased population pressures nor an inadequate agricultural base is a valid reason for limiting economic growth in the United States over the next 50 years. Even if population growth accelerates and the total fertility rate rebounds to 2.5 (the average of the 1960's) as is assumed in Case A, the United States population will not exceed 350 million by 2025.[3] The nation's agricultural capacity can readily adapt to such population trends. A fertility rate of 2.5 causes continuing increases in population, however, and if maintained would result in a national population of over 2 billion people (or about 10 times the current level) by the year 2200. A variety of economic and social pressures might be expected to alter fertility rates long before such population levels were reached.

In 1972 and 1973 the fertility rate in the United States slipped below the replacement level of 2.1, assumed for the moderate-growth case (Case B), and approached 1.8, the rate used for the low-growth case (Case C). The population trends created by these two fertility rates are shown on Charts 6•1 and 6•2 along with that of Case A. In Case B, population will rise to about 315 million and then stabilize, while in Case C it will peak at 270 million and then begin to decline. Social trends in the United States make it likely that actual population growth will approximate Case B, making it unnecessary for the nation to consider any public policy related to population limits.

The nation's farms already have the capacity to produce sufficient foods to sustain a population of 350 million at adequate levels of nutrition. Increases in productivity and acreage have the potential to accommodate the Case A population growth and still continue to increase agricultural exports, at least through the next 50 years. The Case Western Reserve world model indicates that, even with a population growth close to that of Case A, United States agricultural output of proteins can be four times the domestic needs by 2025, in contrast to 1.9 times at present. Under the more likely Case B population levels there may, of course, be additional potential for increased exports.

2. Economic Growth

The potential for further economic growth in the United States will remain strong over the remainder of this century, unless extreme growth limiting policies are instituted by government action. Real growth of gross national product (after inflation effects are removed) will probably average between 3.5 and 3.7 percent per year over the next 25 years. This is approximately one-half percentage point lower than typical growth rates of the post World War II period.

The potential for such a future growth rate lies in

Chart 6•1
UNITED STATES POPULATION

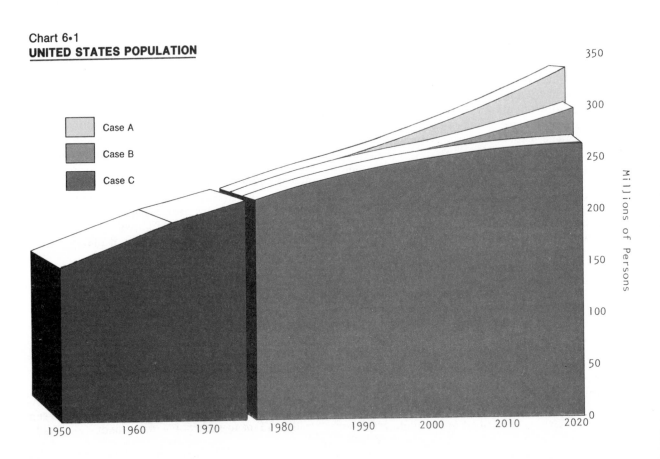

106

Chart 6·2
POPULATION INCREASE FROM 1975

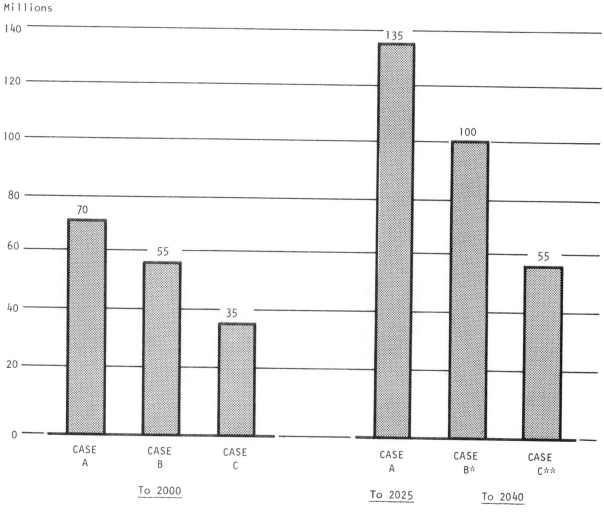

Millions

* Would stabilize at 2040.
** Would peak at 2040, then start to decline.

the combination of the following conditions: (1) continuing growth in the labor force, (2) reasonable incentives to increase investment in productive plant and equipment, and (3) a continuing improvement in productivity.[4] Such conditions are assumed to prevail in the Case B, moderate growth alternative.

Some observers are concerned that historic rates of improvement in productivity cannot be maintained in the future as the shift continues from agriculture and manufacturing to services. However, the scenarios in this study assume that major potentials exist for continued productivity improvement in services as well as in agriculture and manufacturing. Many

services, particularly those with greatest impact on the nation's economic output, exhibit large potentials for productivity improvement, e.g., wholesale and retail trade; finance, insurance and real estate; and government. The problems lie not so much in the absence of potentials for further improvements in productivity, as in society's willingness to adjust existing structural constraints to take advantage of such potentials. This study assumes that such constraints *will* gradually be adjusted.

Chart 6·3 summarizes three different trends in United States economic growth which are forecast for the three scenarios. The Case A growth, at 4.2

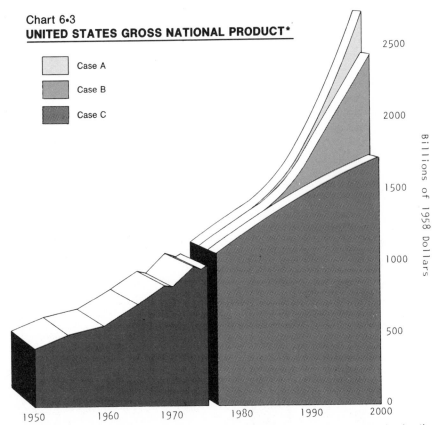

Chart 6•3
UNITED STATES GROSS NATIONAL PRODUCT*

Case A
Case B
Case C

Billions of 1958 Dollars

2500
2000
1500
1000
500
0

1950   1960   1970   1980   1990   2000

* Data Resources, Inc. definition of GNP is equal to GNP on a National Income Accounts basis plus the imputed value of service from consumer durables.

Table 6•1
**CASE A: SOURCES OF ECONOMIC GROWTH; 1975-2000
(Percent per Year)**

Sources[1]	Rate of Increase	Relative Weight[2]	Contribution To Growth
Labor			
Quantity..	1.23%	.63	0.77%
Quality	0.60	.63	0.38
Capital			
Quantity..	2.90	.37	1.07
Quality	0.80	.37	0.30
Total Factor Productivity	1.50	1.00	1.50
Real GNP...			4.02[3]

(1) Land (i.e. resources or "contributions of nature") is not considered to be a restraint on growth except to the degree that society limits its application of labor and capital to resource extraction.

(2) The relative contributions of capital and labor are determined by the average proportions of national income accruing to each during the period 1948-1972.

(3) The 4.02 percent calculated as the growth rate of potential GNP is below the 4.18 percent average growth rate forecast for Case A (See Table 6•5). This is because the GNP at the 1975 starting point for the forecast is significantly below potential GNP.

percent per year is just above the average rate for the 1947-1972 period and only slightly below the 4.3 percent rate experienced between 1961 and 1972. Vigorous public policy support of economic growth combines with a continuing strong increase in population to yield this high-growth forecast. Efforts to improve the environment would be restricted under Case A so that no major new investment programs to reduce pollution would be undertaken in addition to those already mandated. Under this high-growth alternative, the relative contributions of labor, capital, and productivity to economic growth are summarized in Table 6•1. A discussion of the measurement of productivity and other contributions to economic growth is given in Appendix E.

A moderate reduction in growth rates from the Case A scenario will result from the lower population growth and less vigorous public policy support for growth assumed for Case B. A continuation of current ecological concerns would be reflected in further expenditures aimed at environmental improvement. In Case B, energy supplies are assumed to be less readily available than in Case A, and a heightened awareness of resource depletion would probably put moderate supply pressures on other raw materials. The consequence is an average GNP growth of 3.5 to 3.7 percent per year for the Case B—moderate-growth scenario.

Case C anticipates a strong national commitment to the attainment of a steady-state, or low-growth society by the late 1980's. A combination of voluntary actions and compulsory legal restraints is assumed to be necessary. Gradual imposition of limits on resources use is contemplated as a primary method for limiting pollution as well as for conserving natural resources. When these constraints are combined with low population growth, the resulting forecast is an average annual increase in GNP of about 2.3 percent over the period from 1975 to 2000. Much of this growth is concentrated in the years prior to 1985 during the period when the growth-limiting restraints are being designed and implemented. After 1985 the growth rate averages only 1.7 percent per year.

Chart 6•4 compares GNP growth rates for the three scenarios. Table 6•2 compares the relative contributions of labor, capital, and productivity for Cases A, B, and C. Although resources are assumed to be available less rapidly in Cases B and C, the controlling restraints are still assumed to be imposed via limits on labor and capital inputs. Particularly in Case C, the labor and capital inputs are controlled by social and political decisions. The primary object of the Case C control actions is to limit resource depletion.

Chart 6•4
GROWTH RATES OF REAL GROSS NATIONAL PRODUCT
(Based on 1958 Dollars)

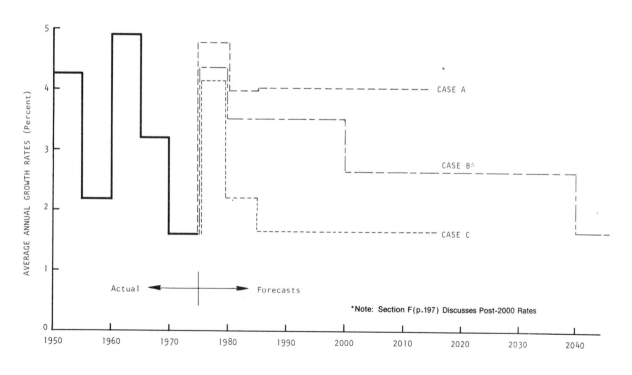

109

Table 6·2
**CONTRIBUTIONS TO ECONOMIC GROWTH
COMPARISON: CASE A, B, C: 1975-2000
(Percent per Year)**

	Case A	Case B	Case C
Labor			
Quantity	0.77%	0.68%	0.03%
Quality	0.38	0.38	0.38
Capital			
Quantity	1.07	0.83	0.29
Quality	0.30	0.30	0.06
Total Factor			
Productivity	1.50	1.50	1.50
Real GNP	4.02	3.69	2.20

The scenarios can also be compared by examining the proportions of families which gain an opportunity to escape from the low income ranges. In Case A, for example, the percentage of all families and unrelated individuals with money incomes below $6,000 per year (in constant 1975 dollars) drops from 25 percent in 1975 to 12.0 percent in the year 2000; a reduction of more than half. In Case C, however, the figure only drops to 17 percent.

The differences in real personal consumption per capita between Case A and Case B are not so significant as to suggest very different lifestyles for Case B than for Case A. Comparing Cases B and C shows a much greater difference. Under Case C conditions there will be a much greater emphasis on activities that consume only small amounts of

3. Personal Consumption

Physical output per capita will vary significantly under the three scenarios. In terms of real personal consumption per capita, Case A will provide an increase from about $4,600 per year in 1975 to about $10,300 in the year 2000 (in constant 1975 dollars). In the moderate-growth scenario, Case B, personal consumption will rise to about $9,980 in 2000 while in Case C the figure will be only $7,090 in the year 2000. Similar relationships can be seen from the trends in real GNP per capita shown in Chart 6·5. Note that in this case the data are plotted in terms of 1958 dollars.

Chart 6·5
REAL GROSS NATIONAL PRODUCT PER CAPITA*

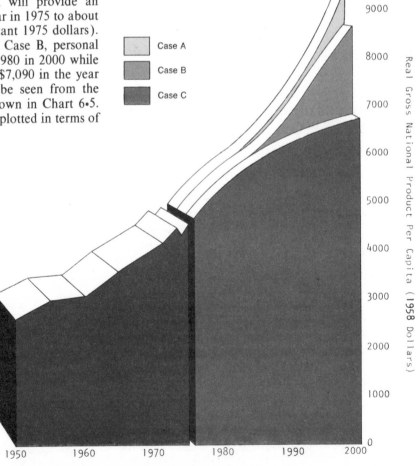

* Data Resources, Inc. definition of GNP is equal to GNP on a National Income Accounts basis plus the imputed value of service from consumer durables

nonrenewable resources; activities such as education, leisure, the arts and nature. There will be fewer material goods, which will tend to be simpler in nature, and more expensive.

Many affluent families may anticipate such changes with relative equanimity. However, few of today's low and moderate income families are likely to be content with such a future. The efforts of these latter families to resist the imposition of Case C conditions could be expected to greatly complicate the task of managing the transition to low growth.

A moderate-growth scenario such as Case B appears to be a preferable compromise. It should provide most of the material goods of Case A as well as many of the non-material advantages of Case C.

4. Non-Energy Minerals

Limited availability of mineral raw materials is not likely to impose a significant restriction on continued economic growth over the next 25 years. Neither the United States nor the world will enter the 21st century bereft of such raw materials if technological development is allowed to continue.

Growth in minerals consumption is a prerequisite for continued economic growth in the United States. However, as the nation moves from an industrial to a post-industrial society its metals consumption will rise less rapidly than its real GNP. This relationship

may be expected under all three alternative growth patterns. In part, it is due to the shift toward a less material-intensive form of economic output in the post-industrial society. It also stems from gradual improvements in the efficiency with which raw mineral resources are turned into useful finished products. In Case A, for example, consumption of the 15 major metals is forecast to rise at 3.2 percent per year over the 1970 to 2000 period in contrast to a real GNP growth rate of about 4.2 percent. Rates of growth of mineral consumption are correspondingly lower for the other two scenarios; averaging 2.8 percent per year for Case B and 1.6 percent for Case C. Similar relationships are evident in the per capita consumption patterns shown on Chart 6•6.

Cumulative consumption of the five major metals

Chart 6•6
UNITED STATES PER CAPITA CONSUMPTION OF FIVE MAJOR METALS*

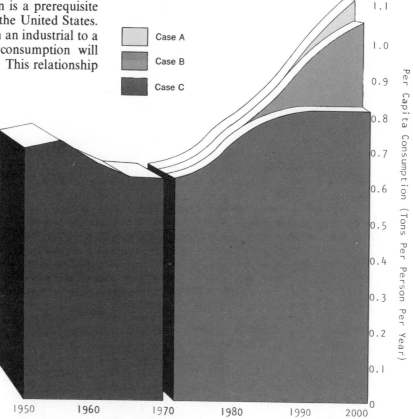

Case A
Case B
Case C

(iron, aluminum, copper, lead and zinc) over the period from 1970 to 2000 will amount to nearly 6.5 billion tons under high growth conditions. Under the gradually increasing incentives for recycling which are forecast, about 45 percent of this tonnage will be recycled, and the remainder, 3.5 billion tons, will be newly mined (primary) metal. Lesser amounts of primary metals will be needed to support economic growth in the Case B and Case C scenarios; i.e., 3.3 and 2.8 billion tons, respectively.

Even under low-growth conditions and with maximum recycling, the cumulative demands through the year 2000 will exceed current domestic reserves for all of the top five metals except copper. Domestic reserves are an inadequate basis for judging the ultimate availability of minerals, however, since they exclude vast resource deposits both here and abroad which have not been sampled or not yet been located. Even larger amounts are dispersed in the earth's crust and under the oceans. Crustal abundances in the top 5/8 of a mile of the earth's surface

range from 100,000 to 1,000,000 times as large as reserves.

Improved technology, in combination with careful use, increased recycling, and selective importing of metals, promises to provide the United States with adequate supplies for many centuries. Over the years technology has permitted the recovery of successively leaner deposits. There is as yet no clear sign that any major technological limits have been reached. The primary incentive for improved technology, as well as for recycling and careful use, should be supplied by a free and responsive price system. The price system is a more efficient allocator of resources than government regulations. Price should also be the measure of when and to what extent importing of minerals would be of mutual advantage to both the United States and the exporting country. The United States should continue to encourage international trade in metals, subject to continuing cautious appraisal of the possible development of OPEC-like cartels in strategic raw materials other than oil.

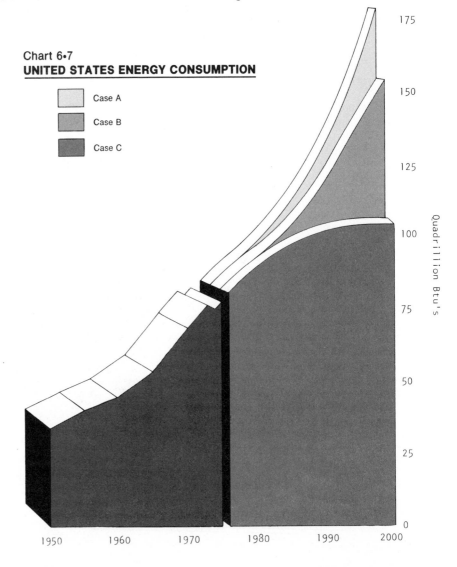

Chart 6·7
UNITED STATES ENERGY CONSUMPTION

Case A
Case B
Case C

Table 6·3
**GROWTH RATES PER GNP AND
ENERGY DEMAND: 1975-2000
(Percent per Year)**

Scenario	GNP	Total Energy	Electric Energy
Case A:			
High Growth	4.2%	3.6%	5.8-6.3%
Case B:			
Moderate Growth	3.7	3.0	5.3-5.8
Case C:			
Low Growth	2.3	1.4	3.7

Research and development into mineral recovery is as important as energy R&D. To date there is no technologically feasible ultimate solution to mineral depletion comparable to the solutions of fossil fuel depletion which are potentially provided by the breeder reactor and solar energy. Mining the seabed and recovery of minerals from "average rock" in the earth's crust would be parts of a comparable solution.

5. Energy Demand

Demand for energy in the United Sates will continue to grow much as it has in the past. The abrupt rise in the prices for oil imposed by the OPEC countries in 1973-74 has no doubt slowed energy growth somewhat. Higher prices, however, will eventually bring forth additional domestic supplies of oil, gas, and competing energy sources. Higher prices will also induce more careful consumption patterns and the development of energy-saving technologies. These developments will slowly bring supply, demand, and price into better balance.

As in the case of minerals, and for somewhat similar reasons, energy demand will continue to grow at a slower pace than real GNP in all three alternative futures. In Case B for example, energy growth over the next 25 years will average 3 percent per year in contrast to 3.7 percent for real GNP. Chart 6·7 compares the Case B forecast with energy growth patterns of the high and low growth scenarios.

Growth in. consumption of electric energy will be much faster than for energy as a whole. This too will represent a continuation of past relationships. The rapid growth in consumption of electricity will result from: (1) superior convenience and versatility, especially for the fast-growing service sectors of the economy; (2) flexibility in being able to use any basic energy source, particularly coal and nuclear fuel which are in good supply from domestic sources; (3) slower rates of price increase than for some competing fuels; and (4) the need for the nation to achieve energy independence. (See Table 6·3.)

In the most probable (moderate growth) future, electric energy demand will grow at an average rate of 5.3 to 5.8 percent per year.[5] The 5.8 percent

Table 6·4
**GROWTH RATES OF ENERGY CONSUMPTION FOR ELECTRICITY
VERSUS OTHER USES OF ENERGY
(Percent per Year)**

	1975-80	1980-85	1985-2000	1975-2000
Case A:				
Energy for Electricity	7.17	5.54	5.49	5.83
Other Uses	3.45	3.05	1.74	2.34
Total	4.51	3.84	3.21	3.59
Case B:				
Energy for Electricity	6.05	5.35	5.01	5.29
Other Uses	2.86	1.79	1.28	1.69
Total	3.76	2.91	2.76	2.99
Case B—HCN:				
Energy for Electricity	6.05	6.60	5.59	5.88
Other Uses	2.86	1.32	0.61	1.20
Total	3.76	3.03	2.79	3.03
Case C:				
Energy for Electricity	5.51	4.32	2.82	3.65
Other Uses	2.38	1.36	-0.96	0.16
Total	3.26	2.28	0.53	1.42

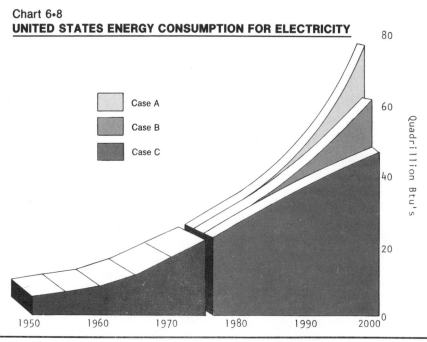

Chart 6•8
UNITED STATES ENERGY CONSUMPTION FOR ELECTRICITY

Case A
Case B
Case C

Quadrillion Btu's

80
60
40
20
0

1950   1960   1970   1980   1990   2000

growth rate was developed under a variant to Case B, designated as Case B-HCN (high coal and nuclear). For Case B-HCN, domestic oil and gas resources were assumed to be less plentiful than in Case B, and public policies to reduce the nation's dependence on imported oil and gas were assumed to be effectively devised and implemented. Several trends, ranging from political to geological in nature, seem to be combining in such a way that the energy forecasts of Case B-HCN appear both more plausible and more advantageous to the nation than those of the basic Case B.

Even under the low growth conditions of Case C, however, demand for electric energy will increase at an average rate of nearly 3.7 percent per year, in contrast to a growth rate of only 1.4 percent annually for total energy consumption. Chart 6•8 depicts the growth in electric consumption graphically for each of the scenarios and Table 6•4 contrasts rates for electricity with growth rates for all other energy types. The study shows a close similarity between Case B-HCN and Case A as regards growth in energy consumption for electricity generation. Consumption of energy for generation of electricity is likely to constitute between 45 and 55 percent of all energy consumption in the year 2000 as against about 27 percent in 1975. This conclusion holds true for all of the alternate futures which were examined.

It should be noted that in the cases of both energy demand and energy supply, the separate forecasting efforts summarized in the paragraphs on "Forecasting Methods" yielded similar though, of course, not identical results.

6. Energy Supply

Energy supplies need not restrict the nation's growth over the long term since the United States possesses adequate resources to become fully self-sufficient, should it choose to be. These resources are primarily in the form of oil and gas (with particular emphasis on untapped resources off-shore and in Alaska), coal, shale oil, and nuclear fuel for breeder reactors as well as for the current fission reactors. Over the longer range future; i.e., well into the 21st century, solar energy and fusion power will provide major additional energy supplies. These will insure continued self-sufficiency should it be deemed necessary. Over the next decade, however, artificial restraints on imports have the potential for causing major disruptions in United States economic growth.

The consumption pattern of various fuels will shift gradually over the forecast period from dominance of oil and natural gas toward increasing use of coal and nuclear power. At present, coal, hydro power, and nuclear fuel provide only 23 percent of the nation's energy. Oil and natural gas provide the remainder. The share of coal, hydro power and nuclear fuel should approach 30 to 35 percent by 1985 and 45 to 55 percent by the end of this century. (See Chart 6•9.) The potentials for sources such as geothermal power, tides, winds and trash are small, although geothermal power may be significant on a local basis in the Western part of the United States. "Novel" sources such as solar and fusion power are not likely to make major contributions until well into the 21st century.

A primary prerequisite to achievement of reasonable self-sufficiency is a free and responsive pricing system. Prices that reflect full costs will encourage exploration and promote wise rather than wasteful energy use. Federal guarantees may be necessary to protect investments in domestic energy facilities against possible sharp cuts in imported oil prices. An enlightened environmental attitude which aims for a reasonable balance between environmental considerations and economic welfare is another prerequisite.

Under such conditions, the forecast of the moderate growth, Case B envisions adequate energy supplies. In Case A, the assumptions of fewer additional environmental restrictions and no importing problems lead to a forecast of plentiful supplies. However, even the sharply reduced demands of the low growth society are unlikely to be met fully under the restraints which were assumed to be imposed under Case C. Rationing and other legal restrictions on energy use would be necessary to close the supply-demand gap under low growth.

The condition of limited energy availability in Case C could have a number of secondary impacts on the economy. For example, agricultural output could be restricted by fertilizer shortages, with consequent adverse effects on the nation's ability to export food. Similar restrictions on manufactured goods output for export would derive not only from process energy shortages but also from restrictions on raw material use.

Energy imports under the moderate growth, Case B are projected to remain essentially constant at about 18 percent of total demand until 1980. After that they will gradually decrease to some 12 percent in 1985 and to 10 percent by the end of the century. A 10-12 percent level of imports is judged to provide a reasonable balance between risks of interruption of

Chart 6·9

UNITED STATES ENERGY SUPPLY PATTERNS FOR CASES A, B, AND C

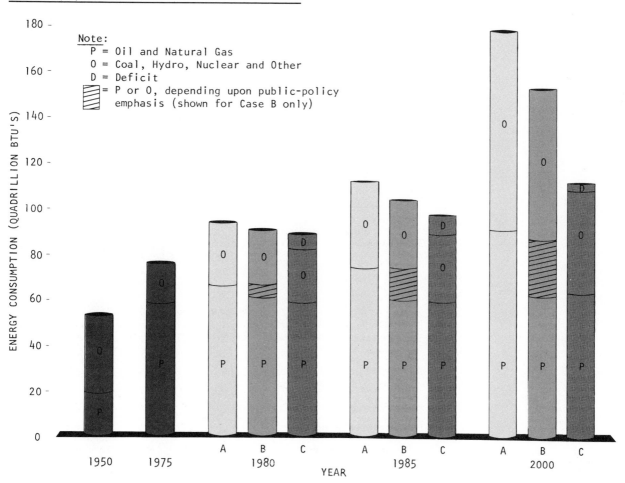

Table 6·5

SUMMARY OF GROWTH PATTERNS FOR 1975-2000: CASES A, B, AND C

Characteristic	1975[1]	2000	Average Annual Percent Change
Population (Millions)			
A	214	286	1.17
B		264	0.84
C		251	0.64
Real GNP (Billions of '58 Dollars)[2]			
A	983	2736	4.18
B		2430	3.69
C		1725	2.27
Real Per Capita GNP ('58 Dollars)[2]			
A	4589[3]	9568	2.98
B		9191	2.82
C		6881	1.63
	1970[4]		
Minerals Consumption (5 Major Metals) (Millions of Short Tons)			
A	126.6	322.6	3.17
B		287.2	2.77
C		202.8	1.58
Energy Demand (Quadrillion Btu) (DRI)			
A	77.0	186.1	3.59
B		160.9	2.99
C		109.5	1.42
Electricity Demand (Billion Kwhr) (DRI)			
A	1963	8079	5.82
B		7103	5.28
C		4806	3.65
Energy Supply (Quadrillion Btu)[5] (EPRI)			
A	77.0	179.1	3.43
B		155.1	2.84
C		104.5	1.23
Energy Supply for Electricity (Quadrillion Btu)[5] EPRI			
A	20.8	77.8	5.42
B		63.4	4.56
C		46.1	3.23
Electricity Demand (Billion Kwhr) (High Coal, Nuclear: DRI)			
A	1963	9084	6.32
B		8240	5.87
C		4880	3.71

(1) The DRI projections of economic growth were developed in mid-1974 when the 1974-75 recession was generally expected to be less severe than it became in actuality. At that time some modest real growth was expected in 1975. It is reasonable to anticipate that the economy will return to the DRI forecast trends well before 1980.

(2) DRI model basis: National Income Accounts basis plus imputed value of service from consumer durables. See Appendix C.

(3) Average of slightly different DRI estimates for 1975 for Cases A, B, and C.

(4) For non-energy minerals only.

(5) Based on EPRI assumption of gradual improvements in heat rate (i.e. generating efficiencies).

the imported energy and costs of providing a higher level of domestic supplies. The feasibility of essentially total self-sufficiency is indicated by an alternate Case A forecast which shows imports down to 5 percent in 1985.

Under the assumed environmental restrictions of Case C, domestic supplies would be so limited that imports would remain high throughout the period. The forecast shows Case C imports rising to 24 percent of total consumption in 1980, staying at that level through 1985 then dropping to 18 percent by the year 2000.

Table 6·5 brings together average annual growth rate forecasts (1975-2000) for: population, GNP, metals consumption, energy demand and supply, energy supply for electricity, and electricity demand (kilowatthour output).

7. After 2000

An evaluation of the prospects for the Case B alternative in the period after the year 2000, shows a gradually declining population growth rate in the early part of the 21st century and a stable population level after 2030 or 2040. It seems reasonable to expect that rates of economic growth will also decrease during this period, and that the composition of economic growth will continue to change toward less resource-intensive output. The result would be a movement toward a stabilization of resource consumption per capita.

As one example of the consequences of such trends, the post-2000 evaluation assumed that by the middle of the 21st century energy and minerals consumption would be stabilized at 2 to 3 times the current levels of use per capita. In addition, it was assumed that, over the same period, recycled metals would rise from the current one-third of total consumption to about two-thirds of total consumption. Under such circumstances the nation's *domestic* recoverable resource potentials, exclusive of nuclear breeder technologies, would be adequate for the nation's resource needs for approximately another 2000 years. Much longer periods of adequate resources—on the order of one-half to one *million* years—are available if developments such as breeder reactor technology, deep seabed mining, and exploiting crustal abundance are pursued successfully.

An evaluation such as this must clearly be understood to be no more than informed speculation. However, it does provide evidence to support the conclusion that the United States has more than adequate time in which to adapt to the future, if it allows presently available adjustment mechanisms a reasonable degree of freedom.

C. Case A: The Future Under High Growth

1. General Description of Assumptions

The first scenario, Case A, corresponds to the continuation of the conditions, attitudes and policies that characterized the 1950's and 1960's. These conditions were generally favorable to growth and, in fact, many government policies were explicitly aimed at promoting faster growth, with particular emphasis placed on assuring adequate levels of consumption. For the high growth scenario this situation is assumed to continue, while the supply of raw materials is not considered to be a binding restraint. Therefore, the one effective constraint on growth is expected to be the productive capacity of the economy. This, in turn, is governed by the current stocks of capital, labor, and technical and organizational knowledge. Specific Case A assumptions for these factors of production as well as for government policies, personal consumption lifestyles, and raw material availability are as follows.

a. Raw Materials

It is assumed that no serious shortages of raw materials occur. To the extent domestic sources of supply are insufficient, imports are assumed to be available at comparable costs. Introduction of "cleaner" technology is assumed to proceed at such a pace that it does not require additional major diversion of capital funds from "productive" effort. Mining methods will not be further restricted, western coal will be available, and nuclear power development will not be inhibited by additional restrictions over those currently in force. Of course, oil, natural gas and other required energy source materials are among the raw materials assumed to be in good supply. Current energy prices, i.e., those of mid 1974 are used as base period prices. Thus, Case A projections incorporate the demand-inhibiting effects of the current high prices. This important development was not generally anticipated by studies done before the late 1973 Arab embargo and price increases.

b. Labor

A fertility rate of 2.5 is assumed, corresponding to the Census Bureau Series D projection.[6] This is next to the highest of four recent Census Bureau projections. The Series D projection results in a population of about 285 million people by the year 2000. Labor force growth will continue approximately in concert with population growth, with continued fluctuations in response to age distribution changes. Current trends in participation by women, part-time employment, and in hours worked per week are expected to continue. Over the long term a constant unemployment rate of 4.6 percent is assumed on the basis that the economy, in conjunction with an improved government stabilization policy, can maintain such a rate while limiting inflation to moderate rates. Higher rates of unemployment are assumed for the period 1974 to 1977, reflecting the down-swing in economic activity.

The choice of a 4.6 percent average unemployment rate over the long term reflects: (a) gradual decrease in the fraction of the labor force composed of low-skill teenagers, (b) better integration of women and minorities into the labor force, and (c) a conviction that structural rigidities in the labor market rather than a Phillips-curve relationship are the primary cause of excessive unemployment in the United States.[7]

c. Capital Services

Private sector capital is assumed to be fully productive at the same general level of efficiency as prevailed during the 1950's and 1960's. This assumes that no major new investment programs, in addition to those already underway or mandated, are undertaken to reduce pollution. (In a market economic sense, such investment is a nonproductive use of capital.) It also assumes that there are no raw material or energy shortages sufficient to depress the average efficiency at which the capital stock can be utilized.

d. Technology

Continued improvement in technology is assumed, with rates of improvement following past trends. This corresponds to an improvement in total factor productivity at around 1.5 percent a year, in labor augmenting technology at 0.6 percent and in capital augmenting technology at 0.8 percent a year. (See Appendix E on Productivity and Chapter 5, "Where We Stand Now," for a discussion of these terms.)

e. Government Policies

A continuation of government policies favorable to economic growth is assumed. It is assumed that there will be no legislation that will: 1) significantly reduce labor input; 2) restrict resource extraction from its 1960's pattern; 3) prevent imports of raw materials and fuels from entering the United States; or 4) further curtail production in order to achieve additional environmental protection. Some inducement, or compulsion, may be given to the introduction of cleaner production techniques but not on a scale which causes a significant drag on general growth.

Government policies in the energy industry, as elsewhere throughout the economy, will attempt to improve the functioning of the price system as a resource-allocation device. In the area of international relations, government policies will continue to favor international trade but be alert to the potential for economic and political pressures being exerted on the United States by its trading partners. When such potential exists, the government will act by stockpiling materials, guaranteeing investment in crucial, though potentially uneconomic, domestic facilities, etc.

The government sector also exerts a major influence on the course of economic growth through its revenue and spending programs. Therefore, explicit assumptions about the budgetary side of government activity must be made. The general assumptions made are: 1) that the gradually increasing share of government purchases in GNP continues; 2) that the increasing relative importance of government transfer programs continues; and 3) that the existing tax and revenue structure is maintained broadly along current lines.

With regard to the international balance of payments, it is assumed that the United States will maintain reasonable competitiveness in world markets through successful control of domestic inflation, and an enlightened policy of encouraging technology and investment in those areas of commerce where the nation enjoys a position of comparative advantage. In addition, agricultural exports will continue to be a major contributor to a positive trade balance while efforts to achieve energy independence will gradually slow the outflow of funds to the OPEC countries.

f. Consumption Lifestyle

The high growth scenario assumes a continuation of the general attitudes toward comsumption which prevailed during the 1950's and 1960's. These attitudes supported a consumption lifestyle based on free consumer choice without serious regard for impending shortages, and with little concern for the environment or for depletion of natural resources. The primary and only significant restraint on consumption for the average household was the budget.

2. Model Outputs—A High-Growth Scenario

a. Economic Growth

With assumed conditions very similar to those which prevailed in the 1950's and 1960's, the macroeconomic forecasts produced by the DRI model for Case A closely approximate a continuation of past growth trends. A slight diminution in economic growth rates might be expected because population

118

growth rates are assumed to be somewhat lower than the average for the 1950's and 1960's. Nevertheless, a significant growth of population continues and, when combined with other assumed conditions, attitudes and policies, the result is continued high rates of overall economic growth. The primary output from the DRI macro model is in terms of: gross national product and its components; prices; population and labor force; and business capital equipment and profits. These characteristics are as follows and as presented in Tables 6·6 and 6·7.

(1) Gross National Product

Real output (GNP with inflation effects removed) is forecast to increase at an average rate of about 4.2 percent a year over the 1975-2000 period. This growth is higher in the late 1970's as the economy recovers from recession and as the labor force increases rapidly. Thereafter, the main structural cause of variations in the rate of real growth is fluctuation in the rate of labor force growth, which dips in the 1980's and then increases in the 1990's.

The average economic growth rate is extremely close to the rates observed in the past. (Average growth of real GNP was 4.0 percent a year over the 1947-1972 period, and 4.3 percent between 1961 and 1972.) This is despite some negative factors such as: (1) slower growth of population and the labor force, (2) high energy prices, and (3) somewhat more environmental protection activities than in the 1950's and early 1960's. Countering these growth depressing factors, at least partially, is the assumption that after the recovery from the 1974-75 recession there will be a significant improvement in the economy so as to allow more evenly balanced growth and a stabilization of inflation. This will permit the economy to operate closer to its true potential than in the past.

(2) Composition of the Real GNP

Although total real output increases at 4.2 percent per year, there is a substantial variation among the growth rates of different components; i.e., personal consumption, private investment and government purchases. Personal consumption increases rapidly at around 4.4 percent per year in real terms, so that its share of total output increases noticeably, from 58.7 percent in 1975 to 61.6 percent in 2000.

Within the overall category of personal consumption, the trend toward relatively more spending on services and relatively less on durable and nondurable goods will accelerate. This conclusion stems from a judgmental forecast of income distribution changes which is discussed later in this section.

Private investment also increases rapidly, at an average rate of 4.5 percent per year, with the result that investment goods output accounts for 23.5 percent of total output in 1975 and for 25.5 percent in 2000. Within the general category of private investment, business capital spending increases more rapidly than the remaining components; i.e., residential construction, non-business capital investment, and inventory accumulation.

The relative increase in the consumption and investment components of output is at the expense of a decline in the real government component. Real government purchases are projected to increase at about 3.0 percent per year, resulting in government claims on real output falling from 17.8 percent in 1975 to 13.4 percent in 2000. This decline, however, is somewhat deceptive. It is due to the fact that a large proportion of government spending is absorbed in direct payments for labor services. Since labor services increase rapidly in price, the average current dollar cost of government purchases increases more rapidly than the current dollar cost of private purchases. Therefore, most of the rapid increase in government purchases reflects pay increases rather than increases in quantity of goods purchased. Even so, government employment is projected to absorb an increasing fraction of the labor force while government purchases of nonlabor goods and services increase a bit less rapidly than real GNP.

(3) Prices (Inflation)

Prices are projected to increase more rapidly than typical past rates although not as rapidly as the rates experienced in the last few years. Inflation (as measured by the GNP price index) is forecast to increase at 4.4 percent a year over the 1975-1980 period. After that, it is expected that the effects of present disruptions and price increases, and the wage-price spiral will have subsided. Somewhat more effective anti-inflationary policies on the part of the government in the future will then permit a reduction in inflation to 3.7 percent a year over the remainder of the forecast period.

Prices of consumption goods and of investment goods move very closely, with each increasing less rapidly than the GNP price index. The price of government purchases, in contrast, rises much more rapidly due to the importance of labor in total government purchases.

(4) Per Capita Income and Consumption

Per capita incomes are projected to increase along trends similar to those observed in the past. Projected real per capita GNP will increase at about 3.0 percent a year over the forecast period (compared to a historical growth of around 2.9 percent). There are

119

Table 6·6
CASE A: MACRO ECONOMIC PROJECTIONS; 1975-2000[1]

	1974	1975[2]	1980[2]	1985	2000
1. Disposition of GNP (Billions of Current $)[3]					
GNP	1544	1714	2689	3978	12329
Personal Consumption	896	995	1553	2287	7040
Private Domestic Investment	337	380	608	906	2705
Government Purchases	309	338	526	785	2584
2. Disposition of Real GNP (Billions of 1958 $)[3]					
Real GNP	944	983	1241	1509	2736
Real Personal Consumption	559	577	734	904	1683
Real Private Domestic Investment	229	231	301	375	696
Real Government Purchases	146	175	203	235	367
3. Price Deflators for GNP Components (1958 = 1.0)					
Price of GNP		1.744	2.162	2.636	4.506
Price of Personal Consumption		1.723	2.116	2.529	4.180
Price of Private Domestic Investment		1.645	2.021	2.417	3.882
Price of Government Purchases		1.932	2.590	3.340	7.043
4. GNP Per Capita (Thousands of Current $)		7.961	11.758	16.310	43.108
Personal Consumption Per Capita (Thousands of Current $)		4.621	6.791	9.377	24.615
Real GNP Per Capita (Thousands of 1958 $)		4.566	5.426	6.187	9.568
Real Personal Consumption Per Capita (Thousands of 1958 $)		2.680	3.209	3.706	5.988
5. Percentage of GNP (Current $ Basis)					
Personal Consumption		58.2	57.8	57.5	57.1
Private Domestic Investment		22.2	22.6	22.8	21.9
Government Purchases		19.7	19.6	19.7	21.0
Government Expenditures		31.5	31.5	31.9	34.1
6. Percentage of Real GNP (1958 $ Basis)					
Real Personal Consumption		58.7	59.1	59.9	61.6
Real Private Domestic Investment		23.5	24.3	24.9	25.5
Real Government Purchases		17.8	16.4	15.6	13.4
7. Population (Million)		215.3	228.7	243.9	286.0
Labor Input (Billion Effective Manhours)		488	535	579	768
Labor as Percent of Total Time		14.2	14.2	14.2	14.3
Net Wage and Salary Index (1967 = 1)		1.660	2.368	3.201	7.371
8. Real Capital Stock (Billions of 1958 $)		2108	2458	2846	4327
Rate of Return on Private Capital (Percent)		8.5	9.9	9.3	10.1
Labor Productivity Index (1967 = 1)		1.328	1.496	1.674	2.262
Unit Labor Cost Index (1967 = 1)		1.740	2.205	2.663	4.536
Corporate Profits (Billions of Current $)		88	126	176	490
Corporate Cash Flow (Billions of Current $)		165	249	362	1077
Private National Wealth (Billions of Current $)		4735	7000	9738	25830

(1) See Appendix B for the definition of GNP used in this table and the correspondence of this definition to the National Income Accounts definition.

(2) The DRI projections were developed in mid-1974 when the length and depth of the 1974-75 recession was generally being underestimated. At that time some modest real growth was expected in 1975. It is reasonable to expect that the economy will return to the DRI forecast trend well before 1980.

(3) Net Exports (a component of GNP) is not tabulated because of its small size. For example, in 1974, net exports were $2 billion in current dollars and $9 billion in 1958 dollars.

some fluctuations in the forecast rate of real per capita income growth in the 1980's. This results from the comparatively rapid population growth in the early 1980's, which requires that a given GNP be spread over more people, in the period before the children mature and become members of the labor force. At the end of the forecast period the opposite occurs as population growth slows but labor force growth increases. The actual growth in per capita income over the forecast period is very substantial: real per capita GNP doubles from $4,566 in 1975 to $9,568 in 2000 while real per capita consumption increases even more rapidly, from $2,680 to $5,988.

Although the DRI model does not forecast income distribution or family formation, a judgmental forecast of these factors, which was made by the EEI staff, concludes that: (1) average family size will continue the gradual decrease which has characterized the 1950's and 1960's; (2) income distribution will at least maintain the very gradual leveling process of the post-World War II years; and (3) government cash transfers to low income groups will account for the same fraction of total money income as at present.[8] By the year 2000 family size may be expected to approach 2.6 or 2.7 persons on average; as compared to just over 3.0 at present. Increasing affluence, fewer children per family, more divorces, more people who remain single and more widows and widowers are among a variety of influences expected to reduce the average size of individual living groups, or families and unrelated individuals to use the Census Bureau term.

On this basis, Table 6•8 and Chart 6•10 show the changes in living-group monetary income which may be expected. By the year 2000, large numbers of families and individuals will have moved into the higher income brackets. Only 26.5 percent will remain in the brackets below $12,000 in contrast to almost half in 1975 and better than two-thirds in 1960.

Non-cash transfers (such as medicaid and rent

Table 6•7

CASE A: MACRO ECONOMIC GROWTH RATE PROJECTIONS: 1975-2000 (Average Annual Percent Growth Rates)

	1975 to 1980	1980 to 1985	1985 to 2000	1975 to 2000
GNP	9.42	8.15	7.83	8.21
Personal Consumption	9.31	8.05	7.78	8.14
Private Domestic Investment	9.86	8.30	7.56	8.17
Government Purchases	9.25	8.34	8.27	8.48
Real GNP	4.77	3.98	4.04	4.18
Real Personal Consumption	4.93	4.25	4.23	4.45
Real Private Domestic Investment	5.43	4.49	4.22	4.51
Real Government Purchases	3.01	2.97	3.02	3.01
Price of GNP	4.40	4.00	3.64	3.87
Price of Personal Consumption	4.19	3.63	3.41	3.61
Price of Private Domestic Investment	4.20	3.64	3.21	3.49
Price of Government Purchases	6.04	5.22	5.10	5.31
GNP Per Capita	8.11	6.76	6.69	6.99
Personal Consumption Per Capita	8.00	6.67	6.65	6.92
Real GNP Per Capita	3.51	2.66	2.95	3.00
Real Personal Consumption Per Capita	3.67	2.92	3.25	3.27
Population	1.22	1.30	1.07	1.14
Labor Input	1.84	1.59	1.90	1.83
Net Wage and Salary Index	7.36	6.21	5.72	6.14
Real Capital Stock	3.12	2.97	2.83	2.92
Labor Productivity	2.41	2.27	2.03	2.15
Unit Labor Cost Index	4.85	3.85	3.61	3.91
Corporate Profits	7.44	6.91	7.06	7.11
Corporate Cash Flow	8.64	7.75	7.54	7.79
Private National Wealth	8.13	6.83	6.72	7.02

Table 6•8
DISTRIBUTION OF MONEY INCOME
OF FAMILIES AND UNATTACHED PERSONS*
(Constant 1975 Dollars and Percentages)

Income Range (1975 Dollars)	1960	1975	Case A 2000
Less than $3,000	16.0%	12.2%	5.0%
3,000 - 5,999	17.0	12.6	7.0
6,000 - 8,999	18.0	11.3	7.5
9,000 - 11,999	18.0	12.2	7.0
12,000 - 14,999	11.0	13.0	9.5
15,000 - 24,999	15.0	26.5	36.0
25,000 - 49,999	4.5	10.2	18.0
50,000 and Over	0.5	2.0	10.0
Total	100.0	100.0	100.0

* Earned income plus government transfer payments in the form of cash (e.g. old age assistance and aid to families with dependent children).

supplements) will at least maintain their present importance as a means for helping low income groups.[9] If the value of these non-cash payments is added to monetary income as a measure of "effective income," the distribution in 2000 is further improved. On an effective income basis, the brackets below $6,000 will be essentially eliminated with the possible exception of a few one-person households. It then would require a relatively small further income redistribution (perhaps 2 percent of total personal income) to assure that no multi-person living groups receive less than $10,000 per year of effective income. To achieve such a goal in 1975 would require a further redistribution of perhaps 12-15 percent of total personal income. Note that all income figures are in 1975 dollars.

(5) Labor and Capital

Economic growth is sustained by increases in labor input, capital input, and technical efficiency. Labor input varies substantially during the scenario period because of changes in the birth rate. Labor productivity, capital productivity, and total factor productivity are assumed to follow past trends. The approximate contributions of these factors to economic growth are summarized in Table 6•9. The factors are developed on the basis that overall labor inputs constitute 63 percent of national income and capital inputs 37 percent.

b. Population

With a fertility rate of 2.5, population growth will continue indefinitely, reaching about 285 million people in the year 2000 and increasing to some 350 million by 2025. This represents a total increase of 65 percent over the next 50 years, and average densities of 80 to 90 people per square mile in the first quarter of the 21st century compared to about 60

Chart 6•10
INCOME DISTRIBUTION
(Percent of Total Families and Unrelated Individuals)

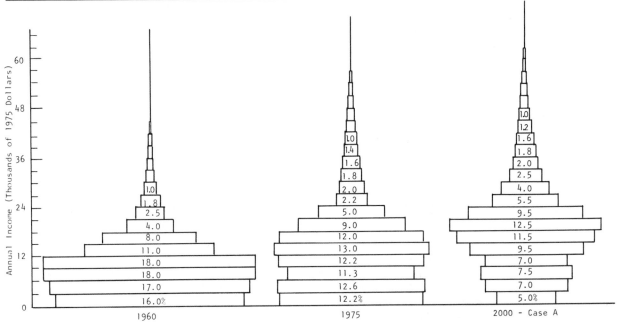

Table 6·9
CASE A: SOURCES OF ECONOMIC GROWTH; 1975-2000[1]
(Percent per Year)

Component	Rate of Increase	Weighting Factor	Contribution to Growth of Real GNP
Labor:			
Quantity	1.23		
Quality	0.60		
Total	1.83	63.	1.15
Capital:			
Quantity	2.90		
Quality	0.80		
Total	3.70	37.	1.37
Total Factor Productivity	1.50		1.50
Real GNP			4.02[2]

(1) See Appendix E for a description of the sources for the productivity assumptions.

(2) The 4.02 percent calculated as the growth rate of potential GNP is below the 4.18 percent average growth rate forecast for Case A. (See Table 6·5.) This is because the GNP at the 1975 starting point for the forecast is significantly below potential GNP.

in 1973. The increase will have to be absorbed at about the same pace as during the last 25 years; i.e., 2.6 million per year.

A large fraction of the additional population will be accommodated within the current urban and suburban regions. The return to the central city can be expected to gain momentum. This need not cause major crowding problems in either urban or suburban regions. For example, if all of the increase between today's 215 million and the 350 million in 2025 were to be accommodated in the urban and suburban regions in the same proportion as these regions now hold population (i.e., 45 percent in urban and 55 percent in suburban), the average density in the cities would rise to 8,500 persons per square mile and in the suburbs to 390 persons per square mile. Today Pittsburgh with 9,400 and Minneapolis with 7,900 persons per square mile are representative cities with similar densities, while the suburbs around Salt Lake City currently have about the same suburban density as mentioned above.

At some point, however, even the relatively low one percent per year population growth which accompanies a total fertility rate of 2.5 will be reduced. A one percent annual growth rate doubles the population every 70 years, and results in a United States population of some 6 *billion* people by the year 2300. Long before such population levels are reached, a variety of natural and social pressures will certainly have reduced the birth rates.

Increases in average life span may also pose

eventual problems. A number of medical and biological experts are convinced that their professions are on the verge of developments which will make possible major increases in longevity. If this occurs, of course, there will be a corresponding increase in population. It is possible, for example, to visualize an increase in longevity, perhaps from 72 years at present to 100 years by the year 2025. An approximate demographic calculation suggests that the United States population in 2025 would then be 65 million people larger than if the current slow increase in longevity is maintained. Such a development would also cause a marked change in the age distribution with 25 percent of the population over 65 years of age in 2025 versus less than 10 percent in 1975.

c. Agriculture

The United States has the most productive agriculture in the world. In terms of total protein output, United States farms currently produce sufficient foods to feed a population of about 350 million at current United States per capita consumption levels. The basis for the agriculture segments of the high growth scenario is the Case Western Reserve University World Model studies.[10] The CWR studies have included rather detailed examinations of the potentials for increased food production in the United States and Canada. They have concluded that, even after accommodating a population growth approximating the Case A situation, North America will be able to continue to increase its protein exports rapidly

Table 6·10
CALORIE AND PROTEIN OUTPUT PER ACRE

Acreage Required for Production of 1 million Calories

Food Source	Acres of Land
Sugar	0.15
Potatoes	0.44
Corn—as corn meal	0.9
Wheat—as whole wheat flour	0.9
Wheat—as refined wheat flour	1.2
Hogs (pork and lard)	2.0
Whole Milk	2.8
Eggs	7.8
Chickens	9.3
Steers	17.0

Source: Frederick Stare, "Fiasco in Food," *Atlantic Monthly*, January 1948.

Protein per acre

Method of Land Management	Method of Recovering Protein	Edible Protein (lbs. per acre per year)
Planted to forage, grain, fed to steers	as beef	43
Planted to forage, silage, fed to cows	as milk	77
Planted to soybeans	as soybeans	450
Planted to alfalfa, United States average crop	as extracted protein	600
Planted alfalfa, Western United States irrigated	as extracted protein	1,500

Source: Harrison Brown, James Bonner and John Weir, *The Next Hundred Years*, p. 71.

at least through the next 50 years. By 2025, for example, the Case Western Reserve studies suggest that North American food exports on a protein basis can be 3 times the domestic consumption. This compares with 1973 exports which were slightly less than domestic consumption. In other words, total output by 2025 will be 4 times domestic consumption while at present it is about 1.9 times domestic needs, again on a protein basis.

The Case Western Reserve results are obtained by a combination of increases in acreage and increases in productivity. Only about half of the 980 million acres of potentially arable land in North America are presently under cultivation or grazing. Major fractions of the "unused" land are in the United States

and are suitable as a base for increasing animal protein, grain, or fiber output.

In addition, there is no sign that agricultural productivity, as regards animal, grain, or fiber output in the United States, has reached a peak, or even that there has been a significant slowdown in productivity growth in recent years. The CWR model, for example, projects that productivity of agriculture in terms of protein output per acre will continue to increase over the forecast period. A variety of developments from higher yielding strains of crops to more effective fertilization can achieve these productivity gains.

Although application of synthetic fertilizers may require certain precautions to prevent ecological damage to adjacent water courses, there is no in-

Chart 6·11
WORLD PROTEIN AND CALORIC INTAKE

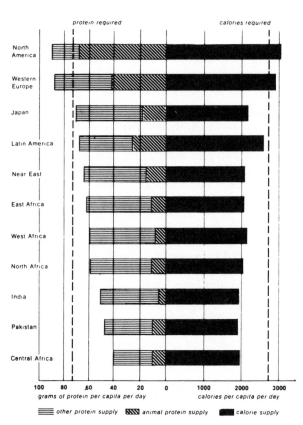

Dash-lines indicate estimated North American protein and caloric requirements, based on diets sufficient to enable people to attain full body weight.

Source: UN Food and Agriculture Organization Provisional Indicative World Plan for Agricultural Development (Rome: UN Food and Agriculture Organization, 1970).

124

dication that intensities of fertilizer use have reached a practical maximum. Agricultural technologies in use in other parts of the world, especially parts of Western Europe, have accommodated much heavier fertilizer use than in the United States.

Many of the higher yielding crop strains are already in existence and proven on test acreage, but not yet in general use. Thus, no major breakthroughs in technology are required to achieve the output figures forecast by Case Western Reserve.

One change that the forecast does assume, is a gradual shift toward grain production and away from meat production. Both protein and calorie output per acre are many times greater if land that is suitable for grain is planted in grains for human consumption than if it is devoted to production of meat or fowl. See Table 6•10. It must be recognized, of course, that major tracts of land now used for grazing may not be suitable for grain production under current technologies. Although meat proteins are generally more "complete" foods than grain proteins for human nourishment, there is evidence that the average United States resident consumes much more meat protein than the body can use effectively, while much of the rest of the world's population consumes too little of both animal and grain protein.[11] See Table 6•11 and Chart 6•11.

The Case Western Reserve studies suggest that the rest of the world will need every bit of nourishment the United States can provide in excess of United States domestic requirements. A combination of economic and humanitarian pressures to increase food exports to the maximum will tend to support United States food prices and will encourage a shift in land use so as to emphasize grain production for direct human consumption.

d. Non-Energy Minerals

As previously noted, the United States with about 6 percent of world population uses 30 percent of its

Table 6•11
GRAIN USED PER CAPITA: 1964-66 AVERAGE
(Kilograms per Year)

Region	Total	Food	Feed
Developed:			
United States	746	91	590
Canada	906	92	689
Australia & New Zealand	428	113	217
U.S.S.R.	556	217	169
EEC-9	404	120	233
Eastern Europe	576	207	283
Japan	241	157	62
South Africa	294	178	61
Other W. Europe	354	128	179
Total	511	152	277
Less Developed:			
Argentina	388	138	173
Mexico & Central America	204	151	36
Other S. America	144	112	15
West Asia	292	185	60
China	197	164	15
Brazil	242	123	88
East Asia & Pacific	161	147	5
North Africa	219	178	19
South Asia	166	150	2
Southeast Asia	197	163	3
Africa So. of Sahara	151	133	2
Total	188	154	16
World	287	153	95

Source: OECD Food Consumption Statistics 1960-68 and FAO Food Balances 1964-66, with adjustments for grains omitted by OECD and FAO. Rice included as milled rice. Compiled by Economic Research Service Foreign and Competition Division, United States Department of Agriculture in *World Food Situation—Trends and Prospects*—March 1974.

total annual energy consumption and 20 percent of its non-energy minerals. Concern over resource depletion has often concentrated on energy, since fossil fuels are both non-renewable and non-recyclable. Depletion of non energy minerals is generally accorded a level of concern somewhat below fossil fuels since the non-energy minerals are at least partially recyclable.

Technological factors associated with energy resources offset the recyclable advantage of non-energy minerals, at least partially. The combination of known fossil fuel reserves (including, coal, tar sands, and oil shale) plus nuclear breeders offers reasonable assurance of an almost limitless energy resource base using largely proven and economic technology.

In contrast, the equivalent solution for non-energy minerals; i.e., an effectively infinite resource base for minerals through the extraction and refining of ores from "average rock" and from the seas, is far from technologically and economically proven. Ore deposits must be of a concentration about 100 times that of average crustal abundance (i.e., "average rock") to be economically recoverable with current technology.

Thus, it appears that any growth study should be as vitally concerned with the minerals availability situation as with the energy supply. A detailed examination of minerals availability and related topics is therefore presented in Appendix F. Some of the information from that study is summarized in the following paragraphs.

(1) Consumption Forecast

Forecasts to the year 2000 under Case A conditions have been developed for consumption of the five major metals: iron, aluminum, copper, zinc and lead. The forecasting technique makes use of persistent patterns in metal consumption which have been observed in the United States and around the world over the past forty years. In many respects these patterns are similar to those observed in the case of energy consumption trends around the world.

As a region changes from an industrial to a post-industrial society, with increasing emphasis on services, its metals consumption rises less rapidly than its real GNP; i.e., the metals consumption per dollar of GNP decreases. The United States has been in this latter situation for at least 40 years for each of

Table 6-12
CASE A: UNITED STATES METALS CONSUMPTION
(Thousands of Short Tons)

	1970	1985	2000	1970 to 2000 Cumulative Growth (Thousands of Short Tons)	1970 to 2000 Cumulative Growth (Rate: Percent/Year)
Iron	116,900	189,500	283,900	5,798,700	3.0%
Aluminum	4,128	11,800	26,800	394,350	6.5
Copper	2,820	4,430	6,390	135,250	2.8
Zinc	1,374	2,185	3,360	67,900	3.0
Lead	1,335	1,785	2,170	53,850	1.6
Subtotal (5 Major)	126,557	209,700	322,620	6,450,050	3.17
Magnesium	1,156	1,790	2,770	56,300	3.0
Manganese	1,327	1,770	2,360	54,200	1.9
Titanium	490	1,015	2,090	34,580	5.0
Chromium	529	815	1,260	25,650	2.9
Nickel	204	335	550	10,700	3.4
Tin	80	105	140	3,200	1.9
Tungsten	8	18	38	600	5.3
Cobalt	8	10	13	300	1.6
Vanadium	7	15	31	500	5.1
Colombium	3	6	10	200	4.1
Total (15)	130,368	215,579	331,882	6,636,280	3.16

Source: Appendix F for iron, aluminum, copper, zinc and lead; Final Report of National Commission on Materials Policy, 1973, for other metals.

the major metals except aluminum. Appendix F illustrates the changing patterns of metal consumption per dollar of GNP for each of the five major metals from 1929 to 1970. It also develops forecasting trends based on these patterns.

Consumption of the five major metals, based on Case A GNP forecasts, is shown on Table 6•12. This table also contains forecasts for some of the minor metals taken from the Final Report of the National Commission on Materials Policy, 1973.

Average growth rates of the major metals range from 1.6 percent per year for lead to 6.5 percent for aluminum over the 30 year period. The weighted average for all 15 metals is 3.16 percent, almost exactly the same as the growth rate of iron and aluminum combined. The GNP growth under the Case A scenario is about 4.2 percent per year over the same 30 year period, with the difference between the growth rates reflecting the gradually decreasing intensity of metals use.

The relative importance of iron decreases gradually over the forecast period, dropping from 90 percent of the total tonnage of the top 15 in 1970 to 86 percent in 2000. Aluminum continues to gain importance, moving from 3 percent of the total in 1970 to 9 percent in 2000. These figures illustrate the relatively slow pace of substitution of one metal for another, and demonstrate the continued dominance of iron over the forecast period. A similar analysis based on value rather than tonnage shows iron in a somewhat less overwhelming position but still clearly dominant. In value terms, iron accounted for about 69 percent of the total in 1970 with copper and aluminum together accounting for another 15 percent. In the next 25 years the relative values will probably follow the same trend as the relative tonnages.

(2) Recycling

The demand for primary metal (i.e., newly mined) will be reduced below the Table 6•12 figures to the extent that secondary, or recycled metal becomes available.

Over the next 25 years, recycled metal will likely become a much more significant supplement to primary metal supplies than it is at present. This will be induced primarily through the price mechanism. If prices of primary metal rise, it will become economically rewarding both to increase the recovery of used metal products and to design new products specifically to facilitate such recovery.

Recycling of metal will ease pressure on finding new deposits and thus help to preserve the environment. It will also: 1) ease pollution problems and

reduce energy consumption by decreasing the amount of future primary smelting; and 2) ease dependency on foreign sources. Recycling will require significant amounts of energy, however.

Adequate data are lacking to estimate recycling potentials under various economic conditions, but it seems unlikely that more than 50 to 60 percent of total annual metal consumption can be derived from previously used materials over the next 25 years, even under the most favorable conditions. The dominance of iron with its many long-lived uses and a current recycling rate in the 30 percent range supports such a conclusion. (The average life of metal products is important in determining recycling potentials because the lower production rates of metal products in earlier years limits the tonnage available for recycling now. For example, if metal consumption is growing 3 percent per year and the average pound of recycled metal is 10 years old, it can fill no more than ¾ of current requirements if every ounce is recovered.) In addition, economic pressures to increase recycling are likely to rise only gradually. Therefore, achievement of a 45 percent level of recovery by 1985 and a 55 percent level by 2000 seem realistic, and perhaps even optimistic.

Table 6•13 presents projections of increased recycling fractions and the degree to which primary metal requirements are reduced as a consequence of the increased recycling effort.

The savings from the additional recycling effort (994,950 thousand short tons) represents primary metal supplies saved for consumption after the year 2000. Under these "maximum" recycling conditions, the primary demand for the five major metals in 2000 is forecast to be about 150,000 thousand short tons. Therefore, the additional recycling effort over the 30 year period will save about 6.7 years worth of primary metal. If consumption after the year 2000 continues to rise about 3 percent per year, the savings will provide needed primary metal until about 2007. Thus, although recycling is important, it cannot alone solve the problem of future metals availability.

(3) Supply

Table 6•14 contrasts current estimates of reserves and resources in the United States for the five major metals: iron, aluminum, copper, lead and zinc, as well as for several others. (See Appendix F for a discussion of the terms "reserves" and "resources.") Briefly, a reserve is a quantity of ore that has been located and sampled and that can be mined economically with current technology. Resources are deposits which are: 1) known but uneconomic, or 2) unknown but inferred from geologic conditions or

127

Table 6•13
CASE A: EFFECTS OF RECYCLING ON METALS REQUIREMENTS
(Thousands of Short Tons)

Major Metals	Cumulative Consumption, 1970-2000		
	Primary Demand plus Secondary Recovery	Primary Demand with Current Recycling*	Primary Demand with Maximum Recycling*
Iron	5,798,700	4,035,500	3,126,500
Aluminum	394,350	335,350	275,680
Copper..	135,250	67,760	51,530
Zinc..	67,900	59,400	55,250
Lead..	53,850	26,500	20,600
Total	6,450,050	4,524,510	3,529,560
		Savings from "Maximum" Recycling	994,950

	Percent of Total Consumption from Recycled Materials			
			Maximum Practical	
	Actual 1967	Estimated 1970	1985	2000
Iron..	31.2	31.2	45	55
Aluminum	18.3	18.3	29	38
Copper	49.7	49.7	60	70
Zinc..	12.6	12.6	18	23
Lead	49.6	49.6	60	70

* Current Recycling and Maximum Recycling Percentages are given in the bottom half of the table.

the presence of nearby reserves. Only in the cases of copper, titanium, and tungsten are presently identified reserves in the United States adequate to meet the cumulative demand for primary metal to the end of the century under present recycling practices.

This reserve situation is not unusual. In fact, known reserves of many materials are now historically high on a worldwide basis, with a number of important ores boasting 50 to 100 years supply.[12] Normally, known reserves are sufficient to satisfy only two or three decades of demand. This is because, if reserves of any material represent more than that, it is not worth hunting for additional supplies. In a real world of limited capital and labor it is not economic to expend either capital or labor in a search for materials that cannot be marketed, and the costs thus recouped, for several decades.

Much greater quantities of metals are known to be distributed through the earth's crust in very low concentrations. In total, the "crustal abundance" of most metals in the top ⅝ mile of the earth is on the order of one hundred thousand to one million times as great as known reserves. Table 6•15 lists crustal abundance, recoverable resource potential, and the ratios of potential to reserve for 12 important metals in the United States. (See Appendix F for a discussion of recoverable resource potential.)

These figures suggest that reserve estimates alone present an inadequate picture of the ultimate availability of minerals. Continued exploration and technological improvement can almost certainly provide domestic supplies of mineral ores sufficient for most United States needs for several centuries.

Nevertheless, it will almost certainly be more economic for the United States to import significant and, in fact, growing fractions of its primary metal needs from abroad over the next 25 to 50 years. Many known deposits around the world permit more economic recovery of ores than do similar deposits in the United States.

In some instances; e.g., manganese and chromium, the United States has essentially no domestic reserves at current prices. Thus, we are almost completely dependent on the continued availability of foreign imports for supplies of these materials. Chart 6•12 shows the relative imports for 38 classes of metals and fuels. In many cases, the import dependence is as high as shown in Chart 6•12 because of the existence of large, low-cost foreign deposits, rather than because the United States is bereft of resources.

Use of low-cost foreign deposits is to be encouraged, so that exploration of more costly ore bodies can be delayed pending the development of im-

Table 6·14
UNITED STATES RESERVES AND RESOURCES VS PRIMARY DEMAND: 1970-2000

	Primary Cumulative Demand: 1970-2000[1]	Reserves at 1971 Prices	Resources Ratios[2]	
			Identified	Hypothetical
Iron	4,036[3]	2,000[3]	2-10	10
Aluminum	335	13	2-10	KDI[4]
Copper	68	81	.75-2	.75-2
Zinc	59	30	2-10	2-10
Lead	27	17	.75-2	.35-.75
Manganese	50	—	.75-2	KDI
Chromium	16	—	0.1	0.1
Titanium	32	33	2-10	2-10
Nickel	10	—	.75-2	KDI
Tungsten	32	175	.35-.75	.35-.75

(1) Assuming 1967 recycling percentages from Table 6·13.

(2) The number of times Primary Cumulative Demand can be supplied.

(3) Millions of short tons.

(4) KDI = known data insufficient to judge.

Source: Appendix F

Table 6·15
CRUSTAL ABUNDANCE AND RESERVES OF METALS IN THE UNITED STATES
(Millions of Metric Tons)

	United States Crust to a Depth of 1 Kilometer	Recoverable Resource Potential[1]	Reserves	Ratio of Potential to Reserves
Iron	1,200,000,000	118,000	1,800	65
Aluminum	2,000,000,000	203,000	8	24,000
Copper	1,230,000	122	78	10
Zinc	2,000,000	198	32	6
Lead	330,000	32	32	1
Manganese	24,900,000	2,450	1	2,450
Chromium	1,920,000	189	2	387
Titanium	1,300,000	13,000	25	516
Nickel	1,500,000	149	0.2	830
Tin	38,000	4	—	Very High
Tungsten	30,000	3	0.08	37
Cobalt	440,000	44	0.03	1,760

(1) As dicussed in Appendix F, the total of identified and undiscovered resources recoverable under present economic conditions is represented by the formula $R = 2.45 \times 10^6 \ A \times 10^6$ where R = recoverable resource potential and A = crustal abundance.

Source: United States Department of the Interior, *United States Mineral Resources,* Geological Survey Professional Paper 820, 1973.

Chart 6•12
UNITED STATES MINERAL IMPORTS: 1974

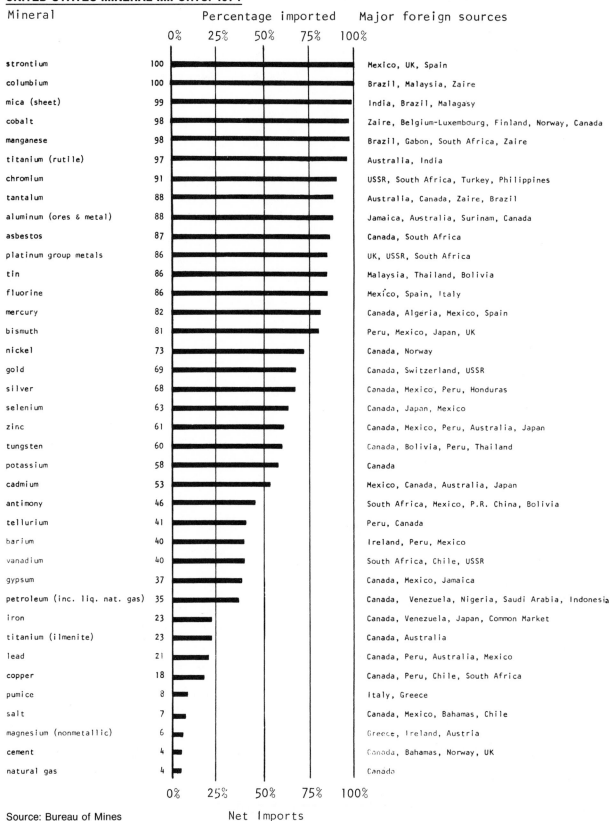

Mineral	Percentage imported	Major foreign sources
strontium	100	Mexico, UK, Spain
columbium	100	Brazil, Malaysia, Zaire
mica (sheet)	99	India, Brazil, Malagasy
cobalt	98	Zaire, Belgium-Luxembourg, Finland, Norway, Canada
manganese	98	Brazil, Gabon, South Africa, Zaire
titanium (rutile)	97	Australia, India
chromium	91	USSR, South Africa, Turkey, Philippines
tantalum	88	Australia, Canada, Zaire, Brazil
aluminum (ores & metal)	88	Jamaica, Australia, Surinam, Canada
asbestos	87	Canada, South Africa
platinum group metals	86	UK, USSR, South Africa
tin	86	Malaysia, Thailand, Bolivia
fluorine	86	Mexico, Spain, Italy
mercury	82	Canada, Algeria, Mexico, Spain
bismuth	81	Peru, Mexico, Japan, UK
nickel	73	Canada, Norway
gold	69	Canada, Switzerland, USSR
silver	68	Canada, Mexico, Peru, Honduras
selenium	63	Canada, Japan, Mexico
zinc	61	Canada, Mexico, Peru, Australia, Japan
tungsten	60	Canada, Bolivia, Peru, Thailand
potassium	58	Canada
cadmium	53	Mexico, Canada, Australia, Japan
antimony	46	South Africa, Mexico, P.R. China, Bolivia
tellurium	41	Peru, Canada
barium	40	Ireland, Peru, Mexico
vanadium	40	South Africa, Chile, USSR
gypsum	37	Canada, Mexico, Jamaica
petroleum (inc. liq. nat. gas)	35	Canada, Venezuela, Nigeria, Saudi Arabia, Indonesia
iron	23	Canada, Venezuela, Japan, Common Market
titanium (ilmenite)	23	Canada, Australia
lead	21	Canada, Peru, Australia, Mexico
copper	18	Canada, Peru, Chile, South Africa
pumice	8	Italy, Greece
salt	7	Canada, Mexico, Bahamas, Chile
magnesium (nonmetallic)	6	Greece, Ireland, Austria
cement	4	Canada, Bahamas, Norway, UK
natural gas	4	Canada

Net Imports

Source: Bureau of Mines

proved technology. In addition, world trade in minerals will benefit both the exporter (in many cases, a developing country) and the importer, if the minerals are properly priced to include all costs of recovery. Raw material exports of all sorts are a valuable source of capital to such exporting regions, which are generally capital-poor.

Charts 6•13 through 6•16 present a picture of the United States demand and supply of 4 major minerals from 1950 to 2000. The projections are based on economic forecasts very similar to those of the High Growth—Case A forecast. Therefore, it is not surprising that the demand forecasts shown on these charts are also very similar to the Case A forecasts on Table 6•12. The charts show imports to be a growing source of United States supplies over the next 25 years.

An obvious danger in relying heavily on imports is the potential for establishment of an OPEC—like cartel by a group of exporting nations. While this potential must be continually re-examined by United States policy makers, it does not appear to be likely in the near future. The international metals markets are analyzed in some detail in Appendix F to assess the probable success of such cartels, and it is concluded that they are unlikely to succeed. Appendix F also recommends several steps, such as stockpiling, to protect the nation against such an eventuality even though it is unlikely, and to help insure against it.

e. Energy Demand

This section will outline the likely energy demand consequences of Case A, the high-growth scenario. This discussion has been separated, from "Energy Supply," in Subsection f, for ease of presentation, although in all of the underlying forecasts, supply and demand were considered simultaneously. Background information on energy demand and supply to supplement this section will be found in Appendix G,

DEMAND AND SUPPLY OF MAJOR METALS TO THE YEAR 2000

Chart 6•13

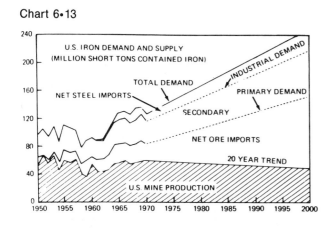

Chart 6•14

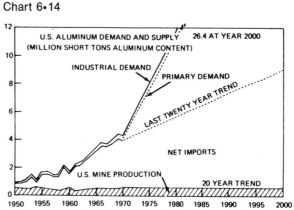

Chart 6•15

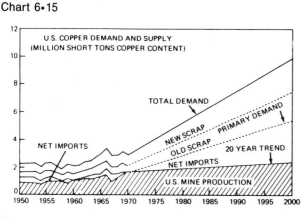

Chart 6•16

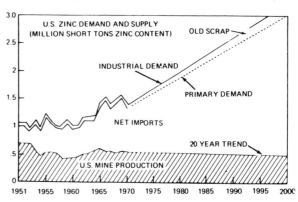

Source: "Material Needs and the Environment Today and Tomorrow," *Final Report of the National Commission on Materials Policy, June 1973*, p.2-9.

"Energy Supply and Demand; General Concepts." Additional summary information on energy is found in Chapter 5, "Where We Stand Now." Two contrasting and largely independent techniques were used to estimate energy demand; i.e., a judgmental forecast by the EEI staff, of demand by each consuming sector, and an inter-industry demand forecast using the DRI model. These are described in Sections (1) and (2) which follow.

(1) Energy Demand by Consuming Sectors

In examining energy consumption, it is useful to divide the overall market for energy into at least four sub-markets: residential, commercial, industrial and transportation. An initial forecast to the year 2000 was made for each sub-market, on the assumption that the OPEC price increases of 1973-1974 had *not* occurred. Instead, oil prices were assumed to continue to rise gradually in response to normal market factors and to inflationary pressures. In all other respects, the high growth assumptions of Case A were employed. This initial forecast was developed to recognize that the DRI forecasts for Case A already reflect some depressing effects on energy

demand relative to the pre-OPEC assumptions which were prevalent in 1972 and early 1973.

The results of the low energy price/high economic growth forecast are presented on Table 6•16. It is not surprising that this forecast is similar to other forecasts made prior to the Yom Kippur War of October, 1973.[13]

With this initial forecast as a point of departure, estimates were made of the likely restraints on energy growth resulting from the higher prices imposed by OPEC in late 1973 and early 1974. Other assumptions were unchanged, thus achieving a situation identical to Case A. A moderately lower trend of energy demand growth was obtained in consequence of the higher energy prices. Table 6•17 summarizes this high energy cost, high economic growth forecast and compares it with the previous low energy costs, high economic growth forecast. The comparison shows reductions of 5 to 10 percent as a consequence of higher prices, even with adequate and reliable energy supplies.

The effects of the higher energy costs are seen to be concentrated in the 1972 to 1985 period when the

Table 6•16
CASE A: LOW ENERGY COSTS—HIGH ECONOMIC GROWTH
(Quadrillion Btu)

Consuming Sector	Energy Demand by Consuming Sector								
	1972 Actual			Case A With Low Energy Costs					
				1985			2000		
	Fuel	Electric	Total	Fuel	Electric	Total	Fuel	Electric	Total
Transportation	18.00	0.02	18.02	31.06	0.04	31.10	45.70	0.08	45.78
Residential	8.56	1.89	10.45	10.95	4.25	15.20	12.04	7.11	19.15
Commercial	6.15	1.55	7.70	9.90	3.30	13.20	10.50	7.70	18.20
Industrial	20.76	2.46	23.22	33.30	5.20	38.50	38.60	14.20	52.80
Sub Total	53.47	5.92	59.39	85.21	12.79	98.00	106.84	29.09	135.93
Energy Conversion			12.41			26.20			58.00
Total			71.80			124.20			193.93

Consuming Sector	Average Annual Growth Rates (Percent)	
	1972-1985	1985-2000
Transportation	4.3	2.6
Residential	2.9	1.6
Commercial	4.3	2.2
Industrial	4.0	2.1
Sub Total	3.9	2.2
Energy Conversion	5.9	5.5
Total	4.3	3.0

Table 6·17
CASE A: EFFECT OF HIGH ENERGY COSTS ON ENERGY DEMAND BY CONSUMING SECTOR
(Quadrillion Btu)

Energy Costs: Consuming Sector	1985 Low	1985 High	2000 Low	2000 High
Transportation	31.10	29.51	45.78	42.50
Residential	15.20	14.50	19.15	17.80
Commercial	13.20	12.00	18.20	17.00
Industrial	38.50	35.00	52.80	49.00
Sub Total	98.00	91.01	135.93	126.30
Energy Conversion	26.20	24.30	58.00	55.00
Total	124.20	115.31	193.93	181.30

Average Annual Growth Rates (Percent)	1972-1985	1985-2000
Energy Cost:		
Low	4.3	3.0
High	3.7	3.0

average annual growth rate is reduced from 4.3 percent to 3.7 percent by the high prices. In the period after 1985 energy growth rates are the same in both cases.

By 1985 the economy has absorbed the effects of the higher prices which occurred early in the period, and is well on the way to making many of the energy saving changes which are economically justified. In addition, the higher prices for all energy sources, and for imported oil in particular, have induced expanded exploration for oil and gas, a re-emphasis on coal as an energy source, and acceleration in nuclear plant construction. By 1985 these efforts have borne sufficient fruit so that energy prices are once more approaching free market levels; i.e., the levels assumed under the low energy costs, high economic growth scenario (Case A without the OPEC action in 1973).

(2) Inter-Industry Model Forecast of Energy Demand

The prime source of the energy demand estimates for the high growth scenario was the combination of the DRI macro-econometric model used to forecast general economic conditions and the DRI inter-industry model. This latter model was specifically developed to estimate energy demand and supply. The energy demand forecast from this modeling effort was independent of the forecast described in the preceding subsection. The DRI models and their interactions are described in some detail in Appendix

B. However, before examining the output from the inter-industry model a few words of explanation may be helpful.

Essentially, the inter-industry model disaggregates the total production and total input figures derived in the macro-model. This disaggregation is of two distinct types. First, the final output predicted by the macro-model is separated into final demands from various sectors of the economy (e.g., personal consumption expenditures). Secondly, the disaggregation delineates those flows of production from one part of industry to another (e.g., from manufacturing to transport) which are necessary to sustain the final demands.

To illustrate the disaggregation, Table 6·18 presents the input-output table arrangement of the DRI model. The "X" in the lower left-hand corner of the inter-industry transactions block represents the location in the input-output table which would contain a measure (perhaps in terms of dollars) of the output from the electric utilities industry which was needed by manufacturing. Similarly, the "X" in the final demand block represents electric utilities output used by individuals (i.e., residential sales in industry parlance).

(a) Energy Demand

The energy demand estimates developed by the DRI model for the high growth Case A are summa-

133

rized in Table 6•19. This tabulation presents the pattern of energy consumption by sector and by type of fuel. For each of the forecast years, it gives consumption by: 1) household and commercial (excluding vehicles), 2) industrial (excluding vehicles), 3) transportation (which includes all travel in all vehicles), and 4) electricity generation. The generation and use of synthetic gas is shown as a separate sector. In a future of high growth, total energy input will increase from 77.0 quadrillion Btu in 1975 to

186.1 quadrillion Btu in 2000. This is an average annual growth rate of 3.6 percent. The actual growth rate varies over time. It is 2.7 percent for the 1970-1975 period when it is depressed by the current energy shortage and the recession of 1974-1975. It is 4.5 percent for the 1975-1980 period when the growth rate is high because of the depressed initial point. It is 3.8 percent from 1980-1985 and 3.2 percent for 1985-2000. These growth rates are within the range of those experienced since World

Table 6•18
INTER-INDUSTRY TRANSACTIONS: DIAGRAMMATIC REPRESENTATION

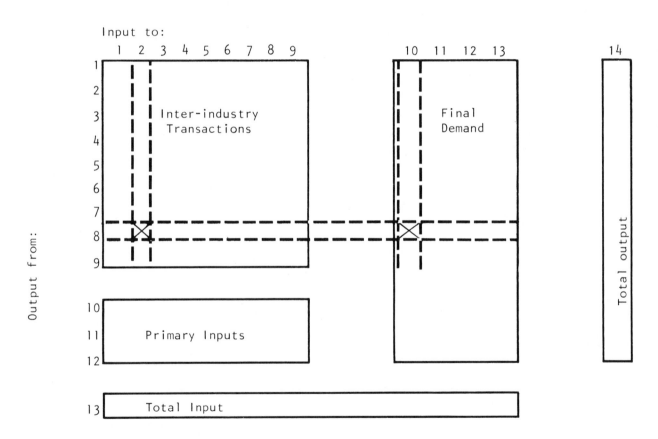

Intermediate sectors:

1. Agriculture, non-fuel mining and construction.
2. Manufacturing, excluding petroleum refining.
3. Transport.
4. Communications, trade, services.
5. Coal mining.
6. Crude petroleum and natural gas.
7. Petroleum refining.
8. Electric utilities.
9. Gas utilities.

Primary inputs, rows:

10. Imports
11. Capital services.
12. Labor services.

Final demand, columns:

10. Personal consumption expenditures.
11. Gross domestic private investment.
12. Government purchases of goods and services.
13. Exports.

War II, (e.g., 3.1 percent per year from 1949 to 1961 and 3.7 percent per year from 1961 to 1974).

The underlying trend of energy use in the future under high economic growth is one of a declining growth rate; i.e., per capita energy use continues to increase but at a declining rate. This is due not only to the recent sharp increases in energy prices but also to the projected change in economic structure due to: 1) the increasing relative importance of service and government industries which are comparatively non-

energy intensive, 2) the expected continuation of rapid technical progress in the energy intensive manufacturing sector, and 3) a trend towards saturation of many energy using items such as cars, space heating and cooling equipment and home appliances. These factors produce a pattern of growth in which growing real incomes do not require comparable increases in energy input.

These trends are reflected in the changing ratio of energy to real GNP. This ratio was 83.1 (thousand

Table 6·19
CASE A: CONSUMPTION OF ENERGY BY SECTOR OF USE; 1975-2000
(Energy Flows in Trillion Btu)

	Household, Commercial	Industrial	Transportation	Electricity Generation	Synthetic Gas	Total Input
1975						
Coal	199.	4353.	0.	8661.	0.	13213.
Petroleum	6835.	6602.	17980.	2380.	0.	33797.
Natural gas	8234.	10976.	934.	4326.	0.	24469.
Hydro, nuclear	0.	0.	0.	5475.	0.	5475.
Total input	15268.	21930.	18914.	20843.	0.	76955.
Electricity	3969.	2739.	22.	0.	0.	6730.
Synthetic gas	0.	0.	0.	0.	0.	0.
Total use	19238.	24669.	18936.	20843.	0.	76955.
1980						
Coal	188.	4035.	0.	11282.	0.	15505.
Petroleum	8562.	8079.	22518.	3097.	0.	42255.
Natural gas	8798.	13394.	1047.	4873.	0.	28111.
Hydro, nuclear	0.	0.	0.	10154.	0.	10154.
Total input	17548.	25509.	23564.	29405.	0.	96026.
Electricity	5837.	3628.	32.	0.	0.	9497.
Synthetic gas	0.	0.	0.	0.	0.	0.
Total use	23385.	29136.	23597.	29405.	0.	96026.
1985						
Coal	178.	3698.	0.	13251.	1136.	18264.
Petroleum	10105.	9304.	26827.	3241.	91.	49567.
Natural gas	8824.	16096.	1109.	5778.	0.	31808.
Hydro, nuclear	0.	0.	0.	16251.	0.	16251.
Total input	19107.	29098.	27936.	38522.	1227.	115890.
Electricity	8127.	4276.	39.	0.	0.	12442.
Synthetic gas	310.	379.	0.	0.	0.	690.
Total use	27545.	33753.	27975.	38522.	1227.	115890.
2000						
Coal	174.	4759.	0.	18556.	5107.	28595.
Petroleum	13434.	14350.	32873.	4770.	409.	65836.
Natural gas	8355.	19670.	1223.	7722.	0.	36970.
Hydro, nuclear	0.	0.	0.	54717.	0.	54717.
Total input	21963.	38779.	34095.	85765.	5515.	186118.
Electricity	19227.	8420.	60.	0.	0.	27707.
Synthetic gas	1638.	2002.	0.	0.	0.	3640.
Total use	42828.	49202.	34155.	85765.	5515.	186118.

135

Btu/1958 dollar of GNP on the DRI basis) in 1960 and 82.9 in 1970. It is forecast to be 78.3 in 1975, 77.4 in 1980, 76.8 in 1985, and 68.0 in 2000. This is a gradually falling trend, although subject to short run fluctuations.

(b.) Electricity Demand

Rapid increase in electricity use is a prominent feature of the energy consumption forecasts shown in Tables 6•19 and 6•20. Over the entire period from 1975 to 2000, electricity consumption grows at an average rate of nearly 6 percent per year. Although this rate is lower than the 7 to 8 percent rates experienced in the past, it is still an extremely rapid rate of increase. It implies a doubling of consumption every 12 years, rather than the 10 year doubling time under 7 percent growth.

Electricity prices are forecast to increase at a rate less than the rate of inflation. This is due to the projection of continued productivity advances of about 3 percent per year in labor productivity in electricity generation and distribution which permits some input cost increases to be absorbed and not passed on in output prices. Even so, the projected productivity increase in electricity generation is expected to be much less rapid than the 6 to 7 percent per year which occurred in the past. A fall in real electricity prices of 24 percent is forecast between 1975 and 2000 which is compared to a 43 percent fall between 1951 and 1971. Forecasting a 24 percent fall in the real price of electricity over a 25 year period is essentially equivalent to anticipating that the current dollar price of electricity will rise about one percentage point per year less rapidly than the general price level.

These price changes play a fundamental role in determining the pattern of energy demand described above. The decline in electricity price relative to the prices of other fuels stimulates electricity use by supplementing the basic increase in demand for

Table 6•20
CASE A: UNITED STATES ENERGY CONSUMPTION; 1975-2000

	1975	1980	1985	2000
1. Energy Consumption (Quadrillion Btu)				
Direct Consumption				
Coal	4.552	4.223	5.013	10.039
Petroleum	31.417	39.158	46.326	61.066
Gas	20.143	23.238	26.030	29.248
Total	56.112	66.619	77.369	100.353
Electricity Generation				
Coal	8.661	11.282	13.251	18.556
Petroleum and Gas	6.706	7.970	9.019	12.492
Hydro, Nuclear, Other	5.475	10.154	16.251	54.717
Total	20.842	29.406	38.521	85.765
Total	76.954	96.025	115.890	186.118

	1975-80	1980-85	1985-2000
2. Energy Consumption Growth (Percent per Year)			
Direct Consumption			
Coal	-1.49	3.49	4.74
Petroleum	4.50	3.42	1.86
Gas	2.90	2.30	0.78
Total	3.49	3.04	1.75
Electricity Generation			
Coal	5.43	3.27	2.27
Petroleum and Gas	3.51	2.50	2.20
Hydro, Nuclear, Other	13.15	9.86	8.43
Total	7.13	5.55	5.48
Total	4.53	3.83	3.21

electricity with additional demand arising from the substitution of electricity for other fuels.

One consequence of the rapid increase in use of electricity is the apparent absorption of increasing proportions of total energy input in "conversion losses." For example, in 1975 electricity conversion losses are projected to amount to 14.1 quadrillion Btu, or 18.3 percent of total energy input, but in 2000 these losses are projected to be 58 quadrillion Btu or 31 percent of total energy input. The concentration of attention on conversion losses in the use of electricity can be misleading for several reasons, however. First it must be realized that similar efficiency losses occur in the use of other energy forms. In the typical application of electrical energy the major losses occur in the generation process, while efficiency at the site of final consumption is often close to 100 percent. In many other forms of energy consumption, however, the major losses occur at the point of final consumption. These losses are less easily measured or estimated since they occur at millions of separate locations (e.g., each automobile) rather than at a few electrical generating stations.

In addition, the significance of the conversion losses is further offset by the favorable implication of the growth in electricity use. This favorable implication is the flexibility in fuel use that characterizes electricity generation, i.e., any fuel can be used as the primary input. Uranium and hydro resources have, at present, no alternative use. Also, electricity generation can use coal, which is in relative abundance in the United States, and residual oil which, for technical reasons, has only limited value as a fuel in other uses. Thus, electricity generation can exploit these fuels which are cheaper and in the greatest abundance, leaving scarcer oil and gas supplies available for direct use.

The projected use of fuels in electricity generation is discussed in more detail in the section on Energy Supply and Prices. In general, however, the trends in fuel use reflect the influences discussed above in that nuclear power provides the bulk of the increase, with coal providing the next largest increase in inputs. Oil and natural gas provide the bulk of the remainder, with only small amounts coming from geothermal and other so-called "novel" sources.

Additional information on the projected use of fuels is provided in a later section which examines the prospects for a "high coal and nuclear" alternate to the moderate growth Case B.

f. Energy Supply and Prices

Using a general approach somewhat similar to that used in forecasting energy demand, two essentially independent forecasts of energy supply and prices were developed for this study. One forecast was that of the DRI models and the second was a judgmental forecast prepared under the direction of personnel from the Electric Power Research Institute with minor editing by the EEI Staff. The DRI energy supply forecast has the benefit of theoretical consistency with the macro-economic and energy demand forecasts, including price change effects. In contrast, the EPRI forecast relies on the conviction that factors affecting energy supply are so diverse and complex (political, social, environmental, geological, etc.), that judgmental forecasts prepared by persons knowledgeable in energy supply matters offer potential advantages over forecasts prepared more mechanically by computer. This conviction led to the decision to depend upon the EPRI work as the primary energy supply forecast.

The ensuing paragraphs summarize the domestic resource picture of the United States and then describe the EPRI forecast in some detail. This is followed by a comparison between the DRI and the EPRI supply forecasts to highlight the areas where they differ.

(1) Domestic Energy Resources

For most of its history the United States has been generally self-sufficient in energy; exporting rather than importing fuels. It was only during the 1960's that a variety of factors combined to change the nation to a net importer and to initiate what has become a rapidly growing dependence on foreign supplies.

Actually, the United States still has an immense energy resource base if it chooses to develop and use it. (These matters are considered in some detail in Appendix G). To set the stage for the detailed

Table 6·21

UNITED STATES ENERGY RESERVES AND RESOURCES
(Quadrillion Btu)

	Reserves	Resources
Coal	9,000	66,000
Oil	300	16,400
Natural Gas	300	6,400
Shale Oil	900	147,000
Uranium—Thermal	220	440,600
Uranium—Breeder	11,000	220,030,000
Total	21,720	220,706,400

Note: Annual Consumption in 1973 was 75 Quadrillion Btu.

supply forecasts which follow, however, a summary tabulation developed from Appendix G is presented here as Table 6•21. These figures suggest that an absolute shortage of resources is not the cause of our present energy problems.

(2) Judgmental Forecasting Technique

Energy supply projections were made for 1975, 1980, 1985 and 2000. The approach used for each period was modified according to differences in degrees of uncertainty and the ability of economic, technological, and policy factors to influence outcomes. For the short run the patterns necessarily represent essentially an extrapolation of recent trends. These were modified only in light of known or likely changes in availability, cost and policy influences.

The intermediate forecasts (1980-85) focused initially on 1985 since major technological and economic changes and new policy initiatives will by then have had time to show significant results, whereas by 1980 this will be the case only where lead times are comparatively short. Therefore, a detailed analysis was first made of possible supplies and prices for 1985. Thereafter, the likely 1980 patterns were determined in light of developing trends, with consideration for lagging responses. For the high growth case (Case A), where the policy framework establishes sufficient flexibility to open up choices of supply options, two sub-cases were developed for 1985: (1) a high self-sufficiency, and (2) a relatively high import alternative. By 1980, however, the high self-sufficiency route would not be likely to show significant results, even if appropriate policies were instituted at an early date.

For the year 2000, any projections are of necessity even more speculative and the results obviously carry a lesser degree of assurance than those for earlier years. In particular, no attempt was made by EPRI to study in detail the most probable mix of coal and nuclear generation in the electrical sector. Instead, two sets of estimates were prepared; one representing a higher coal alternative and the other a higher nuclear alternative.

(3) Estimates for 1975

The results of the judgmental projections for Case A—the future under high growth—are shown on Tables 6•22 through 6•31. For 1975 the Case A projections are identical to those for the other two scenarios. The primary assumptions are an absence of major economic or political disturbances and a continuation of present policies affecting the energy sector. To the extent that some policies may be altered (e.g., decontrol of natural gas prices assumed

in Case A), there will not be sufficient time to evoke a significant supply response.

The growth rates from 1973 to 1975 for both total energy and the electrical sector are below the historical trend. Supply shortages of natural gas combine with a recession and sharp price increases for all energy sources, thus restraining demand. Coal use is up only modestly in view of continued use of gas and low sulfur fuel oil by thermal power plants (because of pollution regulations), supply limitations, and the slow increase in electricity demand.

(4) Estimates for the Intermediate Period (1980-85)

The estimates of supply components for the years 1980 and 1985 are based on the following assumptions:·

For *nuclear power*, availability of 250,000 Mw capacity is estimated in 1985, with a capacity factor of 0.6 and a heat rate of 10,400 BTU/kwhr. The 1980 estimate is 110,000 Mw capacity, with the same capacity factor and a slightly higher heat rate. The 1980 level is somewhat below the AEC's 1974 listing of plants then currently operating, being built or on order and scheduled to be completed through 1980. This reduction is an attempt to consider recent delays in industry construction plans. The 1985 estimate represents an increase of 35,000 Mw over the recent AEC tabulation. However, the nuclear supply industry should have substantial deliverability in excess of current orders during the 1980-85 period and should have little difficulty reaching the estimated level, particularly under the Case A assumptions.

For hydroelectric and geothermal power, projected 1985 capacity is in line with that of the Department of Interior, i.e., 120,000 Mw, and slightly below the NPC's High (Case I).[13] It represents an increase of about 50 percent over the current level, with hydroelectric capacity accounting for about 70 percent of the total and geothermal for the remainder. In accord with the general assumptions regarding Case A, these figures represent considerable success in locating and utilizing sites, especially geothermal sites.

The supply estimate for fossil fuel for *power plant use* rests on the premises: that by 1985 environmental constraints will not materially impede the utilization of coal; that bottlenecks in producing and transporting coal will have been overcome; and that acceptable methods for sulfur removal will have become commercially feasible. Accordingly, use of oil and gas in power plants will be phased down to peak load and other special purposes, and coal will be utilized as the exclusive base load fuel in nonnuclear steam electric power generation. The result-

Table 6·22
CASE A: ENERGY BALANCES
(Quadrillion Btu)

	1973[1]	1975	1980	1985	2000
Total Demand[2]	75.6	77.0	96.0	115.9	186.1
Less Fuel Efficiency Adjustment[3]	—	—	1.5	3.0	7.0
Adjusted Demand	75.6	77.0	94.5	112.9	179.1
				High Coal	**High Nuclear**
Electrical Sector	19.8	20.9	27.7	35.4	77.8	77.8

	1973[1]	1975	1980	High Coal	High Nuclear
Electrical Sector	19.8	20.9	27.7	35.4 77.8	77.8
Hydro/Other	2.9	3.1	3.8	4.3 10.0	10.0
Nuclear	0.9	1.6	6.2	13.7 38.9	46.7
Petroleum[4]	7.3	6.9	5.7	2.6 2.1	2.1
Coal	8.7	9.3	12.0	14.8 26.8	19.0
Net Utility Generation[2] (Trillion Kwhr)	1.86[5]	1.98	2.77	3.63 8.08	

	1973[1]	1975	1980	1985		2000
				High Self-sufficiency	**High Imports**	
Non-Electrical Sector	55.8	56.1	66.8	77.5	77.5	101.3
Coal	4.8	4.9	5.1	5.2	5.2	6.5
Industrial	4.4	4.6	4.8	5.1	5.1	6.5
Other[6]	0.4	0.3	0.3	0.1	0.1	—
Gas	23.6	23.8	29.2	43.8	42.3	52.4
Natural, Lower 48	22.4[7]	25.0	36.8	34.8	39.4	
North Slope, Alaska	—	—	1.5	3.0	1.5	3.0
SNG[8]	0.1	0.2	0.7	1.5	1.0	2.0
Domestic	22.5	22.7	27.2	41.3	37.3	44.4
Imports	1.1	1.1	2.0	2.5	5.0	8.0
Petroleum Liquids Required	27.4	27.4	32.5	28.5	30.0	42.4
Crude + NGL Lower 48[9]	21.9	21.4	23.0	18.9	16.8	21.0
North Slope, Alaska	—	—	1.3	8.4	4.2	8.4
Syncrude	—	—	0.2	1.2	1.0	4.2
Domestic	21.9	21.4	24.5	28.5	22.0	33.6
Imports	5.5	6.0	8.0	0	8.0	8.8

Footnotes to Table 6·22

(1) United States Bureau of Mines Data (preliminary).

(2) Provided by Data Resources, Inc.

(3) Difference between energy inputs of electrical sector under assumption of constant heat rate made by DRI and decreasing heat rate made in this study. See Table 6·31.

(4) Projected figures assumed to be liquids because of non-availability of gas. 1973 actual: 3.9 gas, 3.4 oil.

(5) Estimated from weekly data.

(6) Excludes coal for gasification, which is included with gas (SNG).

(7) Adjusted for extraction losses, stock changes, and transfers.

(8) SNG = Synthetic natural gas

(9) NGL = Natural gas liquids

Table 6·23
CASE A: ENERGY SUPPLIES; PETROLEUM LIQUIDS
(Millions of Barrels) [1]

			1985		
	1975	1980	High Imports	High Self-sufficiency	2000
Lower 48 [2]	3,900	4,182	3,054	3,436	3,818
North Slope, Alaska	0	236	764	1,527	1,527
Syncrude	0	36	182	218	764
Total Domestic	3,900	4,454	4,000	5,181	6,109
Imports	2,345	2,500	1,927	473	1,982
Total [3]	6,245	6,954	5,927	5,654	8,091

(1) Converted at 5.5 million Btu's per barrel. (2) Includes South Alaska

(3) Excludes liquids for gasification (76 million barrels for all years)

Table 6·24
CASE A: ENERGY SUPPLIES; GAS
(Trillions of Cubic Feet) *

			1985		
	1975	1980	High Imports	High Self-sufficiency	2000
Lower 48	21.8	24.3	33.8	35.7	38.3
Alaska	0	1.5	1.5	2.9	2.9
SNG	0.2	0.7	1.0	1.5	1.9
Domestic	22.0	26.5	36.3	40.1	43.1
Imports	1.1	1.9	4.8	2.4	7.8
Total	23.1	28.4	41.1	42.5	50.9

* At 1,030 Btu per cubic foot dry gas excluding transfer and losses.

Table 6·25
CASE A: ENERGY SUPPLIES; COAL
(Millions of Short Tons) [1]

				2000	
	1975	1980	1985	High Coal	High Nuclear
Electrical	387	500	617	1,118	792
Industrial and Other [2]	204	212	217	271	271
Gasification	0	40	98	328	328
Domestic	591	752	932	1,717	1,391
Exports [3]	71	75	87	108	108
Total	662	827	1,019	1,825	1,499

(1) Converted at 24.0 million Btu per ton, except gasification at 23.2 million Btu per ton.

(2) Includes small quantities of other uses in earlier years.

(3) Department of Interior estimates (Dec. 1973).

ing volumes of coal burned in power plants are about 500 million tons in 1980 and 620 million tons in 1985, the latter representing an increase of 70 percent over the 1973 level. Adding domestic coal demand by other sectors, principally the steel industry, of about 215 million tons brings total domestic demand in 1985 to about 835 million tons. Even a sizable increase in exports would result in total demand of well under 1 billion tons, a figure easily within the ability of the coal industry to achieve by 1985, provided appropriate policies are adopted soon enough to overcome the long lead times required for opening new mines and developing ancillary facilities. (A National Academy of Engineering study

suggests that 1.26 billion tons is an attainable objective for 1985.)[14]

The above estimates do not include coal production to support gasification plants. As explained below, however, it is anticipated that development of a synthetic gas industry would be limited during the next 10-15 years. SNG plants thus would not result in straining the availability of coal for power plants or other uses. (See Table 6·25.)

The assumption that wellhead prices of natural gas are freed promptly is critical for the Case A forecast. Assuming liberal leasing policies for the most promising areas (primarily in various offshore regions and

Table 6·26
CASE A: ENERGY SUPPLIES; NUCLEAR POWER

	1973	1975	1980	1985	2000 High Coal	2000 High Nuclear
Installed Capacity (Thousands of MW)	31[1]	50	110	251	740	890
Net Generation (Billions of Kwhr)[2]	80	150	580	1,320	3,890	4,670
Energy Inputs (Quadrillion Btu)	0.85	1.6	6.2	13.7	38.9	46.7

(1) Estimates for Dec. 31.

(2) A conservatively low capacity factor of 0.6 is used for 1980 and beyond. Perhaps more realistic would be a capacity factor which rose gradually as the technology matured. For example, a capacity factor of 0.75 in 2000 would require only 710. thousand MW of capacity to generate 4,670 billions of kwh, as opposed to 890 thousand MW shown under the High Nuclear column.

Heat rates through 1985 from Department of Interior, Dec. 1972 report; *United States Energy Through the year 2000.* This report shows a decrease from 10,560 Btu per Kwhr in 1975 to 9,760 in 1985. For 2,000 a slower rate of improvement was used.

Table 6·27
CASE A: ENERGY SUPPLY SUMMARIES
(Quadrillion Btu)

	1975	1980	1985 High Imports	1985 High Self-Sufficiency	2000 High Nuclear	2000 High Coal
Gas	23.8	29.2	42.3	43.8	52.4	52.4
Petroleum Liquids	34.3	38.2	32.6	31.1	44.5	44.5
Coal	14.2	17.1	20.0	20.0	25.5	33.3
Nuclear	1.6	6.2	13.7	13.7	46.7	38.9
Hydro/Other	3.1	3.8	4.3	4.3	10.0	10.0
Total	77.0	94.5	112.9	112.9	179.1	179.1

Table 6·28
CASE A: SHARES OF ENERGY SUPPLY SOURCES
(Percent)

	1975	1980	1985 High Imports	1985 High Self-Sufficiency	2000 High Nuclear	2000 High Coal
Gas	31.0	30.9	37.5	38.8	29.3	29.3
Petroleum Liquids	44.5	40.4	28.9	27.6	24.8	24.8
Coal	18.4	18.1	17.7	17.7	14.2	18.6
Nuclear	2.1	6.6	12.1	12.1	26.1	21.7
Hydro/Other	4.0	4.0	3.8	3.8	5.6	5.6

Table 6·29
CASE A: SHARES OF PETROLEUM AND GAS IMPORTS
(Quadrillion Btu)

	1975	1980	1985 High Imports	1985 High Self-Sufficiency	2000
Petroleum Imports	12.9	13.7	10.6	2.6	10.9
Petroleum Demand	34.3	38.2	32.6	30.7	44.5
Imports (Percent)	37	36	33	8	24
Gas Imports	1.1	2.0	5.0	2.5	8.0
Gas Demand	23.9	29.2	42.3	43.8	52.4
Imports (Percent)	5	7	12	6	15
Total Imports	14.0	15.7	15.6	5.1	18.9
Total Energy Demand	77.0	94.5	112.9	112.9	179.1
Imports (Percent)	18	17	14	5	11

Alaska), a significant expansion of domestic gas production is likely. Natural gas was severely underpriced even before the recent sharp increase in oil and coal prices. In a free market, gas prices would tend to rise to approximate Btu parity with low-sulfur fuel oil, at least for new contracts, before buyer resistance is felt. Under decontrol, wellhead prices of new gas would then approach $2.00 per MCF, and this would provide the necessary stimulus for a greatly increased exploration and development effort. In time, such an effort would not only arrest the declining trend of gas discoveries but would very probably support a major expansion of production. The projections for the lower 48 states envisage the onset of such a turn-around by the late 1970's and a major increase above current output by 1985.

Seemingly very high from today's perspective, these gas output estimates, as well as those for petroleum liquids, are based on relatively optimistic estimates of total domestic resources and on an in-depth study of the work of the National Petroleum

Council, Professor Henry Steele and others.[15] This study permits the determination of theoretically valid price-quantity relationships, and hence of supply elasticities. (Supply elasticity is the percent change in quantity supplied for each percent change in price.) The assumed elasticities are 1.0 for gas and 1.5 for crude oil. The latter is greater because at higher prices the recovery ratio for crude can be increased by secondary and tertiary recovery methods, whereas for gas the recovery rate generally is high (except in special situations like the tight formations previously referred to).

Along with decontrol of gas prices it is assumed that under the economic climate of Case A, existing controls on prices of both "old" and "new" crude oil and petroleum products will be lifted promptly. Controlled crude oil prices (currently $5.25 per barrel of "old" oil at the Gulf Coast) would then tend to rise toward the "free" market level (currently about $10-12 per barrel), and this increase would further reinforce incentives for exploration and de-

142

velopment of both oil and gas. Under Case A conditions, it is not necessary to assume that wellhead prices would continue to rise further, even under the long-term inflationary conditions expected to prevail, since prices following decontrol would be very substantially above those needed to evoke required oil and gas supplies. Accordingly, the Case A expectations are that oil and gas prices in current dollars will remain constant during the period and be

Table 6·30
CASE A: ASSUMED OIL AND GAS PRICES; LOWER 48 STATES (1975 $)

Crude Oil & NGL[1]

1975

Quadrillion Btu	21.4
Millions of Barrels	3900
Millions of Barrels per day	10.7
Dollars per Barrel	$10.00

1985

Quadrillion Btu	16.8[2]
Millions of Barrels	3055
Millions of Barrels per day	8.37
Dollars per Barrel	$5.60

2000

Quadrillion Btu	21.0
Millions of Barrels	3818
Millions of Barrels per day	10.46
Dollars per Barrel	$8.50

Gas

1975

Quadrillion Btu	22.5
Thousands of Cubic Feet	21.8
Dollars per Thousand Cubic Feet	$1.94

1985

Quadrillion Btu	34.8
Thousands of Cubic Feet	33.8
Dollars per Thousand Cubic Feet	$1.01

2000

Quadrillion Btu	39.4
Thousands of Cubic Feet	38.3
Dollars per Thousand Cubic Feet	$1.58

(1) Natural gas liquids

(2) High import case. High self-sufficiency case yields 18.9 quadrillion Btu's (9.4 millions of barrels per day) at same price.

Table 6·31
CONVERSION FACTORS USED IN TABLES 6·22-6·30

BTU CONTENT OF FOSSIL FUELS

Coal for gasification	23,200,000	Btu per short ton
Other coal	24,000,000	Btu per short ton
Crude oil	5,500,000	Btu per short ton
Residual fuel oil	6,100,000	Btu per barrel
Natural gas	1,030	Btu per cubic feet

HEAT RATES OF ELECTRICAL GENERATING PLANTS
(Btu per Kwhr)

	1975	1980	1985	2000
Fossil fuels	10,575	9,875	9,575	9,250
Nuclear	10,660	10,660	10,400	10,000
Hydro/Other*	10,220	9,500	9,200	9,000
Average	10,560	9,990	9,760	9,600-9,360

* Hydro power outputs are converted to theoretical energy inputs on the basis of heat rates for large fossil-fueled steam-electric plants.

gradually eroded by inflation in "real" terms. By the end of the decade, prices would be such as to produce the indicated volumes under conditions of long-run equilibrium, which imply a normal return on investment for the industry as a whole. These would be in the order of $5.60 per barrel for crude and $1.00 per thousand cubic feet of gas in 1975 dollars. (See Table 6·30.)

Taxes on oil and gas production, and import controls are other important policy issues which will encourage (or discourage) the development of new oil and gas production capacity. For this scenario it is assumed that either current tax provisions will be retained and the 22 percent depletion allowance reinstated, or that crude oil and gas prices will rise further to offset any reduction of the various tax incentives.

As to imports of petroleum liquids, an assumed $2 per barrel reduction in world prices would bring foreign crude prices closely into line with the 1975 price of $10 per barrel in the United States. The impact of world markets on domestic prices, and especially investment incentives, would be very critical if a policy of unrestrained imports were followed. This would be especially serious, of course, if one or more exporting countries were to attempt a major expansion of sales in the United States market, or if large new discoveries by non-OPEC countries were to undermine the existing world price. Such contingencies would tend to act as a negative factor on domestic oil and gas investment unless the industry were assured in advance that the United States market would be sufficiently insulated from foreign competition. The projections assume that, even in the relatively high import case, such assurances will be provided to the extent necessary to encourage increased domestic exploration, development, and production.

The large expansion of conventional oil and gas supplies from the lower 48 states at declining real prices makes it both unnecessary and unlikely that the development of other domestic sources will be very rapid. Under the high-import case, production of North Slope oil and gas is estimated to proceed at the presently scheduled pace, involving the Alaska Pipeline and one gas line, which draw on already proved reserves. Only presently contemplated shale oil projects would be developed by 1985, and synthetic gas, primarily from coal, would emerge quite slowly. Even so, the level of oil imports would fall to about 1.9 billion barrels (i.e., 5.3 million barrels per day) from the current 2.4 billion barrels (6.5 million barrels per day).

Under these conditions, oil imports could be drastically reduced if not completely eliminated, if this were deemed desirable, without major departure from the supply and pricing pattern prevailing under the assumed basic Case A policies. By 1985 the North Slope should be able to support twice the basic levels of oil and gas production, while shale oil and SNG output could be accelerated by financial or tax policies or price-market guarantees. It can also be anticipated that the reduced investment risks under a self-sufficiency policy would evoke somewhat greater exploratory efforts, and thus yield larger oil and gas supplies from the lower 48 states, at similar prices.

(5) Estimates for the Long-Range (2000)

Under the Case A—high growth conditions the United States would have a wide range of choices for meeting its energy needs in the year 2000.

Professor Steele's work includes an extrapolation of oil and gas production in the lower 48 states for the year 2000, with a supply curve which lies about one-third above that for 1985, i.e., a one-third price increase would be required to evoke the same volume of oil and gas. In this view there is no indication that the resource base is a serious constraint on supply (other than through higher prices). On this basis, plus a continued assumption of parity between the price of fuel oil and gas, gas prices in 2000 would be about $1.50 per million BTU and crude oil prices about $8.50 a barrel. Production of natural gas from the lower 48 states would be about 38 trillion cubic

feet, and output of crude and natural gas liquids about 10.5 million barrels per day. (Note that all these prices are in 1975 dollars.)

For the North Slope, it is assumed that the normal pace of development by 2000 would result in about the same volumes as accelerated output under a self-sufficiency policy would have achieved in 1985. Synthetic natural gas production is assumed to double from the basic 1985 case and syncrude production is estimated to reach 2 million barrels per day, a figure sometimes considered to be a limit on shale production under conventional mining technology because of constraints on water availability. Under these conditions, imports of oil and gas combined would rise little from 1985 (high import case) and they would decline as a percentage of total United States energy supplies. (See Table 6·29.)

For the *electrical sector* two cases have been developed; a nuclear case (60 percent of total generation), and a high coal case (nuclear at 50 percent of total). For this judgmental forecast there was no attempt to make an independent analysis of the potential market shares of these two major sources of electricity. These shares will depend on technological, economic, and policy developments whose impact cannot be readily anticipated, even in the absence of serious constraints on either or both sources. It is clear, however, that both coal and nuclear power must play major parts in the nation's energy future. Neither can do the job alone. Even using the optimistic Case A figures for the future availability of oil and gas, about 40 percent of the nation's energy diet in the year 2000 must be derived from coal and nuclear sources.

The contribution of non-fuel energy sources (hydro, geothermal and new sources such as solar power) is estimated to be more than double the 1985 rate. No detailed study of the composition of this component was undertaken, rather the high estimate of the Energy Policy Project has been accepted.[16] The use of oil and gas in the electrical sector would be minimal in 2000 with Case A because of the assumed absence of constraints on nuclear power and coal, and because oil and gas would be relatively high cost fuels for use under boilers at prices expected to prevail in 2000.

(6) Comparison with the DRI Supply Forecast

The DRI forecast confirms the EPRI estimates for energy supplies from coal, nuclear, hydro, and other sources as shown on Chart 6·17 and Table 6·32. Significant differences are seen in the oil and natural gas projections, however, with EPRI being much more optimistic as regards the increase in gas

Chart 6•17
**CASE A: COMPARISON OF ENERGY SUPPLY
FORECASTS
(EPRI vs DRI)**

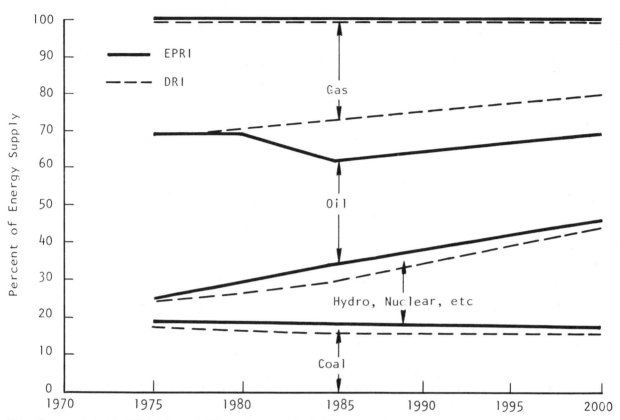

Note: Figures charted for EPRI represent: (1) an average of the high imports and high self-sufficiency cases for 1985 and (2) an average of the high coal and high nuclear cases for 2000.

supplies which will result from a removal of wellhead price controls.

For oil and natural gas, the EPRI forecast sequence is: early decontrol of domestic prices of both; a rapid price increase for natural gas; plentiful supplies and depressed prices of both oil and gas by 1985. Under free market conditions, gas supplies will increase rapidly and customers, when able to choose between liquid and gaseous energy, will prefer gas in many applications. Consequently, gas consumption rises more rapidly than oil.

With the exception of transportation and a few other uses, petroleum liquids are treated somewhat as residuals in the EPRI analysis. The smaller volumes of oil consumption represent demand rather than supply limitations. Initial oil prices are determined by current very high world market prices, but these stimulate a large domestic program to expand production. This program is successful to the degree

that real prices are significantly eroded by 1985, and return to the long-term trend thereafter.

In contrast, the DRI price projections represent more nearly stable expansion paths with trends which do not show any major variations due to temporary disequilibrating forces. Thus, price incentives for expansion of new gas and oil supplies are somewhat smaller in the near term and the response in increased production rates is less dramatic than in the EPRI forecast. In the case of natural gas, for example, prices remain somewhat below a free market equilibrium until perhaps 1985. Thereafter, resource limitations become dominant.

In both versions, supplies are fully adequate to support the Case A demands for energy and, in the EPRI forecast at least, the higher prices create a surplus energy supply situation even with the continued high growth in demand.

The DRI and EPRI supply forecasts and price

Table 6·32
CASE A: COMPARISON OF ENERGY SUPPLY FORECASTS:
(EPRI vs. DRI) [1]

(Quadrillion Btu)	1975 EPRI	1975 DRI	1985 EPRI	1985 DRI	2000 EPRI	2000 DRI
Domestic						
Oil	21.4	20.5	24.1	35.4	31.0	42.4
Natural Gas	22.5	22.2	38.1	27.1	42.4	27.1
Total	43.9	42.7	62.2	62.5	73.4	69.5
Synthetics						
Syncrude	—	—	1.2	—	2.6	9.5
Synthetic Gas	0.2	—	1.2	0.7	2.0	3.6
Total	0.2	—	2.4	0.7	4.6	13.1
Imports						
Oil	12.9	13.3	6.6	14.2	10.9	13.9
Natural Gas	1.1	2.3	3.8	4.0	8.0	6.3
Total	14.0	15.6	10.4	18.2	18.9	20.2
Total Oil and Gas	58.1	58.3	75.0	81.4	96.9	102.8
Other						
Coal	14.2	13.2	20.0	18.3	29.9	28.6
Nuclear	1.6	2.3	13.7	12.0	42.8	44.7
Hydro, Other	3.1	3.2	4.3	4.3[2]	10.0	10.0[2]
Total	18.9	18.7	38.0	34.6	82.7	83.3
Total Energy	77.0	77.0	113.0	116.0[3]	179.6	186.1[3]

(1) EPRI Figures represent an average of the high imports and high self-sufficiency cases for 1985, and an average of the high coal and nuclear cases for 2000. Differences between figures on this table and those on preceding related tables are caused by averaging and rounding.

(2) Hydro, Other taken from EPRI Forecast because DRI forecast aggregates Nuclear, Hydro, Other.

(3) Differences between EPRI and DRI total energy figures stem primarily from the EPRI assumption of gradual decrease in heat rates for electrical generation, while DRI has assumed no such improvement.

forecasts also differ somewhat in the use of petroleum fuels for generation of electricity. However, both foresee the continued use of coal and a rapid expansion in the use of nuclear power. Specifically the two forecasts differ as shown on Table 6·33. EPRI forecasts the almost complete disappearance of oil and gas as boiler fuels by the year 2000 as these energy sources are appropriated in increasing quantities for higher value uses such as transportation, raw materials, etc.

Yet another difference between the two forecasts exists in the assumed average heat rates for electric generation (i.e., Btu per kilowatthour). DRI assumes these rates will remain unchanged over the next 25 years while EPRI foresees a significant improvement (See Table 6·31). The effects of these two different heat rate assumptions can be seen on Table 6·34. The electric generation figures are

Table 6·33
CASE A: ENERGY SUPPLY FOR THE
GENERATION OF ELECTRICITY:
COMPARISON OF EPRI AND DRI FORECASTS
(Percent)

	1975	1980	1985	2000
DRI Forecast				
Oil & Gas	32.2	27.1	23.4	14.6
Coal	41.5	38.4	34.4	21.6
Hydro, Nuclear, Other	26.3	34.5	42.2	63.8
Total	100.0	100.0	100.0	100.0
EPRI Forecast				
Oil & Gas	33.0	20.6	7.2	2.7
Coal	44.5	43.3	42.0	29.4
Hydro, Nuclear, Other	22.5	36.1	50.8	67.9
Total	100.0	100.0	100.0	100.0

identical in both forecasts, but the energy consumed to generate that electricity differs from one forecast to the other. By the year 2000 the higher efficiency generation foreseen by EPRI would save 7 quadrillion Btu per year in comparison to the DRI energy consumption figure. Over the 25-year period, the improving efficiency would reduce the average growth rate of energy consumption for electric generation from 5.8 percent per year to 5.4 percent per year.

Both forecasts are consistent in concluding that supply conditions in the electricity generating sector are not likely to place any long run constraints on electricity generation (this scenario assumes that environmental and safety regulations do not prevent the expansion of capacity). Fuel supply, in the form of coal and nuclear fuels, and to a lesser extent, petroleum and gas fuels for peak load generation, is not expected to provide a binding constraint over the remainder of the century.

The remaining major input is that of capital. Although construction capacity may be a limiting factor at the present time it is not expected to limit consumption of electricity over the long run. This scenario assumes easing of the capital availability problem, prompt reinstatement in utility construction plans of many of the generating stations deferred during 1974, and a timely and adequate expansion of the scale of the construction industry. Reductions in licensing delays, standardized designs and improved construction procedures are also expected to play a significant role. A separate assessment of capital requirements for the electric utility industry is provided in Chapter 10 of this study.

D. Case C: The Future Under Low Growth

1. Assumptions

The low-growth scenario is based on a set of assumptions about the kinds of conditions that might exist if the United States decided to pursue a policy of slowing or stabilizing economic growth. It is unlikely that these conditions would evolve in the short term future. For purposes of this scenario, however, it was assumed that major restrictions on growth could be made operative by the late 1980's; i.e., within perhaps one-half of a generation. It seems unlikely that such conditions would develop so quickly without some artificial constraints to growth such as: (1) resource restrictions which might result from a continuation and intensification of the recent OPEC actions related to oil prices and production rates; (2) the development of similarly effective cartels in other important international raw materials; (3) greatly increased public pressure to clean up the environment and limit the impact of technology without major regard to costs or other effects; or (4) a protracted and severe worldwide depression resulting from the first two previously assumed conditions. Even with these constraints, the assumed actions would require greater use of governmental authority than has characterized past United States history. With these qualifying comments, the following conditions are assumed for the low-growth scenario.

a. Raw Materials

The general assumptions regarding the supply of raw materials (including the supply of air, water, and

Table 6-34
CASE A: COMPARISON OF ELECTRIC ENERGY FORECASTS: (EPRI versus DRI)

	1975		1985		2000	
	EPRI	DRI	EPRI	DRI	EPRI	DRI
Energy Consumption for Electricity Generation (Quadrillion Btu)	20.9	20.8	35.4	38.5	77.8	85.8
Electricity Generated (Trillion Kwhr)	1.98	1.98	3.63	3.63	8.08	8.08

	1975-1985		1985-2000		1975-2000	
	EPRI	DRI	EPRI	DRI	EPRI	DRI
Average Annual Growth Rates (Percent)						
Energy Consumption	5.5	6.3	5.4	5.5	5.4	5.8
Electricity Generation	6.3	6.3	5.5	5.5	5.8	5.8

147

land inputs), are conditioned by the capital productivity assumptions outlined below. The specific assumption concerning the use of raw materials is that per-capita use of materials, including energy, is gradually restricted by public policy prohibitions until the late 1980's. After that time it is assumed that a steady state condition of constant per capita resource use will exist. Unfavorable supply conditions will develop for both domestically produced raw materials and imports. Domestic raw materials supplies are assumed to become increasingly scarce and expensive after currently known reserves are depleted, and major imports are limited to current levels.

The public policy prohibitions, which are assumed to limit resource consumption, could take any one of several forms. Some possibilities are reviewed in Chapter 4 of this report. One consists of government controlled auctions in which the limited resources are auctioned to the highest bidders. Although the specific form of these prohibitions need not be specified for the DRI modeling effort, the auction technique was assumed as the basis for parts of the judgmental forecasting efforts.

b. Labor

A continuation of current trends in average fertility rates is assumed which results in a total fertility rate of 1.8 (this is Census Bureau population projection series F). This may involve government action to limit births. Based on current trends, however, this fertility rate could emerge by individual choice. The assumed 1.8 fertility rate leads to continued population growth until about 2030 or 2040 but thereafter to a decline in the total population. The rate of population increase is 0.8 percent a year until 1985. Then it falls steadily to 0.4 percent in the year 2000, and eventually becomes negative. The labor force follows a similar pattern but with a lag in time of 20 years. In fact, it is not until the late 1980's that the low fertility rate impacts on the size of the labor force. In the interim, per capita income levels are boosted. This is because the labor force is increasing faster than population and the average family income must be spread over fewer people.

It is also assumed that the historical trend towards increasing leisure will accelerate over the 1980-2000 period. The actual change which the modeling work found to be necessary is a 25 percent reduction in per capita labor over this period, e.g., a reduction in the average full-time manufacturing work week from 40 to 30 hours. In terms of the average private sector workweek, the reduction would be from 37 hours at present to about 32 hours by 1985 and 27 hours by

the year 2000. This change exceeds that which could be expected on the basis of historical experience; it must be attributed either to major change in individual attitudes or to government regulations as part of a general conservation plan.

Such a reduction in weekly hours was found necessary to achieve a reasonable balance between labor input and the other inputs (capital and resources) which determine economic growth. An obvious, but unpleasant alternative to the shrinkage in everyone's workweek would be a longer workweek and fewer workers. For example; the same total labor inputs could be achieved by an unchanged workweek and unchanged labor force participation with a 14 to 15 percent unemployment rate by 1985, and a 28 to 30 percent unemployment rate by 2000. Under such conditions, labor force participation might be expected to decrease as more and more unemployed persons became discouraged and left the labor force. Government regulations to limit employed persons to one from each family unit would be conceivable. Another alternative would be purposely to decrease productivity to keep people busy doing things inefficiently.

c. Capital Services

Three types of conditions were assumed for capital stock in the low-growth scenario. All three tend to decrease the productivity of the capital stock in a market sense. The first is an increase in the use of new capital in environmental improvement programs. By market criteria, this investment is unproductive in that it does not contribute to future material output. It is a diversion from the current output of investment goods that has no return in the market system aside from the employment provided by such programs. It is assumed that the increased capital devoted to this purpose (in addition to the amounts already being spent or mandated) will rise from $1 billion per year in 1975 to $10 billion in 1980 (in constant 1958 dollar terms) and each following year.

The second assumption about capital is that increasingly strict regulations on effluents and energy and materials inputs will have the effect of reducing the productivity of existing capital. Specifically, it is assumed that the trend of productivity increase in the use of capital will drop to –0.2 percent a year, a one percentage point reduction from the 0.8 percent a year increase observed historically and used for the Case A high-growth scenario. The implication of this is that production activity is controlled in such a way that environmental damage and resource requirements per unit of output are not only prevented from increasing but actually reversed so that a progressive improvement in environmental quality occurs.

The third change assumed for capital is related to the productivity of new investment. In addition to the devotion of significant capital solely to environmental improvement, it is assumed that new investment will be limited to environmentally clean and resource-efficient techniques which have low productivity. That is, new investment is assumed to follow resource efficiency criteria rather than economic efficiency criteria. Specifically the productivity of new investment is assumed to decline at 2 percent a year for the rest of the century.

These assumptions reflect the view that the objectives of environmental improvement and resource conservation will be pursued gradually to achieve continuing, steady improvement rather than by a sudden, drastic change. Drastic changes could, of course, result in major disruptions of the economic system which would reduce economic growth even further.

d. Technology

The capital productivity assumptions have been discussed above. Labor and total factor productivity growth are assumed to continue at past rates—a 0.6 percent annual rate of improvement in labor productivity and a 1.5 percent rate of increase in total factor productivity.[17] This is based on a consideration of the types of activity that will occur in a low growth economy. The increase in educational, health and research activity in such a society will, if anything, increase these types of productivity growth rather than reduce them. This degree of productivity improvement can probably be sustained through the end of the century. At some point a steady state society, such as we envisage here, might be urged to set absolute zero limits on growth and employ productivity "dividends" to achieve a gradual reduction of resource consumption. For Case C it is assumed that this achievement of true zero growth occurs sometime after the year 2000.

e. Government Policies

Government action would be needed to accomplish some of the changes assumed for the low-growth scenario. There are other changes, such as low population growth, which could occur as the result of individual action. A slowing in the growth of resource use could also occur as the result of physical shortages or bottlenecks in the supplies of materials. In most cases however, government action would be required to ensure that a suitable range of conservation changes was effected. Such action would be required in the areas of rationing raw materials and enforcing a shift from labor to leisure.

Other governmental actions are assumed which would be directed at reducing the incentives for growth and investment. At the national level such actions might include: elimination of the investment tax credit; continuation of high interest rates to discourage investment; selective credit controls to encourage "desirable" investment in, for example, pollution control equipment; and curtailment of government-sponsored or aided "improvements" such as dams, inland waterways, etc. On a local level, controls and limits on land use would be expected to be strengthened.

The nature of the DRI model is such that it cannot incorporate all of these assumptions explicitly as input. They are listed above and in other portions of the report merely as examples of likely policies in a low-growth society. In some cases they are also useful as supplementary assumptions for the judgmental forecasts (i.e., energy demand by consuming sector, energy supply, and non-energy minerals supply and demand).

To occupy the population during its increased leisure time as material production is restricted, it is assumed there will be expanded government support of educational and cultural activities. The role of government is assumed to grow in relation to the private economy, with government purchases accounting for a gradually increasing share of GNP. Other government activities and services, on the other hand, would be expected to follow the generally slower rate of economic growth. In particular, this would mean major reductions (as compared to Case A) in such areas as foreign aid, R&D, and national defense. Existing revenue programs are assumed to be adequate to finance the changing mix of government expenditures so that no major tax changes are required during the period to the year 2000 except, perhaps, as another measure to discourage growth.

f. Consumption Lifestyle

A variety of government-mandated and voluntary social controls on personal consumption is assumed to become effective over the first decade of the period. Consumption patterns are expected to shift from material-intensive and energy-intensive goods and services toward those emphasizing education, leisure, the arts and nature. Consumer durable goods would be designed to maximize useful life and to facilitate repairs. Non-durable goods such as clothing would be designed for simplicity, long-life, and multiple-use applications. Style changes and "planned obsolescence" would be minimized in response to government restrictions.

Table 6·35
CASE C: MACRO ECONOMIC PROJECTIONS; 1975-2000[1]

	1974	1975[2]	1980[2]	1985	2000
1. Disposition of GNP (Billions of Current $) [3]					
GNP	1544	1714	2581	3591	7358
Personal Consumption	896	995	1462	2032	4001
Private Domestic Investment	337	380	629	881	1643
Government Purchases	309	338	484	677	1714
2. Disposition of Real GNP (Billions of 1958 $) [3]					
Real GNP	944	983	1205	1344	1725
Real Personal Consumption	559	577	699	785	1031
Real Private Domestic Investment	229	231	318	361	454
Real Government Purchases	146	175	190	201	235
3. Price Deflators for GNP Components (1958 = 1)					
Price of GNP		1.744	2.144	2.672	4.265
Price of Personal Consumption		1.723	2.091	2.589	3.881
Price of Private Domestic Investment		1.645	1.979	2.440	3.619
Price of Government Purchases		1.932	2.545	3.367	7.295
4. GNP Per Capita (Thousands of Current $)		8.032	11.727	15.552	29.350
Personal Consumption Per Capita					
(Thousands of Current $)		4.663	6.593	8.800	15.959
Real GNP Per Capita (Thousands of 1958 $)		4.606	5.433	5.821	6.881
Real Personal Consumption Per Capita					
(Thousands of 1958 $)		2.704	3.151	3.400	4.112
5. Percentage of GNP (Current $ Basis)					
Personal Consumption		58.1	56.2	56.2	54.4
Private Domestic Investment		22.2	24.2	24.5	22.3
Government Purchases		19.7	18.6	18.9	23.3
Government Expenditures		31.5	30.7	31.1	37.8
6. Percentage of Real GNP (1958 $ Basis)					
Real Personal Consumption		58.7	58.0	58.4	59.8
Real Private Domestic Investment		23.5	26.4	26.9	26.3
Real Government Purchases		17.8	15.8	15.0	13.6
7. Population and Labor Force					
Population (Million)		213.4	221.8	230.9	250.7
Labor Input (Billion Effective Manhours)		488	535	520	548
Labor as Percent of Total Time		14.2	14.2	12.8	10.8
Net Wage and Salary Index (1967 = 1)		1.660	2.214	3.079	5.866
8. Capital Items					
Real Capital Stock (Billions of 1958 $)		2108	2398	2582	2515
Rate of Return of Private Capital (Percent)		8.5	9.3	8.5	8.8
Labor Productivity Index (1967 = 1)		1.328	1.488	1.670	2.009
Unit Labor Cost Index (1967 = 1)		1.740	2.120	2.645	4.274
Corporate Profits (Billions of Current $)		88	117	142	264
Corporate Cash Flow (Billions of Current $)		165	236	316	597
Private National Wealth (Billions of Current $)		4735	6414	8362	11675
Input of Effective Capital Services (Billions of 1958 $)		310	352	380	370

(1) See Appendix B for the definition of GNP used in this table and the correspondence of this definition to the National Income Accounts definition.

(2) The DRI projections were developed in mid 1974 when the length and depth of the 1974-75 recession generally was being underestimated. At that time some modest real growth was expected in 1975. It is reasonable to expect that the economy will return to the DRI forecast trend well before 1980.

(3) Net Exports (a component of GNP) is not tabulated because of its small size. For example, in 1974, net exports were $2 billion in current dollars and $9 billion in 1958 dollars.

2. Model Outputs—A Low-Growth Scenario

a. Economic Growth

The future of economic growth under the conditions assumed for Case C low-growth is reflected in Tables 6•35 and 6•36. These figures are forecasts from the DRI modeling effort. The basic result shown by these tables is that, despite the severe limitations on resource use and production activity, growth of real output and real per capita incomes still continues. The growth rate is greatly reduced from past trends but remains positive. Economic welfare, even as measured by the conventional market-based indicators, can be expected to continue to increase, but only rather slowly. Account should also be taken of the nonmarket benefits such as increased leisure, a cleaner physical environment, and a somewhat reduced rate of depletion of the Earth's nonrenewable resources. In these regards,

overall welfare might be considered to have increased still further.

(1) Gross National Product and Its Composition

In the low-growth scenario real incomes and total output increase until 1980 at rates only slightly below past trends. Starting in 1980, however, growth restricting changes begin to have a major effect and slow the rate of growth. Real GNP growth averages 4.2 percent a year between 1975 to 1980. It drops to 2.2 percent for the years 1980 and 1985 and further to a 1.7 percent annual rate for the remainder of the century.

The composition of real output changes somewhat from current patterns, but not drastically. Real investment increases most rapidly over the 1975-1985 period. It grows from 23.5 to 26.9 percent of real GNP as the capital demands for growth are

Table 6•36

**CASE C: MACRO ECONOMIC PROJECTIONS, GROWTH RATES; 1975-2000
(Average Annual Percentage Growth Rates)**

	1975 to 1980	1980 to 1985	1985 to 2000	1975 to 2000
GNP	8.53	6.83	4.90	6.00
Personal Consumption	8.00	6.81	4.62	5.72
Private Domestic Investment	10.60	6.97	4.24	6.03
Government Purchases	7.44	6.94	6.38	6.71
Real GNP	4.15	2.21	1.67	2.27
Real Personal Consumption	3.91	2.35	1.83	2.35
Real Private Domestic Investment	5.09	2.56	1.54	2.74
Real Government Purchases	2.01	1.13	1.05	1.19
Price of GNP	4.06	4.50	3.17	3.64
Price of Personal Consumption	3.61	4.37	2.74	3.30
Price of Private Domestic Investment	3.30	4.28	2.66	3.20
Price of Government Purchases	5.78	5.76	5.29	5.46
GNP Per Capita	7.86	5.81	4.32	5.32
Personal Consumption Per Capita	7.17	5.94	4.05	5.04
Real GNP Per Capita	3.36	1.39	1.12	1.62
Real Personal Consumption Per Capita	3.11	1.53	1.28	1.69
Population	0.78	0.81	0.55	0.65
Labor Input	1.86	-0.56	0.35	0.46
Net Wage and Salary Index	5.78	6.82	4.39	5.18
Real Capital Stock	2.61	1.49	-0.18	0.71
Labor Productivity Index	2.30	2.34	1.24	1.67
Unit Labor Cost Index	4.03	4.53	3.25	3.66
Corporate Profits	5.86	3.95	4.22	4.49
Corporate Cash Flow	7.42	6.05	4.33	5.26
Private National Wealth	6.26	5.45	2.25	3.68
Input of Effective Capital Services	2.57	1.54	-0.18	0.71

supplemented by the capital required for environmental improvement. After the mid 1980's, however, the lower overall growth rate and the redirection of growth away from capital intensive material production result in some decline in the fraction of total output that is invested. This is despite the capital requirements associated with resource conservation. Thus, over the 1985-2000 period, real private investment increases at 1.5 percent a year, which is more slowly than total output so that its share of the real GNP falls slightly, to 26.3 percent in 2000.

Real consumption follows a growth pattern opposite to investment. Between 1975 and 1985 consumption increases more slowly than output and its contribution to GNP declines marginally as production is drawn off into private investment. After 1985, the slower growth in investment and government permits a more rapid increase of real consumption so that, by 2000, real consumption increases its share of total output to 59.8 percent. Real government purchases show a steady increase, in both total and per capita terms, but the rate of growth is much less than that of total output and the share of real government purchases declines from 17.8 percent in 1975 to 13.6 percent in 2000. Nonetheless, there is a

continuing increase in government services; the slow real growth is due to the dependence of these services on labor services, an input whose supply increases only slowly.

Total output in current dollars is projected to increase at a declining rate, 8.5 percent a year in the 1970's, 6.8 percent between 1980 and 1985 and 4.9 percent over the rest of the century. Personal consumption expenditures increase marginally more slowly so that the consumption share drops slightly over the forecast period. Investment expenditures rise a little more rapidly than total spending until 1985 but then the rate of increase falls and its share in total spending declines slightly. Government purchases are the most rapidly increasing component of spending. These increase at over 6 percent a year in current dollar terms for the entire forecast period, increasing the government share in total spending to 23.3 percent by 2000. The difference between the upward relative trend for purchases in current dollars and the downward trend in real dollars is due to the high wage and salary component in these purchases.

The combination of a slow economic growth rate and an even slower growth of real government purchases may cause major changes in the nation's international relations. This will be almost inevitable

Chart 6•18
INCOME DISTRIBUTION
(Percent of Total Families and Unrelated Individuals)

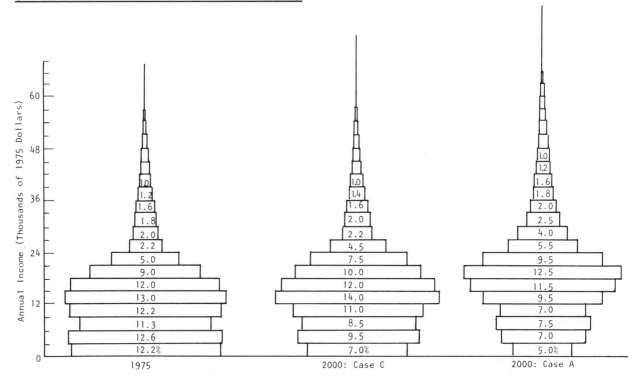

if most of the rest of the world maintains its growth objectives unchanged. A slow growth of research and development expenditures would gradually erode competitiveness in international markets. Lagging growth in domestic living standards might adversely affect the nation's willingness to increase foreign aid.

The nation's defense posture is another example of the potential problems associated with slow growth. If the share of real government expenditures which is allocated to defense remains constant and a Case C environment is assumed, United States defense expenditures in the year 2000 will be about 80 percent larger than in 1974. With continued growth the expenditures of competing nations could expand by a much greater percentage. Such a development could be avoided, of course, if major progress on disarmament were made or if the United States were willing to allocate gradually increasing shares of its output to national defense.

(2) Prices (Inflation)

Prices in the low-growth scenario increase at an average rate of 3.6 percent over the entire 25 year period. In the last half of the 1970's prices increase at just over 4 percent per year. In the early 1980's, the rate increases slightly to 4.5 percent a year. This is due to the pressure of some excess demand caused by anti-growth policies which work to restrict supplies faster than demand. After 1985, however, the rate of inflation would fall to 3.2 percent as the economy adapts to slower growth. The rates of price increases in consumption and investment goods are similar. They accelerate in the early 1980's in response to demand pressure, and then fall back to a rate of increase under 3 percent. The cost of government purchases increases at around 5.5 percent a year over the entire forecast period.

Inflation under low growth is only slightly less than in the high growth case, if the entire period to the year 2000 is examined. The GNP price index figure of 4.265 for the year 2000 under low growth compares with 4.506 for the high growth scenario. (See Table 6•6.) Over the 26-year period from mid-1974 this represents an average annual inflation rate of about ²⁄₁₀ of 1 percent lower for the low growth scenario. During shorter periods within the 26 years, however, the rates differ markedly, with the inflation rates under low growth being significantly higher from 1980 to 1985 and lower thereafter.

(3) Per Capita Income and Consumption

Per capita incomes continue to increase under low growth, although at a slow rate after 1980. Real per capita GNP and consumption each increase by over

Table 6•37

DISTRIBUTION OF MONEY INCOME OF FAMILIES AND UNATTACHED PERSONS*
(Constant 1975 Dollars and Percentages)

Income Range (1975 Dollars)	1960	1975	2000 Case C	2000 Case A
Less than $3,000	16.0%	12.2%	7.0%	5.0%
3,000 - 5,999	17.0	12.6	9.5	7.0
6,000 - 8,999	18.0	11.3	8.5	7.5
9,000 - 11,999	18.0	12.2	11.0	7.0
12,000 - 14,999	11.0	13.0	14.0	9.5
15,000 - 24,999	15.0	26.5	32.0	36.0
26,000 - 49,999	4.5	10.2	14.0	18.0
50,000 and Over	0.5	2.0	4.0	10.0
Total	100.0	100.0	100.0	100.0

* Earned income plus government transfer payments in the form of cash (e.g., old age assistance and aid to families with dependent children).

3 percent a year between 1975 and 1980, then fall to around 1 percent per year. Capital restrictions, resource use limitations, and the enforced move towards increased leisure all contribute to this slowdown. The effects on the family incomes are shown on Table 6•37 and Chart 6•18. This table presents family income distributions in real terms, and compares them with similar projections from Table 6•8 in the discussion of the Case A, high-growth scenario. As noted in the Case A discussion, the income distribution projections are judgmental forecasts developed by the EEI staff rather than direct output from the DRI model. They are consistent with the model, however, to the extent that they correctly reflect the model's total consumption figures.

The chart and table show that Case C produces an income distribution in the year 2000 that is somewhat improved over that of 1975 but not as favorable as for Case A. For example, in the year 2000, some 36 percent of the families and unattached persons will earn less than $12,000 per year, in contrast to only about 26 percent in Case A.

Perhaps more significant than these figures is the evidence that the majority of the modest progress in per capita income that occurs in Case C takes place during the period before 1985. This is evident not only from detailed evaluations of income distribution for the years 1980 and 1985 but also from the real GNP per capita figures shown in Tables 6•35 and 6•36. These show a 26 percent increase in real GNP per capita in the first ten years of the period and an 18 percent increase over the next 15 years.

During the fifteen years from 1985 to 2000, material resource constraints are assumed to be fully effective. These constraints will tend to force up prices of material goods such as appliances, furniture, housing, and automobiles more rapidly than the increase in composite prices of all goods and services. While such a development may not be serious for those segments of the population who are already affluent or near-affluent, it may place a severe restraint on those families which will not yet have been able to obtain an adequate stock of material goods.

Thus, the combination of limited resource use and very slow income gains after 1985 is likely to confine significant numbers of families to living standards well below their expectations as regards material possessions. To offset this lower material standard of living and the prospect of slow improvement, there would probably be somewhat greater environmental cleanliness, lesser resource depletion, and improved availability of leisure, education, the arts and other non-material-consuming services. The attitude with which most lower income families would regard such a trade-off is uncertain.

Therefore, to assess the practicality of a low-growth future, it is important to examine the number of families in the lower income groups. For the purposes of such an analysis, it is convenient to divide the nation's families and individuals into those with incomes of: (a) under $6,000 per year, (b) from $6,000 to $15,000, and (c) above $15,000. Considering that all these figures are in 1975 dollars, these three groups may be said to include the majority of: (a) the low income or poverty-level families, (b) the modest or moderate income families and individuals, and (c) the higher income and affluent groups.[18]

Table 6•38 and Chart 6•19 compare the progress made in reducing the size of the lower and moderate income groups in Case C and in Case A. Of course, the lower growth alternative, Case C, does not do as well as Case A. Specifically, Case C leaves 4.5 percent more of the nation's living groups in the below $6,000 range, and 9.5 percent more in the $6,000 to $15,000 range.

The $15,000 limit may be used as an approximate separation line between those families which feel a real need for more material possessions (e.g., refrigerators, furnitures, etc.) and those which might more readily be persuaded to cut back on additional consumption in the interest of achieving a steady state society. Today, the fact that the under-$15,000 group is still a majority would make the institution of a low-growth society difficult. By 2000 under Case A, the size of the under-$15,000 group will be much diminished, and a sizeable proportion of those remaining in the group will be small families, individuals, and the elderly. Under such circumstances, a low-growth society may seem more acceptable. Under Case C, however, the likelihood of its acceptability would appear to remain much lower through the next 25 years and well into the 21st century.

(4) Labor and Capital

Under the conditions of low growth, the labor force increases until 1980 but then declines by 1.2 percent a year until 1985. This pattern results from the increase in leisure which reduces labor input faster than the entry of new workers into the labor force can make it up. Actual hours of labor input decline less rapidly for the rest of the forecast period. Between 1985 and 2000, the rate of decline is 0.3 percent. However, effective labor input (i.e., the combined effects of changes in both the quantity and the quality of the labor input) which is shown on Tables 6•35 and 6•36, increases very gradually after 1985 as the increases in labor efficiency offset the decline in hours to produce a 0.35 percent annual increase in the effective labor force.

The effective capital stock (i.e., the combined effects of the changes in both the quantity and quality of the capital stock input) increases until the mid 1980's and then begins to decline. The decline occurs despite a continuing increase in real investment because of the absorption of some of the investment in non-productive uses and because the new investment is of declining efficiency. The net result is that, after the late 1980's, depreciation of the existing capital stock exceeds the rate of installation of new capital, leading to a small decline, 0.2 percent a year, in the supply of capital services.

The final productive force, improvements in general technology and organization, is assumed to continue to increase at the past rate of 1.5 percent a year. This is the critical force in securing the continuing increase in per capita incomes despite the slow growth in labor and capital input. The specific contributions to real growth over the 1980-2000 period are shown in Table 6•39. This table also shows that, without technical progress, there would be essentially no increase in real income per capita.

Table 6•38
**INCOME DISTRIBUTION
(Percent of Families and Unrelated Individuals)**

Annual Income (1975 Dollars)	1960	1975	2000 Case C	2000 Case A
Less Than $6,000	33.0	24.8	16.5	12.0
$6,000 to $15,000	47.0	36.5	33.5	24.0
Over $15,000	20.0	38.7	50.0	64.0

Table 6·39
CASE C: SOURCES OF ECONOMIC GROWTH; 1980-2000
(Percent per Year)

Component	Rate of Increase	Weighting Factor	Contribution to Growth of Real GNP
Labor:			
Quantity	-0.05		
Quality	0.60		
Total	0.55	63.	0.35
Capital:			
Quantity	0.78		
Quality	0.17		
Total	0.95	37.	0.35
Total Factor Productivity	1.50		1.50
Real GNP			2.20

Chart 6·19
INCOME DISTRIBUTION
(Percent of Families and Unrelated Individuals)

*Income in Thousands of 1975 Dollars per Year

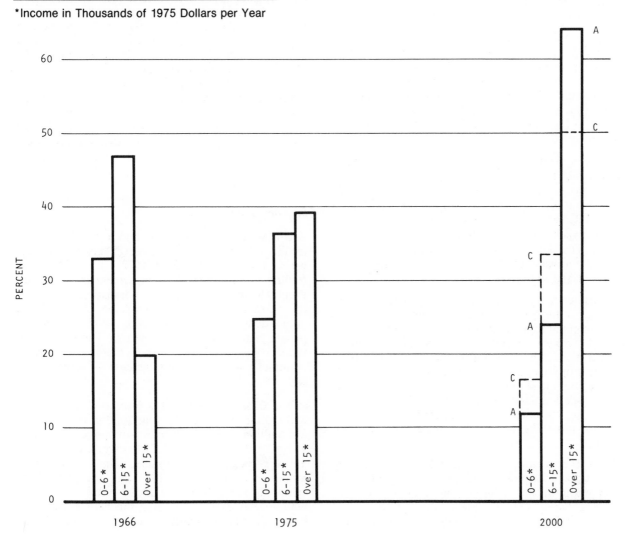

(5) Problems of Distributing National Output

The output from the DRI model summarizes a sequence of equilibrium conditions in the period under examination. It does not attempt to simulate temporary discontinuities in the economic trends, which may be caused by social or political tensions.

The likelihood that such tensions will develop increases as the rate of change in the economic and social environment increases. The probable severity of the resulting discontinuities also increases. In Case A and Case B the assumed changes in the economic and social environment are small and occur rather slowly. In Case C, however, the changes are major and rapid, and the possibilities are much greater that such discontinuities will force the economy to deviate markedly from the expected equilibrium forecasts.

It is not feasible to develop discontinuity scenarios as variants to Case C in any quantitative context. However, it is possible to develop possible Case C variants in a qualitative sense. One such variant is summarized here.

In Case C the model forecasts that the growth rate of real per capita consumption will drop from more than 3 percent per year in the 1975-1980 period to only 1.5 percent in the 1980-85 period and to about 1.3 percent after 1985. This abrupt change in the rate of material improvement of the average citizen is likely to be resisted, particularly by the less affluent sectors of society.

Government responses to the pleas of these citizens could take a variety of forms, many of which might be aimed at reallocating the available national output. Reducing the share of total output which is reserved for capital investment might be one of the more feasible responses from a political point of view. The short-term advantages of such a shift are that the adverse effects on the economy are largely delayed and indirect in nature.

This tendency for a society to be less and less willing to forego current consumption in favor of investment in future output is already visible in many mixed market economies of the world. Unrealistic expectations, which cannot be met by the society in the near future even at its maximum potential growth rate, cause it to shift its output away from investment and toward immediate consumption, thus stunting future growth potentials and deferring even further into the future the date at which the expectations can be met.

The pressures on society to take this essentially short-sighted approach are likely to be in direct proportion to the difference between reality and expectations. Thus, in Case C, the differences between reality and historically conditioned expectations could be very large during the period of the 1980's. The consequence could be to bring the growth rate of the economy down toward zero more rapidly than the society (or an equilibrium forecast such as that of the DRI model) would anticipate. Under such circumstances, the perverse results of the social policy could redouble efforts to improve current and near-future consumption, leading to a spiraling downturn.

This spiraling downturn variant to Case C illustrates what would certainly be a major practical concern for the nation were it to pursue the Case C objectives; namely, the management of slowdown and decline. Few major sectors of our society have had any real experience in managing or adapting to the gradual elimination of growth.[19] If the average growth rate drops toward 1 percent, of course, more and more sectors would experience first zero and then negative growth rates.

Structural rigidities built into the economy are likely to offer strong resistance to such slowdown and decline, thus distorting the path of the slowdown away from the most "efficient" path toward one which recognizes relative strengths of the various economic sectors. The rapidity with which the slowdown will take place under Case C would materially aggravate the difficulties likely to be encountered. To accomplish a successful transition to steady state in the Case C time frame, or in any time frame short of several generations, would likely require not only very stringent but very effective and farsighted government controls over a great many aspects of national life.

b. Population and Agriculture

Under the low growth scenario it is assumed that fertility rates stabilize at 1.8, a level very close to that which was experienced in 1972 and 1973. This fertility rate is below the replacement rate so it will eventually lead to a decline in population. However, the current age distribution of the United States population contains a relatively large number of people in their reproductive years. The children of these young adults will be numerous enough to maintain a slow population increase for several more decades.

The Case C population is forecast to reach some 250 million people in the year 2000 as compared to 210 million in 1973. It will continue to grow until about 2030 (but it is unlikely to exceed 270 million) and then begin a slow decline. The increase of 35 million people between 1975 and the end of the century is only half as great as the 70 million increase which is assumed to occur in the high growth scenario. Population densities too will be lower in Case

Table 6·40
CASE C: UNITED STATES METALS CONSUMPTION
(Thousands of Short Tons)

	1970	1985	2000	1970 to 2000 Cumulative Growth (Thousands of Short Tons)	(Rate: Percent per Year)
Iron	116,900	168,900	179,700	4,760,000	1.45
Aluminum	4,128	10,500	16,900	315,900	4.84
Copper	2,820	3,950	4,040	110,850	1.20
Zinc	1,374	1,948	2,120	55,050	1.45
Lead	1,335	1,592	1,370	44,250	—
Total	126,557	186,890	202,760	5,286,050	1.62

C, reaching an average of no more than 75 persons per square mile in the first quarter of the 21st century versus about 85 for Case A.

Fewer people would appear to mean less pressure on agriculture to expand production for domestic use, and perhaps a greater potential for increasing exports. However, it is at least as likely that less food would be available for export than in Case A. Such an eventuality in Case C would result from the expected reductions in: labor force, availability of capital, returns to capital, rates of technological progress, and availability of energy. It is conceivable, in fact, that the reduced availability of these necessary inputs to agriculture would be severe enough to erode and eventually eliminate the nation's food export potential under Case C. A similar counter-intuitive result is forecast with regard to the availability of energy under Case C.

The potentially adverse effect of the lower population in Case C is related to the consequences of a major increase in longevity. If the average life span reached 100 years by 2025, for example, nearly 33 percent of the population would be over 65 years of age. This compares to 25 percent under the high growth scenario and less than 10 percent at present.

c. Non-Energy Minerals

(1) Consumption Forecast

Forecasts of metal consumption per dollar of real GNP are developed in Appendix F. These have been combined with real GNP estimates for Case C from the DRI model to yield metal consumption projections to the year 2000. The results for the five major metals, iron, aluminum, copper, zinc and lead, are given in Table 6·40.

The average growth rate for the five major metals is about 1.6 percent per year over the period from 1970 to 2000. Most of the increase in consumption occurs in the period prior to 1985, during which the average growth is almost 2.7 percent per year. After 1985 the restraints on resource consumption become increasingly effective and the average growth is reduced to about ¾ of 1 percent per year. Aluminum is projected to increase in use at a relatively rapid rate even after 1985. The forecast for aluminum shows average growth rates of about 6.5 percent from 1970 to 1985 and 3.2 percent thereafter. The trend toward reduced growth in total consumption of the five major metals after 1985 is made evident by Chart 6·20.

(2) Recycling

The prospects for increased recycling of metals are discussed under the high growth scenario. It is reasonable to anticipate that under low growth there will be even stronger pressures to rely as much as possible upon scrap and re-used materials. In a low-growth society these pressures may come primarily from regulations rather than from price pressures, which were assumed to be the main mechanism under high growth. In both societies, however, there will be certain maximum practical limits to recycling. Some of these are imposed by technological factors, as in the case of zinc used for galvanizing.

Two different estimates of recycling potentials have been made for the low-growth case: one assumes that the recycling fraction remains constant at its 1967 percentage for each of the major metals, and the other assumes that the fraction rises gradually to levels somewhat higher than in Case A. The consequences of these two assumptions are shown on Table 6·41 in terms of cumulative primary demand for the years 1970-2000. If the trend toward increased recycling can be achieved, the savings over

Chart 6•20
CASE C: CONSUMPTION OF 5 MAJOR METALS*
(Millions of Short Tons)

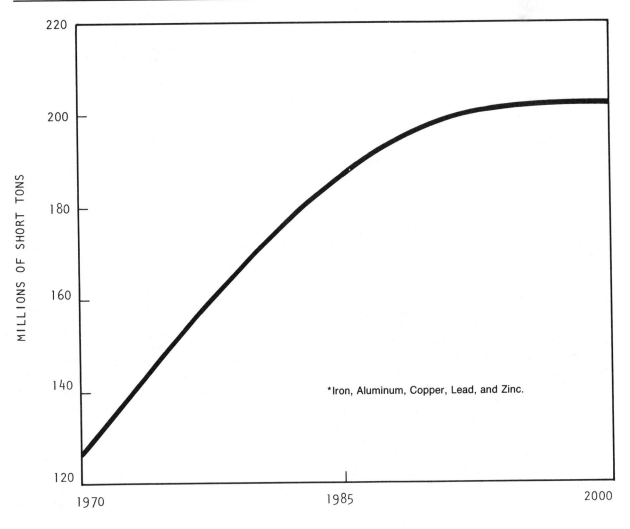

*Iron, Aluminum, Copper, Lead, and Zinc.

the 30-year period will be equivalent to another 10 years of primary demand, which is estimated to be about 83,000 thousand short tons per year.

The difference in metals consumption between Case A and Case C is also of interest. Table 6•13 gives 4,524,510 thousand short tons as the Case A cumulative consumption from 1970 to 2000 under current recycling conditions. In contrast, the Case C cumulative figure with maximum recycling is 2,841,990 thousand short tons, for a difference of some 1,682,520 thousand short tons. This translates into a savings of about 20 years worth of metal at the Case C consumption rate for the year 2000.

d. Energy Demand

(1) Energy Demand by Consuming Sectors

As noted earlier, the consuming sector demand forecasts are judgmental estimates prepared by the EEI staff. These estimates conclude that each of the major energy consuming sectors will be affected somewhat differently by the growth restraints of Case C. The differences are in timing as well as severity. The judgmental examination of each consuming sector produced the energy demand forecast which is summarized on Table 6•42.

Increasingly severe restraints on energy con-

158

Table 6·41

**CASE C: EFFECTS OF RECYCLING ON METALS REQUIREMENTS
CUMULATIVE CONSUMPTION; 1970-2000
(Thousands of Short Tons)**

Major Metals	Primary Demand plus Secondary Recovery	Primary Demand with Current Recycling*	Primary Demand with Maximum Recycling*
Iron	4,760,000	3,283,020	2,538,390
Aluminum	315,900	258,480	200,595
Copper	110,850	55,365	41,850
Zinc	55,050	48,225	44,025
Lead	44,250	22,095	17,130
Total	5,286,050	3,667,185	2,841,990
	Savings from "Maximum" Recycling		825,195

Percent of Total Consumption from Recycled Materials

	Actual 1967	Estimated 1970	Maximum Practical	
			1985	2000
Iron	31.2	31.2	45	60
Aluminum	18.3	18.3	29	50
Copper	49.7	49.7	60	75
Zinc	12.6	12.6	18	30
Lead	49.6	49.6	60	75

* Current Recycling and Maximum Recycling Percentages are given in the bottom half of the table.

Table 6·42

**CASE C: ENERGY DEMAND BY CONSUMING SECTOR
(Quadrillion Btu)**

Consuming Sector	1972 Actual			Case C 1985			Case C 2000		
	Fuel	Electric	Total	Fuel	Electric	Total	Fuel	Electric	Total
Transportation	18.00	0.02	18.02	23.00	0.02	23.02	25.00	0.04	25.04
Residential	8.56	1.89	10.45	9.00	2.90	11.90	6.80	5.80	12.60
Commercial	6.15	1.55	7.70	8.10	2.70	10.80	7.20	6.40	13.60
Industrial	20.76	2.45	23.22	25.30	4.20	29.50	25.50	5.50	31.00
Sub-Total	53.47	5.92	59.39	64.40	9.82	75.22	62.50	17.74	82.24
Energy Conversion			12.41			20.60			35.00
Total			71.80			95.82			117.24

Case C Demand as a Percentage of Case A Demand

	1985	2000
Transportation	78.0%	58.9%
Residential	82.2	70.8
Commercial	90.0	80.0
Industrial	84.5	63.3
Sub-Total	81.5	65.0
Energy Conversion	85.0	63.6
Total	83.0	64.7

sumption are imposed during the latter part of the 1970's and the early 1980's under Case C conditions. The combination of a resource auction system and a government allocations program is assumed to adjust energy consumption patterns so as to: improve efficiency of use, limit discretionary consumption, and favor use of those fuels with the largest and environmentally "cleanest" resource base.

The overall effect of these adjustments on energy use will be to limit consumption to about 96 quadrillion Btu in 1985 and to 117 quadrillion Btu in 2000. These figures represent reductions of 17 percent and 35 percent respectively, as compared to Case A levels. The following paragraphs consider the changing consumption patterns in each sector which will achieve these reductions.

(a) Transportation

Transportation is assumed to be the sector affected first and most severely. It is the only one on which the impact will be major by 1980. A variety of measures with near-term consequences can be devised to: eliminate portions of discretionary travel, improve load factors on airlines, shift transport of goods to railroads, encourage high mileage autos, etc. By 1985 these efforts will have so adjusted transportation modes and lifestyles that energy consumption for transportation will be only 78 percent of that in the high growth case.

Further direct restraints will probably be imposed on the transportation sector in the following 15 years. These will be strongly supplemented and reinforced by the general slow-down in economic growth in the years after 1985. A slower growth in factory output means a slower growth in delivery requirements. With personal income in real terms moving up at a rate of 1.8 to 2 percent per year instead of 4 or 5 percent, there will be slower growth in personal travel of all sorts and, particularly, discretionary travel for pleasure. These and similar effects will limit transportation sector demand by 2000 to less than 60 percent of Case A demand.

(b) Residential

Residential consumption growth is assumed to be moderated over the period prior to 1985 by actions with near term effects such as improving insulation in existing homes and taxing all energy consumption which exceeds that of the previous year. As the need for increasingly severe restraints grows during the 1980's, it is assumed that tax penalties will be increased and absolute prohibitions placed on certain types of energy consumption and energy consuming appliances.

By 1985 the effect of new residential construction standards will begin to be felt. Larger fractions of new construction will be multi-unit buildings of limited square footage and with improved insulation standards. As in the case of transportation, the slower rate of overall economic growth will impact on residential consumption. Housing, energy-using appliances, and all material goods will rise in price relative to non-material-intensive services. With personal income rising only about 2 percent per year, families will be limited in their ability to acquire new energy consuming devices.

These factors will cut residential energy consumption in 1985 to not much more than 80 percent of the Case A consumption, and will restrict usage in the year 2000 to some 70 percent of Case A.

(c) Commercial

Major fractions of commercial consumption are for office and public buildings, hospitals, schools, stores, etc. Significant near-term reductions in energy consumption in these areas are assumed to be achieved through legislation of heating, lighting and air conditioning standards. Over the longer term, changes in building codes can be effective.

It has been assumed that a steady state society would emphasize education, health, recreation, and services rather than goods production and consumption. Such activities will require continued expansion of commercial activities, and thus of commercial energy consumption. Therefore, this consuming sector offers less potential for energy savings than the others. The level of use for this sector is 90 percent of the Case A use in 1985 and 80 percent in 2000.

(d) Industrial

Industrial activity growth is assumed to be gradually curtailed during the late 1970's and early 1980's under Case C. A parallel curtailment will occur in growth of energy consumption by this sector. Over the near term, legislated changes in industrial heating, lighting, and processing standards can cut energy growth. Taxes directed at penalizing production and consumption of energy-intensive products are also assumed to be imposed to slow growth of industrial energy consumption. Enforced recycling of metals can begin over the near term as a means of reducing energy-intensive mining and smelting activities. Of course the rapid pace of development of environmentally "clean" mining and manufacturing processes will be a major source of demand for additional energy consumption. To some extent the introduction of these "clean" processes will offset the energy savings achieved through slower growth and the other changes mentioned above, particularly during the first part of the forecast period.

However, over the longer term the assumed establishment of a ceiling on materials consumption will greatly reduce the growth of energy use for industrial purposes. Consequently, this sector under Case C will show a large reduction in use as compared to Case A. By 1985, for example, consumption will be about 85 percent of Case A and by 2000 it will be only 65 percent.

(2) Inter-Industry Forecast of Energy Demand

(a) Energy Demand

The energy consumption picture for the low-growth scenario, as derived from the DRI model, is presented in Tables 6·43 and 6·44. These figures

Table 6·43
CASE C: CONSUMPTION OF ENERGY BY SECTOR OF USE; 1975-2000
(Energy Flows in Trillion Btu)

	Household, Commercial	Industrial	Transportation	Electricity Generation	Synthetic Gas	Total Input
1975						
Coal	199.	4353.	0.	8661.	0.	13213.
Petroleum	6835.	6602.	17980.	2380.	0.	33797.
Natural gas	8234.	10976.	934.	4326.	0.	24469.
Hydro, nuclear	0.	0.	0.	5475.	0.	5475.
Total input	15268.	21930.	18914.	20843.	0.	76955.
Electrictiy	3969.	2739.	22.	0.	0.	6730.
Synthetic gas	0.	0.	0.	0.	0.	0.
Total use	19238.	24669.	18936.	20843.	0.	76955.
1980						
Coal	200.	4395.	0.	10149.	0.	14743.
Petroleum	7886.	7764.	20924.	2547.	0.	39122.
Natural Gas	8190.	12843.	995.	4471.	0.	26499.
Hydro, nuclear	0.	0.	0.	10018.	0.	10018.
Total input	16275.	25002.	21920.	27185.	0.	90381.
Electricity	5365.	3383.	31.	0.	0.	8779.
Synthetic gas	0.	0.	0.	0.	0.	0.
Total use	21640.	28385.	21951.	27185.	0.	90381.
1985						
Coal	170.	3434.	0.	11571.	1107.	16282.
Petroleum	8918.	8329.	22996.	2829.	89.	43161.
Natural gas	7485.	14121.	969.	5046.	0.	27620.
Hydro, nuclear	0.	0.	0.	14150.	0.	14150.
Total input	16573.	25884.	23965.	33596.	1195.	101213.
Electricity	7127.	3688.	36.	0.	0.	10851.
Synthetic gas	310.	379.	0.	0.	0.	690.
Total use	24011.	29952.	24000.	33596.	1195.	101213.
2000						
Coal	128.	3301.	0.	11079.	5000.	19508.
Petroleum	8171.	8526.	19577.	2821.	400.	39495.
Natural gas	2996.	9711.	624.	4611.	0.	17942.
Hydro, nuclear	0.	0.	0.	32505.	0.	32505.
Total input	11295.	21537.	20201.	51015.	5400.	109450.
Electricity	11731.	4706.	42.	0.	0.	16479.
Synthetic gas	1638.	2002.	0.	0.	0.	3640.
Total use	24664.	28245.	20244.	51015.	5400.	109450.

show a continuing decline in the rate of increase of total energy consumption until 1985, after which per capita consumption remains constant. Total energy input increases from 76.955 quadrillion Btu in 1975 to a projected 109.450 quadrillion Btu in 2000, an average rate of increase of 1.4 percent. The increase in total energy input over the 1975-1980 period is at 3.27 percent a year, only a little below historical trends. After that, the restrictions on growth in general, and energy use in particular, start to have a major effect and the rate of increase slows to 2.3 percent between 1980 and 1985 and 0.5 percent thereafter. The energy/GNP ratio remains stable over the 1975-1985 period. This suggests that the energy conservation achieved in this period results largely from reductions in the general level of economic activity. In many instances the "easy" conservation efforts are assumed to have been taken in the 1973-75 period, and further major effects may not be seen until capital goods with higher energy efficiencies come into use in large quantities. Autos,

with relatively short useful lives of about a decade, may be an exception. After 1985 the energy/GNP ratio falls substantially, reflecting both the opportunities that exist for conserving energy in production and consumption uses and the redirection of economic growth towards the relatively non-energy-intensive service sectors.

The pattern of energy demand, showing use of each fuel by each of four major consuming sectors, is given in Table 6·43. This shows that the principal increases in energy used are in coal, hydro and nuclear energy for electricity generation and that the main increase in consumption takes place in the household and commercial sectors.

(b) Electricity Demand

Electricity assumes an increasingly dominant position in a future of low growth. Electricity consumption increases at 5.5 percent a year between 1975 and 1980, at 4.3 percent until 1985 and at 2.8

Table 6·44

CASE C: UNITED STATES ENERGY CONSUMPTION; 1975-2000

	1975	1980	1985	2000
1. Energy Consumption (Quadrillion Btu)				
Direct Consumption				
Coal	4.552	4.594	4.711	8.429
Petroleum	31.417	36.575	40.332	36.674
Gas	20.143	22.028	22.574	13.331
Total	56.112	63.197	67.617	58.434
Electricity Generation				
Coal	8.661	10.149	11.571	11.079
Petroleum and Gas	6.706	7.018	7.874	7.432
Hydro, Nuclear, Other	5.475	10.018	14.150	32.505
Total	20.842	27.185	33.595	51.016
Total	76.954	90.382	101.212	109.450

	1975-80	1980-85	1985-2000
2. Energy Consumption Growth (Percent per Year)			
Direct Consumption			
Coal	0.18	0.50	3.95
Petroleum	3.09	1.97	-0.63
Gas	1.81	0.49	-3.45
Total	2.41	1.36	-0.97
Electricity Generation			
Coal	3.22	2.66	-0.29
Petroleum and Gas	0.91	2.33	-0.38
Hydro, Nuclear, Other	12.84	7.15	5.70
Total	5.46	4.33	2.82
Total	3.27	2.29	0.52

Table 6·45
CASE C: ENERGY BALANCES
(Quadrillion Btu)

	1975	1980	1985	2000
Total Demand[1]	77.0	90.4	101.2	109.5
Less Fuel Efficiency Adjustment[2]	—	1.2	2.3	5.0
Adjusted Demand	77.0	89.2	98.9	104.5
Electrical Sector	20.9	25.6	30.9	46.1
Hydro/Other	3.1	3.2	3.5	6.0
Nuclear	1.6	5.4	9.8	23.0
Petroleum[3]	6.9	7.1	7.1	6.0
Coal	9.3	9.9	10.5	11.1
Net Utility Generation[1]	1.98	2.56	3.17	5.17
(Trillion Kwhr)				
Non-Electrical Sector	56.1	63.6	68.0	66.8
Coal	4.9	5.1	5.2	5.3
Industrial	4.6	4.8	5.1	5.3
Other[4]	0.3	0.3	0.1	—
Gas	23.8	22.6	19.2	21.6
Natural, Lower 48	22.5	20.0	14.2	11.6
North Slope, Alaska	—	0.8	1.5	3.0
SNG[5]	0.2	0.3	1.5	4.0
Domestic	22.7	21.1	17.2	18.6
Imports	1.1	1.5	2.0	3.0
Petroleum Liquids Required	27.4	35.9	43.6	39.9
Crude + NGL, Lower 48[6]	21.4	21.5	22.4	21.3
North Slope, Alaska	—	1.3	4.2	6.3
Syncrude	—	0.2	0.5	1.0
Domestic	21.4	23.0	27.1	28.6
Imports Required	6.0	12.9	16.5	11.3
Imports Available	6.0	7.0	7.0	8.1
Deficit	0	5.9	9.5	3.2

(1) Provided by Data Resources, Inc.

(2) Difference between energy inputs of electrical sector under assumption of constant heat rate made by DRI and decreasing heat rate made in this study. See Table 6·54.

(3) Projected figures assumed to be liquids because of nonavailability of gas.

(4) Excludes coal for gasification, which is included with gas (SNG)

(5) SNG = Synthetic natural gas   (6) NGL = Natural gas liquids

percent between 1985 and 2000. Thus, per capita electricity consumption increases at over 2 percent a year after 1985, even though total per capita consumption of fuels is constant.

Electricity appears to have the highest income elasticity of demand of any form of energy (i.e., an increase in personal income results in a greater increase in demand for electricity than for any other form of energy). To reinforce this income effect, the slowly declining price of electricity, relative to other fuels, induces users to substitute it for many petroleum and gas uses. Further, electricity demand is stimulated by the relative increase of service and government activities since these activities are comparatively intensive in their use of electricity, relative to other fuels.

e. Energy Supply and Prices

The judgmental forecasts of energy supply and prices as developed by EPRI for Case C—low growth—are summarized in Tables 6·45 to 6·54. Under the Case C environment, several years at a

Table 6·46
CASE C: ENERGY SUPPLIES; PETROLEUM LIQUIDS
(Millions of Barrels)[1]

	1975	1980	1985	2000
Lower 48[2]	3,900	3,909	4,073	3,873
North Slope, Alaska	0	236	764	1,145
Syncrude	0	36	91	182
Total Domestic[3]	3,900	4,181	4,928	5,200
Imports[4]	2,345	2,564	2,564	2,564
Total	6,245	6,745	7,492	7,764

(1) Converted at 5.5 million Btu's per barrel

(2) Includes South Alaska

(3) Excludes liquids for gasification (76 million barrels for all years).

(4) Represents estimated available supplies, which fall short of requirements beginning in 1980.

Table 6·47
CASE C: ENERGY SUPPLIES; GAS
(Trillions of Cubic Feet) *

	1975	1980	1985	2000
Lower 48	21.8	19.4	13.8	11.3
Alaska		0.8	1.5	2.9
SNG	0.2	0.3	1.5	3.9
Domestic	22.0	20.5	16.7	18.1
Imports	1.1	1.5	1.9	2.9
Total	23.1	22.0	18.6	21.0

* At 1,030 Btu per cubic foot dry gas excluding transfer and losses.

Table 6·48
CASE C: ENERGY SUPPLIES; COAL
(Millions of Short Tons)[1]

	1975	1980	1985	2000
Electrical	387	412	437	462
Industrial and others[2]	204	212	217	221
Gasification	0	0	40	213
Domestic	591	624	694	896
Exports[3]	71	75	87	108
Total	662	699	781	1,004

(1) Converted at 24.0 million Btu per ton, except gasification at 23.2 million Btu per ton.

(2) Includes small quantities of other uses in earlier years.

(3) Department of Interior estimates (Dec. 1972).

Table 6·49
CASE C: ENERGY SUPPLIES; NUCLEAR POWER

	1973	1975	1980	1985	2000
Installed Capacity (Thousands of MW)	31[1]	50	105	180	437
Net Generation (Billions of Kwhr) [2]	80	150	505	945	2,300
Energy Inputs (Quadrillion Btu)	0.85	1.6	5.4	9.8	23.0

(1) Estimates for Dec. 31.

(2) Assumes load factor of .60 beginning in 1980.
Heat rates through 1985 from Department of Interior, Dec. 1972 report; *United States Energy Through the Year 2000.* This report shows a decrease from 10,560 Btu per Kwhr in 1975 to 9,760 in 1905. For 2,000 a slower rate of improvement was used.

Table 6·50
CASE C: ENERGY SUPPLY SUMMARIES
(Quadrillion Btu)

	1975	1980	1985	2000
Gas	23.8	22.6	19.2	21.6
Petroleum Liquids	34.3	37.1	41.2	42.7
Coal	14.2	15.0	15.7	16.4
Nuclear	1.6	5.4	9.8	23.0
Hydro/Other.................................	3.1	3.2	3.5	6.0
Available Supply......................	77.0	83.3	89.4	109.7
Deficit	0	5.9	9.5	3.2
Total Demand..........................	77.0	89.2	98.9	112.9

Table 6·51
CASE C: SHARES OF ENERGY SUPPLY SOURCES
(Percent)

	1975	1980	1985	2000
Gas	31.0	25.3	19.4	19.1
Petroleum Liquids	44.5	41.6	41.7	37.8
Coal	18.4	16.8	15.9	14.5
Nuclear	2.1	6.1	9.9	20.4
Hydro/Other.................................	4.0	3.6	3.5	5.3
Available Supply......................	100.0	93.4	90.4	97.2
Deficit	—	6.6	9.6	2.9

Table 6•52
CASE C: SHARES OF PETROLEUM AND GAS IMPORTS
(Quadrillion Btu)

	1975	1980	1985	2000
Petroleum Imports	12.9	14.1	14.1	14.1
Petroleum Supply............................	34.3	37.1	41.2	42.7
Imports (Percent)	37	38	30	29
Gas Imports..................................	1.1	1.5	2.0	3.0
Gas Supply	23.9	22.6	19.2	21.6
Imports (Percent)	5	7	10	14
Total Available Imports	14.0	15.5	16.1	17.1
Total Available Energy	77.0	83.3	89.4	109.7
Imports (Percent)	18	19	18	16
Total Import Demand	14.0	21.3	25.0	20.3
Total Energy Demand......................	77.0	89.2	98.9	112.9
Imports (Percent)	18	24	25	18

minimum will be required to begin a noticeable shift toward a low-growth energy consumption pattern. Therefore, no changes from the Case A situation can be expected initially. Some important differences will be visible by 1980, however.

(1) *Estimates for the Intermediate Period (1980-1985)*

The energy supply patterns during this intermediate period are likely to be as follows. For hydro and geothermal power, an expansion somewhat similar to the National Petroleum Council Case IV as reported in *United States Energy Outlook,*[13] is assumed to be the maximum that can be expected. This represents only a 20 percent increase above the current levels. Nuclear generating capacity is assumed to reach a slightly lower level in 1980 than in the other cases (105,000 MW versus 110,000 MW) and to be operated at a lower load factor (0.55 versus 0.6). Capacity in 1985 is projected at 180,000 MW, which would mean that not all currently announced projects would be fully operational.

For *fossil fuel power plants*, it seems reasonable to assume that units currently required to burn low sulphur fuel oil (or gas) will have to continue doing so, regardless of cost, either because coal burning technology is lagging behind environmental standards or because prohibition of strip mining keeps coal in short supply.

For crude oil, natural gas liquids, and natural gas, the restraints on growth seem certain to reduce the

quantity supplied at any given price to perhaps 20 percent lower than with Case A. This is equivalent to moving the supply function to the left, as illustrated in Chart 6•21. In addition, the natural gas price ceiling is assumed to be kept at 44¢/per thousand cubic feet in constant (1975) dollars, with adjustments allowed only for general inflation. Crude oil price ceilings are assumed to be gradually raised to the level of uncontrolled crude (about $10.00 a barrel) but are not permitted to rise significantly beyond this in constant dollars.

Under these assumptions the volume of natural gas available from the lower 48 states in 1985 falls sharply to about 14 trillion cubic feet (about one-third below the current level), while the volume of crude oil and natural gas liquids at around $10.00 shows little change (about 11 million barrels per day). Alaskan North Slope supplies of oil and gas are assumed to be available prior to 1985, in line with current plans, but development of synthetic natural gas and syncrude is slowed further from the high growth projections because of environmental obstacles.

The result is a sharp increase in import requirements, which continues after 1980 in spite of the slow expansion of demand. By 1985 the deficit between domestic liquid supplies and requirements approaches 4.3 billion barrels (i.e., 11.7 million barrels per day). Under the world conditions prevailing for Case C these imports may not be obtainable, regardless of price. If one assumes that the import volumes are limited to the present level of about 2.5 billion

166

Table 6·53
CASE C: ASSUMED OIL AND GAS PRICES; LOWER 48 STATES (1975 $)

Crude Oil & NGL*

1975

Quadrillion Btu	21.4
Millions of Barrels	3900
Millions of Barrels per day	10.7
Dollars per Barrel	$5.25

1985

Quadrillion Btu	22.14
Millions of Barrels	4073
Millions of Barrels per day	11.16
Dollars per Barrel	$10.30

2000

Quadrillion Btu	21.3
Millions of Barrels	3873
Millions of Barrels per day	10.61
Dollars per Barrel	$10.00

Gas

1975

Quadrillion Btu	22.5
Thousands of Cubic Feet	21.8
Dollars per Thousand Cubic Feet	$0.44

1985

Quadrillion Btu	14.2
Thousands of Cubic Feet	13.8
Dollars per Thousand Cubic Feet	$0.44

2000

Quadrillion Btu	11.6
Thousands of Cubic Feet	11.3
Dollars per Thousand Cubic Feet	$0.44

* Natural gas liquids

Chart 6·21
SUPPLY FUNCTION

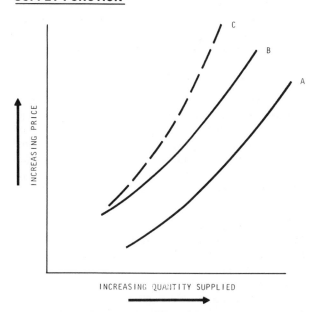

Note: The curves indicate that increasing supplies will be induced by increasing prices. Moving upward or to the left on the chart; e.g., from Curve A to Curve B, means that increased prices will be required under Curve B conditions to provide the same supplies as previously were forthcoming at lower prices under Curve A conditions. If the supply function becomes steeper; e.g., changes from Curve B to Curve C, a given increase in price will result in a smaller increase in supply than previously.

Table 6·54
CONVERSION FACTORS USED IN TABLES 6·45-6·53

BTU CONTENT OF FOSSIL FUELS

Coal for gasification	23,200,000	Btu per short ton
Other coal	24,000,000	Btu per short ton
Crude oil	5,500,000	Btu per short ton
Residual fuel oil	6,100,000	Btu per barrel
Natural gas	1,030	Btu per cubic feet

HEAT RATES OF ELECTRICAL GENERATING PLANTS (Btu per Kwhr)

	1975	1980	1985	2000
Fossil fuels	10,575	9,875	9,575	9,250
Nuclear	10,660	10,660	10,400	10,000
Hydro/Other*	10,220	9,500	9,200	9,000
Average	10,560	9,990	9,760	9,600-9,360

* Hydro power outputs are converted to theoretical energy inputs on the basis of heat rates for large fossil-fueled steam-electric plants.

167

barrels (i.e., 7 million barrels per day) there would be a sizeable shortage of total liquid supplies of between 4 and 5 million barrels per day. Under Case C conditions, such a gap would require a widespread system of rationing, in addition to price controls.

(2) Estimates for the Long-Range (2000)

For the end of the century, it is assumed that development of new energy sources would be much slower than with Case A, that petroleum would have to continue to be burned at roughly the same rate in power plants, and that nuclear generation would constitute half of total electricity output. Coal requirements would then rise relatively little from present levels.

The supply curves for oil and gas from the lower 48 states are assumed to shift up by one-third from their 1985 position. Prices are assumed to be held constant in real dollars. The result is a further decline in production of natural gas (to about 11 trillion cubic feet) while crude and natural gas liquids output falls only slightly from the 1985 rate.

It is further assumed that because of the severe shortage, the flow of gas from the North Slope and the output of synthetic natural gas are increased rapidly, but that for environmental reasons supplies of liquids are allowed to rise only moderately. This would be the case, for example, if a second Alaskan gas pipeline were built but the crude shipments could be increased only by adding additional pumping capacity to the Alyeska line. Also, shale oil output may be severely restricted and coal liquefaction may lag for technological and environmental reasons.

Assuming imports continue to be available at the same rates, the total domestic supply deficit by the year 2000 would be sharply reduced from the 1985 figure. But it would not vanish completely, so that continued controls would be required, unless prices were allowed to rise.

(3) Comparison with the DRI Supply Forecast

As in Case A, the energy supply forecast from the DRI model differs somewhat from the judgmental EPRI forecast. In this low growth case, however, the differences are less significant. The general similarity

Chart 6·22
CASE C: COMPARISON OF ENERGY SUPPLY FORECASTS (EPRI VS DRI)

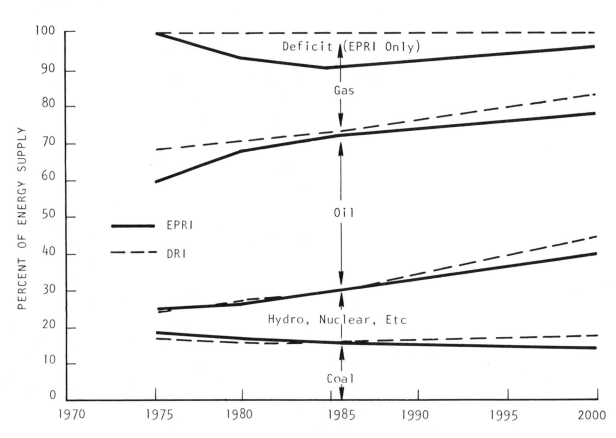

is seen in the fuels supplied to the electric industry as well as in fuels for other uses. See Chart 6·22 and Table 6·55.

The major difference between the two forecasts is that the judgmental EPRI forecast expects a supply deficit while this is not predicted in the DRI outputs. The deficit expected by EPRI develops by 1980 and persists throughout the remainder of the period despite the much lower level of demand under the low-growth conditions.

The difference between the DRI and the EPRI forecasts stems at least partially from differences in assumptions made about prices. As Table 53 shows, the EPRI study assumes continued control of natural gas prices at a constant level in real 1975 dollar terms. Some increases are assumed in the case of domestic crude oil but they are concentrated in the period before 1985. Thereafter, government controls are stringent enough to keep real prices constant. The underlying philosophy of the Case C, low-growth society which would enforce such price controls is assumed to be: consumer "protection" against high energy prices despite adverse supply consequences. Under such a philosophy, rationing and other artificial constraints on demand are assumed to be preferable to high energy prices.

The basis for the DRI Case C forecast was altered slightly from the EPRI assumptions to allow sufficient price increases so that supply was able to satisfy demand. Demand, however, was assumed to be constrained by a variety of non-price restraints including the raw materials auctions mentioned previously.

The price implications derived from the DRI model contrast with the EPRI forecasts as follows. For natural gas, DRI finds that consumer real prices will rise from $1.00 per thousand cubic feet in 1975 to $1.32 in 1985 and to $2.30 in 2000. The EPRI forecast was for constant real well head prices throughout the period. For oil, the DRI model projects that real prices in 1975 dollars will reach $13.36 per barrel by the year 2000 while EPRI restricts prices to $10.30 per barrel in 2000.

Although the DRI forecast projects a balanced demand-supply situation for Case C, it does foresee a *tendency* for demand to outstrip supply. It notes that even under the very severe no-growth constraints assumed for Case C, a certain amount of freedom will be needed to develop and consume coal resources as well as to permit construction of nuclear generating stations. If coal and nuclear power are not allowed to supplement oil and gas as energy sources, even such a modest objective as constant per capita energy consumption cannot be sustained through the year 2000.

Table 6·55

CASE C: ENERGY SUPPLY FOR THE GENERATION OF ELECTRICITY: COMPARISON OF EPRI AND DRI FORECASTS (Percent)

	1975	1980	1985	2000
DRI Forecast				
Oil & Gas	32.2	25.8	23.5	14.5
Coal	41.5	37.3	37.4	21.7
Hydro, Nuclear, Other	26.3	36.9	42.1	63.8
Total	100.0	100.0	100.0	100.0
EPRI Forecast				
Oil & Gas	33.0	27.0	21.0	13.0
Coal	44.5	38.6	32.4	24.0
Hydro, Nuclear, Other	22.5	34.4	46.6	63.0
Total	100.0	100.0	100.0	100.0

E. Case B: The Future Under Moderate Growth

The high growth and low growth alternatives presented as Case A and C have provided a picture of the range of possible economic futures for the United States over the next quarter century. These scenarios are based on sets of assumptions which contemplate two different lifestyles for the average citizen. Parts of each scenario would probably be considered desirable by a cross section of United States citizens, and parts of each would be viewed as unacceptable.

It is the premise of this study that, somewhere between the high-growth and low-growth futures, there is a more probable and more desirable growth path that would allow some moderation of the disadvantages associated with each of the two extremes. This is not to suggest that there is an "optimum" growth path for the nation over the next 25 years. Even if there were an optimum, it could not be charted by a computer model. The value in developing an intermediate scenario is to be able to describe a more probable future of growth which can be compared with the high and low parameters.

1. Assumptions

The Case B scenario is based on assumptions that represent what could be considered the most likely set of conditions determining economic growth. These assumptions incorporate some restrictions on economic activity without going as far as the extreme restrictions used in Case C. It is assumed that the overall desirability of some continued growth is not questioned. However, some constraints on growth are assumed to result from the introduction of policies designed to prevent excesses in resource depletion and environmental damage that have occurred in the past. In the development of this scenario, the basic growth trends are provided by the same factors as in the past—increases in capital input, in labor input and in the level of technological and organizational knowledge. However, the actual growth path is somewhat lower because of the imposition of some restrictions on the environmental impact of economic activity and on the rate of depletion of natural resources. The specific assumptions were as follows:

a. Raw Materials

It is assumed that no serious shortages of raw materials will occur although energy supplies will be less readily available, and more costly to obtain, than in Case A. Nevertheless, a continued growth in the per-capita availability of energy and minerals is assumed. This implies that continued development of coal and uranium reserves, as well as the use of these fuels, will be possible, although reclamation restrictions on mining and emissions restrictions on use will be applicable. Similar changes are assumed to occur in other extractive industries as they move toward inclusion of full social and economic costs in the prices of their refined products. It is assumed that the pace of these changes will be set by a balanced consideration of costs, benefits and available technology.

b. Labor

The very low total fertility rates observed in 1973 are assumed to be a temporary decline from an underlying average fertility rate of 2.1 which is closer to that observed in the five years prior to 1972. The 2.1 rate corresponds to the Series E Census Bureau population projection. This rate implies an ultimately stable population although the actual population total will continue to increase well into the next century because of the large proportion of the population currently in childbearing age groups. The effect of this age composition is that population growth will peak in the mid-1980's at slightly over 1 percent a year, compared to current rates of increase of a little over 0.8 percent, before steadily declining to a 0.65 percent rate of increase by 2000.

The labor force is not affected by the fertility rate assumption until the early 1990's, when today's babies begin to enter the work force. One indirect effect may be felt in the interim, however—the fertility rate and family size can affect the number of married women who enter the labor force on a full-time basis. The assumption was made that previous trends toward increased female participation would continue so that a gradual upward trend in the

average number of hours per year worked by women would result. This trend is sufficient to offset a slight trend towards a shorter average work year for male workers, due to longer vacations and earlier retirements. The result is a stable average work year for the population as a whole. A similar assumption for unemployment rates was made as in the Case A projections, i.e., that the initial rate of unemployment is 6 percent, due to the current economic recession, but that subsequent economic recovery would reduce the unemployment rate to 4.6 percent before 1980. After 1980, no attempt was made to model short-run fluctuations but, instead, a constant unemployment rate of 4.6 percent was assumed. Under this combination of circumstances there would not be the need for the drastic, mandatory curtailment of the average workweek which was found necessary under Case C conditions.

Table 6•56
CASE B: CAPITAL INPUT INTO ENVIRONMENTAL IMPROVEMENT

	Input (Billions of 1958 Dollars)	Input (Billions of Current Dollars)
1975	1	1.6
1976	2	3.3
1977	4	6.7
1978	6	10.5
1979	8	14.4
1980	8	15.1
1981	8	15.7
1982-2000	6 per year	

c. Capital Services

Policies to improve environmental conditions and to economize on the use of raw materials were assumed to affect the use of capital. The first type of policy is the requirement that some additional capital (over that contemplated for Case A) will be devoted to environmental improvement. Such investment is an extraction of capital from the flow of new investment to a use that has no near-term payoff in the market sense. Such uses of capital include scrubbers for stack gas cleaning and reclamation of land that has been strip-mined. The additional capital assumed to be devoted to these uses is shown in Table 6•56.

The use of capital equipment already in place was also assumed to be subject to more stringent regulations, with the objectives of: (1) using energy

Chart 6·23
COST/BENEFIT CURVES

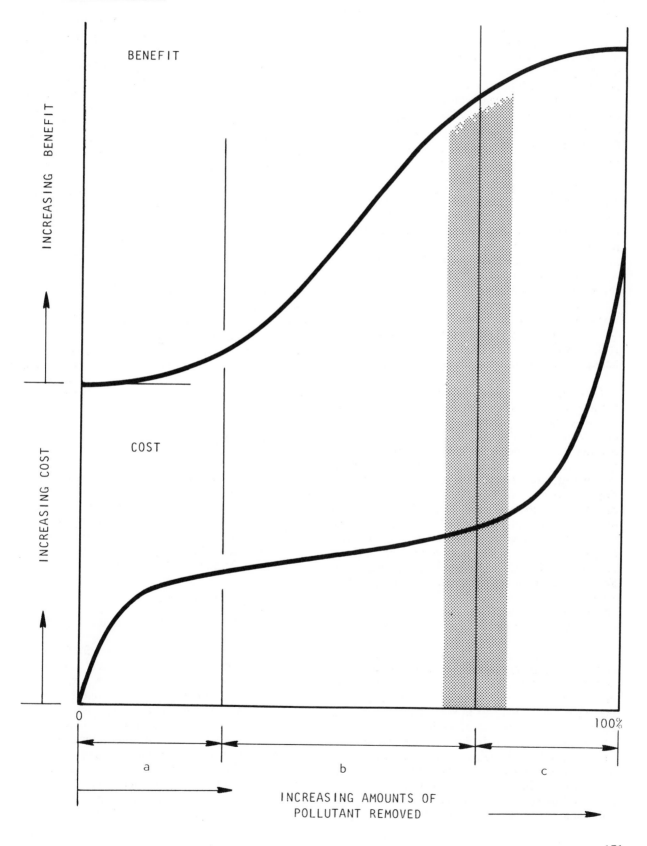

inputs and material throughput more efficiently, and (2) releasing less effluents as by-products of operation. Such restrictions have the effect of reducing the productivity of capital. The assumption was made that the level of productivity of existing capital was 2.5 percent lower than that assumed for Case A for the period between 1975 and 1985. By 1985, existing equipment in most manufacturing industries will be largely replaced with new equipment incorporating more resource efficient and less environmentally damaging technology. Therefore, this constraint on productivity was removed after 1985.

The third assumption on capital use concerns the productivity of new investment. It was assumed that new investment would incorporate technology which is environmentally cleaner and more efficient in resource consumption, even at the expense of some loss in overall efficiency. Such changes could be required by regulation or induced in response to restrictions on production. Therefore, a decline of 0.5 percent a year in the productivity of new investment was imposed for the 1975-85 period. After 1985, it was assumed that the trend towards increased environmental damage would have been halted, so the productivity decline was removed.

These assumptions about capital productivity and use are arbitrary. They may overstate or understate actual capital requirements implicit in current environmental regulations since, at this time, these requirements are not fully apparent. However, the qualitative nature of the assumptions are based on established relationships—the substitution relationships between capital input and market efficiency of capital use on the one hand, and resource efficiency of capital use and environmental damage on the other. Also, these assumptions embody the two central features of the best aspects of current environmental policy: (1) the objective of arriving at and maintaining an environmental balance markedly above current levels while (2) concentrating environmental cleanup efforts on those activities with a high benefit/cost ratio.

For example, Chart 6•23 plots cost and benefit curves for a hypothetical, but generally typical, pollution control effort. The lower curve shows that as increasing amounts of pollutants are removed from the environment, the cost of removal generally goes through three stages: (a) an initial stage where the cost rises sharply as initial investments in even rudimentary control equipment are quite costly; (b) an intermediate stage where relatively modest further capital investments will often be capable of removing large additional amounts of pollutant; and (c) the final stage where very complex and expensive equip-

ment must be provided as the amount of pollutant to be removed approaches 100 percent.

The upper curve on Chart 6•23 shows the manner in which society generally benefits as increasing amounts of pollutant are removed. It is assumed that some objective and practical means for determining these benefits has been devised. Very often the benefits from removing only a small proportion of the pollutant are relatively minor as shown by segment (a) of the benefit curve. However, the benefits are then likely to increase rapidly as increasing percentages of the pollutant are removed in segment (b). Finally, a point is reached where further efforts to approach 100 percent purity yield very small incremental benefits (segment c). It must be emphasized that Chart 6•23 is meant merely as a general illustration of a principle, not a specific example of any actual situation; e.g., the relative lengths of segments (a), (b) and (c) will vary markedly from one pollutant to another.

In Case B, society's environmental efforts would tend to aim at achieving a balance somewhere in the crosshatched band near the juncture of segments (b) and (c) of the curves on Chart 6•23. In Case A, however, society would usually be satisfied to be somewhere well to the left of the crosshatched band, while in Case C the primary objective would be to approach 100 percent removal almost regardless of cost.

d. Technology

Labor and total factor productivity are assumed to grow at past rates—a 0.6 percent per year rate of improvement in labor augmenting technical changes and a 1.5 percent rate of increase in total factor productivity. The capital productivity assumptions have been outlined above under the section on Capital Services. (See Appendix E for definitions of productivity terms.)

e. Government Policies

The role of the government in the economy is assumed to follow present trends. These trends are covered in some detail in the discussion of Case A, and apply to the present projections with only minor changes. Government purchases are expected to grow slightly faster than total output, but the composition of these purchases is taken to continue along current lines. Government transfer programs are assumed to increase in relative importance. Some of this increase will occur within existing programs, particularly the social security programs, as the low fertility rate leads to a steady increase in the average age of the population and, consequently, to increasing claims on pension and health programs. The major change in the thrust of government activity, compared to historical trends or to the Case A conditions, occurs in the area of environment and resources. Current environmental protection programs are assumed to continue in force. Policies to reduce energy demand through regulatory measures, such as insulation requirements for structures and gasoline mileage requirements for automobiles, are assumed for this scenario. With regard to energy supply, government policy is assumed to be oriented toward relaxation of existing oil and gas regulations, together with the leasing of currently undeveloped offshore and other areas for petroleum and gas exploration and development. Steps in these directions will be somewhat slower than in Case A, however.

f. Consumption Lifestyle

No marked changes in lifestyle from Case A are assumed for the moderate-growth scenario. Certainly the adaptive process will be less rapid and less drastic than for the low-growth case.

Many of the changes implied by the scenario assumptions will be accomplished through the workings of established economic and social institutions such as the price system. When government regulations are found necessary to supplement, reinforce, or restrain private enterprise choices, they will be developed and enforced in a balanced manner.

Social, political, and lifestyle changes will reflect greater respect for the nation's natural resource endowment but without major restrictions on personal freedom and without abandoning efforts to achieve continuing technological progress. It is assumed that programs will be developed to assess the impacts of environmental and economic trade-offs.

Improved efficiency of resource utilization is assumed which will enable significant economic growth to continue while slowing consumption of the most limited resources. Again, a properly functioning price system will encourage improved efficiency.

2. Model Outputs—A Moderate-Growth Scenario

a. Economic Growth

The outlines of a future under moderate growth are shown in Tables 6-57 and 6-58. Real output grows steadily over the entire forecast period, although at a slightly slower rate than in Case A. Gross national product per capita increases, although also at rates a little slower than in Case A. The composition of projected economic growth is not greatly different from Case A patterns. In sum, a

continuation of current policies and trends is expected to produce continued real output and income growth and at the same time to permit some economy in resource use and the continued gradual improvement of the natural environment.

(1) Gross National Product

The average rate of growth of real GNP between 1975 and 2000 is 3.7 percent a year in the moderate-growth case. Real output growth until 1980 is 4.4 percent a year. This is more rapid than past trends because it is a period of recovery for the economy from an initial position of recession. After 1980, the economy grows at the rate permitted by the assumptions made about labor and capital inputs and productivity. The 1980-85 period shows a decline in the rate of increase of real GNP to 3.5 percent per year. This decline is produced by the slowing of the rate of increase of the labor force together with the continued restrictive effects of the environmental and energy constraints imposed by a combination of the economic system and the government. In fact, the effects of these changes continue, even after 1985, to produce an average growth rate of 3.5 percent a year over the remainder of the century.

(2) Composition of Real GNP

The composition of real output in a future of moderate growth is similar to existing patterns. The principal change is the increase in the relative importance of the output of consumption goods and services, which increases from 58.7 percent of real output in 1975 to 62.3 percent in 2000. This is equivalent to 4.0 percent annual rate of increase in real consumption. Real per capita consumption therefore increases only fractionally less rapidly than under the historical growth conditions (3.10 percent a year compared to 3.27 percent). This increase in the consumption share takes place at the expense of government purchases.

Real government purchases increase at 2.88 percent a year, substantially less rapidly than total output, with the result that the government share of total output declines from 17.8 percent in 1975 to 14.5 percent in 2000. This still permits a continued increase in real government services per capita.

Real private investment claims an unchanging share of total output over the forecast period— ranging between 23.4 percent and 24 percent. This is somewhat different from investment in Case A conditions, where the fraction of real output devoted to investment rose steadily over the forecast period. This lower rate of capital accumulation, together with the restrictions on capital use and capital effi-

Table 6·57
CASE B: MACRO ECONOMIC PROJECTIONS, 1975—2000

	1975	1980	1985	2000
1. GNP (Billions of Current $)	1714	2632	3834	11292
Personal Consumption (Billions of Current $)	995	1530	2191	6420
Private Domestic Investment (Billions of Current $)	380	581	853	2378
Government Purchases (Billions of Current $)	338	522	787	2490
2. Real GNP (Billions of 1958 $)	983	1217	1452	2460
Real Personal Consumption (Billions of 1958 $)	577	729	870	1532
Real Private Domestic Investment (Billions of 1958 $)	231	287	346	574
Real Government Purchases (Billions of 1958 $)	175	203	234	356
3. Price of GNP (1958 = 1)	1.744	2.163	2.641	4.587
Price of Personal Consumption (1958 = 1)	1.723	2.101	2.518	4.191
Price of Private Domestic Investment (1958 = 1)	1.645	2.024	2.465	4.144
Price of Government Purchases (1958 = 1)	1.932	2.571	3.362	6.995
4. GNP Per Capita (Thousands of Current $)	8.013	11.744	16.266	42.708
Personal Consumption Per Capita (Thousands of Current $)	4.652	6.827	9.296	24.281
Real GNP Per Capita (Thousands of 1958 $)	4.596	5.431	6.135	9.191
Real Personal Consumption Per Capita (Thousands of 1958 $)	2.698	3.253	3.691	5.794
5. Percentage of GNP				
Personal Consumption	58.1	58.1	57.1	56.9
Private Domestic Investment	22.2	27.1	22.2	21.1
Government Purchases	19.7	19.8	20.5	22.1
Government Expenditures	31.5	31.8	32.8	35.8
6. Percentage of Real GNP				
Real Personal Consumption	58.7	59.9	60.1	62.3
Real Private Domestic Investment	23.5	23.6	24.0	23.4
Real Government Purchases	17.8	16.7	16.2	14.5
7. Population (Million)	213.9	224.1	235.7	264.6
Labor Force (Billion Effective Manhours)	488	535	579	740
Labor as Percent of Total Time	14.2	14.2	14.2	14.3
Net Wage and Salary Index (1967 = 1)	1.660	2.262	3.022	7.030
8. Capital Stock (Billions of 1958 $)	2108	2318	2541	3673
Rate of Return on Private Capital (%)	8.5	10.2	10.3	10.7
Labor Productivity Index (1967 = 1)	1.328	1.444	1.572	2.084
Unit Labor Cost Index (1967 = 1)	1.740	2.182	2.676	4.697
Corporate Profits (Billions of Current $)	88	122	168	450
Corporate Cash Flow (Billions of Current $)	165	241	345	987
Private National Wealth (Billions of Current $)	4735	6568	9018	24642

ciency, are major contributors to the lower growth of real per capita incomes.

(3) Prices (Inflation)

Prices continue to increase in a future of moderate growth. The rate of increase of the GNP price index is 3.9 percent a year. Although this is below the rate of inflation experienced in the recent past, it is still above previous trends. The fastest rate of increase is 4.4 percent a year over the 1975-80 period. After that, it is expected that the rate of inflation will slow to an average of 3.8 percent over the rest of the

forecast period. The price of government services is the fastest rising component of total prices, increasing at an average 5.3 percent a year.

(4) Per Capita Income and Consumption

Per capita gross national product increases a little less rapidly than in the past, although the difference is not large. Real per capita GNP increases at an average 2.8 percent a year (compared to a historical growth trend of 2.9 percent). Since consumption absorbs a slightly increasing share of total output, the trend in real per capita consumption is slightly faster, at 3.1 percent a year. The rate of increase varies over the forecast period, being highest in the 1975-80 interval as the economy recovers from the initial recession, then declining between 1980 and 1985. In the five years after 1980, population growth reaches a peak at the same time as capital productivity is low and the rate of increase in the labor force declines. After 1985, population growth slows, capital productivity increases and these, with a small increase in labor force growth, permit per capita incomes to increase more rapidly.

Income distributions improve somewhat less rapidly than for Case A, but much more rapidly than for Case C. Improvement is here defined in terms of the reductions in the proportions of families and individuals in the lower income brackets. (See Chart 6•24.)

(5) Labor and Capital

Labor costs, as measured by the net wage and salary index, will increase at 6.5 percent per year under moderate growth. When direct improvements in labor productivity are taken into account, this represents a 5.9 percent annual increase in the price of labor services. The 1.5 percent a year increase in total factor productivity reduces the rate of increase of unit labor costs to 4.05 percent a year. This rate is fractionally higher than the rate of increase of output prices so there is a slight trend towards labor income and away from capital income. Part of this redistribution is from corporate income as is reflected in the increase of corporate net profits at only 6.8 percent a year over the forecast period.

Table 6•58
CASE B: MACRO ECONOMIC PROJECTIONS, GROWTH RATES; 1975-2000
(Average Annual Percent Growth Rates)

	1975 to 1980	1980 to 1985	1985 to 2000	1975 to 2000
GNP	8.95	7.81	7.47	7.83
Personal Consumption	8.98	7.45	7.43	7.74
Private Domestic Investment	8.86	7.98	7.07	7.61
Government Purchases	9.08	8.56	7.98	8.32
Real GNP	4.36	3.51	3.52	3.74
Real Personal Consumption	4.78	3.60	3.84	3.98
Real Private Domestic Investment	4.44	3.81	3.43	3.71
Real Government Purchases	3.01	2.88	2.84	2.88
Price of GNP	4.40	4.15	3.81	3.94
Price of Personal Consumption	4.08	3.70	3.45	3.62
Price of Domestic Investment	4.23	4.02	3.52	3.76
Price of Government Purchases	5.88	5.51	5.01	5.28
GNP Per Capita	7.94	6.74	6.65	6.92
Personal Consumption Per Capita	7.97	6.37	6.61	6.83
Real GNP Per Capita	3.40	2.47	2.73	2.81
Real Personal Consumption Per Capita	3.81	2.56	3.05	3.10
Population	0.94	1.01	0.77	0.85
Labor Force	1.86	1.59	1.64	1.68
Net Wage and Salary Index	6.38	5.96	5.79	5.94
Capital Stock	1.92	1.85	2.49	2.25
Labor Productivity Index	1.69	1.71	1.90	1.82
Unit Labor Cost Index	4.63	4.17	3.82	4.05
Corporate Profits	6.75	6.61	6.79	6.75
Corporate Cash Flow	7.87	7.44	7.26	7.42
Private National Wealth	6.76	6.55	6.93	6.82

ECONOMIC GROWTH IN THE FUTURE

The overall growth picture is summarized in Table 6·59. Growth is sustained by increases in labor input, capital input and total factor productivity. Labor input, in actual manhours and improved labor quality, contributes 1.06 percent a year. Capital services contribute 1.13 percent a year of the real GNP growth, and total factor productivity provides 1.5 percent of real GNP growth.

b. Population and Agriculture

Population growth in the Case B intermediate growth scenario is assumed to be governed by a total fertility rate of 2.1. This rate results in a population which stabilizes at about 315 million people sometime in the mid-21st century. By the year 2000, there will be about 265 million people in the United States, as compared to 285 million for the high growth Case A and only 250 million for the low growth Case C.

Population densities, pressures on agricultural production, and other population-related characteristics of the nation under Case B will be intermediate to the other two growth situations. All three of the scenarios establish sets of conditions which are well within the nation's accommodative capacity. A

Table 6·59
CASE B: SOURCES OF ECONOMIC GROWTH 1975-2000

Component	Rate of Increase (Percent per Year)	Contribution to Real GNP Growth (Percent per Year)
Labor:		
Quantity	1.08	
Quantity	0.60	
Total	1.68	1.06
Capital:		
Quantity	2.25	
Quality	0.80	
Total	3.05	1.13
Total Factor Productivity	1.50	1.50
Real GNP		3.69

society can be developed with a satisfactory quality of life well into the 21st century under any of the three sets of population conditions. Only under the Case A conditions must some eventual decrease take place in the total fertility rate.

Chart 6·24
**INCOME DISTRIBUTION
(Percent of Total Families and Unrelated Individuals)**

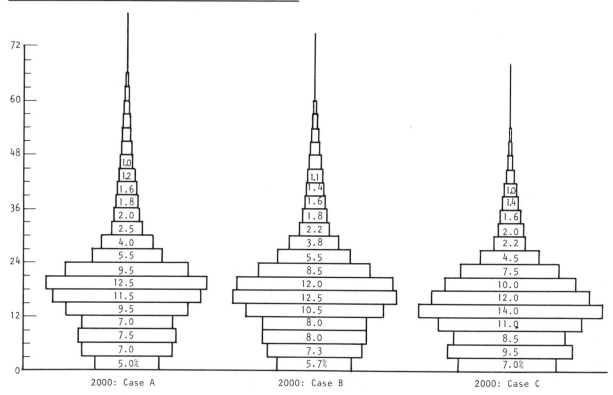

2000: Case A   2000: Case B   2000: Case C

176

c. Non-Energy Minerals

(1) Consumption Forecast

Minerals consumption forecasts in the moderate-growth scenario are based on the DRI forecasts of GNP and on the technique described in Appendix F. This technique results in a gradually decreasing trend of consumption per dollar of real GNP for each of the five major metals except aluminum. Consumption per capita continues to rise, however, and by the year 2000 it is 75 percent higher than in 1970. Table 6·60 presents the resulting consumption forecast for the five major metals.

d. Energy Demand

(1) Energy Demand by Consuming Sector

Judgmental forecasts of energy demand for each of four consuming sectors were prepared by the EEI Staff for the moderate-growth situation. The forecasts are summarized on Table 6·62.

The overall energy consumption under Case B moderate growth was found to be about 10 percent lower than under high growth. This reduction was somewhat more severe in the period prior to 1985 than in the years after 1985. The early period is

Table 6·60
CASE B: UNITED STATES METALS CONSUMPTION
(Thousands of Short Tons)

	1970	1985	2000	1970 to 2000 Cumulative Growth (Thousands of Short Tons)	Rate: (Percent per Year)
Iron	116,900	181,347	252,838	5,493,241	2.6
Aluminum	4,128	11,271	23,776	378,346	6.0
Copper	2,820	4,237	5,682	127,321	2.4
Zinc	1,374	2,094	2,991	64,148	2.6
Lead	1,335	1,710	1,929	50,131	1.2
Total	126,557	200,659	287,216	6,113,187	2.8

The lower GNP figures for Case B result in proportionately lower metals consumption estimates as compared to the high growth scenario. Over the 30-year period, 1970 to 2000, cumulative consumption for Case B is about 5 percent lower than for Case A.

(2) Recycling

Case B recycling figures are assumed to be equal to those of Case A. Table 6·61 shows that cumulative demand for primary metal over the period 1970 to 2000 is about 70 percent of total cumulative demand for primary and secondary metal at 1967 recycling rates. If recycling can be increased gradually to the higher rates shown at the bottom of the table, cumulative primary demand from 1970 to 2000 drops to about 55 percent of total primary and secondary demand. The saving in "unmined" metal by the year 2000 is equivalent to almost 7 years of additional primary consumption.

assumed to be a time of reacting to the OPEC price increases of 1973-74 and of rearranging the nation's energy use patterns to match consumption rates more closely to resources; i.e., to shift from oil and gas toward coal and nuclear fuels. By 1985 the tasks of reacting and rearranging are well underway so that from then on the major determinant of energy consumption is United States economic growth.

In comparing the individual sector forecasts for Case B with those of the high growth future, it is apparent that each sector is affected differently. Transportation experiences the largest drop compared to Case A. Following transportation in decreasing order of severity are: the residential, industrial, and commercial sectors. As in Case C, service activities in the economy are least measureably affected by changing economic growth restraints, and it is within the commercial sector that most service activities are concentrated.

177

Table 6•61

**CASE B: CUMULATIVE UNITED STATES METALS CONSUMPTION; 1970-2000
(Thousands of Short Tons)**

Major Metals	Primary and Secondary Demand	Primary Demand	
		Current Recycling*	"Maximum" Recycling*
Iron	5,493,241	3,790,328	2,954,400
Aluminum	378,346	310,238	255,976
Copper	127,321	63,653	48,788
Zinc	64,148	55,808	51,990
Lead	50,131	25,058	19,606
Total	6,113,187	4,245,085	3,330,760
Savings			914,325
Annual Primary Demand in 2000			133,105
Years of Additional Metal			6.9

Percent of Total Consumption from Recycled Materials

	Actual 1967	Estimated 1970	Maximum Practical	
			1985	2000
Iron	31.2	31.2	45	55
Aluminum	18.3	18.3	29	38
Copper	49.7	49.7	60	70
Zinc	12.6	12.6	18	23
Lead	49.6	49.6	60	70

* Current Recycling and Maximum Recycling Percentages are given in the bottom half of the table.

Table 6•62

**CASE B: ENERGY DEMAND BY CONSUMING SECTOR
(Quadrillion Btu)**

Consuming Sector	1972 Actual			Case B					
				1985			2000		
	Fuel	Electric	Total	Fuel	Electric	Total	Fuel	Electric	Total
Transportation	18.00	0.02	18.02	25.70	0.05	25.75	38.50	0.08	38.58
Residential	8.56	1.89	10.45	9.57	3.15	12.72	9.90	6.30	16.20
Commercial	6.15	1.55	7.70	8.76	2.25	11.01	8.90	7.02	15.92
Industrial	20.76	2.46	23.22	26.65	5.55	32.20	32.30	12.60	44.90
Sub-Total	53.47	5.92	59.39	70.68	11.00	81.68	89.60	26.00	115.60
Energy Conversion			12.41			23.20			51.50
Total			71.80			104.88			167.10

Case B Demand as a Percentage of Case A Demand

	1985	2000
Transportation	87%	91%
Residential	88	91
Commercial	92	94
Industrial	92	92
Sub-Total	90	92
Energy Conversion	95	92
Total	91	92

178

Table 6·63
CASE B: CONSUMPTION OF ENERGY BY SECTOR OF USE; 1975-2000
(Energy Flows in Trillion Btu)

	Household, Commercial	Industrial	Transpor-tation	Electricity Generation	Synthetic Gas	Total Input
1975						
Coal	199.	4353.	0.	8661.	0.	13213.
Petroleum	6835.	6609.	17980.	2380.	0.	33797.
Natural gas	8234.	10976.	934.	4326.	0.	24469.
Hydro, nuclear	0.	0.	0.	5475.	0.	5475.
Total input	15268.	21930.	18914.	20843.	0.	76955.
Electricity	3969.	2739.	22.	0.	0.	6730.
Synthetic gas	0.	0.	0.	0.	0.	0.
Total use	19238.	24669.	18936.	20843.	0.	76955.
1980						
Coal	198.	4329.	0.	10428.	0.	14955.
Petroleum	8104.	7999.	21616.	2617.	0.	40336.
Natural Gas	8363.	13039.	1012.	4594.	0.	27007.
Hydro, nuclear	0.	0.	0.	10303.	0.	10303.
Total input	16665.	25367.	22628.	27941.	0.	92601.
Electricity	5502.	3490.	32.	0.	0.	9024.
Synthetic gas	0.	0.	0.	0.	0.	0.
Total use	22167.	28857.	22660.	27941.	0.	92601.
1985						
Coal	176.	3731.	0.	12234.	1115.	17255.
Petroleum	9309.	8964.	24422.	2992.	89.	45776.
Natural gas	7670.	14248.	1010.	5335.	0.	28263.
Hydro, nuclear	0.	0.	0.	15595.	0.	15595.
Total input	17154.	26943.	25432.	36156.	1204.	106889.
Electricity	7439.	4006.	37.	0.	0.	11682.
Synthetic gas	310.	379.	0.	0.	0.	690.
Total use	24904.	31328.	25469.	36156.	1204.	106889.
2000						
Coal	184.	5389.	0.	16344.	5065.	26982.
Petroleum	11438.	12085.	27904.	4198.	405.	56031.
Natural gas	5617.	16382.	989.	6803.	0.	29791.
Hydro, nuclear	0.	0.	0.	48055.	0.	48055.
Total input	17239.	33856.	28894.	75400.	5470.	160858.
Electricity	17265.	7037.	56.	0.	0.	24358.
Synthetic gas	1638.	2002.	0.	0.	0.	3640.
Total use	36142.	42895.	28949.	75400.	5470.	160858.

179

Chart 6•25
**ENERGY USE AND REAL GNP: ANNUAL GROWTH RATES
(Percent)**

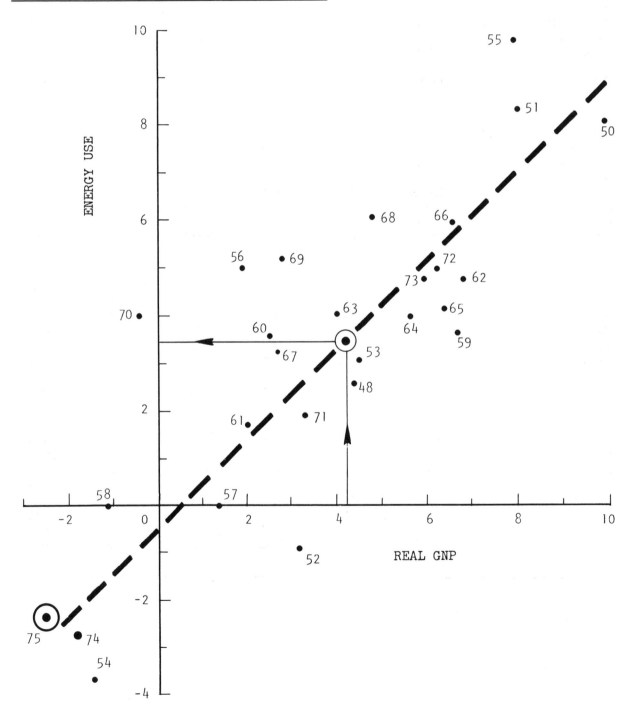

(2) Inter-Industry Forecast for Energy

(a) Energy Demand

The DRI model forecast of energy demand for the moderate-growth alternative is presented in Table 6•63. The major trend in these projections is toward an increase in total energy use, but at a declining rate. Other trends are a rapid increase in the relative importance of nuclear power, an increase in the relative importance of electricity, and a continuing increase in real energy prices.

Total energy input is forecast to increase from 77 quadrillion Btu in 1975 to 160.9 quadrillion in 2000, an average rate of increase of 3.0 percent a year. The rate of growth is initially higher, at 3.8 percent a year, but some of this is due to a catch-up of energy use from its depressed 1975 value. After 1980, an underlying trend of decline in the rate of increase of energy use emerges, with the growth rate slowing to 2.9 percent in 1985 and then to 2.8 percent until 2000. This is caused in part by economy in energy use stimulated by rising energy prices, and in part by structural changes. These changes stem from the increasing relative importance of service industries and a slowing in the growth of space heating and transportation demands for energy. The declining ratio of energy to real GNP reflects the trends towards non-energy intensive activity and towards greater efficiency in energy use in general.

Improving the energy efficiency of the nation is likely to be a long, difficult and expensive process. Most of the energy consuming devices used by society are long-lived; e.g., automobiles have a useful life of about a decade, houses last perhaps 50 years, and industrial equipment is used for 15 or 20 years in many cases. Thus, it is unrealistic to expect rapid reductions in the energy-GNP ratio over a short time, without resorting to arbitrary restrictions on consumption. Such restrictions would almost certainly exert a much more damaging effect on the rest of the economy than will occur if each energy user is guided in his consumption patterns by the signals of a freely responsive price mechanism.

The relationship between energy consumption and economic growth since 1973 is instructive in this regard. The sharp increases in all energy prices after the OPEC actions in late 1973 presented a strong incentive for energy users to cut energy consumption wherever possible. Some actions to reduce energy use could be taken immediately. Among them were reducing automobile speeds, turning off excess lights in homes, stores, and factories, and turning space heating thermostats down. Other actions, such as increasing the thickness of ceiling insulation in homes, could be taken with only a minimum time delay.

It was to be expected that the cumulative effect of these actions on energy consumption would be significant in 1974, and that the relationships between energy consumption and real GNP would, therefore, be measurably different than in earlier years. Chart 6•25 illustrates the relationships between the percent growth of real GNP and the percent growth of energy consumption which have prevailed each year since the end of World War II. The dashed line is a statistical, best-fit relationship based on all the data points to and including 1973. This chart suggests that an average growth rate of 4.2 percent per year for real GNP would have to be sustained by an average increase of 3.5 percent in energy consumption (the point designated by the larger, circled dot).

The chart also shows that this same general relationship between energy and GNP was preserved in 1974 despite the massive disruptions in the energy market and the sincere attempts at conservation which characterized the energy situation in that year. Furthermore, energy consumption fell only modestly in 1975 despite a further decline in real GNP. Thus, in both years the nation failed to improve its energy-efficiency.

(b) Electricity Demand

The dominant feature of the energy consumption forecast shown in Table 6•64 is the rapid increase in the use of electricity. Demand for electricity increases at an average of 5.3 percent a year between 1975 and 2000. Within the forecast period, demand growth slows measurably from 6.0 percent between 1975 and 1980 to 5.0 percent after 1985. Although these demand growth rates are quite rapid, they are still well below the historical trend for growth in electricity demand.

Part of the decline in the growth rate can be attributed to the more rapid increase forecast for future electricity prices than has occurred in the past and thus to the more efficient use of electricity that is expected in the future. And part can be attributed to the approaching saturation of many electricity-using appliances, e.g., home air conditioning and major kitchen appliances.

Compared to other fuels, electricity prices decline and this, together with its ease of use, leads to a substitution of electricity for other fuels in many energy uses. Thus, the rapid increase in electricity use is accompanied by slower increases in the consumption of other fuels. Gas consumption increases at only 0.53 percent and petroleum use increases at 2.04 percent, both well below past trends.

Table 6·64
CASE B: UNITED STATES ENERGY CONSUMPTION; 1975-2000

	1975	1980	1985	2000
1. Energy Consumption (Quadrillion Btu)				
Direct Consumption				
Coal..	4.552	4.527	5.021	10.638
Petroleum	31.417	37.719	42.784	51.833
Gas...	20.143	22.413	22.928	22.988
Total................................	56.112	64.659	70.733	85.459
Electricity Generation				
Coal..	8.661	10.428	12.234	16.344
Petroleum and Gas........................	6.706	7.211	8.327	11.001
Hydro, Nuclear, Other......................	5.475	10.303	15.595	48.055
Total..	20.842	27.942	36.156	75.400
Total...	76.954	92.601	106.889	160.859

	1975-80	1980-85	1985-2000
2. Energy Consumption Growth (Percent per Year)			
Direct Consumption			
Coal..	-0.11	2.09	5.13
Petroleum	3.72	2.55	1.29
Gas...	2.16	0.46	0.02
Total...	2.88	1.81	1.27
Electricity Generation			
Coal..	3.78	3.25	1.95
Petroleum and Gas........................	1.46	2.92	1.87
Hydro, Nuclear, Other......................	13.48	8.64	7.79
Total..	6.04	5.29	5.02
Total...	3.77	2.91	2.76

e. Energy Supplies and Prices

The EPRI judgmental forecast of energy supply under Case B incorporated the assumptions which follow. Intermittent problems will be experienced with energy imports but they will not be so severe as to force an all-out attempt to reach complete energy self-sufficiency. Efforts will be made to guard against a repetition of the 1973 oil embargo by developing storage facilities and alternate sources of foreign supplies. However, the general principle that international trade benefits both trading partners will be the basis for our relations with all other countries—including energy exporters. International trade in nuclear energy resources such as natural uranium and thorium will develop and be encouraged by the United States. In these areas, as in all other contracts with foreign nations, the United States will foster the development of adequate technical and commercial safeguards.

Some difficulties will occur in building United States refining capacity. There will be moderate delays in exploiting offshore oil, Western oil shales, and coal. More expensive environmental protection will represent a moderate drag on economic growth. More serious efforts at conservation will take the form of government jawboning, regulations, and administrative restraints on consumption to supplement the price mechanism.

These restraints will not inhibit the development of United States fuel resources to anywhere near the same degree as in Case C. Although more extensive than in the high growth case, they are not so severe as to cripple resource exploration, extraction, or use.

182

(1) Estimates for the Intermediate Period 1980-85

In the 1980-85 period, Case B differs from the high growth Case A in the manner described in the following paragraphs.

Domestic coal requirements in 1985 have risen to 820 million tons (45 percent over the 1973 level and nearly the same output as in Case A), excluding coal based SNG production. This stems directly from a reduced availability of nuclear, hydro, and geothermal plants, as described below. Technological advance in coal burning and a balanced environmental-energy policy with respect to strip mining are assumed to allow such an expansion. Alternatively, it may be possible to slow the phaseout of petroleum consumption by electric power plants, assuming additional fuel oil imports could be obtained, but this would tend to raise electricity costs to United States consumers and increase import requirements.

For natural gas and petroleum liquids from the lower 48 states and southern Alaska, several important changes from Case A are likely. First, the availability of leases in some areas with high promise (e.g., the Gulf of Alaska) may be delayed; in some areas development may not be permitted at all pending improved technologies for overcoming environmental risks. Second, the general investment climate under Case B would not be as favorable to natural resource development as under historical growth conditions. To reflect these changes, the oil and gas supply functions are assumed to shift from Case A by about 10 percent; i.e., a given price will elicit about 10 percent less supply than in Case A. It is also probable that the slopes of the supply function will be somewhat steeper than for Case A; i.e., a given price *increase* will not cause as large a supply *increase* as in Case A. (See Chart 6·21.) Since actual output will be substantially smaller than with Case A, this may not affect the estimates significantly, and the elasticity assumptions made for Case A have not been altered.

Finally, it is assumed that while crude oil prices would be decontrolled at an early date, natural gas prices would remain subject to Federal Power Commission regulation. The commission is assumed to let the national ceiling price rise, in constant 1975 dollar terms to 66¢ per thousand cubic feet in 1985.

The impact of these assumptions is that natural gas supplies from the lower 48 states would be substantially less than with Case A and that, with prices held below market equilibrium, continued allocation would be required. In addition, even though total energy demand with Case B is lower than with Case A, requirements for petroleum liquids would be sharply increased. Demand for crude oil and natural gas liquids from the lower 48 states is 13 million

barrels per day for Case B. The crude oil price required to elicit this volume goes up sharply to $9.40 per barrel.

Because of the much tighter supply conditions resulting from continued regulation of gas prices, the development of the North Slope and of supplementary sources of gas and liquids under Case B is assumed to be at least as rapid as with Case A. This is despite the slower increases in energy demand. By 1985 these sources are likely to contribute similar volumes, except for synthetic natural gas, which is likely to be developed at a more rapid rate because of the shortage of natural gas. Under these conditions petroleum imports could be reduced from the 1980 level, which would minimize the problems assumed to exist abroad. Therefore, it is unnecessary to develop a separate high self-sufficiency case for Case B.

For nuclear power, it is judged that only those units currently reported by the AEC as licensed to operate, being built, or ordered (about 215,000 MW by 1985) will be in operation. This coincides with the Interior Department's 1972 projection. It allows for substantial slippage from scheduled completion dates into the 1983-85 period.

The estimate for hydro, geothermal power and other energy sources is reduced from 4.3 to 3.8 quadrillion Btu (as compared with Case A) to reflect slower demand increases as well as environmental and/or technological obstacles. This figure corresponds to the National Petroleum Council, Case III reported in *United States Energy Outlook*, 1972. It is below the NPC high growth cases and the Interior Department estimate.[13] It is slightly above a National Academy of Engineering projection.[14]

(2) Estimates for the Long Range (2000)

For the end-of-century estimates, a somewhat slower development is likely for electricity generated by hydro-geothermal and new sources (because of reduced emphasis on technology). This results in a slightly larger use of petroleum in power plants. Case B continues to offer the option of stressing either nuclear power or coal in power generation. In the high-nuclear case, coal demand in 2000 would be little above the 1985 level.

For gas and petroleum liquids from the lower 48 states it was judged necessary to shift the basic Case A supply functions by the same percentage as for 1985. Wellhead prices of gas are assumed to rise sufficiently to double the 1975 level (88¢ per thousand cubic feet in 1975 dollars). Because of increased resource scarcity, however, the quantity produced at this price is below the 1985 volume and is little more than half of that available without price controls. Because of this decline a large increase in synthetic natural gas becomes necessary; i.e., to triple the 1985 level.

Because of the greatly reduced supply of gas, requirements for petroleum liquids are much higher than in Case A. Assuming that supplies from the North Slope and syncrude are the same as with Case A and that imports are held to about the 1985 level, the demand for domestic crude and natural gas liquids from the lower 48 states would be nearly half again as great as Case A demand. This would require prices to rise to $12 a barrel (in 1975 dollars), against $8.50 per barrel in the high growth case. Depending on world market conditions, import restrictions may well be needed to sustain this price, despite unsettled political problems which have been assumed to affect foreign supplies.

Tables 6•65 through 6•74 present the detailed forecasts for Case B in a format similar to that shown earlier for Cases A and C; i.e., Table 6•65, Energy Balances; Tables 6•66 through 6•69, Energy Supplies for Petroleum Liquids, Gas, Coal, and Nuclear Power; three summary tables; a price forecast table; and a list of conversion factors.

(3) Comparison with the DRI Supply Forecast

The comparison of EPRI and DRI supply forecasts on Table 6•75 shows a somewhat closer correspondence between the two than in Case A. This is particularly notable with regard to domestic supplies of oil and natural gas. For Case B, the EPRI forecast assumes that wellhead price controls on natural gas will be retained and prices will be permitted to increase only rather slowly. The forecasted consequence of this continued control is a sharp cutback in available supplies of natural gas as compared to Case A, thus bringing the EPRI estimates very close to those of DRI for 1985 and 2000.

By the year 2000, both forecasts find energy imports at about 9 or 10 percent of total energy consumption. EPRI sees somewhat faster progress toward energy independence, however, with imports down to 12 percent of total consumption by 1985. DRI imports have dropped only to about 17 percent by 1985, in contrast to over 20 percent currently.

f. Case B Variant: Higher Electricity Growth Rates

The Case B analysis immediately preceding foresees average annual growth rates of about 3.7 percent for real GNP and about 3.0 percent for total energy consumption over the next 25 years. This analysis indicates that energy consumption for electricity will grow at about 5.3 percent per year while other energy consumption will grow at only about 1.7 percent per year.

This difference in projected growth rates between electricity and other forms of energy is consistent with past trends and may be expected to persist in future years for a variety of reasons. Among them are: a slower rate of price increase for electricity; its superior convenience and versatility; and the tendency of the service sector (the most rapidly growing part of the economy) to emphasize electric power in its energy consumption patterns. Another very important factor is the relative domestic abundance of fuels, such as coal and nuclear, which are most readily converted to useful energy forms in the generation of electricity. This domestic abundance is in contrast to the relative scarcity of oil and gas.

Thus, the normal free-market pressures (price and value) for increasing the consumption of electricity are likely to be reinforced by specific public policies aimed at achieving energy independence. If these policies are to be effective they *must* be directed at accelerating the shift to coal and nuclear power.

The following paragraphs consider the degree to which modest variations in free market forces and public policies, from those assumed in Case B, may combine to raise the levels of electricity consumption above those projected in Case B. This variation from Case B is designated as Case B-HCN (high coal and nuclear).

The basic economic and demographic characteristics of Case B are assumed to prevail in Case B-HCN. The total consumption of energy is also assumed to be essentially the same as in Case B. Only the fraction of total energy used to generate electricity is increased. This increase is achieved primarily by prices of oil and gas which are assumed to be higher, relative to the price of electricity, than in Case B. In this illustration, the basic environmental restraints of Case B are assumed to remain in force. These restraints prevent coal production from rising significantly above the Case B figures, despite the improved economic incentives associated with increased oil and gas prices. As a result, the shift is primarily to nuclear power.

An equally feasible substitute for Case B-HCN could be developed which would depend upon coal as the energy source for generating much of the additional electricity needed for this alternate to Case B. It would be necessary only to revise the assumptions regarding environmental restrictions and prices sufficiently to provide coal with the necessary economic and technological advantages. These alternatives are not developed in detail here. However, the quantitative implications for coal demand are discussed below for a Case B-HCN future which would concentrate to a greater degree on coal.

Table 6.65
CASE B: ENERGY BALANCES
(Quadrillion Btu)

	1975	1980	1985	2000	
Total Demand[1]	77.0	92.6	106.9	160.9	
Less Fuel Efficiency Adjustment[2]	—	1.3	2.6	5.8	
Adjusted Demand	77.0	91.3	104.3	155.1	
				High Coal	High Nuclear
Electrical Sector	20.9	26.3	32.7	63.4	63.4
Hydro/Other	3.1	3.6	3.8	8.0	8.0
Nuclear	1.6	6.2	11.8	31.7	38.0
Petroleum[3]	6.9	5.7	2.6	2.4	2.4
Coal	9.3	10.8	14.5	21.3	15.0
Net Utility Generation[1] (Trillion Kwhr)	1.98	2.63	3.35	7.11	
Non-Electrical Sector	56.1	65.0	71.6	91.7	
Coal	4.9	5.1	5.2	5.8	
Industrial	4.6	4.8	5.1	5.8	
Other[4]	0.3	0.3	0.1	—	
Gas	23.8	25.3	27.8	35.0	
Natural, Lower 48	22.5	22.0	21.8	21.0	
North Slope, Alaska	—	0.8	1.5	3.0	
SNG[5]	0.2	1.0	2.0	6.0	
Domestic	22.7	23.8	25.3	30.0	
Imports	1.1	1.5	2.5	5.0	
Petroleum Liquids Required	27.4	34.6	38.6	50.9	
Crude + NGL, Lower 48[6]	21.4	22.5	26.1	31.2	
North Slope, Alaska	—	1.3	4.2	8.4	
Syncrude	—	0.3	1.0	4.2	
Domestic	21.4	24.0	31.3	43.8	
Imports	6.0	10.6	7.3	7.1	

(1) Provided by Data Resources, Inc.

(2) Difference between energy inputs of electrical sector under assumption of constant heat rate made by DRI and decreasing heat rate made in this study. See Table 6.74.

(3) Projected figures assumed to be liquids because of non-availability of gas.

(4) Excludes coal for gasification, which is included with gas (SNG).

(5) SNG = synthetic natural gas

(6) NGL = natural gas liquids

Table 6·66
**CASE B: ENERGY SUPPLIES; PETROLEUM LIQUIDS
(Millions of Barrels)** [1]

	1975	1980	1985	2000
Lower 48 [2]	3,900	4,091	4,745	5,673
North Slope, Alaska	0	236	764	1,527
Syncrude	0	36	182	764
Total Domestic	3,900	4,363	5,691	7,964
Imports	2,345	2,963	1,800	1,727
Total [3]	6,245	7,326	7,491	9,691

(1) Converted at 5.5 million Btu's per barrel

(2) Includes South Alaska

(3) Excludes liquids for gasification (76 million barrels for all years).

Table 6·67
**CASE B: ENERGY SUPPLIES; GAS
(Trillions of Cubic Feet)** *

	1975	1980	1985	2000
Lower 48	21.8	21.4	21.2	20.4
Alaska	0	0.8	1.5	2.9
SNG	0.2	1.0	1.9	5.8
Domestic	22.0	23.2	24.6	29.1
Imports	1.1	1.5	2.4	4.9
Total	23.1	24.7	27.0	34.0

* At 1,030 Btu per cubic foot dry gas excluding transfer and losses.

Table 6·68
**CASE B: ENERGY SUPPLIES; COAL
(Millions of Short Tons)** [1]

	1975	1980	1985	2000 High Coal	2000 High Nuclear
Electrical	387	450	604	887	625
Industrial and Other [2]	204	212	217	242	242
Gasification	0	40	98	328	328
Domestic	591	702	919	1,457	1,195
Exports [3]	71	75	87	108	108
Total	662	777	1,006	1,565	1,303

(1) Converted at 24.0 million Btu per ton, except gasification at 23.2 million Btu per ton.

(2) Includes small quantities of other uses in earlier years.

(3) Department of Interior estimates (December, 1972).

Table 6•69
CASE B: ENERGY SUPPLIES; NUCLEAR POWER

	1973	1975	1980	1985	2000 High Coal	2000 High Nuclear
Installed Capacity (Thousands of MW)	31[1]	50	110	215	602	720
Net Generation (Billions of Kwhr) [2]......	80	150	580	1,130	3,170	3,800
Energy Inputs (Quadrillion Btu)...........	0.85	1.6	6.2	11.8	31.7	38.0

(1) Estimates for December 31.

(2) A conservatively low capacity factor of .60 is used beginning in 1980. Heat rates through 1985 from Department of Interior, December, 1972 report; *United States Energy Through the Year 2000.* This report shows a decrease from 10,560 Btu per Kwhr in 1975 to 9,760 in 1985. For 2,000 a slower rate of improvement was used.

Table 6•70
CASE B: ENERGY SUPPLY SUMMARIES
(Quadrillion Btu)

	1975	1980	1985	2000 High Nuclear	2000 High Coal
Gas	23.8	25.3	27.8	35.0	35.0
Petroleum Liquids	34.3	40.3	41.2	53.3	53.3
Coal	14.2	15.9	19.7	20.8	27.1
Nuclear	1.6	6.2	11.8	38.0	31.7
Hydro/Other...................................	3.1	3.6	3.8	8.0	8.0
Total...................................	77.0	91.3	104.3	155.1	155.1

Table 6•71
CASE B: SHARES OF ENERGY SUPPLY SOURCES
(Percent)

	1975	1980	1985	2000 High Nuclear	2000 High Coal
Gas	31.0	27.7	26.7	22.6	22.6
Petroleum Liquids	44.5	44.2	39.5	34.4	34.4
Coal	18.4	17.4	18.9	13.4	17.5
Nuclear	2.1	6.8	11.3	24.5	20.4
Hydro/Other...................................	4.0	3.9	3.6	5.1	5.1

Table 6·72
CASE B: SHARES OF PETROLEUM AND GAS IMPORTS
(Quadrillion Btu)

	1975	1980	1985	2000
Petroleum Imports	12.9	16.3	9.9	9.5
Petroleum Demand	34.3	40.3	41.2	53.3
Imports (Percent)	37	41	24	18
Gas Imports....................................	1.1	1.5	2.5	5.0
Gas Demand...................................	23.9	25.3	27.8	35.0
Imports (Percent)	5	6	9	14
Total Imports.................................	14.0	17.8	12.4	14.5
Total Energy Demand.....................	77.0	91.3	104.3	155.1
Imports (Percent)	18	20	12	9

Table 6·73
CASE B: ASSUMED OIL AND GAS PRICES; LOWER 48 STATES (1975 $)

Crude Oil & NGL*

1975

Quadrillion Btu	21.4
Millions of Barrels..	3900
Millions of Barrels per day	10.7
Dollars per Barrel	$7.00

1985

Quadrillion Btu	26.1
Millions of Barrels..	4745
Millions of Barrels per day	13.00
Dollars per Barrel	$9.40

2000

Quadrillion Btu	31.2
Millions of Barrels..	5673
Millions of Barrels per day	15.54
Dollars per Barrel	$12.00

Gas

1975

Quadrillion Btu	22.5
Thousands of Cubic Feet	21.8
Dollars per Thousand Cubic Feet...............	$0.44

1985

Quadrillion Btu	21.8
Thousands of Cubic Feet	21.2
Dollars per Thousand Cubic Feet...............	$0.66

2000

Quadrillion Btu	21.0
Thousands of Cubic Feet	20.4
Dollars per Thousand Cubic Feet...............	$0.88

* Natural gas liquids

Table 6·74
CONVERSION FACTORS USED IN TABLES 6·65-6·73

BTU CONTENT OF FOSSIL FUELS

Coal for gasification	23,200,000	Btu per short ton
Other coal....................	24,000,000	Btu per short ton
Crude oil......................	5,500,000	Btu per short ton
Residual fuel oil	6,100,000	Btu per barrel
Natural gas..................	1,030	Btu per cubic feet

HEAT RATES OF ELECTRICAL GENERATING PLANTS
(Btu per Kwhr)

	1975	1980	1985	2000
Fossil fuels...............	10,575	9,875	9,575	9,250
Nuclear	10,660	10,660	10,400	10,000
Hydro/Other*	10,220	9,500	9,200	9,000
Average................	10,560	9,990	9,760	9,600-9,360

* Hydro power outputs are converted to theoretical energy inputs on the basis of heat rates for large fossil-fueled steam-electric plants.

(1) Domestic Oil and Gas Availability and Price

A number of developments could combine to raise oil and gas prices above the levels projected in Case B. Generally, these developments might be expected to occur in a future with characteristics somewhere between Case B and Case C. Specifically, the scenario for such a future could differ from Case B by including one or more of the following assumptions: (a) moderately lower availability of domestic oil and gas resources; (b) public policies which provide less effective support to (or place more stringent restraints on) the energy industry in its attempts to expand domestic supplies of oil and gas; and (c) public policies aimed directly at minimizing utilization of less plentiful resources.

The probabilities are reasonably high that one or

more of these assumptions will become reality. The oil and gas resource and production estimates used in developing the Case A and B energy supply scenarios are relatively optimistic, although below the highest of such forecasts. The process of estimating the extent of as yet undiscovered natural resources is necessarily an inexact one, as a review of the literature discloses. Therefore, the quantity of resources available may be less than is anticipated in Case B.

Government intrusion into the private sector has increasingly affected the speed and efficiency with which the energy industry can respond to changes in its economic environment. The degree to which this intrusion expands or contracts in the future, and the extent to which it is aimed at encouraging or frustrating the search for new oil and gas, will be instrumental in determining production capabilities

Table 6.75

CASE B: COMPARISON OF ENERGY SUPPLY FORECASTS:
(EPRI vs. DRI) [1]

(Quadrillion Btu)	1975 EPRI	1975 DRI	1985 EPRI	1985 DRI	2000 EPRI	2000 DRI
Domestic						
Oil	21.4	19.7	30.3	30.7	39.6	35.1
Natural Gas	22.5	22.3	23.3	23.6	24.0	21.3
Total	43.9	42.0	53.6	54.3	63.6	56.4
Synthetics						
Syncrude	—	—	1.0	—	4.2	8.5
Synthetic Gas	0.2	—	2.0	0.7	6.0	3.6
Total	0.2	—	3.0	0.7	10.2	12.1
Imports						
Oil	12.9	14.1	9.9	15.1	9.5	12.4
Natural Gas	1.1	2.2	2.5	4.0	5.1	4.9
Total	14.0	16.3	12.4	19.1	14.6	17.3
Total Oil and Gas	58.1	58.3	69.0	74.1	88.4	85.8
Other						
Coal	14.2	13.2	19.7	17.3	27.1	27.0
Nuclear	1.6	2.3	11.8	11.8	31.7	40.1
Hydro, Other	3.1	3.2	3.8	3.8 [2]	8.0	8.0 [2]
Total	18.9	18.7	35.3	32.9	66.8	75.1
Total Energy	77.0	77.0	104.3	107.0 [3]	155.2	160.9 [3]

(1) EPRI Figures represent an average of the high imports and high self-sufficiency cases for 1985, and an average of the high coal and high nuclear cases for 2000. Differences between figures on this table and those on preceding related tables are caused by averaging and rounding.

(2) Hydro, Other taken from EPRI Forecast because DRI forecast aggregates Nuclear, Hydro, Other.

(3) Differences between EPRI and DRI total energy figures stem primarily from the EPRI assumption of gradual decrease in heat rates for electrical generation, while DRI has assumed no such improvement.

over the next 25 years. Case B assumes that the traditional incentives to private industry activity will remain largely intact. If this assumption is overly optimistic as regards oil and gas exploration and production, the actual oil and gas supplies may well be significantly lower than suggested by Case B.

Governmental policy can also impact strongly on future oil and gas supply rates by way of taxes and subsidies on consumption. These can be designed either to encourage or discourage consumption. If they are developed to encourage moves toward national energy independence, they might well tax those uses of oil and gas for which coal and nuclear power were feasible alternatives. Such taxes could be supplemented by subsidies to encourage use of coal and nuclear energy by sectors of the market formerly dominated by oil and gas.

(2) Price of Electricity

Under the Case B scenario, electricity prices over the next 25 years are forecast to rise at a slightly slower rate than overall prices as expressed in terms of the GNP deflator. This results from an assumed gradual increase in productivity for the electric utility industry. For the purposes of this discussion, productivity is defined as output (i.e., kilowatt hours) per unit real cost of all inputs (i.e., fuel, labor, capital, other expenses). The relationship between historic rates of productivity improvement and those assumed for Cases A, B, and C are shown in Table 6·76. All of the assumed rates of future improvement are conservatively low when compared to past rates.

Table 6·76
PRODUCTIVITY IMPROVEMENT IN ELECTRIC UTILITY INDUSTRY*

Description	Percent per Year
Actual: 1950-1970	3.4
Case A: 1975-2000	1.1
Case B: 1975-2000	0.8
Case C: 1975-2000	0.2

* Based on output per unit cost of all inputs; i.e., kilowatt-hours per dollar, with costs expressed in deflated, constant dollar terms.

If future rates of productivity improvement are more rapid than has been assumed, the demand for electricity will grow somewhat faster than forecast in Cases A, B, and C. If productivity improvement were once again to attain the rates experienced in the 1950's and 1960's, electricity demand growth would probably be limited less by price considerations than by financial and technical restrictions on the pace at which power producing facilities could be built, and the rate at which consuming techniques could be shifted to electricity.

While it may be unlikely that past rates can be regained fully, some improvements above the Case B situation seem quite possible. In this regard, it is interesting to note the rates of improvement which were achieved even during the inflationary period from 1966 to 1972. Table 6·77 suggests that, even during this difficult period, the investor-owned electric utility industry improved its productivity at well in excess of one percent per year.

It must be noted that the calculation on Table 6·77 contains a number of approximations in that it is based on a computation of the cost of electricity in 1972 as it *would have been* if the industry had earned an "adequate" 14 percent return on common equity. (See Chapter 9, Pricing, and Chapter 10, Financing, for discussions of returns on common equity.) The industry actually earned approximately 11.7 percent in 1972. The return on equity in 1966 was within a reasonable range, considering the much lower costs of capital at that time, so no adjustment to the 1966 cost of electricity was necessary. If the Table 6·77 calculation had not been adjusted to compensate for the low return in 1972, the industry would show an *apparent* productivity improvement of 2.2 percent per year from 1966 to 1972.

(3) Limits on Electricity Growth Rates

Under some circumstances, technological and financial factors may limit the rapidity with which the nation can shift to electricity. As noted previously, energy producing and energy consuming technologies are capital intensive and involve the use of equipment which is generally long-lived (e.g., nuclear reactors, oil refineries, steel mills, home heating systems, automobiles). Thus, altering the mix of energy consumption by shifting from on-site combustion of oil and gas to the use of electricity generated by coal and nuclear fuel, is a long and expensive process.

A judgmental forecast of energy demand by consuming sector was developed to assess the maximum practical rate at which such a shift to electricity might take place. For this forecast, the general economic and social conditions of Case B were assumed to prevail, but were supplemented by higher oil and gas prices, and a clear national objective of achieving energy independence. However, the development of emergency situations which would induce a wartime-like response were not included.

This forecast is designated as Case B-ME (maximum electric). It is summarized on Table 6·78.

Table 6·77
ELECTRIC UTILITY INDUSTRY PRODUCTIVITY IMPROVEMENT: 1966-1972[1]

	1966	1972
1) Electric Revenue (Millions of Dollars)	$ 13,373.	$ 25,445.[2]
2) Sales to Ultimate Customers (Billions of Kwhr)	796,317.	1,239,807.
3) GNP Price Index (1958 = 100)	113.94	146.12
4) Average Output per Current Dollar (Kwhr per $)	57.9	48.6
5) Average Output per Constant, 1958, Dollar (Kwhr per $)	65.8	71.1
6) Average Annual Output Improvement (Percent per Year)	1.3%	

(1) Investor Owned Electric Utility Statistics from EEI Statistical Yearbook.

(2) Calculation of 1972 Electric Revenue to yield an "Adequate" Return on Common is as shown below.

Equity Basis: (Millions of Dollars)	1972
7) Average Common Equity	$31,686.
8) Return on Common Equity (percent)	14.
9) Net Income Required	4,445.
10) Actual Net Income	3,721.
11) Incremental Net Income	724.
12) Incremental Net Income from Electric Operations	625.[3]
13) Incremental Revenue (2.1 X Line 12)	1,312.[4]
14) Actual Revenue	24,133.
15) Adjusted ("Adequate" Return) Revenue	25,445.

(3) $724 X .826 where .826 = Electric Operating Revenue/Total Operating Revenue.
(4) Federal, state and local income taxes on incremental revenue assumed at 52.5%.

This tabulation may be compared with figures on Table 6·62 for Case B. The comparison shows that by the year 2000, Case B-ME foresees energy consumption for electricity at about 58.8 percent of total energy use while the comparable figure for Case B is 46.5 percent. In terms of average annual growth rates, Case B-ME shows growth of energy for electricity at 6.2 percent per year in contrast to 5.3 percent per year for Case B.

All consuming sectors contribute to the higher electricity demand figures for Case B-ME, with transportation exhibiting the largest relative increase over Case B by the year 2000. Electric transportation will account for over 2 percent of total energy consumption in 2000 under Case B-ME, while it reaches only about ½ of 1 percent for Case B. As regards other consumption sectors, the Case B-ME residential market is higher by 27 percent in 2000, the industrial market is higher by 13 percent, and the commercial market is higher by only 8 percent.

These increases from the Case B figures represent: (a) a major penetration of the transportation market by electric propulsion for urban vehicles carrying both passengers and freight, and (b) significantly more rapid penetration into the central house heating markets as builders and owners despair of solving the price and availability problems of oil and gas heat. In the industrial market the shift is likely to be concentrated in the iron and steel, paper, cement and petrochemical industries as well as in the general category of process heat in other industries. By 2000 the commercial sector is already heavily electrified under Case B assumptions so that the potential for further shifts is limited in that market.

(4) Most Probable High Electricity Growth Conditions

It is unlikely that circumstances will so combine as to achieve the maximum growth rates for electricity which are technically and financially possible. However, it is possible to visualize a future with electricity growth rates approximately intermediate between Case B and Case B-ME.

To obtain one measure of the likelihood of such an energy future, a sensitivity analysis was performed using the DRI model. The model's Case B output was used as the control solution. The sensitivity study varied the prices of oil and gas upward and the price of electricity downward from Case B prices.

Several alternate combinations of price adjustments were found which were within reasonable

Table 6·78
CASE B: MAXIMUM COAL AND NUCLEAR ELECTRIC FORECAST; DEMAND AND SUPPLY BY CONSUMING SECTOR (Quadrillion Btu)

1972	Transportation	Residential	Commercial	Industrial	Total	Electrical Generation	Total
Electricity	—	1.9	1.5	2.5	5.9	—	—
Natural Gas	0.8	5.3	2.4	10.7	19.2	4.1	23.3
Oil	17.2	3.3	3.4	5.5	29.4	3.2	32.6
Coal	—	—	0.4	4.5	4.9	7.5	12.4
Other	—	—	—	—	—	3.5	3.5
Sub-Total	18.0	10.5	7.7	23.2	59.4	18.3	71.8
Energy Conversion							
Electric					12.4	-12.4	—
Synthetic Fuels					—	—	—
Total					71.8	5.9	71.8
1985							
Electricity	0.4	3.8	3.1	5.9	13.2	—	—
Natural Gas	—	6.2	3.9	9.5	19.6	2.0	21.6
Oil	23.8	1.3	1.3	9.2	35.6	4.0	39.6
Coal	—	—	2.2	5.4	7.6	17.0	24.6
Other	—	0.2	0.2	1.6	2.0	18.0	20.0
Sub-Total	24.2	11.5	10.7	31.6	78.0	41.0	105.8
Energy Conversion							
Electric					27.8	-27.8	—
Synthetic Fuels					0.8	—	0.8
Total					106.6	13.2	106.6
2000							
Electricity	3.4	8.0	7.6	14.2	33.2	—	—
Natural Gas	—	6.3	6.0	5.9	18.2	1.5	19.7
Oil	27.9	1.4	0.7	10.1	40.1	3.5	43.6
Coal	—	—	—	6.6	6.6	25.0	31.6
Other	—	0.3	0.3	3.4	4.0	68.6	72.6
Sub-Total	32.3	16.0	14.6	40.2	102.1	98.6	167.5
Energy Conversion							
Electric					65.4	-65.4	—
Synthetic Fuels					1.6	—	1.6
Total					169.1	33.2	169.1

bounds and which caused electricity demand to grow until its fraction of total energy consumption reached 53 or 54 percent by the year 2000. This is approximately mid-way between the 46.5 percent of Case B and 58.5 percent of Case B-ME. One set of price adjustments which achieves such growth is shown on Table 6·79 where the adjusted prices are compared with price estimates from Case B.

By the year 2000 these adjustments have raised oil prices 24 percent higher, and gas prices 29 percent higher, than in Case B. Although such shifts seem significant, it must be noted that these differences are accumulated gradually over a period of 25 years. The adjustment in electricity prices is in the opposite direction, so that by the year 2000 the price is about 8 percent below Case B. This suggests a slightly more rapid increase in productivity; specifically at an average annual rate of 1.2 percent per year in contrast to a rate of 0.8 percent per year for Case B.

Tables 6·80 through 6·83 show the energy supply

and demand details from the DRI forecast using these alternate prices. This forecast is designated Case B-HCN (high coal and nuclear). Comparing Case B with Case B-HCN as in Table 6•84, it can be seen that oil and gas consumption growth rates differ markedly between the two cases. In Case B the average growth rate from 1975 to 2000 for the total of oil and gas consumption is about 1.6 percent per year. In Case B-HCN, however, it is only 0.9 percent per year. The change in growth rates of the other energy sources (coal, hydro, nuclear, other) is in the opposite direction of course, averaging 5.8 percent per year in Case B and 6.5 percent per year for Case B-HCN.

As noted previously, the Case B-HCN depicted in Table 6•84 emphasizes nuclear power as the primary energy source used to generate the additional electricity needed over and above the Case B requirements. This results, of course, in an even more rapid growth in nuclear power output than for Case B; i.e., about 13.5 percent per year for Case B-HCN versus 12.1 percent per year for Case B. Only modest changes in the environmental and technological assumptions associated with Case B would be necessary to shift much of the burden of the additional electricity generation to coal rather than to nuclear power. If all of the additional electricity were to be generated from coal rather than nuclear power, the

Table 6•79
COMPARISON OF ENERGY PRICE FORECASTS: DRI

	1975	1985	2000
Oil:			
Case B	7.12	7.71	11.44
Case B-Adjusted	7.12	8.18	14.21
Gas:			
Case B	1.00	1.28	1.92
Case B-Adjusted	1.00	1.37	2.46
Electricity:			
Case B	2.07	1.93	1.70
Case B-Adjusted	2.07	1.85	1.56

Note: All prices are in constant, 1975 dollar terms. Oil prices are dollars per barrel; gas prices are dollars per 1000 cubic feet, and electricity prices are cents per kilowatt-hour.

DRI forecast for total coal consumption in the year 2000 would increase from 1150 million short tons (27 quadrillion Btu) for Case B to 1690 million short tons (40.5 quadrillion Btu) for Case B-HCN.

As discussed earlier, the shift from Case B to Case B-HCN could be the result of either: (a) government policy aimed at maximizing energy independence, or

Table 6•80
CASE B—HCN: UNITED STATES ENERGY INPUT; 1975-2000

	1975	1980	1985	2000
1. United States Energy Input (Quadrillion Btu)				
Coal	13.213	14.955	17.313	27.540
Petroleum	33.797	40.336	44.377	49.425
Natural gas	24.469	27.007	27.814	24.498
Hydro, nuclear, other	5.475	10.303	18.011	61.086
Total	76.955	92.601	107.516	162.548
Total Energy Input per capita (Million Btu)	360	413	456	614
Energy Input: Real GNP Ratio (Thousand Btu per 1958 $)	78.3	76.1	74.3	66.9
2. Energy Input, Growth Rates (Percent per Year)				
Coal	0.45	2.51	2.97	3.14
Petroleum	2.68	3.60	1.93	0.72
Natural gas	2.12	1.99	0.56	-0.84
Hydro, nuclear, other	13.72	13.48	11.82	8.48
Total	2.67	3.77	3.03	2.79
3. Energy Input, Composition (Percent of Total)				
Coal	17.17	16.15	16.10	16.94
Petroleum	43.92	43.56	41.27	30.41
Natural gas	31.80	29.16	25.87	15.07
Hydro, nuclear, other	7.11	11.13	16.75	37.58
Total	100.00	100.00	100.00	100.00

Table 6·81
CASE B—HCN: UNITED STATES ENERGY SUPPLY; 1975-2000

	1975	1980	1985	2000
Coal (Million Short Tons)				
United States Production	656	736	852	1319
Exports	85	89	104	128
United States Consumption	571	647	748	1191
Petroleum (Million Barrels a Day)				
United States Crude Output (Including Gas Liquids) ...	10.40	12.40	15.12	14.25
United States Output of Shale, Synthetic Oil	0	0	0	4.29
Imports	6.62	7.85	7.13	6.11
United States Consumption	16.77	20.02	22.03	24.53
Exports	0.25	0.23	0.22	0.12
Gas (Billion Cubic Feet)				
United States Output of Natural Gas	21587	22707	22718	18335
United States Output of Synthetic Gas	0	0	690	3640
Imports	2210	3444	4145	5150
United States Consumption	23717	26096	27509	27107
Exports	80	55	44	18
Total (Quadrillion Btu)				
United States Energy Input	76.955	92.601	107.516	162.548
Exports	2.666	2.669	2.960	3.297
Total Demand	79.621	95.270	110.476	165.845
Imports	16.350	20.308	19.456	18.218
Supplemental (Synthetic Oil, Gas and Shale Oil)	0	0	0.690	12.127
Other United States Production	63.271	74.962	90.330	135.500

Table 6·82
CASE B—HCN: COMPOSITION OF INPUTS TO UNITED STATES ELECTRICITY GENERATION; 1975-2000

	1975	1980	1985	2000
Inputs (Quadrillion Btu)				
Coal	8.661	10.428	12.351	16.844
Petroleum	2.380	2.617	2.913	3.670
Gas	4.326	4.594	5.124	5.229
Hydro, nuclear, other	5.475	10.303	18.011	61.086
Total	20.843	27.941	38.398	86.829
Inputs (Percent of Total)				
Coal	41.6	37.3	32.2	19.4
Petroleum	11.4	9.4	7.6	4.2
Gas	20.8	16.4	13.3	6.0
Hydro, nuclear, other	26.3	36.9	46.9	70.4
Total	100.0	100.0	100.0	100.0

Table 6-83

CASE B (HCN): CONSUMPTION OF ENERGY BY SECTOR OF USE; 1975-2000
(Energy Flows in Trillion Btu)

	Household, Commercial	Industrial	Transpor- tation	Electricity Generation	Synthetic Gas	Total Input
1975						
Coal	199.	4353.	0.	8661.	0.	13213.
Petroleum	6835.	6602.	17980.	2380.	0.	33797.
Natural gas	8234.	10976.	934.	4326.	0.	24469.
Hydro, nuclear	0.	0.	0.	5475.	0.	5475.
Total input	15268.	21930.	18914.	20843.	0.	76955.
Electricity	3969.	2739.	22.	0.	0.	6730.
Synthetic gas	0.	0.	0.	0.	0.	0.
Total use	19238.	24669.	18936.	20843.	0.	76955.
1980						
Coal	198.	4329.	0.	10428.	0.	14955.
Petroleum	8104.	7999.	21616.	2617.	0.	40336.
Natural Gas	8363.	13039.	1012.	4594.	0.	27007.
Hydro, nuclear	0.	0.	0.	10303.	0.	10303.
Total input	16665.	25367.	22628.	27941.	0.	92601.
Electricity	5502.	3490.	32.	0.	0.	9024.
Synthetic gas	0.	0.	0.	0.	0.	0.
Total use	22167.	28857.	22660.	27941.	0.	92601.
1985						
Coal	174.	3674.	0.	12351.	1115.	17313.
Petroleum	8966.	8556.	23852.	2913.	89.	44377.
Natural gas	7623.	14067.	1000.	5124.	0.	27814.
Hydro, nuclear	0.	0.	0.	18011.	0.	18011.
Total input	16762.	26299.	24852.	38398.	1204.	107516.
Electricity	7986.	4379.	37.	0.	0.	12402.
Synthetic gas	310.	379.	0.	0.	0.	690.
Total use	25059.	31058.	24889.	38398.	1204.	107516.
2000						
Coal	182.	5454.	0.	16844.	5059.	27540.
Petroleum	9825.	10593.	24932.	3670.	405.	49425.
Natural gas	4598.	13764.	907.	5229.	0.	24498.
Hydro, nuclear	0.	0.	0.	61086.	0.	61086.
Total input	14604.	29811.	25840.	86829.	5463.	162548.
Electricity	19686.	8310.	54.	0.	0.	28050.
Synthetic gas	1638.	2002.	0.	0.	0.	3640.
Total use	35928.	40124.	25893.	86829.	5463.	162548.

Table 6·84
COMPARISON OF DRI ENERGY SUPPLY FORECASTS: (CASE B vs. CASE B—HCN)

(Quadrillion Btu)	1975 Case B	1975 Case B-HCN	1985 Case B	1985 Case B-HCN	2000 Case B	2000 Case B-HCN
Domestic						
Oil	19.7	19.7	30.7	29.1	35.1	27.9
Natural Gas	22.3	22.3	23.6	23.0	21.3	15.7
Total	42.0	42.0	54.3	52.1	56.4	43.6
Synthetics						
Syncrude	—	—	—	—	8.5	8.5
Synthetic Gas	—	—	0.7	0.7	3.6	3.6
Total	—	—	0.7	0.7	12.1	12.1
Imports						
Oil	14.1	14.1	15.1	15.3	12.4	13.1
Natural Gas	2.2	2.2	4.0	4.2	4.9	5.2
Total	16.3	16.3	19.1	19.5	17.3	18.3
Total Oil and Gas	58.3	58.3	74.1	72.3	85.8	74.0
Other						
Coal	13.2	13.2	17.3	17.3	27.0	27.5
Nuclear	2.3	2.3	11.8	14.2	40.1	53.1
Hydro, Other	3.2	3.2	3.8	3.8	8.0	8.0
Total	18.7	18.7	32.9	35.3	75.1	88.6
Total Energy	77.0	77.0	107.0	107.6	160.9	162.6

(b) lower than expected natural resource endowment. If it were the former, and if production rates of domestic and synthetic oil and gas could be kept at the Case B level, the consequence would be to lower oil and gas import requirements. Table 6·85 summarizes the figures involved, to show that under such circumstances, imports could be reduced to about 5.5 quadrillion Btu by the year 2000; i.e., less than 3.5 percent of total energy consumption.

Table 6·85
POTENTIAL EFFECT OF HIGH ELECTRICITY GROWTH RATES ON ENERGY IMPORTS (Quadrillion Btu)

	1975	1985	2000
Oil and Gas: Domestic and Synthetic	42.0	55.0	68.5
Coal, Nuclear, Hydro, Other	18.7	35.3	88.6
Required Imports	16.3	17.3	5.5
Total Energy	77.0	107.6	162.6

However, the picture may be greatly different if limited domestic resources of oil and gas are the primary pressures accelerating the shift toward a high coal and nuclear electric economy. Some geologists, e.g., M. King Hubbert of the United States Geological Service, are convinced the United States is nearing depletion of these resources, that only moderate production increases are possible and that such increases over the near term will only serve to advance the date of depletion and worsen the energy problem in the 1990's and beyond.[20] Table 6·86 presents some relative figures on domestic oil and gas producibility derived from Hubbert's work. Those figures are then used in conjunction with the Case B-HCN estimates of coal, nuclear, hydro, and synthetic fuels to determine the amount of imports necessary under a "low domestic resources" condition.

Under these circumstances, imported fuels would almost double between 1975 and 1985 and then remain approximately level over the next 15 years. In 1985 imports would constitute about ⅓ of total energy supplies, in contrast to about ⅕ now. By 2000 the imported fraction would have returned only to about ⅕. Additional use of coal resources would certainly be in order under these conditions and environmental restrictions assumed under Case B would probably have to be altered to permit the mining and burning of more coal.

It seems apparent from these two rather extreme versions of Case B-HCN, that there are major national advantages associated with as rapid as possible a shift toward a high coal and nuclear posture: (a) it would provide a safeguard against the possibility that resource limits or public policy constraints may prevent domestic oil and gas from reaching the Case B estimates, and (b) if the Case B oil and gas production rates prove to be achievable, they can be combined with high electricity growth so as to virtually eliminate energy imports.

Additional details of the Case B-HCN electric energy supply situation are given in Chapter 10, Financing.

F. Case B: After the year 2000

No attempt was made to employ computer modeling techniques for examining the period after the year 2000. However, it was possible to evaluate the

Table 6.86

DOMESTIC PRODUCTION OF OIL AND GAS; 1975-2000
(Percent of 1975 Production)

Year	Oil	Natural Gas	Total
1975	1.00	1.00	1.00
1980	1.17	.96	1.05
1985	1.19	.79	.96
2000	1.08	.35	.67

POTENTIAL EFFECT OF LOW DOMESTIC OIL AND GAS RESOURCES ON ENERGY IMPORTS
(Quadrillion Btu)

	1975	1985	2000
Oil and Gas:			
Domestic	42.0	40.3	28.1
Synthetic	—	0.7	12.1
Coal, Nuclear, Hydro, Other ..	18.7	35.3	88.6
Imports	16.3	31.3	33.8
Total Energy	77.0	107.6	162.6

population assumptions of Case B after the turn of the century and to speculate upon the effects that this gradually stabilizing population might have upon economic growth, minerals usage, and energy consumption.

As the population growth rate slows during the years between the turn of the century and 2040, it is assumed that longevity will increase slowly, labor force participation will rise slightly, average hours worked per week will decline gradually, and the retirement age will halt its decline and then begin to rise slowly. The combined effects of these trends will reduce the labor input contribution to growth by a substantial amount.

Under such conditions, the contributions of capital to economic growth might also be expected to decrease in the period after 2000. It is possible that the trend in capital quantity will move approximately in harmony with the trend in labor quantity. However, it seems likely that the decline in the capital quantity factor will be less rapid and less severe than the decline in the labor quantity factor under the Case B environment. Such differential movements in the two factors could be anticipated if society attempted to postpone or minimize the slow-down in economic growth which would otherwise result as the population begins to stabilize. The result of these differential movements would be to accelerate the increase in capital equipment available per worker. This could be supported by the higher savings rate to be expected from an increasingly old and more affluent population.

The quality improvement factors for labor and capital, which also contribute to economic growth, may be expected to continue at close to historic rates, while the pace of total factor productivity improvement might well begin to slacken. The result of all these changes would be to reduce the potential for economic growth significantly in the years after 2000. It must be emphasized that the foregoing are no more than speculation which are of interest primarily as illustrations of the directions in which long term growth rates could go.

Under such conditions, it might be expected that the Case B rates growth in the mid 21st century would be similar to the Case C contributions for the period from 1975 to 2000. This suggests that a major difference between Case B and Case C is the very important matter of timing. The Case B speculations after 2000 show the possibility of a slow and voluntary approach to a lower growth society over a period of several generations, in contrast to the rapid and forced approach described by Case C.

It is interesting to examine the prospects for consumption of mineral and fuel resources over the very long term under this type of post-2000 Case B environment. Again, the attempts to specify consumption rates after 2000 must be designated as informed speculations rather than forecasts. However, it is reasonable to establish the following basis for speculation: (a) both energy consumption and minerals consumption on a per-capita basis will continue to rise, but at a gradually decreasing pace, stabilizing at about two or three times the current rates within a generation after the population stabilizes, and (b) recycling of metals will increase steadily so that the part of current consumption derived from recycled material will rise from about one-third at present to about two-thirds and stabilize thereafter.

The consequences of such speculations for energy and metals consumption were estimated in terms of annual and cumulative consumption, and primary demand to the year 2100. The resulting figures were then compared with domestic recoverable resource estimates to determine the number of years supply remaining *after* 2100. It was found that approximately 2000 additional years of supplies were available for both energy and minerals. It should be emphasized that the resource estimates are for domestic sources only and, thus, do not include any use of imported fuels or minerals.

In addition, the mineral resource figures do not consider any contributions from deep sea mining or from a technology which could extract metals from the "average rock" in the Earth's crust. Similarly, the energy resource estimates do not consider breeder reactor technology, fusion energy, or large amounts of solar energy. If such energy and mineral supplies were to become available, the periods to resource exhaustion would be much longer—on the order of one-half to one million years.

Of course, the results of these calculations are much different from results which have been obtained by others who have assumed that: (a) exponential growth of consumption will continue indefinitely, and (b) growth can be satisfied only until presently known reserves are exhausted.

The primary purpose of such speculations as described above for Case B after the year 2000 is not to estimate a period to resource exhaustion, but rather to support a conclusion that, if *reasonable* projections of the future are made, it may be concluded that the nation has available a *very* long time in which humans can employ technology and social systems to adapt gradually to a changing environment.

FOOTNOTES

1. There has been no attempt in this report to attach subtle differences in meaning to words which are approximate synonyms for forecast. For example, the word 'projection' is sometimes used to refer to a mechanical extrapolation of a past trend.
2. Ex-post tests check accuracy in duplicating the past, i.e., that period whose events guided the construction of the model. Ex-ante tests check accuracy in predicting events which occurred after the model was constructed.
3. Total fertility rate refers to the total number of children per average woman over her entire child-bearing years.
4. Recessions and other short-term fluctuations in investment incentives and productivity do not necessarily signal any changes in secular trends.
5. The word "demand" is used here, and elsewhere throughout the report, in the economic sense rather than in accord with electic utility parlance. The reader's attention will be directed specifically to each occasion where the latter definition is intended.
6. Census Bureau Population Report Series P-25, Number 470.
7. Important among these structural rigidities is an excess of unskilled labor in a job market that is increasingly skill-oriented. This and other rigidities are capable of solution. The Philips Curve thesis associates low unemployment rates with a high rate of inflation. It has been largely discredited except as a temporary phenomenon. That is, an increase in the inflation rate may decrease unemployment *temporarily*, but in the long term, structural characteristics of the society will set the "normal" unemployment rate with but little relationship to the inflation rate.
8. EEI Staff forecast based on National Planning Association data; e.g., Report No. 73-R-1, *Regional Economic Projections: 1960-1985,* and other studies.
9. Chapter 5. "Where We Stand Now," notes that non-cash transfers are approximately equal to 50 percent of money income for the groups below the $5,000 per year level.
10. See Chapter 7 for a description of the Case Western Reserve University World Model.
11. The American Heart Association has recommended a one-third cut in meat consumption: *New York Times,* November 7, 1974.

12. "A Little More Time," *The Economist,* June 29, 1974.

13. National Petroleum Council, *United States Energy Outlook, Energy Demand, 1972,* and related documents. Also, Department of the Interior, *United States Energy Through the Year 2000,* 1972.

14. The National Academy of Engineering, *United States Energy Prospects, An Engineering Viewpoint,* 1974.

15. Henry Steele, unpublished work done for the Ford Foundation Energy Policy Project. Contact Resources for the Future regarding availability.

16. *Ford Foundation Energy Policy Project, A Time to Choose,* and related publications, many by Ballinger & Co., 1974-1975.

17. See Appendix E and the section on Productivity in Chapter 5 "Where We Stand Now," for a discussion of these items.

18. "Poverty Level is $5,050." *Philadelphia Inquirer,* May 7, 1975. A Labor Department announcement set $5,050 as the annual income below which an urban family of four should be considered "low income." The Labor Department definition sets higher levels for larger families and lower levels for: rural families, smaller families and individuals. Thus, the $6,000 cut-off used here encompasses not only most of the low income families, but also some moderate income rural and smaller urban families as well as moderate income individuals. Also, see United States Department of Labor Release 75-190, "August 1974 Urban Family Budgets," April 9, 1975. This document determines $14,300 to be an "intermediate budget" for an urban family of four headed by a "typical wage earner and clerical worker." Updating the $14,300 to account for inflation to mid 1975 would certainly increase the intermediate budget to $15,000 or slightly more.

19. Very little theoretical work seems to have been done in this area. An exception is Oskar Morgenstern's article, "The Compressibility of Economic Systems and the Problem of Economic Constraints," *Zeitschrift fur Nationalokonomie, Vienna,* 1966.

20. M. King Hubbert, "Energy Resources," in *Resources and Man,* National Academy of Sciences, National Research Council, Committee on Resources and Man, Washington, D.C., 1969, and many other references.

CHAPTER 7

World Economic Growth

A. Introduction

This chapter is an analysis of future *global* economic growth in terms of: a) population, b) agriculture and food supplies, c) resources—energy and non-energy, d) general economic growth in regard to the gap between developed and developing countries and the prospects for aid, and e) pollution and the quality of life.

Substantial amounts of this analysis are based on work done at Case Western Reserve University (CWR) using a Multi Level World Model. For some material, other sources such as the United Nations have been used. Unless otherwise noted, however, this chapter is based on the CWR work.

B. Summary of Overall Conclusions

The prospects for world economic growth have been analyzed in terms of several determining factors. The analysis has been highly aggregative and only the barest outlines of the problems have been treated. Despite these limitations, it is important to attempt a synthesis of the individual findings into some overall conclusions. More detailed discussions of the findings are presented at the beginning of each major section, e.g., Population. In summary form, the conclusions are as follows:

1. Undifferentiated exponential growth will not be physically supportable in the future; nor, in fact, has it been truly characteristic of the past.

2. Stopping economic growth will not resolve the problems. In large parts of the world, survival demands rising material standards of living. A redistribution of existing wealth would not be adequate.

3. The most serious threat to continued orderly economic growth is the increase in population. Unless vigorous efforts are made to check population growth, none of the other growth-related problems will be solved.

4. If the world population increase is brought under control, progress in agricultural technology and other measures can assure adequate food supply. This will probably not be achieved, however, without massive investments in the agricultural sectors of the poor economies.

5. In the short run, the world faces a serious energy problem. The situation is particularly difficult for developing countries. Oil and natural gas alone are not adequate sources of energy for the long run. There is a relative abundance of coal but its use requires some recognition that there must be trade-offs with environmental considerations. In addition, like oil and gas, the geographical distribution of coal is uneven. Nuclear energy can solve the problem as breeder reactor technology is perfected, and if there is reasonable concurrence that the safety and environmental problems have, in fact, been resolved satisfactorily.

   Among the other possible sources of energy, geothermal power has limited potential, barring technological breakthroughs. Fusion research and solar power research are still in their infancy, and these sources are not likely to make significant contributions in the remainder of this century. The initial applications of solar power are likely to be for space and process heating. Most of the other energy source technologies, including solar power for electricity, are likely to be complex and expensive, and thus may be beyond the reach of the developing countries. This is an area where international collaboration will be necessary.

   Considerable potential exists for increased efficiency in energy use. This is especially true of the industrialized countries of the Northern Hemisphere. Such efforts may require some changes in consumption habits. Over the long run, rising prices will have a significant influence on patterns of energy use. In some instances government leadership may also be needed to assure that changes are brought about in a timely fashion.

6. Non-energy resources present some problems,

but not of the same magnitude as with energy. Some materials are in short supply, but the situation with regard to the major metals and minerals is relatively comfortable. Technological innovations in this area are capital and energy intensive, and at some point diminishing returns to further capital inputs may be experienced. Recycling has great potential but its use can best be promoted through market forces.

7. The quality of the environment and other non-economic considerations present difficult problems for analysis. Almost all productive and consumptive activities, and thus the mere act of existing, have some adverse impacts on the environment. Research will find ways to minimize environmental impact but technology alone cannot be counted on to eliminate the problem. It must be recognized that serious trade-offs cannot be avoided between material goods, services and many other aspects of the public interest on one hand, and the quality of life and the environment on the other hand. Internalizing the effects of economic activity through taxes or subsidies, thus letting the market forces reflect the structure of priorities, may be the best approach to this problem for the developed economies. The choices are particularly difficult for developing countries.

C. World Models

Before turning to the analysis it is important to summarize the major features of the Case Western Reserve University model. The CWR model is a comprehensive model of the world system designed to capture all the essential relationships in the world economy.[1] Its purpose is to carry out large-scale computer simulations of the behavior of the world system under alternative assumptions.

The first such comprehensive world model was constructed by J. W. Forrester at M.I.T., and was used in *The Limits to Growth* project.[2] The M.I.T. World Model had several shortcomings which were broadly critiqued after *The Limits To Growth* was published. The CWR World Model attempts to avoid some of these weaknesses in the following ways. First, the M.I.T. model attempted to simulate the entire world economy as a monolithic entity. It neglected regional peculiarities that are important because of differences in natural endowments, population pressures, socio-economic institutions and levels of economic achievement. The CWR World Model divides the world into ten regions with approximately similar economic and political environments.

The M.I.T. model is a self-contained forecasting system. The CWR model allows much more interaction between the analyst and the computer, which facilitates experimentation with different sets of assumptions. The CWR model also has a hierarchical structure incorporating various levels of decision making. In contrast to the M.I.T. model which uses a systems dynamics methodology, the CWR model employs a combination of econometric techniques and control theory.

The CWR approach can be summarized as follows. The world system is assumed to be composed of several essential elements, such as population, production and investment, natural resources, agriculture, and environment. The behavior of each of these is simulated as a subsystem with specified linkages with the other subsystems. Relationships among the subsystems are developed based on a combination of historical analysis, and assumptions about the future. These relationships are fed into the computer in the form of mathematical equations. Historic factual data is also fed in to provide the starting values for the model variables. The output of the computer represents the details of alternative futures of economic growth. The purpose of this form of analysis is not to forecast the future but to provide plausible scenarios; i.e., "if... then..." statements, about what might be expected to happen if different courses of action were followed. With this technique the outputs should be looked upon as approximate estimates rather than precise predictions.

It must be emphasized that, although the CWR model represents a major improvement over earlier world models, it still remains only a blurred reflection of reality. The limitations of modeling must be kept continually in mind throughout the following discussion. A somewhat more detailed evaluation of the various forecasting tools used in this study is presented as Appendix A.

D. Population

1. Summary of Findings

This section examines world population growth. The major themes are: the implications of a continuation of past growth rates, the effects of various birth control policies, and the current status of family planning programs around the world.

The conclusions of this analysis can be summarized as follows:

1. At current growth rates and with no major changes in the level of population control

effort, the world population will nearly double by the end of this century and will multiply nearly 20 times by the end of the next century. It is unlikely that such a large population can be adequately provided for, and with such growth, starvation deaths on a large scale in the underdeveloped regions would be a real prospect.

2. Vigorous population control efforts can reduce the burden considerably. Even a delayed and modest effort will yield significant results.

3. The population control programs in various countries have met with varied success. The results have been significant in countries where economic growth also has been relatively more rapid. The attitudes expressed by the developing countries at the 1974 World Population Conference in Bucharest, indicate that they are not enthusiastic about implementing large scale fertility control programs. The question whether economic and social change is a precondition for successful fertility control is unresolved.

2. Analysis

The world population in 1971 was about 3.7 billion and the world growth rate was 1.9 percent per year. The regional distribution of population and growth rates were extremely uneven. (See Table 7.1)

The underdeveloped areas of the world had more than 2½ times as many people as the developed areas. The growth rates showed approximately the same relationship. The U. N. population division has prepared population forecasts for the year 2000. The world population is expected to be around 6.5

Table 7.1
ANNUAL RATES OF POPULATION GROWTH: 1965—1971

Developed Areas		Rest of World	
North America	1.2%	Latin America	2.9%
Japan	1.1	South Asia	2.8
USSR	1.0	Africa	2.6
Europe	0.8	Oceania	2.0
Total	1.0	East Asia	1.8
		Total	2.5

POPULATION PROJECTIONS: 1971—2000

	1971	2000	Amount of increase
Developed Areas		(millions)	
North America	230	333	103
Japan	105	134	29
USSR	245	330	85
Europe	466	568	102
Total	1,046	1,365	319
Rest of World			
Latin America	291	652	361
South Asia	1,158	2,354	1,196
Africa	354	818	464
Oceania	20	35	15
East Asia	841	1,290	449
Total	2,664	5,149	2,485
Total World	3,710	6,514	2,804

Source: United Nations Statistical Supplement: 1972, pp 8, 10.

Chart 7•1
FERTILITY AROUND THE WORLD

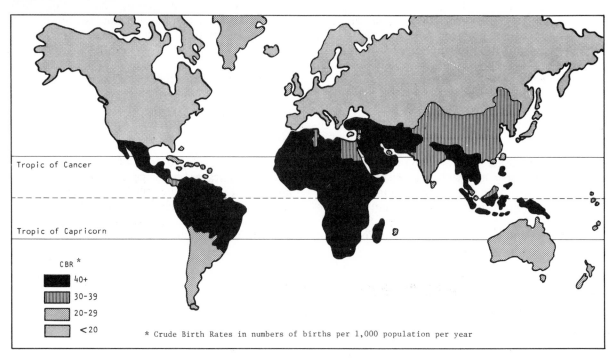

Source: B. Berelson "World population: Status Report 1974", The Population Council Inc. New York, 1974.

billion in 2000. Nearly ⅘ of the people will be in what are today underdeveloped areas.

There is ample evidence that differences in death rates between developed and underdeveloped countries are narrowing, but the same cannot be said about fertility. Chart 7•1 gives a summary picture of fertility around the world.

Along with large populations, the developing countries have a greater proportion of dependent youth. High fertility rates result in a larger per-

Table 7•2
WORLD POPULATION IN 2000, 2050, 2100: Regional Breakdown— (Millions)

Year	N.A.	W.E.	Ja.	R.D.	EU & SU	L.A.	M.E.	M.A.	S.E.A.	Ch.	TOTAL
2000	298.28	469.63	127.31	86.52	417.10	716.74	280.56	488.54	2,494.50	1,306.81	6,685.99
2050	415.08	591.62	129.14	326.57	383.01	3,506.59	890.44	1,500.88	9,366.35	2,705.49	19,815.17
2100	552.85	734.32	127.62	1,239.73	332.02	17,216.83	2,805.57	4,617.85	35,244.77	5,555.05	68,426.60

SOURCE: CWR project, population model (Run 8, normal)

The regions in tables 7•2-7•4 are as follows:

Region 1. N.A.:	North America	Region 6. L.A.:	Latin America
Region 2. W.E.:	Western Europe	Region 7. M.E.:	North Africa and Middle East
Region 3. Ja.:	Japan	Region 8. M.A.:	Main Africa
Region 4. R.D.:	Rest of Developed	Region 9. S.E.A.:	South and Southeast Asia
Region 5. E.U.&S.U.:	Eastern Europe & Soviet Union	Region 10. Ch.:	China

Note: A list of countries in each region is provided in Appendix C, which describes the CWR world model.

centage of the population being in the below-19 age group. Chart 7•2 contrasts the age structures of Mexico and Sweden to illustrate this point. One consequence of such a "bottom heavy" age distribution is that even after instituting an effective birth control policy it will take a long time for these countries to achieve stable populations.

In the CWR World Model, total population is divided into 86 one-year age groups, and age-specific fertilities and mortalities have been estimated from the data for the years 1950-70. Starting from given population and age structures in any year, the model is capable of generating population patterns over time, given various assumptions about fertility and mortality rates. The "standard runs" of the model assume that fertility and mortality will remain constant at the 1970 level, as will the age-specific probability distributions. Under these assumptions the regional distribution of population in the years 2000, 2050 and 2100 are shown in Table 7•2.

In the developing countries nearly exponential growth in population is indicated (i.e., a constant percentage increase in population), while in the developed regions (North America, Western Europe, Japan and Eastern Europe including the Soviet

Union) the pattern is well below the exponential growth curve as evidenced by gradually decreasing growth rates. Table 7•3 shows these differences in growth patterns, as well as crude birth and death rates for selected years up to 2030 for the same regions. These figures show a relentless pressure on the countries which can afford it the least. For example, the percentage of world population in the developed countries of the world (regions 1 through 5) drops from about 30 percent in 1970 to 21 percent in 2000, to less than 10 percent in 2050 and to only about 4 percent in 2100. The drop would be even more rapid were it not for the assumption of continued very high growth rates in region 4.

Obviously these patterns cannot continue as far into the future as is suggested by Tables 7•2 and 7•3. Either natural or man-made checks (e.g., in the form of effective birth control) or both will start working before we reach a "standing room only" condition. If these patterns were to continue, mass starvation or serious protein deficiency would cause millions of deaths in the poor regions of the world. The population submodel of the CWR project has been used in attempts to investigate these possibilities. With respect to population control policies it was

Chart 7•2

COMPARATIVE AGE STRUCTURES IN A DEVELOPED AND A DEVELOPING COUNTRY

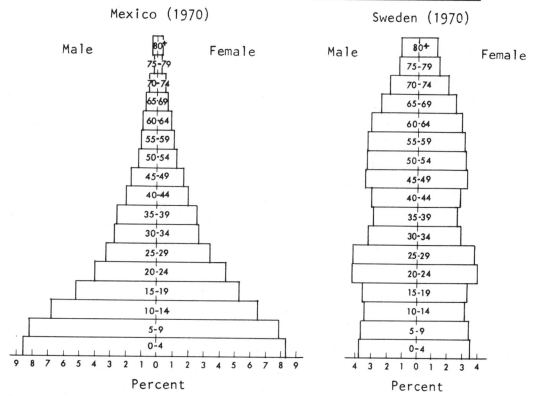

Source: B. Berelson "World population: Status Report 1974", The Population Council Inc. New York, 1974.

Table 7·3

CRUDE BIRTH RATE, CRUDE DEATH RATE & NET GROWTH RATE FOR SELECTED YEARS (Percent)

YEAR	N.A. CBR	N.A. CDR	N.A. NGR	W.E. CBR	W.E. CDR	W.E. NGR	Ja. CBR	Ja. CDR	Ja. NGR	R.D. CBR	R.D. CDR	R.D. NGR	E.U. & S.U. CBR	E.U. & S.U. CDR	E.U. & S.U. NGR
1980	2.06	0.98	1.08	1.78	1.14	0.64	1.66	0.82	0.84	3.28	0.85	2.43	1.77	0.96	0.81
1990	1.84	1.01	0.83	1.76	1.17	0.59	1.38	0.96	0.42	3.13	0.80	2.33	1.51	1.07	0.44
2000	1.81	1.03	0.78	1.70	1.17	0.53	1.53	1.11	0.42	3.34	0.76	2.58	1.43	1.21	0.22
2010	1.82	1.03	0.79	1.71	1.21	0.50	1.37	1.29	0.08	3.32	0.69	2.63	1.41	1.39	0.02
2020	1.74	1.07	0.67	1.70	1.23	0.47	1.35	1.42	-0.07	3.32	0.66	2.66	1.35	1.57	-0.22
2030	1.77	1.15	0.62	1.69	1.26	0.43	1.46	1.45	0.01	3.35	0.67	2.68	1.37	1.67	-0.30

YEAR	L.A. CBR	L.A. CDR	L.A. NGR	M.E. CBR	M.E. CDR	M.E. NGR	M.A. CBR	M.A. CDR	M.A. NGR	S.E.A. CBR	S.E.A. CDR	S.E.A. NGR	Ch. CBR	Ch. CDR	Ch. NGR
1980	4.06	1.01	3.05	3.90	1.39	2.51	4.16	2.00	2.16	4.17	1.61	2.56	3.24	1.51	1.73
1990	4.10	1.00	3.10	3.75	1.37	2.38	4.22	2.01	2.21	4.18	1.61	2.57	3.09	1.52	1.57
2000	4.13	0.99	3.14	3.72	1.37	2.35	4.23	2.00	2.23	4.23	1.60	2.63	3.10	1.57	1.53
2010	4.14	0.97	3.17	3.75	1.40	2.35	4.23	1.99	2.24	4.22	1.58	2.64	3.10	1.62	1.48
2020	4.14	0.96	3.18	3.71	1.42	2.29	4.24	1.99	2.25	4.22	1.58	2.64	3.06	1.63	1.43
2030	4.14	0.96	3.18	3.71	1.42	2.29	4.23	1.99	2.24	4.23	1.58	2.65	3.07	1.64	1.43

Note: The Regions are the same as in Table 7·2   CDR = crude death rate
        CBR = crude birth rate   NGR = net growth rate

SOURCE: CWR project, population model (Run 6, normal)

assumed there would be no change in mortality after 1970, and population policies would be directed at achieving equilibrium fertility (i.e., zero net growth). Each policy has two critical features—the time at which it is instituted and the amount of time it takes to achieve equilibrium fertility. By choosing different values of these features, a variety of futures can be simulated. Some of these are summarized in Table 7·4 which shows the tremendous changes that can be achieved by a vigorous population control policy. If such a policy is instituted world wide in 1975, and the transition period is only 14 years—certainly an unrealistic hope—the world population in 2100 would be less than one-tenth of what it could theoretically be without any checks (see Table 7·2). The reductions in population are especially impressive in South East Asia, China and Main Africa where figures for the year 2100 would be 2.2 billion, 1.26 billion and 428 million instead of 35.24 billion, 5.55 billion and 4.61 billion. Even if the start of control is delayed as much as 20 years (i.e., 1995) and transition time is 35 years, the world population would be 11.82 billion in 2100 as against a theoretical 68.4 billion without any policy and without any natural checks. Again the changes are most impressive in the

poorest and most heavily populated areas of the world today. It is interesting to note that policies aimed at achieving a worldwide equilibrium population in the long run, result in larger populations than current trends would suggest for Japan and Eastern Europe including the Soviet Union since population in these regions is expected to decline in the absence of any policy.

What if the population continues to grow at the current rates? It is almost certain that food shortages—especially protein deficiency—will cause mass deaths in at least the poorer areas of the earth. Such a possibility was investigated by the CWR team, for South East Asia, assuming no large increase in food imports. From the food submodel, figures were available for the probable growth of protein yield. Certain mathematical functions were postulated relating age-specific sensitivity to protein deficiency, daily protein consumption and consequent changes in mortality.

The results are frightening. In one of the studies, (the various studies assume different values for the parameters in the mathematical relationships), South

East Asia's population in 2100 is estimated to be nearly 6 billion even though nearly 18 billion deaths have previously occurred between 1970 and 2100 due to lack of protein. The crude death rate climbs to an annual rate of 4.59 percent as compared to current values of about 1 percent in the United States and 1.6 percent in South East Asia. Other studies give similar orders of magnitude of deaths due to malnutrition. The combined effects of varying degrees of population control and malnutrition also were simulated for the same region. Depending upon the control and transition parameters and the other parameters mentioned above, the population for South East Asia in the year 2100 varies from about 1.4 to 3.75 billion, and the total number of deaths over the period from now to 2100 varies from about 4.5 to 7 billion.

It is impossible to "predict" what will actually happen. The U.N. projection prepared in 1963 does not differ much from the one prepared in 1972 (summarized in Table 7•1) as regards world population in the year 2000. Both place it around 6 billion, suggesting that (in the U.N. view) little had been accomplished between 1963 and 1972 to alter world population prospects for the year 2000. Some unpublished data from the Population Council suggest a population of nearly 7 billion in the year 2000 if current family size is extended into the future.[3] Some experts agree that this is a reasonable projection.[4]

The message is clear—if the world (and particularly the underdeveloped part of the world) does not take vigorous positive actions to curtail rapid population growth and thus reduce the demands on the earth's carrying capacity, nature will trigger its own mechanisms to achieve the same ends, but with immeasurably more disastrous consequences.

Table 7•4
WORLD POPULATION UNDER VARIOUS POPULATION POLICIES— (Millions)

CONTROL: 1975, Transition: 14[(1)]

YEAR	N.A.[(2)]	W.E.	Ja.	R.D.	EU & SU	L.A.	M.E.	M.A.	S.E.A.	Ch.	TOTAL
2000	285.32	453.91	127.55	66.79	426.02	496.97	214.79	372.16	1,828.68	1,116.73	5,388.95
2050	319.57	483.83	130.65	85.75	437.08	637.90	256.27	429.22	2,219.18	1,267.14	6,266.58
2100	319.77	483.77	130.82	85.64	437.03	635.94	255.71	428.90	2,217.8	1,264.18	6,259.56

CONTROL: 1975, Transition: 35

YEAR	N.A.	W.E.	Ja.	R.D.	EU & SU	L.A.	M.E.	M.A.	S.E.A.	Ch.	TOTAL
2000	292.05	462.03	127.43	76.53	421.34	603.57	247.20	428.83	2,151.26	1,211.27	6,021.51
2050	338.53	505.69	130.32	113.96	424.56	906.24	329.76	548.55	2,970.56	1,474.99	7,743.16
2100	340.03	506.61	130.47	115.56	424.21	915.85	330.84	551.16	2,990.13	1,479.33	7,784.20

CONTROL 1985, Transition: 14

YEAR	N.A.	W.E.	Ja.	R.D.	EU & SU	L.A.	M.E.	M.A.	S.E.A.	Ch.	TOTAL
2000	292.39	462.35	127.43	76.47	421.05	600.54	246.81	427.65	2,141.47	1,211.13	6,007.80
2050	338.05	505.16	130.33	111.23	424.64	874.22	322.86	536.63	2,890.51	1,461.10	7,594.72
2100	338.91	505.27	130.49	111.67	424.63	874.17	321.93	536.87	2,885.98	1,458.13	7,588.05

CONTROL: 1995, Transition: 35

YEAR	N.A.	W.E.	Ja.	R.D.	EU & SU	L.A.	M.E.	M.A.	S.E.A.	Ch.	TOTAL
2000	298.07	469.37	127.32	86.13	417.24	712.11	279.23	486.09	2,480.20	1,303.06	6,658.82
2050	371.71	543.38	129.76	178.46	404.75	1580.87	498.18	825.98	4,768.39	1,907.40	11,208.69
2100	381.21	552.32	129.79	196.99	400.70	1729.54	523.27	863.89	5,079.23	1,972.34	11,829.28

Notes:

(1) "CONTROL" specifies year of start of population control policy.
"TRANSITION" specifies the number of years required to achieve equilibrium fertility.

(2) The Regions are same as in Table 7•2   SOURCE: CWR Population Model Run 7

The CWR model considers only two influences on birth and death rates and hence on population: birth control policies and the availability of nutrition. Other influences could conceivably become important. Rising per capita incomes have generally been accompanied by reduced birth rates, even in the absence of any deliberate policies. Increasing longevity can significantly raise population levels, other things being equal. On the other hand, it is possible that high levels of pollution which might result from poorly planned worldwide industrialization could tend to increase the death rates in spite of adequate nutrient supplies.

A decreasing birth rate with rising per capita incomes has been historically observed in what are today the developed countries. But a positive or negative correlation establishes no causal relationship. It is more or less universally accepted that rising per capita incomes go hand in hand with better education, increased urbanization, increased participation by women in the labor force, better social legislation for the care of the aged, and so on. It is quite plausible that these factors automatically act to reduce the birth rate and average family size. Unfortunately, for much of the underdeveloped world, efforts at stimulating economic growth have barely been adequate to compensate for the increasing population and consequently per capita economic growth has been very slow. At the same time, progress in medical science and mass manufacture and distribution of effective drugs continue to reduce the mortality rates and raise population. On balance, economic development may have a gradual restraining effect on the population growth rate, as seems to have occurred generally throughout the developed world. However, social, psychological and cultural factors may affect the relationship between population growth and economic development. Therefore, it is not clear that the experience of the developed countries in this regard can be used to predict events in the underdeveloped world. At present it seems doubtful that economic development alone will be enough and in time.

The current status of population policies in various countries is not greatly encouraging.[5] In most of the developed countries the policies are not "population policies" in an explicit sense. Most often they are part of more general social policies. In fact, some advanced countries (e.g., France, Japan, Romania) have, at times, regarded their problem as too little population growth. In only about one third of even the most advanced countries is modern fertility control widely available and practiced.

In the developing countries the situation is very different. Only in recent years have most of them established explicit population policies and programs

in the form of family planning programs. The programs have met with varied success. Table 7·5 shows the spread of family planning in various countries. Table 7·6 summarizes a range of developments relating to acceptance of family planning.

E. Agriculture and Food Supplies

1. Summary of Findings

This section investigates food availability as a potential constraint on world economic growth. The discussion will be oriented towards answering questions related to land use and the possibilities of expanding food supplies both by cultivating more land and by increasing productivity through modern-

Table 7·5
SPREAD OF FAMILY PLANNING

Country & Year	Contraceptive Users* as a Percentage of Married Women Aged 15-44	
	Public Programs	Private Sources
Fiji 1973	28.9	4.4
South Korea 1972	28.0	4.0
Taiwan 1973	27.0	30.0
Hong Kong 1973	25.2	27.1
Thailand 1973	17.7	8.0
West Malaysia 1972	16.8	4.3
Mauritius 1972	16.8	4.3
Egypt 1973	15.8	4.8
India 1972	13.6	u**
Philippines 1973	11.0	u
Iran 1972	9.0	u
Tunisia 1973	6.4	u
Indonesia 1972	3.3	u
Guatemala 1973	2.7	1.0
Turkey 1973	2.0	25.0
Nepal 1971	2.5	u
Kenya 1971	2.2	u
Morocco 1973	2.1	3.5
Mexico 1973	1.0	12.2

* "Users" are couples using some means of contraception or terminating latest pregnancy with induced abortion.

** Unavailable

Source: Berelson, B., "World Population: Status Report 1974". The Population Council.

ization of the agricultural practices in the under-developed countries. The technical and financial problems that are likely to be encountered in such modernization programs are discussed. The focus of the analysis is on the underdeveloped regions of the world where the adequacy of food to feed expanding populations is going to be the most acute problem, at least over the next few decades.

The conclusions that emerge from the analysis can be summarized as follows:

1. One of the most definite potential constraints on growth is food supply. The effect of food shortages is direct and absolute. In large areas of the world today, producing food occupies almost all the working time of large fractions of the population.

2. There is hope for expanding the area under cultivation and for multiple cropping, except for the regions of South East Asia, China, and Western Europe.

3. The major limitation on increasing food supplies in this manner is availability of water. The uneven distribution of river run-off gives rise to technical problems in expanding irrigation. Even where the technical problems are not too difficult, the capital requirements will be considerable.

4. In addition to land and water, advanced cultivation practices require enormous inputs of fertilizers and pesticides which translate into substantial outlays on the part of the under-developed countries either to import them or to create the capacity to manufacture them.

5. As an illustration of the magnitude of the financial burden, it has been estimated that, provided South East Asia succeeds in controlling its population, annual investment aid of the order of $7 billion from advanced nations would be needed to help that region gradually achieve self-sufficiency over a period of 50 years, while maintaining a balanced economic structure.

2. Analysis

Most of the underdeveloped economies are agricultural economies. Table 7·7 shows the percentage of the labor force employed in agriculture and related activities in several countries.

How many people can be fed adequately if all the potential sources of food are exploited? It has been estimated that enough food can be grown to provide a minimum diet for 104 billion people.[6] On the other hand, incipient famines have been predicted time

Table 7·6
GROWTH OF ACCEPTANCE OF FAMILY PLANNING

	Countries
Sustained performance at 8-12 percent of MWRA* per year	Singapore, South Korea, Taiwan
or at 6-8 percent year	Hong Kong, Mauritius
An upward trend since 1968 to a 1972 level of 8-12 percent	Costa Rica, Iran, Philippines, Thailand
or 4-7 percent	Colombia, Honduras, Indonesia, Mexico, Nicaragua, Venezuela
Stable or erratic performance at 3-5 percent	Bangla Desh, Chile, Dominican Republic, Egypt, India, Jamaica, Pakistan, SriLanka, Tunisia, West Malaysia
Stable performance at a low level (0-2 percent)	Ecuador, Ghana, Kenya, Morocco, Nepal, Nigeria, Turkey

* MWRA means "Married Women of Reproductive Age." The figures thus indicate growth rates of acceptance of some family planning practice in this group.

Source: Same as Table 7·5

and again starting with Malthus.[7] Large-scale famines have struck in the past and severe, though localized, famines occur even today.

For the world as a whole at this time, about 1.4 billion hectares (a hectare equals 2.47 acres) are cultivated to provide the food, fibers and other agricultural products needed by about 3.5 billion human beings, or 2.5 people per hectare. The distribution of land use is very uneven, and the land available per capita varies widely between countries. Table 7·8 gives a picture of the regional distribution of ultimate maximum arable land and presently cultivated land. In South East Asia and China, almost all of the ultimately arable land is already under cultivation. The utilization in Western Europe is also quite high, but in most other areas there seems to be potential for expanding land usage.

A nearly minimum subsistence diet for human beings is about 2500 kilocalories per person per day.

Table 7•7
PERCENTAGE OF LABOR FORCE EMPLOYED IN AGRICULTURE, FORESTRY AND FISHING IN SELECTED COUNTRIES

Country		Number of People Employed in Agriculture, Forestry, Fishing etc.	Percentage of Economically Active Population
Australia	(1971)	386,407	7.2%
Brazil	(1970)	13,090,358	44.4
Bulgaria	(1965)	1,891,398	44.4
Canada	(1973)	621,000	6.7
Czechoslovakia	(1961)	1,615,999	24.9
Egypt	(1966)	4,446,913	53.3
India	(1971)	129,963,000	72.0
Japan	(1970)	10,163,680	19.1
Niger	(1960)	743,850	96.9
Peru	(1967)	1,772,520	46.9
Philippines	(1970)	6,332,071	51.4
Thailand	(1970)	13,399,000	31.4
United States	(1972)	3,701,000	4.2
West Germany	(1971)	2,203,000	8.2

Source: International Labor Office. Year Book of Labor Statistics 1973.

On this basis, one hectare of land with a level of technology equivalent to that of corn farmers in Iowa can produce the food energy required by 24 human beings. This is essentially ten times the average world productivity of agricultural land. Thus there is considerable potential for expanding food output by increasing both the area under cultivation and the productivity.

In addition, it is possible to increase the total yield by multiple cropping; i.e., raising more than one crop on the same land in a year. Table 7•9 gives some indication of the possibilities opened by multiple cropping. Note that the Table 7•8 figure of 2,425 million hectares of potentially arable land world wide agrees closely with the Table 7•9 figure of 2,427 million hectares which is described as areas outside the humid tropics which have available water.

Of course, land is only one of the inputs in food production. Complementary inputs—other than human labor—require investment in irrigation facilities, agricultural machinery, fertilizer and pesticide manufacturing plants, agricultural research, training and information transmittal to spread the best practices. The capital requirements and technical knowledge needed to develop these complementary inputs in a timely manner will be available to most of the underdeveloped regions of the world only with massive aid from the developed regions.

Table 7•8
REGIONAL DISTRIBUTION OF ARABLE AND CULTIVATED LAND—(Thousands of Hectares) *

	(a) Ultimate Maximum Arable Land	(b) Land in the Cultivation Cycle	(c) (b) as percent of (a)	(d) Land Harvested per Year	(e) (d) as percent of (b)	(f) Average Growth Rate Harvested Land
N. America	392,000	219,844	56.1%	111,499	50.7%	-1.51%
W. Europe	155,000	127,318	82.1	88,707	69.7	0.53
Japan	8,000	5,603	70.0	5,858	104.6	-1.57
Rest of Developed	150,000	57,779	38.5	19,474	33.7	2.82
E. Europe	382,000	279,894	73.3	193,260	69.0	0.98
Latin America	429,000	128,206	29.9	76,587	59.7	2.83
Mideast	86,000	52,606	61.2	28,676	54.5	1.14
Africa	423,000	166,997	39.5	73,080	43.8	1.77
S. & SE Asia	278,000	267,798	96.3	235,156	87.8	1.54
China	122,000	117,774	96.5	100,000	84.9	—
World	2,425,000	1,423,819	58.7	1,000,390	70.3	1.08

*1 hectare = 2.47 acres

Source: CWR Food Model

210

Irrigation is one example. When data on water availability and its regional distribution are examined, it must be concluded that the figures in Table 7·9 under potential gross cropped area are misleadingly high. The magnitude of technical problems has been suggested by Revelle:

"...The potential for irrigation development is thus very large but is limited by the uneven distribution of river runoff between the different continents and within different climatic zones on each continent. About a third of the total runoff comes from South America with less than 15% of the earth's land area while Africa which contains 23% of the land yields only 12% of the runoff. Runoff from Southwestern United States, temperate South America, and Australia is less than 5%, yet these

Table 7·9
POTENTIALLY ARABLE AND IRRIGABLE LANDS AND POTENTIAL GROSS CROPPED AREAS (Millions of Hectares)

	(1) Potentially Arable Land	(2) Potentially Arable Without Irrigation	(3) Potentially Arable Only With Irrigation	(4) Total Irrigable Area	(5) Without Irrigation	(6) With Full Irrigation	(7) With Available Water
					Potential Gross Cropped Area		
Africa	730	600	130	610	820	1980	1110
	(620)*	(490)	(130)	(610)	(500)	(1660)	(790)
	[500]**	[490]	[10]	[290]			
Asia	620	530	90	410	830	1460	1340
	(540)	(450)	(90)	(410)	(590)	(1220)	(1100)
	[465]	[450]	[15]	[335]			
Australia	150	120	30	110	150	330	152
	(150)	(120)	(30)	(110)			
	[122]	[120]	[2]	[2]			
Europe	170	170	—	30	230	270	270
	(170)	(170)	—	(30)			
	[170]	[170]	—	[30]			
North America	460	440	20	170	280	490	440
	(450)	(430)	(20)	(170)	(240)	(450)	(400)
	[450]	[430]	[20]	[160]			
South America	670	640	30	310	1420	1900	1500
	(370)	(340)	(30)	(310)	(520)	(1000)	(600)
	[370]	[340]	[30]	[80]			
USSR	350	320	30	30	370	400	400
	(350)	(320)	(30)	(30)			
	[350]	[320]	[30]	[30]			
World Total	3150	2820	330	1670	4100	6830	5212
	(2650)	(2320)	(330)	(1670)	(2600)	(5330)	(3712)
	[2427]	[2320]	[107]	[1027]			

Note:
   * Numbers in parentheses are areas outside the humid tropics.

   ** Numbers in brackets are areas outside the humid tropics with available water.

Source: R. Revelle, "Will the Earth's land and water resources be sufficient for future populations?" UN Stockholm Symposium, Oct. 1973.

regions contain 25% of the total area...The total potentially arable area is thereby reduced to 2,925 million hectares and the potential gross cropped area to 5,212 million hectares..."[8]

In some respects, the capital availability problems are as difficult as the technical ones. Regarding irrigation, the possibilities vary from country to country and there is little reliable data. The range of problems is indicated by these comments about India and Bangla Desh.

"...the Indian Irrigation Commission has estimated that 84.2 million gross cropped hectares could ultimately be put under irrigation in India...The Commission's estimated total cost of future irrigation is approximately $14 billion...the present cropped area would be increased by 158%..."

About Bangla Desh on the other hand:

"...Studies have shown that with a total new investment of $1.78 billion, yields of food grains could be more than doubled during the next 20 years...the annual wheat and rice production available for human consumption would be about 20 million tons, barely enough...for a minimum diet for the 134 million people anticipated in 1993...we are faced with an urgent and potentially tragic problem..."[9]

Conclusions about Sub-Saharan Africa are even more pessimistic.

Investments in fertilizer and pesticide production, agricultural research, etc., would also require enormous outlays on the part of the developing countries. It is clear that such large scale investment programs cannot be carried out successfully without considerable assistance from the developed countries. Also, some parts of the world may need direct food aid for a long time to come.

The CWR project investigated some alternatives for the world food problem using their integrated food policy model. The model considers both the production of foodstuffs and allocation of this production to various uses within a given region. Production is considered in three different sectors; field crops, livestock, and fisheries. The model is driven by the economic and population models integrated into the food model. The population model, along with dietary requirements, determines the demands made on the food sector in terms of volume and composition of total production. The economic sector helps to determine the amount of capital that can be allotted to the three food sectors to increase their capacity. The horizon extends to the year 2020, and the focus is on South East Asia where the shortage of land and other inputs along with exploding populations are likely to create the most

acute problems. The analysts have examined three issues:

1. Possibilities of attaining self-sufficiency without significant outside aid during the period 1975-2020.

2. Contributions which could be made by a program of foreign aid to the attainment of self-sufficiency.

3. Capabilities of a single developed region comprising the United States and Canada to provide the needed aid, assuming no additional demands or contributions from the rest of the world.

The model is quite detailed since it considers 26 different foodstuffs, and dietary requirements are calculated in terms of per capita needs for calories, total protein and animal protein. In the field crops production sector it considers: short-term technological changes in terms of fertilizer inputs, and long-term effects of technical change in terms of capital investment in the infrastructure.

The analysts have constructed a large number of alternatives corresponding to various combinations of possibilities. It is interesting to examine a few illustrative scenarios that bring out the nature and magnitude of the problems involved.

Scenario 1: Continuation of past trends.

It is assumed that economic priorities of the last twenty years will prevail. Population control is given consideration, but only a modest policy is implemented over a fifty year period.

Chart 7·3 depicts what will happen if, in addition, it is assumed that the food imports to meet the growing domestic deficits are available from somewhere so that no starvation occurs. Over fifty years the cumulative deficit would amount to about 1200 million tons of protein. About ten times as much food would be needed to provide this amount of protein, assuming that about 10 percent of the total weight of the average foodstuff is useful protein. This 12,000 million tons of food may be compared to total United States grain exports in 1974 of about 60 million tons.[10]

Chart 7·4 represents what may happen if food aid in such huge quantities is not forthcoming. Regional per capita protein supply falls sharply, reaching starvation levels in about 1985. Starvation deaths, especially among children, occur with increasing frequency.

Chart 7·3
PROTEIN NEEDS AND POPULATION GROWTH IN SOUTH ASIA

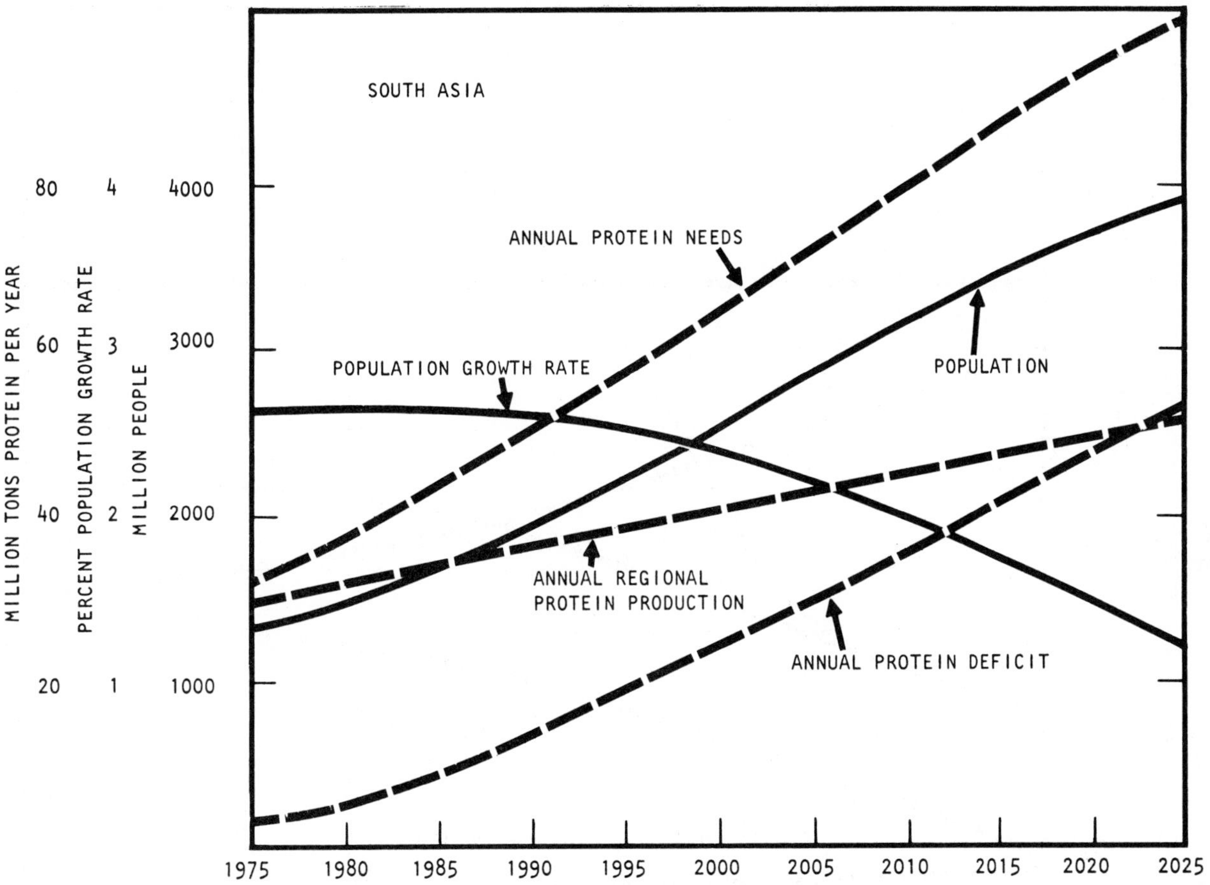

Source: CWR Food Model

Scenario 2: Population control plus shifting priorities.

In this scenario a population policy is combined with shifts of investment to agriculture, thus making South East Asia essentially an agricultural region.

The result is that the protein deficiency is alleviated in the short run but starts increasing after about 2005. (See Chart 7·5.) The economic consequences of such an unbalanced development policy are also disastrous. As a result of the failure of the industrial sector to grow normally, gross product for the region in 2020 drops from $1,100 billion under balanced growth conditions to about $500 billion. (See Chart 7·6.) There is no substantial gain in agricultural production either, over the long run.

Scenario 3: Population control plus food aid.

This scenario assumes population control in South East Asia, while North America attempts to meet the need for food. The aid program affects consumption, investment and government expenditure significantly in North America. Chart 7·7 shows that about 60 percent of North America's total potential agricultural surplus is required to meet South Asia's food needs while self-sufficiency is attained. The consequences for aggregate output and capital stock in North America are shown in Chart 7·8. Output in North America is reduced by about 6 percent in 1990 and by almost 25 percent in 2025 as compared to a situation which merely maintained historical relationships.

Scenario 4: Population control plus investment aid.

This examines the possibility of meeting South Asia's agricultural investment needs through aid from North America. The conclusion is that, in order for South Asia to avoid starvation and gradually attain self-sufficiency, the total amount of aid re-

213

Chart 7•4
POPULATION GROWTH AND FOOD NEEDS IN SOUTH ASIA—NO FOREIGN AID

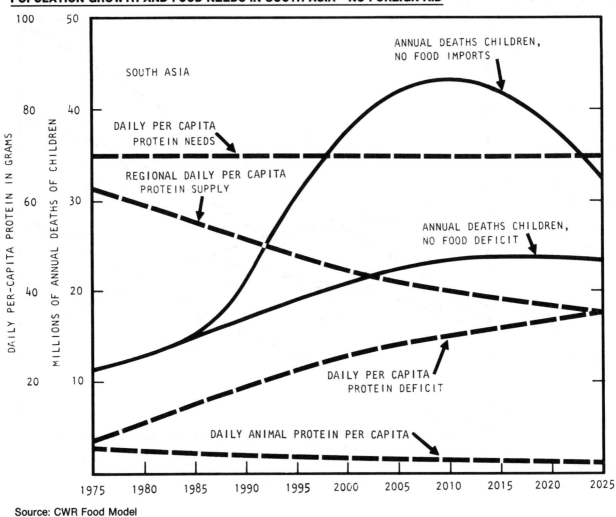

Source: CWR Food Model

quired over the period to 2025 is about $350 billion in constant dollars. While such an amount is substantial, it is not beyond the realm of practicality. In fact, the average of $7 billion per year is small in some contexts; e.g., the increase in annual OPEC oil revenues since 1972.

Other detailed scenarios for South Asia have also been prepared. The conclusions that emerge from all these exercises can be summarized as follows:

1. In the absence of any action, large regions of the world are almost sure to face a severe food problem.

2. Population control should be a major priority objective for large portions of the underdeveloped world.

3. With substantial assistance from the developed

countries and vigorous population control policies, not only can starvation be avoided in the poor areas of the world, but eventually these areas can become self-sufficient.

4. The amount of aid required is far greater and for a longer term than anything undertaken so far. But, if all the developed countries cooperate, it is economically feasible.

The present discussion has not considered the problems of political feasibility—whether the governments of the developed countries can persuade their electorates to support such large-scale foreign assistance programs. Another problem is to determine whether the underdeveloped countries will have the political and administrative apparatus necessary to utilize the aid effectively. The present international climate and historical effectiveness of

214

Chart 7•5
PROTEIN NEEDS, PRODUCTION AND DEFICIT IN SOUTH ASIA—INVESTMENT MAINLY IN AGRICULTURE

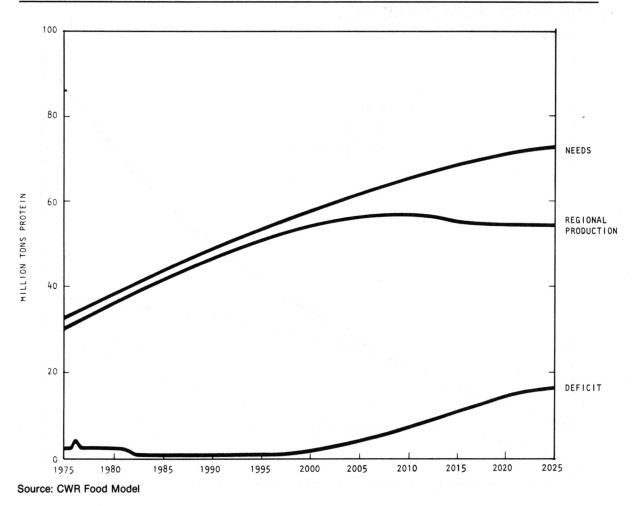

Source: CWR Food Model

United States foreign aid efforts—except the Marshall plan—are not encouraging. Also, the present discussion has not touched upon the related logistical problems such as the transportation, storage and distribution of food.

In conclusion, the constraints presented by food and agriculture can be overcome by increased effort and technology, but much more effective international cooperation than has existed up to now will be required.

F. Resources: Energy and Non-Energy

This section examines the future of natural resources. Energy resources and non-energy minerals will be discussed separately.

1. Energy Resources—Summary of Findings

The purpose of this section is to examine the relation between world economic growth and energy use and to explore the future of energy supplies. Although each of the ten CWR world regions is considered separately, the analysis is less detailed than is desirable. Some important aspects such as interfuel substitution and constraints arising out of geographical distribution of energy resources have not been treated in depth. However, this assessment of energy resources as a potential constraint on economic growth provides the following conclusions:

1. Reasonable assumptions about growth in energy consumption yield a demand projection for the year 2000 that is between two and four times the world's present energy use.

215

Chart 7•6
CONSEQUENCES OF UNBALANCED DEVELOPMENT FOR GROSS REGIONAL OUTPUT OF SOUTH ASIA

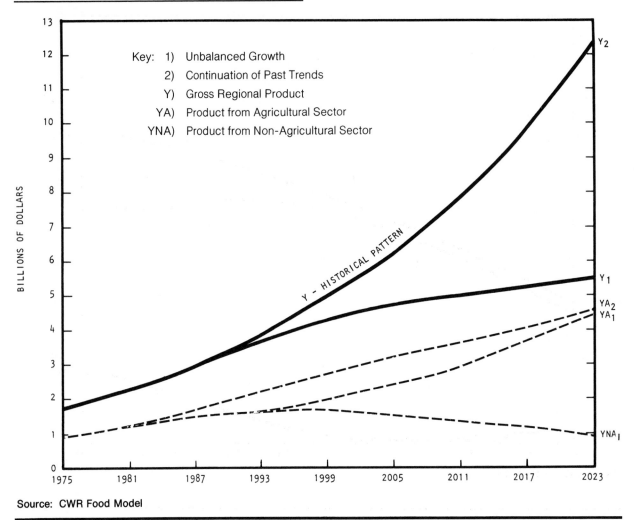

Key: 1) Unbalanced Growth
2) Continuation of Past Trends
Y) Gross Regional Product
YA) Product from Agricultural Sector
YNA) Product from Non-Agricultural Sector

Source: CWR Food Model

2. Constraints will emerge most clearly in the case of fossil fuels. They cannot alone form the basis of long-term economic growth.

3. Continuing improvements in nuclear technology, leading to a safe and environmentally acceptable breeder reactor, could eliminate the energy shortage for centuries to come. For countries abundantly endowed with coal, its direct consumption plus synthetic fuels based on coal are partial alternatives. In the very long run, today's speculative technologies like fusion and solar energy to generate electricity may become commercially feasible. In the short and medium terms—to 20 or 25 years—however, a serious shortage of con-

ventional fuels could threaten the process of economic growth in many parts of the world —developed as well as underdeveloped.

4. Environmental problems connected with either nuclear energy or coal-based energy systems must be considered by underdeveloped countries. Preventing diversion of nuclear fuels to weapons uses and providing safe storage for radioactive wastes are two examples.

5. The capital requirements of any major new technology or even the exploitation of new reserves of traditional fuels will be large. Many developing countries lack both the resources and the technological sophistication required to employ the new technologies.

6. Careful use of energy must be given a high priority, particularly in advanced countries where consumption habits and production processes tend to be more highly energy intensive. In addition to eliminating inefficiencies, changes in lifestyles may be required in some countries to save energy and thus conserve capital. It may take considerable political skill and courage to make needed conservation efforts effective.

2. Energy Consumption Analysis

This assessment considers energy demand, resources and supplies; the relationships between energy use and economic growth; and future energy technologies.

The patterns and levels of energy use differ widely from nation to nation. Table 7•10 gives some historical data on energy consumption by source and major regions. Chart 7•9 pictorially represents some of this information. Somewhat more recent information of a similar nature is set out in Table 7•11. Both the levels and patterns of energy use are intimately connected with the region's economic status, natural endowments, geographic factors and the nature of its political and economic institutions. The United States, with less than 10 percent of world population, uses more than 30 percent of the world's energy. The

Chart 7•7
FOOD REQUIREMENTS IN SOUTH ASIA AND FOOD SURPLUS IN NORTH AMERICA

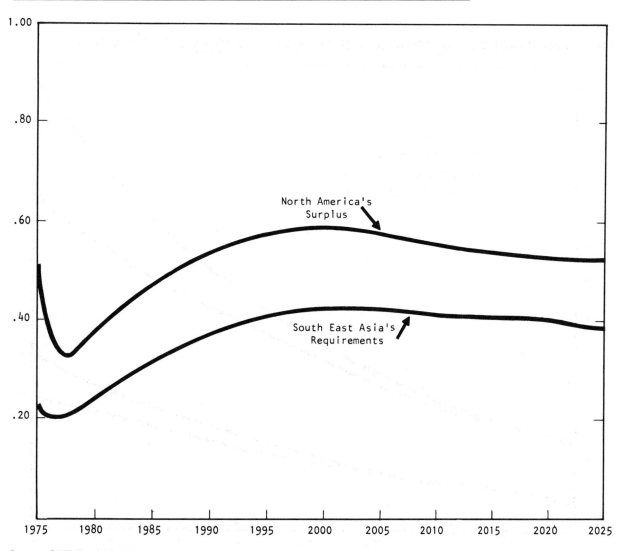

North America's
Surplus

South East Asia's
Requirements

Source: CWR Food Model

217

United States uses about ⅔ of world gas; Japan uses almost twice as much oil as coal; the USSR and Communist Asia rely heavily on coal; many of the poorer countries still burn substantial amounts of vegetation and animal wastes for fuel.

Although these energy consumption relationships are continually in flux, the pace of change is relatively slow, limited as it is by the capital-intensive nature of both energy producing and energy consuming technologies. Over the 40-year period from 1925 to 1965, however, a major shift from solid to liquid and gaseous fuels took place on a nearly worldwide basis. (See Chart 7·9.)

In view of the complex relationships between energy use and all other facets of human existence, detailed forecasting is an enormously difficult task. Systematic energy modelling is relatively recent and is being undertaken on a major scale only in some developed countries. Our understanding can be considerably advanced, however, by analyzing simple relationships between aggregates like total energy use and one or more of its determinants—e.g., economic activity. One such relationship is depicted in Chart 7·10. This shows how per-capita energy use was related to per-capita income at a particular time for different countries. The equation implies a 1.21 percent increase in energy consumption per capita for every 1 percent increase in GNP per capita.

However, Chart 7·10 fails to reveal some significant differences in the energy use/GNP relationship around the world. (In the following discussions it is not always possible to distinguish between gross national product, and gross regional product. This occurs particularly in comparing regions of the world

Chart 7·8
NORTH AMERICA—EFFECTS OF PROGRAM TO MEET NEEDS OF SOUTH ASIA UNDER SCENARIO 3

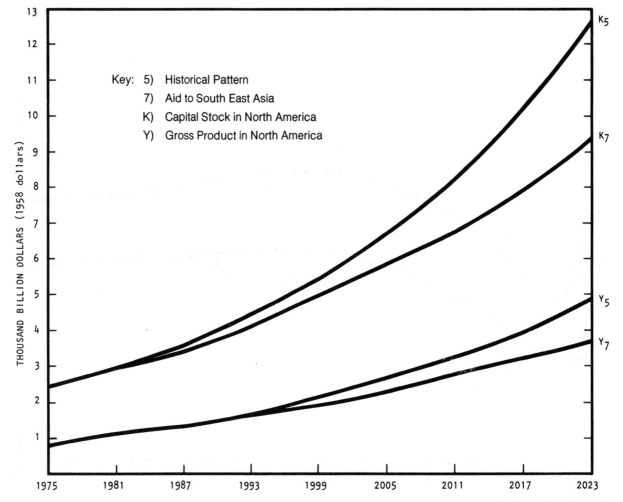

Key: 5) Historical Pattern
7) Aid to South East Asia
K) Capital Stock in North America
Y) Gross Product in North America

Source: CWR Food Model

Table 7·10
WORLD ENERGY CONSUMPTION, PERCENTAGE DISTRIBUTION BY SOURCE AND MAJOR REGION, 1925, 1950, 1965

A. As percent of each region's total energy consumption

Region	Solid fuels 1925	1950	1965	Liquid fuels 1925	1950	1965	Natural gas 1925	1950	1965	Hydroelectricity 1925	1950	1965	Total 1925	1950	1965
North America	74.5%	43.0%	23.6%	18.9%	37.5%	43.4%	6.0%	18.0%	31.1%	0.6%	1.5%	1.9%	100.0%	100.0%	100.0%
of which:															
United States	74.2	42.3	24.3	19.2	37.7	42.9	6.2	18.9	31.5	0.5	1.1	1.3	100.0	100.0	100.0
Western Europe	96.0	83.8	47.1	3.2	13.5	47.1	—	0.3	2.5	0.7	2.4	3.3	100.0	100.0	100.0
Oceania	92.6	72.0	51.7	6.9	26.1	44.7	—	—	—	0.5	1.9	3.5	100.0	100.0	100.0
U.S.S.R. & Communist															
E. Europe	82.9	82.5	58.7	15.2	14.8	25.1	1.7	2.3	15.2	0.1	0.4	0.9	100.0	100.0	100.0
U.S.S.R.	64.9	76.9	48.9	34.2	20.0	30.7	0.7	2.5	19.3	0.1	0.5	1.1	100.0	100.0	100.0
Comm. E. Europe	91.2	93.0	81.9	6.5	4.8	12.0	2.2	2.0	5.7	0.1	0.2	0.4	100.0	100.0	100.0
Communist Asia	94.0	98.1	94.1	6.0	0.3	5.1	—	—	—	—	1.5	0.8	100.0	100.0	100.0
Latin America	37.6	13.0	6.4	56.6	73.2	70.9	4.2	11.0	19.5	1.6	2.7	3.2	100.0	100.0	100.0
Asia	83.1	68.4	37.6	14.4	24.8	54.2	0.8	1.8	5.0	1.7	5.1	3.2	100.0	100.0	100.0
Japan	92.4	83.2	35.5	4.4	6.1	58.4	0.1	0.2	1.4	3.1	10.4	4.7	100.0	100.0	100.0
Other Asia	73.7	57.0	39.6	24.6	39.0	50.2	1.5	3.0	8.4	0.2	0.9	1.8	100.0	100.0	100.0
Africa	91.6	67.7	57.2	8.3	31.9	39.4	—	—	1.6	0.1	0.4	1.8	100.0	100.0	100.0
WORLD	82.9	61.0	41.8	13.3	27.7	39.4	3.2	9.7	16.7	0.7	1.7	2.1	100.0	100.0	100.0

B. As percent of world consumption of each energy source

Region	Solid fuels 1925	1950	1965	Liquid fuels 1925	1950	1965	Natural gas 1925	1950	1965	Hydroelectricity 1925	1950	1965	Total 1925	1950	1965
North America	45.4%	34.4%	21.0%	71.9%	66.3%	41.0%	93.9%	91.3%	69.5%	45.0%	44.1%	34.8%	50.4%	48.9%	37.3%
of which:															
United States	43.3	31.9	20.0	69.9	62.7	37.3	92.6	90.2	65.0	34.0	29.6	21.9	48.3	46.0	34.4
Western Europe	40.4	30.7	23.0	8.5	10.9	24.4	—	0.7	3.1	39.2	32.0	32.6	34.8	22.4	20.4
Oceania	1.2	1.3	1.4	0.5	1.1	1.3	—	—	—	0.8	1.3	1.9	1.1	1.1	1.1
U.S.S.R. & Communist															
E. Europe	5.4	24.0	32.2	6.2	9.5	14.6	2.9	4.3	20.9	0.8	4.3	10.1	5.4	17.8	22.9
U.S.S.R.	1.3	14.6	18.8	4.4	8.4	12.5	0.4	3.0	18.6	0.3	3.7	8.9	1.7	11.6	16.1
Comm. E. Europe	4.1	9.4	13.4	1.8	1.1	2.1	2.5	1.3	2.3	0.4	0.6	1.2	3.7	6.2	6.9
Communist Asia	1.8	2.7	13.3	0.7	—	0.8	—	—	—	—	1.5	2.3	1.6	1.7	5.9
Latin America	0.8	0.5	0.6	7.1	6.7	6.6	2.1	2.9	4.3	4.0	4.1	5.7	1.7	2.5	3.6
Asia	4.1	4.5	6.3	4.4	3.6	9.7	1.0	0.8	2.1	10.1	12.3	11.1	4.1	4.1	7.0
Japan	2.3	2.4	2.9	0.7	0.4	5.1	0.1	—	0.3	9.7	11.0	7.8	2.1	1.8	3.4
Other Asia	1.8	2.1	3.4	3.7	3.2	4.6	0.9	0.7	1.8	0.5	1.3	3.2	2.0	2.3	3.6
Africa	1.0	1.8	2.3	0.6	1.9	1.7	—	—	0.2	0.1	0.4	1.5	0.9	1.6	1.7
WORLD	100.0	100.0	100.0	100.0	100.0	100.0	100.0	100.00	100.0	100.00	100.0	100.0	100.0	100.0	100.0
WORLD (mill. met. tons coal equiv.)	(1,230.0)	(1,593.2)	(2,290.8)	(196.7)	(722.2)	(2,159.1)	(47.9)	(252.1)	(912.1)	(9.8)	(43.4)	(112.6)	(1,484.5)	(2,610.9)	(5,474.6)

Source: Joel Darmstadter et. al., "Energy in the World Economy", RESOURCES FOR THE FUTURE, 1971.

Chart 7•9

WORLD ENERGY CONSUMPTION BY SOURCE AND MAJOR REGION—1925 AND 1965

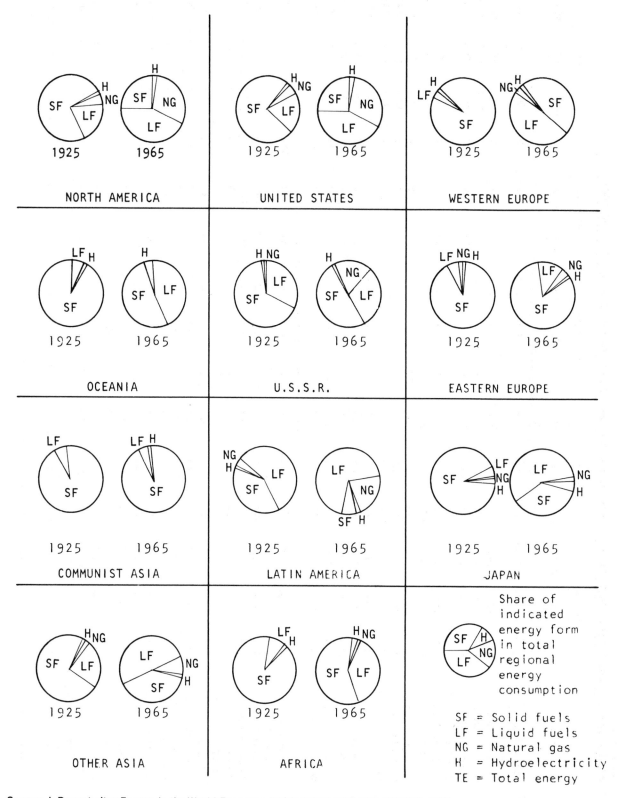

Source: J. Darmstadter *Energy in the World Economy*, RESOURCES FOR THE FUTURE, 1971.

Chart 7•10
RELATION BETWEEN ENERGY PER CAPITA AND GNP PER CAPITA

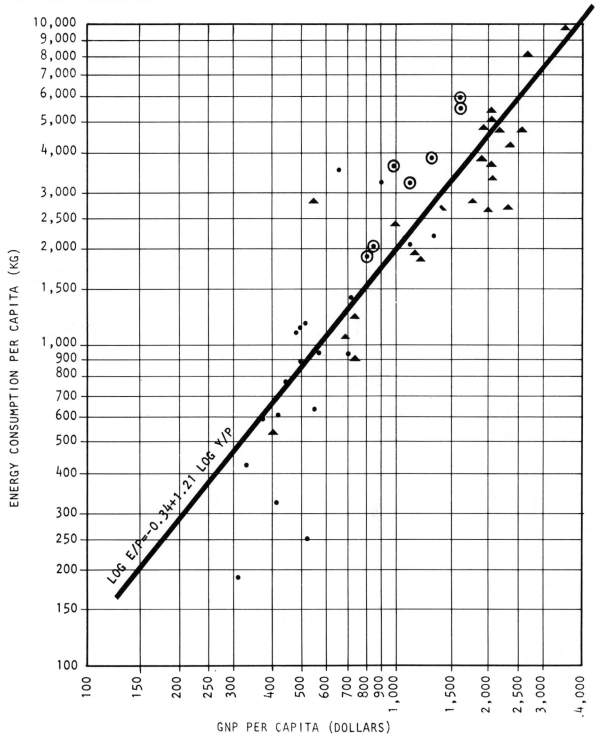

Country Legend:
▲ North America, Western Europe, Oceania, South Africa, Japan
⊙ East European Communist countries and U.S.S.R.
• Latin America, Other Africa and Non-Communist Asia

Source: Case Western Reserve University World Model

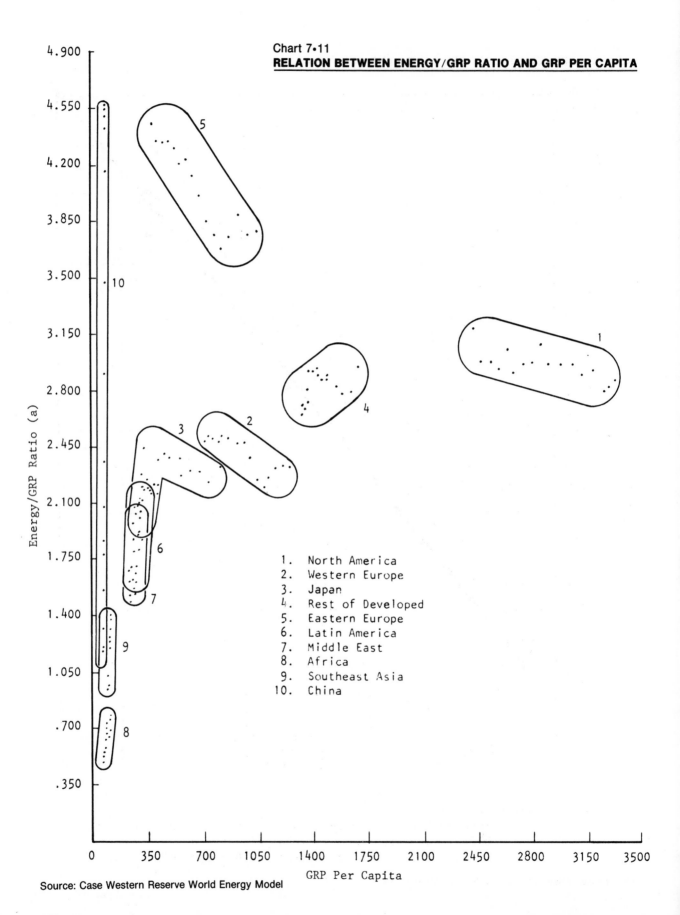

Chart 7•11
RELATION BETWEEN ENERGY/GRP RATIO AND GRP PER CAPITA

Energy/GRP Ratio (a)

GRP Per Capita

1. North America
2. Western Europe
3. Japan
4. Rest of Developed
5. Eastern Europe
6. Latin America
7. Middle East
8. Africa
9. Southeast Asia
10. China

Source: Case Western Reserve World Energy Model

with the United States or Japan. Efforts have been made however, to insure that the meaning is clear.) The CWR project examined this relationship for a number of years in each of the ten major regions, and charted the behavior of the energy/GRP ratio for each region against its GRP per capita, as on Chart 7•11.

In the developing regions, the energy/GRP ratio rises rapidly as development and industrialization proceed. At some state in the development process, however, the situation reverses and further increases in GRP per capita become possible with gradually smaller increments of energy input. The data for Japan are particularly pertinent since it has experienced this reversal within the time period shown on the chart.

A variety of factors such as resource availability and population density appear to affect both the energy/GRP ratio and the per-capita GRP at which this reversal occurs. In addition, the composition of industries, the effects of rising fuel prices, and rates of improvement in energy conversion technology may all differ from region to region and contribute to the inter-regional differences shown on Chart 7•11.

The significance of the chart can be seen by noting that both Western Europe and Japan currently can generate an additional unit of GRP per capita with only about 2.3 additional units of energy, while the United States uses almost 3 units of energy. If the trends shown for Japan and Western Europe continue, those countries will achieve energy/GRP ratios between 1.0 and 1.5 by the time their GRP per capita equals that of the United States at present. While there are no assurances that the relationships will remain linear, the chart does demonstrate a wide diversity around the world in the present and probable future intensity of energy use. More importantly, it suggests that other regions may hope to approximate United States levels of GRP per capita with lower energy use than the United States.

The CWR project has prepared forecasts of growth trends of GRP per capita for each of the ten world regions and then used the Chart 7•11 relationships to compute energy/GRP ratios and, thus, energy consumption estimates for the future. Using this technique, alternative paths of energy demand in the future can be constructed based on different assumptions about the growth of GRP.

Implicit in this approach to energy forecasting is the assumption that the price of energy relative to other goods remains stable. Since energy prices have risen sharply in recent months, the forecasts discussed here may be somewhat high. Tables 7•12 and 7•13 summarize the results of a CWR energy analysis for selected years. The medium growth rate of GRP

Table 7•11

WORLD ENERGY CONSUMPTION BY SOURCE AND MAJOR REGION, 1968

Region	Percent of The Region's Total Energy Consumption			
	Coal	Oil	Natural Gas	Hydro & Nuclear
United States	21.3	43.3	31.3	4.0
Canada	10.4	43.5	23.8	22.3
Western Europe	32.6	51.8	3.8	11.9
Oceania	42.8	48.5	0	8.7
Latin America	5.2	68.2	14.4	8.0
Japan	26.0	64.6	1.0	8.4
Other Asia (Non Communist)	27.5	59.7	7.8	5.1
USSR	42.9	32.0	21.4	3.6
Eastern Europe	76.2	15.2	7.5	1.1
Communist Asia	90.4	7.2	—	2.5
Africa	45.8	47.4	1.4	5.5
World	33.8	42.9	16.8	6.5

Source: J. Darmstadter in *Energy, Economic Growth and the Environment*. Resources for the Future, 1972.

for each region reflects the actual growth experience in the last decade, with some judgmental modifications—such as in the case of Japan where it was thought unlikely that the high growth rates of the recent past could be maintained for an extended period.

For the world as a whole, the three paths of energy demand are shown in Chart 7•12 over the interval 1975-2025. For the low-growth alternative, energy demands increase nearly five fold in this period while the increase is about 12 fold in the case of the high-growth assumption. This corresponds to increases in income which are of the same order. The doubling time for energy use is roughly 14 years for the high-growth assumption, implying an annual growth rate of about 5 percent; and 23 years for the low-growth assumption, with a growth rate of about 3 percent per year.

The inter-regional pattern of energy use should change somewhat between 1975 and 2025 with the share of the developed world (Regions 1-5) decreasing from 86 percent to 77 percent. The growing share of the underdeveloped regions results from their somewhat higher economic growth rates and their rising energy/GRP ratios. The share of the underdeveloped regions is likely to rise even more

Table 7·12
REGIONAL ENERGY DEMAND WITHOUT BIRTH CONTROL (Million Tons of Coal Equivalent)

	North America			West Europe			Japan			Rest of Dev.			East Europe		
	Low	Med	High	Low	Med	High	Low	Med	High	Low	Med	High	Low	Med	High
GNP Growth Rates (percent)	2.5	3.5	4.5	2.5	3.5	4.5	4.5	5.5	6.5	2.5	3.5	4.5	3.0	4.0	5.0
1975	3,152	3,152	3,152	2,062	2,062	2,062	695	695	695	173	173	173	1,919	1,919	1,919
1980	3,566	3,743	3,928	2,352	2,480	2,614	1,020	1,029	1,039	196	207	220	2,189	2,279	2,371
1985	4,035	4,446	4,895	2,684	2,988	3,327	1,336	1,394	1,454	222	249	277	2,489	2,691	2,900
1990	4,565	5,280	6,100	2,067	3,609	4,194	1,665	1,821	1,992	251	298	348	2,817	2,149	3,512
1995	5,165	6,271	7,601	3,508	4,312	5,226	2,074	2,381	2,729	284	355	438	2,169	3,702	4,482
2000	5,843	7,448	9,472	4,017	5,121	6,512	2,585	3,112	3,739	321	423	551	3,541	4,504	5,720
2010	7,479	10,506	14,709	5,142	7,223	10,113	4,015	5,315	7,018	410	602	872	4,753	6,666	9,318
2025	10,832	17,600	28,464	7,447	12,100	19,569	7,769	11,865	18,048	591	1,019	1,707	7,405	12,005	19,370

	Latin America			Middle East			Africa			So. East Asia			China		
	Low	Med	High	Low	Med	High	Low	Med	High	Low	Med	High	Low	Med	High
GNP Growth Rates (percent)	4.0	5.0	6.0	6.0	7.0	8.0	3.0	4.5	6.0	3.0	4.5	6.0	3.0	4.5	6.0
1975	379	379	379	146	146	146	60	60	60	211	211	211	492	492	492
1980	462	487	512	201	210	221	70	77	85	245	269	295	570	613	658
1985	564	626	694	272	295	327	82	99	121	286	344	415	661	763	880
1990	689	806	943	371	411	480	96	128	173	333	441	587	766	951	1,178
1995	841	1,038	1,282	506	565	700	112	166	249	388	566	836	888	1,186	1,580
2000	1,027	1,337	1,747	693	776	1,020	131	215	362	452	728	1,197	1,029	1,478	2,071
2010	1,532	2,225	3,262	1,313	1,477	2,113	180	366	743	613	1,207	2,498	1,384	2,268	3,495
2025	2,791	4,805	8,259	3,340	3,727	6,051	289	824	871	969	2,616	6,722	2,156	4,147	7,014

Source: Case Western Reserve World Model

Table 7·13
WORLD ENERGY DEMAND WITHOUT BIRTH CONTROL (Million Tons of Coal Equivalent)

	World Energy Demand		
Year	Low	Med	High
1975	9,290	9,290	9,290
1980	10,873	11,398	11,946
1985	12,634	13,899	15,293
1990	14,622	16,898	19,510
1995	16,939	20,545	25,127
2000	19,644	25,145	32,394
2010	26,824	37,859	54,144
2025	43,590	70,710	117,076

Source: Case Western Reserve World Model

rapidly if: (a) the speculations in Chapter 6 relative to post-2000 growth rates for the United States are correct, (b) the rest of the developed world follows a similar path, and (c) the economic efficiencies of the underdeveloped regions can gradually be increased. For example, it was assumed that all regions follow the medium growth paths to 2000, with a shift to the low paths for the developed regions and to the high paths for the underdeveloped regions after 2000. The resulting energy split in 2025 would be 67 percent for the developed regions and 33 percent for the underdeveloped.

The analysis described so far has assumed that there will be little or no effort to control population in the less developed regions. The CWR project has also investigated the consequences of a gradual stabilization of world population on energy demands. Table 7·14 shows the assumed values of rates of population growth in 1975 and 2025 with the process of fertility reduction starting in 1975. Tables

Table 7·14

AGGREGATE POPULATION CHANGE RATES IN 1975 AND 2025 WITH BIRTH CONTROL BEGINNING IN 1975

Region	1975	2025
North America	1.0	.3
Western Europe	.7	.2
Japan	1.1	.2
Rest of Developed	2.4	.9
Eastern Europe	.9	.1
Latin America	3.1	.9
Mideast/North Africa	2.5	.6
Africa	2.4	.8
South Asia	2.6	.7
China	1.8	.4

Source: Case Western Reserve World Model

Chart 7·12
WORLD ENERGY CONSUMPTION 1975-2025—NO BIRTH CONTROL

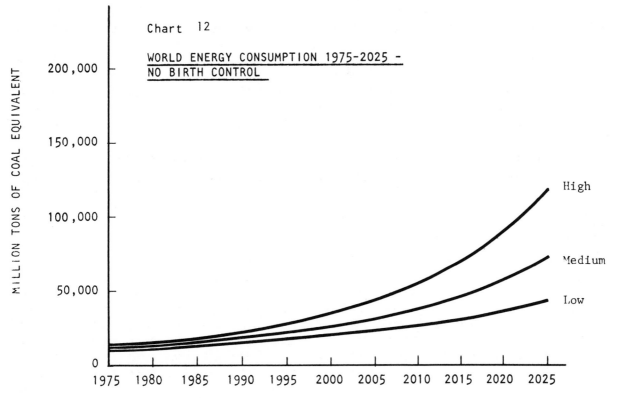

Source: Case Western Reserve World Model

7·15 and 7·16 present estimates of energy demand under these conditions. It appears from a comparison of Tables 7·13 and 7·16 that population control may lead to increased energy demand because effects of improving living standards (GRP per capita) in less developed countries will outweigh the impact of slower population growth. Chart 7·13 depicts the growth in world energy demand for low, medium and high economic growth assumptions with birth control in less developed regions.

For purposes of comparison, a projection of world energy demand from an alternative source is presented in Table 7·17. The time horizon is only to 2000. The total consumption figure is an approximate compromise between the medium and the high projections given in Tables 7·13 and 7·16.

Table 7·16
WORLD ENERGY DEMAND WITH BIRTH CONTROL (Million Tons of Coal Equivalent)

Year	World Energy Demand		
	Low	Medium	High
1975	9,290	9,290	9,290
1980	11,212	11,865	12,556
1985	12,640	13,907	15,302
1990	14,640	16,921	19,534
1995	16,979	20,588	25,190
2000	19,715	25,241	32,554
2010	27,013	38,186	54,555
2025	44,241	71,708	117,790

Source: Case Western Reserve World Model

Table 7·15
REGIONAL ENERGY DEMAND WITH BIRTH CONTROL (Million Tons of Coal Equivalent)

	North America			West Europe			Japan			Rest of Dev.			East Europe		
	Low	Med	High	Low	Med	High	Low	Med	High	Low	Med	High	Low	Med	High
GNP Growth Rates (percent)	2.5	3.5	4.5	2.5	3.5	4.5	4.5	5.5	6.5	2.5	3.5	4.5	3.0	4.0	5.0
1975	3,152	3,152	3,152	2,062	2,062	2,062	695	695	695	173	173	173	1,919	1,919	1,919
1980	3,566	3,743	3,928	2,352	2,480	2,614	1,020	1,029	1,039	196	208	220	2,189	2,279	2,370
1985	4,035	4,446	4,895	2,684	2,988	3,327	1,336	1,394	1,454	222	250	277	2,489	2,691	2,900
1990	4,565	5,280	6,100	2,067	3,609	4,194	1,665	1,821	1,992	253	299	349	2,817	2,149	3,510
1995	5,165	6,271	7,601	3,508	4,312	5,226	2,074	2,381	2,729	288	357	441	2,169	3,702	4,482
2000	5,843	7,448	9,472	4,017	5,121	6,512	2,585	3,112	3,739	329	428	558	3,541	4,504	5,720
2010	7,479	10,506	14,709	5,142	7,223	10,113	4,015	5,315	7,018	424	616	882	4,753	6,666	9,310
2025	10,832	17,600	28,464	7,447	12,100	19,569	7,769	11,865	18,048	627	1,055	1,707	7,405	12,005	19,370

	Latin America			Middle East			Africa			So. East Asia			China		
	Low	Med	High	Low	Med	High	Low	Med	High	Low	Med	High	Low	Med	High
GNP Growth Rates (percent)	4.0	5.0	6.0	6.0	7.0	8.0	3.0	4.5	6.0	3.0	4.5	6.0	3.0	4.5	6.0
1975	379	379	379	146	146	146	60	60	60	211	211	211	492	492	492
1980	462	487	513	201	210	221	70	77	85	246	269	295	570	613	658
1985	566	628	696	273	295	327	82	100	121	288	347	418	661	763	880
1990	693	811	949	372	412	483	97	130	176	338	449	599	766	951	1,178
1995	850	1,050	1,300	511	571	709	115	171	258	398	584	868	888	1,186	1,573
2000	1,044	1,364	1,790	705	791	1,044	137	227	385	471	766	1,276	1,029	1,478	2,054
2010	1,590	2,339	3,426	1,357	1,511	2,169	197	412	758	669	1,361	2,760	1,384	2,233	3,399
2025	3,069	5,228	8,664	3,431	3,787	6,051	352	894	2,006	1,177	3,252	7,164	2,129	3,920	6,747

Source: Case Western Reserve World Model

Chart 7·13
WORLD ENERGY CONSUMPTION 1975-2025—WITH BIRTH CONTROL

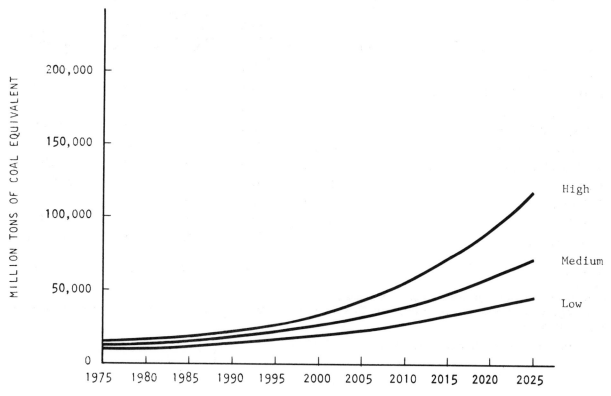

Source: Case Western Reserve World Model

Table 7·17
FORECAST OF WORLD ENERGY CONSUMPTION

Energy Source	Units	1980		2000	
Coal...........................	percent & MTCE	20.0%	2,450	12.0%	3,550
Oil.............................	" "	48.6	6,000	44.1	13,100
Natural Gas................	" "	19.5	2,400	18.0	5,520
Hydro........................	" "	5.7	700	5.3	1,560
Nuclear......................	" "	6.2	760	20.7	6,110
Total.......................	" "	100.0%	12,310	100.0%	29,640

Note: MTCE is Million Tons of Coal Equivalent. Conversion factor is 1 MTCE = 28 trillion BTU.

Source: J. Darmstadter in *Energy, Economic Growth and the Environment*, RESOURCES FOR THE FUTURE, 1972.

Table 7·18
OIL RESERVES (Thousands of Barrels)

Region	Proven Reserves [2]	Percentage of World's Total	Life-Index:[1] Static Consumption	Life Index with 5% Growth Rate	Production In 1972
NORTH AMERICA (1)	47,023,271	7.1%	12	9	4,011,350
WESTERN EUROPE (2)	12,632,000	1.9	80	33	157,680
JAPAN (3)	23,000	0.003	4	4	5,475
REST OF DEVELOPED (4)	2,354,460	0.3	15	11	157,206
EASTERN EUROPE (5)	78,500,000	11.8	26	17	3,066,000
LATIN AMERICA (6)	32,601,750	4.9	19	14	1,739,079
MIDDLE EAST (7)	438,894,000	65.8	58	28	7,519,110
MAIN AFRICA (8)	22,801,000	3.4	30	19	754,638
SOUTH EAST ASIA (9)	12,553,800	1.9	23	16	543,084
CHINA (10)	19,500,000	2.9	105	38	186,150
WORLD	666,883,281	100	37	21	18,140,122

1) Numbers given for life indexes are rounded to integers.

2) The data on proven reserves was reported by the *Oil and Gas Journal;* Dec. 1972, and the annual oil production was taken from the same source.

Source: Case Western Reserve World Model

3. Energy Supply Analysis

Over the next 50 years, world energy consumption may rise by a factor of between 5 and 12, depending upon the rate and extent of economic development, and upon the availability and price of energy. This rapid growth is likely to place severe strains on both reserves and productive capacities of fossil fuels. Accelerated introduction of new energy technologies will be necessary if energy is not to be a restraint on economic growth. It is probable that any major, new technological breakthrough will take at least two decades before it becomes commercially feasible and broadly applied. Some of the new energy technologies currently under investigation may take much longer than that. Thus, it appears that the conventional fossil fuels—oil, natural gas, coal—must meet the bulk of the increasing needs over the medium term. A serious shortage of any one of these fuels will disrupt the process of economic growth somewhere.

The pattern of potential constraints on growth emerges most clearly in the case of oil and natural gas. Table 7·18 presents estimates of known oil reserves as of 1972. The table also shows static life indices for the ten regions as well as the whole world. The static life index is the number of years the reserves will last if consumption continues at a given

level (in this case the 1972 level). For the world this index is 37 years. If the consumption grows at 5 percent per year, the known reserves will be exhausted in about 20 years. Even with generous estimates of ultimately recoverable oil resources, a 5 percent growth rate will lead to exhaustion in 50 years. An estimate of ultimate oil in place and recoverable reserves and resources is given in Table 7·19, which also gives some life indices. Natural gas reserves are also limited. Tables 7·20 and 7·21 show that the life indices are of the same order of magnitude as for oil. Additional discoveries of both oil and gas, such as the recent North Sea and Alaska finds, will continue to be made. They are unlikely to change the life index situation in a major way, however. Many of the new discoveries will be offshore and in regions where both capital and operating costs are high.

There are large amounts of oil in unconventional sources like tar sands and oil shale with more than 2,000 billion barrels of shale resources and a similar magnitude of tar sands having been identified. Here too, both capital costs and unit production costs will be high, perhaps even higher than for offshore oil. At current oil prices these production costs are by no means prohibitive but the amount of investment required to build the needed capacity will be enormous. The higher cost sources of conventional oil as well as the shale oil and tar sands resources are likely to be needed over the next 50 years if the share of oil in total world energy consumption is to be maintained.

World fossil fuel reserves are not limited to oil and gas. Coal and lignite resources an order of magnitude higher are available. Even at a 5 percent growth rate of consumption the life index for these fuels is more than a century. Estimates of total coal reserves are given in Table 7.22. Both the mining and burning of coal have associated with them some serious environmental problems. The environmental problems of burning coal can be lessened, and its flexibility of use increased by synthesizing gaseous and liquid fuels from it. The technologies for producing these synthetic gaseous and liquid fuels are known, but they are only marginally economic in most regions of the world and they are very capital intensive.

The present patterns of energy consumption with heavy reliance on oil and gas cannot be sustained for long. Returning to coal is a partial solution, as is the utilization of oil from shale and tar sands. However, conventional fossil fuels alone cannot form the resource base of the world economy in the long run, even assuming that there is a willingness to accept a reasonable balance between environmental considerations and the need for fossil fuel consumption.

Nuclear energy has received considerable attention in the last few years. The total potential of this source depends on whether the thermal reactor or the fast breeder is assumed to be the dominant technology of the future. It also depends on future exploratory results. The search for uranium has only been pursued in earnest for a decade or two. Therefore, estimates of ultimate resource availability on a worldwide basis are potentially subject to large er-

Table 7.19

OIL: ESTIMATED ULTIMATE IN PLACE AND ULTIMATE DISCOVERIES[1] (Billions of Barrels)

Region[2]	Ultimate Oil In Place	Possible Ultimate Discoveries	Recoverable Reserves and Resources[3]		Production[4] (Thousands of Barrels)	Life Indexes[5]			
						Static		5% Growth	
			0.3	0.6		0.3	0.6	0.3	0.6
1	2	3	4	5	6	7	8	9	10
CANADA, MEXICO, CENTRAL AMERICA AND CARIBBEAN.....	500	300	90	180	705,728	128	256	41	54
SOUTH AMERICA........	800	500	150	300	1,577,202	95	190	36	48
EUROPE......................	500	300	90	180	133,955	672	1,344	73	87
AFRICA......................	1,800	1,100	330	660	2,068,017	160	320	45	58
MIDDLE EAST..............	1,400	900	270	540	6,273,255	43	86	24	34
SOUTH ASIA...............	200	100	30	60	173,704	173	346	46	60
USSR, CHINA, AND MONGOLIA..............	2,900	1,800	540	1,080	3,252,150	166	332	46	59
AUSTRALIA, EAST IN-DIES, AND PACIFIC ISLANDS..................	300	200	60	120	488,261	123	246	40	53
UNITED STATES.........	1,600	1,100	300	600	3,467,500	87	174	34	46
WORLD	10,000	6,200	1,860	3,720	18,140,000	103	206	37	50

1) Data was taken from T. A. Hendricks, "Resources of Oil and Gas," U.S. Geological Survey Circular 522, 1965.
2) Regions are not comparable to those of CWR-World Model. They are taken from the original source.
3) Columns 4 and 5 refer to recoverable reserves-resources assuming recoverability of 0.3 and 0.6.
4) Production data are taken from *Oil and Gas Journal*, Dec. 1972.
5) Columns 7,8,9, and 10 refer to static and dynamic life-indexes, assuming a recovery factor of 0.3 and 0.6 respectively and either static or a 5 percent annual production growth rate.

Source: Case Western Reserve World Model

rors. Table 7·23 gives one estimate of uranium reserves for different grades of ore. The lifetime of these reserves also depends on the future growth of nuclear energy. This in turn depends on how the patterns of energy use shift in response to relative scarcities, environmental and safety considerations. However, with thermal reactors alone, the apparent long-term potential of nuclear energy is not impressive. For example, with a growth rate of 10 percent per year the life index of world uranium reserves now appears to be about 40 years. This includes the following grades of uranium ore in deposits which have been located and evaluated to the extent necessary to qualify as reserves at 1973 prices:[11]

A. More than 2 pounds of U308 per short ton of ore at a cost of $10 per pound of U308.

B. 0.6-2 pounds of U308 per short ton at a cost of $10-15 per pound,

C. Less than 0.6 pounds of U308 per short ton at a cost of $15 and more per pound.

Fast breeder reactors alter the picture dramatically, multiplying the potential energy from uranium many times and greatly extending the range of ore

concentrations which can be economically mined; i.e., concentrations well below grade C. will be useful.[12] Accordingly, nuclear breeders can provide a viable source of energy for thousands of years, in contrast to perhaps 100 years for fossil fuels.

Aside from the continuing debate over the safety of nuclear power, the most severe restraint on its use by the developing countries is the huge capital investments required to build such facilities. Without major assistance from the developed world, the shift to nuclear power by the developing countries will be extremely slow. Of course, if nuclear power substantially replaces fossil fuels in advanced countries, the developing countries may not have to "go nuclear" in the very near future. Also, as with other technological developments, they will be able to utilize the technologies from the advanced countries and will not have to incur development expenditures.

There are other possible sources of energy that have not been discussed. Of these, fusion and solar energy could virtually eliminate the energy shortage forever. Nuclear fusion research is in elementary stages. Sustained, power producing fusion has not been achieved even in laboratories. It is possible that

Table 7·20
GAS RESERVES (Billions of Cubic Meters)

Region	Proven Reserves [1]	Percent of World's Total	Life Index Static	Life Index 5% Growth	Production (1972) [2]
1	2	3	4	5	6
NORTH AMERICA (1)	9 244	17.3%	13	10	713.471
WESTERN EUROPE (2)	5 056	9.5	41	22	123.670
JAPAN (3)	11	0.02	4	4	2.577
REST OF DEVELOPED (4)	1 509	2.8	438	64	3.442
EASTERN EUROPE (5)	18 219	34.2	69	31	263.935
LATIN AMERICA (6)	2 243	4.2	24	16	92.655
MIDDLE EAST (7)	13 733	25.8	248	53	55.316
MAIN AFRICA (8)	1 359	2.5	648	72	2.097
SOUTH EAST ASIA (9)	1 348	2.5	101	37	13.292
CHINA (10)	595	1.1	150	44	3.968
WORLD	53 317 [3]	100[4]	41	23	1 298.628[5]

1) Data on proven reserves was reported by the *Oil and Gas Journal*, Dec. 1972.
2) Production numbers are taken from Felix Fremont, "The Future of Energy Supply: The Long Haul," 1973.
3) Estimates reported by Felix Fremont, "The Future of Energy Supply: The Long Haul" totals to 53,719 billions of cubic meters.
4) When added, total of column 3 may not equal 100 percent on account of round-off errors in individual numbers.
5) When added, total of column 6 may not equal the world total as some individual figures are not available.

Source: Case Western Reserve World Model

the technology will be mastered in the next 50 years or so but it seems certain to be exceedingly complex and within the reach of only a few countries.

As to solar energy, units that yield hot water and hot air for single dwellings are in use in many countries. Such devices can probably become competitive with conventional energy sources in some areas (with sufficient development efforts) and the technology can be applied to heating larger structures as well. At present the efficiencies of these solar systems are exceedingly low. Engineering studies of large centralized power generating systems are still embryonic but suggest that much research will be needed before costs approach competitive levels.[13]

Solar energy would be clean and safe. However, its impact on the environment would depend in large measure on the development of collection devices. With present technology, large centralized systems require collection devices covering large areas. Even the more feasible use of solar energy for heating and cooling buildings requires major architectural and engineering changes. These are likely to be undertaken primarily on new structures. Such problems

indicate that solar power is unlikely to become a major energy source for many years.[14]

Other "new" sources of energy such as geothermal energy and tidal power are unlikely to be of major significance during the next 25 years. In the case of geothermal energy for example, the total potential available in the United States has been estimated to be 30,000 MW, a small fraction of the total energy requirements. Geothermal energy might become an important source in some small areas of the world but its overall impact will be minimal. Tidal power presents severe engineering difficulties. Total power available from tides on a worldwide basis is immense, but it is so diverse that it would require engineering projects too huge and costly to harness a significant fraction.[15]

Synthetic fuels from coal were mentioned earlier. The basic technology for many fossil fuel conversion processes is quite old and well known. Some processes have been commercially used. The current research efforts are directed towards selecting the most promising technology, a major consideration being environmental restrictions. It seems almost certain that in areas with abundant endowments of

Table 7·21
NATURAL GAS: ESTIMATED ULTIMATE IN PLACE AND ULTIMATE DISCOVERIES[1]
(Trillions of Cubic Meters)

Region	Ultimate Gas In Place	Possible Ultimate Discoveries	Recoverable (Trillions of Cubic Meters)	Static	Life Index[2] 5% Growth	7.5% Growth	10% Growth	Prod. (1972) (Billions of Cubic Meters)
CANADA, MEXICO, CENTRAL AMERICA, CARIBBEAN	99	62	49.6	491	66	50	41	100.916
SOUTH AMERICA	71	45	36	517	67	51	42	69.666
EUROPE...............................	37	23	18.4	110	38	31	26	166.695
AFRICA....................................	153	96	76.8	8 691	125	90	71	8.837
MIDDLE EAST	102	62	49.6	1 065	82	61	49	46.57
SOUTH ASIA	17	11	8.8	735	74	56	45	11.978
USSR, CHINA AND MONGOLIA..............................	241	150	120	534	68	51	42	224.878
AUSTRALIA, EAST INDIES, PACIFIC ISLANDS................	31	20	16	2 219	97	71	57	7.211
UNITED STATES	113	71	56.8	89	35	28	24	635.544
WORLD	864	540	432	333	59	45	37	1,298.628

1) Data was taken from Hendricks, "Resources of Oil and Gas," U. S. Geological Survey Circular 522, 1965.
2) The average growth rate of production amounts to 7.5 percent in the past decade, and 5 percent growth rate was estimated to be true for world total primary energy demand in the future.

Source: Case Western Reserve World Model

Table 7·22
COAL RESERVES, PRODUCTION AND LIFE INDEXES [1]
(Millions of Tons)

Region	Measured Reserves	Identified Reserves	Production[2]	Static (measured reserves)	Static (reserves)	Dynamic (measured reserves) 2%	Dynamic (measured reserves) 5%	Dynamic (reserves) 2%	Dynamic (reserves) 5% [4]
1	2	3	4	5	6	7		8	
North America (1)	62,713	688,025	566.106	113	1,237	60	39	164	85
Western Europe (2)	63,088	70,673	384.826	164	184	73	45	78	48
Japan (3)	2,921	10,057	39.759	73	253	46	32	91	54
Rest of Developed (4)	32,192	68,652	109.794	293	652	97	56	131	71
Eastern Europe (5)	122,156	2,457,348	821.060	149	2,993	70	44	207	103
Latin America (6)	2,127	11,097	9.141	233	1,214	87	52	163	84
Middle East (7)	12	58	0.771	16	75	14	12	46	32
Main Africa (8)	2,385	6,588	4.237	563	1,555	127	69	175	89
South East Asia (9)	7,821	56,855	88.065	89	646	52	35	133	72
China (10)	35,280	786,303	395.589	89	1,988	52	35	187	94
World	330,695	4,155,656	2,409.348	137	1,725	67	42	180	118

P. Averitt Estimates	Identified Reserves-Resources	Ultimate Coal in Place	Static (Column 2)	Static (Column 3)	Dynamic (Column 2) 2%	Dynamic (Column 2) 5%	Dynamic (Column 3) 2%	Dynamic (Column 3) 5%
	8,618,400	15,300,176	3,577	6,350	216	106	245	118
	Identified Reserves	Recoverable Reserves Resources						
	4,309,200	7,650,088	1,789	3,175	182	92	210	104

1) In this table, coal is defined as the total of coal and brown coal. Detailed description of calculating this number is given in the source document.
2) Coal production data (1970) are taken from: World Energy Supplies 1961-1970, U.S. Series J.No. 15.
3) Numbers given for life indexes are rounded to integers.
4) Percent growth rate.

Source: Case Western Reserve World Model

coal this form of energy will become important in the very near future. Many discussions of coal-based synthetic fuels technologies can be found in the literature.[16] [17]

Efforts to increase world energy supplies must be balanced by efforts to use energy wisely. Undoubtedly, higher energy costs will encourage wise use and result in somewhat lower consumption rates than those projected by the CWR project. However, large reductions in the intensity of energy use (i.e., a sharply lower ratio of energy/gross output) are unlikely unless there are major changes in the production and consumption practices in the developed countries. The production methods, both in agriculture and industry, are highly energy intensive in the advanced countries. As the developing countries industrialize along similar lines, they will unavoidably increase the total consumption much in the manner predicted by the CWR studies. Technological developments in industry for many years have been in the direction of more energy intensiveness. Pollution abatement calls for further inputs of energy.

Economic growth in developing countries need not mean exact repetition of the experience of developed countries, although the transfer of technology and knowledge has usually been accompanied by a transfer of lifestyles. Concerted political action on the part of national governments may be necessary if the objective is to limit or modify such transfers of lifestyles.

4. Non-Energy Minerals — Summary of Findings

Non-energy minerals are perhaps as important as energy resources, although an average citizen feels their impact only indirectly. This section is an assessment of the availability of metals and minerals as a factor in economic growth. The relationship between economic activity and material use will be examined, some estimates of future requirements of major materials will be presented, and these will be compared with the availability estimates of reserves and resources. Although material availability is the main concern of this section, the discussion will also briefly touch upon economic and environmental aspects of mineral resource exploitation. Chapter 6 and Appendix F contain additional information on non-energy minerals.

The analysis in this section leads to the following conclusions:

1) Material use is intimately related to the volume and composition of GNP. Material use per dollar of GNP generally tends to decline as an economy matures and importance of the service sector increases. This decline eventually levels off.

2) The rising intensity of use in the developing countries and the sustained high absolute levels of use in the developed countries combine to produce rapidly rising absolute amounts of world consumption.

Table 7·23
WORLD URANIUM RESERVES [1]

REGION	Price Category I [2]		Price Category II [2]	
	Proven Reserves	Probable and Possible Reserves	Proven Reserves	Probable and Possible Reserves
USA..........................	355	590	172	327
CANADA	210	209	118	153
SOUTH AFRICA.................	272	—	—	—
SWEDEN.......................	—	—	318	—
AUSTRALIA	100	5	7	5
FRANCE.......................	35	19	7	12
NIGERIA......................	20	29	10	10
OTHERS.......................	49	73	296	146
WORLD [3]	1,041	925	928	653

1) Uranium 71, J. T. Sherman in *Jahrbuch der Atomwirtschaft 73*.
2) Includes price categories as listed in subsection F.3.
3) World total includes only western world.

Source: Case Western Reserve World Model

3) Material reserves and resources are dynamic concepts. How much can be extracted from the earth's crust depends upon the economic incentives and the state of knowledge.

4) Increased exploitation of mineral resources, although technically feasible and economically advantageous, may involve rising environmental costs and social disruptions. These tradeoffs cannot be overlooked, and the choices have to be made in a political and social context.

5) Demand reduction measures such as recycling could make a significant difference, but their material saving potential and their economic impact are not clear.

6) On the whole, shortages of major metals and minerals are not likely to emerge as a potential threat to continued economic growth.

5. Non-Energy Minerals—Analysis of Demand

The demand for metals and minerals is intimately related to the level of economic activity; e.g., the gross national product. Most efforts to project future demand make use of these relationships. Other approaches are possible—e.g., deriving the demands for various broadly grouped metals and minerals from input-output relationships. The data requirements for such an analysis far exceed the data availability except in the advanced countries. The method using the GNP-materials requirement relationship is simpler and data requirements are moderate.

One such study was recently completed for the National Commission on Materials Policy by W. Malenbaum.[17] The methodology used had two components:

1) Projecting GDP (Gross Domestic Product) growth to the year 2000, using past data.

2) Projecting the "intensity of use" parameter for the minerals under consideration. Intensity of use is the same as the requirement per dollar of GNP. The projection uses past trends in this parameter to estimate future values.

This procedure was applied to ten regions of the world. The regions are defined at the end of Table 7·24. Tables 7·24 through 7·30 show the material requirements for some selected materials to the year 2000. Table 7·31 shows the ratios of requirements for these materials in 2000 to the average annual requirements over the period 1966-69, for the whole world. The ratios are in the neighborhood of 3.0 except for primary aluminum with a ratio of 5.5 and

Table 7·24
CRUDE STEEL: REQUIREMENTS
(millions of metric tons)

REGION*	1951-55	1966-69	2000
1. W E	50.6	120.3	361
2. Japan	6.2	49.4	203
3. O D L	9.5	20.7	61
4. USSR	37.8	98.9	319
5. E E	23.2	34.6	104
6. Africa	1.3	2.7	16
7. Asia	5.6	12.1	68
8. L A	5.2	13.3	68
9. China	2.2	16.2	86
10. United States	91.1	133.8	266
NON-UNITED STATES TOTAL	141.6	368.2	1,286
WORLD TOTAL	232.7	502.0	1,552

Source: W. Malenbaum et al, "Material Requirements in the United States and Abroad in the Year 2000," University of Pennsylvania, 1973.

*Regions:
1. Western Europe (includes OECD countries, Spain, Portugal, Greece, Turkey)
2. Japan
3. Other Developed Lands (Canada, Australia, New Zealand, Israel, South Africa)
4. Union of Soviet Socialist Republics
5. Eastern Europe (also includes Albania and Yugoslavia)
6. Africa (excludes South Africa)
7. Asia (excludes Israel, Japan, mainland China and related areas)
8. Latin America
9. China (includes Mongolia, North Vietnam, North Korea)
10. United States

fluorspar at 4.65. These ratios suggest average annual growth rates of about 3.5 percent.

It is also important to look at the underlying trends that lead to these estimates. The intensity of use approach rests on the following general considerations:

a) Demand forces influence the composition of gross domestic product—i.e., shares of agriculture, industry and services. The common feature of all developed economies is the rising share of the service sector, which is less material intensive

Table 7·25
IRON ORE: REQUIREMENTS
(millions of long tons)

REGION*	1951-55	1966-69	2000
1. W E	39.2	85.1	232
2. Japan	2.6	40.3	161
3. O D L	5.5	17.4	49
4. USSR	28.1	73.5	235
5. E E	6.0	20.3	58
6. Africa	0.1	1.6	9
7. Asia	2.2	7.2	41
8. L A	1.5	9.6	50
9. China	2.3	22.6	110
10. United States	59.1	74.8	141
NON-UNITED STATES TOTAL	87.5	277.6	945
WORLD TOTAL	146.6	352.4	1086

Source: W. Malenbaum et al, "Material Requirements in the United States and Abroad in the Year 2000," University of Pennsylvania, 1973.

*See detailed description of regions on Table 7·24.

Table 7·26
REFINED COPPER: REQUIREMENTS
(thousands of metric tons)

REGION*	1951-55	1966-69	2000
1. W E	1163	2063	5354
2. Japan	97	650	2996
3. O D L	168	358	1078
4. USSR	367	872	2940
5. E E	125	312	920
6. Africa	6	12	111
7. Asia	34	62	476
8. L A	79	145	589
9. China	9	150	840
10. United States	1297	1887	4339
NON-UNITED STATES TOTAL	2048	4624	15,304
WORLD TOTAL	3345	6511	19,643

Source: W. Malenbaum et al, "Material Requirements in the United States and Abroad in the Year 2000," University of Pennsylvania, 1973.

*See detailed description of regions on Table 7·24.

Table 7·27
PRIMARY ALUMINUM: REQUIREMENTS
(thousands of metric tons)

REGION*	1951-55	1966-69	2000
1. W E	611	1965	10,320
2. Japan	40	581	6420
3. O D L	94	322	2009
4. USSR	286	1183	6552
5. E E	75	507	2358
6. Africa	1	18	167
7. Asia	13	180	1088
8. L A	25	154	1116
9. China	3	133	1056
10. United States	1213	3424	15,657
NON-UNITED STATES TOTAL	1148	5043	31,086
WORLD TOTAL	2361	8467	46,743

Source: W. Malenbaum et al, "Material Requirements in the United States and Abroad in the Year 2000," University of Pennsylvania, 1973.

*See detailed description of regions on Table 7·24.

Table 7·28
ZINC: REQUIREMENTS
(thousands of metric tons)

REGION*	1951-55	1966-69	2000
1. W E	752	1326	3483
2. Japan	86	493	1846
3. O D L	121	259	772
4. USSR	240	471	1470
5. E E	115	353	1006
6. Africa	1	7	46
7. Asia	29	154	663
8. L A	44	132	620
9. China	8	133	720
10. United States	859	1209	2822
NON-UNITED STATES TOTAL	1396	3328	10,626
WORLD TOTAL	2255	4537	13,448

Source: W. Malenbaum et al, "Material Requirements in the United States and Abroad in the Year 2000," University of Pennsylvania, 1973.

*See detailed description of regions on Table 7·24.

Table 7·29
FLUORSPAR: REQUIREMENTS
(thousands of metric tons)

REGION*	1951-55	1966-69	2000
1. W E	270	852	3870
2. Japan	23	412	2675
3. O D L	76	204	858
4. USSR	166	495	2604
5. E E	31	109	589
6. Africa	NA**	3	56
7. Asia	2	25	136
8. L A	11	39	310
9. China	61	149	696
10. United States	513	1121	4076
NON-UNITED STATES TOTAL	640	2288	11,794
WORLD TOTAL	1153	3409	15,870

Source: W. Malenbaum et al, "Material Requirements in the United States and Abroad in the Year 2000," University of Pennsylvania, 1973.

* See detailed description of regions on Table 7·24.

** NA = not available.

Table 7·30
SULFUR: REQUIREMENTS
(thousands of metric tons, sulfur content)

REGION*	1951-55	1966-69	2000
1. W E	4630	7823	24,510
2. Japan	1242	2006	7490
3. O D L	1204	2631	8085
4. USSR	NA**	2663	10,920
5. E E	NA**	2365	7763
6. Africa	52	391	1388
7. Asia	81	746	3570
8. L A	199	1039	4650
9. China	NA**	1167	5400
10. United States	5246	8712	26,648
NON-UNITED STATES TOTAL	NA**	20,831	73,776
WORLD TOTAL	NA**	29,543	100,424

Source: W. Malenbaum et al, "Material Requirements in the United States and Abroad in the Year 2000," University of Pennsylvania, 1973.

* See detailed description of regions on Table 7·24.

** NA = not available.

Table 7·31
WORLD: MATERIAL REQUIREMENTS
(thousands of metric tons)

Commodity	1966-69	2000	Ratio
Crude Steel	502,000	1,552,000	3.05
Iron Ore*	352,000	1,086,000	3.10
Refined Copper	6,511	19,693	3.02
Primary Aluminum	8,467	46,761	5.50
Zinc	4,537	13,448	2.98
Fluorspar	3,409	15,870	4.65
Sulfur	29,543	100,424	3.40

*Thousands of long tons

Source: W. Malenbaum et al, "Material Requirements in the United States and Abroad in the Year 2000," University of Pennsylvania, 1973.

than industry. This would lead one to expect a falling trend in intensity of use after a certain level of per capita gross product is reached, eventually stabilizing as the share of services stabilizes. In the developing countries on the other hand, the share of industry is expected to continue to rise, leading to rising intensity of use.

b) Technological progress has an important influence on the intensity of use. On the whole, this tends to reduce the intensity of use. Developments in alloys, precision designing and similar improvements have been responsible for such declines in the United States.

c) Economic growth will continue to be characterized by the displacement of natural material by synthetic substitutes. There will be a continuation of the gradual processes of developing substitute materials and different use patterns, in response to technological developments and price changes. As in the United States, however, iron will continue its worldwide dominance, at least through the end of this century.

Charts 7·14 through 7·16 illustrate what has happened to intensity of use in the case of crude steel, refined copper and primary aluminum. In the case of refined copper and crude steel the intensity of use has either already started to decline or is expected to do so soon in most of the developed regions. The intensities in the developing regions are rising and will continue to rise. The picture for aluminum is quite different. The intensity of use shows no signs of reversing the rising trend in the near future. This could be the manifestation of rapid growth of intensities in the developing countries, reflecting the tremendous range of uses of aluminum, and growth in developed countries due to substitution of aluminum for steel and copper.

Comparable analyses of some other important metals and minerals—e.g., manganese, nickel, silica—are not available but it seems plausible that their behavior will not be radically different from the ones already described.

A limitation of the Malenbaum study is that no account is taken of possible scarcities. GDP growth is not assumed to be subject to any material constraints. This seems to be a reasonable assumption as far as non-energy resources are concerned, at least through the year 2000. However, there is the possibility that limits on the availability of energy may limit economic expansion and the use of materials to values lower than projected here.

Chart 7·14

RELATION BETWEEN INTENSITY OF USE AND GNP PER CAPITA—CRUDE STEEL

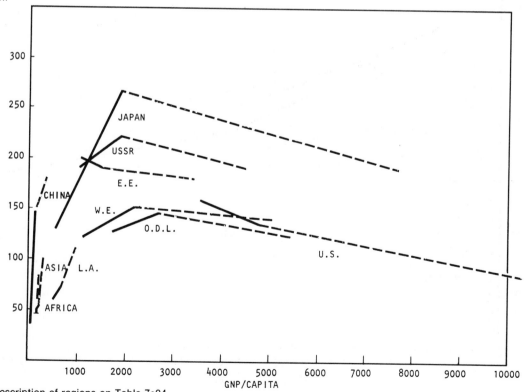

See detailed description of regions on Table 7·24.

Source: Malenbaum, W. et. al., "Material Requirements in the United States and Abroad in the Year 2000." A Research Project carried out at the University of Pennsylvania for the National Commission on Materials Policy, 1973.

6. Non-Energy Minerals—Analysis of Supply

In Appendix H, the current resource position of some commonly used metals and minerals has been summarized. These estimates include only land resources. Most of these should be regarded as tentative as they are based on the current state of the art in geological exploration and estimation. From these and the earlier demand estimates it appears that, with the possible exception of sulfur, no metal listed is likely to be scarce even well beyond 2000.[18]

As with energy resources, a physical inventory of metal and mineral resources is most useful when it provides a range of quantities recoverable at different costs, similar to that shown earlier for uranium.

In general, the occurrence of minerals rises rapidly as concentrations decrease. Probably, absolute physical limitations exist in some cases—mercury is an often quoted example. However, most minerals are present in the earth in huge quantities at very low concentrations. For example, a single cubic mile of average crustal rock contains approximately a billion tons of aluminum, 500 million tons of iron, a million tons of zinc and 600,000 tons of copper. Similarly large quantities of several minerals are present on the seabed. Thus, in a practical sense mineral availability is limited only by the rate of technological improvement in mining and refining processes. In 1880, for example, the lowest grade of copper ore that could be economically handled was 3 percent;

Chart 7•15
RELATION BETWEEN INTENSITY OF USE AND GNP PER CAPITA—REFINED COPPER

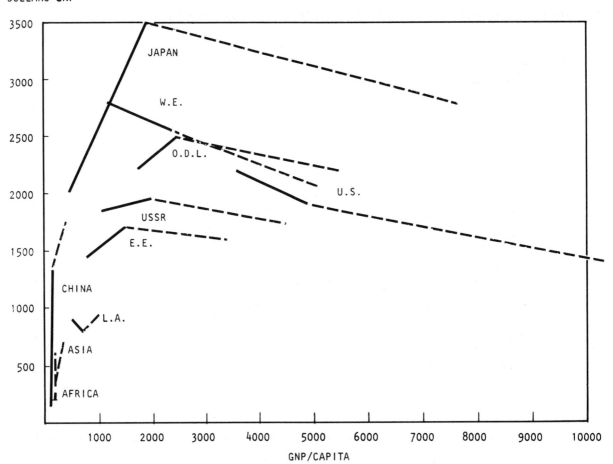

METRIC TONS
PER BILLION
DOLLARS GNP

GNP/CAPITA

Source: Malenbaum, W. et. al., "Material Requirements in the United States and Abroad in the Year 2000." A Research Project carried out at the University of Pennsylvania for the National Commission on Materials Policy, 1973.

238

Chart 7•16
RELATION BETWEEN INTENSITY OF USE AND GNP PER CAPITA—PRIMARY ALUMINUM

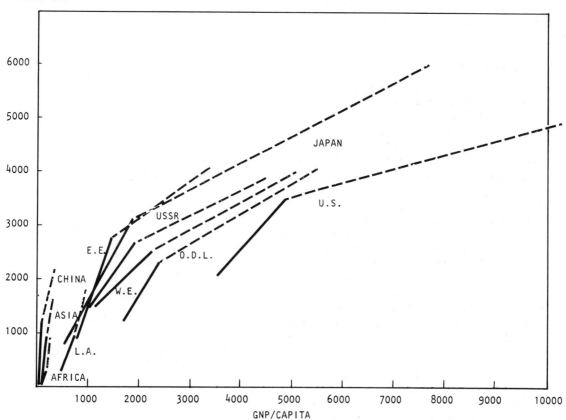

Source: Malenbaum, W. et. al., "Material Requirements in the United States and Abroad in the Year 2000." A Research Project
        carried out at the University of Pennsylvania for the National Commission on Materials Policy, 1973.

today it is 0.6 percent. Nickel can now be economically extracted from lower concentrates in laterite
mines which are much more widespread than the
sulfide deposits used earlier. There seems to be no
particular reason why the growth of knowledge in
this field should halt, as long as the economic system
continues to provide incentives. Even now, several
international consortiums have begun to evaluate the
potential for mining manganese nodules on the floor
of the Pacific Ocean.[19]

No reliable estimates of the capital requirements
to undertake the exploitation of more and more
mineral reserves are available. As the grades of ores
drop and mines become deeper, large additional
capital investments may be necessary. The developing regions may lack both the technology and the

capital resources necessary to exploit newly found
reserves. These questions are both economic and
political since international collaboration will be
necessary to exploit the world's mineral wealth.
Commercial exploitation of the seabed is a prime
example.

In addition to the economic and political implications, there is the issue of environmental damage. In
the past, the opening and closing of a mine has often
been an event with tremendous sociological impacts
on the local communities involved. Land damage is
a sensitive issue, as demonstrated by the considerable
opposition to strip mining of coal in the United
States. Also, mining operations often use large
amounts of energy and can create large volumes of
wastes and pollutants.

G. General Economic Growth

One of the features of economic growth in the past—and which seems likely to characterize growth in the future—was its extreme unevenness in different parts of the world. This pattern of growth poses many conditions and potential problems which will be considered in this section.

1. Summary of Findings

1) The historical pattern of development extended to 2025 suggests that the economies of the developed regions other than Eastern Europe (regions 1-4 in the CWR project) will be nearly 5 times as big as in 1975. The per capita income will reach some $22,000 in 1975 dollars (about $12,000 in 1958 dollars). In contrast, some of the poorer regions will grow slowly and they will be starting from a much lower base. It is possible, however, that past growth rates in both areas may not persist. There is some evidence that the growth rates of the developed areas will slow over the next 25 to 50 years for a variety of reasons (see Chapter 6). Correspondingly, there is a hope that per capita growth rates can accelerate in the underdeveloped world if birth rates are brought under control and efficiencies of their economic organizations improve.

2) The gap between the developed and developing worlds could be reduced through aid. A policy of early and substantial aid would reduce the overall burden on the developed world and

Chart 7•17
PER CAPITA GNP IN SELECTED COUNTRIES—1971

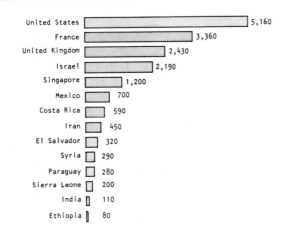

Source: "United States and the Developing World."
Overseas Development Council, 1974.

Chart 7•18
TWO MEASURES OF ECONOMIC WELL BEING

Infant Mortality in Selected Countries
(per thousand live births)

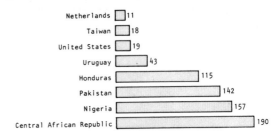

Per Capita Daily Protein Consumption,
in Selected Countries (grams)

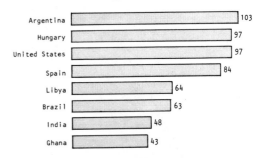

Source: "United States and the Developing World."
Overseas Development Council, 1974.

speed attainment of self-sufficiency on the part of the underdeveloped regions.

3) The costs of this course are considerable. An early action scenario predicts a total aid contribution from the developed world of about $2.5 to 3.0 trillion over 50 years without considering the effects of inflation. This is about 2-½ times the current United States GNP.

4) Political disruptions and resource scarcities could threaten orderly world development. If this were to occur, the gap could widen unless growth in the industrial nations were retarded. Such possibilities cannot be adequately analyzed in an economic framework alone.

2. Analysis

The gap between the rich and poor nations is widening in absolute terms and, in some cases, in relative terms as well.[20] Such enormous differentials in living standards may endanger world stability. The nature of the gap is illustrated by Chart 7•17 which shows the wide range of per capita gross national product in 1971. The ratio of the highest (United States $5,160), to the lowest (Ethiopia $80) on this chart is more than 60. There are some countries—e.g., Bangla Desh, Burundi, Rwanda—which are poorer than Ethiopia. Chart 7•18, showing infant mortality rates and per capita daily protein consumption, also demonstrates the dis-

GNP, of course, is not the ideal measure of welfare. It is not reasonable to conclude from these figures that an average American lives 60 times as well as an average Ethiopian. But despite valid criticism of GNP as a measure of well being, the figures suggest the degree of differences.

The CWR project has developed some growth scenarios which consider the gap between industrialized and developing parts of the world. The analysis

Chart 7•19
ECONOMIC GROWTH IN SELECTED REGIONS—HISTORICAL PATTERNS CONTINUED

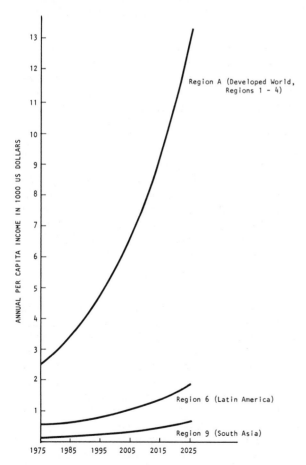

Source: Mesarovic and Pestel, *"Mankind at the Turning Point,"* E. P. Dutton Co., New York: 1974.

focuses on questions concerning the amount and time pattern of aid required by the developing countries to reduce the disparities to some specified extent.

The first scenario depicts how the gap would change if the historical pattern of development were to prevail. In this scenario the level of foreign aid to developing countries does not increase substantially over the presently prevailing level and the world trade cooperation between the Northern and Southern hemispheres follows national and regional interest. The scenario incorporates a somewhat optimistic assumption concerning the success of population policies. Namely, it was assumed that the fertility rate in all regions of the world will reach an equilibrium rate in no more than thirty-five years.

In this first scenario the gap between rich and poor regions increases both in absolute and relative terms. For example, the disparity between per capita incomes in the industrialized countries (regions 1-4 of the World Model) and in Latin America (region 6) will increase from 5 to 1 to almost 8 to 1 or in absolute terms from about $2,000 to more than $10,000 per capita. In the year 2025 per capita incomes in South Asia will be about one twentieth as large as in the developed regions, and in absolute terms the difference will increase from $2,500 to $13,000. Chart 7•19 depicts the complete paths of GNP growth.

The next three scenarios investigate the effects of various aid policies. These policies are designed to achieve a pre-specified target—namely to reduce the gap to 5 to 1 in the more underdeveloped regions such as tropical Africa and South Asia and to approximately 3 to 1 in the relatively more advanced regions such as Latin America, by the year 2025. The aid flows from North America, Western Europe, Japan and the rest of the developed world (i.e., regions 1, 2, 3, and 4) to South Asia, Tropical Africa and Latin America (regions 8, 7 and 6). One important assumption underlying these scenarios is that the disposition of economic resources in the underdeveloped countries—i.e., division between consumption, investment etc.—follows the same pattern as in 1970.

Scenario two assumes that continuous aid is provided to the developing regions starting in 1975 over a period of 50 years. The results indicate the amount of necessary aid would be substantial and would require sacrifice on the part of the developed world. The annual aid would have to reach $500 billion toward the end of the period and the accumulated amount of aid would reach nearly $7.5 trillion. The burden on the developed region would mean an almost $3,000 decrease in per capita income compared with scenario one. The time paths of GRP, annual aid and accumulated aid are given in Charts 7•20, 7•21 and 7•22.

These results raise serious doubts about the political feasibility of implementing such aid programs. However, at a later date, when the consequences of the widening gap have become more clear, attitudes in both the developed and the underdeveloped countries may change. Such a delay, however, is bound to aggravate the problem and impose some extra burden if the hypothetical target is to be achieved.

The third scenario is designed to give some idea of the magnitude of the cost of delay. It is assumed that the historical pattern of development prevails up to the year 2000 and that efforts are then made to attain the target by 2025. It turns out that the total aid required would be more than $10 trillion as compared to about $7 trillion in the continuous aid scenario. Charts 7•21 and 7•22 show the time paths

Chart 7•21
ANNUAL INVESTMENT AID TO LATIN AMERICA, SOUTH ASIA AND AFRICA

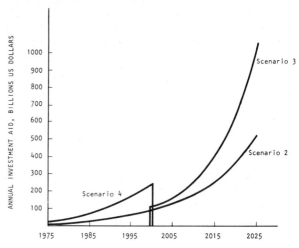

Source: Mesarovic and Pestel, *"Mankind at the Turning Point"*, E. P. Dutton Co., New York: 1974.

Chart 7•20
ECONOMIC GROWTH IN SELECTED REGIONS—WITH AID TO DEVELOPING REGIONS

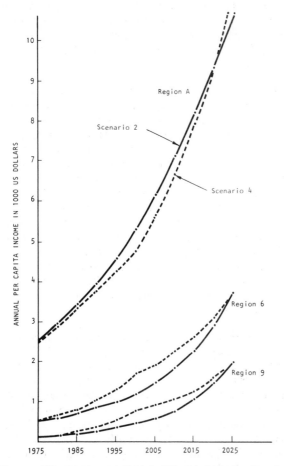

Source: Mesarovic and Pestel, *"Mankind at the Turning Point,"* E. P. Dutton Co., New York: 1974.

of annual investment aid and accumulated aid for this scenario.

The fourth scenario is designed to answer the question: if it does not pay to wait, would it pay to act early? It is assumed that increased aid is provided from 1975 to 2000 so that no aid is necessary thereafter and the target can still be attained by 2025. The cumulative aid burden of such a policy is considerably smaller—$2.5 trillion. The maximum annual aid is $250 billion. The total cost of the early action scenario is about ⅓ that of continuous aid and about ⅕ that of delayed action. Thus, early action would reduce the total burden on the developed regions and also make the developing regions self-sufficient by the year 2000. Chart 7•20 shows the time paths of Gross Regional Product and Charts 7•21 and 7•22 show time paths of annual and accumulated aid for this fourth scenario.

The CWR scenarios serve only to illustrate the dimensions of the problem and should not be considered precise forecasts. There are several limitations which must be kept in mind. First, as noted earlier, GNP is not an adequate measure of a nation's achievement. Secondly, the various strata of the multi-level world system are highly interdependent. In the real world in times of multiple crises the interdependence feature becomes all the more important. Shortages of a few critical raw materials, for example, can alter the cost/price structures so extensively that figures of per capita income in deflated dollars may not reflect the real living standards. Thirdly, economic development as described above may not take place at all in the face of institutional, political and resource constraints. Some of the potential constraints have been discussed in earlier sections. It appears that institutional and political constraints are likely to be more important than true resource scarcity. Of course, these institutional and political constraints can adversely affect resource availability and may, at times, create shortages of resources.

Chart 7•22
ACCUMULATED INVESTMENT AID TO LATIN AMERICA, SOUTH ASIA AND AFRICA

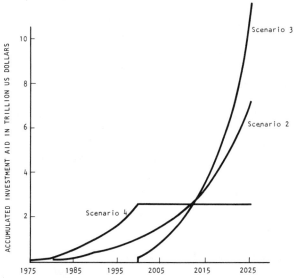

Source: Mesarovic and Pestel, *"Mankind at the Turning Point,"* E. P. Dutton Co., New York: 1974.

H. Pollution and Quality of Life

1. Summary of Findings

In this section an attempt is made to develop an assessment of the relationship between economic growth and environmental quality at the global level. The overall conclusions can be summarized as follows:

1) There are definite trade-offs between material advancement and environmental quality and the non-material aspects of life. It also seems apparent that some growth and economic advancement are essential for a nation to be able to provide effective protection and enhancement of the environment.

2) The trade-offs between the material and the non-material aspects of life are particularly difficult for the developing countries where economic growth

is almost synonymous with survival. Growth does not necessarily mean increasing amounts of goods and services along with increasing amounts of the attendant "bads," but in the underdeveloped countries it is very difficult to pursue both economic and environmental goals at the same time.

3) The environmental impact of economic growth can be considerably moderated by changing the patterns of growth.

2. Analysis

Environmental effects can be roughly classified into direct effects and indirect effects.[21] Direct effects include dangers to human health (lead poisoning, lung diseases due to air pollution), damage to goods and services (corrosive effects on buildings), social disruptions (displacement of human populations due to industrial operations, etc.), and impairment of quality of life (congestion, noise, garbage). Indirect effects are those which may impinge on human welfare through interference with services provided by the natural biological systems—e.g., falling ocean productivity due to polluted coastal waters and land erosion due to logging or overgrazing. Most attention has been focused on direct effects, and on their acute impacts rather than their long-term, chronic manifestations.

Contemporary man is an important ecological force through his production, consumption and leisure activities. For example, agriculture is an essential human activity, but it creates environmental problems. Some of these are:

1) As the area under cultivation expands, unexploited tracts disappear. These tracts have served as reservoirs of species diversity and as regions in which the functions of natural ecosystems can be continued undisturbed.

2) Areas unsuitable for cultivation are being brought under cultivation at the expense of serious and perhaps irreversible land damage.

3) Dramatic increases in inputs such as inorganic fertilizers and pesticides may have far reaching ecological consequences.

4) The quest for higher agricultural yields has led to enormous expansion of "monoculture"—vast areas being planted with a single variety of wheat or rice. Such monocultures are very sensitive to insects and disease, increasing the possibility of large-scale, epidemic crop failures.[22]

As indicated by the earlier analyses, these trends are very likely to continue. In fact, the major hope of the hungry areas seems to be adoption of advanced

243

farming practices—high yielding varieties, fertilizers, insecticides, multiple cropping—and expansion of area under cultivation wherever possible.

The oceans are an important source of animal protein, but half the productive potential of the oceans is concentrated in coastal areas. These amount to only 0.1 percent of the total ocean surface. Oil spills, fallout from atmospheric pollutants generated on the adjacent lands, and river outflow bearing fertilizer and pesticide residues, heavy metals, and industrial chemicals have already endangered marine life in some coastal areas. Over-fishing is also a problem, though it is difficult to separate the two effects. Some biologists estimate 100 million tons as the maximum sustainable yield of food from the oceans, while the present yield is already 60 million tons. Declining returns from further fishing efforts are already observable, and there are political problems connected with fishing rights. In view of all these factors, the theoretical maximum may be difficult to reach.

The enormous flows of material and energy in industries all over the world have raised great concern. Every act of energy conversion, mineral extraction, and material fabrication has side effects in the form of air or water pollution, land damage or waste creation. While reliable data are lacking, some studies estimate that: (a) civilization is now contributing half as much as nature to global atmospheric sulfur and may be contributing as much as nature by the year 2000, and (b) combustion of fossil fuels has increased the global atmospheric concentration of carbon dioxide by nearly 10 percent since the turn of the century. Contributions of human activities to global particulate matter is uncertain but probably considerable. Equally as serious as the lack of reliable data on the *quantities* of pollutants being generated, is the lack of information on the *effects* of various pollutant levels on man and nature. Until reliable data can be developed—and in some areas it will take many years—there can be no firm basis for comparing benefits and costs of proposed environmental protection actions. Under such conditions the relatively affluent, developed nations may tend to over-emphasize clean-up efforts while the pressures in underdeveloped regions may lead them to ignore pollution problems wherever possible.

Population growth has been and is likely to remain a significant contributor to environmental damage.[23] It has been estimated that damaging inputs to global environment in 1970 would have been only about ⅔ as large if population had not grown between 1950 and 1970, other things remaining the same. Population has "multiplicative" effects which may increase environmental impacts disproportionately as population grows. An example of this is the growth of suburbs at the expense of central cities with an associated increase in the use of automobiles. Another example is the potential for diminishing returns to agricultural inputs such as additional fertilizers and pesticides. The incremental inputs to feed an additional million mouths are more than the inputs required to feed the previous million, after a certain state has been reached. Multiplicative effects taken together exert considerable environmental pressure even in the absence of economic growth.

The sources and consequences of environmental effects have not been traced in detail. However, the broad outlines of the problem are clear. In man's productive activity, every act of resource recovery and conversion gives rise to certain environmental effects, many of which are generally undesirable. On the other hand it must be recognized that economic and technological progress have achieved any number of desirable environmental effects; e.g., eliminating particular forms of disease. In any event the use of energy and other resources is certain to expand considerably in the future. Though the intensity of use (e.g., Btu per dollar of GNP or per capita) may eventually decline, absolute amounts will surely be very large. Much additional scientific information must be obtained regarding environmental effects of pollution, and continued vigilance will be needed to assure that proper benefit-cost information is available from which to judge "good" growth from "bad."

Some forms of environmental disruption are amenable to elimination or drastic reduction through technology. There are other types of effects which may not have any technological solution—climatic changes or other effects due to continuously increasing absorption of waste heat in the atmosphere, for example. As suggested, earlier, technological "solutions" may only be temporary.

There is thus a clear trade-off between more growth and a more natural environment. This choice is particularly harsh for the poor countries where survival *demands* economic growth. In the economically advanced countries, current trade-offs can be made much less severe by shifting priorities, but it may be no less difficult in terms of political action. It is not surprising that in international conferences and symposia, the developing countries do not appear to be particularly enthusiastic about solving environmental problems. This is understandable in view of their immediate goals.

In addition, there are those who feel that higher material living standards have not led to a "better life." Increased urbanization, crowding, noise, pollution, loss of contact with nature, destruction of communities, and, finally, alienation of human beings are beginning to be looked upon as "costs." Such costs are not normally deducted while calculating per capita GNP.[24] Economic growth has meant all these conditions in the advanced countries, and the commonly used indicators of economic achievement take no account of them.

However, economic growth need not mean "more material goods" and "more environmental bads." In addition to providing adequate nutrition and at least a minimum level of material possessions, it can also mean better education; more leisure; more devotion to music, art, and other things of the mind and spirit; greater accessibility to nature; better recreational facilities, etc. It can also provide the financial support needed for effective environmental control, and for continuing that technological progress which over the years has made innumerable positive changes to the human environment. In large parts of the world today and for many years to come, however, growth will have to be synonymous with increased amounts of material goods—more food, more water, more houses, steel, electricity, hospitals and basic education.

FOOTNOTES

1. See Appendix C

2. Forrester, J., *World Dynamics.* Cambridge, Mass.; Wright-Allen Press, 1971, and Meadows, Donella H. et. al., *The Limits to Growth.* New York; Universe Books, 1972.

3. Berelson, B., *World Population: Status Report 1974.* The Population Council Inc., New York, 1974.

4. The American Assembly, *"Overcoming World Hunger"* Prentice-Hall Inc., New Jersey, 1969.

6. Berelson, as above.

6. Revelle, R., "Will The Earth's Land and Water Resources be Sufficient for Future Populations?" U. N. Symposium on Population, Resources and Environment. Stockholm, 1973.

7. For example, see Paddock & Paddock, Dumont and Rosier, 1969 translation to come by Linell and Sutcliffe.

8. R. Revelle, as above.

9. R. Revelle, as above.

10. *Survey of Current Business,* May 1975.

11. Case Western Reserve World Model-1973 prices.

12. Ross, P. N. "Development of the Nuclear Electric Energy Economy," Westinghouse Electric Corporation, Pittsburgh, Pa., 1973.

13. U. S. Congress, House of Rep. "Solar Energy Research," Staff Report of the Committee on Science and Astronautics; 1973.

14. Seaborg, G. T. "The Erehwon Machine: Possibilities for Reconciling Goals by Way of New Technology," in Schurr S. (ed) *"Energy, Economic Growth and the Environment,"* Resources for the Future Inc.; 1972.

15. Seaborg, as above.

16. Linden, H. R. "Review of World Energy Supplies," International Gas Union London: 1973, and Squires A. M, "Clean Fuels from Coal Gassification," *Science,* vol. 184, p.340, 1974.

17. Malenbaum, W. et. al., "Material Requirements in the United States and Abroad in the Year 2000." A Research Project carried out at the University of Pennsylvania for the National Commission on Materials Policy, 1973.

18. For detailed estimates of resources of a wide variety of metals and minerals see Brobst & Pratt. (Eds) "United States Minerals Resources," Geological Survey Professional Paper 820, U. S. Dept. of the Interior.

19. *Business Week,* October, 1974.

20. Case Western Reserve World Model Study.

21. Ehrlich, P. & Holdren, J., "Human Population and the Global Environment." U. N. Stockholm Symposium, 1973.

22. Ehrlich & Holdren, as above.

23. Ehrlich & Holdren, as above.

24. See Part 1 of this report for a discussion of the costs and benefits of growth.

CHAPTER 8

Recommendations

A. Introductory Comments

In Part I of this report the arguments for and against growth were stated and general conclusions were drawn on specific issues. Part II has presented the results of an analysis of alternative futures of growth. The general conclusions of Part I and the analysis of Part II provide the basis for a number of recommendations for public policy consideration. The focus of the recommendations is on dealing with the problems which pose potential constraints to economic growth in the United States over the long-term future (e.g., the next 25 years and more). Consideration, but less emphasis is given to the more immediate and shorter-term problems of economy management.

The recommendations are in the form of broad public policy guidelines and objectives, with some suggestions for specific actions. A general problem-solving approach is described first, followed by recommendations concerned with economic growth, energy and materials resources, population, agriculture, environment, and international relations. These are followed by a discussion of the changing priorities of growth.

B. A Problem-Solving Approach

A comprehensive and coordinated approach to problem solving is required to develop public policies dealing with the problems of growth. The approach to be outlined is an attempt to apply management concepts to the task of dealing with these complex, interrelated problems. The thrust of the approach is toward direct attacks on problem conditions within a framework provided by problem specifications and statements of objectives.

The proposed approach would combine three activities. A comprehensive approach is suggested for *problem specification* and *objective setting*. An incremental approach is recommended for *direct attacks on specific problems*. The three activities could proceed simultaneously.

1. Problem Specification

The first element is problem identification and description. A broad, inclusive perspective is required for this task. This report represents an attempt to use such a perspective. It is hoped that the report will lead to additional constructive efforts to produce specific problem definitions.

Problem specification in the growth issue must proceed on two levels. At the broadest level the problem is one of determining, "What kind of society the United States (and the world) should be." At this level, growth and the economy are viewed as means. The questions concern what benefits the economy should provide and for whom. The resolution of such "questions of basic principle" must be resolved through the political process.

The second level of problem specification is concerned with defining the boundaries of the specific problem conditions associated with growth, identifying the alternative means of dealing with them, and charting plans for problem solution. The concern at this level is with what must be done to resolve the problem and at the same time maintain the economy. What is required are decisions on *priorities* and *methods* to achieve generally agreed upon goals.

The two main problems at the second level are those associated with assuring adequate supplies of resources to sustain the economy, and preserving a clean and healthy environment. Related problems are: inflation, balance of payments, adequacy of investment capital, environmental protection costs, declining public confidence, and reliability problems in technical systems.

Problem specification must include an overall process of priority ranking. It must also identify linkages between problems and potential means of resolution. This requires a pragmatic assessment of the general problem-solving environment which includes the chain of events which led to the current conditions as well as prior attempts at problem resolution.

A major factor in the problem-solving environment is global interdependency. Any effort to develop a national growth policy or to deal effectively with the related problems will require some degree of international cooperation. No major policies affecting rates of economic growth can be pursued without consideration and conferral on international impacts.

Finally, an assessment of the problem-solving environment must include an awareness of limits and constraints to action. In dealing with the problems of growth, it must be recognized that for any given technical or resource area there are limits to the rates of technical advance and resource availability that can be realized over a set period of time. This is also true for the amounts of capital and labor that can be made available. The current problem of inflation stems in part from a failure to recognize such limits.

2. Goal Setting

The second component of the recommended problem-solving approach is goal setting. This task also calls for a broad perspective. Goals are essential to problem-solving. They provide a basis for planning and action and serve to focus and coordinate human effort. What is required are medium and long-range achievable goals to guide individual problem-solving efforts.

Before listing some examples of general goals, it should be emphasized that the process of setting goals need not result in the centralizing of power and control over problem resolution. Indeed, a set of broad objectives will include aims which are in conflict. The pursuit of conflicting objectives will require trade-offs at the point of problem-solving action. This is illustrated in the following set of general goals which would provide a framework for more specific objectives and plans.

(1) Preserve an economic system capable of accommodating a number of diverse and changing wants; that is, *preserve freedom of choice.*

(2) Maintain a relatively stable economy; that is, *minimize wide fluctuations in prices and employment.*

(3) Provide political and economic systems which *maximize opportunities and market choices for the individual* and provide incentives for exercising individual responsibility.

(4) *Balance the requirements for a clean and healthy physical environment and a healthy economy.*

(5) Maintain production levels which will *provide improvements in the standard of living and the quality of life.*

(6) *Assure national security.*

(7) Pursue *rates of economic growth* which will allow the accomplishment of the other general goals, now and for future generations.

It should be noted that these objectives avoid the value-laden terms of "progress" and "growth" as ends in themselves. *Goals* should be directed at expressing desired end results and, where appropriate, time frames for achievement. However, this does not suggest that the *ideas* of progress and advance are not valid as human values. Promoting human progress and social advancement remain valuable aspirations.

3. Problem Resolution

The third activity in the problem-solving approach is directed at problem resolution. Direct attacks on problems should proceed simultaneously with the activities of problem specification and objective setting. An incremental approach is suggested for attempts at problem resolution. By an incremental approach it is meant that individual problems should be attacked step-by-step with the means most readily at hand. Also, the most critical aspects of the problems should receive the most effort and resources. With this approach, actions are adapted to each situation and potential solutions are improvised on a trial-and-error basis. Success requires experimentation, innovation, and adaptability. The effectiveness of solutions must be tested, and there must be a willingness to abandon unsuccessful investments. This is the sort of pragmatic, results-oriented approach which characterizes management behavior.

The suggestion of an incremental approach for problem resolution rests on the recognition that the problems of growth are too complex to be resolved by objective analysis alone. Thus, there can be no overall action plan beyond the framework provided by the problem specifications and statements of objectives. Solutions to the problems of growth will require changes and accommodations among many conflicting interests. This will only be accomplished through negotiation and incremental adjustments over time. The needed changes and improvements must grow out of interactions and mutual adjustments among policy makers and interested parties.

The thrust of the suggested incremental approach for problem resolution is toward direct action. The actions may be partial, tentative, and occasionally unproductive, but the accumulation of incremental actions will lead to problem resolution.

Attacking the problems of growth directly and on

an incremental basis will require new and more adaptable organization structures. There may be need for institutional restructuring. In any case, more effort will have to be directed at conferral and bargaining in addition to the emphasis traditionally placed on competition and personal initiative. The incremental mode could be expected to be sensitive and responsive to changing directions in social values.

An incremental approach applied to problem resolution is compatible with a comprehensive perspective required in problem specification and objective setting. However, attempts to apply a comprehensive approach to problem resolution result in plans which are so complicated and cumbersome they defy implementation.

With this overall problem-solving approach as background, attention is now turned to recommendations for each of the specific problem areas.

C. Economic Growth

Much of the analysis done for this report was based on the use of econometric models. As has been noted, such models are valuable forecasting and analytical tools, but they are also only crude representations of reality. The limitations of this analytical tool must be kept in mind in the formulation and consideration of policy recommendations.

Based on the analysis and findings of this study, it would be unnecessary to attempt to limit economic growth in the United States during the remainder of this century. The nation possesses agricultural, energy, and mineral resources in adequate supply to support a continuing, although changing, pattern of economic growth.

It is also clear that "growth for growth's sake" is an obsolete objective. The directions of growth should be guided by the conclusions drawn on the specific issues as discussed in Chapter 4 of this report.

Overall rates of economic growth can be recommended on the basis of the analyses done. Recommendations of this type can be considered public policy targets. Although they are stated as specific numbers, they are meant to designate the center of a desirable and achievable range. As planning targets, they could, of course, be adjusted to changing circumstances.

An average real GNP growth rate of 3.5 to 3.7 percent per year could be sustained over the next 25 years under policies which sought a balance between economic and environmental priorities. The following set of policy objectives would allow the recom-

mended growth rate and promote the balancing of economic and environmental needs.

(1) Continue the development of natural resources within guidelines which minimize environmental damage and give consideration to costs and benefits.

(2) Account for social and environmental costs that can be identified for all industries.

(3) Encourage improvements in technology.

(4) Rely on a freely functioning price system to provide adequate supplies of resources and allocate them among competing uses in an optimum manner.

(5) Devote additional capital in gradually increasing amounts over the remainder of the 1970s and early 1980s, to the objectives of improving the environment and economizing on the use of raw materials. Concentrate this capital in areas where benefits are high relative to costs.

D. Resources

1. Energy

An average growth rate for energy use of 2.8 to 3.0 percent per year can be expected through the year 2000 if the overall economic growth rate of 3.5 to 3.7 percent is realized. Rates of energy growth in this range are compatible with a vigorous, carefully balanced plan to achieve greater energy independence.

Arbitrary restrictions on energy consumption should be avoided as unnecessary and unwise. Moderate energy growth will be required to sustain economic growth as well as for processing lower grade mineral resources, recycling, and for environmental clean up and protection activities. Over the next several years the economy will be hard pressed merely to accommodate the energy price increases which have occurred since October 1973. Efforts at further restraining demand, by arbitrary consumption ceilings or punitive consumption taxes, run the serious risk of crippling the economy at a critical period when the nation must make major investments in new energy supply sources. An economy suffering a prolonged recession will be preoccupied with short-term problems and unable to develop the long-range perspective necessary to make these major investments.

Energy policy should be directed at assuring a reliable source of supply and reducing growth of demand by eliminating waste. To achieve these dual objectives it is recommended that the United States energy policy contain the following elements. First, dependence on foreign oil must be reduced, not to the point of total self-sufficiency, but to provide a posture of "energy independence." To accomplish this, it is recommended that national objectives be established to: 1) reduce energy imports to about 10 percent of total consumption by the latter half of the 1980s, 2) develop fuel storage capacities sufficient to offset the effects of a six-month embargo, and 3) prepare a plan for curtailing oil use by 10 percent during the same period. Reasonable targets for 1985 are 9.9 quadrillion Btu of oil imports and 2.5 quadrillion Btu of natural gas imports. However, it should be recognized that in the intervening years imports may well follow first an increasing and then a decreasing trend, both in absolute amounts and as percentages of total energy consumption.

It is recommended that, during this intervening period, every effort be made to diversify supply sources among as many producer countries as possible. It is also recommended that at all times, but especially during this intervening period of unavoidable excess dependence on imports, United States foreign policies be concentrated on finding positions of mutual accommodation with producer nations. Searching for positions of mutual accommodation has always been a cardinal principle of international trade. Its importance rises in proportion to the importance of the item of trade.

The choice of a 10 percent maximum as the objective for energy imports is arbitrary. However, it is estimated to represent an amount by which United States consumption could be reduced without major harm to the nation, in case one or a group of foreign suppliers cut off supplies. The threat of such a cut-off could be further reduced, both in the years before the 10 percent level is reached and thereafter, 1) by building fuel storage capacities, 2) by developing standby producing capacity, and 3) by preparing contingency plans for curtailing the nation's consumption promptly and sharply for short periods of up to 6 months.

Storage and standby production facilities are expensive, and nonproductive in normal circumstances. Therefore, careful consideration should be given to choosing the proper balance between investment in such "defensive" facilities, and investment in developing new domestic sources of long-term supply. In the period of capital scarcity which seemingly lies ahead, there is the danger that the costs of responding to near-term fears may prevent the nation from ever tackling the long-term problems.

An objective of total United States self-sufficiency in energy supply may be desirable, but it is not

realistic. What is needed is an explicit policy and action plan to achieve "energy independence." A recent report of the Committee for Economic Development (CED) deals with *Achieving Energy Independence*.[1] There is an important distinction between "independence" and "self-sufficiency." "Independence" means the capacity to forego the use of unreliable supply without unacceptable economic dislocations. "Self-sufficiency" implies a closing of our borders as soon as possible to imported energy from any source irrespective of price differentials between domestic and foreign energy. An independent posture contemplates the kind of contingency plan suggested above for stand-by supplies and curtailments of consumption in the event the flow of foreign oil is cut off.

In order to achieve energy independence, it will be necessary to make a basic shift to coal and nuclear fuels. The ultimate aim should be to limit oil and gas consumption to those applications where coal and nuclear power are not feasible alternatives; e.g., petrochemical raw materials. It is recommended that accelerating the shift from oil and gas to coal and nuclear be given the highest possible priority in the nation's energy policy. A suitable policy target is the estimate of coal and "other" (essentially hydro and nuclear) energy source proportions embodied in the "High Coal and Nuclear" version of the moderate growth scenario described in Chapter 6. In this scenario coal and "other" energy sources together constituted 23 percent of total energy consumption in 1974, and would be about 33 percent in 1985 and about 54 percent in 2000. Although these figures may be on the high side of the practical range, the importance of accelerating the shift to coal and nuclear is such that a challenging objective should be set.

A major effort should be undertaken jointly by government and industry to resolve remaining questions in the public's mind about nuclear safety. The recent Rasmussen report will be very helpful in reducing the remaining uncertainty about the possibility of serious accidents.[2] Similar documentation can be assembled and should be publicized broadly to respond to the concerns over waste disposal and storage, and diversion of nuclear material to weapons use. Only when such concerns are dispelled from the mind of the average citizen can the electric utility industry and the nation proceed to develop nuclear power at the pace needed. A specific policy target by which to measure the pace of such development is available from the High Coal and Nuclear version of the moderate-growth scenario described in Chapters 6 and 10. The recommended targets for installed nuclear generating capacity thus obtained are 236 million kilowatts in 1985 and 820 million kilowatts in

2000. An alternate approach to a high coal and nuclear version of the moderate-growth future would place greater emphasis on coal and less on nuclear fuel. Under, these circumstances, the installed nuclear capacity might be as much as 100 to 200 million kilowatts lower in the year 2000, with a corresponding addition to coal capacity.

Much depends on the pace and success of energy research and development. Established private institutions should be encouraged to continue and expand their research and development activities, thus relieving the general taxpayer of as much of the research and development effort as possible. The Electric Power Research Institute is an example of a nongovernment, nonprofit organization established to coordinate research and development for the electric utility industry. This organization provides a direct linkage between those who fund the research and those who are potential beneficiaries (the electric utility customer). The major utility companies and electrical manufacturers all sponsor research and development efforts in ways which maintain the linkage between support and benefit.

The government's contribution to energy research and development should emphasize long-range technology and the investigation of potentially low-payout research and development which cannot be justified by private organizations. Government contributions may also be necessary where there is a pressing national interest, or where market forces which would encourge research and development are inhibited by unavoidable government actions and regulations.

The existence of a large number and variety of research organizations, ranging from business through the academic community to government, provides both opportunities and problems. The opportunities lie in joint efforts such as in current fusion research. These efforts are to be encouraged as providing benefits through cooperation and interchange. The problems lie in coordinating the various efforts and minimizing duplication. It is recommended that joint program reviews be conducted periodically among all major energy researchers.

In past years, government-sponsored energy research in the United States has been heavily concentrated in nuclear technologies. This work clearly met the primary criterion for government research and development proposed above. Under circumstances which have developed in the last few years, projects such as coal gasification, shale oil recovery, solar, and geothermal energy are other instances where additional government assistance may be justified on the basis of a pressing national interest.

Research and development to increase the efficiencies of energy conversion processes and end-use devices should also be accelerated. Efficiencies of end-use devices have been given relatively little attention in the past because of the low cost of energy. With the advent of higher prices, such research and development will increase in response to normal market forces, but these efforts should be encouraged and accelerated wherever possible by public policy.

It is recommended that oil and gas prices be deregulated as rapidly as possible without causing major disruptions to the domestic economy, such as were caused by the abrupt increases in oil prices in 1973-74. Deregulation would allow the price allocation process to work more effectively. Specifically, it would: a) encourage exploration, b) encourage the use of secondary and tertiary recovery schemes which maximize oil and gas flows from existing wells, c) reduce the tendency for misallocation of resources which results from artificially low prices, and d) eliminate the need for administratively complex government allocation schemes which are necessary under the current price regulations.

A second main thrust of energy policy must be toward conservation and elimination of waste. This is an area in which immediate action is possible and in which significant near-term results are achievable. Eliminating energy waste would work to further the objective of independence, reduce the environmental effects of energy production and consumption, and lower inflationary pressures caused by high oil prices. Conservation efforts should include a joint effort by industry and government to provide consumers with information on which to make energy-efficient choices.

If allowed to function efficiently, the price mechanism can be relied upon as the primary means for promoting wise use and discouraging wasteful use of energy. Government actions in the transportation and residential areas could supplement price pressures, and cause further moderate reductions in consumption with little or no adverse effects on either economic conditions or lifestyles. One such action is the expansion of mass transit. Over the near term, emphasis must be placed on expansion of bus lines and improvement of existing rail lines. Government assistance is required to achieve any major increases in mass transit systems.

A related conservation measure is the continuation and strict enforcement of the 55 mph speed limit. In addition, action should be taken to provide greater flexibility in government regulations on freight rates and freight movements. Some current regulations artificially reduce the railroads' ability to compete, and require inefficient truck scheduling or routing.

Government action should also be taken to aid consumers in making energy-efficient choices. Publishing mileage estimates for automoblies is an example of an action of this type already taken by the government. Requiring the labeling of energy using appliances with relative efficiency measures is another. Dissemination of recommended insulation and construction standards for homes and commercial buildings is a third.

Localities should be encouraged to strengthen those aspects of building codes which are energy related. Federal assistance should be made available to local agencies which determine building codes so as to assure that the technical basis for code changes is adequate and that the changes have met cost-benefit criteria. Changes that add significantly to first costs of residential construction should be examined with particular care to avoid pricing more low- and moderate-income purchasers out of the housing market.

Efforts to assure energy supplies and promote conservation must be carefully coordinated. The diverse government agencies whose actions impact on energy supply and demand must be monitored and focused toward consistent and compatible national goals. The parochial interests of individual agencies must be subordinated to and coordinated with the overall national goals of: continued economic growth, wise energy use, environmental improvement, greater energy independence, and enhancement of the overall quality of life. For these reasons it is recommended that the Energy Resources Council be continued and strengthened to give it authority and responsibility for carrying out United States energy policy.

2. Materials

Continued moderate economic growth will require continued growth in consumption of materials. However, the rate of growth of consumption of nonenergy resources will be slower than the rate of growth of GNP. This is because the services component of GNP is growing faster than the production component and because efficiency of metals utilization is improving. It can be expected that the increase of consumption of the five major metals (iron, aluminum, copper, zinc, and lead) will average 2.8 percent per year, in conjunction with a 3.5 to 3.7 percent per year growth in real GNP. Increases in recycling metals will reduce the growth rate of newly mined metal somewhat below the 2.8 percent figure.

Such a growth in consumption is well within the resource capacity of the United States, as supplemented by reasonable levels of imports. For a few strategic metals such as manganese, chromium, and nickel, the United States must depend almost entirely on imports from a relatively few countries. In most other cases, however, United States import policies reflect the existence of large, low-cost mineral deposits dispersed among a number of foreign countries. In these cases, imports benefit both the United States and the exporting countries whenever prices are set to cover all costs adequately. There is no need for ceilings on mineral imports. Prudence would suggest, however, that contingency planning should provide for alternatives if there should be an embargo by any of the exporting countries.

It is recommended that primary reliance be placed on the combination of rising prices and improving technology to make increasing quantities of materials available. These factors will also cause the percentages of recycled metal to increase. As prices of newly mined metals rise, separation of scrap metal will become more economical as will redesign of products to facilitate recovery.

Technological progress must also be pursued to aid in making resources available at reasonable costs. Transfer of such technology to resource-rich developing countries may be one form of compensation to induce these countries to share their resources. For these reasons, research and development into mineral recovery and recycling techniques will be equally as important as energy research and development over the next 25 years. Undersea mining as well as underground and surface mining techniques must be improved.

The development of stable, balanced, and consistent government policies is as crucial as technological progress in determining the future of the United States minerals industry. Government policies with regard to mining, pollution controls, and reclamation must be reviewed from a cost-benefit viewpoint. The resulting regulations must be instituted so that there is assurance as to their stability and permanence. Without such stability, private investment cannot be expected either in research and development or in new full-scale mining operations.

The establishment of government policies is particularly important as a prerequisite to undersea mining. Here, international agreements are lacking, and government policy intentions and assurances are needed to back up private initiative. Some efforts to mine manganese nodules in the Pacific Ocean are currently being planned, and equipment is already being procured. For such activities to proceed on a large scale, however, general international agreements are necessary.

Some authorities believe that the establishment of

minerals cartels with the strength and determination of OPEC is improbable. (See Appendix F material on Non-Energy Minerals.) Nevertheless, it is recommended that the United States develop contingency plans adequate to counter the threat of an import embargo of any of the important minerals. These plans should include such alternatives as stockpiling, recycling, development of consumption cutbacks, and examination of substitution possibilities.

As in the case of oil, any shortages in supplies of minerals will more likely result from artificial causes than from depletion of ore reserves or other natural causes. The ultimate solution to such artificial shortages must be improved international cooperation and a world organization with some degree of power to prevent unilateral actions in defiance of previously ratified multinational agreements. The United States should consider the establishment of such an organization to be of prime importance as an objective in all international trade negotiations.

E. Population

There are two aspects of the population problem in the United States—overall size and distribution. The status of both aspects is clouded by recent apparent reversals of long-standing trends. In the last decade the birth rate in the United States has declined past the replacement level. Also, recent surveys suggest that the historic trend of population movement from rural to urban areas may have ended. It is, of course, uncertain whether these patterns will continue. As long as they do, however, the ability of the United States to accommodate its population need not be a matter of concern. It is unnecessary to adopt measures to control population size as long as population patterns develop along the lines of the moderate-growth scenario described in Chapter 6.

In regard to population distribution, no measures to limit further concentrations are necessary. It remains important, however, to encourage efforts to rejuvenate central cities so that middle and upper income families will be induced to return. Efforts by the private sector to participate in this rejuvenation should be facilitated. Rising energy costs, especially in the area of transportation, may provide an impetus to city renewal efforts.

F. Agriculture

United States agricultural output should be maximized so that food can be sold in world markets to help meet the needs of developing nations and to help overcome the United States balance of pay-

ments problems arising from the importation of oil and other raw materials. Agricultural product pricing practices should permit average price levels to reflect full costs of production and should be freely competitive to encourage efficient production practices. Farm subsidies, acreage allotments, and incentives to limit output are inconsistent with current national objectives and should be discontinued.

Agricultural research and development should focus on developing high yielding strains and pesticides which do not have undue effects on ecological balances. Additional efforts are needed to expand arable land and maximize the usage of renewable fertilizers.

G. The Environment

Economic growth can be compatible with continuing improvements in environmental quality, although capital diversion from "productive" facilities to pollution-control devices will tend to slow growth somewhat. The degree of slowdown need not be major, if the costs and benefits of proposed environmental standards are carefully balanced and the status of technological developments is properly assessed.

Environmental quality standards will have to be enforced by regulation supplemented by financial incentives. Over the long term, a combination of regulations, pollution taxes or fees, and tax credits for pollution control expenditures will provide the most equitable solution to environmental problems.

Environmental quality regulations should be subjected to cost-benefit analyses which consider all aspects of the public interest. Once adopted on this basis, standards should not be subject to frequent changes. Uncertainty in this area inhibits the development of new energy supplies. For example, mining and land reclamation regulations should be determined on the basis of reasonable compromises between the nation's need to make use of its coal resources and its desire to maintain and improve the environment. Once the determinations have been made, the regulations should be stabilized.

H. Finance

Recommendations concerning financing and electric utility pricing are included in the sections on those subjects in Part III.

I. International Relations

The analysis of world growth patterns presented in

Chapter 7 provides the basis for some observations and suggestions related to international relations.

Population growth and food supplies represent major problems for developing countries. These problems will only be overcome through aid and assistance from the advanced countries.

Some form of international economic organization would be useful in assuring that environmental costs are accounted for and that unilateral, sharp price changes are avoided. Other objectives would be reducing the gaps between the developed and developing world and tapping the pool of investment capital being concentrated in the oil producing countries.

J. The Changing Priorities of Growth

It is the conclusion of this report that some form of economic growth will continue and that a "new concept of growth" is called for. To develop a new concept of growth does not mean completely eliminating old ideas. Growth has two connotations: one is the process of producing *more*. The second and more important meaning is *change*. Economic growth causes change in resource availabilities, patterns of production and consumption, technologies, and social values and preferences. A new view of growth can emphasize the value of change without discounting the traditional value assigned to having more.

New weight will be given to diversity, collective capacity, and wealth of the overall society. There must also be a merging of economic and ecological concepts. The holistic/systemic perspective of ecology can be employed to broaden the economic conception of growth beyond material production and consumption and population. Likewise, the economic view of resources as being relative to the forces of markets, prices, and the expansion of knowledge can moderate the ecologists' vision of resources as absolute, and thus "limited," physical quantities.

The idea of "limits" is pertinent for the new concept of growth, but it applies more to the needs of individuals for material things than to the amounts of resources available to meet those needs. Growth in consumption to bring all people up above the pov-erty level is necessary and desirable, while consumption which is wasteful is uneconomic. The merging of economic and ecological concepts would reflect a broadened view of the human and environmental condition.

Other elements to be incorporated in a new concept of growth are the notions of durable production and provident consumption. As the costs of resource flows through the economy increase, the use of disposable goods and goods which employ designed obsolescence will decline. Rising costs for essentials will also reduce purchases of things that are not really needed and promote the notion of "making do."

The new concept of growth calls for greater reliance on individual responsibility and action. Growth will be defined in terms of the enlargement of shared interests among individuals and their economic, ecological, political, and technological subsystems.

The terms "clean growth," "quality growth," or "optimal growth" might be used to describe a new concept of growth, although none of these terms really captures the sense of continuous change and multiplicity of forces being experienced. The concept of "betterment" may be a useful alternative. "Betterment," that is, growth in good, is elusive, but it may suggest the beginning of some new measures with which to test the value of the other forms of growth. Unfortunately, there is no single indicator for what is "good." Each case has to be evaluated on its own merits, and there may be disagreement about the evaluation. "Goodness" represents an evaluation of the total system, and if this evaluation is estimated to be better tomorrow than today, then there is betterment.

On balance, it may be inappropriate to try to characterize a new concept of growth in one term or phrase. Such terms tend to suggest a finality which does not exist in a world which is constantly changing and evolving.

FOOTNOTES

1. Commitee for Economic Development. *Acheiving Energy Independence.* New York, Committee for Economic Development, 1974.
2. Atomic Energy Commission. *Reactor Safety Study.* Washington, D.C., Atomic Energy Commission, Aug. 1974.

PART III

Growth and the Electric Utility Industry

ARTS I and II of this study presented first a general and then a specific analysis of the problems and prospects for economic growth in the future. Although the study concentrates primarily on the United States, a substantial analysis of world growth problems is also included.

The bulk of Part II is devoted to describing the results of a broadly based analysis of prospects for growth in the United States over the next 25 years and more. A number of different aspects of the growth phenomenon; e.g., population, agriculture, national income, personal consumption, minerals demand and supply, energy demand and supply, electricity demand and supply, etc., are considered. These aspects of growth are examined in terms of the impacts of growth on the society, the economy, and the private citizen in the United States.

Part III concludes the study by relating the findings of Parts I and II to the electric utility industry in the United States. In particular the pricing and financing problems of the industry in the future are evaluated in the light of the conclusions of Parts I and II. Recommendations are made concerning future developments in the pricing of utility services and the financing of utility facilities. Action on these recommendations would improve the ability of the industry to serve the nation over the next 25 years.

CHAPTER 9

Electric Power Pricing

A. Introduction

Earlier portions of this report have examined the prospects for economic growth in the United States during the balance of the century. This provides a basis for estimating probable energy demand and supply. An important factor in the relationship between demand and supply is price.

In the theoretical world of pure competition, price is automatically determined by the interaction of supply and demand. In the real world we have a mixed economy with partly free and partly government-controlled markets. Price still remains an important factor, but it is not the sole determinant of supplies. When supply is controlled by non-market forces, price generally helps to adjust demand to match the available supply. When price is controlled, supply and demand tend to get out of balance.

Much of the energy industry operates under controls. Oil prices are currently determined largely by the pricing practices of the Organization of Petroleum Exporting Countries while interstate gas prices are set by the Federal Power Commission. In the electric utility industry, prices are set primarily by state regulatory commissions.

Price determination is a matter of substantial concern to both the consumer and producer. This concern has increased in the energy industry as energy prices have escalated over the last few years. Some observers believe that the only practical solution to the energy demand-supply-price dilemma lies in eliminating price controls whenever possible, or at least making them hew more closely to a cost-based control system where decontrol is impractical. There are others who continue to believe that the solution lies in imposing more and stricter controls to reinforce those already in existence.

During this debate, it is natural that one of the most common areas of discussion has been the pricing of electricity. Pricing practices in the electric utility industry are necessarily complex for a variety of reasons: (a) the industry is fragmented into a large number of companies having different costs;

(b) state regulatory commissions deviate from one another in their approaches to price regulation; (c) each company serves a number of different types of customers some of whom impose far different cost burdens on the company than others; (d) service to these customers is provided by plant and equipment used under joint cost conditions,[1] making proper allocation of costs to various customers a difficult task; (e) the industry is the most capital-intensive in the world so that adequate payments for the use of capital are a substantial part of total costs and are of extreme importance; (f) electricity storage is impractical in large quantities so that in a very real sense a kilowatt hour sold, for example, on a hot, mid-week summer afternoon may have a very different cost than one sold at midnight on an autumn weekend; and (g) electricity may, in many cases, be of such essential importance and value to the user that price is not a primary determining factor.

In addition, the industry consumes large quantities of nonrenewable resources, and the production, transmission, and distribution of electricity affects the environment. As a result, revision of industry pricing policies has been urged by some observers as a means for restricting consumption to that amount which they judge to be "desirable." Others view alterations in prices to some customer classes as a way to achieve unrelated "desirable" social objectives. Still others see the more rapid growth of electrical energy than of other energy forms as a reason for restricting consumption to some "average" rate.

For these reasons it is important that a comprehensive review of past, current, and prospective pricing practices be provided as a part of this study.

The following paragraphs attempt to present such a review by: considering the rationale for past and current policies; evaluating some of the major criticisms now being raised; discussing the need for and availability of information about the effects of price changes on consumption; and proposing several developments in pricing which merit consideration in meeting the future needs of society.

B. The Economic Nature of Utilities

In some respects, the investor-owned electric utility company in the United States is essentially the same as any other privately owned business.[2] The utility obtains funds in the competitive capital market to build its facilities; it hires employees in the competitive job market to operate these facilities; it competes for the customer's dollar with suppliers of all other goods and services including alternate forms of energy such as oil and gas; it pays taxes on its receipts, its real estate, its income, etc.; and it must make a fair return on its invested capital if it is to stay in business, compensate present owners adequately, and continue to attract new capital as required.

However, there are several important differences between the electric utility and the conventional private enterprise: (a) the utility company is afforded a monopoly for its basic service in the sense that, generally, only one electric utility is permitted to operate in a particular area; (b) the utility is subject to government regulation of its prices and service; (c) the utility has an obligation to serve all within its franchise territory who apply for service under the established rate structure; and (d) the utility may not withdraw from the business of selling electric service without prior regulatory approval.

The concept of government regulation of public utilities derives from English common law as modified by a series of landmark United States judicial decisions over the period from 1877 through 1943.[3] These decisions gradually determined the criteria for a public utility to be: (a) a business whose activities are essential to the public welfare (i.e., in legal terms, "affected with a public interest:"), and (b) one which operates at lowest average cost in supplying a particular market when it is free from competition of others selling the same service.

The second criterion, defining what economists call a "natural monopoly,"[4] stems from the basic economic and technological characteristics of the business rather than from legal pronouncements. The most important of these characteristics is that the supplying of electricity requires very costly capital equipment with a very high ratio of investment to annual revenue. Efficient utilization of this expensive capital equipment requires that the facilities be operated as close to full capacity as possible, thus dividing the fixed costs of these facilities among the maximum number of the units of output. In this context, duplicate facilities such as would be present in the usual competitive situation, would result in substantially higher costs.

Despite the absence of direct competition in the form of rival companies vying to sell electric service within a given territory, the electric utility company in the United States has faced a variety of indirect competitive forces. Natural gas and oil are potential substitutes for electricity in residential cooking, water heating and space heating services, as well as for a wide variety of commercial and industrial heating and processing applications. Industrial and large commercial customers can always consider the alternative of generating their own electricity rather than purchasing it from the local utility company. Competition with electric utility companies, and with government power projects in other areas is sometimes a significant factor in determining where new industrial plants and office complexes will be located.

However, it has generally been concluded that the forces of indirect competition cannot alone be relied upon to protect the public interest. Therefore, a combination of local, state and federal regulatory bodies has been established throughout the United States to supplement those restraints on investor-owned electric utility operations which are imposed by the indirect competitive forces. The dominant form of regulation of investor-owned utilities is on a statewide basis with essentially all of the states having public utility commissions charged with regulating the production and intrastate retail sale of electricity by investor-owned companies. In Texas, municipal governments regulate within city boundaries. In South Dakota, a mediation board is available to settle disputes. And in Nebraska, all electric utility facilities are government-owned or government-financed. The Federal Power Commission is charged with regulatory responsibilities regarding all interstate transactions and sales at wholesale.

C. Regulation and Pricing

Responsibilities of the typical utility commission, relative to electric utility regulation, encompass a wide variety of activities having to do, principally, with construction, rates, service, and financing. One of the most important tasks of regulation is rate making. The basic criteria which govern the rate-making process are that rates shall be just and reasonable to both the consumer and the company, and that they shall not involve unfair discrimination among customers similarly situated. To qualify for a "just and reasonable" label, electric rates must meet several important, but sometimes conflicting criteria. Well-designed rates should:

(a) Provide for prices which will compensate producers for expenses incurred and services rendered.

(b) Allocate costs fully and fairly among classes

of customers, within the limits of reasonable practicality.[5]

(c) Compensate fairly the owners of all capital funds employed in the business, and provide earnings which will attract the capital necessary to finance the new facilities needed for continued production.

(d) Reward efficiency of production and high quality of service.

(e) Promote efficient utilization of the fixed plant facilities of the utility company.

(f) To the extent possible, provide reasonably stable trends in revenues over time to facilitate both customer and company planning for the future.

(g) Be simple enough to be administered efficiently by the utility company and understood by the customer.

In endeavoring to set rates which perform all of the foregoing functions, the typical regulatory process involves two distinct steps: (a) setting an adequate *level* of rates in the aggregate, and (b) developing an appropriate *structure* of rates.

The *level* of rates determines the degree to which total revenues cover all reasonable operating expenses, provide a fair return on invested capital, and are adequate to attract the new capital required. The *structure* of rates determines the way in which total costs, including the cost of capital, are apportioned among the various customers.

Although the criteria listed above are essentially the same as those which govern prices generally in a market economy, the method of pricing under regulation is far different from that which prevails in a competitive industry. In the economist's neatly theoretical world of pure competition, the price of a product is automatically determined at the point of intersection of the industry supply and demand curves for that product. Under these circumstances the average individual producer has absolutely no effect on the price. Even in the admittedly less than perfectly competitive conditions which characterize the great bulk of United States industry, it is the interplay of demand and supply forces which predominates in the price setting process.

In the real world of electric utility economics, however, rate setting is the last of several complex steps in the regulatory process, at each of which human intervention and judgment are necessary to balance conflicting social, technical, and financial considerations.

The remainder of this chapter on pricing and rate

structure is divided into three parts: a discussion of factors which primarily affect the setting of rate *levels;* a summary of rate *structure* considerations; and an outline of probable future trends in rate regulation.

D. Rate Levels

In setting rate levels, two primary questions should be addressed. The first is: What is the company's total revenue requirement considering both operating expenses and the cost of capital; i.e., return on investment? The second is: What is the company's incremental cost situation? It is important to emphasize that the rate levels being set by current regulation will be applied in a future period.

A satisfactory answer to the first question is required if the utility company is to: continue to provide satisfactory service, maintain financial integrity, provide a reasonable return to its present investors, and continue to attract the capital needed to support future construction. A satisfactory answer to the second question is needed if the rates which have been authorized are to continue for any length of time to serve the functions just enumerated and to allocate in an optimum manner those natural and capital resources consumed by the utility, considering the competing needs of other segments of the United States economy. Unfortunately, the rate levels associated with each question will, in general, be different; sometimes greatly different.

1. Revenue Requirements

The total revenue requirement, also often called the total cost of service, can be defined as the sum of: (a) necessary operation and maintenance expenses; (b) annual depreciation; (c) taxes; and (d) a reasonable return on the net valuation of the property used for the supply of electric service. Therefore, it will reflect the total costs of operating the utility's physical plant as it exists at the time the rates are to be in effect.

In equation form this total revenue requirement can be summarized as:

$$RR = OM + D + T + (G - AD) R$$

where:

RR = revenue requirement
OM = operation and maintenance
D = annual depreciation
T = taxes
G = gross value of the property
AD = accrued (or sometimes observed) depreciation on the property
R = rate of return (a percentage)

In the process of determining the total revenue required, the regulatory agency may dispute any of the company's figures. For example, it may decide that a specific type of expense (part of OM in the formula) is unreasonable and excessive and therefore may disallow part or all of it. When such items are disallowed they are, in effect, charged to the company's stockholders.

The regulatory agency must also ascertain an appropriate value for (G - AD), or rate base as it is normally called. The rate base is the depreciated value of the tangible and intangible property "used and useful" in the business. This suggests that (G - AD) is determined primarily from the left-hand or asset side of the balance sheet and from such other valuation as may be required under the law applicable to the particular regulatory agency. As in the case of expenses, the regulatory agency may disallow, or eliminate, certain items of property from the rate base, on the grounds that they are not used or useful in the business.

A variety of techniques can be used to determine (G - AD) but two are most common. One, called "original cost," is based on the company's accounting records showing what each piece of property cost when first put into utility service, less its accumulated depreciation. Another, variously called "reproduction cost," "current cost," or "fair value," is an attempt to recognize changes in the value of facilities since their initial construction.

Finally, a fair rate of return, R, must be determined. An appropriate value for R is at least partially dependent on: (a) the company's capitalization; i.e., its mixture of outstanding bonds, preferred stock and common equity and (b) the interest and preferred dividend rate payable on securities in the company's capitalization.

In actual regulation, the combined tasks of determining appropriate values of (G - AD) and R can be accomplished in many ways, each of which is capable of achieving a result that is fair both to the customer and the company.

If the problem is viewed from the right-hand part of the balance sheet, specifically that part termed the capitalization, the rate of return must reflect interest payments on bonded indebtedness, dividends on preferred stock, and earnings on common stock equity. The first two components are specified exactly in the bond indenture and the preferred stock certificates. The third component is a residual amount which becomes available to the common equity holders only after all other legitimate claims on the company have been settled. Determining the fair and reasonable level of this residual amount is generally the most difficult task.

The Supreme Court, in a 1944 decision called the Hope Natural Gas Case,[6] developed the following two general criteria to aid regulators in this task: (a) the return to the equity owner should be commensurate with returns on other investments having corresponding risks and (b) the return should be sufficient to ensure confidence in the financial integrity of the enterprise so that it can maintain its credit and attract new capital when needed. In applying these general criteria to specific situations it is, of course, necessary to define the terms "corresponding risks" and "financial integrity." An extensive literature on these aspects of rate making has developed over the years; a sampling from which is presented in the Selected Bibliography which follows the footnotes for this section, and by many of the documents referenced in the footnotes themselves.

2. Adequate Return on Common Equity

The Hope Natural Gas Case criteria can be thought of as establishing a range of reasonableness for the proper rate of return for an electric utility company. The "proper" position within this range for a specific utility company will be influenced by a wide variety of factors including the efficiency of management and the policies of the regulatory commission.

In the past much attention has been directed toward establishing appropriate upper limits for return on common equity by attempting to quantify the concept of "risk." These attempts have included the very simple approach of assuming that the only companies with corresponding risks were other electric utility companies with similar capitalization ratios. This approach can be criticized on the basis of "circularity," i.e., if it is first applied when returns on utility stocks in general are low, the returns must always remain low, and vice versa.

At the other extreme are some very sophisticated ventures into portfolio theory and other aspects of financial analysis to assess relative risks in different industries. Such methods are perhaps more logical than comparing each utility company with all other utility companies, since each utility company must compete for capital not only with its "sister" companies but with all companies in all industries. Unfortunately, the techniques for measuring relative risks across industry boundaries are often complex, difficult to interpret, and open to criticism from other "experts" with other techniques.

Describing such techniques is beyond the scope of this study. Three excellent examples of the voluminous literature in this field are listed as Footnotes 7, 8 and 9. Each, in turn, provides suggestions for further reading in the field.

In the current environment for most electric utilities, however, it seems more reasonable to concentrate attention on the other criterion of an adequate rate of return which, according to the Hope decision, must not be breached if utility companies are to maintain financial integrity and thereby be able to attract new capital as required. The characteristics of the current environment which direct attention to this criterion are: inflation; heavy construction programs with rapidly rising costs; coverage requirements in indentures which must be satisfied before particular kinds of new securities can be issued; severe regulatory lag; and an extremely uncertain fuel supply situation. All of these could be with us for many years into the future, and together they have pushed many utility companies to or below the limits satisfying the Hope criterion.

Establishing the limits for the "financial integrity—capital attraction" criterion is, in one sense, somewhat easier than in the case of the "corresponding risks" criterion. Two common financial measures: market-to-book ratio and interest coverage ratio are appropriate for this purpose. The first ratio is defined as the average market value of a share of common stock divided by the book, or accounting, value per common share. The denominator of the ratio can, of course, be determined by dividing the total common equity of the company by the number of shares outstanding. This ratio is important to any company desiring to raise new capital by selling additional common shares. Whenever the ratio is below 1.0, the sale of new common shares will dilute[10] the equity of existing shareholders.[11]

The second ratio has particular relevance when specified minimum coverage ratios appear as a legal provision in a company's bond and debenture indentures. A typical provision in a bond indenture requires pre-tax operating income to be at least twice the total interest charges on existing bonds and on proposed bonds, before those proposed bonds can be issued.

Most preferred stock issues contain similar restrictions on the issuance of additional preferred, so that the earnings coverage for the preferred stock constitutes a third limit.

Together these represent three measures of return which relate to a company's financial health and to its ability to attract capital to finance new facilities. When a market-to-book ratio is less than 1.0, it reflects a return which has so discouraged common stock investors that they have forced the company's stock price down until it is less than the book value. The other two measurements relate to whether earnings will or will not be sufficient to cover legal minimums to permit the sale of new debt or pre-

ferred stock. If the limit for one measure (e.g., interest coverage ratio) is reached before that of the other two, the utility management may be able to switch to one of the other methods of raising new capital (e.g., common or preferred stock). However, such financings can continue only for a relatively short time before severely distorting the company's capitalization ratios.

Once all three limits have been reached, common stock financing becomes more and more difficult and, eventually, only such funds, if any, as may be internally generated (e.g., depreciation, retained earnings and tax deferrals where these are normalized rather than "flowed through")[12] remain available to support the utility's construction programs. For essentially all electric utility companies the combined effects of growing demand for electricity and rising construction costs make the total of internally generated funds woefully inadequate as a basis for current construction programs. Over the period from 1969 through 1973, for example, internally generated funds covered less than 33 percent of the new construction expenditures for the industry as a whole.

The technique of regulation which keeps earnings barely sufficient to cover embedded interest and dividends and minimum earnings for common stock may appropriately be called the "bare-bones" technique. This frequently ignores coverage ratios and makes it impossible to meet coverage tests.

Unfortunately, the bare-bones technique can be a very dangerous one in an uncertain world. The combination of adverse effects on earnings, coupled with regulatory lags, can cause abrupt drops in coverage ratios. This in turn can force the company to postpone or cancel new securities issues and consequently to delay or halt construction projects. Extended lows in the stock market can similarly depress market-to-book ratios. In recent months the oil shortage and huge price increases for imported oil and for other fuels combined with a depressed stock market to trigger just such unanticipated consequences for several companies. The closer they were to their minimum coverage ratios on the eve of October 17, 1973, the more likely it was that their efforts to raise needed amounts of new capital would be frustrated, and the more severe the consequent disruption in their operations was likely to be in the following months.

Because of the long-term commitments involved in most utility construction programs, it is impossible to stop or start them overnight. Momentum once lost because of the unavailability of capital is difficult and costly to regain, for example, in the construction of a one-half billion dollar 1000 MW nuclear station. The final consequences of such stop-and-go construc-

Chart 9·1
UTILITY INDUSTRY FINANCIAL RATIOS

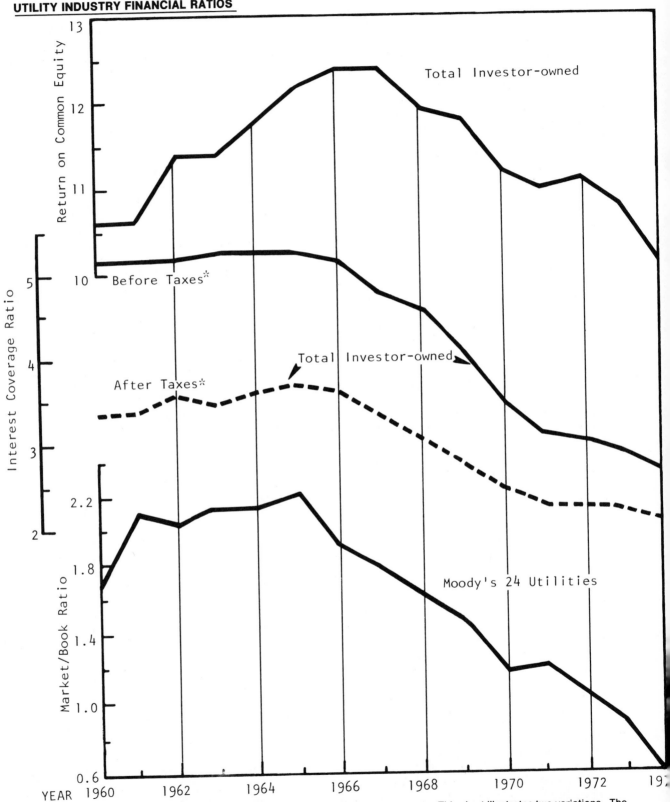

*Note: There are several methods for calculating interest coverage ratio in common use. This chart illustrates two variations. The solid line is based on net income before taxes while the dashed line is based on net income after taxes and after subtracting allowance for funds used during construction. This second version was also used to develop Table 10·5.

262

Chart 9•2
MARKET-TO-BOOK RATIO

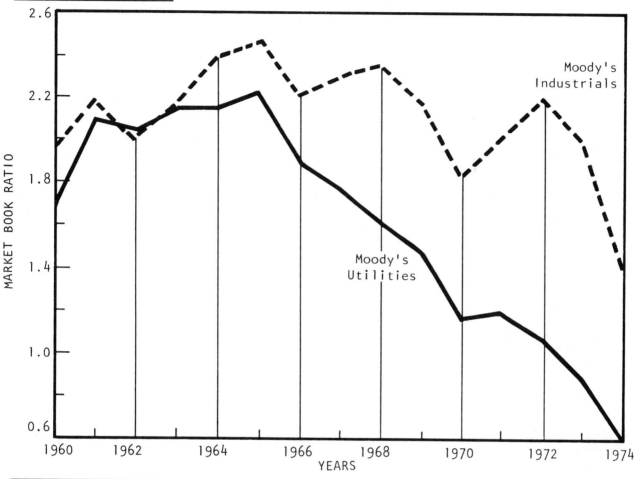

tion are: (a) higher costs of facilities and (b) the danger of inadequate capacity in future years.

Even if regulation could respond instantly so as to assure that minimum coverage ratios were never violated, a bare-bones approach would be inimical to the long-term interests of the customers and to the common shareholders as well. This is a consequence of the fact that such an approach typically yields a return on common equity which so discourages common stock investors that they allow market-to-book ratios; i.e., the first financial measure mentioned earlier, to fall well below 1.0.

For the aggregate of all investor-owned companies, the trends of return on common equity and bond interest coverage are shown on Chart 9•1 for the last few years. The same chart presents market-to-book ratios for the 24 typical utilities which constitute Moody's index. Note that over the last half of this period the return on year-end common equity dropped gradually from about 12½ percent to 10 percent, while coverage ratios dropped from 5 to 2.7,

and the market-to-book ratio went from about 2 down to well below 1.0.

A utility company—or any other company—in such straits cannot be considered in a healthy financial condition. In fact, a number of studies, such as that by George E. Phelps[13] and others, extending over several past stock market cycles, suggest that a market value of no less than 1.25 to 1.5 times book value is necessary for reasonable financial health (i.e., a market/book ratio of 1.25 or more).

Over these same several stock market cycles, an average return on common equity of 12½ to 15 percent would have sufficed for most electric utility company common stock market prices to reach 1.50 times book value. Of course, all utility companies are not alike, and for some with prospects for continued high load factor, rapid load growth, and earnings growth it may be reasonable to expect them to command significantly higher market-to-book ratios than 1.5 under normal conditions. Chart 9•2 presents a 10-year history of market-to-book ratios for a standard group of 24 electric utility stocks followed by Moody's Investors Services[14] and, for comparison, the same ratio for a group of industrial companies compiled by Moody's.

Since common stocks must compete with other forms of investment such as bonds, it is generally conceded that an adequate return on common equity must be higher in periods of high interest rates than in periods of low interest rates. On such a basis a common equity return of 12½ percent might have been judged adequate five years ago when interest rates were 5-6 percent, while 15 percent or more might be necessary in the current environment with interest rates as high as 10 to 12 percent.

Fortunately, a relatively small increment in revenue requirements is sufficient to raise the return on common equity of a typical electric utility company from an inadequate 11 percent to a more nearly adequate level; e.g., 15 percent in 1973.[15] Using aggregate statistics for all investor-owned electric utilities in the United States, for example, it is simple to calculate that the difference between total revenues needed to yield the actual 11 percent return in 1973, and those revenues which would have yielded 15 percent in that year, is a rather modest 7.6 percent. For the ten largest investor-owned utility companies the increment needed to reach a 15 percent return ranged from 0.5 to 14 percent. Of course, these figures represent the increases in revenues necessary to correct, in one year, a worsening situation which developed over a period of six or seven years.

Another way to illustrate the difference between sickness and health—between inadequate and adequate returns—is to calculate how much additional revenue (beyond those amounts actually obtained) would have been needed by the industry *each year* after 1966 to allow returns on equity to rise from 12.7 percent in 1966 to 15 percent in 1973, instead of dropping to 11 percent as they did in actuality. The calculation shows that 0.6 percent more would have been needed in 1967; another 2.4 percent more would have been needed in 1968; another 1.3 percent in 1969; another 2.0 percent in 1970, another 0.9 percent in 1971, another 0.2 percent in 1972 and another 0.7 percent in 1973. See Appendix I for calculations.

These figures indicate that the difference between inadequate and adequate returns would have been almost insignificant in terms of its cost to the average customer, while it would almost certainly have made a great difference to the industry, in terms of its ability to raise new capital and its ability to provide for the future requirements of its customers. It should also be noted that with adequate returns, the costs of financing would have been significantly less than they actually were. This would have saved the customer a certain amount in interest charges, thus partially offsetting the incremental revenue needed to produce the adequate return.

In a long-term sense the interests of the customers, the regulators, the company, and its investors are compatible, if not identical. All groups benefit from a healthy company and suffer from a sick one. Other parts of this report indicate that the electric utility industry, as well as other parts of the energy industry, will require major additional funding over the next 10-15 years. Since only a fraction of these funds can be derived from internal sources, the remainder must come from the competitive capital markets. If the electric utility industry can offer competitive returns and an outlook for future earnings gains competitive with other companies seeking funds, it will be able to obtain what it needs. If electric utility companies cannot compete on these terms for new capital, investors will provide it only at a very high cost or will not provide it at all.

The problem lies not only in regulatory decisions which fail to allow adequate returns on equity but also in the regulatory lags which prevent companies from earning what has been allowed. Inflation, of course, is the basic culprit. In a period of rapid inflation, a rate filing based on a past test year which must then endure up to a year or more of waiting periods, staff analyses, hearings, and commission deliberations is almost certain to be woefully out of date on the first day it becomes effective.

Some solutions to this basic problem of regulatory lag are available in most jurisdictions right now, without any changes in the legal basis of regulation. The use of forward test years is an obvious example. Another is to allow tariff changes to become effective immediately, subject to refund to the customers of any portions of the rate increase which later hearings show to be excessive.

Other possible solutions to the problem may require some changes in the legal basis of regulation in some jurisdictions. In this area it would be particularly valuable to develop techniques for reducing the length of hearings by eliminating the repetition of matters which were fully covered in earlier hearings. In many cases a simple update is all that is required. Another method for reducing the complexity as well as the length of hearings is to extend the concept of automatic adjustment clauses to components of capital costs, including environmental expenditures, as well as to other expense categories in addition to fuel.

3. Accounting for Social Costs

Social costs and private costs are two separate and

distinct parts of the overall burden imposed on society by the production of all goods and services. Private costs are those which are recognized, levied, and paid within the normal operation of the economic system. Thus defined, private costs associated with the production and sale of electricity would include: fuel costs, labor costs, real estate taxes, etc. On the other hand, social costs (or externalities, to use the economists' term) derive from activities which impose a cost or burden on society, but are external to the operations of the economy in such a way that no recompense is normally obtained.

Most agricultural and industrial processes, including the production and distribution of electric power, contribute to the imposition of a wide variety of costs on society, in the form of deterioration in air and water quality, high noise levels, etc. Farming, for example, imposes a social cost on society at large when fertilizer components leach from the fields into streams or lakes and thereby disrupt the normal ecological balance of the marine life. Individuals and communities also impose vast social costs on one another without any balancing of accounts. An obvious example in the case of communities is dumping of sewage into rivers, lakes, and the oceans.

In theory, the attempt to use the price system to allocate scarce resources (as discussed in the sections on Marginal Costs, and Long Run Incremental Costs) will be unsuccessful to the extent that significant social costs are ignored. If social costs are excluded from consideration, the market price of goods will reflect private costs only and, it is argued, be too low. The low market price will lead to an output which, from the standpoint of society as a whole, is too high.

On the other hand, techniques for including social costs which exaggerate the true effects on society, will result in prices which are excessive and consumption which is lower than optimum. Similarly, including social costs in the prices of some items and not others will distort the resource allocation process in unknown ways. The tendency, of course, will be to reduce the output below the optimum level for those commodities whose social costs have been included in the market price and to increase the output of other commodities to an unwarranted extent. It seems obvious, then, that without adequate means for measuring social costs accurately and imposing them broadly throughout the economy, attempts to include them in the prices of one or a few commodities may well produce an overall adverse impact on society.

Measuring actual social costs presents a multitude of extremely difficult problems. Considering the particulate and sulfur emissions from fossil fuel combustion, for instance, the social costs could conceivably range from: (a) higher cleaning bills for clothes and house furnishings of people in the affected area, to (b) the need for more frequent painting of houses, and to (c) higher medical costs for people with a susceptibility to respiratory disease. Assessing these effects quantitatively for several given levels of pollution and a variety of weather conditions is impossible in any practical sense, even if only a single installation were the source of the pollution. In the typical situation the local power plant may be only one of a multitude of sources, among which are other industries, municipal facilities such as incinerators, and tens of thousands of automobiles.

The current attempts to deal with this complexity have, in general, taken the form of government regulations on maximum allowable levels of pollution either at the point of release (regulation of the effluent) or in the general environment (regulation of ambient conditions). Such regulations result in additional costs for stack gas cleanup, cooling towers, use of higher cost fuel, and water treatment facilities. These costs are added to the other costs of producing and distributing electricity. The inclusion of these costs in the price of electricity is, in effect, one way of internalizing social costs and thus transforming them into private costs.

Other methods of dealing with social costs are to: (a) tax pollution and (b) grant pollution discharge permits. Under the first method, the tax would rise in direct proportion to the severity of the pollution, thus giving the polluter the choice of reimbursing society through the tax payment for the consequences of the pollution, or of paying for facilities to eliminate the pollution and so avoid the tax. Under the second method, the responsible government agency would grant permits to pollute, up to a maximum within the ability of the environment to accommodate the releases. Such permits could be obtainable based upon payment of a fee or upon proof of some social or economic "need" to pollute.

Unfortunately, with all such techniques for quantifying social costs, there has generally been an inadequate basis for setting allowable levels of pollution or for determining appropriate tax levels. As other sections of this study suggest, the scientific community is just beginning to discern some of the complexities of ecological interactions, and to appreciate the widely varying tolerances of the environment for different pollutants.

As such knowledge accumulates, a logical basis can be formed for studies which will balance the economic and social benefits of any given level of environmental cleanliness against the costs of achieving such a level. The methodology of cost-benefit analysis which has been used by various government agencies to examine the consequences of public improvements such as dams, internal waterways, etc. has of late begun to be applied more widely to environmental protection problems. While much progress has been made in applying this methodology to new types of problems, much more remains to be done if such analysis is to provide a satisfactory guide to decision making.

During this learning period, there is the danger that over-zealousness to clean up the environment at almost any cost will place severe impediments in the path of economic progress and social well-being. There is evidence, for example, that the single-minded pursuit of elimination of sulfur from generating station stack gas during the period from 1968 to 1973, severely aggravated the oil crisis in the autumn and winter of 1973-74.

This conclusion stems from the fact that if utilities had been burning the same mix of fossil fuels in 1973 as they burnt in 1967 (rather than having switched in the interim from coal to a higher proportion of oil), the nation's total oil consumption would have been nearly 1 million barrels per day lower than it was.

Despite the difficulties, the electric industry has been pressed further than other industries to internalize its environmental costs. This is illustrated in Chart 9·3. The primary authority for establishing allowable pollutant levels for the utility industry is in the hands of specific agencies such as the Environmental Protection Agency at the national level, and similar state agencies at the local level. The responsibility for transforming these EPA regulations into action rests with the individual companies, while the responsibility for incorporating the resultant costs into the price of electricity is shared by the companies and the regulatory authorities. Thus, normal regulatory action is limited to: (a) evaluating the reasonableness of the costs incurred or estimated by the utility companies to bring their activities into compliance with the laws; and (b) permitting prompt incorporation of such costs into the utility's rate structure.

E. Rate Structure

Criteria for well-designed rates were presented in Section C of this Chapter in somewhat general terms, and from a point of view which concentrated on rate *levels*. A restatement of these criteria to emphasize their application to rate *structure* considerations may be of value at this point. The following list is taken largely from Bonbright:[16]

(a) Simplicity, understandability, public acceptability and feasibility of application.

(b) Freedom from controversy as to proper interpretations.

(c) Effectiveness in yielding adequate total revenues.

(d) Stability from year to year in revenues and rates.

(e) Fairness in apportioning costs of service.

(f) Efficiency of rate classes and rate blocks in approximating the true costs to serve, thus guiding the customer toward optimum use of limited resources, both in terms of total usage and in terms of distributing consumption between peak and off-peak periods.

The single criterion of an adequate rate structure which generally has been held to outrank all others in importance is that requiring a close correspondence between rates and cost of service, thus preventing unfair discrimination. For a variety of reasons, which will be discussed in the following paragraphs, it has been impossible to match rates exactly to costs for each particular customer. However, much of the history of cost analysis and rate structure determination in the United States has been aimed at achieving a closer approximation to that ideal while still meeting a variety of practical constraints and conflicting objectives.

1. Differential Pricing

If the only objective of a rate structure were to be the development of a fair total revenue, then a countless number of different rate structures would each be satisfactory for the purpose. One such structure might charge the same rate to all customers, regardless of the purpose for which, or the extent to which energy was used. While such a structure might have surface appeal as being 'fair' it would violate the most basic principles of service at cost and consequently be economically wasteful.

One simple example of differences in the costs of serving two types of customers is available in the comparison of a large industrial customer with the typical residential customer. The large industrial customer who accepts service at a relatively high load factor,[17] and accepts it directly from the utility company's high-voltage transmission lines by providing his own transforming, switching and other receiving equipment, represents a far different cost burden to the utility than does the residential customer whose use generally varies widely from time to time, and who requires the use of expensive step-down transformers, and an elaborate low voltage distribution system. It would be unfair to allocate to

Chart 9·3
EXPENDITURES FOR AIR AND WATER POLLUTION CONTROLS AS A PERCENT OF TOTAL CAPITAL EXPENDITURES BY BUSINESS

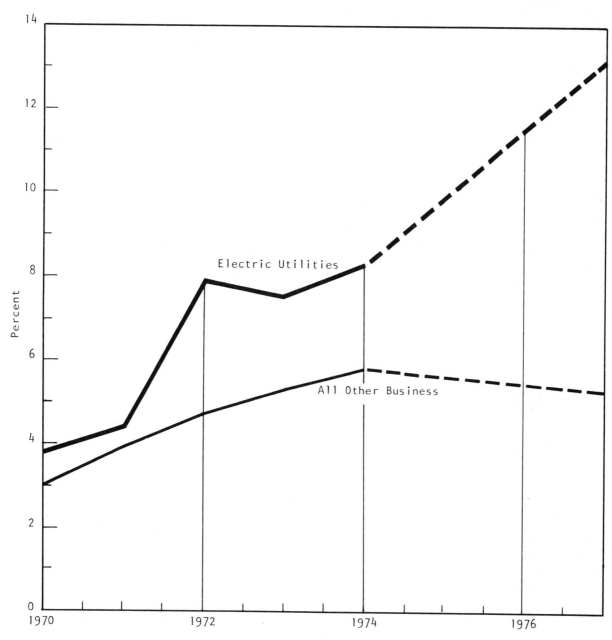

Source: McGraw-Hill Surveys

the large customer, either that part of the fixed costs (30 to 40 percent of the typical utility capital investment) represented by the distribution system required to serve the residential customer, or that part of the generation, transmission and distribution facilities necessary to assure the system's ability to meet the widely varying load of the residential customers.

Although cost differences have been the primary justification for rate structure differences, an ancillary consideration has sometimes been the value of, or demand for, the service. Again, the large industrial customer will provide a good example. A high load factor industrial customer served on an interruptible rate ensures a higher utilization of plant facilities, most of which were already required to serve other customers. If he, nonetheless, is charged for a share of the fixed costs of the utility, he is instrumental in reducing the cost of serving all other customers. In such a case, a net benefit to all customers results as long as the revenues from the industrial customer exceed the incremental (i.e., additional) costs of serving him.

If such a customer is charged more than these incremental costs but less than the value of the service, it would be beneficial to him as well as the other customers. If, on the other hand, prices to this customer were set higher than the value of the service, he might turn to self-generation; i.e., develop an electric generating plant of his own to meet his needs.

2. Customer Classes

The establishment of customer classes in the ratemaking process has as its primary objective the grouping or classifying of customers with similar service requirements and cost-causing responsibilities, i.e., the costs of serving them. Another important criterion determining customer classes is the need to limit customer classes to a manageable number, each with clearly discernible characteristics that are understandable by the average customer. In actuality, customers are like fingerprints in that no two are exactly alike, so that the last factor necessitates certain compromises.

Consideration of such factors over the years in the United States has led to the following typical customer service classifications: residential, farm, general service, commercial, industrial, transit, street lighting, and public authorities. Further sub-classification in the residential class, for example, is common with separate rates for water heating and house heating. Commercial and industrial customers may also be subclassified to provide different rates for those who

may wish to provide transforming, switching and other receiving equipment.

3. Cost of Service

The cost of supplying electricity to different customers is a function of many variables. The most frequently used division of total costs is a threefold one: (a) demand,[18] capacity or load costs; (b) energy, output, or volumetric costs; and (c) customer costs. Comparing this breakdown to the common industrial classifications of fixed and variable costs, we find that demand and customer costs are approximately equivalent to fixed costs while energy costs are essentially variable costs.

a. Demand or Capacity Costs

Demand or capacity costs vary with the quantity of plant and equipment and the associated investment. They consist primarily of capital costs; i.e., return on investment, taxes, and depreciation expense. However, part of the capital costs of the secondary distribution system may be assigned to customer costs as discussed under Subsection c which follows. Demand costs also include those operating and maintenance expenses which do not vary with the quantity of service supplied in kilowatthours, or with the number of customers, as well as part of administrative and general expenses. Finally, the portion of the fuel expense incurred to maintain readiness to serve may be included.

b. Energy Costs

Energy costs are those which vary with the quantity of kilowatthours produced. They are largely made up of the cost of fuel, fuel handling and labor. A portion of the fuel and labor costs, however, may be regarded as demand-related because some costs are incurred merely to keep the plant in readiness to serve.

c. Customer Costs

Customer costs are those operating and capital costs found to vary directly with the number of customers served, rather than with the amount of utility service supplied. Customer related expenses include meter reading, billing, collecting, and accounting expenses. Customer related capital costs include the investment in meters, customer service connections and a portion of the costs related to the primary and secondary distribution systems. Portions of administrative and general expenses and general plant may also be assigned to customer costs.

Part of the costs related to the primary and

secondary distribution systems are sometimes included in customer related costs because of the recognition that there must be a minimum sized distribution system just to connect the customer into the generating and transmission pool of the utility supplying service. There are two methods utilized in developing the cost of this minimum sized distribution system; i.e., the zero intercept (minimum intercept or positive intercept) and the minimum practical size methods. Details of the zero intercept method are described in Appendix J.

Particularly important to the level of demand or capacity costs for an electric utility are two basic features of electricity supply. First, it is technologically and economically infeasible to store electric energy in commercially significant quantities except through the use of pumped storage.[19] Second, demand for electric energy normally fluctuates widely during each day and over the year as a whole. As a result of these two features the capacity of an electric utility system must be large enough to satisfy the anticipated maximum composite demand of all customers during the normal peak use period while still allowing for normal maintenance and adequate reserve capacity in the case of equipment failure.

In other words, demand costs reflect the costs of providing facilities and constant preparedness to supply as much power and energy as may be required instantaneously by all the customers. Therefore, with sufficient capacity in physical plant manned by competent employees and an adequate fuel supply, economic efficiency dictates that energy output should be maximized so long as the price for additonal output is high enough to cover all energy costs and make some contribution to fixed cost.

Application of these principles leads to the development of low rates for interruptible customers taking load at off-peak times with the understanding that such service may be interrupted when the system load increases. Similarly, a utility with a strong summer peak due to air conditioning load, can offer lower rates to electric heat customers, thereby increasing the use of the facilities during off-peak winter months and, if they are charged a portion of demand costs, decreasing average costs for all customers.

4. Joint Costs

The process of allocating costs to specific customer classes presents a variety of difficulties. One of the most serious of these difficulties relates to the demand costs which generally constitute about one half of the total costs, and which to a large extent may be classified as joint costs.

Electric utilities operate under joint or common cost conditions because substantial portions of their facilities are used jointly to supply service to all or most classes of customers. In addition, the production facilities are such that without major alterations, they can generally accommodate significant shifts in the fractions of total output sold to each of the various customer classes. Under such conditions, only a part of the total costs can be identified as relating directly and entirely to a given class of customer. The sizeable proportion of total cost which cannot be so identified must be allocated insofar as possible in accordance with cost causation factors such as contributions to peak demands. However, this allocation process necessarily involves the use of assumptions and judgments.

The problems of proper allocation of costs have been a subject of investigation within the electric utility industry almost since its founding. In 1892 Dr. John Hopkinson devised the basic two part rate, consisting of separate customer charges for maximum demand (kilowatts) and for total energy consumption (kilowatthours). The Hopkinson rate assumes that fixed costs attributable to a customer are proportional to his peak kilowatt demand and that variable costs are proportional to kilowatthour consumption.

A three-part rate was suggested by Henry Doherty in 1900 as a refinement of the Hopkinson rate. The three-part rate did not change the method of assessing the customer for his share of variable costs, but divided the fixed costs component into two parts, one of which is a measure of so-called customer costs. For a large customer, these customer costs would constitute a very small part of the total cost to serve him, but for a small customer, such costs could be a significant part of the total costs to serve him.

Neither of these rate forms measures the degree to which the customer's maximum demand coincides with (occurs at the same time as) the maximum demand on the entire system. The latter, of course, is the combined result of the demands of all customers.

It is generally conceded that, from the point of view of allocating costs more precisely, a larger share of fixed costs should be allocated to a customer or class of customers whose maximum demand coincides with the peak demand being imposed upon the utility system by all customers, in contrast to a similar maximum demand imposed by a customer at a time when the total system load is well below its normal peak. Consider, for example, two industrial customers each with a peak demand of 1,000 kw: Customer A, whose peak demand occurs on week days at 4:00 pm near the time of the system peak; and Customer B with a peak demand at 4:00 am on week days when the total system load is well below peak. It would generally be conceded that a larger share of fixed costs could properly be allocated to Customer A. Similar arguments can be developed with regard to loads with a marked seasonal variation such as air conditioning.

In some instances the duration, as well as the time, of a customer's peak demand may have an important effect on his responsibility for sharing joint costs. For example, let us consider two customers, A and C, each with a peak demand of 1,000 kw occurring at or near the time of the system peak. The duration of Customer A's peak demand is two hours, however, while that of Customer C is only one half hour. A rational pricing policy might require determining the extent to which the demand-related costs to serve A are greater than those to serve C, and reflecting any significant cost differences in the rates.

5. Methods of Allocating Demand Costs

The determination of proper methods for allocating demand costs, and the closely associated problems of peak versus off-peak pricing, have concerned the industry at least since the 1920s. A large number—approaching 30—of different methods have been developed over the years, but none has proven to be both completely sound from a theoretical view and entirely practical when factors such as metering costs, customer understanding and simplicity of administration are considered.[20] Three of the more common methods are: (a) the peak responsibility method, (b) the noncoincident demand method, and (c) the average and excess demand method.

a. Definition of Terms

Even a summary discussion of these cost allocation methods requires definition of six important terms.

(a) Coincident demand—the sum of two or more individual group demands which occur in the same time interval.

(b) Maximum non-coincident demand—sum of two or more individual group maximum demands which do not necessarily occur in the same time interval.

(c) Diversity factor—the ratio of the sum of the non-coincident maximum demands of two or more groups to their coincident maximum demands.

(d) Coincidence factor—the inverse of the diversity factor.

(e) Load factor—the ratio of the average load

in kilowatts supplied during a given period to the peak or maximum load occurring in that period.

(f) Excess demand—the difference between group maximum demand and group average demand.

b. Load Factor—Coincidence Factor Relationships

A high load factor is conducive to low average costs per kilowatthour since a relatively high kilowatthour output can be obtained from a relatively small investment in capacity. Similarly, a low coincidence factor (high diversity factor) is also conducive to low average costs per kilowatthour. In this instance the low costs derive from being able to serve a relatively large number of customers with a relatively small investment in capacity, when the requests for service from each customer are so spaced over time that they do not overlap to a large degree. Thus, low average costs result either from: (a) a group of customers with high load factors, or (b) a group with lower load factors but a high diversity factor.

A great deal of empirical work has been done over the years to measure the relationships between load factors and coincidence factors for actual customer groups.[21] One of the most familiar of these relationships is reproduced as Chart 9•4. Essentially all of the empirical work, which began in the 1930s and has continued to date, suggests the shape and location of the curves are remarkably stable over time for a given sample size and customer class. Work has also been done to derive inter-class coincidence factors and similar curve shapes have resulted, but lying closer to the lower limit line as shown by the dashed line in Chart 9•4.

A primary application of these curves has been to assist in the allocation of diversity benefits among customer groups. The shape of the curve suggests a way in which diversity benefits should be distributed between low load factor and high load factor customers.

c. Peak Responsibility Method

Under strict application of this method of cost allocation, the entire demand costs are allocated in proportion to the kilowatt demand of each class at the time of peak load. Generally, this cost allocation method concentrates on generation demand costs. Since the various parts of the distribution system may peak at different times, their demand costs would be allocated according to their own peaks. Services rendered off-peak are not charged with any demand costs. The basic justification for this method rests in the premise that all capacity costs are incurred to meet the needs of the peak demand placed on the system. In addition to asserting that this method of pricing achieves a closer approximation to the cost of service, proponents point to the slower growth in peak demand, and thus in the need for new facilities, which will result if the method does cause consumers to shift parts of their load to off-peak periods.

Critics point to several aspects of this method of allocation which are said to cause difficulties in its use. Among the difficulties are: (1) the distribution system peaks may occur at different times than the generation peak, (2) periods of peak demand are subject to change over time, thus requiring more frequent changes in rate structure, (3) off-peak demands should be assessed demand costs if the timing of their off-peak requirements is such as to restrict maintenance and thus require additional capacity, and (4) serving off-peak customers requires installation of more durable and more expensive base load equipment than would be necessary if all customers needed service only during the peak period and could be served using less expensive peaking capacity.

Finally, if such a costing technique is to be fully effective, its application must eventually be extended

Chart 9·4
EMPIRICAL RELATIONSHIP BETWEEN LOAD FACTOR AND COINCIDENCE FACTOR
Based on Integrated 30-Minute Demands in December for Groups of 30 Customers

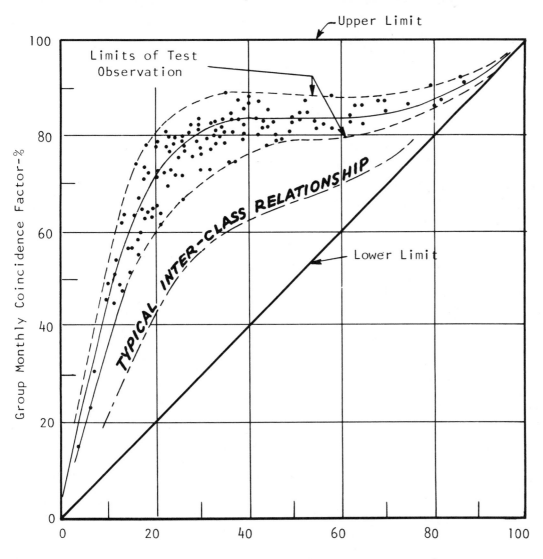

to individual residential customers as well as to individual commercial and industrial customers, with consequent major additions in metering and recording expenses. Effectiveness in discouraging on-peak usage would be negligible if rates were based on the *class* use at peak. Only if the *individual* customer could reduce *his* bill by altering *his* consumption patterns would the desired result be achieved. Extension to residential customers also involves the utility company in a difficult educational program to convince the average customer of the equity of charging him rates per kilowatthour which may vary by a factor of two or more between one hour of the day and the next, or between the same hours in successive days of the week (e.g., Sunday and Monday).[22]

For other customer classes (e.g., large commercial), the increases in metering and billing costs associated with peak-hour pricing would be less significant in proportion to the total costs of the service. Nevertheless, experimental determination of the relative benefits and costs of peak-hour pricing should precede the incorporation of such pricing provisions in all rate classes.

Some compromise approaches to peak period pricing have been justified and incorporated on a practical basis in many situations. Recognizing broad peaks as in the case of summer-winter differentials has been found to be practical on many systems. Special space heating rates on summer peaking systems are another example of applying the general principle of peak responsibility. Indeed, all off-peak rates are premised on peak responsibility pricing.

d. Non-Coincident Demand Method

Under this method, allocation of demand costs is made in accordance with each group's maximum demand regardless of when that maximum demand occurs. Three steps are involved. The sum of the maximum demands of each customer class is obtained. The percentage of this sum that is attributable to each class is calculated. Demand costs are then allocated in accordance with these percentages.

The philosophy underlying this method is that each group or class would require facilities sufficient to meet the group maximum demand if that group were served independently, and each group, therefore, should share in the total system demand costs in the same *proportion* as they would if each were served by its own mini-system.

Opponents claim that this method is largely unrelated to bulk power supply costs and that it is inequitable to the off-peak customer groups. Proponents for this method of allocation argue that it

distributes the benefits of diversity between classes equally to all classes; that is, in the same way that diversity benefits among individual customers in each class are normally distributed. It seems clear to the proponents that the benefits of diversity among classes can be occasioned only by the existence of more than one class of service. No single class of service should have primacy in obtaining the benefits of this diversity, but rather each class should share equally.

e. Average and Excess Demand Method

In this method demand costs are divided into two parts. One part considers only that part of the company's capacity which would be needed if all customer classes were taking their power uniformly over time, i.e., at 100 percent load factor. The second part considers the additional plant capacity, i.e., that which is needed because customer classes are not at 100 percent load factor. The first part of the demand costs are divided among customer classes in proportion to their average loads, i.e., on a kilowatthour basis. The second, or excess, part of the demand costs are allocated by either the non-coincident demand or the peak responsibility method.

One of the objections to the peak responsibility method, as noted previously, is that in its "pure" form it allocates no capacity charges to off-peak customers although even off-peak service requires *some* capacity. The average and excess demand method avoids this criticism by allocating capacity to off-peak customers in proportion to their average demands. It also recognizes individual class load factors, unlike the other two allocation schemes. This, then, is a compromise method.

f. Concluding Remarks

No formula of apportionment is perfect from a theoretical standpoint and, at the same time, practical from an administrative point of view. The National Association of Regulatory Utility Commissioners (NARUC) in their Cost Allocation Manual[23] do not specify one method to the exclusion of all others. They state on page 79 that, "it is suggested that coincident demands (peak responsibility method) be used where *feasible.*" To some extent it *has* been found feasible and its principles have been and are being applied in such varied instances as summer-winter differentials, special rates for off-peak space heating and water heating, and interruptible rates for a variety of types of customers. However, in its strictest interpretation (no demand costs allocated to any but the peak period customers along with a sharp, short definition of the peak), it is impractical and may be discriminatory. At the same time, desirable characteristics of other allocation methods, such as recognition of class load factors and diversities, suggest that continued compromises will be in order in determining the best practical cost allocation method in any given circumstance.

A large body of literature has developed over the years in an effort to analyze the various characteristics of each method. The 1955 study by the Cost Allocation Committee of NARUC[24] and the book by Davidson[25] are examples of such studies.

6. Block Rates

Exact segregation and allocation of customer, energy and demand costs to individual customers requires very detailed metering, record-keeping, and billing. The cost of such detailed operations for small customers has generally proven prohibitively high, so that more economical approximations to the three-part rate have been sought for the small customers, especially the residential customers.

Over the years the declining block rate form has proven the most equitable compromise between cost, accuracy, and simplicity in approximating costs to serve the residential customer. However, some variation of a two-part rate, with separate charges for demand and energy, and perhaps with declining blocks for demand charges, has come to predominate in the case of larger customers. For those latter customers, the demand charge is applied to the maximum kilowatt demand established during a short time interval such as a 30-minute or one-hour period during the month, as measured by a demand meter. In the case of very large customers the demand meter records the time of occurrence. The energy charge is applied to the total kilowatthour consumption for the month. Maximum demand is the best known, but still only an approximate measure of the customer's responsibility for the fixed costs associated with providing his service.

Over the years, declining block rate structures have been developed and justified by numerous cost of service and rate design studies. These have necessarily taken a wide variety of forms. However, a simple but illustrative example is provided by the study prepared in 1970 and 1971 by the Rate Research Committee of the Edison Electric Institute. An abbreviated summary of this study is included as Appendix K.

This appendix outlines the development of rate forms for large and small commercial and industrial customer classes as well as for residential customers. Typical relationships between capacity costs, load factors and kilowatthour consumption are illustrated, and the use of load factor-coincidence factor curves is shown for the commercial and industrial rate classes. The resulting rate forms include a decreasing block rate structure for the capacity costs, as shown on Chart 9•5.

A similar approach to rate design is possible in the case of the residential class of customers, although these customers may be more homogeneous in their use patterns so that the potential diversity benefits may be less. The appendix outlines the development of a rate form for residential customers, beginning with a survey and analysis of groups of typical customers. Such surveys are designed to include groups which represent the full range of customer kilowatthour consumption, from low to high. From this analysis the relationship between the diversified maximum demand for the average weekday and the annual use (i.e., a measure of load factor) is determined for each test group. In this way the demand cost component of the residential rate can be developed.

However, for residential customers the rate design typically incorporates customer and energy costs as well as capacity costs into one overall rate form. Again, the final result is a blocked rate with the initial high block being due to a combination of customer costs and capacity costs.

Another technique for residential rate design is illustrated by Chart 9•6 which shows a fundamental cost curve for residential service in 1972 for a New England company. This cost information was developed by determining the cost to serve a hypothetical customer who adds appliances in the indicated sequence at the average consumption and load characteristics for each appliance. The solid lines depict the cost to serve at various rates of return while the dashed line shows the revenue obtained from this hypothetical customer under the company's residential rates. Details of the rate structure are presented in the box underneath the figure.

Table 9•1 shows one of the detailed calculations from which the cost data were derived. The bottom line is of particular interest since it demonstrates the degree to which average costs per kilowatthour decreased as the customer and capacity charges were spread over larger amounts of consumption and with improving load factor.

In many systems in recent years the last step for the typical residential customer in adding appliances

273

has been the addition of air conditioning units. Generally the effect of this last addition has been to decrease the typical customer's load factor. In a number of cases, utility companies have responded to this development by adding a summer-winter differential to the tariff to recognize the additional capacity costs associated with serving those customers with air conditioning units.

The rapid increase in fossil fuel prices over the last several years has significantly shifted the balance between customer, capacity, and energy costs for many utilities. As energy costs become a larger

Chart 9•5
DEMAND COMPONENT OF COST—SMALL COMMERCIAL AND INDUSTRIAL CUSTOMER CLASS

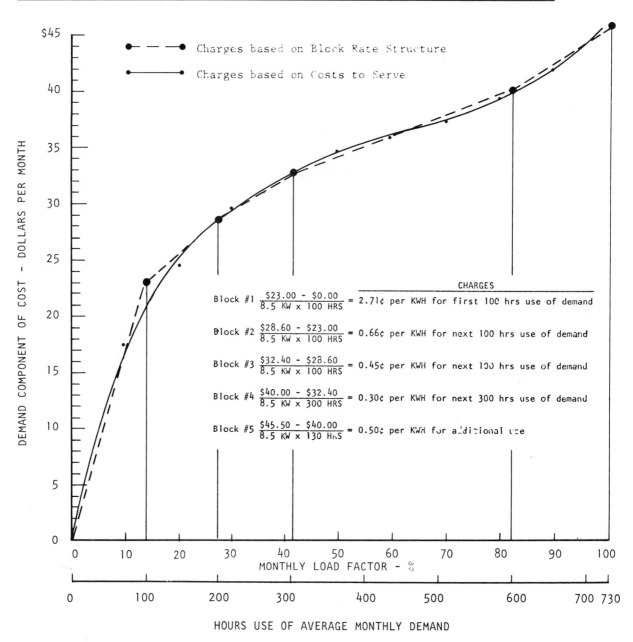

Chart 9·6
FUNDAMENTAL COST CURVE-CLASS I 1972

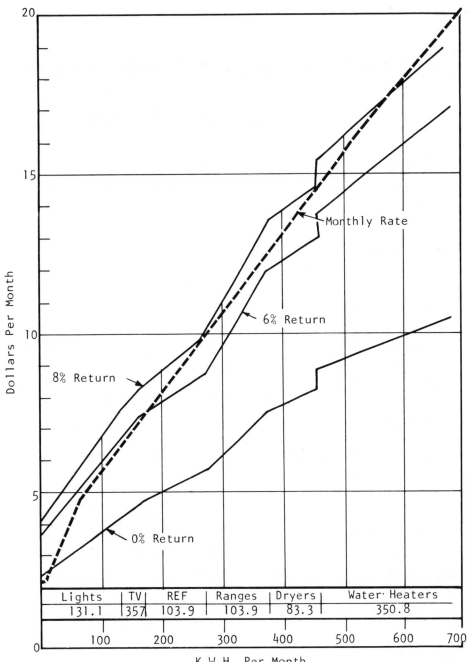

Lights	TV	REF	Ranges	Dryers	Water Heaters	
131.1	357	103.9	103.9	83.3	350.8	

K.W.H. Per Month

	Per Kilowatt-Hour
First 14 KWH or Less $2.30	
Next 50 "	5.10¢
Next 436 "	2.50¢
Over 500 "	2.15¢
+ A Fuel Adjustment Charge	

Table 9·1
1972 COST ANALYSIS—COORDINATES FOR FUNDAMENTAL COST CURVE—CLASS I

	No Use	Lts. & Misc. Appliances	Plus TV	Plus Refrigerators & Freezers	Plus Ranges	Plus Dryers	Plus Uncontrolled No Use	Water Heaters Full Use
Characteristics								
Average Monthly KWH		131.1	166.8	270.7	374.0	457.3	457.3	808.1
Annual KWH		1,573.1	2,001.2	3,247.7	4,487.7	5,487.7	5,487.7	9,697.7
Demand-KVA		.615	.702	.895	1.507	1.622	1.622	2.306
Demand-KW		.525	.602	.739	1.339	1.449	1.449	2.119
Investment Responsibility ($)								
Customer @ 163.59/ Customer	163.59	163.59	163.59	163.59	163.59	163.59	163.59	163.59
KVA @ 224.81/KVA		138.26	157.82	201.20	338.79	364.64	364.64	518.41
KW @ 67.74/KW		35.56	40.78	50.06	90.79	98.16	98.16	143.54
Energy @ .007445/KWH		11.71	14.90	24.18	33.42	40.86	40.86	72.21
Special Investment		(6.56)	(6.56)	(6.56)	(6.56)	(6.56)	19.10	19.10
Total Investment Responsibility	163.59	342.56	370.53	432.47	619.94	660.69	686.36	916.85
Operating Expenses— Monthly ($)								
Customer @ 3.02/Customer	3.02	3.02	3.02	3.02	3.02	3.02	3.02	3.02
KVA @ 2.01/KVA		1.24	1.41	1.80	3.03	3.26	3.26	4.64
KW @ .977/KW		.51	.59	.72	1.31	1.42	1.42	2.07
Energy @ .006443/KWH		.85	1.07	1.74	2.41	2.95	2.95	5.21
Special Expenses		(.18)	(.18)	(.18)	(.18)	(.18)	.45	.45
Total	3.02	5.44	5.91	7.10	9.59	10.47	11.10	15.39
Total Cost to Serve at 0% Return ($) (-.003439/Month On investment)	2.46	4.26	4.64	5.61	7.46	8.20	8.74	12.24
Total Cost to Serve at 6% Return ($) (.003970/Month On Investment)	3.67	6.80	7.38	8.82	12.05	13.09	13.82	19.03
Total Cost to Serve at 8% Return ($) (.00643/Month On Investment)	4.07	7.66	8.30	9.89	13.58	14.73	3.40	21.30
Average Cost to Serve at 8% Return (¢/KWH)	—	5.8	5.0	3.7	3.6	3.2		2.7

fraction of total costs, the percentage changes in cost between the initial blocks of consumption and the final block decrease. As an example of this "flattening effect," let us assume that the energy charge incorporated in the Chart 9•6 rate was a uniform 0.7 cent per kilowatthour in 1972. It is not unreasonable to assume that these fuel costs tripled in the next three years and reached 2.1 cents in 1975. Under these circumstances (and assuming no other cost changes), the ratio of the tail block rate to that of the 15-65 kilowatthour block would have changed from 42 percent (2.15/5.10) in 1972 to 55 percent (3.55/6.50) in 1975.

If fossil fuel cost increases abate in future years, the trend toward nuclear plants, with high capital costs and low fuel costs, will tend to reverse the flattening of rates which has occurred in many areas of the nation in recent years.

7. Marginal and Incremental Cost Pricing and Inflation

A utility's rate *level*, as determined by a regulatory agency, is obtained by adding allowable operating costs (expenses, depreciation and taxes) and a fair return on the rate base (with the latter determined by depreciated original cost, replacement cost, or some variation of these methods). This total, called the revenue requirement, in turn, becomes the figure which all rates, in the aggregate, must be designed to yield. Emphasis in this section is on the application of marginal or incremental cost concepts to develop appropriate rate *structures*, and on the impact of inflation.

a. Marginal Costs

It is a well-established doctrine in economics that when prices of goods and services are set equal to the costs of production of the marginal (or "last") unit, there results a socially optimum allocation of resources, i.e., a situation in which each resource is being put to its best use, with a consequent maximization of satisfaction yielded by these limited resources.

This doctrine can be illustrated by reference to Chart 9•7, in which the solid line represents the demand curve for a product and the interrupted line denotes the marginal cost of producing that product; i.e., the cost of producing the "last unit" of that product. If output is set at 10 units, each can be sold for 3.2 cents, but the marginal cost (i.e., the cost of producing the 10th unit) is only 3.0 cents. If the production rate were to be raised to 20 units, the selling price for each unit would be 2.8 cents, the

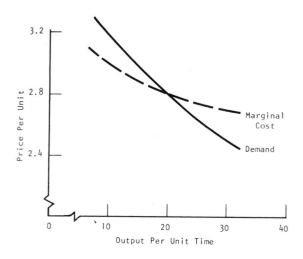

Chart 9•7
MARGINAL COSTS

same as the cost of producing the 20th unit. At production rates above 20, however, the marginal unit (and thus the total production) could only be sold at a unit price less than the cost of producing that marginal unit. Therefore, selling more than 20 units of the product involves providing the consumer additional units which he values less than the cost of production to society; producing less than 20 involves foregoing units for which the consumer would be willing to pay more than the cost of production. Only when price is equal to marginal cost is consumer satisfaction maximized.

Despite the obvious desirability of electric rates which would serve, in theory, to allocate resources properly, marginal cost pricing has not been put into general practice by electric utilities in the United States. The primary reason that it has not stems from the relationship between marginal costs and average total costs. When a company operates under decreasing cost conditions, marginal costs are lower than average costs (see Charts 9•8 and 9•9), and pricing each unit sold at marginal costs would force the firm to operate at a deficit.

Decreasing cost conditions are those which prevail when average costs decline as output increases, all other things remaining equal. For example, consider a fictitious utility company which is providing 1 billion kilowatthours at 3 cents per average kilowatthour while maintaining an adequate rate of return on investment. If this company could expand instantaneously, using the same technology, and sell 2 billion kilowatthours to the same or a similar mix of customers at 2.5 cents per average kilowatthour

Chart 9•8
DECREASING COST INDUSTRY

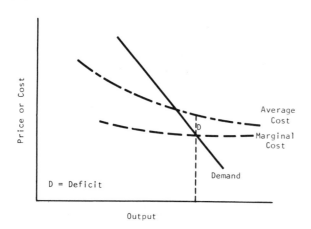

Price or Cost

Average
Cost

Marginal
Cost

D

Demand

D = Deficit

Output

Chart 9•9
INCREASING COST INDUSTRY

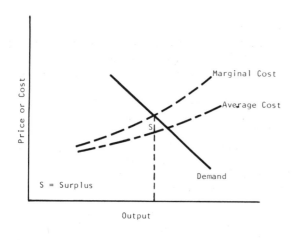

Price or Cost

Marginal Cost

Average Cost

S

Demand

S = Surplus

Output

b. Long-Run Incremental Costs

There is a variant of the theoretical marginal cost principle, however, which has greater practical application, namely, the long-run incremental cost concept. This concept, unlike the concept of marginal cost, recognizes that electric utilities add capacity in discrete units and on a continuous basis. The long-run incremental cost concept thus includes the future costs of supplying electricity, as opposed to the average cost of serving existing customers.[26]

Some have argued that the long-run incremental cost concept cannot be used because of the general reluctance on the part of regulators, and many of the regulated companies as well, to set rates on the basis of future, projected costs rather than on the basis of past, experienced costs. In the past, when fossil fuel generating stations could be constructed in four or five years, and with transmission and distribution construction times of two to three years, such a pricing scheme would have required a four or five-year forecast. Now, with nuclear plant construction times extending over a decade the necessary forecast period would be doubled.

Thus, the forecasting period involved in the application of long-run incremental cost pricing is generally much longer than the period involved in the application of future test year pricing. The fact remains, nevertheless, that electric rates are being set for the future and not for the past. Unless such rates reflect costs that are expected to be incurred in the foreseeable future, electric utilities (in an inflationary economy) will continue to experience difficulties in meeting their revenue requirements. Considering long-run incremental costs in the rate-setting process, like the use of a future test year, offers an opportunity to overcome the adverse effects of inflation.

Indeed, it is perfectly possible that rates based on primarily long-run incremental costs will permit the utility to earn more than its revenue requirement (as determined by the regulatory authorities). In such cases, some proponents of long-run incremental pricing maintain that economic theory provides a suitable guideline for deviating from the basic pricing concept so as to: (1) prevent the utility company from collecting more than its revenue requirement, while (2) still preserving a great measure of the resource allocation potential of the concept. This guideline would set rates below true incremental costs by a sufficient amount to eliminate the "excess" revenues, but concentrate the reductions in those markets where demand is inelastic (i.e., where a price decrease would do little to increase consumption).

There are at least three problems with these cost

while maintaining the adequate rate of return, then the company is operating under decreasing cost conditions.

In contrast, when a firm is operating under increasing cost conditions (the reverse of the above fictitious situation), pricing electricity at marginal cost would result in excess profits to the utility. To avoid the operating deficits under decreasing cost conditions or the excess profits under increasing cost conditions, it is necessary to subsidize or to tax the utility. In the United States, neither of these avenues has proven practical, since the regulatory agencies charged with setting electricity prices do not have the authority either to tax or to subsidize the utilities they regulate.

concepts. First is the fact that any significant deviations from true incremental costs on the basis of demand elasticities could be defined as inconsistent with regulatory requirements that rates be just and reasonable for all customers. Second, and closely related, is the need for knowledge of the price elasticity of each customer class. Further discussion on elasticity, which is provided in Section E.8., indicates that the currently available methods for estimating price elasticities are approximate at best, so that all that can be expected is an informed judgment about relative elasticities among customer classes.

Finally, as long as other competitive forms of energy, such as natural gas, are not priced by using long-run incremental cost principles, there is no basis for judging whether incremental cost pricing of electricity alone would move the overall energy markets toward or away from an optimum use of resources. If electricity that is too low in price causes an undue expansion of energy-intensive activities, the effect on the economy could be significant. But it should be recognized that adverse results are highly uncertain. If the effect of prices below long-run incremental costs is simply to cause a substitution of electric energy generated with coal or nuclear fuel for the use of oil or natural gas, the effect on the total energy economy may actually be beneficial.

c. Inflation Effects

For many years the electric utility industry was clearly a decreasing cost industry in that its average costs (per kilowatthour) declined as its total kilowatthour output increased. In other words, the industry enjoyed economies of scale so that larger facilities generated and distributed electricity more economically than smaller ones. During most of the period since World War II, those economies of scale were sufficient to overwhelm the relatively slow rates of inflation which then prevailed, and to permit utilities gradually to lower the price for the average kilowatthour.

During the last few years, however, several factors have combined to force the price of electricity upward. The primary factors are: (a) higher inflation rates, especially in field construction costs, (b) much higher costs of capital, (c) much higher fuel costs, and (d) an apparent slowdown in achieving economies of scale, at least in the generation aspects of the business. These factors have led some observers to conclude that utilities are no longer a decreasing cost industry, but instead have become rather suddenly an increasing cost industry.

However, the mere presence of inflation, or a shift to a more rapid rate of inflation, is not a proper basis for judging whether an industry has changed from decreasing to increasing cost conditions. The failure to exclude inflationary effects before judging the cost situation in the utility industry, has led some observers to what are probably erroneous conclusions. Dr. Paul Joskow[27] employs a chart somewhat like Chart 9•10 to illustrate the problems of interpretation which have arisen. The figure depicts declining average cost curves AC_1 through AC_7, each applicable during a time period $t = 1$ through $t = 7$. Each curve depicts a declining cost industry in which average costs decrease as output increases and marginal costs are below average costs. With the passage of time, however, inflation causes the cost curves to shift upward from $t = 1$ toward $t = 7$.

The heavy line PAC_1 (pseudo average cost) depicts a situation where output grows from Q_1 to Q_4 while a relatively slow rate of inflation pushes the cost curve from AC_1 to AC_4. The line labeled PAC_2 shows the results of a more rapid rate of inflation in which the cost curve moves to AC_7 while output grows to Q_4. Superficially, PAC_2 appears to represent an increasing cost industry. Similarly PAC_3 shows a more slowly growing output coupled with the same inflationary environment as for PAC_1. Superficially PAC_3 also appears to have taken on increasing cost characteristics.

However, one should not infer from either PAC_2 or PAC_3 that economies of scale have been replaced with dis-economies of scale. PAC_2 and PAC_3 are both meaningless representations of the average resource costs of producing different levels of output. The industries represented by PAC_2 and PAC_3 are both still in a decreasing cost situation and the optimum pricing rules as well as the rate *structures* at any point in time should be identical to those which are proper for PAC_1.

Note also from Chart 9•10 that the less growth there is, the faster nominal average costs rise and the more slowly real average costs fall. Consequently, if Chart 9•10 is representative of reality, pricing devices such as inverted rates, which aim specifically at slowing growth, are inconsistent with the basic principles of pricing. Similar reasoning can be applied to dispute currently popular arguments that growth in consumption should be discouraged by charging higher prices for: (a) consumption by all new customers or (b) increased consumption by old customers. In addition, in the regulated electric utility industry, such arguments are wholly inconsistent with the regulatory requirements for "just and reasonable" rates and the regulatory prohibition against different rates for customers similarly situated.

Chart 9•10
AVERAGE COST CURVES

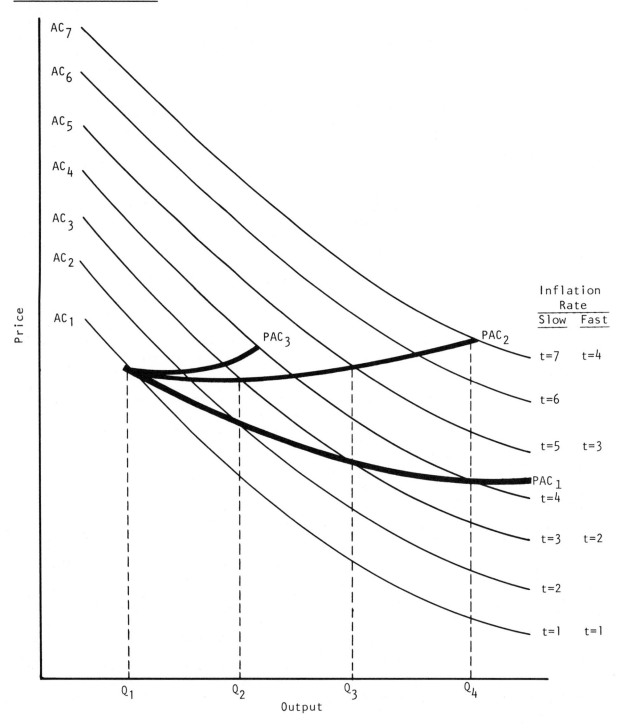

8. Elasticity Studies

Earlier parts of this section discussed the need for accurate estimates of the price elasticity of demand by customer classes. The price elasticity of demand is an economic concept developed to describe certain characteristics of demand curves such as illustrated in Chart 9·11. In this case, elasticity simply measures the relationship between a percentage change in price and the ensuing percentage change in the quantity of electricity which customers desire to purchase. At the point Y on the curve of Chart 9·11, the elasticity is $(\Delta q/q)(p/\Delta p)$. Normally, if the price increases, the quantity demanded will decrease so that the sign of the price elasticity of demand is negative.

It is interesting to note that for a linear demand curve such as pictured in the example, the elasticity varies continually along the curve, ranging from 5.0 at X, to 1.0 at Y, and to 0.2 at Z. In those regions of the linear demand curve above and to the left of Y, where elasticities are greater than one, a one percent increase in price causes a greater than one percent decrease in demand. As a result, total revenues after a price increase are somewhat less than before the increase. When the elasticities are less than one, the opposite is true; i.e., one percent increase in price causes less than a one percent decrease in demand, and total revenues are greater after the price increase. Only in those cases when the demand curve is in the shape of a power function (as shown approximately by the dashed line on the figure) does

Chart 9·11
DEMAND CURVES AND ELASTICITIES

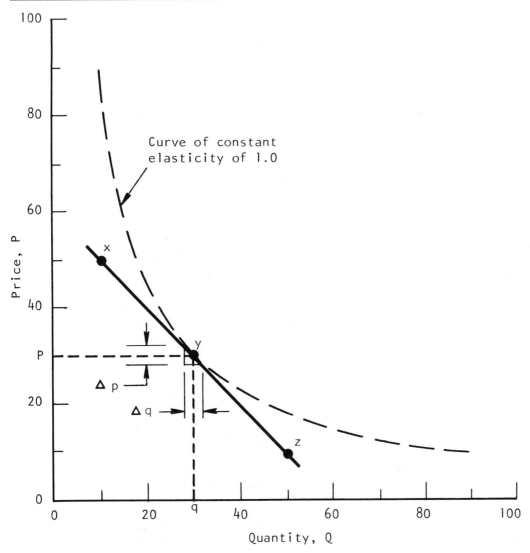

the elasticity remain constant over the length of the curve.

A number of serious statistical studies have been performed in recent years to determine experimental values of price elasticities of demand for electricity by various customer classes.[28] Such experimental determinations face many formidable problems, so the comments which follow should be taken as an attempt to describe some of these problems rather than to be unduly critical of the specific studies referenced here. In general the studies attempt to relate demand for electricity to one or more of the following factors: the price of electricity, the price of competing fuels, income levels, population, climate and other variables felt to be significant.

a. Short versus Long-Run Elasticities

It has been generally conceded that, over the short run, the demand for electricity by all customer classes is quite inelastic. Consumption over the short-term is assumed to be dependent primarily on existing equipment and processes in the case of the industrial customer and on the existing stock of appliances in the case of the average residential customer. Most previous statistical studies have confirmed these assumptions. Over the longer run, however, demands might be expected to be more elastic, since changes in industrial processes, additional insulation in buildings and alterations in lifestyle may be expected in response to price changes. Some studies confirm the higher long-run elasticity expectations and others do not. For both marginal pricing and forecasting purposes it is the long- rather than the short-run elasticities that are more significant. Unfortunately, the statistical problems associated with measuring long-run elasticities are even more vexing. One approach is to use complex, statistical techniques to measure lagged responses to price change, as was done by Chapman et al.[29] Another approach is to use cross-sectional data techniques in which data is recorded at one point in time for groups of customers in different regions with different income and price characteristics. The regional differences are used as a proxy for time differences. Both of these techniques are subject to major difficulties of interpretation.

b. Decreasing versus Increasing Prices

Essentially all of the major studies examined time periods during which the average current dollar price of electricity was gradually but consistently decreasing, while the price in purchasing power terms was dropping even more rapidly. The results from these studies must now be applied to an environment in which electricity prices have recently been increasing rather rapidly both in current dollar and in purchasing power terms. Furthermore, in some instances current prices are well beyond the range covered by the studies. Thus, if the available studies are to be used as a guide to the future, it must be assumed that the demand processes observed in the past are applicable in circumstances far different from that in which the processes were observed. However, there is no statistical evidence available to confirm this applicability. In fact, the continued steady growth in total United States consumption during the period from 1968 to 1973, when electric rates had already experienced major increases, argues that the demand processes observed in the past may not be fully applicable now.

One particular area of concern is that of air conditioning demand. Some scattered evidence has already been accumulated to show that attempts to limit electricity consumption, whether prompted by fear of shortages or by price increases, show up in the form of significant reductions in consumption on warm days but with little or no reduction on the hottest days. This, of course, reduces total revenues to the utility company but requires it to maintain the same capacity with the same fixed charges to meet the hot-day peak demand. Generally, elasticity studies, as currently designed, cannot develop data with sufficient detail to contribute answers to problems such as are posed by the "hot day" phenomenon.

c. Reduced Ability to Substitute

All of the elasticity studies have examined time periods when substitute forms of energy such as oil and gas were readily available. During these same periods, prices of these substitutes were nearly unchanging in current dollar terms, and were decreasing slowly in purchasing power terms. Oil was in excess supply during most of the period between 1957 and 1972 and natural gas prices were under wellhead price control. Consequently, purchase of oil and gas as well as the purchase of electricity on a per-unit basis gradually came to be a smaller and smaller proportion of the average customer's total expenditures. This situation has altered remarkably, however, since 1972. Now, and probably for the foreseeable future, some of the substitute forms of energy are less readily available and their costs are likely to rise more rapidly than that of electricity.

d. Further Evaluations

Several good overall critiques of elasticity studies have been made; e.g., by the Electric Power Research Institute[30] and National Economic Research

Associates, Inc.[31] The latter document discusses the difficulties of conducting such studies and examines eight studies of residential demand elasticity in some detail. NERA concludes that all are, "...inadequate as support for government or business policy decisions." A summary of the flaws they discern in the studies is as follows:

(a) Several of the studies use statewide averages for consumption and price. In so doing they combine areas within the state which differ widely from one another in climate, population density, per capita income, etc.

(b) The price of electricity faced by an individual customer is not a single average value per unit but rather a structure of rate blocks. In general, the studies do not adequately consider the effects of decreasing unit costs with increasing consumption.

(c) Some of the studies ignore the effects of income on consumption and do not examine the potential effects of income distribution.

(d) Several studies do not include the price of competing fuels as a consideration and none considers competition from fuel oil as a relevant factor.

(e) A few consider climate variables in the analysis although statewide averaging tends to dilute the potential effects of climate. Most of the studies do not consider climate at all.

(f) Most of the studies do not examine the differences between urban and rural consumption patterns, nor do they attempt to differentiate customers in terms of their housing characteristics, e.g., single homes versus apartments.

(g) The studies have almost completely disregarded the existence of two different residential markets for electricity: one for uses where no competing fuel exists such as lighting; and a second for uses where substitutes are available such as space heating.

e. Outlook for Future Studies

In the space available here, it is impossible to evaluate these pioneering studies completely. Each, though imperfect to some degree, is an important step forward. The flaws are summarized above to highlight some of the very major difficulties involved in such studies and thereby urge caution in applying the results in real-life pricing and forecasting decisions. Another important conclusion which can be drawn is that much more attention must be directed by individual utility companies to the tasks of examining price elasticity within their own territory. If the statistical and econometric techniques developed and used in some of the referenced studies are used as a point of departure, supplemented with further refinements, and combined with the detailed knowledge which each utility company has of its own territory, the resulting elasticity estimates may be of significant use in guiding future actions. This task will be long and difficult. It must include: (a) assembling adequate mathematical and statistical techniques; (b) designing adequate data collection methods; (c) obtaining experimental data from statistically significant samples of consumers over reasonable time periods; and (d) analyzing the results.

F. Recommendations for Future Pricing and Rate Structuring

The previous pages describe a number of concepts and practices which relate to the pricing of electricity. Some have withstood the tests of time and others have yet to be widely accepted. The following paragraphs summarize those concepts and practices which appear best suited to meet the needs of society in the future.

1. Cost to Serve

Rates should be based primarily on cost to serve. In periods of rapidly changing prices, this may necessitate more frequent and more detailed cost studies than during periods of relative price stability. While rate design should strive to move ever closer to the cost to serve objective, it is also important to maintain a reasonable balance with the subsidiary but still important practical objectives of pricing: stability, simplicity, understandability, public acceptability, and feasibility of application.

2. Revenue Requirements

The utility's total rate structure should produce sufficient revenues to cover all necessary expenses of doing business, and provide a rate of return on all investment to compensate present owners fairly and attract additional capital at reasonable costs. Current conditions in the capital markets, rather than complex theoretical calculations, must be the final judge of a proper rate of return on investment. Sufficient flexibility in rate of return deliberations should be maintained via the "zone of reasonableness" concept so that efficiency is recognized and rewarded. Both customer and investor interests are best served over the long run by a financially healthy industry.

3. Regulatory Response

Regulatory lag should be reduced so that it becomes possible for the efficiently managed utility company to earn the return authorized by the regulatory process. Innovations are required to adapt regulation promptly to changing economic conditions. In the current climate of rapidly changing fuel prices and virulent inflation, several innovations which should be considered are: using forward test years; expanding the scope of automatic adjustment clauses; and allowing tariff changes to become effective without suspension, subject to refund to the customers of any portions of the rate increase which subsequent hearings show to be excessive.

4. Long-Run Incremental Costs

Careful consideration should be given to long-run incremental cost principles in designing rates. Particularly important is the aspect of incremental cost pricing which emphasizes that rates which will be used in the future must be designed for the future. At the same time, it must be recognized that practical implementation of these principles requires the solution of several problems; e.g., total revenues which are produced are, in general, different from the revenue requirements associated with an adequate return on investment as determined through regulatory proceedings.

5. Customer Classifications

The utility's customers with similar service requirements, market demands, and load characteristics should be grouped together and served under a specific schedule for rates which reflects the costs to serve that class of customer. In general, rates should move toward equalizing rates of return from all classes of service, though this too must be done in such a way as to prevent sudden and drastic adjustments to rates. In this regard, attention must also be paid to the degree to which pricing practices of competitive forms of energy move toward more logical economic principles. Uneven progress throughout the energy industry could cause damaging shifts away from the use of relatively plentiful coal and nuclear resources and toward the use of scarce oil and gas resources.

6. Rate Blocks

Block structuring of energy and demand charges for large customers should be eliminated where such blocks are no longer justified by cost considerations such as load factors, coincidence factors, and customer costs. Until more complex rate structures for residential customers are shown to be economically, technically and practically feasible, rate blocking for these customers should continue as the best practical approximation to costs to serve.

7. Peak Period Pricing

Rate structures should move toward more accurate reflection of differences in the costs of serving on-peak and off-peak customers. However, this movement should not progress so far as to relieve off-peak customers from any and all responsibility for capacity costs. Over the near term, emphasis in rate design should concentrate on rates which promote off-peak uses of energy while still contributing at least partially to demand costs. The use of a summer-winter differential which (in the case of summer peak systems) encourages off-peak uses such as electric heat, is an example of such pricing techniques.

8. Social Costs

The gradual incorporation of measurable social costs into the pricing of all goods and services throughout the economy would be beneficial. The incorporation of such costs by only one industry (e.g., the electric utility industry) or one segment of the economy (e.g., the energy industry) may, however, significantly distort resource allocations. Cost-benefit analyses should precede the incorporation of social costs into the price system. This is necessary to assure that a reasonable balance is struck between the benefits to society and the costs (or penalties) of incorporation—some of which may be hidden from view since they occur only in the form of secondary or tertiary reactions.

9. Inverted Rates

A proper regard for the distribution of customer costs, capacity costs and energy costs has in the past produced a rate structure in which the average price paid for energy declined with increasing use. In today's environment, high fuel costs have at least temporarily made energy costs a higher, and demand costs a lower, fraction of total costs than they formerly were. This has, in effect, tended to flatten, but not to invert, rates. If the shift is made to nuclear generation, with low fuel and high capital costs, it would reverse this trend. As costs and technologies change, rate structures should also change so as to continue to reflect costs to serve. The idea of inverted rates as a device to check demand growth and redistribute income should be rejected as inconsistent with the primary guiding principle of basing rates on costs to serve.

10. Accomplishing Sociological Goals

Using energy pricing to reallocate income among various groups would be inappropriate for several reasons. It is an unwieldy tool, the impact of which is uncertain and not determinable even on an after-the-fact basis. For example, studies have shown that there is not a high degree of correlation between income and electricity use; i.e., some low-income families are heavy consumers of electricity and some high-income families are small consumers. Changes have also been proposed to decrease residential rates and increase industrial rates. To the extent that such changes are not cost-related, the effect would be to distort resource allocation by shifting part of the costs of residential electricity from the consumers of that electricity to the unknown consumers of the products of the affected industry.

Redistribution of income is a governmental responsibility best discharged through the public systems of taxation and welfare. Using energy pricing to discourage "unnecessary" or "undesirable" consumption of electricity is questionable since it is impossible to determine, other than on a completely subjective basis, what or whose uses of electricity are desirable or undesirable. Under normal circumstances, there is no better allocator of energy resources than the price system when it is allowed to work. Conservation objectives are best pursued not by artificial, subjective constraints on consumption—whether it be of electricity or of any other resource-consuming product—but rather by a fully responsive, all-inclusive pricing system. Achievement of sociological goals should be the subject of direct legislative action.

11. Research Efforts

Research efforts into various aspects of rate design are an ongoing industry activity. These efforts in fact, have been increased in recent years.

In-depth studies are needed to examine the technological and economic feasibility of time-of-day metering and associated on peak-off peak pricing to all customer classes. These studies should include surveys of representative samples of customers to determine the effectiveness of such rate structures in reducing system peaks and encouraging off-peak consumption.

Empirical studies should also be aimed at: (a)

determining the impact on rates of long-run incremental cost pricing principles; and (b) assessing the shifts in energy consumption and resource allocation if other parts of the energy industry do not simultaneously revise their pricing structures.

To bring rates into more exact correspondence with costs, studies should examine the economic and social impacts of revising residential rates to include customer charges as a separate and distinct part of the tariff rather than include them in the initial rate blocks.

A serious effort to improve techniques for determining elasticity of demand by customer classes should be undertaken. The program should be coordinated so as to bring to bear the theoretical knowledge of the economic and statistical professions as well as the practical knowledge of the industry and its customers which is available only within the operating utility companies.

FOOTNOTES

1. Joint cost conditions are discussed in Section E.4. of this Chapter.

2. Russell E. Caywood, *Electric Utility Rate Economics*, New York, McGraw Hill, Inc., 1972.

3. Garfield & Lovejoy, *Public Utility Economics*, Englewood Cliffs, New Jersey, Prentice-Hall, Inc., 1964.

4. Alfred E. Kahn, *The Economics of Regulation*, New York, John Wiley & Sons, 1970.

5. Accurate allocation of costs will permit prices to fulfill the basic economic function of distributing limited labor, capital and material resources in an optimum manner.

6. Charles F. Philips, Jr., *The Economics of Regulation*, Homewood, Ill., Richard D. Irwin, Inc., 1969.

7. M. Miller and F. Modigliani, "Some Estimates of the Cost of Capital to the Electric Utility Industry: 1954-57," *The American Economic Review*, vol. 56 no. 3, June 1966, pp. 333-391.

8. Stewart C. Myers, "The Application of Finance Theory to Public Utility Rate Cases," *The Bell Journal of Economics and Management Science*, vol. 3 no. 1, Spring 1972, pp. 58-97.

9. Myron J. Gordon, *The Cost of Capital to a Public Utility*, Michigan State University Press, 1973.

10. Dilution may be said to occur when the net proceeds to the company per share of newly issued stock are below book value. These proceeds are generally less than the market value just before the sale because of: (a) expenses of the sale and (b) temporary downward pressure on the market price (and thus on the price realized on the new share) as a result of the imminence of the sale of new shares. Thus a pre-announcement market price perhaps

10 percent higher than book value is required to avoid dilution on a net proceeds basis.

11. The concept of dilution is discussed in Chapter 10 under "Current Conditions for Common Stock."

12. Normalizing and flow-through are terms used to describe two different accounting methods used by utility companies to relate book (i.e. financial) accounting to tax accounting particularly as regards the treatment of depreciation expenses and investment tax credits. A full description of these matters is provided by James E. Suelflow in *Public Utility Accounting: Theory and Application*, Michigan State University Public Utilities Studies, 1973. East Lansing, Michigan. A summary description is provided in Appendix M.

13. George E. Phelps, "A Research Report on the Subject of Rate of Return on Common Equity," Phelps Utility Advisory Service, Fountain Valley California, 1972.

14. *Moody's Public Utility Manual*, 1973, Moody's Investors Service, Inc., New York, N. Y., 1973.

15. See Chapter 10 for further discussions of adequate returns on common equity.

16. James C. Bonbright, *Principles of Public Utility Rates*, New York, Columbia University Press, 1961.

17. Load factor is the ratio of the average load in kilowatts supplied during a designated period to the peak or maximum load in kilowatts occurring in that period. Load factor, in percent, also may be derived by multiplying the kilowatt-hours in the period by 100 and dividing by the product of the maximum demand in kilowatts and the number of hours in the period.

18. Demand is defined as the rate at which electric energy is delivered to or by a system, part of a system, or a piece of equipment expressed in kilowatts or other suitable units at a given instant or averaged over a designated period of time. For a more extended definition, see *Glossary of Electric Utility Terms*, Edison Electric Institute, New York, N.Y.

19. Pumped storage is an arrangement whereby additional electric power may be generated during peak-load periods by hydraulic means using water pumped into a storage reservoir during off-peak periods.

20. Cost Allocation Committee of Engineering Committee of National Association of Railroad & Utilities Commissions, "Comparison of Methods of Allocating Demand Costs, *Electric Utilities*," June, 1955.

21. Constantine W. Bary, *Operational Economics of Electric Utilities*, New York, Columbia University Press, 1963.

22. John J. Doran, et al, *Electric Utility Cost Allocation Manual*, Washington, D. C., National Association of Regulatory Utility Commissioners, 1973.

23. John J. Doran, et al, as above.

24. Cost Allocation Committee of Engineering Committee of NARUC, as above.

25. Ralph K. Davidson, *Price Discrimination in Selling Gas and Electricity*, Baltimore, Johns Hopkins Press, 1955.

26. R. G. Lipsey and Kelvin Lancaster, "The General Theory of Second Best," *Review of Economic Studies*, 1956, vol XXIV, 11-32. For further discussion of "second best" pricing concepts see Footnote 4 and H. M. Trebing, *Essays on Public Utility Pricing and Regulations*, Michigan State University Press, 1971.

27. Paul L. Joskow, "Public Utility Rate Structures in a World of Rapid Inflation and Environment Concern," M.I.T. Energy Conference, February 1973.

28. F. M. Fisher and C. Kaysen, *The Demand for Electricity in the United States*, North Holland Publishing Co., 1962.

L. D. Chapman, T. J. Tyrell and T. D. Mount, "Electricity Demand in the U.S.: An Econometric Analysis," Oak Ridge National Laboratory Report, ORNL-EP-49. This same study is discussed in "Electricity Demand Growth and the Energy Crisis," *Science, vol. 178, no. 4062, November 17, 1972.*

R. Halvorsen, "Sierra Club Conference on Power and Public Policy," Public Resources Inc., Burlington, Vermont, 1969.

J. W. Wilson, *Residential and Industrial Demand for Electricity: An Empirical Analysis*, University Microfilms, Ann Arbor, Michigan, 1969.

The Rand Corporation, *Some Implications of Policies to Slow the Growth of Electricity Demand*, R990-NSF/CSA, June, 1972.

Stanford Research Institute, *Meeting California's Energy Requirements* 1975-2000, SRI Project No. ECC-2355, May, 1973.

29. L. D. Chapman, T. J. Tyrell, and T. D. Mount, as above.

30. Lester D. Taylor, "The Demand for Electricity: A Survey," *The Bell Journal of Economics*, Spring 1975, p 74.

31. National Economic Research Associates, Inc., "The Studies of Residential Demand for Electricity: A Critique," August, 1973.

Selected Bibliography

a) Charles E. Olson, *Cost Considerations for Efficient Electricity Supply*, Michigan State University Press, 1970.

b) W. J. Samuels and H. M. Trebing, *A Critique of Administrative Regulation of Public Utilities*, Michigan State University Press, 1972.

c) H. M. Trebing, *Performance Under Regulation*, Michigan State University Press, 1972.

d) H. M. Trebing, *Essays on Public Utility Pricing and Regulation*, Michigan State University Press, 1971.

e) H. M. Trebing and R. H. Howard, *Rate of Return Under Regulation: New Dimensions and Perspectives*, Michigan State University Press, 1969.

f) United Nations Department of Economic and Social Affairs, St/ECA/156, *Electricity Costs and Tariffs: A General Study*, United Nations, New York, 1972.

g) Edwin Vennard, *The Electric Power Business*, New York, McGraw-Hill, Inc. 1970.

CHAPTER 10

Financing the Capital Requirements of the Electric Utility Industry

A. Introduction

In Chapter 6 several alternate patterns of future economic and energy growth were evaluated. It was concluded that the moderate-growth, Case B conditions seemed to represent a more desirable balance of competing considerations, and to be more likely of achievement than the other two sets of conditions. Therefore, it is desirable to examine the long-range financial implications of the Case B conditions for the electric utility industry.

The objectives of this study are primarily of a long-range nature. For those readers desiring an overview of the short-range economic and energy situation in the United States, a wide variety of references are available. A similarly broad choice of papers can be found which deal with the short-range financial problems of the economy in general and of the electrical industry in particular. Here, however, attention is concentrated on the longer-range aspects of the financing requirements of the electric utility industry.

This Chapter is organized as follows: (1) summary and conclusions; (2) discussion of "the current financial situation;" (3) assumed future financial and operating conditions in the electric utility industry; (4) description of the financial forecasting model used; (5) summary of output from the model runs; and (6) an overview of the financing needs of the rest of the United States economy.

It must be emphasized that the financial model outputs, like the scenarios of Chapter 6, are attempts to describe a range of possible future conditions rather than to define a single, specific future. It must also be emphasized that individual utility company situations may vary widely from the average industry conditions discussed here.

B. Summary and Conclusions

The capital requirements of the investor-owned electric utility industry were examined over the period to 1990. The examination was primarily based on the economic and total energy demand conditions of the moderate-growth scenario, Case B—HCN as developed in Chapter 6. The moderate-growth energy demand conditions were altered by shifting slightly more energy demand to the electric utility sector than the Case B scenario envisioned in order to create a variant called Case B—HCN (high coal and nuclear.)

A long-range financial planning model was adapted and used as a calculating tool for this financial examination. The projected needs of the electric utility industry were compared with other contemporary estimates of future capital needs in the United States.

The conclusions of the study may be summarized as follows:

(1) The primary prerequisite for a financially healthy industry is prompt rate relief designed to: (a) permit electric utility companies to earn an adequate rate of return on common equity; and (b) to attract the necessary new capital. A number of revisions to regulatory procedure, which would aid in achieving this objective, are discussed in Chapter 9, Electric Power Pricing.

(2) Accounting, tax and regulatory changes are recommended to supplement but not replace the effort to attain adequate after-tax returns on equity. Among these changes are: higher depreciation rates; inclusion of construction work in progress (in whole or in part) in the rate base; raising the investment tax credit to the 10 percent range; normalizing tax deferrals; and allowing tax-free reinvestment of dividends in new issue stock.

(3) Some emergency provisions may be necessary to assist the industry over a short-term crisis period. Among these are financial aid for specialized needs such as pollution control. It must be emphasized, however, that such devices do not eliminate, or even reduce significantly, the basic and continuing need for fair and proper electric rates.

(4) As the nation develops a program for greater energy independence there will be a strong tendency to shift, where possible, from oil and gas to electricity generated with coal and nuclear fuel. This will tend to increase the growth rate of electricity from the 5.3 percent per year forecast of Case B to a range nearer to 5.8 percent.

(5) With demand for electricity growing about 5.8 percent per year, and assuming moderate inflation in a range close to 4 or 5 percent per year, utility construction expenditures will grow at an average rate of 12 to 13 percent per year from 1970 to 1980 and at a rate of about 9 percent per year in the following decade. Greater inflationary pressures will result in even more rapidly growing expenditures.

(6) Limited capital availability over the near term will require compensatingly higher expenditures in later years, probably during the 1980-85 period.

(7) Total current dollar requirements for capital during the period from 1975 to 1990 inclusive will approximate $735 billion dollars.

(8) By 1990 the total electric plant investment of the investor-owned segment of the industry will approximate $900 billion dollars on an original cost basis. This is almost 9 times the investment in 1970.

(9) Inability to raise the required new capital funds will result in slowing the nation's economic growth, and delaying or rendering impractical its efforts to achieve greater energy "independence."

(10) External funds will continue to be the source of nearly two-thirds of the industry's total capital needs, although this fraction may decline significantly during the 1980's.

(11) Between $400 and $450 billion of funds will have to be raised in the securities markets over the period from 1974 to 1990. This is about 4.7 times as much as was raised over the preceding 15 years for similar purposes. Of the $400 to $450 billion, over $100 billion will be in the form of common stock.

(12) Average industry returns on common equity in the range of 15 percent or more must be *realized* if the large volumes of new common stock are to be marketed successfully. To *realize* these earnings rates, the returns *allowed* in regulatory proceedings must be several percentage points higher to compensate for the earnings erosion due to inflation. The difference between allowed and realized rates of return will depend on many factors; e.g. the rate of inflation, the regulatory lag, the use of forward test years, etc.

(13) The key to successful marketing of new common equity will continue to be the investor's estimate of the likely total return (i.e., dividends plus market value appreciation) on his investment. With common equity returns in the range of 14 to 15 percent or more, per-share growth of real earnings (and dividends) in the range of 3 to 6 percent per year is feasible. Such rates of growth may be marginally sufficient to induce investors to return to utility securities.

(14) If rates of return on equity remain at the 10-12 percent level, however, earnings are likely to decrease, in real terms, at a rate of from 3 to 4 percent per year. Only nominal increases of 1 to 2 percent per year can be expected even on a current dollar basis. Under such conditions, equity issues of many companies may become essentially "unmarketable."

(15) The nation may be entering a period of chronic capital scarcity as a number of economic and social developments combine to increase the demand for funds. In addition to the demands of the electric utility industry, demand pressures may be expected from financing requirements for: (a) environmental protection efforts, (b) development of petroleum and coal resources and associated technologies such as coal gasification and liquefaction, and recovering oil shale and tar sands, (c) the need to recover and refine successively leaner grades of metallic ores, (d) improving existing mass transit facilities and building entirely new networks, (e) satisfying requirements for new housing as the population age distribution shifts toward a greater concentration in the young adult age brackets—the groups with the highest rate of household formation, (f) investment in plant and equipment with higher energy consumption efficiency, and (g) higher public expenditures for social welfare.

(16) The capital shortage will be felt in the form of a whole collection of lower-priority demands for capital which will not be met. A major decision society must make over the remainder of this decade is the choice of techniques for determining these priorities. A free market is the most efficient and equitable means for allocating capital. Public policy should be directed toward eliminating those controls which presently distort the allocation process, instead of attempting to spread similar controls over ever-wider sectors of the economy.

(17) The future quality of life in this country will be significantly affected by the quantity of capital formation. It will be even more seriously affected by the allocation of such capital. Allocation of capital based on fluctuating waves of political sentiment can be highly detrimental over the long run.

(18) Regulation of the electric utility industry must recognize the necessity for allowing utilities to compete for capital on more nearly even terms with other institutions. Unregulated industrial companies can react freely and promptly to changing conditions in the capital markets by raising prices or by postponing expansion. Government agencies have special privileges which improve their access to capital. Electric power companies have neither of these options or privileges. The single most important regulatory step toward improving utility company competitiveness in the capital markets will be to allow companies to earn adequate returns on common equity.

(19) The difference between a sick industry with a 10-11 percent average return on equity and a healthy one with at least a 14 or 15 percent return, will remain in the 6 to 12 percent range in terms of the necessary additional price per kilowatthour to the average customer. The model shows a difference of 8 percent in 1980 and 10 percent in 1985.

C. The Current Financial Situation

The electric power industry in the United States is about 100 years old, having started as a street lighting and electric railway business. Today it has become one of the largest groups of business enterprises in the nation. It has always been predominantly an investor-owned industry. In 1932 electric companies owned about 93 percent of the generating capacity in the United States, while municipal and other government power agencies owned the rest.

Beginning in the 1930s, government ownership assumed greater importance until the early 1950s, when the investor-owned proportion of the industry had dropped to about 80 percent of generating capacity. At present there are five distinct classes of ownership in the electric power industry: (1) investor-owned companies accounting for 78 percent of sales to ultimate customers; (2) federal government power agencies with 11 percent of the output, most of which is marketed through locally owned distribution entities; (3) state and district power agencies with 4 percent; (4) municipal electric systems with 6 percent and; (5) rural electric cooperatives with 1 percent.

The remainder of this analysis will concentrate on the investor-owned segment of the industry because it is predominant in size. While the government and government-financed power segments enjoy a number of advantages, such as access to public tax revenues, their financing problems are generally sim-

ilar to those of the investor-owned sector. The overview of financing needs of the rest of the United States economy, at the end of this section, will touch upon the government power segments of the industry.

1. Capital Investment

At the end of 1974, the investor-owned electric utility industry had a total gross investment in electric plant and equipment of approximately $150 billion, which was larger than any other industry in the United States. The petroleum industry, the next largest in terms of physical investment, reported an aggregate figure which was only about two-thirds as large, with significant portions representing overseas assets.

The size of this investment relative to the industry's annual revenues from sales and to its total employment, clearly justifies the description, "capital intensive." Table 10·1 compares 1973 figures for electric utilities with similar figures for other industries, and with median figures for all manufacturing companies.

Electric utilities require about $4.00 of capital assets to generate each annual dollar of sales, while the average manufacturer requires only about 80¢ of capital assets to generate an annual dollar of sales. For this reason, the cost of capital (i.e., interest charges, preferred dividends, common equity return and income taxes) plays a very material part in determining the price the electric utility industry must charge its customers. Likewise, the other "fixed

Table 10·1
INVESTMENT PER DOLLAR OF ANNUAL SALES AND PER EMPLOYEE (December 31, 1973)

	Assets/ Revenues	Estimated Assets/ Employee
Electric Utilities	$4.18	$279,000
Telephone	2.85	84,000
Railroads	2.54	62,000
Oil	1.15	240,000
Steel	.86	42,000
Automobiles	.57	54,000
All Manufacturing	.73	37,000

Source: *EEI Statistical Yearbook, Fortune* Magazine, and the Federal Power Commission National Power Survey Advisory Committee Report: *The Financial Outlook for the Electric Power Industry.*

charges" associated with investment; i.e., depreciation, insurance and property taxes, weigh heavily in the total cost of delivered energy. In past years, roughly half of the total cost of electricity could be associated with these investment and investment-related charges. The proportion has dropped from about 58 percent in the mid-1960s to about 40 percent in 1973, and to an even lower figure in 1974. This drop results from the combined effects of inadequate returns on capital investment, correspondingly low income taxes, and high fuel costs.

Present trends are likely to keep fixed costs at 30 to 40 percent of revenue in the next few years. Thereafter, they can be expected to climb. As new and more expensive plant is added to utility systems, as nuclear energy supplies an increasing share of total generation, and as returns on common equity become more nearly adequate, the relative importance of plant costs will increase and that of fuel costs will decrease, once again approaching the half-and-half position.

2. Proportion of Total United States Capital Funds Used by Electric Utilities

A high degree of capital intensity, plus a particularly heavy reliance in recent times on external financing for the major part of its capital expansion, have led to the investor-owned electric utility industry becoming a material factor in the nation's capital markets and in the overall process of capital formation. This significance can be measured in a number of ways. Over the past 25 years, electric utilities have annually taken the equivalent of from 5 percent to 16 percent of all personal savings to finance their construction programs. Over the past decade this percentage has displayed a persistent tendency to rise. Over the period 1947-1972 the share of personal savings (measured on a national income basis) absorbed by investor-owned electric utility stock and bond sales averaged 9.9 percent annually. During the five years 1968-1972, however, the average was 13.4 percent, and the annual values have been rising steadily.

Another measure of the role of electric utilities in the nation's capital requirements is the ratio of investor-owned electric utility expenditures to the total capital expenditures of all United States industries. Over the past decade the investor-owned electric companies have doubled their proportion of the annual creation of new plant and equipment in the United States, from 7.6 percent in 1964 to 15.2 percent in 1972. (See Table 10·2.) A variety of factors have contributed to this trend. Important among them are: (a) a rate of increase of electricity

Table 10·2
CAPITAL OUTLAYS IN ELECTRIC UTILITIES AND OTHER INDUSTRIES

Year	All U.S. Industries	Investor-Owned Elec. Utilities	Investor-Owned Utilities as Percent of Total U.S. Industry
	($ Billion)	($ Billion)	(%)
1964..........	47.0	3.6	7.6
1965..........	54.4	4.0	7.4
1966..........	63.5	5.0	7.8
1967..........	65.8	6.1	9.4
1968..........	67.8	7.2	10.6
1969..........	75.6	8.3	11.0
1970..........	79.7	10.2	12.8
1971..........	81.2	10.9	14.7
1972..........	88.4	13.4	15.2
1973..........	99.7	15.0	15.0
1974..........	112.4	16.4	14.6

Source: United States Department of Commerce, Bureau of Economic Analysis, *1971 Business Statistics*, October 1971, p. 9; *Survey of Current Business*, July 1972, p. S-2; November 1973, p. S-2.

usage which has been nearly twice the rate of growth of the real GNP (i.e., typical growth rates have been 8 percent and 4 percent per year respectively), (b) environmental protection requirements which have impinged heavily on this industry, and (c) the growing commitment to nuclear power, a particularly capital-intensive form of generation which substitutes capital for fuel expense.

3. Trends in Capital Costs of New Plant

Over most of the history of the electric utility industry, plant costs per kilowatt of capacity remained reasonably stable or showed a downward trend. Economies of scale available in production, transmission, and distribution were normally sufficient to offset the effects of inflation. Today economies of scale still exist. Since the late 1960s, however, the gains from advancing technology and increasing plant size have been more than offset by the costs arising from inflation. The current dollar cost of additional capacity is well above the embedded or historical costs of facilities already in service.

Some of the increase in plant investment per kilowatt is due to the installation of more complex, and still more capital-intensive plant. These upward pressures would exist even in the absence of inflationary forces. In effect, they result from the construction of facilities which are noticeably different from existing equipment. Nuclear power stations are a primary example of such new plant. Fossil fuel stations equipped with elaborate environmental protection facilities can also be considered as belonging to a new class of plant. The same can be said of underground distribution facilities in areas where, in the past, less expensive overhead lines would have been considered satisfactory.

4. Effects of Inflation

In addition to boosting the cost of new facilities, inflation affects utilities adversely in several other ways. It raises the price which investors demand in payment for the use of their funds; i.e., it raises the interest rate on new bonds, the acceptable dividend rate on new preferred stock, and the return on common equity which common stock investors consider necessary before they will purchase common stock.

Inflation also makes woefully inadequate the depreciation dollars which accumulate as existing plant and equipment are used and worn out. Without inflation, the funds generated through depreciation accumulations on a piece of equipment by the time its useful life has passed would be sufficient to pay for its replacement. With inflation, accumulated depreciation is often insufficient to cover even one-half the cost of a replacement.

Finally, inflation coupled with regulatory lag makes it effectively impossible for a utility company to realize the rate of return approved by the regulatory authorities, when that approval is based on a so-called historic test year and is obtained through the normal regulatory process. Chart 10•1 illustrates that up to two years can easily elapse between the middle of the test year and the middle of the first year during which the new rates are collected.

The effects of an inadequate return are concentrated upon the common stockholder who is entitled only to what remains after bondholders, preferred stockholders and taxing authorities are given their due. Thus, both dividends and retained earnings are put under pressure. This tends to increase the need for external funding since retained earnings are those earnings not paid out as dividends but rather re-

Chart 10•1
REGULATORY LAG

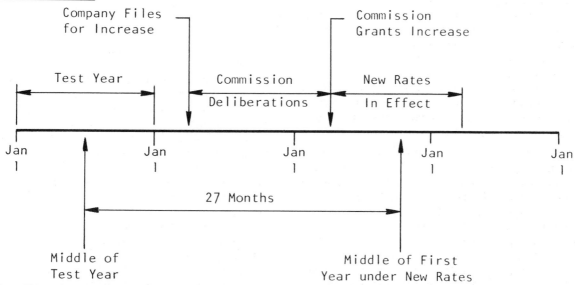

Notes: This example assumes 3 months are required for the company to ascertain final and accurate statistics for the test year and then to prepare the filing documents. It also assumes commission deliberations consume 12 months. Deliberation times vary from one company's filing to another's.

The middle of the test year and the middle of the first year under new rates are highlighted. This reflects the fact that, when costs are rising more or less continuously, the costs and revenues at each mid-year point are reasonable approximations to the average costs and revenue for that year.

This chart is merely illustrative.

tained in the business to pay for new plant and equipment. Consequently, inflation causes a compounding of the financial problems of utilities.

5. Recent Developments in Regulation

In recent years progress has been made in reducing regulatory lag in some jurisdictions. For example, steps have been taken to reduce the length of rate proceedings, to grant interim and emergency increases, to adjust for post-test-year changes, and to allow for test periods which reflect projections of probable future operating conditions.

Unfortunately, these signs of progress are far from uniformly evident across the United States. Regulation in some states is constrained by outdated statutes and legal precedents. In many cases regulation is particularly ill-suited to the inflationary environment which prevails today and may continue in the foreseeable future.

6. Capital Structure of the Electric Utility Industry

The investor-owned electric utility industry is characterized by a highly leveraged capital structure; i.e., a far higher proportion of debt to stockholder's investment than is present in most other industries (but lower than some; e.g., gas pipelines and commercial credit). Reliance on long-term debt plus preferred stock has been justified historically to achieve a lower over-all cost of capital and, therefore, lower rates for the consumer. It has been made possible by stability of net income growth. This is a characteristic which, at least in the past, has been associated with regulated utilities. As a general proposition, shareholders of a company are wary of large amounts of debt because the payment of interest on this indebtedness takes precedence over the payment of dividends.

Hence, the stability in earnings growth for utilities was quite important. It allowed the common equity investor to view high debt ratios with little concern because of his confidence in the availability of adequate earnings. Other industries, which lack stable growth in their net income, have depended less on debt financing and normally are able to generate a larger portion of their new capital internally. When outside financing is needed, firms in these other industries generally have more flexibility built into their capitalization ratios so that they can concentrate either on debt or equity offerings depending on relative market conditions. For example, during periods of stock market weakness, non-utility companies can often resort temporarily to heavier than normal reliance on debt capital, intending to return to equity financing when market conditions improve.

In contrast, the electric utility industry has limited capability for internal funds generation and limited flexibility in its choice of funding. The factors which limit its internal funds generation are: (1) long-lived plant facilities; (2) low equity base in the capital structure; and (3) a stockholder group largely concerned with obtaining a high payout in current dividends.

The long-lived plant facilities provide low book depreciation rates, averaging only about 2.5 percent per year at present, and yielding annual depreciation charges which are small compared to original cost and even smaller when compared to replacement cost. The low common equity base, typically 35 to 40 percent of capitalization, provides a relatively small earnings flow even when adequate returns on common equity are realized. For a given return on equity, the earnings flow to a typical utility will be half that of a non-utility company of equal size with a 70 or 80 percent equity ratio.

Moreover, much of utility company common stock is held by investors who bought the stock because of its reputation for a combination of relatively high current yield, safety, and modest but steady growth in market value. These investors were attracted by payout ratios (dividends as a percent of earnings) in the range of 70 percent which, of course, allow only 30 percent of earnings to be retained in the business. Again, this is about half as large a fraction as is typical for earnings retention in many non-utility companies.

The factors which limit a utility company's flexibility in its choice of debt, preferred or equity as the source of its new capital are: (1) the high proportion of debt in the capital structure; (2) a total return on common equity which is not adequate to entice investors to buy the large quantities of new equity which would permit increases in the equity ratio; and (3) regulatory reluctance to permit equity ratios to rise much above historic norms. Together these factors almost require that utilities continue to market new long-term securities issues in about the same proportions as their current capitalization. Overlong concentration on new debt or preferred issues will hasten the fall of the coverage ratios to legal minimums as described later. Excessive reliance on new common stock issues will reveal an inadequate pool of investors interested in the particular combination of total return (dividend yield plus growth rate of market price) for which utility common stock has become known. This is particularly true today, after several years of static dividends and strongly negative trends in market price. Finally, regulators wish to limit equity ratios to conventional levels because the combination of earnings rates and taxes on

Table 10·3
PERCENTAGE DISTRIBUTION OF CAPITAL SOURCES, ELECTRIC UTILITY INDUSTRY
(Percentage Distribution)

Year	Total Long Term Debt	Preferred Stock	Common Stock	Total Capital- ization
1964......	51.8%	9.6%	38.6%	100.0%
1965......	51.7	9.5	38.8	100.0
1966......	52.5	9.5	38.0	100.0
1967......	53.3	9.7	37.0	100.0
1968......	54.1	9.6	36.3	100.0
1969......	55.0	9.5	35.5	100.0
1970......	55.3	9.8	34.9	100.0
1971......	54.7	10.7	34.6	100.0
1972......	53.7	11.7	34.6	100.0
1973......	52.9	12.0	35.1	100.0
1974......	53.3	12.3	34.4	100.0

Source: Moody's Investor Service.

common stock make it normally a more expensive form of capital than either debt or preferred stock.

Over the past few years, electric utilities have seen their interest and preferred dividend burdens increase rapidly because: (1) long-term interest rates and preferred dividend rates have both risen dramatically and (2) steadily expanding construction programs at inflated costs have required more capital. Since 1964, yields on utility bonds have nearly doubled while annual capital outlays have more than quadrupled. (See Table 10·2.) Preferred stock dividends rates rose at about the same pace as yields on bonds. Nevertheless, managements had to maximize both types of financing to hold down capital costs and to avoid the over-dilution associated with

Table 10·4
COMPOSITION OF NEW LONG-TERM CAPITAL
(Percentage Distribution)

Year	Long Term Debt	Preferred Stock	Common Stock	Retained Earnings	Total
1969.....	64.4%	7.3%	11.1%	17.2%	100.0%
1970.....	57.3	13.1	18.8	10.8	100.0
1971.....	48.7	17.2	23.4	10.7	100.0
1972.....	45.0	19.5	23.4	12.1	100.0
1973.....	45.9	15.1	26.6	12.4	100.0
1974.....	56.5	15.2	18.9	9.4	100.0

Source: Edison Electric Institute.

too-frequent common stock offerings. As a result, the total of debt and preferred stock grew from just over 61 percent of total outstanding capital in 1964, to nearly 66 percent in 1974. (See Table 10·3.)

The shifts in emphasis between long-term debt, preferred stock and common stock as sources of *new* capital are particularly interesting over the last six years as shown in Table 10·4. In the years just before 1969, long-term debt was the favored financing vehicle, accounting for some 64 percent of *new* capital in 1969 versus only 54 percent of *total outstanding* capital at the end of the preceding year. Between 1969 and 1971 the emphasis shifted to preferred stock and then to common equity (new common stock issues plus retained earnings). As retained earnings became less able to carry their accustomed part of the burden, and as coverage ratios for debt and preferred stock decreased, utilities turned to more frequent and larger issues of new common stock as the preferable source. In 1974, stock market conditions forced a return to the bond market.

7. Coverage Ratios

A primary impetus causing the shifts from debt to preferred stock, and more recently from preferred to common stock, has been the coverage ratio.

In virtually all utility mortgage indentures there is a limitation on the issuance of additional long-term debt securities imposed by the "coverage requirement." The general effect of these limitations is that the company is legally prohibited from issuing new bonds or debentures if the ratio of pre-tax earnings to interest charges (adjusted to reflect the effect of the new issues) is less than 2.0.[1] The purpose of such provisions is, of course, to protect the existing bondholders and the company's continued ability to meet its interest payments. Thus, as debt financing was increased at progressively higher interest rates, the interest coverage ratio of the typical utility began to fall, suggesting the need for a shift to preferred and common stock for larger portions of subsequent new capital. The consequence of such a shift, of course, was the increase of preferred dividend payouts until, here too, a coverage ratio limit was approached. Provisions similar to the interest coverage ratio limits are commonly associated with preferred stock issues, though in this case they are usually based on earnings after taxes and after bond interest payments.

Table 10·5 shows the fall of the bond interest coverage ratio for the investor-owned electric utilities over the period since 1965. In addition to their legal implications, bond and preferred stock coverage ratios have long been used by the investment community as a primary measure of the quality and safety of any given company's securities. A high

293

Table 10·5
INCOME AND INTEREST OF ELECTRIC UTILITIES

Year	Income before Interest Charges* ($ Million)	Interest on Long-Term Debt ($ Million)	Ratio
1965	3,454	953	3.62
1966	3,692	1,040	3.55
1967	3,948	1,180	3.35
1968	4,179	1,373	3.04
1969	4,548	1,621	2.81
1970	5,009	2,010	2.49
1971	5,545	2,447	2.27
1972	6,302	2,849	2.21
1973	7,134	3,271	2.18
1974	8,089	3,916	2.07

* Less allowance for funds used during construction.

Source: Edison Electric Institute.

coverage ratio meant high safety, low risk, and consequently a lower interest rate. Decreasing coverage meant decreasing safety and, at some point, a decrease in the quality rating accorded to that company's issues. This is exactly what has happened in the past several years.

From early 1970 through 1974, the credit ratings of securities of approximately 70 major investor-owned electric utility companies have been reduced. During 1974 alone, the ratings of about 43 securities were decreased (while those of six were increased).[2] These derating actions were taken by either Standard and Poors or Moody's or both. These are two of the principal firms involved in credit evaluation of securities. Each derating signals a higher cost of debt for the utility affected, and restricts more severely the potential market for future debt issues of that company.

8. Dependence on External Financing

The dependence of the electric utility companies on external financing, through the issuance of new securities, is shown on Table 10·6. While all non-financial corporations, on average, obtained some 55 percent of their funds from internal sources in 1972, the far more capital-intensive electric utilities got only 31 percent of the funds they required in that fashion. It is important to note that the bulk of the

electric industry's relatively modest internal funds are obtained via depreciation allowances. In striking contrast, the great bulk of the internal financing of other companies is through retained earnings; in fact, earnings are their major single source of all financing—both internal and external.

When the subject of external financing is considered, it is found that other companies generally obtain a substantial portion of their funds via bank loans and other short-term indebtedness. Electric utilities do not. The dominance of utilities in the long-term capital markets (for stocks and long-term debt) is shown by the fact that this one industry absorbed 25 percent of all new long-term business capital generated (i.e., $9.6 billion out of $38.2 billion, as shown on Table 10·6).

Thus, the great and rather unique dependence of electric utilities on capital markets—for 66 percent of their capital requirements in 1972—arises from a combination of factors:

1. The highly capital-intensive character of the

Table 10·6
RELATIVE DEPENDENCE ON CAPITAL MARKETS IN 1972 (Dollars in Billions)

Source of Funds	Electric Utilities Amount	Electric Utilities Per-cent	All Non-Financial Corporations Amount	All Non-Financial Corporations Per-cent
Internal Sources:				
Depreciation and amortization	$ 2.9	20%	$ 62.8	40%
Retained earnings	1.6*	11	21.6	15
Subtotal	$ 4.5	31%	$ 84.4	55%
External Sources:				
Stocks and long-term debt	$ 9.6	66%	$ 38.2	25%
Loans and other short-term items	.4	3	30.7	20
Subtotal	$10.0	69%	$ 68.9	45%
Total	$14.5	100%	$153.3	100%

* Includes reserves for deferred income taxes.

Source: Federal Reserve System Flow of Funds
Edison Electric Institute.

industry and hence its continual need for new capital.

2. The modest availability of retained earnings and other internal sources, and hence the industry's primary dependence on external sources for financing its large capital programs.

3. The minor extent to which the industry uses, or could be expected to use, short-term financing for its long-term capital projects, and thus its great dependence on continually attracting new long-term capital into the industry.

4. High leverage, which limits the industry's flexibility in choosing among debt, preferred stock or common stock as the source of its new capital.

Thus, despite its massive size, the industry has neither the internal financial reserves nor the external financing flexibility which would permit it to continue financing the required new facilities during extended periods of stress in the capital markets.

9. Current Conditions for Common Stock

As coverage ratios have approached legal minimums, first for debt and then for preferred stock, the common stock market has become the final recourse for utility companies seeking new funds. However, the market for utility common stocks has progressively weakened for almost a decade. Chart 9•2 in Chapter 9, Electric Power Pricing, demonstrates the long decline which has occurred in utility stocks as compared to industrial stocks.

Until late 1973, the decline was due primarily to a long history of unexciting earnings performance. This performance can be illustrated by noting that the average return on common equity for the industry was virtually the same in 1973 as in 1962; i.e., about 11 percent. During the same period, however, embedded interest rates on outstanding debt rose from about 3.7 percent to well over 6 percent, and interest rates on newly issued debt at times rose to 10 percent or more, thus drastically shifting the relative attractiveness of the two investment vehicles.

With the advent of the Arab oil price increases in late 1973 and the dividend omission by Consolidated Edison in the spring of 1974, investor confidence in electric utility stocks plummeted still further. The Standard and Poor's index of 35 utilities which had declined 25 percent in 1973 fell another 25 percent in the first half of 1974. Although market prices recovered modestly in late 1974 and early 1975, they remained generally below book value, a situation which makes the sale of new common stock unattractive.

Selling common stock at substantial discounts below book value results in a reduction in average book value of all outstanding shares, and creates dilution of the ownership of existing shareholders. Dilution occurs in all such sales unless existing shareholders purchase all the new shares being offered. The diverse nature of the owners of utility common stock, and the frequency of new issues of common make dilution unavoidable. The dilution results in a direct loss of capital for earlier shareholders. It is discouraging to new investors, as well as to existing stockholders, since it raises the possibility that they, too, may suffer future similar losses.

In many cases such dilution causes a permanent reduction in the earnings and dividend growth potential of all common stock. A recent study suggests that selling 5 to 10 percent additional common stock each year, when the market price is in the range of 50 to 70 percent of book value, will lead to declining earnings per share, barring substantial increases in net income.[3] The study also concludes that a very real point is reached, perhaps just below the 50 percent of book value level, where additional common stock simply cannot be sold.

At such a point the only recourse which remains available to a utility company is to tailor its construction program to fit its internal generation of funds. This would mean a cut-back to perhaps one-third of its planned construction, if its internal generation potential were similar to that of the industry as a whole.

Particularly in the context of the nation's effort to achieve energy independence, it is apparent that serious disruption of the electric utility industry's construction program could be disastrous for the national economy.

D. Forecasting Financial Needs of the Industry

The remaining sections examine the future financing needs of the electric utility industry on a quantitative basis. This is followed by an analysis of financing needs of the nation as a whole and, finally, by a discussion of methods which are available to improve the financial strength of the electric utility industry so as to permit it to meet the future electric power needs of the nation.

The analysis described in Chapter 6 concludes that the moderate-growth alternative designated as Case B-HCN is more likely and more desirable than any of the other alternatives considered. Therefore, Case B-HCN was chosen as the primary foundation for this forecast of electric utility industry financial requirements. Supplementary estimates were also made of the industry capital needs for the high-and low-growth cases.

In specific terms, Case B-HCN foresees average annual growth rates over the next 25 years of about 3.5 to 3.7 percent for GNP, 2.8 to 3.0 percent for total energy consumption and 5.8 percent for consumption of energy for electricity generation.

1. Assumptions for the Financing Forecasts

To employ the financial model to forecast the financing needs of the electric utility industry under these growth conditions, it was necessary to make a number of assumptions to supplement those listed in Chapter 6 for Case B-HCN. A summary of the most important of these supplementary assumptions is given in the following paragraphs.

a. Price Conditions

The general price environment of Case B is assumed to prevail; i.e., a gradually decreasing rate of inflation over the next few years, leading to an average rate of price increase of about 4 percent per year after 1980. Similar patterns are assumed for interest rates and preferred stock dividend rates on new utility issues. Long-term debt interest, for example, is assumed to level out at 7.5 percent per year.

The inflation effects on costs of new generation, transmission and distribution plant are assumed to follow roughly similar trends; moving down from 8 percent per year increases in the 1975-76 period to 4 or 5 percent per year in the early 1980s and maintaining that rate. An individual series of capacity cost estimates was prepared for each major type of capacity; i.e., nuclear, hydro, coal-fueled steam plants, internal combustion turbines, and combined cycle plants.

It is important to emphasize that the possible futures discussed here do not assume a run-away inflation, but rather assume a prompt return to inflation rates below 5 percent. Should inflation rates remain at or above the 8 to 10 percent range, the industry's, as well as the rest of the nation's, financing problems would be greatly increased. Individual savings would be discouraged by the anticipation of chronic inflation, regulatory lag would remain a severe problem, and depreciation charges would continue to be very far below true replacement costs.

b. Capacity Additions

Energy consumption by fuel source (e.g., coal, oil,

etc.) for Case B-HCN was developed in Chapter 6. The results are summarized in Table 10·7. This information was combined with forecast values of load factor and capacity factor to obtain estimates of capacity installed. Load factor may be defined as: actual output from the generating system of a company divided by the potential generation from that system if it were to be run at the actual maximum kilowatt demand for the entire period. Capacity factor may be defined as the "load factor" for a given generating unit or class of generating units in that system.[4] Load factors are determined primarily by the timing of customer demands for electricity (although the utility company can have some impact through its pricing and public information policies), while capacity factors are controlled by the company in response to economic and technical factors (e.g., fuel prices, operation and maintenance costs, suitability of a unit for peak, intermediate or base load service, and installed capacity available for service).

The general trends in generating capacity additions disclosed by the estimating process were:

(1) The bulk of additions will be coal and nuclear fueled steam plants. By the year 2000 these units together will account for almost three-fourths of total installed capacity. The Case B environmental assumptions placed a restraint on the coal fired additions.

(2) Conventional oil and gas fired steam plants will be retired gradually through the forecast period.

Table 10·7
ENERGY CONSUMPTION FOR ELECTRICITY GENERATION— CASE B-HCN

Quadrillion Btu	1975	1980	1985	2000
Coal	8.66	11.22	12.35	16.84
Oil and Gas	6.70	7.47	8.04	8.90
Nuclear	2.28	5.75	14.20	53.09
Hydro and Other	3.20	3.50	3.80	8.00
Total	20.84	27.94	38.40	86.83
Billions of Kilowatthours				
Coal	821	1,065	1,170	1,598
Oil and Gas	636	708	762	844
Nuclear	216	545	1,342	5,040
Hydro and Other	304	332	366	758
Total	1,977	2,650	3,640	8,240

Table 10·8
INSTALLED GENERATING CAPACITY— CASE B-HCN (Average for the Year— Capacities in Millions of Kilowatts)

Energy Source	1975	1980	1985	2000
Coal	205	253	302	456
Oil and Gas	172	200	229	254
Nuclear	45	100	236	820
Hydro and Other	67	79	87	179
Total	489	632	854	1,709

A significant number of combined cycle plants will be added.

(3) Hydro power capacity will continue to grow but the bulk of additions will be on publicly-owned systems. By the year 2000 hydro capacity will account for some 6 percent of the nation's total, in contrast to almost 15 percent at present.

Table 10·8 shows the specific estimates of installed generating capacity which were derived for the period from 1975 to 2000. The nuclear estimate of 820 million kilowatts in the year 2000 is close to the low AEC estimate of 850 million kilowatts.[5] Appendix L summarizes load factor, capacity factor, and reserve margin forecasts associated with the Table 10·8 capacity figures.

Transmission, distribution and other miscellaneous capital additions were forecast in current dollar terms as percentages of total direct costs of the generation additions. The percentages were based in part on recent trends and in part on Federal Power Commission estimates.[6]

c. Government-Owned Generation

The financing problems of the government-owned and financed segments of the industry are distinct from, and somewhat less constraining than, those of the investor-owned companies. Therefore, it is necessary to forecast the capacity additions and the total output of each segment of the industry separately. In the recent past, government-owned and financed utilities have generated about 23 percent of total output using an approximately equal percentage of total installed capacity. However, the government utilities have employed a significantly different mix of generation facilities than the investor-owned companies. For example, government systems in 1972 accounted for about two-thirds of all hydro and internal combustion capacity, but only about 15 percent of the total fossil steam capacity.[7] These

general capacity relationships between the two segments of the industry were forecast to continue and, in addition, it was assumed that government-owned and financed systems would account for close to 15 percent of the nation's growing nuclear capacity.

d. Revenue and Expense Forecasts

With the preceding assumptions it was possible to forecast the construction expenditures of the investor-owned portion of the electric utility industry. However, additional information had to be developed before the sources of the funds needed to finance this construction could be estimated. Specifically, the forecast of retained earnings required the development of figures such as normally appear on an individual company's income statement and its sources and uses of funds statement. However, in this case the figures needed were those for the entire investor-owned industry. A number of additional assumptions were necessary before such figures could be derived by the model. Some of the most critical of those assumptions are summarized below.

Estimates of future fuel costs were based on the fuel price trends developed in Chapter 6. Past and current fuel prices were obtained from the Edison Electric Institute and the Department of Commerce.[8] Industry employment and labor expenses were estimated as follows. EEI employment data for past years were examined along with wage rate data from the Bureau of Labor Statistics.[9] From this data, relationships were developed between employment, labor expense, and kilowatthour output. These relationships were projected into the future with the use of regression techniques and then adjusted to account for the different inflation rates expected in the future. Similar techniques were used to develop forecasts of other operating and maintenance, administrative and general, and customer-related expenses. Federal Power Commission statistics were the source of most of the historical data series used in developing these expense trends.[10]

e. Financial Ratios

The discussions in Section C, "The Current Financial Situation," and in the initial parts of Chapter 9 suggest that the financial health of the electric utility industry will be closely tied to the reception given its new common stock issues in the capital markets of the future. This in turn will depend on factors such as the industry's record of returns on common equity. If the industry can obtain, and then maintain, a satisfactory rate of return on common equity, its new issues will command favorable price-earnings ratios, market prices will be higher, and the number of new shares which must be issued will be less. If returns on common equity continue to be unsatisfactory to investors, they will be willing to purchase new shares only at low price-earnings ratios, market prices will be materially less than book value and the industry will be forced to issue much larger numbers of new shares, with greater dilution, in order to provide required new equity capital.

To examine the quantitative effects of these variables on the future of the industry, several forecasts were developed by the financial model. All of them incorporated the single set of assumptions summarized above. In addition, all of them assumed that new capital would be added in the fixed proportions of: 50 percent debt, 12 percent preferred stock and 38 percent common equity (new stock issues plus retained earnings). However, the forecasts differed from each other in the assumptions used for: (1) return on common equity, (2) price-earnings ratio, and (3) payout ratio. Here, the assumptions ranged from 11 to 15 percent for return on common equity, from 8 to 15 for price-earnings and 60 to 80 percent for payout ratios.[11]

2. Description of the Forecasting Model

The model provides a means for forecasting the financial and operating characteristics of an electric utility company (or industry) for 20 years. Included in the output for each of the 20 forecast years are: (1) a statement of operations; i.e., an income statement; (2) a balance sheet; (3) a source and application of funds statement; (4) a capitalization statement; (5) a balance sheet items statement which lists certain details of the plant and depreciation accounts, and (6) a statement of sales and output statistics. A more detailed description of the model is provided in Appendix D.

3. Output from the Forecasting Model

The most significant results to be obtained from the financial model forecasts are the estimates of required construction expenditures and, thus, of the new capital requirements of the industry. In addition, the model output contains estimates of the breakdown of the capital requirements between internal and external sources of funds, and the components of internal funds; i.e., retained earnings, depreciation, and deferred items.

a. Construction Expenditures

Chart 10•2 presents estimates for electric construction expenditures and electric utility plant (original cost basis, i.e., before depreciation). The solid lines reflect actual data from past years and projections for

Case B-HCN which would be likely under reasonably normal capital market conditions. The dashed lines depict the likely response of the industry to: (1) limited capital availability over the near term and (2) the need to compensate in the early 1980s for the construction delays in the middle and late 1970s.

The dashed utility plant line rises above the solid line in the early 1980s, and remains somewhat above it thereafter, to reflect the fact that construction during the "compensation" period will be at inflated prices compared to the construction foregone in the 1970s. The construction expenditures projected by the dashed line on Chart 2 increase at an average annual rate of 13.1 percent from 1970 to 1980 and then rise at 8.7 percent annually over the 1980 to 1990 period. The slowdown in the latter period reflects a variety of factors including: (1) a gradual slowing in growth of electricity consumption; and (2) some reduction in the rate of inflation as compared to the 1970s.

Table 10•9 lists the annual capital needs required by the construction program pictured as the dashed line on Chart 10•2. The total current dollar requirements from 1974 to 1990 inclusive will approximate $750 billion. Similar estimates were made for the high-and low-growth alternatives (Cases A and C respectively). It is estimated that the high-growth future would require about $820 billion and the low-growth future about $480 billion over the same period: 1974 to 1990.

b. External Funds

In Section C, "The Current Financial Situation," it was noted that electric utilities have traditionally had

Table 10•9
ELECTRIC UTILITY INDUSTRY CAPITAL NEEDS
(Billions of Current Dollars)

Year	Capital Needs	Year	Capital Needs
1974	$17.5	1983	$47.0
1975	17.3	1984	50.5
1976	19.2	1985	54.0
1977	22.8	1986	58.0
1978	27.0	1987	64.0
1979	31.0	1988	69.5
1980	35.0	1989	75.0
1981	39.5	1990	80.5
1982	44.0		

1974 through 1985: $404.8

1974 through 1990: $751.8

Chart 10·2

INVESTOR-OWNED ELECTRIC UTILITY PLANT AND ELECTRIC CONSTRUCTION EXPENDITURES
(Billions of Dollars)

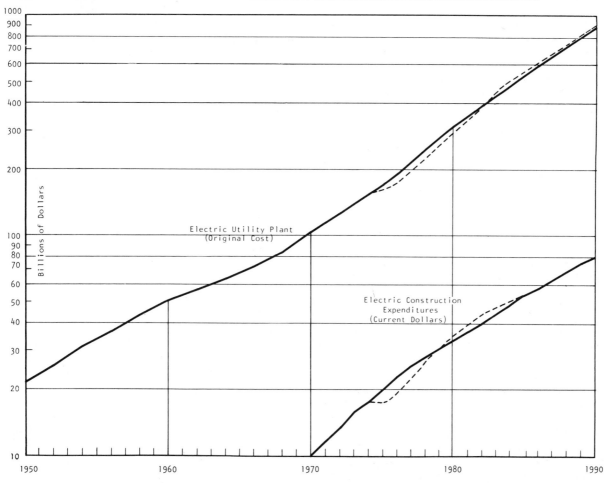

to rely more heavily on external sources of funds to finance new construction than have manufacturing corporations. Large increases in construction budgets over the past several years have made external sources even more important than in earlier year. Table 10·10 shows the changing proportion of funds from external sources for the period from 1966 to 1973.

The forecast of financing requirements for Case B-HCN indicates that external funds must continue to provide from 60 to 70 percent of the new capital needs of the industry over essentially all of the forecast years (1974-1990). However, the construction slowdown expected in the last half of the 1970s will probably be sufficient to cut external funds requirements sharply. Under these circumstances, however, the low external funding period of the next few years is likely to be followed by several years of

Table 10·10

TOTAL AND INTERNALLY GENERATED FUNDS OF ELECTRIC UTILITIES
(Millions of Dollars)

	Total Funds Provided	Internally Generated	Percent Internally Generated	Percent Externally Generated
1966	$5,565	$2,694	48.4%	51.6%
1967	6,726	2,954	43.9	56.1
1968	8,058	2,962	36.8	63.2
1969	8,728	3,392	38.9	61.1
1970	11,306	3,472	30.7	69.3
1971	13,147	3,927	29.9	70.1
1972	14,530	4,585	31.6	68.4
1973	16,000	5,250	32.8	67.2

Source: EEI Economics and Statistics Department.

299

very high external financing while the industry is engaged in "catch-up" construction.

c. Internal Funds

Internally generated funds are derived from three principal sources: (1) retained earnings, (2) depreciation and amortization, and (3) deferrals of normalized items. Of the three internal sources, the second (depreciation and amortization) is the largest, typically providing 60 to 70 percent of the total in recent years. See Table 10•11.

The relative contribution of retained earnings has been decreasing in recent years, while deferred items have risen from a negligible position to over 10 percent of the total. A fourth source, decrease in working capital, is one which is available only sporadically and in small amounts.

Increasing the proportion of funds obtained from internal sources decreases a company's dependence on external funds and thus on the vagaries of the capital market. There are good possibilities for increasing the contributions of all three major sources of internal funds.

A number of industry observers see the need for book depreciation rates higher than the 2.4 to 2.6 percent figures which have been common in the past. (See Table 10•12.) A 2.5 percent rate implies a useful life of 40 years. While these, or even longer, lives are applicable to some categories of utility plant (e.g., hydro installations), a composite rate this low may be less appropriate today than in the past. Rapidly changing technologies in the energy industry and the greater importance of the obsolescence factor suggest that increases in the depreciation rate may be prudent. For example, some utilities have moved to higher rates (shorter lives) in the case of nuclear installations in view of the fact that nuclear technology is improving rapidly. The rapidly changing situation with regard to environmental protection devices also argues for a shorter useful life estimate for such equipment. Many industry observers argue for a 4 or 5 percent overall rate, thus implying a useful life of 20 or 25 years.

The importance of retained earnings as an internal source of funds is materially affected by the return on common equity which the industry is able to realize. If realized returns move upward from the 11 percent range of recent years toward a more nearly adequate level of 15 percent, for example, the importance of retained earnings can be markedly increased.

Currently, only about half of the investor-owned companies normalize tax deferrals, while the remainder flow-through the benefits of tax deferrals to current customers. (See Appendix M for definitions of these terms.) If all companies were to normalize such tax deferrals there would be a measurable increase in internal funds available.

The relative significance of alterations in these three major sources of internal funds can be seen on Table 10•13. This table presents 1973 figures both in actual terms and as they would have appeared if depreciation rates and returns on common equity had been higher (as shown) and if all companies had normalized their tax deferrals. This table shows that under such circumstances, internal funds would have accounted for about 53 percent of the industry's total required funds rather than only 33 percent as is the actual case for 1973.

Table 10•11
INTERNALLY GENERATED FUNDS OF ELECTRIC UTILITIES (Percent)

Year	Retained Earnings	Depreciation and Amortization	Deferred or Future Income Tax	Net Decrease In Working Capital and Misc Sources	Total Internal Funds
1966	32.0	66.1	1.9	—	100.0
1967	30.2	64.4	2.0	3.4	100.0
1968	28.5	69.0	2.5	—	100.0
1969	27.8	65.0	2.8	4.4	100.0
1970	27.4	69.4	3.2	—	100.0
1971	27.8	67.2	5.0	—	100.0
1972	28.8	63.7	7.5	—	100.0
1973	27.2	61.7	11.1	—	100.0

Source: EEI Economic and Statistics Department.

Table 10-12
ELECTRIC UTILITY PLANT AND ANNUAL DEPRECIATION
(In Millions of Dollars)

Year	Total Utility Plant	Depreciation and Amortization	Average Depreciation Rate
			%
1966	$ 69,260	$1,782	2.57
1967	74,640	1,902	2.55
1968	81,040	2,044	2.52
1969	88,470	2,206	2.49
1970	97,690	2,411	2.47
1971	108,910	2,639	2.42
1972	121,480	2,920	2.40
1973	135,240	3,240	2.40

Source: EEI Economics and Statistics Department.

Table 10-13
ELECTRIC UTILITY FUND GENERATION: 1973
(Billions of Dollars)

	Actual	Revised*
Depreciation	$ 3.23	$ 5.38
Retained Earnings	1.43	1.95
Deferred Items and Other Sources	.57	1.14
External Funds	10.67	7.43
Total	$15.90	$15.90

* Depreciation rate: 4 percent
  Return on common equity: 15 percent
  All companies normalizing
  Payout ratio: actual

E. Financing Needs of the Nation

A number of knowledgeable observers have forecast that the nation is entering a period of chronic capital scarcity. In addition to the needs of the investor-owned electric utility industry, a variety of other industries and institutions will be competing for new capital funds.

The public segment of the electric utility industry will be but one of many government needs for capital. Others will be related to: environmental protection efforts such as sewage treatment plants, public housing and government support of borrow-ings to finance private housing ventures, mass transit facilities, and government operating deficits.

In the private sector, the petroleum industry and, to a lesser degree, the coal and natural gas industries will be major consumers of capital as the nation struggles to regain energy independence. The minerals mining and refining industries are likely to require increasing inputs of capital as they find it necessary to recover successively leaner grades of ores. If foreign minerals exporters succeed in establishing OPEC-like cartels, capital needs of the domestic mining industry could soar. The communications industry has for many years been a large factor in the capital markets and this is expected to continue.

Finally, the need has been foreseen to modernize much of the nation's manufacturing facilities which are now somewhat older, on average, than those of our major international competitors. The impetus to shift to manufacturing processes which use energy more efficiently will reinforce the need for renewing our manufacturing facilities.

A recounting of these and other needs raises the specter of possible capital shortages. Of course, in the final analysis there will be no shortages. In a potential shortage situation, demand and supply will be equated through: (a) the withdrawal of some capital seekers from the market and, (b) the offer of additional funds in response to increased interest rates.

The following paragraphs attempt to quantify some of the nation's various capital needs and compare them with: (a) those of the investor-owned electric utility industry and (b) likely supplies of investment capital.

1. Publicly-Owned Electric Utility Industry

It has been assumed for this financing study that the government owned and financed portion of the industry will continue to account for about 23 percent of total output and an approximately equal percentage of installed capacity.

A major portion of the most expensive generating capacity additions to these systems (i.e., nuclear and hydro installations) will probably be made by the Federal systems. Non-Federal segments may participate in future nuclear projects in cooperation with each other or with investor-owned companies. In general, however, the capacity additions of the non-Federal segment will probably emphasize smaller, less capital-intensive internal combusion and combined cycle units, plus the needed distribution and transmission facilities.

301

The various sectors of the government owned and financed utility industry (Federal, non-Federal, and cooperatives) meet their financing needs in different ways. Much of the Federal system, comprising about 11 percent of the total electric utility industry, relies on congressional appropriations to fill its capital needs. Only the Tennessee Valley Authority is authorized to use the private capital markets to sell debt instruments. The non-Federal segment of the government utility industry (about 10 percent of the total industry) relies primarily on internal generation of funds, supplemented as necessary by tax-exempt debt issues. Cooperatives, which constitute some 2 percent of the total industry, depend mostly on internally generated funds with the remainder coming largely from Rural Electrification loans or guarantees. When these characteristics of the government owned and financed sectors are combined with

Table 10·14
FINANCING NEEDS OF THE GOVERNMENT OWNED AND GOVERNMENT FINANCED SEGMENTS OF THE ELECTRIC UTILITY INDUSTRY*

1. *Federal Systems*

    Size: Approximately 11 percent of the total industry.

    Source of Funds: Congressional appropriations. Only TVA is empowered to sell bonds and notes in the private capital market.

    Fund Requirements: Approximately $9 billion in current dollar debt for the TVA system over the period to 1985.

2. *Non-Federal Systems*

    Size: Approximately 10 percent of the total industry.

    Source of Funds: Internal generation (about 60%) supplemented by tax exempt debt (about 40%).

    Fund Requirements: Approximately $15 billion in current dollar tax exempt debt over the period to 1985.

3. *Cooperatives*

    Size: Approximately 2 percent of the total industry.

    Source of Funds: Internal generation (about 75%) supplemented by borrowings, primarily Rural Electrification loans.

    Fund Requirements: Approximately $1 billion in current dollar borrowings over the period to 1985.

* Source: Adapted from Hass, Mitchell, Stone, *Financing the Energy Industry*, 1974, Ballinger Press.

Table 10·15
ENERGY INDUSTRY CAPITAL NEEDS
(Billions of Current Dollars)

Year	Electric Utility Industry	Petroleum Industry	Other	Total
1974............	$17.5	$10.6	$6.5	$34.6
1975............	17.3	12.3	7.1	36.7
1976............	19.2	13.7	7.8	40.7
1977............	22.8	15.3	8.7	46.8
1978............	27.0	17.2	9.7	53.9
1979............	31.0	19.2	10.8	61.0
1980............	35.0	21.6	12.7	69.3
1981............	39.5	23.7	13.6	76.8
1982............	44.0	25.9	14.5	84.4
1983............	47.0	28.5	15.5	91.0
1984............	50.5	31.2	16.5	98.2
1985............	54.0	34.3	17.4	105.7
1986............	58.0	37.4	18.5	113.9
1987............	64.0	40.9	19.6	124.5
1988............	69.5	44.6	20.7	134.8
1989............	75.0	48.7	22.0	145.7
1990............	80.5	52.6	23.5	156.6
1974-85........	$404.8	$253.5	$140.8	$799.1
1974-90........	$751.8	$477.7	$245.1	$1,474.6

the Case B—HCN forecast of electric demand, the financing needs can be estimated. This estimate is shown on Table 10·14.

2. Petroleum Industry

A number of forecasts of the capital needs of the petroleum industry have been made by such organizations as the National Petroleum Council, the Chase Manhattan Bank, and other banks. These are well summarized and analyzed in a recent publication of the Ford Foundation Energy Policy Project.[12]

The general conclusions of the Energy Policy Project (EPP) study have been used as a point of departure for the estimate which follows. The Case B: HCN scenario foresees a somewhat slower rate of growth of petroleum consumption and a different proportion of imports than did the EPP study, much of which was done prior to the Arab oil embargo and the price increases of 1973-74. The Case B—HCN analysis also includes an inflation projection and, therefore, makes it possible to predict current dollar capital requirements rather than the constant dollar estimates of the EPP. In order to adapt the EPP estimates to the basis of this study, they were adjusted to compensate for slower growth of consumption and for inflation. Thus, the resulting figures, as shown on Table 10•15 are generally consistent with the Case B—HCN, analysis.

3. Remainder of the Energy Industry

The remainder of the energy industry consists of natural gas transmission and distribution, coal production and transportation, and nuclear fuel processing. In the eleven-year period 1961-71 these portions of the energy industry aggregated some $31 billion of capital expenditures, thus accounting for just under 17 percent of the $185 billion expended by the entire energy industry during those years.[12] Nuclear fuel processing will undoubtedly grow rapidly in importance, while the capital needs of gas transmission and distribution will grow much more slowly. Much of the growth in coal consumption necessary to fuel the Case B—HCN future will come from western strip mines where capital requirements are less than for underground mines. On the other hand, significant quantities of capital will be needed to develop synthetic fuels capacities, particularly toward the end of the period under examination. These various factors have been considered and their effects combined into the forecasts shown on Table 10•15.

4. Rest of the United States Economy

Recently the New York Stock Exchange compiled estimates of capital needs and savings potentials of the United States economy for the period 1974 through 1985. The estimates of capital needs were derived from specific industry forecasts and from projections made by respected research organizations.[13]

The projected value of business saving was derived from a regression of such saving on GNP, using data from 1950 to 1973. Implicit in this technique are assumptions that there will be no drastic changes during the next ten years in profit margins, depreciation rates, corporation taxes, etc. Personal saving estimates were developed by examining past ratios of personal saving on GNP and estimating these ratios in the future based on expected economic and demographic changes in the next decade. Among the factors felt to be significant were: (1) the shifting age distribution toward the low-saving young adult brackets; (2) rapid increases in forced savings via the social security system; and (3) the erosion of real wealth by the recent severe inflation. All these

factors were judged to be likely to depress the personal saving rate gradually over the forecast period, moving it from 4.25 percent in 1973 to 3.9 percent in 1985. Finally, estimates of governmental demands for funds were estimated.

The individual forecasts and projections were adjusted by the Stock Exchange to insure comparability with respect to general factors such as assumed rates of growth of real GNP and assumed inflation rates. In these two critical areas the assumptions used were: 3.6 percent average annual rate of growth of real GNP and a 5 percent average annual inflation rate. Both figures are just a bit higher than assumed for the Case B forecast, as shown on Table 10•16.

Table 10•16
COMPARISON OF NY STOCK EXCHANGE AND EEI CASE B GROWTH RATES (Percent Per Year)

Factor	Stock Exchange (1974-85)	EEI Case B			
		1974-75	1975-80	1980-85	1974-85
Real GNP...	3.6%	-1.5%	4.36%	3.51%	3.44%
Inflation	5.0	9.0	4.40	4.15	4.68
Total ...	8.6%				8.12%

The results of the Stock Exchange forecast are presented on Table 10•17. It will be noted that the estimate of $824 billion for the total energy industry is quite close to the $799 billion shown on Table 10•15 for the period 1974 to 1985. There is closer correspondence between the Stock Exchange total of $400 billion for the electric utility industry and the $405 billion figure on Table 10•15.

Next to energy, the Stock Exchange report attributes the largest capital spending needs to the basic materials industries such as iron, steel, aluminum, paper, and cement.

The transportation sector will concentrate large sums on solving the nation's mass transit problems. Significant increases in spending in the remaining industries will be required to enable them to parallel the growth in the general economy. Included here are the communication, services, food, electrical machinery, non-electrical machinery, textiles and other basic parts of the nation's industrial establishment.

Huge and growing volumes of capital must be funneled into housing. Over the next ten years the age distribution of the United States population will shift to a heavier proportion of young adults, 20 to 35 years of age. This is the age group which has the highest rates of marriage and household formation. To meet the housing needs of this group, while also continuing to replace the nation's substandard dwellings, has been estimated to require as many as three million new units per year by 1985.

The category of non-profit, agriculture, and inventories includes a diverse group some with accelerating growth prospects and others whose growth seems to be slowing. Among the latter are hospitals and universities. Agriculture is primary among the groups that are likely to be growing rapidly in response to growing export needs.

Finally, it is interesting to examine the estimate of government needs. After the Stock Exchange forecast was published in September 1974, the recession worsened rapidly and the current Federal budget outlook is such that cumulative budget deficits over the next two years alone are likely to amount to $100 billion or more. It thus appears that, for the Federal deficit to total only $42 billion over the 1974-85 period, surpluses of $7 to 8 billion per year will be necessary for the last 8 years of the forecast period. From today's vantage point, such surpluses seem very unlikely, and the $42 billion seems much too low.

At present, it seems more likely that the Federal deficit will average at least $50 billion each year for the next two years and then in the neighborhood of at least $15 billion per year for the remainder of the period. Under these circumstances the total governmental demands would aggregate between $350 and 400 billion over the forecast period, instead of $175 billion as shown on Table 10·17.

Even with only $175 billion for total governmental demands, the savings gap is estimated to be about $650 billion. With a less optimistic estimate of government performances, e.g., $350 billion in total demands for capital, the savings gap increases to over $800 billion.

Of course the existence of such a gap does not mean there will, in fact, be a shortage of capital. However, it does suggest that there will be spirited competition for funds and that the actual balance of supply and demand may have to be achieved somewhere between the $4,032 billion and the $4,678 billion figure shown in Table 10·17. In other words, there will be a whole collection of lower priority demands for capital which will not be met. Since the Federal government can get essentially all the capital it wants, the effects of the savings gap will be felt in the private sector in the form of unsatisfied demands. Similarly, Table 10·17 suggests that the competition for funds will encourage personal savings by keeping interest rates high, even after inflation slows, and by inducing government changes in tax and depreciation rules to encourage higher internal cash generation by corporations. Other possible consequences are government enforced personal saving and government allocation of credit.

The DRI econometric forecasting model, by its very nature, does not predict *desired* levels of savings and investment, as did the Stock Exchange. Rather, it forecasts equilibrium conditions in which savings

Table 10·17

SOURCES AND USES OF INVESTMENT FUNDS IN THE UNITED STATES; 1974-1985 (Billions of Current Dollars)

Sources of Funds		
Business		
Depreciation Allowances.....	$2,359	
Retained Earnings...............	564	$2,923
Personal Saving.......................		1,109
Total Sources...........................		$4,032
Uses of Funds		
Business		
Electric Utilities....................	$ 400	
Other Energy Industries......	424	
Basic Materials....................	238	
Transportation and Transport Equipment.................	225	
Communication and Services................................	772	
Other......................................	419	2,568
Residential Construction........		1,085
Non-Profit, Agriculture, and Inventories...........................		850
Government		
Federal Deficit Financing.....	42	
Federal Credit Agency Borrowing.......................	103	
State and Local Governments...............................	30	175
Total Uses..............................		$4,678
Savings Gap..............................		($646)

Source: New York Stock Exchange

and investment are forced into equality by adjusting interest rates and real rates of economic growth. For the period 1974 to 1985 the DRI model forecasts non-government capital needs of $4,172 billion (the development of this figure is shown in Table 10·18). This compares with Stock Exchange figures of $4,032 billion of supplies and $4,503 billion of non-government demands ($4,678 less $175). Thus, the Case B projections are shown to be reasonably close to the Stock Exchange figures for total non-government capital needs, as well as for the electrical utility industry, and the energy industry as a whole.

Table 10·18
CASE B FORECAST OF GROSS PRIVATE DOMESTIC INVESTMENT—NIA*
(Billions of Current Dollars)

Year	Private Domestic Investment (DRI) (**)	Consumer Durable Investment (**)	Private Domestic Investment (NIA)
1974	$ 349	$134	$ 215
1975	380	147	233
1976	414	159	255
1977	451	173	278
1978	491	188	303
1979	535	204	331
1980	581	222	359
1981	627	258	369
1982	677	276	401
1983	731	296	435
1984	789	317	472
1985	853	340	513
1986	914	364	550
1987	979	389	590
1988	1,048	416	632
1989	1,122	445	677
1990	1,202	476	726
		1974-1985	$4,172
		1974-1990	$7,347

* DRI estimates of private domestic investment include purchases of consumer durables while NIA (national income accounts) statistics do not. Therefore, to derive an estimate of private domestic investment consistent with normal usage (i.e., basis used by the Stock Exchange), it is necessary to subtract estimates of consumer durable purchases.

** 1975, 1980, 1985 values are taken from DRI model output. Other values are obtained by interpolation; those after 1985 with the aid of DRI estimates for 2000.

F. Improving the Financial Health of the Electric Utility Industry

From this evaluation of the capital needs of the electric utility industry, and of the nation as a whole, the following conclusions may be drawn:

1) There will continue to be vigorous competition for a limited supply of capital investment funds in the United States over at least the next decade.

2) The electric utility industry will continue to need a significant portion (roughly 10 percent) of the total available funds in the nation, and will continue to depend on the competitive capital markets rather than on internal cash generation for the bulk of these funds (nearly two-thirds of its total needs will have to be satisfied from external sources). This heavy dependence on external funds means that about 25 percent of all new bond and stock issues will be those of electric utility companies.

3) The competition for funds will keep interest rates high even after inflation has been brought under control. If inflation is not brought under control, the financing problems of all institutions, the electric utility industry included, will be immensely difficult.

4) The present outlook for government deficit financing suggests that the government's requirements for investment funds to cover these deficits will be very large. *All* of the government requirements must be met by the private capital markets or by Federal Reserve creation of money. There are no government internal sources of funds to cover net deficits. A primary objective of long-term government policy should be to reduce the need for deficit financing by balancing the budget, either through decreases in spending or increases in taxes.

5) The size of the gap between desired saving and desired investment is likely to be larger if inflation is not brought under control (i.e., brought down to the 4 to 5 percent range). The gap will be smaller if the war on inflation is extremely successful (i.e., reducing it to the 2 to 3 percent range).

6) The existence of a gap between desired saving and desired investment suggests the need for supplementary government action (in addition to efforts to reduce inflation) to encourage saving. Among these efforts are the removal or reduction of a number of *dis*incentives to capital investment such as the capital gains tax and the double taxation of dividends.

7) A number of devices which have been suggested for encouraging capital formation and investment in productive facilities can be useful as

remedies for emergency situations. However, they may well be harmful in the long run since they attack the symptom rather than the illness. Such devices include government guarantees; capital allocation rules; and government loans.

8) The primary approach to encouraging investment should be to develop an environment which provides the opportunity to earn an adequate return on the capital invested. This is equally true for all productive business activities, electric utilities included.

9) Electric utility regulatory practices should be revised to permit utilities to earn adequate returns on common equity investments. Chapter 9 discusses some possible regulatory changes which would help to attain this objective. Primary among these changes is an acceleration of regulatory hearings and other procedures so as to reduce regulatory lag.

10) A number of other regulatory, tax, and accounting changes can be recommended which would improve the current critical financial condition of electric utility companies. Among them are: (a) increasing allowable book depreciation rates by decreasing estimated useful lives for most classes of property; (b) normalizing tax deferrals; (c) including construction work in progress in the rate base; (d) increasing the investment tax credit rate and increasing the percentage of income tax against which it can be credited; and (e) encouraging equity investment by allowing tax-free reinvestment of dividends in new issue stock.

FOOTNOTES

1. In a few indentures, the ratio is as low as 1.75 and in some cases over 3.0. In the majority of cases, the required coverage ratio is 2.0.

2. Federal Power Commission, The National Power Survey, Advisory Committee Report. *The Financial Outlook for the Electric Power Industry,* December 1974.

3. Federal Power Commission, as above.

4. Capacity factor = Generation in Kilowatthours ÷ (Installed Capacity in Kilowatts × Hours per Year).

5. Atomic Energy Commission *Nuclear Power Growth 1974-2000,* WASH 1139 (74), United States Atomic Energy Commission Office of Planning and Analysis.

6. Federal Power Commission, *1970 National Power Survey, Volume 1,* p I-19-5.

7. Edison Electric Institute, *Statistical Yearbook,* 1973.

8. Edison Electric Institute, *Pocket Handbook of Industry Statistics,* 1973; and Department of Commerce, Office of Business Economics, *Business Statistics, 1971* and *Survey of Current Business,* various issues.

9. Department of Labor, Bureau of Labor Statistics, *Monthly Labor Review,* various issues.

10. Federal Power Commission, *Statistics of Privately Owned Electric Utilities in the United States,* 1973.

11. Price/earnings ratio is the market price of a share of common stock divided by annual earnings applicable to each common share. Payout ratio is the percentage of common earnings paid out as dividends.

12. Hass, J. E., Mitchell, E. J., and Stone, B. K., *Financing the Energy Industry,* 1974, Ballinger Publishing Co., Cambridge, Mass.

13. New York Stock Exchange, *The Capital Needs and Savings Potential of the United States Economy: Projections through 1985,* September, 1974.

Appendices

APPENDIX A

Forecasting Tools: Techniques and Limitations

1. Introductory Remarks

Many improvements have been introduced to the arts of quantitative economic and social forecasting during the last half century, yet they still remain merely imprecise arts rather than sciences. Tracing the threads of these improvements in the United States would reveal: the development of national income accounting by Kuznets in the 1920 s; the initial work on input-output analysis by Leontieff in the 1930 s; the development of linear programming and other operations research techniques as an outgrowth of wartime studies by Morse and many others in the 1940s; the development of simultaneous equation econometric models by Tinbergen and others in the 1940s and later, major advances in mathematical statistics by Haavelmo, Koopmans and others in the 1940s and 1950s; the formulation of multi-equation forecasting models of the United States economy in the 1950s by Klein and others; the development of high speed, high capacity electronic computing devices in the 1950s; and the formulation of non-linear, feedback modeling techniques, called systems analysis, by Forrester and others in the 1960s.[1]

It is impossible, of course, to single out any one of these developments as the primary one. However, it is possible to identify the high speed electronic computer as the single factor without which most of the others would have been unable to reach their full potential as forecasting tools. The immediate followers of Tinbergen, for example, were severely hampered by the computational machinery at their disposal. The general practice among early econometricians was to single out an isolated equation from the system of several equations which they had developed to simulate the economy. They would then attempt to evaluate the selected equation by use of least-squares regression techniques without considering the interactions which might exist between that equation and others in their system. The computational burden of evaluating such equations for a reasonably complex economic system, even when taking one equation at a time, was extremely heavy when only a desk calculator was used. This burden also limited the number of alternate sets of input assumptions which could be investigated within practical manpower limits. Similar limits to the usefulness of input-output analysis and linear programming were gradually eased as ever more sophisticated computers were devised.

Despite major advances in the theory, techniques, and "machinery" of forecasting, the results are often far from accurate even when the forecast period is limited to one or two years. Even the most complex economic models are but pale reflections of reality, employing gross aggregation of data as well as severe theoretical simplifications, and then largely basing forecasts on the presumption that the future economic and social structure of the nation will be like the past, or at least will vary from the past only in terms of gradual change. A number of other important criticisms and limitations of various modeling techniques are summarized in section 3 which follows.

While giving adequate recognition to the limitations of forecasting models it is also important to realize that any thinking about any subject is done within the framework of a conceptual model which reflects the thinker's knowledge of the subject. Many of these mental models are vague and ill-defined; some are intuitive since they are based on accumulations of experience rather than the result of a conscious formulation; and others are logical structures formed in a systematic way. The human mind is capable of developing logical structures which are reasonably accurate reflections of segments of a complex socio-economic system. This same mind is capable of interpreting the types of interactions which occur between the various segments. The products of such human mental activity are models. When developed in equation form and buttressed with statistical or other quantitative mathematical verification they become mathematical models.

The human mind is also capable, at times, of making some surprisingly accurate intuitive judgments about such complex systems. However, in general, the mind, unaided, is severely limited in interpreting the quantitative consequences of a change in one variable in a complex system on all the other variables. When the potentials for dynamic interactions or feedbacks exist, as they do in most socio-economic systems, the human mind is likely to be led astray. Forrester, for example, develops convincingly his thesis that complex social systems often behave counterintuitively, so that the intuitive thinker is sometimes led to exactly the wrong conclusion.[2]

Therefore, in complex systems, be they social or economic, mathematical models capable of computer solution do have distinct advantages. One, that was merely alluded to above, is the practicality of developing a wide range of solutions in terms which are capable of answering "what if . . ." questions. Thus, it is in the area of futures analysis that mathematical models exhibit their greatest strengths.

2. Methods of Forecasting

The following reviews of forecasting techniques concentrate on those used at one or more points in this study, rather than attempting to provide an all-inclusive review. Naive forecasts in the sense of trend extrapolations, are also mentioned in passing. The purpose of these reviews is to provide those readers unfamiliar with such techniques with enough information to judge the quality and the limitations of the output derived from the use of the techniques in this study.

a. Naive

The simplest approach to forecasting is to assume that what is happening at present will continue to happen unchanged in the future. Such forecasts are often given the description "naive." It is useful to identify two distinctive variations of naive forecasting. One assumes that a variable whose value is growing will continue to increase by a constant arithmetic increment each year; a second assumes a constant percentage growth each year. While naive forecasts may be useful over relatively short periods of time in interpreting growth phenomena, they become increasingly suspect as the length of the forecast period increases. No natural phenomena (with the possible exception of the size of the universe) follow trends of either continued arithmetic or continued exponential growth. It seems safe to draw similar conclusions regarding economic and social phenomena.

b. Econometric Models

The word econometric is a combination of the words economic and mathematical; so in general terms, an econometric model is any model expressed in mathematical terms which deals with economic subject matter. In common parlance, however, such models are developed to forecast economic statistics of the type which appear in the national income accounts; e.g., gross national product, personal income, personal consumtion expenditures, business investment, government spending for goods and services, and net exports.

These models focus attention on the total output of the economy in terms of the final goods that are produced and the incomes and other payments generated as a consequence of the production. The roles of producers, consumers, the government, and the rest of the world as both receivers of income and purchasers is shown in relation to the activity of the economy as a whole.

Each of the variables to be forecast by such a model is called an endogenous variable, and is assumed to be determined by: (1) an earlier, or lagged, value of that same variable; (2) other endogenous variables; (3) exogenous variables, which are those determined by factors beyond the scope of the model structure such as population or government spending; and (4) unknown influences.

These variables are arranged in a series of equations, generally linear in nature, with the qualitative relationships in the equations derived from economic theory. Two equations from the DRI econometric growth model are presented here as an example. In these equations, the model builders have assumed that the "independent" variables: personal consumption demand (PC) and personal leisure demand (PL), are related to several "independent variables": a lagged value of wealth (W); and three other economic variables: PL, LH, and EL.

Consumption demand:

$$PC \times C = a \times W(\text{-}1) + b \times (PL \times LH + EL).$$

Leisure demand:

$$PL \times LJ = c \times W(\text{-}1) + d \times (PL \times LH + EL).$$

This example illustrates the inter-connected nature of such equation systems, in that the first equation requires current values of PL, LH, and EL before PC can be estimated. However, the estimate of PL can be obtained only by solving the second equation. In like manner, EL may be another variable determined by yet another equation of the model. Thus, a consistent solution can be obtained only by simultaneous solution methods.

Once the equations have been derived, they are tested by inserting past, known values for the variables over a period of several years and solving for the coefficients, i.e., the lower case letters a, b, c, and d. Statistical techniques are available for determining these coefficients so that the resulting equations minimize the errors in the calculated values of the dependent variables. If the model builder decides that the equations are not satisfactorily accurate; i.e., they do not explain a high proportion of the period-to-period changes in the dependent variables, another economic theory must be sought which will make the dependent variable "dependent" on other independent variables. Once the equations have been verified in the sense that they would have provided adequate forecasts of the past (ex-post tests), they can then be tested as time passes to check their accuracy in predicting current conditions (ex-ante tests).

The above description has been simplified. A more detailed description of the DRI model is contained in Appendix B. A wide variety of books on econometrics is also available to the interested reader: e.g., Klein[3] and Johnston.[4]

c. Input-Output Models

Econometric models which concentrate on national income account statistics can forecast only the external features of an economic system. Different and more detailed information is required if the flows of goods, services, and money through the economy are to be measured and predicted. Money and credit flows through the economy are determined by an economic accounting system known as the flow-of-funds accounts, while flows of goods and services are established through the input-output or inter-industry accounts. Input-output models of the United States economy are of direct use in any attempt to forecast energy consumption in the nation, because they can show energy use by industrial sectors as well as by households, government and other final demand sectors.

For an individual firm the meaning of the words input and output are clear. The firm uses raw materials, labor, capital, and energy as inputs to its productive process. The output of this process is one or more goods or services which are sold to other manufacturers or to final consumers. Similarly, for the economy as a whole, input-output accounts divide the market value of the production of each industry among: (1) the purchases of goods and services from other firms and (2) the payments for land, labor, and capital services which the industry requires. The output pattern for each industry shows how the output of that industry is purchased by other industries or used to satisfy final demands. The focus of such a scheme is on inter-industry relationships, so that the classification of inputs and outputs is primarily in terms of standard industrial classifications; e.g., agriculture and fisheries, food and kindred products, chemicals, primary metals, etc.

Input-output models generally are developed in tabular form similar in appearance to the very simple model depicted in Table A•1.

Table A•1
SIMPLE INPUT-OUTPUT MODEL

Output of These Industries	Input to These Industries			
	Agriculture	Manufactures	Final Demand	Total Output
Agriculture...............	25	20	55	100
Manufacturers.........	14	6	30	50
Households, etc.......	80	180	40	300

In this illustrative example, the horizontal row labeled "Agriculture" shows that this sector delivers 25 units of its output to itself (e.g., feed grains), 20 units as raw materials to manufacturing industries such as cotton for textiles and 55 units to householders and other sources of final demand. The vertical row labeled "Agriculture" shows that this sector requires inputs of 25 units from itself, 14 units from manufacturing industries (e.g., farm machinery) and 80 units from households, capital services, etc.—if it is to produce the total output of 100 units shown in the right-hand column.

The detailed input-output tables for the United States compiled by the Department of Commerce provide information for some 370 industries.[5] When stored in a computer, such an input-output table becomes a working model of the economy. When provided with estimates of final demand, in terms of the major components of GNP for example, such a model can develop estimates of the required inputs to each industry and the resulting outputs from each industry. A more adequate description of input-output models and some of their applications is available in a series of *Scientific American* articles.[6] A description of the DRI input-output model is provided in Appendix B.

d. Linear Programming Models

Linear programming refers to mathematical techniques for solving a general class of optimization problems dealing with the interaction of many variables and subject to certain restraining conditions. In solving these problems a certain objective, such as maximum output, is to be obtained in the best possible manner, eg. at minimum cost, while subject to limits on certain input items such as raw materials or production processes. For example, certain steel products may be obtained in a steel mill by various combinations of raw materials and hot-rolling, cold-rolling, annealing, normalizing and slitting operations. The restrictions imposed in such a problem might be capacity limits for each production process, limitations of raw materials, a minimum required output and a set of delivery time requirements. The objective to be optimized might be maximum profit, or minimum cost. To to able to reach the

best feasible set of conditions, all feasible combinations of these operations and limits must be considered. Thus, there is a problem somewhat like the simultaneous solution of a series of econometric equations.

However, in the typical linear programming problem the relations are expressed in terms of inequalitites rather than normal equations. The following two examples will illustrate the difference.

$$y + 1 = x$$
$$y + 1 \geq x$$

The first is, of course, an equation while the second is an inequality which is read y plus 1 is equal to or greater than x. In a graphical form the equation can be represented by the line in the left-hand figure of Chart A•1 while the inequality would encompass all the area to the left and above the line, as well as the line itself. In a complex linear program there may be many such inequalities where one variable or a combination of variables can be "no bigger than" or "no smaller than" some limit. For illustrative purposes we can add two more very simple inequalities to the first one mentioned above to carry the example a bit further:

$$y + 1 \geq x$$
$$y - 2 \leq 3x$$
$$y - 10 \leq -x$$

These additional inequalities are graphed on the right-hand section of Chart A•1. Together, all three inequalities define the area *within* the triangle ABC. *Any* point within that triangle meets the limits set by the inequalities. Finally, however, an optimization rule might be set which requires that the value of y should be as large as possible without violating the other conditions; i.e., the inequalities. In this example, of course, the single, optimum answer would then be point A. With several inequalities and several variables, graphical representation and graphical solution become impossible, and for most real-life problems a computer solution is the only practical approach.

Oil refinery operations have been a very important application of linear programming. Each refinery must produce a variety of products under fixed limits of processing equipment. Some variations in the crude oil input to the refinery may be possible or necessary. Demands for refinery output change as time passes depending on product inventories and market conditions. Processing equipment can be used in different combinations to yield different output mixes.

The Pace Co linear programming model of the energy conversion industry is in one sense merely an extension of the refinery model with: (1) greater choices in input; i.e., coal, gas, oil, nuclear power, instead of merely oil; (2) a wider variety of output requirements; e.g., energy demands for transportation, residential needs, industrial requirements, and petrochemicals, and (3) a multitude of restraints on supplies, demands, and processing capabilities.

e. Systems Analysis Models

Man lives and works within a hierachy of systems.

311

Chart A·1
EQUALITIES AND INEQUALITIES

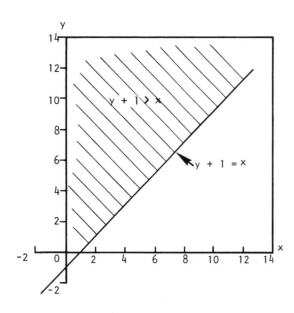

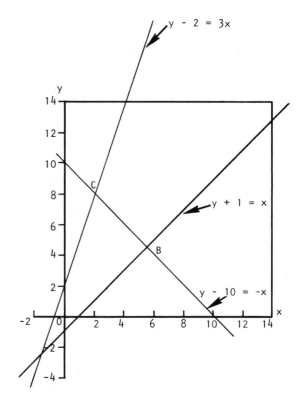

Natural systems control his environment; socio-political systems impose legal limits on his actions; economic systems guide his acquisitive nature; and complex technological systems are a primary consequence of his science and engineering. In this context a system is any grouping of parts, persons, or institutions operating together for a common purpose.

Some rather simple systems can be characterized as "open" systems in that their outputs are isolated from, and have no effect on future inputs. Most systems of interest, however, are "feedback" systems since they are influenced by their own past behavior; i.e., results of past actions will be sensed by the system in such a way as to influence future behavior. One example of an open system is a watch, which by itself cannot sense its inaccuracy and adjust itself. In contrast, a house heating system with a thermostat is an example of a feedback system.

Systems analysis is the art of simulating the major elements of systems in quantitative terms, and of using mathematical modeling techniques to examine their dynamic characteristics. Forrester,[7] Mesarovic,[8] and others have been instrumental in adapting earlier work on the analysis of engineering systems to the fields of social, political, and economic analysis.

A major advantage of systems analysis techniques is the ease with which feedback effects can be simulated and examined. Of course, an econometric model which includes lagged variables (e.g., the W(-1) in the sample equations listed in section b.) as a partial explanation of current period events, has also incorporated feedback effects. However, systems models possess distinct advan-

tages in this regard, as well as in the somewhat greater freedom with which non-linear effects can be simulated. Generally, the importance of both non-linearities and feedback effects in socio-economic models increases as the length of the forecast period increases.

One of the most widely publicized examples of the use of systems models in socio-economic forecasting was that sponsored by the Club of Rome and described in the book, *Limits to Growth.*[9] Another is the more recent and still-continuing modeling work at Case Western Reserve which combines econometric techniques and control theory, and which forms the basis for much of the analysis in Chapter 7 of this study. Appendix C describes and compares both of these models.

f. Judgmental Models

All models, from the simplest mental construction to the most complex mathematical representations, contain some elements of judgment and intuition. In the mathematical models discussed above, such elements are present in the choice and arrangement of variables in the equations, as well as in the forecasts of exogenous variables such as tax rates. In some attempts to examine the future, the mixtures of social, political, economic and technological factors which impinge on the problem are so complex; the possibilities of major shifts in social or economic structures are so great; or time constraints are so limiting; that a combination of quantitative and "informed" judgmental forecasting may be the only practical alternative to what would be a forbiddingly complex econometric or systems forecast.

A large number of judgmental forecasts come easily to

mind. The technique of Delphi forecasting which combines the qualitative judgments about the future of a number of experts into a rough consensus is one example. Such judgments, of course, can be scientific, social, political or economic in nature. One example of a Delphi forecast is described by Gordon and Ament.[10] Other notable examples of primarily judgmental projections in the social-political areas are the examinations of the possible shape of the future by Kahn and Wiener,[11] and Bell.[12]

In an area more directly related to one of the subjects of this study, i.e., energy, the work of the National Petroleum Council[13] is particularly notable as a blend of quantitative and judgmental forecasting. Exercises in energy forecasting have become understandably popular in the last few years, and many of them have been heavily judgmental. Both a summary and a critical review of some of the recent major energy forecasting efforts were prepared as a preliminary to the forecasting efforts specifically sponsored by this study. The Summary[14] and the Critical Review[15] are available from EEI as separate supplements to this study.

3. Deficiencies of Forecasting Models

Deficiencies of forecasting models are discussed in general terms in the Introductory Comments to this appendix. Two deficiencies mentioned there are the need to: (a) oversimplify and (b) assume that the future structure of society will be similar to the past. A third deficiency stems from the need to make separate predictions of exogenous variables (i.e. those aspects of the future which the models can not forecast).

It is important not only to emphasize that the models used in this study suffer from these three general deficiencies, but also to summarize certain specific limitations of the models.

a. Over-Simplification

The DRI macro economic growth and inter-industry models employ the most advanced methodology available for integrating macro demand, macro production, and micro production structure components into a single framework suitable for long-term predictions. In addition, the inter-industry model focuses on energy supply and demand, with five of its nine intermediate sectors being subdivisions of the energy industry; i.e., coal mining, crude petroleum and natural gas, petroleum refining, electric utilities, and gas utilities. These characteristics make the DRI models particularly appropriate tools for the EEI growth study. (Note that Appendix B presents a summary description of the models, while a more detailed description is available from Data Resources, Inc.)

Nevertheless, the models are relatively small, as can be seen by reviewing Appendix B. The macro economic growth model consists of approximately 20 equations and 60 variables, while the inter-industry model incorporates 9 intermediate sectors and 4 final demand sectors. Representing the complex United States economy with such models may be a source of some inaccuracy in the model forecasts. For example, the difficulties experienced by the economy in adapting to a restricted energy growth rate may be underestimated by a model which aggregates all the manufacturing industries in the nation except petroleum refining into one sector of its inter-industry calculations.

The model formulation provides both producing and consuming sectors with adjustment processes, by which reduced energy availability causes other inputs (i.e., labor and capital) to be substituted for energy. Changes in relative prices trigger these adjustment processes. However, with only one inter-industry sector to encompass all the diverse manufacturing industries in the United States, there is some danger that an average adjustment process will not accurately reflect the wide variety of ways in which labor and capital will be substituted for energy in an energy-scarce environment.

In a future where energy availability is forecast to be not greatly different than in the recent past (Cases A and B), the model may be expected to provide satisfactory predictions concerning the ability of the economy to adjust. However, as the assumed energy scarcity becomes more severe and the distortions imposed on the economy become greater, the models may not fully reflect the adjustment difficulties which various parts of the economy will experience. In particular, certain critical industries may be no longer able to adjust to less energy-intensive industrial processes after a certain level of restriction is exceeded. The inability of these industries to adjust completely, could create bottlenecks and reduce the growth potential of the entire economy below the rates forecast by the models.

For this reason, the low growth, Case C, results may be overly optimistic. However, even in Case C the *distortion* of the economy is not great, since this scenario assumes that other resource inputs as well as energy are restrained, and that labor and capital inputs are correspondingly limited. For example, by the year 2000 there is a 33 percent reduction in energy input per capita in Case C as compared with Case A. This is made up primarily of a 28 percent reduction in real GNP per capita and only a 7 percent reduction in energy input per dollar. The reduction in real GNP per capita is caused by similar reductions in the assumed inputs of all production factors. Thus, Case C envisions a *balanced* restraint on growth, a situation which the model should be well equipped to handle. It is rather in forecasting the consequences of scenarios which project an *unbalanced* restraint (e.g., only energy), where the aggregate nature of the model might be expected to yield overly optimistic results.

b. Structural Rigidities

All formal models project future developments on the basis of current and past economic and social structures. The cost of using past structures can be reduced by incorporating information on assumed future structural developments into particular components of the model to simulate changes in the economy and society over the forecast period. This was done in many areas of the DRI projections (e.g., capital inputs, capital efficiencies, government expenditures, labor hours per week).

Each of the three scenarios is, in fact, an attempt to

present a different view of the ways in which the economic and social structure of the economy may change over the next 25 years. The basic deficiency of using a model based on past structure can be reduced or eliminated in this way if the model is sufficiently flexible to permit the inclusion of changing assumptions. The DRI models appear to be satisfactory in this regard.

A more significant weakness has to do with the assumptions used for each scenario about the speed and direction of structural changes in society and in the economy. If the scenario assumptions with regard to structural changes are wrong, the forecasts will be wrong. Once more, it should be emphasized that the prime purpose of the forecasts in this study is to improve the quality of current decisions by exploring *possibilities* for the future, rather than to predict accurately what specific future will occur. Thus, the primary concern of the modeler—and the reader—should be for the internal consistency of the sets of assumptions used for each scenario.

c. Competitive Conditions

Another structural constraint embodied in the DRI models concerns the competitive conditions built into the model relationships. The models are *not* predicated upon a perfectly competitive economy. The assumption concerning pricing is that the underlying relationships between input and output prices continue along the lines of past structure. Thus, if regulatory constraints were present in the past, a similar degree of regulation is generally assumed to continue in the future.

Different markups of prices over direct costs may have been characteristic of different industries in the past, depending on competitive conditions in each industry. Since the models were developed and tested using these past conditions, some implicit assumptions about competitive conditions are certainly imbedded in the models, but they generally correspond to a continuation of past conditions rather than to a condition of perfect competition. Of course, changes in competitive conditions can be built into the model in response to assumptions made by the modelers, just as in the case of other structural restraints. A number of such changes were incorporated in the scenarios, as described in Chapter 6.

d. Short-Run Constraints

With the exception of the 1974-75 recession, the model does not attempt to take account of short term fluctuations in the economy. The projected growth paths are trends, based on the structure of society and the economy, around which the actual growth paths may be expected to fluctuate. At times temporary supply bottlenecks may hold activity below trend; demand pressures may push activity above the trend during boom periods; or the economy may experience periods of under-utilization during a recession. A long-term model may be expected to trace out average trend paths but it should not be expected to forecast short-term fluctuations around this trend path.

e. Technology and Productivity

The economic growth predictions of the models are

dependent on the productivity assumptions provided to the models as input. Appendix E discusses the productivity concepts used in the modeling, and various tables in Chapter 6 summarize the productivity figures used for each of the three alternative futures.

Productivity growth factors include improvements in: (a) the quality of labor input, (b) the quality of capital input and (c) the effectiveness with which labor and capital are combined in the productive processes (i.e., total factor productivity). For all three scenarios, the first and the third of these factors are assumed to maintain their historic (post, World War II) rates of improvement. For Cases A and B, the capital quality is assumed to continue its historic rate of improvement but for Case C, concerns about environmental quality are assumed to be so strong that the capital quality deteriorates (from a market standpoint).

Some observers are concerned that historic rates of improvement in productivity can not be maintained in the future as the shift continues from agriculture and manufacturing to services. They sometimes refer to a barber and a musician as examples, asking how the output of haircuts and music per man-hour can be increased.

The scenarios in this study assume that major potentials exist for continued productivity improvement in services as well as in agriculture and manufacturing. Many services, particularly those with greatest impact on the nation's economic output, exhibit large potentials for productivity improvement; e.g., wholesale and retail trade; finance, insurance and real estate; and government. As these service activities loom larger in the economy and in the average person's budget, increasing attention will be paid to the productivity levels associated with them.

The problems lie not so much in the absence of potentials for further improvements in productivity, as in society's willingness to adjust existing structural constraints to take advantage of such potentials. This study assumes that these constraints *will* gradually be adjusted.

FOOTNOTES

1. Descriptions of these techniques can be found in the following references:
   (a) Tinbergen, J. *Statistical Testing of Business Cycle Theories, II. Business Cycles in the U.S.A., 1919-1932,* League of Nations, Geneva, 1939.
   (b) Kuznets, S. *National Income and Its Composition, 1919-1938,* National Bureau of Economic Research, New York, 1941.
   (c) Leontieff, W. *Input-Output Economics,* Oxford Univ. Press, London, 1966.
   (d) Morse, P. M. & Kimball, G. E., *Methods of Operations Research,* John Wiley & Sons, New York, 1951.
   (e) Johnston, J. *Econometric Methods,* McGraw Hill, New York, 1963.
   (f) Klein, L., *Econometrics,* Row, Peterson & Co, Evanston, Ill, 1953.
   (g) Klein, L., *Economic Fluctuations in the United States,* John Wiley, New York, 1950.
   (h) Forrester, J. W., *World Dynamics,* Wright-Allen Press, Cambridge, Mass, 1971.

2. Forrester, J. *Urban Dynamics*, MIT Press, Cambridge, Mass, 1969.

3. Klein, as cited above.

4. Johnston, as cited above.

5. United States Dept of Commerce, *Input-Output Structure of the United States Economy: 1963*, Office of Business Economics, Washington, D. C., 1969.

6. Leontieff, W. *"The Structure of the United States Economy,"* Scientific American, April 1965, pp 25-35, for example.

7. Forrester, J. *Principles of Systems*, Wright Allen Press, Cambridge, Massachusetts 1968.

8. Mesavoric, M. *Theory of Multi-Level Hierarchical Systems*, Academic Press, New York, New York, 1970.

9. Meadows, Dennis et al, *Limits to Growth*, Universe Books, New York, 1972.

10. Gordon, T. and R. H. Ament, *"Forecasts of Some Technological and Scientific Developments and Their Societal Consequences,"* Institute for the Future Report R-6, September, 1969.

11. Kahn H. and A. J. Wiener, *The Year 2000*, Macmillan Co, New York, 1967

12. Bell, D. *The Coming of Post-Industrial Society*, Basic Books Inc, New York, 1973.

13. National Petroleum Council, *United States Energy Outlook*, 1972 and supporting documents which deal in detail with energy demand, energy supply, nuclear energy, new energy forms, etc. Washington, D.C., 1972.

14. Taussig, R. *"Bibliography and Digest of United States Electric and Total Energy Forecasts: 1975-2050,"* 1974.

15. Taussig R. and P. G. Apte, *"United States Energy Forecasts: A Critical Review of Forecasting Methods,"* 1974.

APPENDIX B

Description of DRI Models

1. The Macro-Economic Growth Model

The general macroeconomic relationships over the forecast period are obtained from a macro model of United States economic growth. This is a dynamic model of aggregate demand and supply in which the activities of four sectors—households, production, government, and rest of world—are distinguished and reconciled within a simulated market system.

The central component of this model is a macroeconometric production function, relating the output of consumption and of investment goods to the inputs of capital and labor services and the level of production efficiency. This enforces the basic constraint that demand cannot exceed supply. Also, this function determines the supply capacity of the economy and provides the means of introducing into the model the three fundamental growth producing forces—the supply of capital services, the supply of labor services, and the level of production efficiency.

The capital services variable is obtained from the capital accumulation equation which expresses one year's capital in terms of the previous year's capital, depreciation, and new investment. The amount of investment is based on household preferences between present and future consumption, which determine the allocation of income between consumption and saving. Exogenous population growth, together with an endogenous work-leisure choice simulated in the submodel of household behavior, determine the growth of the labor force which then enters the production function through the labor input variable. Finally, disembodied, capital-embodied and labor-embodied technical progress are incorporated directly into the production function, the rates of each type of progress being extrapolations of past trends. In this way the basic dynamic forces permitting economic growth are directly incorporated into the model.

The next step is to introduce submodels of producer and household behavior to determine demand and supply for each type of product. The producer submodel derives supply of output functions; i.e., supply of consumption goods and of investment goods, and demand for input functions on the basis of profit maximization in response to prices within the constraint of the production function. Household behavior is modeled to simulate consumer response to market forces as consumption and labor decisions are made by the household in an attempt to promote its own preferences. These are expressed in consumer demand and labor supply functions in terms of prices, wealth, time and preference parameters. The remaining elements in the demand-supply picture are government and rest of world net demands. These are introduced, exogenously, to give a demand and supply function for each aggregate good—consumption goods, investment goods, labor services and capital services.

These different demand and supply conditions are then integrated within a simulated market process. There are two types of market clearing requirements. First, quantity demanded and supplied in each market must be brought into equality (with the exception that the labor market does not clear, this is recognized by the incorporation of an unemployment variable). Second, the value of expenditure on each type of good must equal the total value of receipts derived from the sale of the good. Market clearing conditions of both types are included in the model. They lead to prices, and hence quantities, to adjust until demand-supply is achieved. In this way both prices and quantities for each of consumption goods output, investment goods output, labor input and capital input are generated.

Once these basic production and price variables are determined, the national income accounting framework can then be used to determine variables such as GNP, real GNP, the GNP price deflator, labor productivity, unit labor costs and so on. (One difference between the GNP concepts used in this study and the national income accounts, this study includes purchases of consumer durables in investment and includes an imputed value of services obtained from consumer durables in personal consumption.)

2. Specification of the Macro Model

The econometric growth model is summarized in the following series of tables. In Table B•1 notation for the variables that appear in the model are presented.

The first group of variables convert aggregates from one basis of classification to another. For example, the index of total factor productivity (A) converts input to output. The index of (AW) converts investment weights for capital formation to the weights appropriate for the measurement of wealth. All of the aggregation variables are taken to be exogenous.

The second group of variables appearing in Table B•1 comprises the quantities of products and factors of production, broken down by sector of origin and destination. Variables beginning with (C) are quantities of consumption goods. Similarly, variables beginning with (I) are quantities of investment goods. Variables beginning with (L) are quantities of labor services, while variables beginning with (K) are quantities of capital services. The third group of variables includes prices corresponding to the quantities of products and factors of production. Each price begins with (P) and continues with the corresponding quantity. For example, the variable (C) is personal consumption expenditures, and the variable (PC) is the price of personal consumption expenditures.

The fourth group of variables are financial variables: rates of depreciation and replacement, the nominal rate of return, gross private national saving, and private national wealth. Finally, the fifth group of variables are tax and transfer variables. The variable (EL) represents government transfer payments to persons other than social insurance funds, an expenditure category. The variables beginning with (T) are tax rates. Each of the products and factors included in the model—consumption goods, investment goods, capital services, and labor services—is associated with an effective tax rate. The variable (TP) is the effective tax rate for capital stock.

Table B•1
MACRO-ECONOMETRIC GROWTH MODEL: NOTATION

a. Aggregation variables.

A	Total factor productivity (input to output).
ACI	Investment to change in business inventories, consumption goods.
AI	Investment to capital stock.
AL	Investment to capital stock, lagged.
AK	Capital stock, lagged to capital service.
APC	Implicit deflator of consumption goods to implicit deflator of change in business inventories, consumption goods.
AW	Investment to wealth.

b. Quantities.

C	Personal consumption expenditures, including services of consumers' durables.
CE	Supply of consumption goods by government enterprises.
CG	Government purchases of consumption goods.
CI	Change in business inventories of consumption goods.
CR	Net exports of consumption goods, less income originating, rest of the world.
CS	Supply of consumption goods by private enterprises.
G	Net claims on government.
R	Net claims on rest of the world.
I	Gross private domestic investment, including purchases of consumers' durables.
IG	Government purchases of investment goods.
IR	Net exports of investment goods.
IS	Supply of investment goods by private enterprises.
L	Supply of labor services.
LD	Private purchases of labor services.
LGE	Government enterprises purchases of labor services.
LGG	General government purchases of labor services.
LH	Time available.
LJ	Leisure time.
LR	Net exports of labor services.
LU	Unemployment.
K	Capital stock.
KD	Capital services.

c. Prices.

PC	Implicit deflator, personal consumption expenditures, including services of consumers' durables.
PCE	Implicit deflator, supply of consumption goods by government enterprises.
PCG	Implicit deflator, government purchases of consumption goods.
PCI	Implicit deflator, change in business inventories of consumption goods.
PCR	Implicit deflator, net exports of consumption goods, less income originating, rest of the world.

PCS   Implicit deflator, supply of consumption goods by private enterprises.

PG   Implicit deflator, net claims on government.

PR   Implicit deflator, net claims on rest of the world.

PI   Implicit deflator, gross private domestic investment, including purchases of consumers' durables.

PIG   Implicit deflator, government purchases of investment goods.

PIR   Implicit deflator, net exports of investment goods.

PIS   Implicit deflator, supply of investment goods by private enterprises.

PL   Implicit deflator, supply of labor services.

PLD   Implicit deflator, private purchases of labor services.

PLGE   Implicit deflator, government enterprises purchases of labor services.

PLGG   Implicit deflator, general government purchases of labor services.

PLR   Implicit deflator, net exports of labor services.

PKD   Implicit deflator, capital services.

d. Financial variables.

D   Rate of depreciation, private domestic tangible assets.

M   Rate of replacement, private domestic tangible assets.

N   Nominal rate of return, private domestic tangible assets.

S   Gross private national saving.

W   Private national wealth.

e. Tax and transfer variables.

EL   Government transfer payments to persons other than social insurance funds.

TC   Effective tax rate, consumption goods.

TI   Effective tax rate, investment goods.

TK   Effective tax rate, capital services.

TL   Effective tax rate, labor services.

TP   Effective tax rate, capital stock.

In Table B•2 the equations for the macroeconometric growth model are presented. The model includes five behavioral equations, describing the behavior of household and business sectors.

The demand for labor is determined by the total level of production, the amount of capital services available, and the relative prices of capital and labor services. Output of investment goods is determined by the price of investment goods, the prices of capital services and the available supply of capital services, and the amount of productive capacity being devoted to the output of consumer goods and services. The production that takes place in the United States private sector, whether of consumption or of investment goods, is limited by the total productive capacity which in turn depends on available supplies of capital and labor services as well as on the level of technology.

The level of household expenditure on consumer goods and services is determined by the wealth and resources held by the household sector, including the time endowment of the sector. The desired amount of work input provided by the household sector is determined by the total amount of time available, the wage rate, and the extent of other resources available to the household sector in the form of wealth and transfer payments.

The behavioral equations of the macro-econometric growth model have been estimated from historical data for the United States for the period 1929-1971. In addition to the five behavioral equations, the model includes: accounting identities for capital stock, investment and capital services; the value of input and output; saving and wealth; and for the value of consumption goods, investment goods, capital services, and labor services. These accounting identities incorporate the budget constraints for household and business sectors and the flow of each product and factor of production in current prices.

The model is completed by balance between demand and supply of products and factors of production in

Table B•2
MACRO-ECONOMETRIC GROWTH MODEL: EQUATIONS

a. Behavioral equations.

Investment supply:

$$\frac{PIS \times IS}{PKD \times KD} = 1.1717 - 0.5006 \times (\log CS - \log IS).$$

Labor demand:

$$\frac{PLD \times LD}{PKD \times KD} = 1.5655.$$

Production possibility frontier:

$$0 = -\log KD - 1.5655 \times \log LD + 1.3938 \times \log CS - 2.5655 \times \log A + 1.1717 \times \log IS + 0.2503 \times (\log CS - \log IS) \times 2.$$

Consumption demand:

$$PC \times C = 0.0034 \times W(-1) + 0.1469 \times (PL \times LH + EL).$$

Leisure demand:

$$PL \times LJ = 0.0196 \times W(-1) + 0.8403 \times (PL \times LH + EL).$$

b. Accounting identities:

Capital stock and investment:

$$K = AI \times I + (1 - M) \times K(-1).$$

Capital service and capital stock:

$$KD = AK \times K(-1).$$

Value of output and input:

$$PIS \times IS + PCS \times CS = PKD \times KD + PLD \times LD.$$

Value of consumption goods:

$$(1 + TC) \times PCS \times CS + PCE \times CE = PC \times C + PCG \times CG + PCI \times CI + PCR \times CR.$$

Value of investment goods:

$$(1 + TI) \times PIS \times IS + PCI \times CI = PI \times I + PIG \times IG + PIR \times IR.$$

Value of capital services:

$$(1 - TK) \times (PKD \times KD - TP \times PI(-1) \times AW(-1) \times K(-1))$$
$$= N \times PI(-1) \times AW(-1) \times K(-1) + D \times PI \times AL \times K(-1) + PI(-1) \times AW(-1) \times K(-1) - PI \times AL \times K(-1).$$

Value of labor services:

$$(1 - TL) \times (PLD \times LD + PLGE \times LGE + PLGG \times LGG + PLR \times LR) = PL \times L.$$

Saving:

$$S = PI \times I + PG \times (G - G(-1)) + PR \times (R - R(-1)).$$

Wealth:

$$W = PI \times AW \times K + PG \times G + PR \times R.$$

c. Balance equations.

Consumption:

$$CS + CE = C + CG + CI + CR.$$

Investment:

$$IS + CI = I + IG + IR.$$

Time:

$$LH = L + LJ.$$

Labor:

$$L = LD + LGE + LGG + LR + LU.$$

d. Aggregation equations.

Implicit deflator, change in business inventories, consumption goods:

$$PCI = PC \times APC.$$

Change in business inventories, consumption goods:

$$PCI \times CI = PI \times I \times ACI.$$

constant prices and by aggregation equations that determine inventory accumulation of consumption goods. Although gross private domestic investment is determined in the model, the allocation of investment between fixed investment and inventory accumulation is not determined in the model. An allocation between inventory accumulation in the form of consumption goods and other components of gross private domestic investment is required for the balance between demand and supply of consumption and investment goods.

In Table B•3 the working of the macro-econometric growth model is outlined by means of a diagram.

3. The Inter-Industry Model

The interindustry or input-output model is used in conjunction with the macro model to link the general variables in the macro model to more detailed aspects of primary inputs, intermediate production, and final demand. Essentially, the interindustry model disaggregates the total production and total input figures derived in the macro model, breaking the final output into sectoral demands and tracing the primary and intermediate production flows required to sustain these demands. In the reverse direction, if resource constraints defined at the sectoral level and introduced into the interindustry model prevent the initially defined mix of final demand from being satisfied, then the interindustry model simulates a process of adjustment in which the specific shortages give rise to price changes which, in turn, induce an adjustment in production and consumption patterns to minimize, within the limits of production possibilities and of consumer preferences, the dislocation caused by this shortage.

The interindustry model is based on a sectoral classification of activity in the United States economy. The classification scheme used is shown in Table B•4. This is an input-output tableau which permits the entire chain of production to be traced through the economy, from the purchase of primary inputs through the various intermediate stages of production to the emergence of final products to be absorbed in consumption, investment, government or export final demand. The structure of production includes all of United States domestic supply of goods and services but breaks out the energy sectors in detail to permit a close study of the interaction between energy and nonenergy sectors of the economy.

The input-output framework serves to integrate the various parts of the economy together to form a consistent whole. This is achieved by the use of balance equations between the quantity supplied and demanded in each of the nine sectors included in the model. Supply is the gross output of the domestic producing sector; demand is the demand for intermediate inputs by all nine producing sectors together with demand for sectoral output by the four final use categories: personal consumption, investment, government purchases and exports. Competitive imports of nonfuel goods are regarded as inputs into United States production and are endogenous; imports of fuels are regarded as perfect substitutes for the domestic product and so enter directly to supplement the domestic supply in these sectors. The model also includes accounting identities between the value of domestic availability of

Table B·3
MACRO-ECONOMETRIC GROWTH MODEL: DIAGRAMMATIC REPRESENTATION

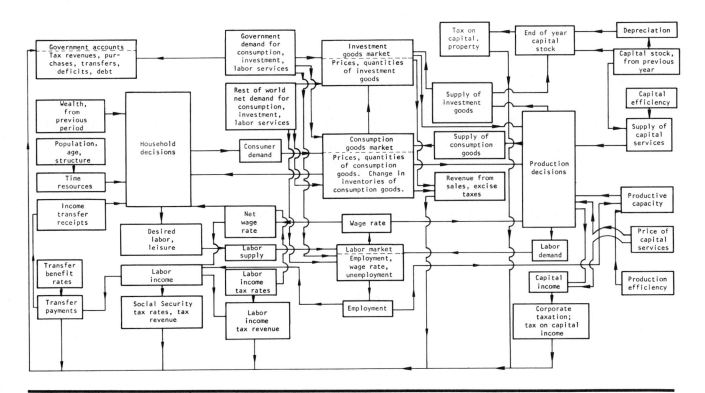

each type of product and the sum of the values of all purchases of inputs, including capital and labor, used in its production. In short, the input-output system is a type of simulated market economy in which simultaneous clearance of all markets is required. (In this role it is a tool of long-run analysis for it does not address market clearance problems that can arise from short-run capacity constraints.)

The segments of the model that fit into this input-output framework come from two sources: a detailed model of producer behavior and a detailed model of final demand. The model of final demand is based on the expenditure components that emerge from the macro model and has the function of allocating these expenditures over the supplying sectors. Producer behavior is modeled by nine simultaneous submodels, one for each producing sector. These models relate sectoral output to inputs into the sector, incorporating information on input requirements and interrelationships derived from actual data for the 1947-1971 period. These submodels are used, as described below, to simultaneously determine the prices that producers must charge to cover costs, given primary input prices from the macro model and given production constraints in each sector, and also to determine the pattern of inputs into each sector which, of all feasible patterns, minimizes unit costs of production given the prices of each input. The result of this is a long-run, average cost price for each of

the nine producing sectors and a set of input-output coefficients for each sector. In short, the input-output pattern in each producing sector is endogenous. This feature enables the model to capture a critically important feature of the modern economy—its flexibility in adapting to changing price and supply circumstances. This flexibility arises from the ability of producers to change input patterns, substituting, within technical limits, the relatively less expensive or abundant input for the relatively expensive or scarce input. It also arises from the responsiveness of final demand to these same forces. Both types of flexibility are explicitly considered in the model.

At this point, the interindustry model is equivalent to a conventional input-output model—it has a set of input-output coefficients, a final demand vector, and a set of demand-supply balance conditions. The system can now be solved to find the gross output required from each sector. Also, prices are part of the solution so the resulting transactions matrix can be expressed in both current and constant dollars.

The energy sectors are treated simultaneously with the nonenergy sectors in this analysis. Once the transactions matrix has been found, however, further analysis of the energy sectors takes place. The first area of extension concerns fuel supply and prices, the second concerns energy flows in Btu's and in physical units. The supply of each fuel comprises domestic production, which is endogenous, and imports, which make up the difference between United States demand and domestic supply at the prevailing price.

A judgmental estimate of the domestic supply function is used for each of the fuels. Imports then make up the supply deficit. But if imports are not free to vary to make up the gap between domestic demand and supply, an iterative procedure is used to increase the average price of fuel, both domestic and imported, until the supply gap is eliminated by increasing supply and/or decreasing demand. The second type of extension concerns the generation of physical energy data from the interindustry flows. The interindustry transaction quantities are expressed in constant dollars (i.e., in 1971 prices) so, by applying Btu per constant dollar ratios obtained from historical data, the fuel flows can be expressed in terms of Btu's. Similarly, the price indices can be combined with base period dollar prices to obtain fuel prices in dollar terms and the constant dollar fuel quantities can be scaled to derive these quantities in physical units such as tons, barrels, kilowatt hours and cubic feet.

4. Producer Behavior

The interindustry model is based on models of producer behavior for each of the nine producing sectors. The production relationships within each sector are represented by price possibility frontiers which give the relation between input prices and the sectoral output price. Although expressed in terms of prices, these frontiers embody the

Table B.4
INTER-INDUSTRY TRANSACTIONS: DIAGRAMMATIC REPRESENTATION

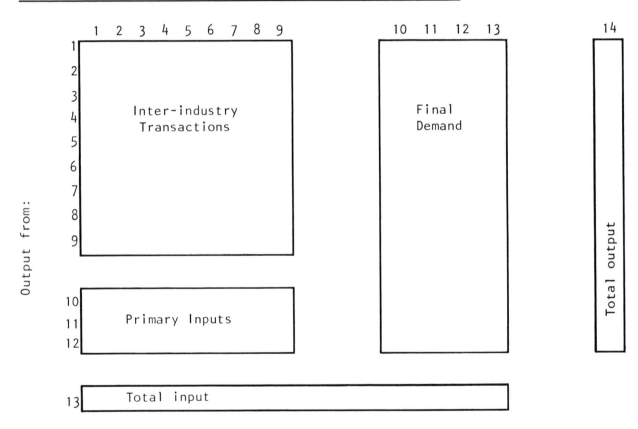

Primary inputs, rows:

10. Imports.
11. Capital services.
12. Labor services.

Final demand, columns:

10. Personal consumption expenditures.
11. Gross domestic private investment.
12. Government purchases of goods and services.
13. Exports.

Intermediate sectors:

1. Agriculture, non-fuel mining and construction.
2. Manufacturing, excluding petroleum refining.
3. Transport.
4. Communications, trade, services.
5. Coal mining.
6. Crude petroleum and natural gas.
7. Petroleum refining.
8. Electric utilities.
9. Gas utilities.

same information as the standard production function or production possibility frontier, i.e., information covering input requirements and substitutability and complementarity between inputs. These price frontiers are used to determine the sectoral output prices as well as the demand functions for each input into each production sector; these demand functions are, in fact, the input-output coefficients which express demand for each input relative to the level of that sector's output. These sectoral output prices and input demand functions are independent of final demand, depending only on the price frontiers, the sectoral efficiency levels and the prices of competitive imports, capital services and labor services. Finally, once prices are known, final demands for each sector's output are calculated and the total level of output from each sector and the interindustry transactions are then found by standard input-output techniques.

A primary objective in implementing an ecometric model of producer behavior is to explore the interrelationships between relative demands for the various inputs. At a general level the relationships between inputs of capital, labor, energy, and materials are investigated. Similarly, we wish to investigate the interrelation between the five types of fuels within the energy category as well as between the five types of materials included in the materials aggregate. To simplify this investigation, a two-tier structure is imposed on inputs into each sector. First, the twelve individual inputs are aggregated into four broad groups—capital services, labor services, energy and materials. Second, an overall production model for each sector is defined in terms of these four aggregates. In more detail, the four input groups are:

(a.) Capital services (K)

(b.) Labor services (L)

(c.) Energy input (E)

(The overall energy price in each sector is expressed in terms of the five fuel prices, i.e., prices of coal, of crude petroleum and natural gas, of refined petroleum products, of electricity, and of gas supplied by gas utilities.)

(d.) Materials input (M)

(The aggregate price of materials input into each sector is represented as a function of its five component prices—prices of agriculture, nonfuel mining and construction, of manufacturing, of transport, of communications, trade and services, and of competitive imports (except imports in the fuel sectors are taken as exogenous and not included in the materials functions).)

A model of producer behavior for each sector is then defined. This involves representing the price of sectoral output as a function of the production efficiency of the sector, i.e., an index of total factor productivity, and of the prices of the four input aggregates. The price frontiers for all sectors at both levels of aggregation, i.e., those covering the energy and the materials sub-aggregates and those covering the overall capital, labor, energy, materials submodels, are represented by a functional form that is quadratic in the logarithms of the prices. The resulting

frontier provides a local second-order approximation to any price possibility frontier. This functional form is referred to as the transcendental logarithmic frontier, or more simply as the *translog price possibility frontier* and was introduced by Christensen, Jorgenson and Lau.[1]

As an example, the price possibility frontier for the aggregate (capital, labor, energy, materials) submodel takes the form:

$$\ln P_i = -\ln A_i + \alpha_O^i + \alpha_K^i \ln PK_i + \alpha_L^i \ln PL_i$$
$$+ \alpha_E^i \ln PE_i = \alpha_M^i \ln PM_i$$
$$+ \frac{1}{2} \left(\gamma_{KK}^i (\ln PK_i)^2 + \gamma_{KL}^i \right.$$
$$\left. \ln PK_i \ln PL_i + \cdots \right)$$

where P_i = output price for sector i

PK_i = price of capital service inputs to sector i

PL_i = price of labor services inputs to sector i

PE_i = price of energy inputs into sector i

PM_i = price of materials inputs into sector i

A_i = level of efficiency (or Hicks neutral technology) of sector i

This allows solving for the nine sectoral output prices. Each sector purchases inputs from twelve sources—the nine producing sectors, competitive imports, capital services and labor services. The prices of these last three inputs—imports, capital and labor—are inserted exogenously into the interindustry model. Also, the technical efficiency index A_i is inserted as an exogenous variable. The only remaining variables are the prices of intermediate inputs into each sector. These are defined in terms of the output prices simply by inserting the historical average factor of proportionality between this input price and the average price of output from the supplying sector. For example:

$$P_{ij} = F_{ij} \times P_i \qquad i = 1,12; j = 1,9$$

gives the price of the i_{th} input into sector j as a proportion of the average price of output i; the F variable is exogenous. Now, all nine price possibility frontiers are expressed in terms of nine endogenous prices—the sectoral output prices. These price frontiers must all be satisfied simultaneously if the production sector is to be in an internally consistent configuration, so we can solve this price system simultaneously to determine the nine equilibrium sectoral output prices.

It is possible to solve for prices independently of any knowledge of final demand by appealing to a class of nonsubstitution theorems first introduced by Samuelson (1966).[2] These theorems state that when production takes place under constant returns and when primary input prices are given, output prices are determined solely by supply considerations, independent of final demand. The intuitive justification for this result is illustrated by the simple supply-demand situation shown in Chart B•1.

The horizontal supply curve rests on two considerations. First, the assumption of constant returns; and second, the implicit assumption that the time frame involved is long

Chart B·1

SUPPLY-DEMAND CURVE

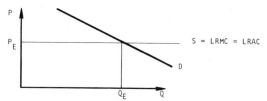

enough for short-run bottlenecks to be removed and for the underlying constant cost characteristics to emerge. Given the supply curve, the demand curve determines the quantity produced and sold. Thus, the equilibrium point ($P_E Q_E$) has price determined solely by supply and quantity determined solely by demand.

The next step is to apply the prices already found, together with the production information embodied in the price possibility frontiers, to determine the specific input patterns adopted in each producing sector. This step is accomplished by determining the input-output coefficients endogenously as functions of prices. This procedure rests on the following derivation. Consider the profit function for each producing sector. This function gives the maximum level of profit attainable under specified input and output prices as a function of these prices. Under constant returns, the value of this function will always be zero. Let $\pi_j(P_j, P_{ij} \ldots P_{12j}) = 0$ be the profit function for the jth sector, where P_j is the price of output and P_{ij} are the prices of its inputs. For variations in prices we have:

$$d\pi_j = \frac{\partial \pi}{\partial P_j} dP_j + \sum_{i=1}^{12} \frac{\partial \pi_j}{\partial P_{ij}} dP_{ij} = 0$$

If all input prices except P_{ij} are constant then:

$$\frac{P_j}{P_{ij}} = -\frac{\partial \pi_j}{\partial P_{ij}} \Big/ \frac{\partial \pi_j}{\partial P_j}$$

But, the theory of the profit function includes the result that the partial derivative of the profit function with respect to a price is the supply function for the corresponding quantity. Therefore:

$$\frac{\partial \pi_j}{\partial P_j} = X_j \quad \text{and} \quad \frac{\partial \pi_j}{\partial P_{ij}} = -X_{ij}$$

where X_{ij} is the quantity of input from sector i to j and X_j is the total input and total output quantity of sector j. Using these results gives:

$$\frac{\partial P_j}{\partial P_{ij}} = \frac{X_{ij}}{X_j} = a_{ij}$$

where a_{ij} is the input-output coefficient. The price possibility frontiers enable evaluation of the price partial derivative. These frontiers give prices in logarithmic form so:

$$\frac{\partial \ln P_j}{\partial \ln P_{ij}} = \frac{\partial P_j}{\partial P_{ij}} \cdot \frac{P_{ij}}{P_j}$$

is used to obtain the results

$$\text{share i in j} = \frac{X_{ij}P_{ij}}{X_j P_j} = \frac{\partial \ln P_j}{\partial \ln P_{ij}}$$

and

$$a_{ij} = \frac{\partial \ln P_j}{\partial \ln P_{ij}} \Big/ \frac{P_{ij}}{P_j}$$

Thus, both input shares and input-output coefficients can be determined endogenously as functions of, inter alia, prices. For example, the input-output coefficient for capital services into sector i is, using the translog functional form:

$$a_{Ki} = \left(\alpha_K^i + \gamma_{KK}^i \ln PK_i + \gamma_{KL}^i \ln PL_i + \gamma_{KE}^i \ln PE_i + \gamma_{KM}^i \ln PM_i\right) \Big/ (PK_i/P_i)$$

Similar expressions can be obtained for the input-output coefficients for labor services, energy and materials. Similar reasoning applies to finding input shares within the energy and the materials subaggregates. Then, the individual input-output coefficients for energy and materials components can be found. For example, for services input to manufacturing:

A services, manufacturing = (share of services in the materials input into manufacturing) × (share of materials input in manufacturing) ÷

Price of Services, Manufacturing

Price of Manufacturing

This derivation of the input demand functions simulates the reaction of producers to prices with the behavioral objective of cost minimization. In addition this behavioral submodel ensures that the accounting identity between the value of output and the total value of inputs holds, or, equivalently, that the input value shares sum to unity.

For each of the nine producing sectors, all three submodels—aggregate (KLEM), energy (E) and materials (M)—were fitted to annual time series data. These data are input-output tables covering the period 1947-71 giving, for each year, the entire interindustry transactions matrix in both current and constant dollars as well as the full matrix of price indices. (The data are presented in Faucett (1973).[3] The method of estimation was the minimum distance estimator for nonlinear simultaneous equations. This method can handle the estimation of the equation systems including the nonlinearities in the variables and the linear restrictions on the coefficients.

The estimated parameters for the nine sectoral production models are presented in Tables B·5 to B·7. These tables give the free parameters in each submodel; the full array of parameters can be obtained from these by applying the homogeneity and symmetry restrictions. The notation used in the tables is as follows. The nine sectors are:

1. Agriculture, nonfuel mining, construction.
2. Manufacturing, except petroleum refining.
3. Transportation.
4. Communications, trade, services.
5. Coal mining.
6. Crude petroleum and natural gas extraction.
7. Petroleum refining and related industries.
8. Electric utilities.
9. Gas utilities.

322

The notation in the energy submodels is:

1. Coal mining.
2. Crude petroleum and natural gas extraction.
3. Petroleum refining.
4. Electric utilities.
5. Gas utilities.

The notation in the materials submodels is:

1. Agriculture, nonfuel mining, construction.
2. Manufacturing, except petroleum refining.
3. Transportation.
4. Communications, trade, services.
5. Competitive imports.

(The import coefficients in the fuel sectors are set to zero since imports are inserted into these sectors exogenously to the production submodels, being set equal to the gap between United States demand for and supply of each fuel at the prevailing price.)

Final demand totals, from the macro model, now have to be allocated over the supplying sectors. The total investment expenditure is allocated over the nine supplying sectors in fixed proportions, these proportions being the average historical shares for these expenditure categories. Similarly, government expenditures are allocated in fixed proportions over the supplying sectors. Export demand for each type of product is also exogenous.

Personal consumption demand covers ten sectors. These are eight of the domestic producing sectors (the personal

Table B.5

ESTIMATES OF THE PARAMETERS OF THE TRANSLOG PRICE POSSIBILITY FRONTIER FOR THE AGGREGATE (KLEM) SUB-MODEL FOR NINE INDUSTRIAL SECTORS OF THE UNITED STATES ECONOMY, 1947-71.

Parameter	Sectors								
	1	2	3	4	5	6	7	8	9
α_K^I	.1785	.1149	.1799	.2994	.1277	.4272	.1373	.3458	.2165
α_L^I	.2354	.2940	.4096	.4171	.4139	.0987	.0978	.1925	.1085
α_E^I	.0244	.0202	.0380	.0182	.1857	.1101	.4553	.2120	.5547
α_M^I	.5616	.5708	.3726	.2653	.2727	.3640	.3096	.2496	.1204
β_{KK}^I	.0851	.0590	.1018	.0595	.0280	.2447	.0849	.1330	.0749
β_{KL}^I	-.0366	.0030	-.0601	.0114	-.0357	-.0422	-.0242	.0288	-.1181
β_{KE}^I	-.0052	-.0055	-.0137	.0011	.0099	-.0470	-.0772	-.1682	-.0941
β_{KM}^I	-.0434	-.0565	-.0280	-.0719	-.0022	-.1555	.0165	.0064	.1373
β_{LL}^I	.0287	.0737	.0582	.0848	-.0751	-.0131	-.0174	-.0968	-.2773
β_{LE}^I	.0023	.0054	-.0180	.0098	.1145	.0459	-.0122	.0239	.1318
β_{LM}^I	.0056	-.0821	.0199	-.1059	-.0037	.0093	.0538	.0441	.2636
β_{EE}^I	.0072	.0188	.0198	.0020	.0087	.0184	.2282	.0638	.1413
β_{EM}^I	-.0044	-.0187	.0119	-.0129	-.1332	-.0173	-.1388	.0805	-.1790
β_{MM}^I	.0022	.1573	-.0038	.1907	.1392	.1635	.0685	-.1311	-.2219

Table B·6
ESTIMATES OF THE PARAMETERS OF THE TRANSLOG PRICE POSSIBILITY FRONTIER FOR THE ENERGY (E) SUB-MODEL FOR NINE INDUSTRIAL SECTORS OF THE UNITED STATES, 1947-71.

Parameter	Sectors								
	1	2	3	4	5	6	7	8	9
α_1^{EI}	.0053	.2040	.0799	.1142	.8510	.0738	.0448	.3165	.0909
α_2^{EI}	.0021	.0002	.0000	.0111	.0000	.1464	.2131	.0000	.1408
α_3^{EI}	.8389	.3384	.8107	.3520	.3997	.0894	.2289	.1173	.0940
α_4^{EI}	.1212	.2858	.0406	.4136	.1062	.6904	.5132	.3829	.6743
α_5^{EI}	.0325	.1716	.0688	.1091	.0029	.0000	.0000	.1829	.0000
β_{11}^{EI}	.0052	.1624	.0735	.1011	-.0118	-.0557	-.0165	.0762	-.0752
β_{12}^{EI}	.0000	.0000	.0000	-.0013	.0000	.1098	.0483	.0000	.1850
β_{13}^{EI}	-.0068	-.0690	-.0648	-.0402	.0220	-.0255	.0005	.0833	-.0192
β_{14}^{EI}	.0011	-.0583	-.0032	-.0472	-.0100	-.0286	-.0323	-.0578	-.0906
β_{15}^{EI}	.0005	-.0350	-.0055	-.0125	-.0002	.0000	.0000	-.1017	.0000
β_{22}^{EI}	.0010	-.0029	.0000	.0110	.0000	.0077	.1113	.0000	-.1416
β_{23}^{EI}	.0007	-.0001	.0000	-.0039	.0000	.0053	-.0592	.0000	.0455
β_{24}^{EI}	-.0007	.0073	.0000	-.0046	.0000	-.1228	-.1003	.0000	.0889
β_{25}^{EI}	-.0010	-.0043	.0000	-.0012	.0000	.0000	.0000	.0000	.0000
β_{33}^{EI}	-.0252	.2239	.1534	.2281	-.0287	-.0418	.0680	.0001	-.0553
β_{34}^{EI}	.0128	-.0967	-.0329	-.1456	.0064	.0620	-.0092	-.0966	.0289
β_{35}^{EI}	.1854	-.0581	-.0557	-.0384	.0003	.0000	.0000	.0162	.0000
β_{44}^{EI}	-.0410	.1868	.0389	.2425	.0055	.0894	.1418	.2077	.1505
β_{45}^{EI}	.0278	-.0390	-.0028	-.0451	-.0019	.0000	.0000	-.0502	.0000
β_{55}^{EI}	-.0458	.1364	.0640	.0972	.0018	.0000	.0000	.1357	.0000

Table B·7
ESTIMATES OF THE PARAMETERS OF THE TRANSLOG PRICE POSSIBILITY FRONTIER FOR THE MATERIALS (M) SUB-MODEL FOR NINE INDUSTRIAL SECTORS OF THE UNITED STATES, 1947-71.

Parameter	Sectors								
	1	2	3	4	5	6	7	8	9
α_1^{MI}	.2578	.1348	.1221	.0819	.0193	.0779	.0562	.1134	.1759
α_2^{MI}	.3777	.5933	.1373	.2548	.4270	.0869	.1656	.1046	.1546
α_3^{MI}	.0653	.0472	.1932	.0532	.0675	.0501	.1736	.1200	.1453
α_4^{MI}	.2674	.1643	.4382	.5774	.4839	.5517	.4659	.6620	.4426
α_5^{MI}	.0318	.0603	.1091	.0327	.0023	.2334	.1388	.0000	.0815
β_{11}^{MI}	.0799	.0376	.1072	-.0454	.0190	.0718	.0530	.0170	-.0407
β_{12}^{MI}	-.1012	-.0200	-.0168	.0848	-.0083	-.0068	-.0093	.0755	.0845
β_{13}^{MI}	.0629	.0043	-.2360	-.0094	-.0013	-.0039	-.0097	-.0292	-.0703
β_{14}^{MI}	-.0672	-.0571	-.0535	-.0806	-.0094	-.0430	-.0262	-.0633	-.0899
β_{15}^{MI}	.0256	.0352	-.0133	.0506	-.0000	-.0182	-.0078	.0000	.1164
β_{22}^{MI}	.2349	.1958	.1185	.0973	.2447	.0794	.1382	.0023	-.0070
β_{23}^{MI}	-.0219	-.0361	-.0265	-.0091	-.0288	-.0044	-.0288	.0037	-.0123
β_{24}^{MI}	-.1009	-.0710	-.0602	-.1179	-.2066	-.0480	-.0772	-.0815	-.0895
β_{25}^{MI}	-.0109	-.0687	-.0150	-.0550	-.0010	-.0203	-.0230	.0000	.0243
β_{33}^{MI}	.0039	.0435	.1559	.0502	.0629	.0476	.1434	.1027	.1095
β_{34}^{MI}	-.0187	-.0030	-.0847	-.0321	-.0327	-.0276	-.0809	-.0773	-.0739
β_{35}^{MI}	-.0263	-.0087	-.0211	.0005	-.0002	-.0117	-.0241	.0000	.0471
β_{44}^{MI}	.1959	.1218	.2462	.2348	.2497	.2473	.2488	.2221	.2346
β_{45}^{MI}	-.0090	.0093	-.0478	-.0042	-.0011	-.1287	-.0646	.0000	.0187
β_{55}^{MI}	.0206	.0329	.0972	.0081	.0023	.1789	.1195	.0000	-.2065

consumption demand for crude oil is zero) together with capital services (supplied by owner-occupied residential structures and by the stock of consumer durables) and those imports that enter directly into consumption. Total personal consumption expenditure, from the macro model, is allocated over these sectors by an econometric model of consumer behavior. This model is based on an indirect utility function that can be represented as:

$$\ln V = \ln V \left(\frac{P_1}{PC \times C} , ..., \frac{P_{10}}{PC \times C} \right)$$

where V is the level of utility, P_i is the price of the ith sectors output and $PC \times C$ is total personal consumption expenditure. For each sector the budget share is taken as given; this corresponds to the assumption of a linear logarithmic indirect utility function.

Final demand, in constant dollars, for each sector's output is now determined:

$$Y_i = \frac{FC_i}{P_{iC}} + \frac{FI_i}{P_{iI}} + \frac{FG_i}{P_{iG}} + \frac{FE_i}{P_{iE}}$$

where Y_i = constant dollar final demand for output of sector i

FC_i = current dollar final demand by personal consumption for

FI_i output of sector i. Similarly for investment, government

FG_i and export final demand

FE_i

P_{iC} = price of sector i's output to personal consumption

P_i purchases. Similarly for prices to investment,

P_{iG} government and export purchases.

P_{iE}

The input-output model can now be solved:

$$X_j = \sum_{i=1}^{9} X_{ij} + Y_j$$

where X_j = total constant dollar output of sector j

X_{ij} = constant dollar input from sector i to j

Y_j = constant dollar final demand for sector j

$X_{ij} = a_{ij}X_j$ i,j=1,9

$$X_j = \sum_{i=1}^{9} a_{ij}X_j + Y_j \qquad j=1,9$$

These equations can be solved for the nine total outputs X_j. This is the standard input-output system, usually expressed in the equivalent matrix form

$$X = AX + Y$$

with the solution

$$X = (1 - A)^{-1}Y$$

The transactions matrix can now be calculated. The constant dollar interindustry transaction between sector i

and sector j is $a_{ij}X_j$ and the current dollar value of this transaction is

$$P_{ij} \times a_{ij}X_j = F_{ij}P_i \times a_{ij}X_j$$

The entire current and constant dollar transactions matrices can be built up in this way.

The structure of the interindustry model is summarized in the flow chart, Table B·8.

Table B·8
INTER-INDUSTRY ECONOMETRIC MODEL: DIAGRAMMATIC REPRESENTATION

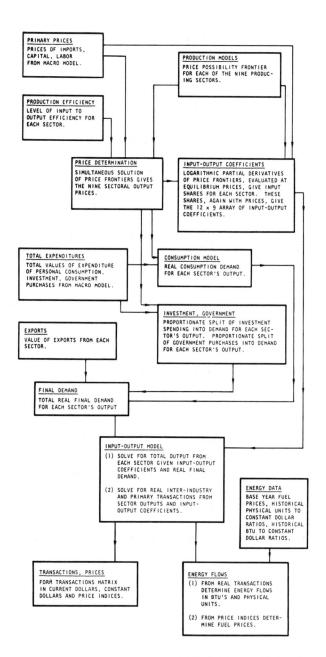

5. Concluding Note

The GNP concepts used in the DRI macrogrowth model differ from the conventional National Income Accounts definitions in two ways:

(a) the stock of consumer durable goods is treated analogously to the stock of owner-occupied residential structures in NIA in that the services flowing from the stock are imputed a value and this imputed value is included in consumption (and GNP); and

(b) this imputation means that consumer durable purchases are viewed as an investment, adding to the existing stock of durable goods. Therefore, durable purchases are included in investment, not in consumption expenditure.

These differences are shown as follows:

NIA DEFINITIONS	DRI GROWTH MODEL DEFINITIONS
C = personal consumption expenditure	$\bar{C}$ = C — CD + SCD
I = investment expenditure	$\bar{I}$ = I + CD
G = government purchases	$\bar{G}$ = G
X-M = net exports	$\bar{X}$ - $\bar{M}$ = X — M
GNP = C + I + G + X — M	$\overline{GNP}$ = $\bar{C}$ + $\bar{I}$ + $\bar{G}$ + $\bar{X}$ — M
	= C + SCD + I + G + X — M
	= GNP + SCD

CD = purchases of consumer durables

(SCD = imputed value of services from the stock of consumer durables)

The 1975 forecasts of the macro economy shown in Chapter 6 can be reconciled to the NIA forecasts as shown below. (The 1975 NIA forecasts are taken from The Data Resources Review, August 1974, Table Control 7/31.)

NIA FORECASTS

C	973($bn)
I	231
G	344
X — M	0.5
GNP	1548
PGNP (1958 = 1)	1.815
Real GNP ($1958 bn)	853

The reconciliation uses the data

CD ($bn)	147
SCD ($bn)	163
price of SCD (1958 = 1)	1.272
real SCD ($1958 bn)	128

The expenditure totals on the growth model concepts derived from the NIA definitions and those simulated in the growth model are:

	From NIA forecasts	From growth model
$\bar{C}$	989($bn)	995($bn)
$\bar{I}$	378	380
$\bar{G}$	344	338
$\bar{X}$ — $\bar{M}$	0.5	0.5
$\overline{GNP}$	1712	1714

The reconciliation of the price deflators is as follows:

$\overline{PGNP}$ = 1.744	(on 1958 = 1)
real $\overline{GNP}$ = 983	($1958 bn)
real $\overline{GNP}$ — real SCD = 855	($1958 bn)
real GNP = 853	($1958 bn)

(The remaining differences between GNP in the DRI Quarterly Macro Model and the DRI Macro Growth Model are due to forecast differences between the models.)

FOOTNOTES

1. Christensen, L. R., Jorgenson, D. W., & Lau, L. J., "Transcendental Logarithmic Production Frontiers," *Review of Economics and Statistics,* February, 1973.

2. Stiglitz, J., (ed.), *The Collected Scientific Papers of Paul A. Samuelson,* vol I, pp 513-536, MIT Press, Cambridge, Massachusetts, 1966.

3. Faucett, J., and Associates, *Data Development for the I-O Energy Model,* Final Report to the Ford Foundation Energy Policy Project, Washington, D. C., May, 1973.

APPENDIX C

Description of Case Western Reserve World Model

1. Introductory Comment

The Case Western Reserve Multi Level World Model was developed within the context of multi-level, hierarchical systems theory. The principal features are:

a. Regionalization; to take account of the differences in problems, resources, characteristics and environments between different areas of the world.

b. A multi-level, multi-goal structure: to incorporate all the essential relations between men, their social and political organizations and their physical environment in the context of a multiplicity of goals.

c. A man-computer interactive mode: to allow decision makers to be an explicit part of the simulation efforts.

2. Regionalization

The world is divided into 10 regions or groups of countries which are similar with respect to their major political and economic characteristics. They are not necessarily geographically contiguous but are at approximately the same stage of economic development and share similar political structures. The regions are interlinked with trade flows, population migration and other movements across their boundaries. A list of the countries in each region is given in Table C·1.

Table C·1
DESCRIPTION OF WORLD MODEL REGIONS

Region 1. North America

Canada
United States of America

Region 2. Western Europe

Andorra	Luxembourg
Austria	Malta
Belgium	Monaco
Denmark	Netherlands
Federal Republic	Norway
of Germany	Portugal
Finland	San Marino
France	Spain
Great Britain	Sweden
Greece	Switzerland
Iceland	Turkey
Ireland	Yugoslavia
Italy	
Liechtenstein	

Region 3. Japan

Region 4. Rest of the Developed Market Economies

Australia	South African Republic
Israel	Tasmania
New Zealand	

Region 5. Eastern Europe

Albania	Hungary
Bulgaria	Poland
Czechoslovakia	Rumania
German Democratic	Soviet Union
Republic	

Region 6. Latin America

Argentina	Guyana
Barbados	Haiti
Bolivia	Honduras
Brazil	Jamaica
British Honduras	Mexico
Chile	Nicaragua
Colombia	Panama
Costa Rica	Paraguay
Cuba	Peru
Dominican Republic	Surinam
Ecuador	Trinidad and Tobago
El Salvador	Uruguay
French Guiana	Venezuela
Guatemala	

Region 7. North Africa and the Middle East

Abu Dhabi	Lebanon
Aden	Libya
Algeria	Morocco
Bahrain	Masqat-Oman
Cyprus	Qatar
Dubai	Saudi Arabia
Egypt	Syria
Iran	Trucial Oman
Iraq	Tunisia
Jordan	Yemen
Kuwait	

(continued)

Table C·1 (continued)
DESCRIPTION OF WORLD MODEL REGIONS

Region 8. Main Africa

Angola	Niger
Burundi	Nigeria
Cabinda	Portuguese Guinea
Cameroon	Republic of Congo
Central African Republic	Reunion
Chad	Rhodesia
Dahomey	Rwanda
Ethiopia	Senegal
French Somali Coast	Sierra Leone
Gabon	Somalia
Gambia	South Africa
Ghana	South West Africa
Guinea	Spanish Guinea
Ivory Coast	Spanish Sahara
Kenya	Sudan
Liberia	Tanzania
Malagasy Republic	Togo
Malawi	Uganda
Mali	Upper Volta
Mauitania	Zaire
Mauritius	Zambia
Mozambique	

Region 9. South and Southeast Asia

Afghanistan	Malaysia
Bangladesh	Nepal
Burma	Pakistan
Cambodia	Philippines
Ceylon	South Korea
India	South Vietnam
Indonesia	Taiwan
Laos	Thailand

Region 10. Centrally Planned Asia

Mongolia

North Korea

North Vietnam

People's Republic of China

3. Multi-level Structure

Chart C·1 shows the multi-level structure of the system. The causal structure comprises variables and relations which are related to the technological and physical environment. The organizational structure takes account of intervening actions taken by governments and other socio-political organizations. It is a true control system that strives to maintain equilibrium in the causal structure. The normative structure takes account of cultural influences as well as values and beliefs of the decision makers.

4. Interactive Mode

The CWR model is intended to be a flexible decision-making tool rather than a self-contained forecasting model. Interaction between the policy analyst and the computer is an essential part of exercises using this model as a tool. The analyst can interconnect or aggregate the components and levels of the model in different ways to answer different questions.

5. Detailed Description

Chart C·2 shows the model structure for any one region as a systems analyst would see it. It attempts to show the linkages between various components of the model. The arrows indicate the direction of influence, e.g., variables in agriculture, health, and demography submodels affect labor, which in turn is an input to the economic submodel, which also interacts with energy, resources etc., within the same stratum and with variables from the other two strata.

The economic submodel is constructed at three levels of aggregation. At the lowest level a nine sector micro-economic model is included, using methods of input-output analysis. The next level is that of the macro-economic model which describes the economy of each region in terms of production and consumption relations. The production and consumption functions are similar but not identical for the various regions. The third level specifies world trade relationships as the most important link between the regions.

Two population submodels have been developed for use in different situations. One of them is a simple regional growth model which is used where the total population estimates are the only important input from the population submodel. The more sophisticated population model projects population by age levels and is used to examine population policy and the impact of other submodels upon population.

The energy submodel is divided into three subsections: energy demand, primary energy supply, and conversion and transmission of primary energy to users. For energy demand, the primary determinant is economic activity. Many variations of the relationship between GRP (Gross Regional Product) and ED (Energy Demand) have been examined. The relationships examined fall into two general classes. First are those that predict total ED from total GRP on the basis of a constant or time variant relationship.

Chart C·1
LEVELS OF THE WORLD MODEL

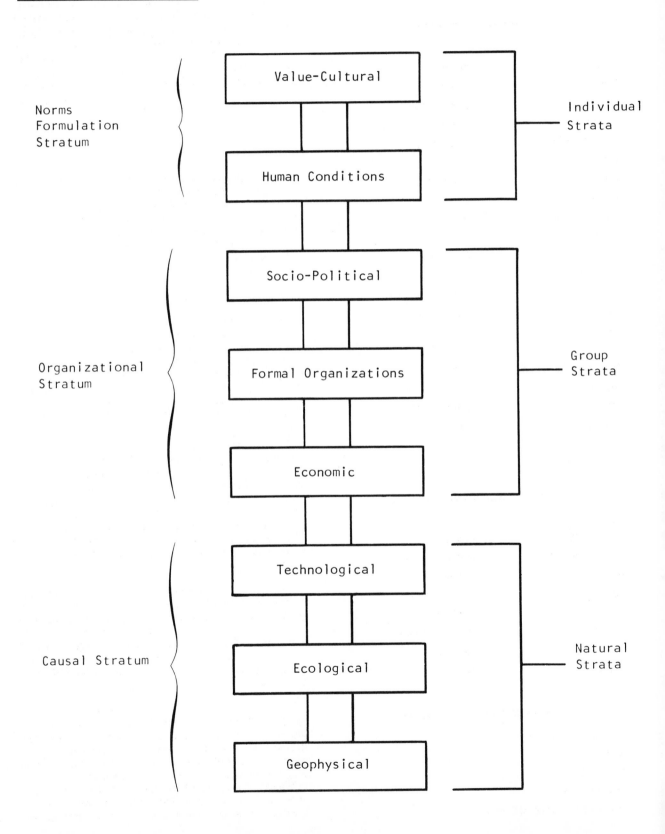

Chart C•2
PROJECTED STRUCTURE FOR ONE REGION OF THE WORLD MODEL
(Regionalization and Coupling Between Regions are Issue-Dependent)

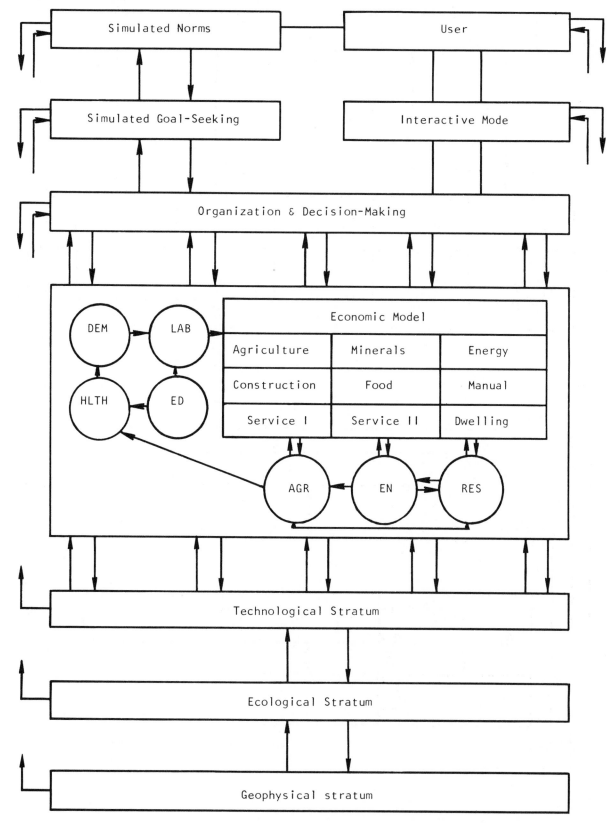

Chart C•3
THE SEQUENCE OF OPERATION IN THE DECISION STRATUM

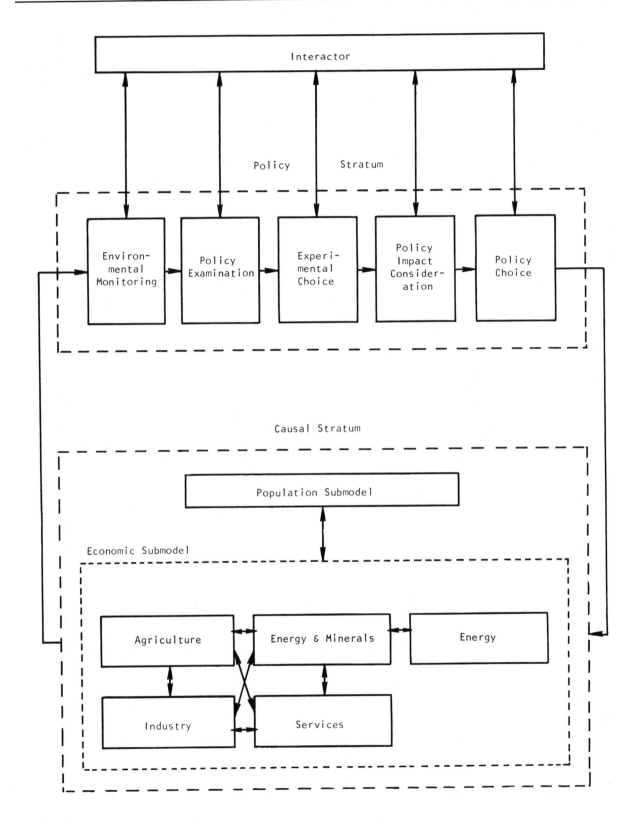

The second class contains models which relate changes in ED to changes in GRP. These energy models were further refined to include (1) the effects of political considerations and (2) the concept of ED/GRP as a function of time for each world region. This sort of a generic approach to demand prediction appears to fit historic data very well but it does not recognize the influence of factors other than GRP growth. Shifting composition of GRP as well as some region specific factors need additional research before they can be incorporated into energy demand prediction.

Predicting energy supplies is more difficult. Besides economic and technological factors, other variables affecting supply are levels of reserves, their location, and political decisions. The basic approach of the world model project is to develop supply models for various energy types which take into account physical factors like reserve, production capabilities, etc., but leave political considerations to be specified as conditioning assumptions. A world oil model has been constructed which makes oil supply projections under various assumptions about political decisions of Middle Eastern Nations. Decisions on regional energy conservation, energy investment policies, company policies and so on can hardly be forecast with any degree of precision and hence it was thought to be better to omit them and incorporate their effects as exogenous factors. The last component of the energy model is a conversion and transmission model. This part of the energy model converts primary energy into useable energy and transmits it to three user sectors: transportation, industrial and residential-commercial. Scenarios can be constructed under various assumptions about technological progress.

A food submodel has been constructed only for South East Asia. The demand side of the food model is linked to the population submodel. The supply side considers both land-based and water-based foods. Growth in the availability of arable land and in yields per acre are two critical supply parameters. The latter depends in turn on non-land inputs. Government policies affect food availability in two ways: indirectly by controlling the availability of non-land inputs and directly by decisions on import and export of food. The South East Asia model has been simulated under various assumptions concerning population growth, arable land availability and yields. Models for other regions are being constructed.

In addition to the causal stratum of the system, there are two more strata in the system: the organizational and the normative. The organizational or policy-making stratum interacts with the causal stratum in two ways. The first is called the interactive approach. Here the man-computer system works together to evaluate a set of policies. The decision makers monitor the environment, perceive policy options, and evaluate each of these with the help of the computer. A simplified sequence of operation is shown in Chart C•3. The second is called simulated norms approach. There will be situations in which the interactive imposition of norms and values will be inadequate. No single group of decision makers (interactors) can control policy making in the world model. There is thus a need to fully simulate the decision processes under circumstances in which no interactor makes policy.

Fairly general values are decided upon in the norms stratum. These lead to operating tools and then to policies in the organization stratum. Norms are altered by changes in environment or by changes in the causal stratum (e.g., increasing "dependence" on foreign sources of energy leads to increased investment in exploration for domestic sources). A simple block diagram of this approach is shown in Chart C•4.

Chart C•4
THE STRUCTURE OF THE NORMS-GUIDED DECISION PROCESS

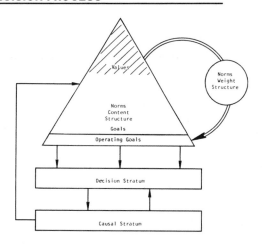

This completes a brief review of the CWR world model project. The work is continuing and many of the submodels described above will eventually be replaced by more sophisticated versions. In its present form, the model can be used in examining a wide variety of policy questions.

APPENDIX D

Description of the Financial Model

The financial model used in this project provides a means for forecasting the financial and operating characteristics of an electric utility company (or industry) for 20 years. It was originally developed for a company providing gas and steam service as well as electricity. When revised for industry calculations only electric service, with its associated costs and revenues, was considered. Included in the output for each of the 20 forecast years are: (1) a statement of electric operations; (2) an income statement; i.e., statement of all operations; (3) a balance sheet; (4) a

Chart D•1
SALES + OUTPUT STATISTICS • 1993

SALES + OUTPUT STATISTICS
1976.

	TOTAL SALES (MKWH/MMCF/MMLB)	TOTAL CUSTOMERS	SALES/CUSTOMER (KWH/MCF/MLB)	CENTS/UNIT SOLD (KWH/MCF/MLB)	TOTAL REVENUE (000)	DOLLARS/CUST
ELECTRIC						
RES–REGULAR						
RES–RATE RH						
SUB–TOTAL						
SMALL CCM & IND						
LARGE CCM & IND						
OTHER						
DISC REVENUE						
TOTAL						
GAS						
RESIDENTIAL						
HOUSE HEATING						
SMALL CCM & IND						
LARGE CCM & IND						
OTHER						
SUB–TOTAL						
INTERRUPTIBLE						
FIRM CONTRACT						
DISC REVENUE						
TOTAL						
STEAM						
DISC REVENUE						
TOTAL STEAM						

COPY OF A
COMPUTER
OUTPUT SHEET
WITH DATA
DELETED

OUTPUT

ELECTRIC(MMKWH)

GAS(MMCF)

STEAM(MMLB)

COPY OF A
COMPUTER
OUTPUT SHEET
WITH DATA
DELETED

SYSTEM DATA – ELECTRIC

OUTPUT(MMKWH)

LOAD FACTOR

PEAK(MW)

source and application of funds statement; (5) a capitalization statement; (6) a balance sheet items statement which lists certain details of the plant and depreciation accounts; and (7) a statement of sales and output statistics. Charts D•1 through D•7 illustrate the format and the level of detail available for each output statement.

The model programming is segmented into three routines which calculate: (1) sales and revenue statistics; (2) plant, depreciation and financing; and (3) operating expense and income items. Information is transferred from routine to routine within a given year, and from year to year. Within a given year an iterative procedure is employed to move from an initial estimate of tariffs to the tariffs necessary to achieve any desired return on common equity.

The versatility of the model is exemplified by its treatment of capital additions. The plant and depreciation routine accepts capital additions input in the form of service date and total direct cost for each project. Length of construction period and distribution of construction expenditures over the construction period can be specified separately for each project. This allows the user to establish different construction periods for nuclear plants than for fossil steam plants, for example. It also permits

construction expenditures to be spread evenly over the construction period or to be concentrated more heavily in the middle years of the construction period according to the user's best estimate of how expenditures will actually be sequenced.

The model calculates and cumulates allowance for construction funds on each project throughout its construction period, and transfers the accumulated amount to the plant account along with the direct cost when the plant goes into service. Once in service, the plant addition is depreciated at a rate specified in the input. Different rates can be applied to nuclear generation; to distribution; to fossil steam generation, etc. Both straight line and double declining balance tax depreciation calculations are made.

A set of flow charts of the model is included here as Charts D•8 through D•13.

It will be noted that the industry version of the model permits breaking tax deferrals into two segments, one of which can be normalized and the other "flowed-through." The proportionate size of the two segments can be varied from year to year. For the runs described in Chapter 10 a 50-50 split was assumed to characterize the industry in the initial years of the forecast period with the split moving gradually to an 80 percent normalized position in the 1980s.

Chart D•2
STATEMENT OF OPERATIONS-ELECTRIC[1] • 1993

ACTIVE CUSTOMERS
REVENUE SALES-MKWH
SALES PER CUSTOMER-MKWH

AMOUNT (000)   PCT.OF OPER.REV.

OPERATING REVENUE
  ELECTRIC SALES REVENUE
  FUEL CHARGE REVENUE
  STATE TAX ADJ REVENUE
  OPERATING REVENUE
  TOTAL ELEC.SALES REV.
  OTHER ELECTRIC REVENUE
TOTAL OPERATING REVENUE

OPERATING EXPENSES
  STM POW GEN-FUEL
           -OPER+MAINT
    SUB-TOTAL
  NUCLEAR GEN-FUEL
           -OPER+MAINT
    SUB-TOTAL
  PURCHASES
  INTERCHANGE
  OTHER
    SUB-TOTAL
  TRANSMISSION
  DISTRIBUTION
    SUB-TOTAL
  CUSTOMER ACCOUNTS
  SALES
  ADMINISTRATIVE+GENERAL
TOTAL OPER + MAINT
BALANCE AFTER OPER+MAINT
  DEPRECIATION - ST LINE
  WRITE-OFF OF TAX SAV-
    ING A/C OF LIB DEP
  AMORT-ANTI-TRUST STLMT
    SUB-TOTAL
PROVISION FOR TAXES
  FEDERAL INCOME
  STATE + LOCAL INCOME
  INVEST.TAX CREDIT ADJ.
  DEFERRED INC TAXES
INCOME TAXES
  CAPITAL STOCK
  GROSS RECEIPTS
  UNEMP.,AGE,TEL.
  STATE REAL ESTATE
  OTHER
NON-INCOME TAXES
TOTAL TAXES

TOTAL OPERATING EXPENSES
OPERATING INCOME
OPERATING INCOME CO
OPERATING INCOME SUBSID.
OTHER INCOME
  AFUDC
  INCOME TAX CREDITS
  OTHER INC OR DED - NET
INCOME DEDUCTIONS
  LONG TERM DEBT CHARGES
  INTEREST ON BANK LOANS
  OTHER
NET INCOME
DIVIDENDS ON PREF.STOCK
COMMON EARNINGS

COPY OF A COMPUTER OUTPUT SHEET WITH DATA DELETED

ELECTRIC GENERATION TABLE
1978.

MKWH   FUEL EXPENSE

ELECTRIC GENERATION

LESS:NET INTERCHANGE
  PUMPED STORAGE
  PURCH

  SUBTOTAL

  NUCLEAR

  FOSSIL

  RESIDUAL OIL
  INTERNAL COMBUSTION
  SYSTEM COAL
  MINE MOUTH COAL
  GAS

COPY OF A COMPUTER OUTPUT SHEET WITH DATA DELETED

[1] Similar statements are available for gas and steam operations.

Chart D•3
STATEMENT OF ALL OPERATIONS[1] • 1993

AMOUNT (000)   PCT. OF OPER.REV.

OPERATING REVENUE
  FUEL CHARGE REVENUE
  STATE TAX ADJUSTMENT
  ELECTRIC SALES
  GAS SALES
  STEAM SALES
  OTHER REVENUE
TOTAL OPERATING REVENUE

OPERATING EXPENSES
  ELECTRIC-PRODUCTION
          -TRANS + DIST
  GAS   -PROD + PURCH
          -DIST
  STEAM   -PROD + DIST
  ALL   -CUST ACCOUNTS
          -SALES
          -ADMIN + GEN
TOTAL OPER + MAINT
BALANCE AFTER OPER+MAINT

DEPRECIATION + AMORT
PROVISION FOR TAXES
  FEDERAL INCOME
  STATE + LOCAL INCOME
  INVEST.TAX CREDIT ADJ.
  DEFERRED INC TAXES
INCOME TAXES
  CAPITAL STOCK
  GROSS RECEIPTS
  UNEMP.,AGE,TEL.
  STATE REAL ESTATE
  OTHER
NON-INCOME TAXES
TOTAL TAXES
TOTAL OPERATING EXPENSES
OPERATING INCOME
OPERATING INCOME(SUBSID)
OTHER INCOME
  AFUDC
  INCOME TAX CREDITS
  OTHER INC OR DED - NET
INCOME DEDUCTIONS
  LONG-TERM DEBT CHARGES
  INTEREST ON BANK LOANS
  OTHER
TOTAL INCOME DEDUCTIONS
NET INCOME
DIVIDENDS ON PREFER STK
BALANCE FOR COMMON STK
DIVIDENDS ON COMMON STK
RETAINED EARNINGS

COMMON STOCK
  SHARES OUTSTANDING
  EARNINGS PER SHARE
  EARNINGS PER AVG SHARE
  DIVIDENDS PER SHARE

COPY OF A COMPUTER OUTPUT SHEET WITH DATA DELETED

[1] This statement combines electric, gas, and steam operations into a corporate (or industry) income statement.

335

Chart D•6

CAPITALIZATION • 1993

```
                                            RETAINED
                        1/1 BAL.    NEW    EARNINGS   12/31 BAL.
LONG-TERM DEBT
PREF. STOCK
COMM. STOCK
TOTAL
COMM.ST.SHARES
```

COPY OF A
COMPUTER
OUTPUT SHEET
WITH DATA
DELETED

```
SHORT-TERM DEBT
```

```
                                    RATIOS
                                    1978.

GROSS INCOME/NET PLANT (SYSTEM)(PER CENT)
NET PLANT/REVENUE (PECO)
GROSS PLANT/REVENUE (PECO)
ELEC REV/SALES (PECO)(C/KWH)
GAS  REV/SALES (PECO)(C/MCF)
STM  REV/SALES (PECO)(C/MLB)
```

Chart D•4

CONSOLIDATED BALANCE SHEET • 1993

```
ASSETS
UTILITY PLANT IN SERVICE
CONSTR. WORK IN PROGRESS
PLANT HELD FOR FUTURE USE
   TOTAL UTILITY PLANT
LESS:ACCUM PROV FOR DEPR
   TOTAL UTIL PLT LESS RESERVE
INVESTMENTS
CURRENT ASSETS:
   CASH
   TEMP CASH INVESTMENTS
   ACCOUNTS RECEIVABLE
   MATERIALS & SUPPLIES
   OTHER CURRENT & ACCRUED ASSETS
   POLLUTION CONTROL FUNDS
      TOTAL CURRENT ASSETS
DEFERRED DEBITS
   TOTAL ASSETS
```

COPY OF A
COMPUTER
OUTPUT SHEET
WITH DATA
DELETED

```
LIABILITIES
CAPITALIZATION:
   LONG-TERM DEBT
   PREFERRED STOCK
   COMMON STK EQUITY(INCL R.E.)
      TOTAL CAPITALIZATION
CURRENT LIABILITIES:
   BANK LOANS
   TAXES ACCRUED
   ACCOUNTS PAYABLE
   OTHER CURRENT LIABILITIES
      TOTAL CURRENT LIABILITIES
DEFERRED CREDITS:
   ACCUM DEF INCOME TAXES
   ACCUM DEF ITC
   OTHER DEFERRED CREDITS
      TOTAL DEFERRED CREDITS
OPERATING RESERVES
CONTR IN AID OF CONSTRUCTION
   TOTAL LIABILITIES
```

Chart D•7

BALANCE SHEET ITEMS • 1993

```
                          AMOUNT(000)
UTILITY PLANT
  PLANT AT ORIGINAL COST
     ELECTRIC
     GAS
     STEAM
     COMMON
     C.W.I.P.
     SUBSIDIARY PLANT
        TOTAL
LESS RESERVE FOR DEPR
  S/L PORTION OF RES
     ELECTRIC
     GAS
     STEAM
     COMMON
     SUBSIDIARY PLANT
        SUB-TOTAL
  SUPPLEMENTAL RES A/C
  LIBERALIZED DEPR
     ELECTRIC
     GAS
     STEAM
     COMMON
        SUB-TOTAL
        TOTAL DEPR RES
NET UTILITY PLANT -12/31
     ELECTRIC
     GAS
     STEAM
     COMMON
     C.W.I.P.
     SUBSIDIARY
        TOTAL
```

COPY OF A
COMPUTER
OUTPUT SHEET
WITH DATA
DELETED

Chart D•5

CONSOLIDATED STATEMENT OF
SOURCE AND APPLICATION OF FUNDS • 1993

```
SOURCE OF FUNDS

NET INCOME
CHARGES(CREDITS) TO INCOME NOT
  AFFECTING FUNDS
     DEPRECIATION
     INV.TAX CREDIT ADJ-NET
     DEFERRED INCOME TAXES
        FUNDS PROVIDED FROM OPNS
SALE OF:
     LONG-TERM DEBT
     PREFERRED STOCK
     COMMON STOCK
INCREASE(DECREASE) IN
     NOTES PAYABLE
        TOTAL
```

COPY OF A
COMPUTER
OUTPUT SHEET
WITH DATA
DELETED

```
APPLICATION OF FUNDS

ADDITIONS TO UTILITY PLANT
DIVIDENDS ON COMMON STOCK
DIVIDENDS ON PREFERRED STOCK
RETIREMENT OF LONG-TERM DEBT
OTHER
        TOTAL
```

Chart D•8
FIOSST (Sales and Operating Statistics)

Chart D•9
FIPREP (Depreciation Print Routine)

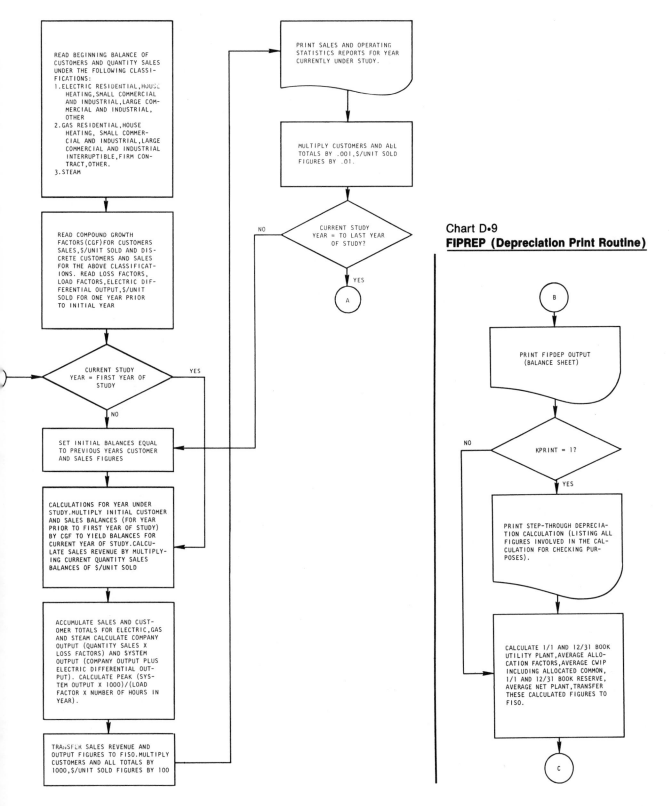

Chart D·10
FIPDEP (Depreciation and Plant)

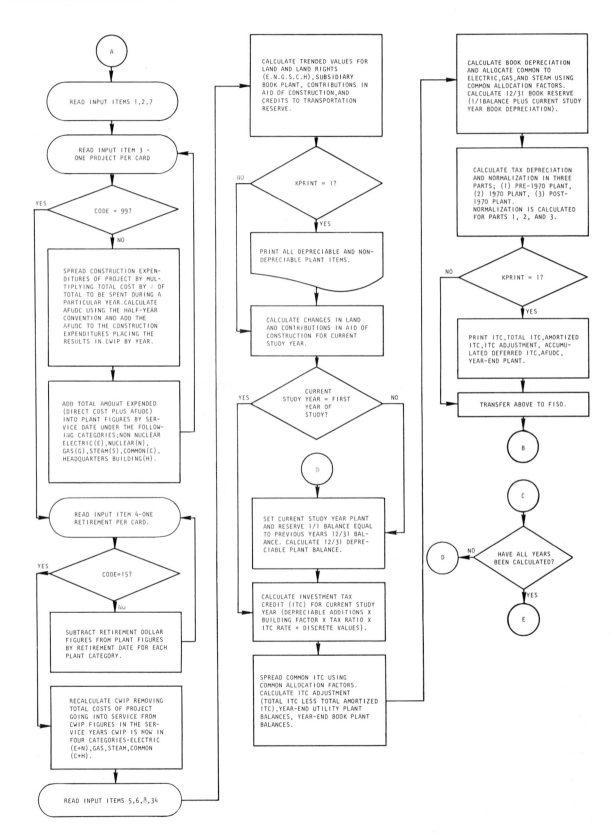

A

READ INPUT ITEMS 1,2,7

READ INPUT ITEM 3 - ONE PROJECT PER CARD

CODE = 99? — YES / NO

SPREAD CONSTRUCTION EXPENDITURES OF PROJECT BY MULTIPLYING TOTAL COST BY % OF TOTAL TO BE SPENT DURING A PARTICULAR YEAR. CALCULATE AFUDC USING THE HALF-YEAR CONVENTION AND ADD THE AFUDC TO THE CONSTRUCTION EXPENDITURES PLACING THE RESULTS IN CWIP BY YEAR.

ADD TOTAL AMOUNT EXPENDED (DIRECT COST PLUS AFUDC) INTO PLANT FIGURES BY SERVICE DATE UNDER THE FOLLOWING CATEGORIES: NON NUCLEAR ELECTRIC(E), NUCLEAR(N), GAS(G), STEAM(S), COMMON(C), HEADQUARTERS BUILDING(H).

READ INPUT ITEM 4-ONE RETIREMENT PER CARD.

CODE=15? — YES / NO

SUBTRACT RETIREMENT DOLLAR FIGURES FROM PLANT FIGURES BY RETIREMENT DATE FOR EACH PLANT CATEGORY.

RECALCULATE CWIP REMOVING TOTAL COSTS OF PROJECT GOING INTO SERVICE FROM CWIP FIGURES IN THE SERVICE YEARS CWIP IS NOW IN FOUR CATEGORIES-ELECTRIC (E+N), GAS, STEAM, COMMON (C+H).

READ INPUT ITEMS 5,6,8,34

CALCULATE TRENDED VALUES FOR LAND AND LAND RIGHTS (E.N.G.S.C.H), SUBSIDIARY BOOK PLANT, CONTRIBUTIONS IN AID OF CONSTRUCTION, AND CREDITS TO TRANSPORTATION RESERVE.

KPRINT = 1? — NO / YES

PRINT ALL DEPRECIABLE AND NON-DEPRECIABLE PLANT ITEMS.

CALCULATE CHANGES IN LAND AND CONTRIBUTIONS IN AID OF CONSTRUCTION FOR CURRENT STUDY YEAR.

CURRENT STUDY YEAR = FIRST YEAR OF STUDY? — YES / NO

D

SET CURRENT STUDY YEAR PLANT AND RESERVE 1/1 BALANCE EQUAL TO PREVIOUS YEARS 12/31 BALANCE. CALCULATE 12/31 DEPRECIABLE PLANT BALANCE.

CALCULATE INVESTMENT TAX CREDIT (ITC) FOR CURRENT STUDY YEAR (DEPRECIABLE ADDITIONS X BUILDING FACTOR X TAX RATIO X ITC RATE + DISCRETE VALUES).

SPREAD COMMON ITC USING COMMON ALLOCATION FACTORS. CALCULATE ITC ADJUSTMENT (TOTAL ITC LESS TOTAL AMORTIZED ITC), YEAR-END UTILITY PLANT BALANCES, YEAR-END BOOK PLANT BALANCES.

CALCULATE BOOK DEPRECIATION AND ALLOCATE COMMON TO ELECTRIC, GAS, AND STEAM USING COMMON ALLOCATION FACTORS. CALCULATE 12/31 BOOK RESERVE (1/1 BALANCE PLUS CURRENT STUDY YEAR BOOK DEPRECIATION).

CALCULATE TAX DEPRECIATION AND NORMALIZATION IN THREE PARTS; (1) PRE-1970 PLANT, (2) 1970 PLANT, (3) POST-1970 PLANT. NORMALIZATION IS CALCULATED FOR PARTS 1, 2, AND 3.

KPRINT = 1? — NO / YES

PRINT ITC, TOTAL ITC, AMORTIZED ITC, ITC ADJUSTMENT, ACCUMULATED DEFERRED ITC, AFUDC, YEAR-END PLANT.

TRANSFER ABOVE TO FISO.

B

C

HAVE ALL YEARS BEEN CALCULATED? — NO → **D** / YES

E

Chart D•11
FISO (Statement of Operations)

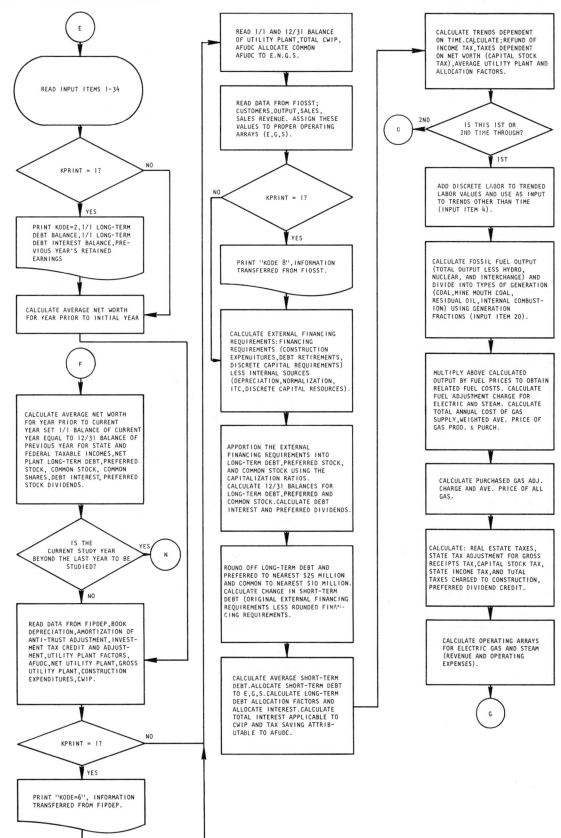

Chart D•11
FISO (Statement of Operations)

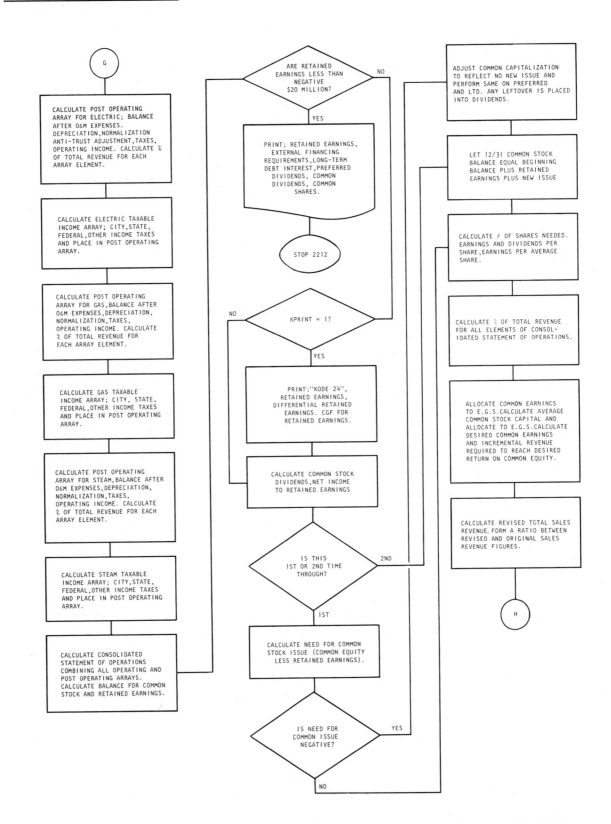

Chart D·11
FISO (Statement of Operations) (continued)

SOURCL
H

CALCULATE SOURCES AND USES OF FUNDS STATEMENT.

I

FIREPS
I

PRINT ELECTRIC STATEMENT OF OPERATIONS.

J

FIREPI
J

PRINT GAS STATEMENT OF OPERATIONS.

K

FIRES
K

PRINT STEAM STATEMENT OF OPERATIONS.

L

FIREPC
L

PRINT CONSOLIDATED STATEMENT OF ALL OPERATIONS.

CALCULATE AND PRINT CAPITAL-IZATION TABLE.

CALCULATE RATIOS-REV/SALES (E.G.S).GROSS INC/NET PLANT, GROSS PLANT/OP.REV.DEP. RESERVE/GROSS PLANT INT. COVERAGE RATIO.

PRINT OUT ABOVE RATIOS.

M

FISOR
M

PRINT SOURCES & USES OF FUNDS STATEMENT.

F

FISO STATEMENT OF OPERATIONS

N

IS THIS 1ST OR 2ND TIME THROUGH? — 2ND → END

1ST

MULTIPLY ORIGINAL $/UNIT SOLD FIGURES BY SALES REVENUE RATIO.

P

APPENDIX E

Productivity Measurement

1. Introductory Comments

The United States for many years has been justly proud of the efficiency with which it is able to produce a vast quantity and seemingly endless variety of material goods. United States productivity has been high. In addition to being a major contributing factor in making possible a high standard of living for the average citizen, high productivity has enabled the United States to export a variety of goods to foreign countries despite much higher labor costs on average in the United States than in most other countries.

Since the end of World War II, however, the nation's productivity advantages compared to other developed nations have been gradually shrinking. In part this has been due to the growth in foreign productivity made possible by the modern industrial plants built essentially from the ground up in Western Europe and Japan to repair the devastation caused by World War II. These new facilities generally incorporated the most modern technology available, often "exported" from the United States along with grants or loans which provided a significant fraction of the funds used to construct the new facilities. In competing with these new foreign factories it became more and more difficult for the United States manufacturers to support the high labor cost differentials between United States and foreign workers. Dollar devaluations in the last few years have once again made some of our products more competitive in international markets, yet the rate of productivity improvement remains a major source of concern in the United States, not only as it affects our competition with other exporting countries, but also as a measure of the rate of further improvements to be expected in our domestic living standards.

2. Measurement

When properly measured and interpreted, productivity can be an excellent indicator of the efficiency with which a society mobilizes its productive capacity toward producing a "more bountiful" life for its citizens. Like GNP, however, it is a purely quantitative measure of material output, unsuitable as a basis for making quality-of-life distinctions among various classes of production.

Productivity is generally measured as a ratio of physical output per unit of input; e.g., tons of aluminum per man-hour, or kilowatt hours per man-hour. The movements of such ratios over a period of time, rather than their absolute level at any given moment, are important pieces of evidence in the puzzle of how effectively society is developing and changing in a material sense. It is in this sense that productivity increases are often used in testing the economic soundness of wage changes.

The absolute levels of productivity—at a given moment—are important, of course, when the efficiency of one company's productive processes are being compared with another's, or when one nation's exporting potential is being judged in the world markets against a competitor nation.

3. Labor Productivity

Ease of measurement, as well as the predominance of labor input in many productive processes, has led to the use of some measure of labor input as the denominator of most productivity ratios. Labor interests have done nothing to discourage this technique of measuring productivity and, in fact, have sometimes maintained that there is no need to seek more refined techniques. A notable exception to the use of labor input as the criterion is in agriculture, where productivity is commonly measured in terms of output per acre as well as per man-hour.

One consequence of the emphasis on labor almost to the complete exclusion of other productive factors, has been the tendency to maintain that wage increases are non-inflationary so long as they do not exceed productivity increases in a given industry. However, to the extent that such productivity improvements derive from increases in capital or land input rather than from additional labor effort, the wage increases may be excessive. The inflationary impact of such wage increases occurs when product prices are raised to obtain some return for the owner of the incremental capital as well as to recover the increased wage costs. In some situations, essentially all of the improvement may be due to better plant and equipment with little or no necessary change in the intensity, the quality, or the quantity of the labor input.

In actuality, of course, in almost all significant productive processes in an industrialized nation, there are three major classes of input factors: land, labor, and capital, each of which contributes in some way to the production process, and each of whose contributions has been altered when overall productivity is seen to have been improved.

An ideal productivity measurement would permit the evaluation of the separate contributions of the various factors of production. Much excellent work has been done in the United States over the past 15 years to develop just such productivity measurements.[1]

4. Rate of Growth of Labor Productivity

An earlier study by Sumner Slichter[2] examined the information then available and concluded that the rate of productivity growth in the United States has been increasing over the long term, when measured in the conventional terms of output per manhour. He concluded that from 1800 to 1850 the annual rate of increase was close to ½ of 1 percent per year; from 1850 to 1900 it was perhaps 1.2 to 1.3 percent per year, and from 1900 to 1950 it was well over 2 percent per year. An examination of the post-World War II record suggests the current normal potential rate of improvement is in the range from 2.6 to 3.0 percent per year. Of course, to the extent that labor, capital goods, and land are being allocated in increasing amount to efforts that are not directly productive in a market sense (e.g.,

eliminating industrial pollutants from the air and water) the productivity improvement potential of the nation is reduced.

5. Factor Productivity

The more sophisticated productivity measurement techniques developed by Denison, Kendrick, Jorgenson and others are of great interest because of their usefulness in economic analysis. The following information is derived primarily from Commerce Department publications and from Denison's book, *Accounting for United States Economic Growth, 1929-1969.*

Both Gorman[3] and Denison measure changes in economic growth in terms of: (1) increases in total factor input; i.e., increases in the *amounts* of land, labor, and capital applied to productive efforts; and (2) increases in the *efficiency* of application. Total factor input is generally a composite of an index of labor input and one of capital input.[4] The labor input index is usually in terms of the number of man-hours worked, and the capital input index is in terms of the deflated dollar value of total useful plant and equipment. These two indices are combined by assuming that the relative shares of national income which have accrued to capital and labor over the last 20 years or so, are valid measurements of the relative importance of the two factors of production. This results in weighting factors of about 60-70 percent for labor and about 30-40 percent for capital. Changes in this weighted index of total factor input are then compared with changes in the deflated dollar value of total output. To the extent that total output is increasing faster than total factor input, there is said to be an increase in productivity.

This productivity increase can be allocated to labor and capital in one of several ways. The technique used in the DRI model is based on the development of a production function of the nature:

$$Q = A \times f(K,L)$$

where Q = real output (GNP)

A = index of total factor productivity

K = input of capital services

L = input of labor services

From this, the proportionate rate of change of real output can be written as:

$$\frac{\Delta Q}{Q} = \frac{\Delta A}{A} + S_K \frac{\Delta K}{K} + S_L \frac{\Delta L}{L}$$

where S_K and S_L are the shares of capital and labor in total income. A description of the methods used to derive total factor productivity and the shares of capital and labor is given by Christensen and Jorgenson.[5]

Using these methods over the period 1961-1972, the composition of United States economic growth was calculated by DRI as shown in Table E•1.

6. Components of Factor Productivity

In Denison's work, a more detailed breakdown of both

the total factor input and the productivity increases are presented. His analysis of the increases in *amounts* of labor permits him to segregate the effects of changing: education, age-sex distribution in the employment force, and hours per week, from the overall increase in numbers of employed persons. Similarly, the increases in the *amounts* of capital are separated into two classifications: (1) inventories and (2) structures and equipment.

In measuring the effect of increased *efficiencies;* i.e., changes in output per unit of input, Denison's analysis identifies the separate effects of: (1) advances in knowledge, (2) improved resource allocation, (3) economies of scale, and (4) other "irregular" factors. Table E•2, summarized from the Denison book, page 111, shows the relative importance of each one of these factors over the period from 1948 to 1969.

Over this period, the contributions to the average annual growth in national income were found to be: (1) advances in knowledge, 38.7 percent; (2) quantity of labor, 13.4 percent; (3) education of labor, 13.4 percent; (4) quantity of capital, 15.6 percent; (5) improvements in resource allocation, 10 percent; (6) economies of scale 13.7 percent; and (7) all others—4.8 percent.

To a significant degree, these results depend upon the measuring techniques chosen and upon some arbitrary breakdowns of factors which the author has developed. For example, the education effect is measured in accordance with average earnings differentials among persons who differ only with respect to their education levels. As another example, changes in output which result from

Table E•1
AVERAGE ANNUAL RATE OF UNITED STATES ECONOMIC GROWTH
(Percent)

Factor	Factor Growth	Factor Share	Contribution to Growth
Capital			
Increase in capital stock	2.8%	37%	1.04%
Increase in capital productivity	1.2	37	0.44
Labor			
Increase in man-hours	1.5	63	0.95
Increase in labor productivity	0.8	63	0.50
Total Factor Productivity			
Total			1.35
Total Economic Growth			4.28%

Table E•2
SOURCES OF GROWTH IN NATIONAL INCOME: 1948-1969
(Percent per Year)

Total Factor Input			
Labor			
Employment	0.84		
Hours	-0.22		
Age-sex composition	-0.12		
Education	0.50	1.00	
Capital			
Inventories	0.15		
Structures & Equipment	0.43	0.58	
Land		0.00	1.58
Output per Unit of Input			
Advances in Knowledge		1.44	
Improved Resource Allocation		0.37	
Economies of Scale		0.51	
Other (Irregular) Factors		-0.18	2.14
Total Increase in National Income			3.72

improvements in the *design* of capital goods are included as advances in knowledge rather than as improvements in capital.

FOOTNOTES

1. (a) Denison, E. F., *Accounting for United States Economic Growth, 1929 - 1969,* The Brookings Institution, Washington, D. C., 1974.
   (b) Kendrick, J. W., *Postwar Productivity Trends in the United States,* 1948-1969, Columbia University Press, New York, 1973.
   (c) U. S. Department of Commerce, "The Measurement of Productivity," *Survey of Current Business, Part II,* May 1972; a compilation of articles by E. F. Denison, D. W. Jorgensen and Z. Griliches.
2. Slichter, S. H., *Economic Growth in the United States, It's History, Problems and Prospects,* Louisiana State Univ. Press, 1961.
3. Gorman, J. A., "Non-financial Corporations: New Measures of Output and Input," *Survey of Current Business,* March 1972.
4. An example of the use of this type of productivity measurement is in the DRI model. See Chapter 6.
5. Christensen, L. R., and Jorgensen, D. W., "United States Real Product and Real Factor Input, 1929-1967," *Review of Income and Wealth,* March 1970.

APPENDIX F

Non-Fuel Minerals as a Limit to Growth

CONTENTS

1. Consumption and Supply of Metals in the United States

a. An Overview

The successful rise of the United States as an industrial and economic power must be credited to many favorable circumstances and conditions; one of those was the endowment of high quality, well-located metal and fuel deposits. These metal deposits first provided exports of ore and concentrates, but later were either consumed by the growing industrial complex for the manufacture of consumer and producer goods or were exported as refined metals. The amount of metals consumed by the United States industry has grown to impressive quantities. Consumption of refined metal for the major metals (plus a minor one, nickel) are tabulated in Table F·1. Steel, with a consumption of 162 million short tons, continues to dominate metals consumption both in terms of quantity, value, and economic importance to the economy. Aluminum has displaced copper as the second most heavily used metal, copper falling to the position of third. Examination of quantities of imports of the major metals relative to the quantities consumed indicates that with the exception of zinc, the United States in 1973 was not a heavy importer of refined metal. Those metals consumed in the greatest quantities were, for the greater part, refined domestically.

In terms of ultimate raw materials (ore) for smelting and refining, the import position of the United States in 1973 was less favorable in terms of self-sufficiency than is suggested by refined metal. Examination of Table F·2 indicates that the United States imported 39,300,000 tons of iron ore, 27.3 percent of the ore consumed in that year. The percentage of bauxite consumption that was imported

Table F·1
CONSUMPTION, PRODUCTION AND NET IMPORTS: REFINED MAJOR METALS IN 1973 (Thousands of Short Tons)

Metal	Consumption	Supply			Net Imports	Imports as Percent of Consumption
		Production				
		Total	Primary	Secondary		
Aluminum[1]	6,600	5,650	4,500	1,150	50	0.8%
Copper	2,350	2,190	1,830	360	31	1.4
Raw Steel[1]	162,000	151,000	151,000	[3]	12,000	7.4
Lead	1,550	1,400	755	645	165	10.6
Zinc[2]	1,520	576	500	76	593	39.0
Nickel	195	45.5	15.5	30	160	82.1

[1] Apparent consumption—does not account for changes in stocks.
[2] Slab zinc only.
[3] Not reported as steel from secondary materials.

Source: United States Bureau of Mines, "Commodity Data Summaries," Appendix I to *Mining and Minerals Policy*, 1974.

Table F·2

CONSUMPTION, PRODUCTION AND NET IMPORTS OF SELECTED METALLIC ORES IN 1973
(Thousands of Tons)

| Metal | Consumption | Supply | | Imports as Percent of Consumption |
		Production	Net Imports	
Iron (Long Tons)....................	142,800	88,000	39,300	27.3%
Chromite (Short Tons)	1,400	0	790	56.4
Manganese (Short Tons)......	1,900	0	1,540	81.1
Bauxite (Long Tons)	15,500	1,850	15,300	98.7

Source: United States Bureau of Mines, "Commodity Data Summaries," Appendix I to *Mining and Materials Policy,* 1974. Data on consumption is "apparent consumption" so that it does not account for changes in consumer stocks or Government stockpiles. The bauxite figures include 3.4 million long tons of imports of alumina and 10,000 tons of alumina exports.

was much greater, at 98.7 percent. Thus, in 1974, a considerable amount of the raw materials for the two most heavily used metals in the United States economy came from foreign sources. The full extent of the dependency of the United States iron and steel industry on foreign sources of ores is more fully appreciated by examination of the ferro alloys. Besides iron, these alloys require molybdenum, tungsten, manganese, chromium, and nickel. As indicated in Table F·1, 82.1 percent of the nickel consumed in the United States in 1974 was imported. Similarly 81.1 percent of the manganese ore and 56.4 percent of the chromite ore were imported. (See Table F·2.)

An examination of trends in the import position of the United States from 1950 to 1970 was made by the National Commission on Materials Policy.[1] Table F·3 reproduces the Commission's data. Examination of Table F·3 reveals a generally increasing dependency on foreign supplies from 1950-1970. There are notable exceptions to this rule, however, such as vanadium, lead and copper.

Heavy reliance on imports of metal raw materials is not in itself a serious situation, given that there is reasonable assurance that imports will not be interrupted or withheld, and given that there are no serious balance-of-payments effects. Experience with the recent oil embargo raises some concern over both provisional conditions for metals imported in large quantities. This concern is strengthened by assessments of future metal requirements, such as the projections made by the National Commission on Materials Policy. (See Table F·4.) Forecasts of metal requirements to the year 2000 indicate quantities ranging from about a 50 percent increase (cobalt, tin and mercury), to nearly a 700 percent increase (aluminum). With current heavy dependency on imported metals raw materials, does this mean nearly total dependency in 30 years? Before contemplating this question further, it is necessary to examine United States reserves and resources of metals, the components of growth in United States metals consumption, and the mineral position of the rest of the world.

Table F·3

CHANGING NET IMPORT REQUIREMENTS OF THE UNITED STATES
(Percent of Domestic Use)

Metal	1950	1960	1970
Iron Ore..................................	5%	25%	30%
Chromium	110	94	100
Cobalt	92	75	96
Columbium	100	100	100
Manganese	77	92	94
Nickel	99	88	91
Tungsten	80	40	*
Vanadium...............................	W	41	1
Aluminum (Bauxite)..............	71	77	86
Beryllium	89	96	W
Copper	35	9	8
Lead.......................................	59	59	40
Magnesium	0	1	0
Mercury..................................	92	36	38
Platinum.................................	91	95	98
Tin..	100	100	100
Titanium	32	30	47
Zinc	37	54	60

W - withheld for disclosure reasons.

* - stockpile transactions distort proportions.

Source: The National Commission on Materials Policy, *Material Needs and the Environment Today and Tomorrow,* 1973.

b. A More Critical Examination of Trends in Metals Consumption

Manufacturing consumes metals in the production of consumer and producer goods that are consumed by man. Thus, metal isn't consumed directly as is food. Nevertheless, consumption of metal on a per capita basis is examined as a means of neutralizing the population-growth effect.

Growth in consumption has two components:

1. A growing population.
2. An increased consumption per capita of metal products.

In order to examine the relative contribution of these two components, data available in literature on the value of per capita consumption of groups of metals and nonmetals for the period of 1902-1962 have been graphed in Chart F•1. During this period, United States population increased from 79.4 million to 186.7 million. Thus, a metal

Chart F•1

UNITED STATES PER CAPITA CONSUMPTION OF METALS

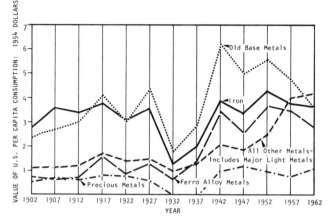

Source: Raw materials in the United States Economy: 1900-1966, United States Bureau of Census and United States Bureau of Mines, 1969.

Table F•4

INDUSTRIAL DEMAND FOR METALS IN THE UNITED STATES: 1970 AND 2000[1]

Metal	Consumption (Thousands of Short Tons)		Growth Rate (Percent per Year)
	1970	2000	
Iron (Millions of Short Tons)	116.9	220	2.1
Chromium	529	1,260	2.9
Manganese	1,327	2,360	1.8
Nickel	204.4	550	3.3
Tungsten	8.4	38.2	5.0
Aluminum	4,128	28,400	7.2
Copper (Total Demand)	2,820	9,700	4.2
Lead	1,335	2,730	2.4
Magnesium	1,156	2,770	2.9
Mercury (76-pound Flasks)	61,503	102,000	1.7
Platinum (Thousands of Troy Ounces)	516	1,295	3.1
Tin (Thousands of Long Tons)	73.1	130	1.9
Titanium	490	2,090	5.0
Zinc	1,374	3,200	3.0
Cobalt	8.1	12.6	1.5
Columbium	2.5	9.6	4.5
Vanadium	7.1	31.0	5.0
Beryllium	.38	1.8	5.3

[1] Industrial demand = apparent primary demand plus secondary recovery.

Source: The National Commission on Materials Policy, *Material Needs and the Environment Today and Tomorrow,* 1973.

Chart F•2
UNITED STATES PER CAPITA CONSUMPTION OF LIGHTWEIGHT METALS

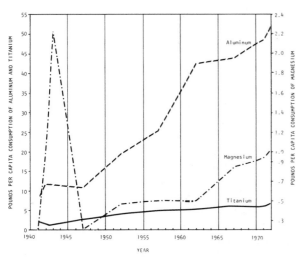

Source: Minerals Yearbook, United States Bureau of Mines, except for 1972 magnesium consumption, Engineering and Mining Journal, March, 1973, 1974.

Note: Data are 5 year averages, except for ends of series, which are single year figures, except for Titanium, 1942-1943 midyear, a 4 year average and Aluminum, 1943, a three year average.

Chart F•3
UNITED STATES PER CAPITA CONSUMPTION OF COPPER, LEAD, AND ZINC

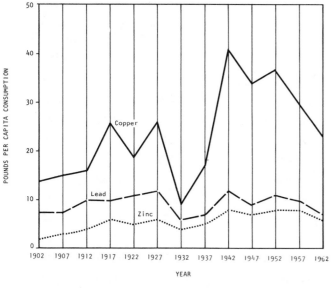

Source: Raw Materials in the United States Economy; 1900-1966, United States Bureau of Census and United States Bureau of Mines, 1969.

that shows no growth in per capita consumption over this period has increased in absolute consumption by a factor of 2.35.

Apart from the cyclical nature typical of economic time series and the decrease in consumption attendant to the Great Depression of the 1930s, Chart F•1 shows that growth in per capita iron consumption is very minor. Old base metals and precious metals show only a slight long-term growth, but two categories of metals show a considerable increase in per capita consumption. These are: all other metals and ferro alloy metals. The catch-all class of all other metals has increased in particular. In order to examine the source of the strong growth in per capita consumption of all other metals, per capita consumption was graphed for the lightweight metals, aluminum, magnesium, and titanium, which are included in this class, Chart F•2. This chart shows the striking growth in per capita consumption of aluminum from less than 9 pounds in 1941 to approximately 52.5 pounds in 1972, a multiple of approximately 5. Considering that population increased by a factor of about 1.4 during this period, total consumption of aluminum increased by a factor of approximately 7.0.

Ignoring the anomalous consumption of magnesium during World War II, magnesium also exhibits a growth trend in per capita consumption, not as rapid as that for aluminum but still a strong trend. On the other hand, the trend in per capita titanium consumption shows a very slow growth.

Per capita consumption for metals of the old base metals group—copper, lead, and zinc—are shown in Chart F•3. From this chart, it can be seen that the trend to growth of the old base metals was primarily due to copper during the period 1902-1962. However, the decline in per capita consumption since 1942 raises the question as to the continuance of the overall upward trend. Similar comments apply to lead and zinc, with the exception that lead shows less growth than zinc, and the time series for zinc implies a more stable market.

Including per capita consumption of recent years confirms the suggestion of Chart F•3, that since the 1940s per capita consumption of copper, lead, and zinc follows a declining trend. Per capita consumption data for some metals were computed for selected years, including 1971. (See Table F•5.) From these data growth rates were computed. From Table F•5, it can be seen that per capita consumption of copper from 1929-1971 increased at a rate of only .71 percent as compared to 3.25 percent for 1903-1929 and 1.63 percent for 1903-1971. Similarly, the growth rate in per capita consumption of lead was 1.71 percent for 1903-1929; .75 percent for 1903-1971, and approximately 0 percent for 1929-1971.

The high growth rate in per capita consumption for aluminum, molybdenum, and nickel for 1929-1971, 7.0 percent, 6.23 percent, and 2.00 percent respectively, contrast markedly with the low ones for lead and copper.

Based upon data on industrial demand reported in the first interim report of the National Commission on Materials Policy, growth rates for per capita consumption were calculated for the 1951-1970 period. (See Table F•6.)

347

Table F·5

PER CAPITA CONSUMPTION OF SELECTED METALS: QUANTITIES AND GROWTH RATE; 1903-1971.

Metal*	Consumption (Pounds per Capita)			Growth Rate (Percent per Year)		
	1903	1929	1971	1903-29	1929-1971	1903-1971
Aluminum............	NA	2.87	49.0	—	7.00	—
Copper...............	6.51	14.50	19.50	3.25	0.71	1.63
Lead...................	7.42	11.55	11.99	1.71	Approx. 0	.75
Molybdenum.......	Negligible	.02	.19	—	6.23	—
Nickel.................	.42	.66	1.50	1.75	2.00	1.88

* Data for copper refer to consumption of refined metal. Aluminum and nickel data are for apparent consumption; i.e., figures are not corrected to remove effects of changes in inventories. Lead and molybdenum figures refer to metal consumed in concentrate form.

Sources: Data for 1903 are from Neal Potter and Francis Christy, *Trends in Natural Resource Commodities*, Resources of the Future, Johns Hopkins University Press, Baltimore, 1962. Data for 1929 and 1971 are from various issues of United States Bureau of Mines, *Minerals Yearbook* and from the National Commission on Materials Policy, *Material Needs and the Environment Today and Tomorrow*, 1973.

The data in Table F·3 for the more recent time period (1950-1970) confirm the negative growth rates in per capita consumption of copper, lead, and zinc indicated in Chart F·1 for 1947-1962. Additionally, these data show that iron has the largest of all negative rates of growth. Since the main use of manganese is in the production of steel and ferro alloys, it is hardly surprising that its per capita rate of growth is also negative. As one might suspect from previous discussion, the metals exhibiting the highest positive rates of growth in per capita consumption are lightweight metals, aluminum and titanium, followed closely by nickel. The negative growth rate in per capita magnesium consumption during this period contrasts with the high positive rates for the other lightweight metals, aluminum and titanium.

2. Consumption and Supply of Metals for the Rest of the World

a. General

The rest of the world is considered to consist of two blocks of countries: developed countries exclusive of United States, and developing countries. Whenever the term developed countries is used in this section, it is to be understood that the United States is excluded. Data in this section are primarily drawn from various "Metall-gezelshaft" publications.

b. Aluminum

The time series of consumption for the period of 1950-1972 exhibits a nonlinear, exponential-type trend for both

Table F·6

PER CAPITA INDUSTRIAL DEMAND OF SELECTED METALS: QUANTITIES AND GROWTH RATES, 1951-1970

Metal	Consumption (Pounds per Capita)		Growth Rate (Percent per Year)
	1951	1970	1951-1970
Iron	1342.8	1124.4	-.91
Chromium...............	4.0	5.08	1.25
Manganese.............	13.35	12.76	-.25
Nickel......................	1.35	1.96	2.0
Tungsten.................	.073	.080	.52
Aluminum	12.89	39.69	6.0
Copper....................	28.18	27.11	-.25
Lead........................	13.91	12.83	-.42
Magnesium	12.29	11.11	-.58
Zinc........................	13.78	13.21	-.25
Titanium..................	3.0	4.71	2.4

Source: The National Commission on Materials Policy, *Interim Report*, 1972.

Table F•7
ALUMINUM STATISTICS

	Developed Countries			Developing Countries		
	Quantity (Thousands of Metric Tons)		Percent Growth	Quantity (Thousands of Metric Tons)		Percent Growth
	1950	1972		1950	1972	
Consumption....................	700	5,778.9	10.1	61	1,463	15.6
Metal in Ore......................	2015	28,493	12.8	5,047	38,383	9.7
Refined Metal...................	840	6,435	9.7	15	1,326	22.6
Scrap..............................	205	1,339	8.9	3	62	4.7

Source: Metallgezelshaft

the developed and developing countries. (See Chart F•4.) The salient features of this series are summarized in Table F•7. Although consumption in 1972 was 5,778.9 thousands of metric tons for the developed countries, as compared to only 1,463 thousands of metric tons for the developing countries, the rate of growth of consumption was greatest for the developing countries, 15.6 percent compared to 10.1 percent.

Although the quantity of metal in mine production of developing countries exceeded in 1972 that of developed countries, the rate of growth in mine production was highest for the developed countries, 12.8 percent compared

Chart F•5
MINE PRODUCTION AND REFINED METAL PRODUCTION OF ALUMINUM

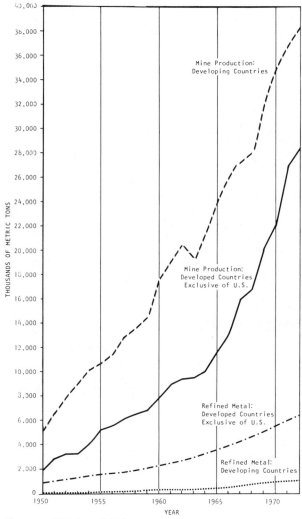

Source: Metallgezelshaft

Chart F•4
ALUMINUM CONSUMPTION

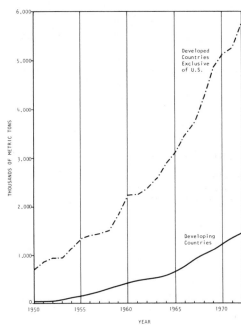

Source: Metallgezelshaft

to 9.7 percent. (See row titled "Metal in Ore" in Table F•7.) Conversely, although the production of refined metal was greatest for developed countries, the rate of growth in production of refined metal was greatest for the developing countries, a high 22.6 percent compared to only 9.7 percent. (See Chart F•5 and Table F•7.)

c. Copper

The consumption series for copper exhibits trends that are approximately linear, having average rates of growth of 5.4 percent and 7.6 percent for the developed and developing countries, respectively. (See Chart F•6 and Table F•8.) Of course, the magnitude of consumption of copper by developed countries far exceeds that of the developing countries, by a multiple of approximately 5. On the other hand, the quantities of metal in ore produced in 1972 were nearly the same for both blocks of countries, although the rate of growth was highest for the developed countries, 6.0 compared to 4.8 percent. (See also Chart F•7.) Production of refined metal by the developed countries in 1972 was double that of developing countries, however, the rates of growth were nearly the same. Overall, the rates of growth in copper consumption and production are about half that for aluminum. That the rates are lower is of no surprise, for substitution of aluminum for copper is taking place both in established markets of developed countries and in new markets of developing economies.

d. Lead

The time series of consumption of lead in developed countries exhibits an essentially linear pattern, while that for developing countries exhibits a slight nonlinearity. (See Chart F•8.) Growth rates of consumption in developed and developing countries (Table F•9) averaged 4.3 and 7.8 percent, respectively. The trend in mine production of lead in developed countries appears essentially linear, while that for developing countries shows an initial sharp increase followed by a leveling off of production. (See Chart F•9.) Average rates of growth in mine production for the developed and developing countries were 4.0 percent and 3.4 percent, respectively. The trends in refined metal parallel those of mine production, except that for developed countries refined metal production exceeds mine

Chart F•6
COPPER CONSUMPTION

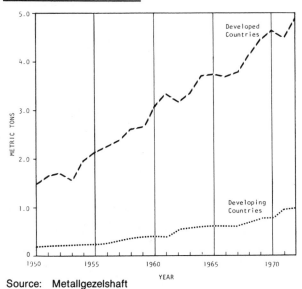

Source: Metallgezelshaft

Chart F•7
MINE PRODUCTION AND COPPER PRODUCTION OF REFINED METAL

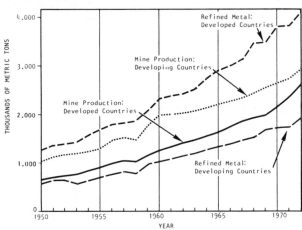

Source: Metallgezelshaft

Table F•8
COPPER STATISTICS

	Developed Countries			Developing Countries		
	Quantity (Thousands of Metric Tons)		Percent Growth	Quantity (Thousands of Metric Tons)		Percent Growth
	1950	1972		1950	1972	
Consumption	1524	4890	5.4	193	971	7.6
Metal in Ore	660	2609	6.0	1040	2934	4.8
Refined Metal	1274	4077	5.4	568	1930	5.7
Scrap	238	407	2.4	40	188	7.3

Source: Metallgezelshaft

Chart F•8
LEAD CONSUMPTION

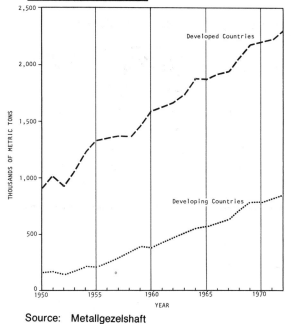

Source: Metallgezelshaft

production; the opposite relationship prevails for developing countries.

e. Zinc

The time series of consumption for zinc exhibit nonlinear trends, having average growth rates of 5.3 percent, and 9.1 percent for developed and developing countries, respectively. (See Chart F•10 and Table F•10.) Although the rate of growth of consumption for developing countries is nearly twice that for the developed countries, the magnitude of consumption in the latter is approximately three times the former (3199 thousand metric tons compared to 957 thousand metric tons).

The time series for mine production and refined metal production for developed countries follow each other so closely that they overlap, except towards the end of the

series. (See Chart F•11.) Both are increasing at similar rates, 5.5 and 6 percent, and both exhibit an exponential-like trend. On the other hand, the trends in these two series for developing countries tend to linearity. Average rates of growth across this period are 4.8 and 7.5 percent for mine production and refined metal respectively. Although the growth rate is higher for refined metal in developing countries than in developed ones, the magnitude of production is far greater in developed countries, 3753 compared to 985. (See Table F•10.)

f. Iron and Steel

Consumption of crude steel in developed countries increased from 83,264 thousands of metric tons in 1950 to 334,023 thousands of metric tons in 1971, or at the annual

Chart F•9
**MINE PRODUCTION AND REFINED METAL
PRODUCTION OF LEAD**

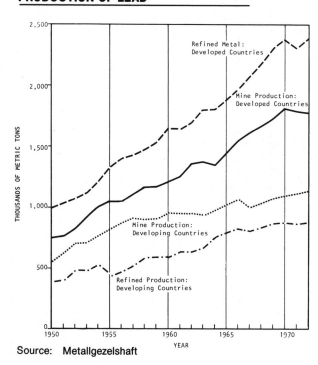

Source: Metallgezelshaft

Table F•9
LEAD STATISTICS

	Developed Countries			Developing Countries		
	Quantity (Thousands of Metric Tons)		Percent Growth	Quantity (Thousands of Metric Tons)		Percent Growth
	1950	1972		1950	1972	
Consumption	913	2,289	4.3	162	842	7.8
Metal from Mine Production	753	1,774	4.0	542	1138	3.4
Refined Metal	990	2,386	4.1	388	877	3.8
Scrap	278	361	1.2	255	495	3.1

Table F·10
ZINC STATISTICS

| | Developed Countries | | | Developing Countries | | |
| | Quantity (Thousands of Metric Tons) | | Percent Growth | Quantity (Thousands of Metric Tons) | | Percent Growth |
	1950	1972		1950	1972	
Consumption	1020	3199	5.3	141	957	9.1
Metal in Ore	1018	3285	5.5	626	1765	4.8
Refined Metal	1032	3753	6.0	202	985	7.5
Scrap	230	337	1.8	75	120	2.2

Source: Metallgezelshaft

Chart F·10
ZINC CONSUMPTION

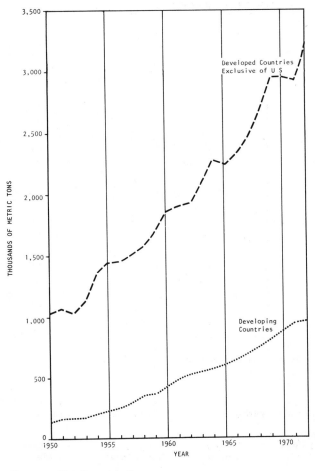

Source: Metallgezelshaft

Chart F·11
MINE PRODUCTION AND REFINED METAL PRODUCTION OF ZINC

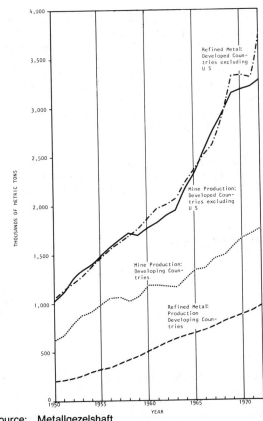

Source: Metallgezelshaft

rate of growth of 6.8 percent. Consumption in developing countries was at considerably lower levels, 9,687 and 105,314 thousands of metric tons. However, the rate of growth in consumption was higher; i.e., 12 percent. (See Chart F•12 and Table F•11.)

The trends in mine and pig iron production, like that of consumption are of an exponential form. (See Chart F•13.) Throughout the series for developed countries, the production of pig iron exceeded that of metal in mine production. Mine production in developed countries increased from 55,841 thousands of metric tons in 1950 to 235,416 thousands of metric tons in 1971, an annual rate of growth of 7.1 percent. Mine production in developing countries was 10,753 and 140,577 thousands of metric tons; giving a high rate of growth of 13 percent. Pig iron production increased from 64,653 to 289,164 thousands of metric tons and from 8,836 to 72,259 thousands of metric tons for developed and developing countries, respectively, yielding growth rates of 7.4 percent and 10.5 percent. Production of crude steel exhibits similar trends (exponential form), increasing from 89,704 thousands of metric tons to 382,198 thousands of metric tons and from 11,748 to 83,598 thousands of metric tons for developed and developing countries, respectively, yielding growth rates of 7.1 percent and 9.8 percent. (See Chart F•14.)

g. Secondary Metal

From Table F•12, it can be seen that from 1951 to 1971 the amount of metal from scrap (secondary metal) has increased for all metals in both developing and developed countries. Note that throughout this section the data on scrap for developed countries do not include scrap from the Soviet Union. The increase in use of lead, zinc and copper scrap by developed countries has been moderate over the period 1951 to 1971, ranging approximately from 25 to 83 percent of the 1951 quantity. With regard to aluminum, this increase in developed countries has been much larger than for the other metals, an increase of about 500 percent. The increase in production of secondary copper, lead, and zinc for developing countries ranged from approximately 50 percent to 330 percent over the same time period. In the case of aluminum, the increased production from scrap in 1971 was approximately 1600 percent of production from scrap in 1951. (See Charts F•15, F•16, F•17, and F•18.)

The production of secondary metal as a percentage of consumption decreased in developed as well as developing

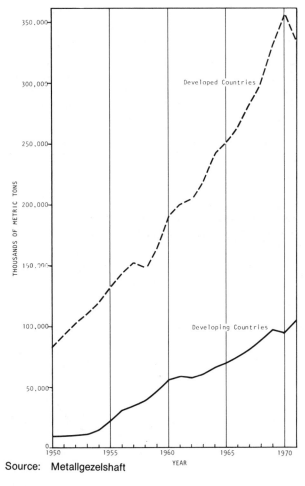

Chart F•12
CONSUMPTION OF CRUDE STEEL

Source: Metallgezelshaft

| Table F•11 | Developed Countries | | | Developing Countries | | |
| **IRON AND STEEL STATISTICS** | Quantity (Thousands of Metric Tons) | | Percent Change | Quantity (Thousands of Metric Tons) | | Percent Change |
	1950	1971		1950	1971	
Consumption	83,264	334,023	6.8	9,687	105,314	12
Metal in Ore	55,841	235,416	7.1	10,753	140,577	13
Pig Iron	64,653	289,164	7.4	8,836	72,259	10.5
Steel	89,704	382,198	7.1	11,748	83,598	9.8

Source: Metallgezelshaft

countries over this time period, with the exception of copper for developing countries, which stayed the same. Similarly secondary aluminum as a percentage of aluminum consumption in developed countries decreased only by one percentage point, and that for developing countries by less than one percentage point. Thus, in the case of aluminum the relationship appears remarkably stable for each of the blocks of countries. However, the magnitude of the percentage for developed countries is approximately five times that for developing countries.

For metals other than aluminum, this pattern is reversed, the percentage of consumption comprised by secondary metal production being greater for developing than for developed countries.

The National Commission on Materials Policy has estimated the percentage of total comsumption of specific metals which was derived from recycled materials in the United States in 1967. It is interesting to compare these figures for the United States with the data on Table F•12. For the United States the percentages of consumption from recycling were: copper, 49.7 percent; lead, 49.6 percent; zinc, 12.6 percent; and aluminum, 18.3 percent. With regard to copper and lead, the secondary metal production in the United States was a much greater percentage of 1967

Chart F•13
MINE PRODUCTION AND PIG IRON AND FERRO ALLOY PRODUCTION OF IRON

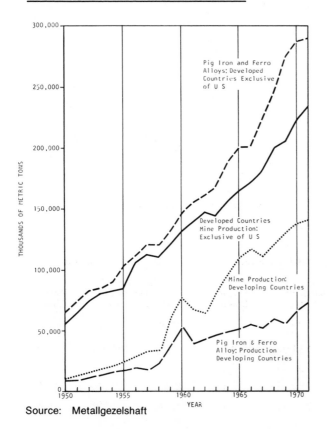

Source: Metallgezelshaft

Chart F•14
CRUDE STEEL PRODUCTION OF IRON AND STEEL

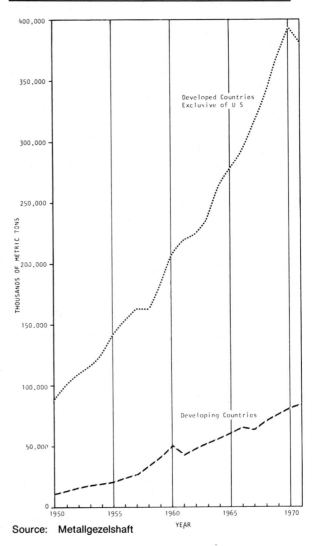

Source: Metallgezelshaft

Chart F•15
SCRAP ZINC PRODUCTION

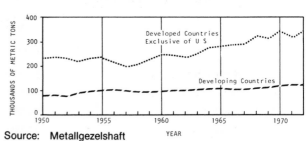

Source: Metallgezelshaft

Table F·12

SECONDARY METAL PRODUCTION IN DEVELOPED AND DEVELOPING COUNTRIES—1951 AND 1971

Metal	1951		1971	
	Quantity (Thousands of Metric Tons)	Consumption (Percent)	Quantity (Thousands of Metric Tons)	Consumption (Percent)
Aluminum				
Developed............................	205.5	24	1250.2	23
Developing..........................	3.5	5	58.3	4.3
Lead				
Developed............................	279.2	29	349.4	16
Developing..........................	238.2	146	502.5	61
Copper				
Developed............................	238.1	15	435.3	9
Developing..........................	45	21	195.3	21
Zinc				
Developed............................	234.3	23	331.5	11
Developing..........................	78.7	50	120	13

Source: All data are from *Metallgezelschaft*. Data are for three year averages: 1950, 1951, and 1952; and 1970, 1971, and 1972. Developed country data exclude United States production. Scrap figures for the Soviet Union are not included.

Chart F·16
ALUMINUM PRODUCTION FROM SCRAP

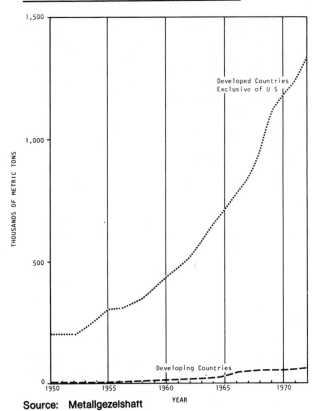

Source: Metallgezelshaft

Chart F·18
LEAD PRODUCTION FROM SCRAP

Source: Metallgezelshaft

Chart F·17
COPPER PRODUCTION FROM SCRAP

Source: Metallgezelshaft

355

consumption than it was in the other developed countries in 1971, and in the case of copper greater than developing countries. Recycling of zinc appears to be approximately the same in the United States in 1967 as it was in developing and developed countries in 1971. Of course, recycling of aluminum was a smaller percentage of consumption in the United States in 1967 than it was for other developed countries in 1971, but much greater than that for developing countries.

3. Reserves, Resources, and Crustal Abundance

a. *Terminology*

An understanding of the usage of the terms reserves and resources is necessary for a clear picture of potential metal supplies. Reserves are not an absolute, but a variable. *A reserve of ore is a quantity of material from which a metal can be mined and extracted at a profit.* Such a definition embodies two basic concepts: 1) the occurrence of metalized rock within the earth's crust (metal endowment), and 2) the discovery and profitable extraction of the ore from the ground and the metal from the concentrate or ore. Consequently, reserves are a function of economic variables as well as a reflection of natural endowment. As prices and technology change, reserves are constantly being redefined. Thus, reserves exist at a point in time and under specified conditions.

In addition to reflecting favorable economics, the term reserves implies that the deposit has been well sampled, sufficiently so that the quantity and quality (grade) can be estimated with some degree of reliability. Categories of reserves are recognized by virtue of the completeness of sampling of the deposit.

For example, one classification designates proved, probable, and possible categories, the proved having been sampled in three dimensions, probable in two, and possible in one. Another classification designates measured, indicated, and inferred categories, with measured reserves corresponding to proved reserves but also requiring that tonnage and grade can be estimated with less than 20 percent error.

A resource is a quantity of rock material that is metalized and has been explored and evaluated but from which metal cannot be profitably produced. A resource is also a hypothetical deposit that could be exploited economically but has not been located. Modifiers of the term, resources, are often used to differentiate material within the resource category. These modifiers are: *identified resources,* i.e., deposits that are known and evaluated but uneconomic; *hypothetical resources,* i.e., deposits believed to exist in areas of known reserves, but are not themselves known; *speculative resources,* i.e., deposits that are inferred from generally favorable geologic conditions; and *conditional resources,* i.e., deposits that are known but not economic.

While reserves and resources refer to accumulations of metals in deposits under specified conditions, *crustal abundance* of a metal is a much more general concept and refers to the concentration of a metal in the earth's crust, or some portion thereof, not to an absolute quantity of metal. A measure often used as a description of crustal abundance is the *Clarke,* which is referred to as the average concentration of a metal in the crust of the earth, usually expressed as a percentage.

b. *Reliability of Stated Reserves and Resources*

Man is continuing to make new discoveries about the ways metal deposits are formed and the environments favorable to their occurrence. For example, not many years ago, little thought was given to the possible occurrence of large stratabound copper deposits. Now, the copper deposits of Zaire and Zambia alone make up 15 percent of the world's identified resources, and enormous deposits are known in the U. S. S. R.[2] About 5 percent of United States copper production comes from a stratabound copper deposit in the White Pine district of Michigan, and stratabound copper deposits occur in Precambrian rocks of Western Montana and adjacent parts of Idaho.

Resource studies often rely upon published data for numerical estimates of quantity and quality of reserves. It is important to realize that these data often are understated. The measures of reserves published by mining companies are sometimes not a true measure of the actual reserves that are present. It has been stated by one industry expert (Personal Communications, **COMRATE** Colloquim on Copper Resources) that reserve figures for some of the large porphgy copper deposits of the Western United States and Chile are understated by as much as a factor of 10.

At any given point in time, we have only a rough estimate of reserves and resources. Even for a given mode of occurrence and in areas that have been mined for an extended time, there exist deposits that have been passed over and will be found at a later date. Furthermore, as economic variables and technology change, reserves and potential reserves are created. Add to this the fact that deposits probably exist in new, unexplored environments and a case can be made for exercising caution in predicting either the exhaustion of metal resources or that a nation's affluence is in jeopardy because of depletion of metal reserves and resources.

With the foregoing serving as a caution, an examination can be made of the reserve position of the United States today with respect to selected metals.

c. *Known Reserves and Resources Compared to Current and Projected Requirements*

Reserve and resource estimates for metals and nonmetals were prepared by The National Commission on Materials Policy. Some of its estimates are provided in Table F•13. The reserve estimates have been divided by 1973 production and by 1973 consumption to give two measures of the duration of these stated reserves.

(1) Ferro Alloys

Perhaps the feature of Table F•13 that is first to catch the eye is the status of the three ferro alloy metals —manganese, nickel, and chromium—for which reserves are nonexistent. In the case of manganese there are large

Table F·13
RESERVES AND RESOURCES OF SELECTED METALS

| | | | Life of Reserves | | | |
| | | | | | Resources* | |
Metal	Reserves At 1971 Prices	Probable Cumulative Mineral Demand: 1970-2000	Based Upon 1973 Mine Production	Based Upon 1973 Consumption, Including Secondary Metal	Identified	Hypothetical
(Millions of Short Tons)						
Aluminum	13	370	31	4	Very Large	KDI
Chromium................................	—	19	0	0	Insignificant	Insignificant
Copper..	81	93	47	34	Large	Large
Iron	2,000	3,000	39	24	Very Large	Huge
Lead..	17	34	28	11	Large	Moderate
Manganese...............................	—	50	0	0	Large	KDI
Titanium....................................	33	32	120	67	Very Large	Very Large
Zinc...	30	62	63	20	Very Large	Very Large
(Millions of Pounds)						
Molybdenum	6,000	3,000	54	100	Huge	Huge
Nickel..	—	14,000	0	0	Large	KDI
Tungsten...................................	175	1,000	22	10	Moderate	Moderate
(Millions of Troy Ounces)						
Gold..	82	293	67	11	Large	KDI
Silver..	1,300	4,400	35	7	Moderate	Large
(Thousands of Flasks)						
Mercury	75	1,730	34	1	Small	KDI

* Identified resources are defined as including reserves and materials other than reserves which are essentially well known as to location, extent and grade and which may be exploitable in the future under more favorable economic conditions or with improvements in technology.

Hypothetical resources are undiscovered, but geologically predictable deposits of materials similar to identified resources.

Resource Appraisal Terms are as follows:

Huge — Domestic resources are greater than 10 times Minimum Anticipated Cumulative Demand (MACD) between 1971 and 2000.

Very Large — Domestic resources are 2 to 10 times the MACD

Large — Domestic reserves are approximately 75 percent to twice MACD.

Moderate — Domestic reserves are approximately 35 to 75 percent of the MACD.

Small — Domestic reserves are approximately 10 to 35 percent of MACD.

Insignificant — Domestic resources are less than 10 percent of MACD.

KDI — Known Data Insufficient. Resources are not estimated because of insufficient geological knowledge of surface or subsurface area.

Sources: Data for mine production and consumption are from the U. S. Bureau of Mines, "Commodity Data Summaries," Appendix 1 to *Mining and Minerals Policy*, 1974. Data on reserves are from The National Commission on Materials Policy, *Material Needs and the Environment Today and Tomorrow*, 1973. Data for tungsten mine production and consumption are from The Department of Commerce, *Statistical Abstract of the United States*, 1973. Estimates of probable cumulative primary mineral demand from 1971 to 2000 are adapted from U. S. Bureau of Mines forecasts.

Mine production of aluminum is based on domestic mine production of bauxite and the assumption of 20 pounds of aluminum per 100 pounds of bauxite. Consumption of aluminum in 1973 is based upon an estimate of the aluminum in the bauxite consumed. Iron ore data was converted to iron by assuming that ore contained 51.5 percent iron on average. Zinc consumption in 1973 was based on slab zinc data.

identified resources. However, the National Materials Policy Commission (NMPC) has estimated that a four-fold price increase would be necessary to transform these resources into reserves. World reserves have been estimated to be 3.8 billion tons of ore, with an additional 15 billion tons of potential reserves. The United States Bureau of Mines' (B/M) estimate of reserves is somewhat smaller than that of NMPC, being only 1.5 billion tons, but still considered sufficient to meet cumulative world requirements for the rest of the century.[3] Of this 1.5 billion tons, 860 million are held by Free World countries: Brazil, 110 million; Gabon, 220 million; India, 25 million; South Africa, 1125 million; and other Free World countries, 380 million. According to B/M statistics, 35 percent of United States imports are currently derived from Gabon, 33 percent from Brazil, 7 percent from South Africa, 7 percent from Zaire, and 18 percent from other countries. With large world reserves and approximately 60 percent of these reserves held by Free World countries, foreign supplies appear reasonably secure and sufficient for quite some time. In the long, long term, recovery from extensive deposits of sea nodules may provide an economic supply of manganese.

Short term security from disruptions in supply are provided by the United States stockpile program. For example, it contains about 4 million tons of metallurgical ore, which is about a two-year supply. Additionally, quantities of ferro-manganese, silicomanganese, manganese metal, and battery and chemical grade ores are held in reserve.

Although domestic reserves of nickel are negligible, e.g., about 200,000 tons under current prices, NMPC has estimated that a 50 percent increase in nickel price would transfer approximately 5 million tons of domestic identified resources to reserves. This quantity is equal to approximately 70 percent of the cumulative requirements to 2000 forecast by B/M. According to B/M estimates, known world reserves at present prices are about 46.2 million tons of nickel, of which 32 million are held by Free World countries in the following amounts:

United States.........................	200,000
Canada.................................	6,300,000
New Caledonia....................	15,400,000
Other Free World................	10,100,000

Currently, 82 percent of United States imports are obtained from Canada. With sizable known reserves in Canada, a supply of nickel through imports of currently known reserves is reasonably secure. The long-run picture for nickel supplies is even brighter, for world resources from deposits of nickel sulfides and nickel laterities are estimated by B/M to total 70 million tons of nickel in ores with an average grade of about 1 percent nickel. Disseminated nickel in peridotites and serpentines, with grades between .2 and .4 percent, represent quantities several orders of magnitude greater than 70 million tons; while nickel in manganese nodules constitutes a resource of similar size. However, B/M indicates that new technology will be required to recover nickel successfully from these deposits.

The outlook for chromium is poor. Not only are current reserves nonexistent, but identified and hypothetical re-

sources are insignificant. The only large, known deposit in the United States is the Stillwater Complex of Montana, but this resource is of low grade and even under favorable economics B/M estimates that it would constitute only 4 to 5 years domestic supply. World reserves have been estimated at about 1.7 billion tons of chromium ore, a quantity about 250 times the 1973 world production. Over one billion tons of these reserves lie in South Africa. South Rhodesia holds 550 million tons, most of the remaining reserves. Currently B/M statistics show that United States imports are constituted as follows: U. S. S. R., 32 percent; South Africa, 30 percent; Turkey, 18 percent; Philippines, 14 percent; and other, 6 percent. World resources are estimated at approximately 10 billion short tons of chromium ore, mostly in South Africa and Rhodesia. Some insurance against interrupted supplies exists in the United States stockpile, which contains 3.4 million tons of metallurgical grade chromite plus 1.5 million tons of chemical and refractory grades and about one-half million tons of metal and alloys.

(2) Copper

Although our reserve and resource positions on the ferro alloys are not ideal, effects of shortages and interrupted supplies would not be as serious as it would be for the major metals: iron, aluminum, copper, lead, and zinc. Examination of Table F•13 reveals that in the case of copper, known reserves are sufficient to meet projected requirements for more than 30 years under 1973 consumption levels. Domestic reserves come close to meeting the cumulative consumption (considering reasonable growth rates) projected to year 2000. The size of our known reserves combined with the fact that the western United States is considered to have excellent potential for discoveries of new copper porphyries gives considerable assurance of adequate future supplies of copper.

World reserves also are large, as shown by the B/M estimates of 370 million tons of metal. Hypothetical resources are estimated to be 400 million tons, and speculative resources should account for 320 million additional tons. At least 380 million tons of copper are expected to exist in currently subeconomic, copper-nickel deposits and deep sea nodules according to Cox et al. Thus, there is reason to be optimistic about future domestic and world copper supplies.

(3) Iron

In the case of iron, the metal consumed in the greatest quantity, domestic reserves are large, sufficient to meet consumption at the current rate nearly to the end of the century, and sufficient to meet two-thirds of cumulative requirements for primary metal to the year 2000, considering reasonable growth rates. Subeconomic, identified resources in the United States have been estimated by the B/M at 88 billion tons of ore. These resources are mainly in the low-grade ores of the Lake Superior region and require benefication and aglomeration for commercial use.

World reserves have been estimated at 249 billion short tons of ore or 96.7 billion short tons of iron. Compared to 1973 production of 907 million short tons of ore, this is about 300 years of production. Identified world resources of iron ore have been estimated by the B/M to exceed 760 billion tons.

(4) Aluminum

If the United States were forced to supply its own requirements of aluminum ore (bauxite), within less than four years the nation would have consumed all its domestic reserves currently known at 1972 prices. For the metal that is second only to iron in the quantities consumed, these reserves appear alarmingly small. An even greater concern arises when the projected cumulative consumption to the year 2000: i.e., of 370 million tons of aluminum, is compared to a reserve of 13 million tons. Such an imbalance implies a great dependency upon imports unless new reserves of aluminum are created by changing prices and technology.

While the prospects for large bauxite deposits in the United States are poor, even with price increases, aluminum reserves could be created from other materials, given appropriate conditions: alunite, aluminum phosphate rock, aluminous shale and slate, high-aluminum clays, nepheline syenite and anorthosite, dawsonite, saprolite, copper leach solution, and sapprolite. Alunite is a present source of aluminum in the U. S. S. R., and plans for processing alunite are well advanced in Mexico.[4] In the United States, exploration has delineated four deposits of alunitized valcanic rock, each with over 100 million tons of material consisting of 35-45 percent alunite. High alumina clays are generally considered the most favorable, nonbauxite source of aluminum. The total amount of high alumina clay in the United States containing 25 percent Al_2O_3 or more and under no limits on availability, overburden, or mining costs may be as much as 10 billion tons according to United States Geological Service (USGS) estimates.[5] With the drive to develop shale oil production initiated by Project Independence, alumina could be recovered as a by-product of shale oil. Oil shale deposits in the Piceance Basin of Colorado are estimated by USGS to contain 1.5 percent acid extractable aluminum, constituting a resource of about 3.6 billion tons of aluminum.

World reserves of bauxite have been estimated at 17.36 billion tons of ore, equivalent to 223 years of world production of bauxite in 1973. Approximately 60 percent of these reserves are held by three countries: Australia, 5.26 million tons; Guinea, 3.92 million tons; and Jamaica, 1.12 million. Other Free World countries hold 36 percent, and the remaining 4 percent is in Communist countries, according to B/M estimates. It has been calculated by the NMPC that world resources at a price of 37 cents per pound aluminum are virtually unlimited. Interpretation of this statement must recognize that 37 cents represents an increase of approximately 9 cents over prevailing prices in 1972.

(5) Lead

Considerable disagreement exists in estimates of lead reserves in the United States. For example, the estimates of the NMPC, the B/M, and the USGS are, 17,56, and 39 million tons of lead, respectively. If the intermediate estimate of 39 million tons is used, domestic reserves could satisfy forecasted cumulative primary metal requirements to the year 2000.

World reserves of lead are estimated by the B/M at 144 million tons which is equivalent to 38 years of 1971 mine production. The B/M also believes that lead in subeconomic deposits on land and on the ocean basins could be as high as 1.5 billion tons. These large low grade deposits include the famous bedded deposit of the Kupferschiefer and lead in manganese nodules.

(6) Zinc

As indicated in Table F•13, known zinc reserves could adequately meet domestic requirements at the 1973 level of consumption for 20 years, and longer if scrap and recycling is considered. However, with the growth in consumption allowed for in the forecasted cumulative requirements to 2000, zinc reserves of the United States are only half as large as are needed. Zinc reserves are estimated by the USGS to be 45 million tons, somewhat nearer the forecasted requirements. Subeconomic, but identified resources are estimated at 75 million tons, and undiscovered but economic resources at 60 million tons. Thus, the potential for adequate future zinc supplies is considerable. World reserves have been estimated at 235 million tons of zinc, equivalent to 38 years of supply at the 1971 mine production level, according to USGS figures. Identified, but subeconomic resources of zinc are estimated at 1,275 million tons and undiscovered but economic resources of lead at 345 million tons.

(7) Concluding Remarks

At this point it is appropriate to restate the dynamic nature of reserves and resources and note that at any point in time our view of the true state of nature is incomplete. With few exceptions, reserves and resources predictions are on the conservative side, partly because of incomplete data and sampling of the earth's crust and partly due to changing technology. In summary, our reserves and resources are undoubtedly greater than suggested by the estimates provided. Even if the estimates are correct, with exception to a few minor metals and aluminum, shortage of future domestic metal supplies does not appear to be a real threat.

4. Estimation of Unknown Reserves and Resources

a. Perspective

By their very nature, studies of resource adequacy require estimates of the quantity of metal that might be supplied in response to forecasted demands. If the forecast period is long, metal requirements may overwhelm known reserves. Furthermore, a long forecast must allow for technological change and adjustment in prices and costs. Consequently, a resource adequacy, or "limits to growth", study begs the question of how much metal might be supplied if: (1) economics encourage more extensive and intensive exploration, and (2) technology and prices allow recovery of deposits of lower grades and different modes of occurrence than are currently economic. There is no elegant and ultimately definitive means of answering this question short of direct sampling of the crust of the United States by drilling at a spacing sufficient to locate the metal deposits. Of course, such a procedure would be extremely costly and it is questionable that the value of information could justify such a cost, although some scholars view the matter differently.[6]

There are several different approaches to inference and different ways in which these approaches could be classified to aid discussion. Three such approaches will be considered in the following paragraphs:

(a) Implicit estimation of production time series.

(b) Crustal abundance.

(1) Abundance-reserve relationship.

(2) The lognormal distribution as a metal resources model.

(c) The cumulative tonnage-average grade relationship.

b. Implicit Estimation

The implicit approach is well demonstrated by Hubbert in his analysis of trends in petroleum production and future supply.[7] The basic assumption made harkens back to the thesis of Hewett, that metal production for an economy through time ultimately describes a "bell-shaped" curve.[8] Exponential increases in production occur as rich deposits are discovered and exploited. This period is followed by a declining rate of increase in production as deposits become more difficult to locate, then by a leveling off of production as premium deposits are depleted, and finally by a decline in production as total resources are depleted.

This method of forecasting is based upon having a history of production sufficient to estimate the parameters of the curve. In practice, it is customary to convert the time series of production to one of cumulative production and fit an asymptotic curve, such as the logistic curve (the integral of the bell-shaped curve) to the series:

$$\text{Cumulative production} = f(t),$$

$$\text{where } t = \text{time.}$$

By evaluating the function at infinity, $f(\infty)$, total potential supply plus past cumulative production is estimated. Subtracting cumulative production from the estimate of the function at infinity yields the potential supply remaining.

Obviously, the reliability of such estimates is no better than the implicit assumption that trends of the past will continue in the future. This general assumption covers a wide spectrum of specific conditions, some of which are that: (1) technological change will continue in a pattern similar to that of the past; (2) the effectiveness of technological innovations in translating resources to reserves will be similar to that of the past; (3) tonnage and grade characteristics will change over time in accordance with patterns reflected in the production time series; and (4) changes in the structure of the economy will continue along

past trends. This last condition, in turn, assumes that new demands so large as to drive up metal prices to unexpectedly high levels will not occur, and changes in economic policies, such as the oil embargo, will not be so severe as to disturb the structure of the economy violently.

In the short or intermediate run, forecasts by this method are quite reliable since the economy is locked in to present technology. However, in the long run, technology and economic structure could be modified considerably, making the assumptions of this method somewhat restrictive as a means for forecasting potential supply.

c. Crustal Abundance

(1) General

The alternatives to the implicit method require the estimation of reserves and resources independently of economics and technology. An examination must then be made of the impact of specified economic and technological conditions on the process of translating resources to reserves and to potential supply. A basic reference for metal concentration that is independent of economic influence is crustal abundance. It is not surprising that in broad speculation about resources attention turns to this ultimate measure of endowment.

As an example, look at copper from the perspectives of reserves, resources, and crustal abundance. The concentration of copper in the crust of the United States has been estimated to be 50 grams per metric ton.[9] This is equivalent to a concentration of about .005 percent. This concentration, combined with the quantity of rock in the crust of the earth within the United States to one kilometer of depth, gives the huge quantity of approximately 1,356 billion tons of copper as an estimate of total copper abundance. Compare this quantity with reserves of 83 million tons and resources (the sum of the estimated hypothetical, speculative, and conditional resources) of about 400 million tons. These figures of reserves, resources and crustal abundance can be restated in relative terms as: 1, 5, and 16,300 respectively.

It is easy to reach erroneous conclusions by considering only crustal abundance measures. For this quantity of copper to be a reserve would require prices of metal and mining and extractive technologies that could extract it from the average rock of the earth's crust at a profit. Of course, this is not the situation. Currently, economically minable deposits must be of a grade approximately 100 times that of crustal abundance. Nevertheless, crustal abundance helps to broaden our perspective and to view reserves of a metal as a dynamic entity: a quantity that can be increased by raising prices or lowering costs or both.

In addition, the consideration of crustal abundance provokes the following questions. If there are approximately 500 million tons of metal (reserves plus resources) at .5 percent copper, and 2,700 times as much as that at .005 percent, what would be the resources at an intermediate grade of .15 percent or .05 percent? Will deposits necessarily occur at these grades? If so, how many and of what size? Answers to these questions are vital in the appraisal of resources. Even if there existed a smooth, continuous relationship between total metal availability and grade down to concentrations at the level of crustal abundance, little can be said as to the economic importance of deposits of low grades, unless something is also said about the tonnage of metal or ore in these low grade deposits. The usefulness of inference motivated by crustal abundance is one thing if, as the grade of deposits decreases, there is, on average, a geometric increase in the tonnage of ore and quite another if there is no necessary relationship between tonnage of ore and grade. In the latter case, the lower grade deposits could contain proportionately smaller amounts of metal, necessitating extremely high prices for their economic exploitation.

(2) The Abundance-Reserve Relationship

A method for making rough estimates of recoverable reserves of metals from crustal abundance data was suggested by McKelvey.[10] McKelvey plotted recoverable reserves in the United States for various metals against their crustal abundance and proposed that there was a general relationship:

$$R = A \times 10^k$$

where

k = a number from 9 to 10,
A = crustal abundance in percent and
R = short tons of domestic reserves of metal currently minable.

In essence, this relationship states that the more abundant the element in the earth's crust, the greater are the recoverable reserves of that element.

However, examination of McKelvey's plot of R versus A shows a very wide scatter, even though data are plotted in logarithms, which normally tends to reduce the apparent magnitude of variation (as appraised by visual inspection of such a plot). To include all the data points within an envelope on an R versus A plot requires that the exponent, k, vary from 6 to 10; i.e., by a factor of 10,000. Obviously, the relationship between abundance and currently recoverable reserves when examined across all metals is a very weak one. By restricting the set of metallic elements to those that form the chief constituents of their ores and have been sought the longest and most intensely, the scatter is considerably reduced. It is upon this restricted set of elements that McKelvey's abundance-reserve equation is predicated.

Erickson,[11] observed that the current reserves of lead were 2.7 times that indicated by McKelvey's relationship. Therefore, he standardized the relationship on lead, modifying it appropriately to describe reserves in metric tons instead of short tons:

$$R = 2.45 \times A \times 10^6$$

where

A = crustal abundance in parts per million, and
R = metric tons of recoverable metal resources.

Since this equation was standardized on lead, the metal for which the reserves to abundance ratio was the largest, the relationship describes for all other metals some part of potentially recoverable resources instead of reserves, because it includes materials not yet known. Recoverable resources for selected metals for the United States and for the world as estimated by Erickson are shown in Table F·14. Additionally, this table shows the ratio of predicted recoverable resources to known reserves.

Table F·14
RECOVERABLE RESOURCES BY ABUNDANCE-RESERVE RELATIONSHIPS

Metal	United States Quantity (Millions of Short Tons)	United States Ratio of Resource to Known Reserves	World Quantity (Billions of Short Tons)	World Ratio of Resource to Known Reserves
Copper	136.6	1.6	2,374.4	10
Lead	35.6	1	616	10
Molybdenum	3.0	1	52.2	1,631[1]
Nickel	166.9	830	29,001	38
Zinc	221.8	6.3	3,808	42
Tungsten	3.2	37	57	42
Tin	4.4	Very High	76.2	12
Manganese	2,744	Indeterminate	4.4	NA[2]
Chromium	211.7	Indeterminate	3.65	NA

[1] Based upon identified resources as listed in United States Bureau of Mines, *Commodity Data Summaries,* 1974.

[2] NA = not available.

Source: Erickson, Ralph (1973) "Crustal Abundance of Elements, and Mineral Reserves and Resources", U. S. G. S. Professional Paper 820, 1973.

While this abundance-reserve relationship may be useful in providing a first approximation of recoverable resources for large unexplored areas, it is of limited use in appraising the long-term resource adequacy of the United States or any other area with established production. This conclusion must follow from the fact that the entire relationship is based upon known reserves at a point in time. Obviously, for lead, the metal of standardization, the relationship predicts only what is already known. Resource predictions of other metals are based upon an obviously weak overall relationship of reserves to abundance and the questionable, implicit assumption that the ratio of known reserves to reserves predicted by McKelvey's equation for lead applies to other metals. For the common metals, especially those that are sulfophile, McKelvey's resource estimates will be seriously underestimated. For those that are lithophile, estimates may be extremely large and of questionable use, for in most cases silicates are not yet economic sources of metals.

(3) The Lognormal Distribution as a Mineral Resources Model

One of the most repeated findings in research on various aspects of metal occurrence, such as quantity, value, or concentration, is the suitability of the lognormal distribution law. Simply stated, this law states that when relative frequency of some feature of metal occurrence is plotted against the magnitude of that feature, as measured on the logarithmic scale, the distribution follows the normal (Gaussian) probability law.

This result has been observed for: (a) the concentration of metal in geochemical samples;[12] (b) the value of production per mine for an individual metal or for the aggregate of several metals; (c) the value of aggregate metal production from mining districts; (d) the distribution of grades in a deposit[13]; (e) the distribution of grade and of tonnage of ore for copper deposits irrespective of type and for specific kinds, such as porphyry deposits[14]; and (f) for the distribution of quantity of U_3O_8, the tonnage of rock containing U_3O_8, and grade of resources in percentage of U_3O_8 for the State of New Mexico.[15]

Brinck considered evidence such as that stated above in formulating a general model.[16] The Brinck model presumed that metal in ore and metal in geochemical samples all derive from the same metal environment. Under such conditions an ore deposit is a rare and special event because of its size and concentration, but not different in kind from the metal concentration in a hand sample or in the rock of a specified region. He proposed that the ultimate environment could be considered the continental crust of the earth, having as its mean the crustal abundance measure. The logarithmic standard deviation of this model (i.e., the distribution of a given metal) is estimated either from geochemical surveys or from the inventory of reserves of the metal. Given these parameters and the use of linear equivalents, probabilistic statements can be made for the occurrence of deposits of any specified median grade and size by the use of normal probability tables.[17]

Based upon world production and reserves data in 1963,

Brinck estimated that the median grade of copper ore was 1.7 percent Cu (range = .6 — 4.55 percent) and that the median ore reserve was 65 million tons of copper. The estimate of crustal abundance was taken to be 70 parts per million.[18] From the inventory of known reserves, Brinck estimated the standard deviation with respect to the median ore reserve to be 1.057. With these parameters, Brinck calculated the probability for the occurrence of copper deposits having a median grade of at least 17,000 parts per million (1.7 percent) in the ultimate metal environment to be 9.35×10^{-8} (93.5 chances out of a billion). Taking the weight of the continental crust of the earth to be 1×10^{18} tons (one quintillion tons), the world's estimated endowment in copperized material having a grade of at least 1.7 percent is estimated by multiplication of these two quantities:

$$T = (9.35 \times 10^{-8}) \times (1 \times 10^{18}) = 9.35 \times 10^{10}$$
metric tons = 93.5 billion metric tons

where
$$T = \text{estimated tonnage of metalized rock.}$$

The estimated average grade of the estimated endowment can then be calculated from the lognormal distribution as 2.34 percent. This and subsequent calculations with regard to the lognormal distribution were made using normal probability tables; consequently, for large standard scores, the numerical answers should be considered approximations. Thus, the estimated endowment of copper resources of the continental crust in deposits having grades of at least 1.7 percent can be calculated to be 2.2 billion metric tons of copper. This quantity is an estimate of orginal endowment; therefore, it includes copper already mined. Brinck estimated in 1967 that the sum of cumulative production and known reserves in 1963 was 219 million metric tons of copper. Between 1963 and 1973, world production amounted to approximately 42 million metric tons of copper. If it is assumed that the production over the last decade was included in estimated reserves in 1963, it may be concluded that remaining resources in deposits having grades of at least 1.7 percent are approximately 2 billion tons of copper. This is approximately twice the estimated tonnage of copper in identified plus hypothetical plus speculative reserves, according to estimates by D. P. Cox.[19]

If the median grade of the individual reserve were .6 percent (rather than 1.7 percent), but with the same median tonnage of 65 million metric tons of ore, world copper resources would increase tremendously. Rather than 2 billion tons, resources would rise to approximately 100 billion tons of Cu, approximately 100 times the world's presently identified plus hypothetical plus speculative reserves (excluding sea nodules). Obviously, a median reserve of 65 million metric tons of ore having a median concentration of only .6 percent copper would require very favorable economic conditions to be exploited profitably. Such low grades often require larger tonnages of ore to be economic. If economic factors restricted commercial interest to those deposits with a quantity of recoverable metal no less than that in the median deposit when concentration was 1.7 percent, this would imply ore tonnage per median recoverable deposit of 184 million metric tons instead of 65 million metric tons. The tonnage of world copper resources occurring in these larger concentrations is calculated to be approximately 17 billion tons, approximately 17 times total reserves as seen today.

For zinc, Brinck found the median grade to be 4.3 percent zinc (ranging from 2.0 to 19.0 percent) and the median ore tonnage per deposit to be 174 million metric tons of ore. The crustal abundance was taken to be 80 parts per million and the standard deviation to be 1.152. Based upon these data and the weight and linear equivalents of the continental crust and the median deposit, Brinck estimated that the probability for the occurrence of deposits having a median grade of 4.3 percent or more is 2.24×10^{-8}. From this probability figure it can be inferred that the world's resources of zinc ore in deposits of at least this concentration are 22.4 billion metric tons. The average grade of the inferred metalized rock of the continental crust having a grade of at least 4.3 percent is estimated to be 5.9 percent zinc, giving 1.3 billion metric tons of zinc metal. This quantity is approximately the same as the estimated total economic resources (identified plus undiscovered ore having at least 4 percent zinc). Suppose that the world resource estimate were to include deposits of the same median ore tonnage but grades of at least 2 percent instead of 4.3 percent. World resources of zinc would be 840 billion tons of metalized rock with an average grade of 2.5 percent giving about 21 billion tons of zinc instead of 1.3 billion.

It is important to keep the proper perspective with regard to these estimates. Obviously, the estimates are only as good as the underlying assumption that metal concentrations of all sizes are distributed lognormally, the mean concentration being the logarithm of the crustal abundance measure, and the variance being modified appropriately to reflect the influence of the sizes of the concentrations and the environment.

The smooth continuous relationship of grade to tonnage implied by the lognormal distribution model has been questioned on the basis of empirical data.[20] These data suggest that the transition from economic concentrations to concentrations near crustal abundance may not be smooth and continuous, but rather may be a step function, with possible discontinuities, in which the steps represent abrupt changes in geologic environments and the combinations of geologic processes required to concentrate a metal in a particular mode. Such a relationship is certainly possible. However, data on grades and tonnages of reserves are not only incomplete but reflect the influence of economic and technological factors on the sampling process. Consequently, it is possible to be misled by apparent relationships. It is possible that if more complete information were available concerning the entire spectrum of modes of occurrence of a given metal, it would support the lognormal distribution as a model of the total metal environment of the earth's crust. Firm conclusions must await more and better data.

The use of crustal abundance as a parameter of the lognormal distribution means that resources estimated by the model include concentrations in all possible modes of occurrence: modes with which we are familiar and modes

about which we have little or no knowledge. Therefore, such estimates, in theory, should be larger than the quantity of the metal that occurs in only the known modes of occurrence.

However, theory and application may not agree, especially if the variance of the element distribution is based upon the inventory of known deposits. The procedure demonstrated by Brinck for estimating world metal resources uses the tonnage of ore produced plus reserves, the ore tonnage and concentration of the median deposit, and the measure of crustal abundance to estimate the variance of the distribution. Obviously, cumulative production plus reserves change with time. Even for known modes of occurrence, the inventory may be quite incomplete. To compound the problem further, the potential reserves of current economic grades that reside in unidentified, or at least unexploited, modes of occurrence, may make the size of the true inventory and the statistics of the typical deposit quite different from those determined from present information.

Consequently, while use of crustal abundance and the lognormal element distribution appear to present a simple means of estimating metal endowment directly, the fact that estimation of the variance is based upon production and reserves clouds the issue by relating physical attributes of the earth's crust to time-dependent variables. Just as important as the presence of time effects is the fact that the data used to estimate the mean of the lognormal distribution and that used to estimate the variance, in a sense, are not consistent. The mean is based upon geochemical data from all rock types at various locations, hence it represents the total environment for the metal in question, while the inventory of reserves plus cumulative production represents the consequences of economic activities which were concentrated on *only those modes* of occurrence that have been *recognized in the past*.

d. The Cumulative Ore Tonnage—Average Grade Relationship

The pioneering work on grade-tonnage relationships is credited to Lasky, who showed that a plot of the cumulative tonnage of ore against the average grade of ore for the typical copper porphyry deposit defined an exponential relationship.[21] Subsequently, Musgrove developed the theory of exponential grade-size relationships and explored their relevance for resource estimation for large regions for each of a number of metals.[22] Using this method for copper, Musgrove estimated there would be 49.45 billion tons of copper ore in the U. S. with an average grade of .224 percent copper, and containing 111 million tons of copper metal. This amounts to only about 1.4 times currently proven reserves. (See Table G·13.) Musgrove acknowledges and discusses the effects of incomplete information upon resource estimates by this procedure.

A recent report documents the use of a subjective probability survey, including: (a) a second round Delphi; (b) known reserve and production data; and (c) grade-tonnage extrapolation, to appraise the uranium resources of New Mexico.[23] Contrary to the broad, general approach described by Brinck, resource estimates in this case are limited to resources of known modes of occurrence. In a sense, the two approaches can be viewed as complements.

In the New Mexico study a distribution of known reserves and cumulative past production by grade class was combined with a similar distribution resulting from a Delphi polling of 36 experts. These experts were queried concerning the magnitude and characteristics of unknown uranium deposits in New Mexico. This combined information was considered an estimate of the totality of uranium oxide occuring in recognized modes and having economic grades.

The relationship between cumulative tonnages of ore and average grade implied by the combined information is indicated by Chart F•19. A mathematical relationship was fitted to all but the circled points (circled points were ignored in the fitting because of their suspected unreliability). This equation was then manipulated to provide estimates of ore tonnage within specified grade intervals. For example, extrapolation and manipulation indicated 296 million metric tons of uranium oxide ore having grades falling in the interval of .10 to .15 percent uranium oxide. This quantity can be compared to negligible tonnage in this concentration interval, as reported from known reserves and estimated to be present in undiscovered deposits by the explorationists. No one knows whether this mathematical model or the exploratory results is correct. However, when one examines the regularity of the pattern made by the logarithm of cumulative tonnage of ore for grades that are economic, one becomes suspicious of the

sudden break in that pattern at the transition to subeconomic grades. Add to this suspicion the fact that concentrations of uranium appear to be lognormally distributed and that a pattern like the one of Chart F•19 can result from a lognormal distribution, and a reasonable case can be made for the credibility of the estimates made by the model.

e. Summary Statement on Resources and Reserves

In a study of resource adequacy, it is necessary to project beyond past and current experience, for almost without fail, reserves and resource estimates have been proven by history to be very conservatively low. Although the conceptual framework for resource appraisals is anything but well defined, there is good argument for the use of resource availability models for selected conditions, not because estimates of these models are necessarily correct, but rather because they provide a means of expanding thinking about resources and prevent the myopia that may result from examination only of published reserve estimates.

5. Resources From Non-Conventional Sources

a. Sedimentary Deposits of Metals

Sedimentary metal deposits, once thought to be a rarity, appear to be a mode of occurrence that may expand considerably our metal resources. Not until recently has

Chart F•19
PLOT OF AVERAGE GRADE VERSUS TONS OF URANIUM ORE

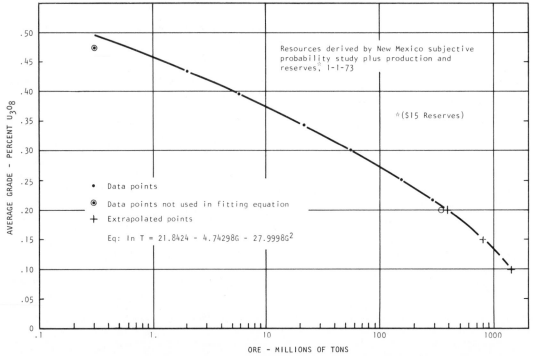

Source: Ellis, Harris, and Van Wie, "Probability Appraisal of the Uranium Resources of New Mexico," U.S., AEC, 1974.

this mode of occurrence received significant attention in exploration, particularly in the United States. An example of this mode of occurrence for copper, lead, and zinc has been known for quite some time, i.e. the Kupferscheifer bed of Germany. The Kupferscheifer bed, first mined for copper, is a bituminous shale approximately one meter thick which lies near the base of the Zechstein Formation. This bed is reportedly mineralized over an area of 4560 square kilometers, the ore minerals commonly consisting of finely disseminated bornite, chalcocite, galena, sphalerite, and tetrahedrite.[24] The grade of the Kupferscheifer that was mined for its copper content is 2-3 percent copper, 1-3 percent zinc, about 1.5 percent lead, and approximately 4 ounces per short ton of rock in silver.[25] That portion of the bed occurring between Magdeburg and Richelsdorf had been estimated to contain 100-150 million tons of lead, 200-250 million tons of zinc and 50 million tons of copper.[26]

Sedimentary copper deposits have been discovered in Western U.S. and the U.S.S.R., and evidence indicates that those of the U.S.S.R. may be of very large tonnage and attractive grades. Sedimentary copper resources of subeconomic grades in the Pre Cambrian Superbelt group of Idaho and Montana may be very large.

Nonconventional, subeconomic resources for lead and other metals are the mineralized sediments that occur in the thermal deeps of the seas. One such thermal deep is the Red Sea Basin. The upper ten meters of the Atlantis Deep in this basin contains 50 million metric tons of mineral bearing sediment, being 3.4 percent zinc, 1.3 percent copper, .10 percent lead, and about 1.6 ounces per ton silver.[27] Similar sediments, but of lower concentration, have been detected in the adjacent Discovery and Chain Deeps, according to Morris, H.T. et al.[28] Recognition of this mode of occurrence not only raises the possibility of exploitation of mineralized sediments in current thermal deeps but also suggests an environment that could have generated similar deposits in paleodeeps, deposits that are now rock bound in sediments.

Table F·15
RATIOS OF METAL CONCENTRATIONS OF PELAGIC SEDIMENTS AS COMPARED TO NORMAL SEDIMENTS

Metal	Range of Concentration[1]	Median Concentration[2]
Manganese	2-30	8
Copper	2.5-30	10
Lead	?-11	7.5
Molybdenum	10-80	12
Barium	1.5-35	7

1 Interpreted from graph, Goldberg and Arrhenius.
2 Geometric mean of limits of range.

Source: E.D. Goldberg and G. Arrhenius, "Chemistry of Pacific Pelagic Sediments," Geochimica et Cosmochimica, Octa 13 pp. 153-212, 1958.

Extensive deposits of pelagic ocean sediments have been found to be richer in metals than the average igneous rock. This enrichment appears anomalous in view of the fact that sedimentary rocks in general have lower metal concentration than the average igneous rock. Goldberg and Arrhenius found the concentrations of manganese, nickel copper, cobalt, lead, molybdenum, ytterbium, yttrium, lanthanum, scandium, barium, and boron to be 5 to 10 times the concentrations in igneous rocks.[29] Interpretation of Goldberg's information shows the range of the concentration of copper to be from 2.5-30 times normal, having an average of approximately 10. (See Table F·15.)

The extent of these pelagic sediments is tremendous, indicating a very large concentration of metals. However, even at enriched levels, the concentrations of these sediments is low. For example, if we take Goldschmidt's estimate[30] of 70 parts per million, as the average concentration of copper in the earth's crust, and assume it is also the average concentration in igneous rocks, the median concentration of these sediments would be 700 PPM = .07 percent. This grade is approximately one order of magnitude below the cutoff grade of economically exploitable deposits in rocks of the continental crusts. Given the higher concentration reported, approximately 30 times that in igneous rocks, a pelagic deposit of this concentration would have a grade of approximately .2 percent Cu, still subeconomic, but approaching a grade close to that of exploitable land deposits, particularly if other metals were present.

Copper concentrations in excess of 1000 ppm and concentrations of several heavy metals were reported along the crest of the East Pacific rise by Bostrom and Peterson.[31] As indicated by Cloud, the importance of these findings to us today is not that the pelagic sediments will be mined for their metals.[32] The depths of these sediments range from bathyl (200 to 4,000 meters) to abyssal (greater than 4,000 meters) so that mining is not currently practical, although it may become practical in the more distant future. More importantly, however, these findings provide evidence of a geologic environment that may give rise to extremely large, though perhaps low grade, deposits of metals. Should man, through the exercise of his science, learn to identify paleo environments of this kind, extremely large deposits might be located on land. These deposits may be exploited by large scale, low unit cost mining operations. Obviously, such an eventuality would greatly augment our resources for some metals.

b. Seabed Mining

Deposits of manganese nodules have been observed on the seabed of all oceans. Although data are meager on the lateral distribution, depth of occurrence in sediments of the sea floor, and metal concentration of the nodules, evidence suggests that deposits are more abundant in the Pacific Ocean than elsewhere. These deposits generally occur within a depth range of 3000 to 6000 meters, although Cloud indicates that some occur in a much shallower depth of water; e.g., 200 to 1000 meters on the Blake Plateau of the Atlantic Ocean offshore of the Carolinas.

An estimate of the average concentration of the more abundant metals in nodules from the Pacific Ocean, based

Table F·16

**COMPOSITION OF PACIFIC MANGANESE
NODULES BY WEIGHT PERCENTAGES
(Dry Weight Basis)**

Element	Average	Maximum	Minimum
Manganese	24.2%	50.1%	8.2%
Iron	14.0	26.6	2.4
Silicon	9.4	20.1	1.3
Aluminum	2.9	6.9	0.8
Sodium	2.6	4.7	1.5
Calcium	1.9	4.4	0.8
Magnesium	1.7	2.4	1.0
Nickel	.99	2.0	.16
Potassium	.8	3.1	.3
Titanium	.67	1.7	.11
Copper	.53	1.6	.028
Cobalt	.35	2.3	.014
Barium	.18	0.64	.08

Source: Cardwell, Paul H.; "Extractive Metallurgy of Ocean Nodules," *Mining Congress Journal,* Nov., 1973.

upon samples from 54 different locations is provided in Table F·16.

Because of imcomplete sampling and meager information, estimates of quantities of nodules must be considered highly speculative. Mero estimates that there are 1.5 trillion tons of manganese nodules on the Pacific Ocean sea bottom and that nodules are forming at the rate of 10 million tons per year.[33] Another estimate, attributed to Mero by Cloud, is that there are between .09 and 1.7 trillion metric tons of manganese nodules averaging 32 percent manganese dioxide. Cloud points out that the silica content of the nodules is often as great as the manganese, rendering them unavailable under current metallurgical techniques. Furthermore, he postulates that if a metallurgical process were developed for treating the high silica nodules, such a process would make available large reserves of low-grade silicious manganese deposits on land.

Appraisals of the economic potential for metal production from nodules are, to say the least, confusing, as they range from an implied cornucopia of metal wealth to the conclusion that their exploitation is in the distant future. In 1967, Mero estimated that the cost of producing nodules to recover the copper and nickel and associated metals would fall in the neighborhood of $4-$5 per ton of raw nodules. Kaufman and Rothstein estimated that a nodule operation on the Blake Plateau would require an investment between 100 to 200 million dollars, and would yield 1 to 2 million tons of nodules annually.[34] Their evaluation indicated a cost per ton of $28 to $53 for a one-million-ton operation, yielding recoverable value between $6 to $130 per ton of nodules, depending upon the assay values of the nodules.

Their calculations were based upon 12 percent rate of return, 5 percent royalty, and a tax rate of 50 percent. A more recent estimate for mining nodules at a depth of 15,000 feet is $5 to $10 per ton.[35]

In appraising the progress and prospects for ocean mining, Archer believes certain facts and relationships are becoming clear.[36] One of these is the likely scale of nodule mining operations. He proposes that each operation seems likely to recover 1 to 3 million metric tons (dry weights) of nodules annually and that, allowing for losses, a one-million-ton operation would yield 13,000 metric tons of nickel, 11,000 metric tons of copper, 2,500 metric tons of cobalt, and 270,000 metric tons of manganese. Archer concludes that, allowing for variations in abundance, grade, dredge pickup performances, and the proportion of a deposit that is likely to be covered, a favorable site to sustain a 20 year operation would require an area of 10,000 square kilometers. He speculates that ore grade deposits of nodules may occur on 1 percent of the area of the ocean seabed, allowing for 250 to 300 mine sites, each of which could yield 20 million metric tons of nodules. On the other hand, Schulze-Westrum of Metallgesellschaft's Ocean Technology Department, as quoted by Ingersoll, states that there are only a few deposits in the Pacific that contain sufficiently high concentrations of copper and nickel to be commercially interesting.[37]

In spite of mixed views on current or near future economic feasibility, private and public firms throughout the world continue to pursue exploration, research, and development activities that may lead to commercial exploitation of nodules. The formation of a consortium consisting of Kennecott Copper Corporation, Rio Tinto Zinc Corporation, Limited, Consolidated Gold Fields Limited, Mitsubishi Corporation, and Noranda Mines Limited was recently announced.[38] The purpose of this consortium was to conduct a fifty million dollar feasibility study on ocean mining. Similarly, Ingersoll relates that a consortium, Arbeitsgemeinschaft Meerestechnishch-Gewinnbare Rohstoffe (AMR), has been formed for ocean mining by three German firms: Metallgesellschaft AG, Preussag AG, and Salzgetter Ag.

There can be little doubt that the quantity of subeconomic resources of manganese, copper, nickel, and cobalt in ocean nodules is very large, and it seems likely that metals from this source will be a significant factor in future metal supply. Just when ocean mining of nodules will become economic and how fast the industry will grow is not at all clear at this time.

On the basis of three assumptions, Rigg concludes that "the new industry will be small for the foreseeable future and that ocean production of nickel, copper, and manganese will represent only minor shares of total world output. Hypothetically, a three-firm industry will be operating by 1978, and its production will meet a projected increased demand of 3.5 to 6 percent per year." The assumptions made by Rigg were:

1. The total cost structure of the industry will at least be competitive with costs from land-based sources.

2. The growth of the ocean mining industry will be determined solely by world market conditions and will not be restricted through international regulations different from those imposed on land-based producers.

3. For the foreseeable future, nickel markets will play the predominant role in limiting the growth of the ocean mining industry.

c. Metal Extraction from Seawater

The sea contains 50 quadrillion tons of dissolved substances in 1500 quadrillion metric tons of water according to Cloud.[39] Currently, only magnesium, bromine and common salt are being extracted economically and in any significant quantities. These elements are among those having the highest concentrations. Cloud suggests that other elements with concentrations sufficiently high that they afford potential for the future are: sodium, sulfur, potassium, and, possibly, strontium, boron, and flourine.

Of the metals sought most by onshore mining (copper, lead, zinc, iron, tin, molybdenum, silver, and gold), the one having the highest concentration in seawater is zinc, estimated at .09 pounds per million gallons; and the one having the lowest concentration is gold, .00004 pounds per million gallons. In terms of percentage by weight, zinc is the most highly concentrated metal in sea water. The concentration of zinc in commercial ores is roughly 10 million times the concentration in sea water. Of course, the ease of mining of seawater is one of the attractive features of seawater as a source of metals. Nevertheless, it would require the processing of approximately 22 billion gallons of seawater to recover 1 ton of zinc metal. Thus, approximately 93 million tons of water would yield 1 ton of zinc. As suggested by Cloud, the practicality of such an operation is not impressive. The concentrations for iron, aluminum, and molybdenum are similar to that of zinc, but the copper concentration is only about one-third that of zinc, according to Goldberg.[40]

There is evidence that other natural brines may provide a more attractive source of metals than does ordinary seawater. Element concentration in the Dead Sea is approximately 10 times that of ordinary seawater, and it is reported that there are places in the Red Sea where waters issuing from fracture zones beneath the sea floor have relatively high concentrations of certain elements.[41]

6. Some Issues of Mineral Economics

a. Costs of Domestic Supplies

The generally favorable reserves and resources position of the United States appears to conflict with the trend toward increasing reliance on imports. The conflict is resolved very simply by economics; at present, many metals can be obtained more cheaply from foreign sources than from domestic reserves. In many instances this is a consequence of early depletion of domestic premium, high grade, deposits and the fact that similar high quality deposits still exist in less well explored areas of the earth. Naturally, many of these premium deposits are in devel-

oping countries, countries that are not highly industrialized and have not had a great internal demand for their domestic resources.

The United States could turn to domestic reserves through the use of tariffs, quotas or subsidies, but to do so would increase the cost of our raw materials. This cost would be passed on to the cost of finished products and worsen the competitive position of many United States metal products. Additionally, an unsound mining industry is created by contrived economic incentives. However, care should be given to keeping proper perspective about the magnitude of the increased product costs due to higher raw materials costs. Some of the minor metals are used in such small amounts that a doubling of the costs of the metal would have an imperceptible effect upon product costs. For the major metals, such as iron and aluminum, an increase in raw material costs would be more noticable, but even here, relative to all costs of the finished product, the increase may be a small percentage of the total cost of the product.

In a few instances, such as chromium, the United States has never had a domestic supply. It is generally accepted that the geologic environment does not appear favorable for the generation of domestic reserves. The geology and metalization of the earth are not homogeneous; consequently, deposits of some of the metals, as currently known, are unequally distributed. Such may be the case for chromium, at least in the form of chromite. In such cases, emphasis must be placed upon securing foreign supplies, upon developing substitutes, and upon searching new geologic environments for chromium.

b. The Likelihood of a Successful Metals Cartel

The Arab embargo of oil supplies and subsequent events have caused concern that markets for other raw materials might be similarly exploited. In a very short time, the OPEC countries greatly increased oil prices and forged a new image for themselves as an economic power, a power on which many industrial countries found themselves highly dependent. The effects of the embargo are many and complex and will not be fully appreciated for years; nevertheless as a result of the embargo the developed countries have had to accept a new perspective of their economic position and the cost of energy, while developing countries have formed a stronger conviction that they are being under-rewarded for the exploitation of their mineral resources. Such conviction will feed the fever of nationalism that was already rampant in some areas of the world. Additionally, the success of the oil embargo can't help but encourage the formation of cartels in other mineral markets.

The oil embargo was successful for several reasons:

1. The Arab nations controlled a major source of supply and reserves.

2. The Arab nations were similar in philosophy and economic structure; there was not a great divergence in the level of economic development.

3. Energy is an essential in economic pursuits as well as survival, and pervades all human activity.

4. Because of the previous history of low prices of Arab oil for many years, and an apparent excess supply, many nations had become dependent upon imports of Arab oil.

5. Although substitute forms of energy exist, conversion and the generation of supply capability take years. In the short run, few alternatives were available.

6. The Arab nations were financially quite strong and able to survive a decrease in exports, even if the decrease generated reduced revenue.

7. Prices were increased to the point that reduction in revenue was not an issue.

8. Oil export was the chief source of revenue for the Arab Nations, thus binding them to a common cause.

First of all, in order for a metal cartel to be an issue of concern, it must develop either in the supplies of a metal so vital that we cannot physically do without it, or in supplies of a major metal for which elevated prices would create an economic hardship. With respect to the physical shortage of a critical metal, there are few metals that are really critical in the sense that there are no substitutes. For those metals that have such characteristics, the United States is assured a supply to withstand such emergencies. Some of the stockpile reserves would meet United States needs for up to two years; for example, manganese and chromite ores.

Thus, the concern about metals cartels must concentrate on the major metals: iron, aluminum, copper, lead, and zinc. The comments to follow examine copper, aluminum, and iron.

A cartel of copper producers, CIPEC, composed of Zambia, Chile, Peru and Zaire, has been in existence for years. So far, it has had little effect on the control of copper production and prices. The combined share of export trade of CIPEC in 1972 was 52 percent.[42]

It is questionable that CIPEC could maintain prices during a depressed market, with only 52 percent of the export trade under its control. There are features of copper use that discourage pressures for price increases. One of them is the ready substitution of aluminum for copper and the other one is the abundance of reserves and resources of copper, which would encourage mine investment and expansion of production capability outside of the cartel. Increased prices would also encourage more reclaiming and recycling of scrap, an activity that would be detrimental to the success of an embargo of copper. In an emergency, such as that of the energy crisis, copper supplies could be increased by relying heavily upon copper scrap and substitution. Additionally, CIPEC does not have the financial stability necessary for a long embargo, one of sufficient duration to pressure consuming countries significantly.

Even if the copper cartel were to act to control production and prices, the effects would be minor and indirect upon the United States, for the nation is nearly self-sufficient in copper, and with increased copper prices it would find incentives to become self-sufficient.

The formation of a cartel of bauxite exporting countries would be a cause of greater concern than would a cartel in copper, for the United States dependence on bauxite from foreign sources is in excess of 90 percent. Indeed, because of speculation that the calling of a meeting of bauxite producers would result in increased prices, the United States Secretary of the Interior recommended in 1974 that steps be taken to develop United States resources to assure domestic supplies of bauxite.[43] In March of that year the International Association of Producers of Bauxite (IAPB) was formed, with Guinea, Australia, Guyana, Jamaica, Sierra Leone, Surinam, and Yugoslavia as members. However, contrary to earlier speculation, the IAPB did not call for a bauxite embargo, but instead agreed to increase their incomes primarily through forward integration into production of alumina, primary aluminum, and fabricated products.

Spokesmen of the aluminum industry had predicted that an attempt by bauxite producing nations to form a cartel would fail for the following reasons:

1. The ore producing countries lack common bonds.

2. United States sources of bauxite and other ores are available.

3. United States aluminum companies are producing alumina from non-bauxite sources on an experimental basis.

4. There are enormous world resources of bauxite yet to be developed.

5. The United States is insulated from an embargo by the stockpile.

6. There is no world price of bauxite.

7. The less developed bauxite producing countries are too dependent on revenue from bauxite.

An embargo on bauxite would undoubtedly cause the United States to turn to the development of its own bauxite and non-bauxite sources of alumina, such as high alumina clays, anorthosite, alunite and laterite ores. At present, alumuna from these sources is not competitive with that from bauxite, but elevated prices could close the gap. Besides, rather than becoming vulnerable to the whims of a cartel, the United States would seek new technology and processes for non-bauxite ores. Additionally, there are large areas in countries not now included as bauxite suppliers for which there is a high potential for bauxite deposits. Finally, copper could be substituted for some uses of aluminum, and aluminum supplies could be augmented by a greater use of aluminum scrap.

A cartel of iron ore producers has an even smaller chance of succeeding than one in bauxite or copper. Both production and reserves are widespread, with many countries of differing interests involved. Many of the iron ore producing countries have developed economies and produce steel. These countries have interests that would conflict with those of developing countries that rely heavily upon revenue from ore. Originating an embargo carries certain political and economic risks. To be willing to undertake such risks, the country would have to be highly dependent upon revenue from the ore. Developed ore-producing countries such as Sweden and Canada most likely could find more profitable activities than engaging in an embargo on iron ore, particularly when there is a large possibility for failure of the embargo.

Among the developing countries that produce iron ore, the largest producers are Brazil, Venezuela, and Liberia. In 1973, these three countries produced only 11 percent of the world production. On the other hand, five industrial countries (United States, Canada, Australia, France, and Sweden) produced 37 percent of the world iron ore.

Also mitigating against an embargo on iron ore is the great use of scrap. Industrial countries have developed a large resource through scrap accumulations and could turn more heavily to such supply in the event of an embargo.

In conclusion, because of the lack of financial strength, common interests, majority control of production and reserves, the availability of other metal substitutes, and the reserve of scrap, a successful embargo on ore supplies by a cartel of exporting countries is not likely development.

c. Recycling of Metals

Metal from secondary recovery constitutes an important part of domestic metal supply, as indicated by the percentage of total consumption in 1967 that was comprised by recycled metal. (See Table F•17.)

Table F•17
RECYCLING OF MAJOR METALS, 1967

Metal	Percentage of Total Consumption
Iron and Steel	31.2%
Aluminum	18.3
Copper	49.7
Lead	49.6
Zinc	12.6

Source: The National Commission on Materials Policy, *Material Needs and the Environment Today and Tomorrow*, Washington, D. C., 1973

If it were not for the metal from secondary sources, there would be much more concern about the adequacy of our primary domestic reserves and resources to meet future metal requirements. As primary metal is produced each year, a greater reserve of secondary metal is accumulating. Developing sound programs for scrap recovery will allow for the reuse many times of the same metal. Such a program would ease pressures on finding new deposits and at the same time would improve the environment. A higher utilization of scrap would decrease the amount of future primary smelting (pollution), ease dependency upon foreign sources for those metals for which resources are negligible, and conserve energy.

d. Energy Consumption and Costs in Metal Production

As high grade deposits have been depleted, the mining industry has turned to large low-grade deposits and the application of large scale mining methods and equipment. In order to observe the effects of the leaner ore bodies and more capital intensive mining, data on energy consumption in mining were acquired from the census of mineral industries for years 1929, 1939, 1954, 1958, and 1963. In addition, data on mine output was obtained for the same years for iron ore, manganese, molybdenum, copper, lead, zinc, bauxite, mercury, gold, and silver. Production of these metals was converted to a value for each year using 1954 metal prices. From these data, the value of metal mined in each year per kwh was computed. These data are plotted in Chart F•20. From 1929 to 1939, there was a sharp increase in value of output per kwh, but since 1939, the output has been following a declining trend. This trend probably reflects the greater quantities of rock mined per pound of metal as industry was forced to leaner ore bodies. However, metal prices in constant dollars declined over this same period. Therefore one must conclude that energy was being substituted profitably for capital or labor.

In view of the relationship of energy consumption and output for metal mining, the recently greatly increased costs of energy are likely to be a heavy burden for mining, unless metal prices rise sufficiently to offset cost increases or some new energy-saving method of mining is adopted.

The trend in output per kilowatthour in nonmetallic mining contrasts markedly with that in metal mining. Output of nonmetals per kilowatthour has increased in an exponential-like pattern from 1944-1958, suggesting energy economizing equipment and procedures have been minor, if not altogether absent.

A similar exercise was performed for refined metal and energy consumption, as shown in Table F•18. In the case of copper refining, there has also been a decline in refined metal output per kilowatthour, with the exception of the

Table F•18
TRENDS IN PRODUCTION OF REFINED COPPER AND ALUMINUM
Pounds per Kilowatthour

Year	Copper	Aluminum
1971	.152	(*)
1967	.173	.0603
1962	.183	.057
1954	.205	.064
1947	.181	.058

* 1971 data on energy consumption in aluminum refining is incomplete

Sources of Data: Census of Manufacturing, Bureau of Census; and Minerals Yearbook, United States Bureau of Mines

first year. For aluminum, however, there doesn't appear to be a trend, but instead a cyclical character. There is a danger of overinterpreting the data because of inconsistencies in reporting of data in the census reports of the various years.

e. Energy Costs for Producing and Recycling Metals

Aluminum is our fastest growing metal in terms of consumption, both in the United States and world in general. This fact, when considered along with the large amount of energy required to produce aluminum from its ores, causes some concern about the impact of energy shortages and high energy prices. A study by Oak Ridge National Laboratory estimated that 64,000 kilowatthours were required per ton of primary aluminum.[44] At a price of $560 per ton of aluminum and 2 mills per kilowatthour energy requirements constitute about 23 percent of the 1973 price of aluminum. This high percentage contrasts with 4 percent for steel (steel valued at $184 per ton). Costs for copper, magnesium, copper from scrap, and

titanium from scrap are shown in Table F•19 over the period from 1947 to 1971. Since 1971, of course, the price of energy has risen significantly and energy inputs are even more significant to all metals refining operations.

The savings in energy consumption that can be achieved by the use of scrap are obvious from Table F•19. According to the Oak Ridge National Laboratory data shown in that table, the energy component of the cost of copper obtained from 98 percent scrap recycle was only 0.1 percent. In contrast, about 4.2 percent of the cost of copper refined from a 0.3 percent sulfide ore was traced to the energy input. The National Commission on Materials Policy reported that using secondary sources of metal and recycling saved 62,000 kilowatthours per ton of aluminum and 7,500 kilowatt hours per ton of steel. This same report estimates the amount of aluminum and steel scrap available for recycling in 1969 as 1.0 and 27 million tons, respectively. If energy costs remain high, savings in energy may be an incentive to greater use of scrap. Such a development would conserve energy as well as extend our domestic metal reserves.

Chart F•20
PRODUCTIVITY OF FUELS AND ELECTRIC ENERGY IN MINING, 1929-1963.

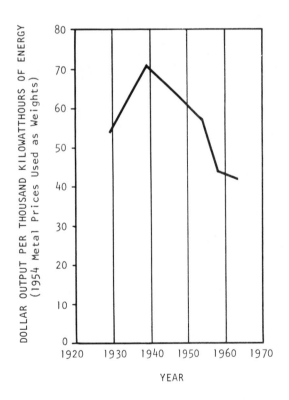
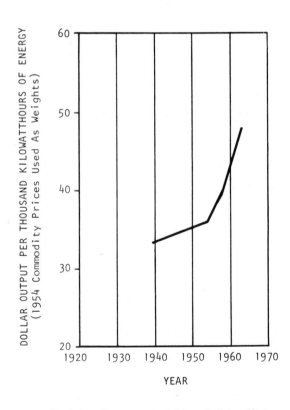

Note: Metal mining output includes: iron ore, manganese, molybdenum, copper, lead, bauxite, mercury, gold, and silver. Nonmetal mining output includes: stone, cement raw materials, sand and gravel, clays, gypsum, phosphate rocks, potash, sulfur, fluorspar, and salt.

Sources: United States Departments of Commerce and Interior, *Raw Materials in the United States Economy, 1900-1966,* Bureau of Census Working Paper No. 30, Washington, 1969, and Potter, Neal and Christy, Francis, *Trends in Natural Resource Commodities,* Resources for the Future, Johns Hopkins Press, Baltimore, 1962.

Table F·19

EFFECTS OF ENERGY COSTS ON MATERIALS PRICES

Metal	Source	Value of Metal (Dollars Per Ton)	Equivalent Energy		Percent of Total Price of Metal
			(Kilowatthours per Ton)	(Kilowatthours per Dollar)	
Copper	1% sulfide ore	1177	13,530	11.50	2.30%
	.3% sulfide ore	1177	24,760	21.00	4.20
	98% scrap recycle	1177	590	.50	.10
	Impure scrap recycle	1177	1,560	1.33	.27
Magnesium	Sea water	765	90,930	118.9	23.4
Titanium	High-grade rutile ore	2840	126,280	44.46	8.9
	Ilmenite sands	2840	153,330	54.0	10.8
	Titanium metal recycle	2840	39,000	13.7	2.8
Aluminum..............................	Anorthosite	560	72,360	129.2	25.8

Source: Oak Ridge National Laboratory (reported in *Engineering & Mining Journal*, April, 1974)

7. Relationship of Metal Consumption and Gross National Product

a. Perspective

Manufacturing is one sector that contributes heavily to the nation's Gross National Product. Manufacturing requires a great variety of metallic raw and semi-finished materials. It is in this sense that metal is consumed, as it undergoes transformation by technology to a product that is used (consumed) by man. The amount of a metal consumed in a country is ultimately determined by many factors, some of which are: 1) the preferences of the consumers for the products containing metals, 2) prices of consumer products, 3) the transformation function of technology, 4) the size of the population, 5) disposable income, and 6) factor prices. Obviously, these things are interrelated in complex ways through the dynamics of general economic equilibrium. In theory, a prediction of metal demand at some future time must account for all of these factors and their dynamics. This section, however, is less conceptually complete than economic theory would dictate.

Proper perspective of the relationships to be examined in this section requires recognition that a general economic measure, GNP, was forecast for various years in the future by the Data Resources, Inc., model. (See Appendix B.) The objective of the following paragraphs is to examine and specify relationships of metals consumption to GNP. This section examines first a broad-gaged view of metal consumption across the major market countries in 1970 and then looks at trends in metal composition relative to GNP.

b. The Relationship Apparent in 1970 Data on Major Market Economics and the Block of Developing Countries

(1) Measures

Per capita consumption of metals, and per capita GNP are preferred measures to use in relating metal demands to the output of the DRI model. Use of per capita measures makes no assumption exterior to the basic model about the dynamics of population growth. Data for 1970 are employed for this initial broad-gauged view because that year is the latest one for which the required data are available. GNP data were transformed to a basis of 1972 dollars, and the following 1972 prices of metals were used: steel, $.0375 per pound; copper, $.506 per pound; aluminum, $.264 per pound; zinc, $.178 per pound; and lead, $.150 per pound.

(2) Aggregate Metal

Data for the year 1971 show that the United States had the highest per capita GNP at $5,152 and the highest per capita consumption of the five major metals (copper, lead, zinc, steel, and aluminum) at $76.45. Canada was second in per capita GNP at $4,299 and Japan was second in aggregate metal consumption having a value of $73.40—a quantity very nearly equal to that of the United States. The metal consumption of Japan is exceptionally high in light of the fact that its per capita GNP of $2,825 was only about one-half of that of the United States.

Per capita metal consumption and GNP for each of the countries or blocks of countries considered to be developed by standards established by the United Nations, and for the block of countries that comprised the United Nation's class of less developed (developing countries) are plotted in Chart F•21. This plot (logarithmic scales) exhibits an overall linear relationship. Regression analysis yielded the following linear equation:

$$\ln V = -2.45433 + .797885 \ln GNP,$$

where V = per capita value of consumption of the five major metals
GNP = per capita gross national product
R^2 = .945
$F^{1.5}$ = 86.5

Close examination of Chart F•21 suggests that there may be two groups of countries with respect to patterns of metals consumption: 1) Japan, South Africa, and Developing Countries; and 2) United States, Australia and New

Zealand, Canada, and Europe. Each group appears to define a linear relationship having a similar slope but different intercepts. If this relationship is valid, a dollar of GNP for Japan, South Africa, and Developing Countries implies greater metal requirements than it does for the other countries. Of course, with limited data, there is a risk of over-interpreting apparent patterns.

(3) Copper

Although Canada ranked second in terms of per capita GNP, it had the highest per capita copper consumption in 1970, while the U. S. and Japan were second and third in per capita copper consumption. A plot of per capita consumption and GNP on a logarithmic scale in Chart F•22 exhibits a general linear pattern, although there is

Chart F•21
VALUE OF METALS CONSUMPTION VERSUS GNP, 1970

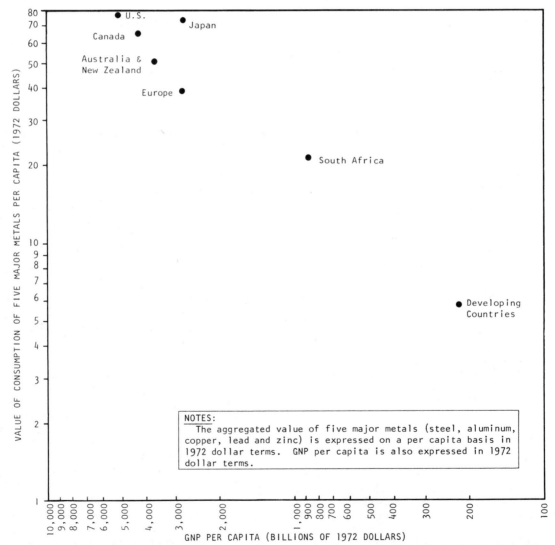

Source: Ellis, Harris, and Van Wie, "Probability Appraisal of the Uranium Resources of New Mexico," U.S., AEC, 1974.

some scatter among the developed countries. Regression analysis yielded the following equation:

$$\ln Cu = -5.37938 + 1.00353 \ln GNP,$$

where
Cu = pounds of copper per capita
GNP = per capita gross national product in 1972 dollars
R^2 = .979
$F^{1.5}$ = 233.7

The per capita consumption of the United States falls somewhat below the least squares estimate, with an actual value of 19.63 pounds compared to a calculated value of 24.46 pounds. In contrast, Canada's per capita consumption lies above the estimate: 23.59 pounds compared to 19.81 pounds. This least squares line is of particular interest because the coefficient of per capita GNP is nearly 1.000, meaning that in this data set for 1970, per capita copper consumption is approximately a constant fraction of per capita GNP, that fraction being $e^{-5.37938} = .0046107$ (approximately .46 percent). Thus, according to this data set, per capita copper consumption could adequately be described by the following linear equation:

$$Cu = .0046 GNP$$

(4) Aluminum

In per capita aluminum consumption, the United States, with 39.7 pounds, exceeds by a multiple of nearly two, the country with the next highest consumption; i.e., Canada with 22.7 pounds per capita. Japan is third, and Australia and New Zealand fourth, having 20.35 pounds and 19.94 pounds, respectively. These high consumptions stand in marked contrast to the consumption of the block of developing countries, a 1.55 pounds per capita.

As indicated in Chart F·23, the plot of per capita GNP and per capita aluminum consumption in logarithmic scale exhibits a strong linear pattern. Regression analysis yields the following least squares line:

$$\ln Al = 4.83113 + .960146 \ln GNP,$$

where
Al = lbs per capita aluminum consumption
GNP = per capita gross national product in 1972 dollars
R^2 = .970
$F^{1.5}$ = 160.2

The per capita consumption of the United States lies slightly above this line (36.93 pounds, compared to 29.22

Chart F·22
COPPER CONSUMPTION VERSUS GNP, 1970

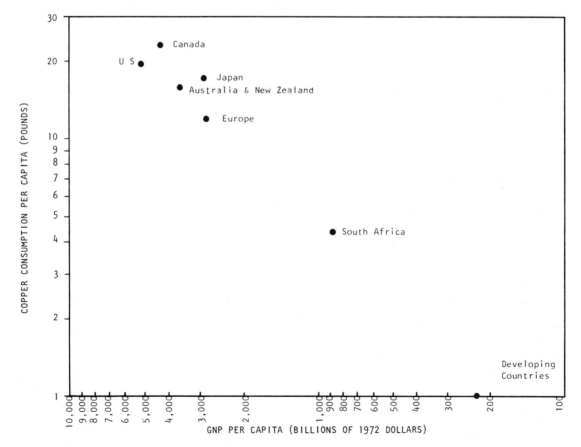

Source: Ellis, Harris, and Van Wie, "Probability Appraisal of the Uranium Resources of New Mexico," U.S., AEC, 1974

373

Chart F•23
ALUMINUM CONSUMPTION VERSUS GNP, 1970

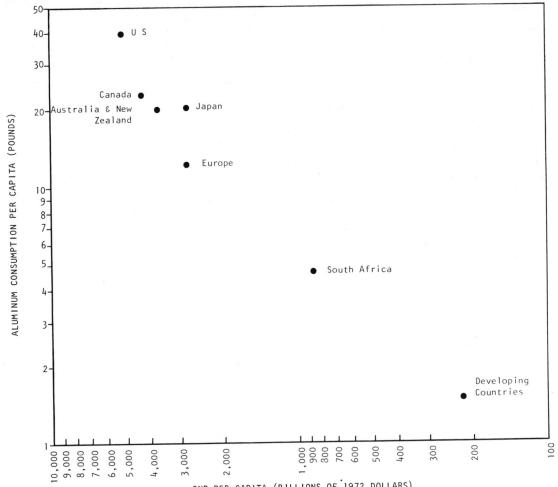

Source: Ellis, Harris, and Van Wie, "Probability Appraisal of the Uranium Resources of New Mexico," U.S., AEC, 1974.

pounds) while Europe falls somewhat below it (12.34 pounds compared to 16.41 pounds).

(5) Crude Steel

Chart F•24 shows that Japan, with a per capita GNP only $2,794, leads the nations of this group in the per capita consumption of crude steel with 1,496 lbs. The United States is second with 1370 lbs, and Canada third with 1,156 lbs. Although the relative positions of the United States and Japan are reversed, the plot of per capita crude steel and per capita GNP in logarithmic scale exhibits an overall pattern similar to that of aggregate metal, exhibiting the same two subsets of linear plots. The presence of this same pattern reflects the large influence of crude steel consumption upon the value of aggregate metal consumption. In the case of the United States, the value of per capita crude steel consumption constitutes 67.2 percent of the total value of the five metals: steel, copper, aluminum, lead, and zinc.

Regression yielded the following equation for crude steel:

$$\ln S = .862564 + .751896 \ln GNP,$$

where S = per capita consumption of crude steel

GNP = per capita GNP in 1972 dollars

R^2 = .922

$F^{1.5}$ = 59.3

The least squares estimate for the United States is just slightly above the actual consumption (1,464.11 pounds compared to 1,370.60 pounds) while the estimate for Japan is considerably below actual consumption (924.27 pounds compared to 1,495.18 pounds), and the estimate for Developing Countries is somewhat above actual consumption (136.95 pounds compared to 120.42 pounds).

374

Chart F•24
CRUDE STEEL CONSUMPTION VERSUS GNP, 1970

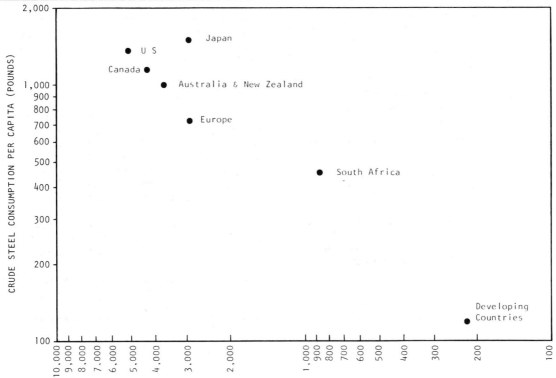

Source: Ellis, Harris, and Van Wie, "Probability Appraisal of the Uranium Resources of New Mexico," U.S., AEC, 1974

Chart F•25
LEAD CONSUMPTION VERSUS GNP, 1970

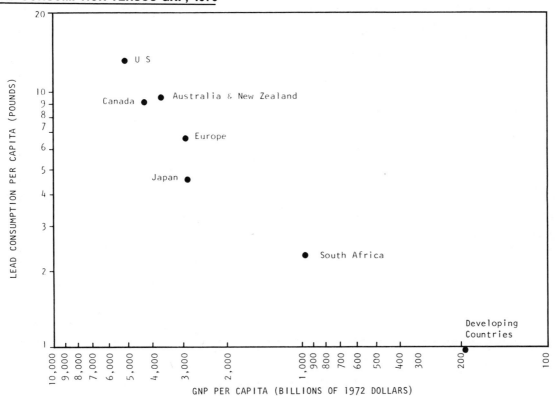

375

(6) Lead

The United States per capita consumption of lead in 1970 at 13.08 lbs. was considerably higher than that of the area having the next highest consumption; i.e., Australia and New Zealand with 9.44 lbs. The overall pattern of the plot of per capita lead consumption and per capita GNP in logarithmic scale appears more nonlinear than linear (See Chart F•25.). This apparent nonlinearity appears to be due primarily to the data representing the Developing Countries, although the point for South Africa appears to lend weight to the nonlinearity.

Regression analysis examined both linear and nonlinear forms:

$$\ln Pb = a + b \ln GNP$$
$$\ln Pb = a + b \ln GNP + C \ln (GNP/100)^2$$

However, the high collinearity of the $\ln GNP$ and $\ln (GNP/100)^2$ prevented reliable matrix inversion, and $\ln (GNP/100)^2$ was eliminated. The linear equation resulting from the regression analysis is as follows:

$$1b\ Pb = -4.38119 + .787165 \ln GNP,$$

where Pb = per capita lead consumption
       GNP = per capita gross national product in 1972 dollars
       R^2 = .945
       $F^{1.5}$ = 86.5

The estimate of per capita consumption for the United States is somewhat below actual consumption (10.45 pounds compared to 13.08 pounds), while that for South Africa was above actual consumption (2.58 pounds compared to 2.28 pounds), and the estimate for the developing countries is below actual consumption (.87 pounds compared to .99 pounds).

(7) Zinc

Although the per capita GNP for the United States, Canada, and Australia and New Zealand differ quite a bit ($5152, $4299, and $3692, respectively) the per capita consumption of zinc for these three countries is fairly similar, 15.11 pounds, 16.49 pounds, and 16.31 pounds, respectively. (See Chart F•26.) In contrast, Japan and Europe have very similar per capita GNP, $2825 and $2794, respectively, but differ considerably in per capita zinc, 4.49 pounds and 6.47 pounds, respectively.

The overall pattern of the plot of per capita zinc consumption and per capita GNP in logarithmic scale appears to be linear, although there is considerable scatter in the plot.

Regression analysis yielded the following relationship:

$$\ln Zn = -4.28083 + .839345 \ln GNP$$

where Zn = per capita zinc consumption
       GNP = per capita gross national product in 1972 dollars
       R^2 = .937
       $F^{1.5}$ = 74.8

Chart F•26
ZINC CONSUMPTION VERSUS GNP, 1970

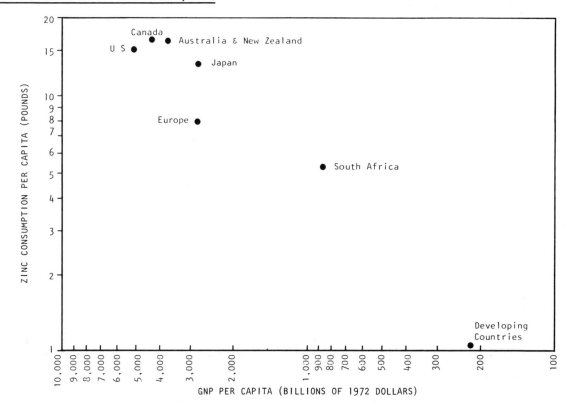

The regression estimate for the United States is somewhat above actual consumption (18.05 pounds compared to 15.11 pounds) while the estimate for Japan is considerably below actual consumption (10.79 pounds compared to 13.33 pounds). The estimate for the Developing Countries is above actual consumption (1.28 pounds compared to 1.12 pounds).

c. The Composition of GNP

(1) Why Important

In the previous section it was demonstrated that in 1970, per capita consumption of a metal and per capita GNP are closely related when viewed across the set of countries selected for this study. While these models could be used for broad-gauged forecasting of metal requirements in the short run, use of them for longer range studies would be valid only if it could be assumed with a reasonable amount of prudence that there will be no significant change in the composition of GNP, as regards the consumption of metals vis a vis the consumption of other resources, of labor, and

of capital. One way of appraising the likelihood for changes in the composition of future GNP is to examine GNP for previous years for trends in composition.

(2) Trends in Composition

In order to look for trends in composition of GNP, the consumption of metal in a given year was divided by the GNP in constant 1972 dollars to give pounds of metal per dollar of real GNP. This measure was plotted for the United States for the years 1929, 1950, 1960, and 1970, for other developed countries for the years 1950, 1960, and 1970, and for developing countries for 1950, 1960, 1963, 1968, and 1970. (See Chart F·27.) The inconsistent sampling years were dictated by availability of data on metal consumption and GNP. In the case of developing countries a consistent series for GNP is not available for years previous to 1950. The date points for these years were connected by straight lines to draw attention to patterns; obviously, the regularity of the time series primarily reflects the sparse data and plotting procedures, rather

Chart F·27
METAL CONSUMPTION PER DOLLAR OF GNP

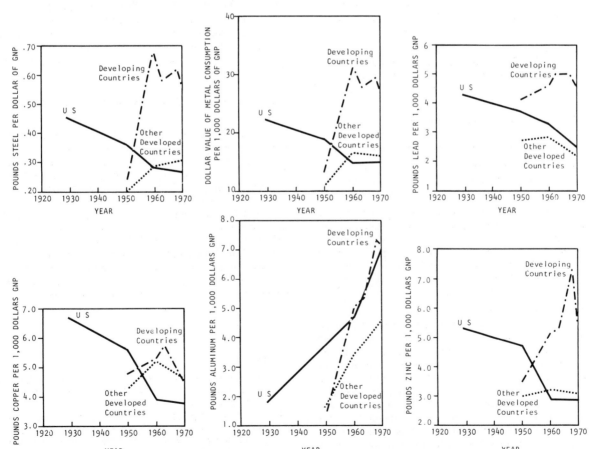

Note: Gross domestic product is used for developing countries. GNP is measured in constant 1972 dollars.
Source: Ellis, Harris, and Van Wie, "Probability Appraisal of the Uranium Resources of New Mexico," U.S., AEC, 1974

Table F•20

FORECASTING RELATIONSHIPS FOR UNITED STATES: POUNDS OF METAL CONSUMPTION PER DOLLAR OF GNP[1]

Metal	Based on Entire Time Series 1929-1970 t = 0, 1929	Based Upon 1960-1970 t = 0, 1960
Copper	$Cu = .0068065 - .00007777t$	$*Cu = .0039 - .00001t$
Aluminum	$Al = .00152 + .0001216t$	$*Al = .0047 + .0024t$
Zinc	$Zn = .00546 - .000065t$	$*Zn = .0029$
Lead	$*Pb = .0044172 - .0000416t$	$Pb = .0033 - .00008t$
Steel	$S = .4525 - .004818t$	$*S = .280 - .0014t$

[1] GNP is measured in 1972 dollars.

* An asterisk appears next to that equation of the two for each metal that forecasts the greatest future metal consumption.

than the state of nature.

The first and obvious conclusion to be drawn from Chart F•27 is that there are definite trends in the historical relationship of pounds of metal per dollar of GNP.

With the exception of aluminum, the overall pattern in the United States has been for metals consumption to be an ever smaller part of GNP. On the other hand, aluminum consumption per dollar of GNP exhibits a strong rising trend. Reasons for these trends are three-fold:

1. As our society and economy mature, needs for services rather than material goods are reflected in greater contribution from the services sector and a proportionately smaller contribution from industrial products.

2. Substitutions of nonmetal for metals in the manufacture of consumer and producer goods displaces metals from some markets (e.g. plastics for lead).

3. Substitution of lightweight abundant metals for traditional metals increases the consumption of the lightweight at the expense of the other metals.

Nonmetals substitutions have affected the consumption of many metals; of those in the set here examined, the consumption of steel, lead, and zinc have been considerably affected by nonmetals substitution. Substitution of one metal for another is partly responsible for the increasing consumption of aluminum and the decreasing consumption of copper, zinc, and steel.

Again, with the exception of aluminum, the patterns in consumption of metal per dollar of GNP for the developing countries and the other developed countries are similar over the twenty-year period represented by the data; however in the level of consumption and in detail there are differences. Both groups showed a large increase in consumption from 1950-1960, and (with the exception of steel for other developed countries) a leveling-off and decline during 1960-1970. Steel consumption by other developed countries continued to increase during 1960-1970, but by a smaller amount than during the previous decade.

Consumption of aluminum per dollar of GNP by devel-oping countries increased at a rate higher than that of the United States, except for the period of 1968-1970 during which there occurred a decrease. The level of consumption per dollar of GNP by developing countries also exceeded that by other developed countries throughout the period, except for the year 1950, and in 1960 and 1968 the consumption per dollar GNP by the developing countries exceeded that by the United States. The evidence seems unanimous and persuasive that aluminum is the metal of the future. Developing as well as developed countries have turned to increasingly heavy use of aluminum. This trend is likely to continue, and may even become stronger in the future.

(3) Forecasting Relationships for the United States

Selecting forecasting relationships from a time series raises the question as to whether to employ the overall trend of the series, hoping that recent developments are merely variation around a long term trend, or to emphasize the most recent part of the series on the premise that this past testifies of the present and most likely future. Two sets of forecasting equations have been prepared: one that is based upon the entire time series and the other one based only upon the last ten years (1960-1970). These equations are listed in Table F•20. They were used to develop the forecasts of metals consumption reported in Chapter 6. This appendix serves as the detailed backup for the quantitative analysis of materials in that chapter.

FOOTNOTES

1. The National Commission on Materials Policy, *Material Needs and the Environment Today and Tomorrow,* Washington, D. C., 1973.

2. Cox, D. P., Schmidt, R. G., Vine, J. D., Kirkemo, H., Tourtelot, E. B., and Fleischer, M., "Copper," chapter in *United States Mineral Resources,* Professional Paper 820, United States Geological Survey, Washington, D. C., 1973.

3. United States Bureau of Mines, "Commodity Data Sum-

maries'', Appendix I to *Mining and Minerals Policy,* Washington, D. C., 1974.

4. Metals Week, ''Aluminum'', June 5, 1971.

5. United States Geological Survey, *United States Mineral Resources,* Professional Paper 820, Washington, D. C., 1973.

6. U. S. Department of Interior, ''A Drill Hole Every 20 Miles Urged by Penn State Scientist to Uncover U. S. Mineral Wealth,'' News Release, Washington, D. C., September, 16, 1974.

7. Hubbert, M. King, ''Energy Resources,'' *Resources and Man,* W. H. Freeman & Co., San Francisco, 1969.

8. Hewett, D. F., ''Cycles in Metal Production,'' *American Institute of Metallurgical Engineers Transactions,* Pub. 183, 1929.

9. Erickson, Ralph, ''Crustal Abundance of Elements, and Mineral Reserves and Resources'', *United States Mineral Resources,* Professional Paper 820, United States Geological Survey, Washington, D. C., 1973.

10 McKelvey, V. E., ''Mineral Resources Estimates and Public Policy'', *United States Mineral Resources,* Professional Paper 820, United States Geological Survey, Washington, D. C., 1973.

11. Erickson, Ralph, as cited above.

12. Coulomb, R., ''Contribution à la Giochimie de l'uranium dans les Granites Intrusifs,'' Rapport C.E.A., No. 1173, 1959.

13. Krige, D. G., ''A Statistical Analysis of Some of the Borehole Values in the Orange Tree Goldfield,'' *Journal of Chemistry, Metallurgy and Mining Society of South Africa,* vol. 53, no. 2, 1952.

14. Singer, D. A., Cox, D. P., and Drew, L. J., ''Grade and Tonnage Relationships Among Copper Deposits,'' United States Geological Survey, forthcoming publication.

15. Ellis, J., Harris, D. P., and Van Wie, N., ''A Subjective Probability Appraisal of the Uranium Resources of New Mexico,'' United States Atomic Energy Commission, 1974, and Harris, D. P., unpublished manuscript.

16. Brinck, J. W., ''Note on the Distribution and Predictability of Mineral Resources,'' EUR 3461e, European Atomic Energy Community, Brussels, 1967.

17. Matheron, G., ''The Theory of Regionalized Variables and Its Applications,'' Les Cahiers de Morphologic Mathematique De Fontainebleau, 1971.

18. Green, G., ''Geochemical Table of the Elements for 1959,'' *Bulletin of the Geological Society of America,* vol. 70, 1959.

19. Cox, D. P., et. al., as cited above.

20. Lovering, T. S., ''Mineral Resources from the Land,'' Chapter 7, *Resources and Man,* W. H. Freeman & Company, San Francisco, 1969.

21. Lasky, S. G., ''How Tonnage and Grade Relations Help Predict Ore Reserves,'' *Engineering and Mining Journal,* pp 81-85, April, 1950.

22. Musgrove, P. A., ''The Distribution of Metal Resources (Tests and Implications of the Exponential Grade-Size Relations),'' *Proceedings of the Council of Economics,* American Institute of Metallurgical Engineers, 1971.

23. Ellis, J., Harris, D. P., and Van Wie, N., as cited above.

24. Bauchau, Christian, ''Essai de typologie quantitative des gisements de plomb et de zinc avec la repartition de l'argent,'' Bur. Recherches Geol. et Minières Bull., sec. 2, no. 3, pp 1-72 and no. 4, pp 1-47, 1971.

25. Morris, H. T., Heyl, A. V., and Hall, R. B., Lead Chapter in *United States Mineral Resources,* Professional Paper 820, United States Geological Survey, Washington, D. C., 1973.

26. Richter-Bernburg, Gerhard, ''Geologische Geselzmässigkeiten en der Metallführung des Kupferschiefers,'' Lagerstättinforschung (Reichstelle für Bodenforschung, N. F., no. 73, p. 61, 1941.

27. Bischoff, J. L., and Manheim, F. T., ''Economic Potential of the Red Sea Heavy Metal Deposits,'' in Degens, E. T., and Ross, D. A., editors, *Hot Brines and Recent Heavy Metal Deposits in the Red Sea,* pp. 535-549, Springer-Verlag, Berlin, 1969.

28. Morris, H. T., Heyl, A. V., and Hall, R. B., as cited above.

29. Goldberg, E. D., Arrhenius, G., ''Chemistry of Pacific Pelagic Sediments,'' Geochimica et Cosmochimica, Octa 13, pp 153-212, 1958.

30. Goldschmidt, V. M., *Geochemistry,* Oxford University Press, N.Y., 1954.

31. Bostom, Kurt, and Peterson, M. N. A., ''Precipitates from Hydrothermal Exhalations on the East Pacific Rise,'' *Economic Geology,* vol 61, pp 1258-1265, 1966.

32. Cloud, Preston, ''Mineral Resources from the Sea,'' *Resources and Man,* W. H. Freeman & Company, San Francisco, 1969.

33. Mero, John L., ''The Outlook for Mining in the Ocean,'' *Proceedings of the Council of Economics,* American Institute of Metallurgical Engineers, 1967.

34. Kaufman, R., and Rothstein, A. J., ''The Oceans: Future Source of Minerals,'' *Proceedings of the Council of Economics,* American Institute of Metallurgical Engineers, 1971.

35. Rigg, John B., ''Minerals from the Sea,'' *Ocean Industry,* p. 213, April, 1974.

36. Archer, A. A., ''Progress and Prospects of Marine Mining,'' *Mining Magazine,* pp. 150-163, March, 1974.

37. Ingersoll, Robert, ''A Mixed View of Seabed Mining,'' *Interocean 73, 1974.**

38. *Engineering and Mining Journal,* March, 1974.*

39. Cloud, Preston, as cited above.

40. Goldberg, E. D., ''The Oceans as a Chemical System,'' in Hill, M. N., editor, *The Sea,* vol. 2, pp. 2-35, John Wiley & Sons, New York, 1963.

41. Miller, A. R., Densmore, C. D., Degens, E. T., Hathaway, J. C., Mannheim, F. T., McFarlin, P. F., Pocklington, R., and Jokela, A., ''Hot Brines and Recent Iron Deposits in Deeps of the Red Sea,'' Geochimica et Cosmochimica Acta 30, pp 341-359, 1966.

42. Straus, Simon, ''Does the Pattern of Oil Prices Set a Precedent for Metals?'' *Mining Congress Journal,* vol. 60, no. 14, pp 43-52, 1974.

43. *Engineering and Mining Journal,* April, 1974.

44. Oak Ridge National Laboratory, ''Energy Expenditures Associated with the Production and Recycle of Metals,'' ORNL-MIT-132, 1971.

APPENDIX G

Energy Supply and Demand: General Concepts

1. Introductory Comments.

Almost since the first settlers arrived from Europe, North Americans have enjoyed relatively cheap and abundant energy. At first, the main sources were wood and work-animal feed. The new nation was primarily a solar-energy-based economy. Even then energy consumption was high. There was a vast continent, much of which was covered with virgin forests available for the cutting, while almost unlimited land areas were available for tilling. Fortunately, before this rudimentary solar-energy-economy was overwhelmed by population pressures, a combination of resources and technology came to the rescue. Coal was the first substitute, followed later by oil, gas, and now nuclear power. Chart G·1 shows the great energy substitution processes which have been under way for well over 100 years, and which almost certainly are destined to continue.

At the time when the first of our fossil fuels, coal, was coming into prominence just before the Civil War, statistics show that the per capita energy consumption rate in the United States was fully 40 percent of the current rate.[1] In other words, over 100 years ago United States citizens were using more energy than 80 percent of the world's popu-

lation uses today.[2] Despite the continued abundance and low cost of energy through the years, as shown in Chart G·2, per capita consumption in the United States has grown at the rather modest average rate of under 1 percent per year over the last 100 years. During this same 100 years the average annual growth rate for real GNP per capita was about 2.2 percent. In recent years, however, per capita energy growth has accelerated so that over the period from 1953 to 1973 it has averaged about 1.9 percent per year, while per capita growth of real GNP remained at about 2.2 percent.

At present the nation requires some 30 percent of world energy consumption to fill the needs of only 6 percent of world population. A variety of reasons can be advanced for this world-wide imbalance in energy consumption. One of the major reasons certainly seems to have been the low-cost and ready availability of energy in the United States. Another is probably the very size of our nation and its generally low population density which encouraged more and longer distance movement of both people and goods, just as it encouraged a unique type of agriculture.

One conventional device used to examine energy use per capita in different countries is to relate it to real GNP per capita as shown on Chart G·3. In addition to the United States, Canada is also a relatively heavy energy consumer, probably for much the same reason as suggested for the United States. With the possible exception of Czechoslovakia and East Germany,[3] most of the other nations of the world appear to be following a somewhat different energy-GNP path than do the United States and Canada.

Chart G·1
ENERGY SUBSTITUTION PATTERNS

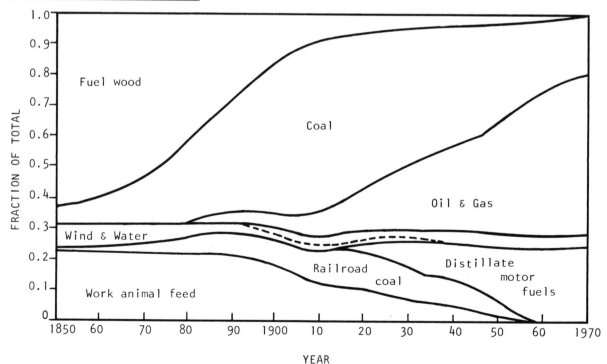

Source: John C. Fisher, *Energy Crises in Perspective*, John Wiley, New York, 1974.

Chart G·2
PER CAPITA ENERGY CONSUMPTION

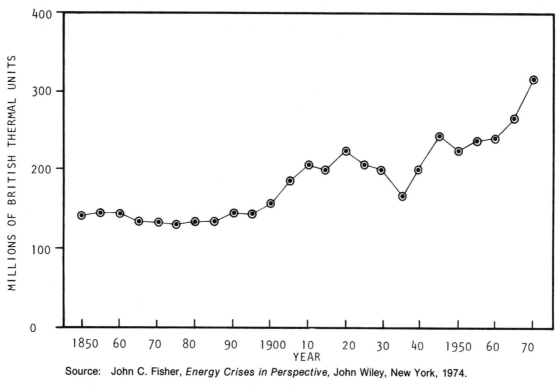

Source: John C. Fisher, *Energy Crises in Perspective,* John Wiley, New York, 1974.

2. Energy Supplies

For most of its history the United States has been generally self-sufficient in energy; exporting rather than importing fuels. Finally, in the 1960s a variety of factors (e.g., more rapid growth in energy consumption; shifts away from coal to oil and gas; increased difficulty in domestic oil and gas exploration; and the availability of very low cost foreign oil) combined to change the nation to a net importer of energy and to initiate what has become a rapidly growing dependence on foreign supplies. Had this trend continued, and had the Arabs not shocked us out of our complacency, some recent energy supply analyses suggest that as much as 40 percent of our total energy supplies could have been imported by the 1980s.

Actually the United States still has an immense energy resource base if we wish to use it. However, even a casual look at generally accepted resource figures suggests that another major shift in the pattern of energy consumption is inevitable and is in fact, already under way. Chart G·4 contrasts the current consumption breakdown with the resource position for the major fossil fuels. It shows, for example, that while oil and gas together constitute more than 75 percent of current United States annual consumption, they account for less than 25 percent of currently "useful" fossil fuel resource base. In contrast, coal fulfills only about 18 percent of our current demands despite a resource base many times larger than that of oil and gas. This disparity between current use and resource availability is greatly magnified if: (1) nuclear fuel in light water reactors is considered; and (2) the technological

feasibility of the breeder reactor is acknowledged. A picture of the United States reserve-resources position is presented graphically on Charts G·5, G·6, and G·7.

With current annual energy consumption at about 75 quadrillion Btu and with such a resource base at our command, there is no doubt that the United States can once again become self-sufficient in energy. In fact, eventual self-sufficiency based on coal, nuclear fission, and ultimately on fusion and solar power seems inevitable. In this case, however, the inevitable is a long way off. Lags in turning decisions into reality are unavoidably long in the energy industry. They have, in fact, become much longer today than they were just a decade ago. The capital intensity and mechanical complexity of the equipment needed for efficient energy production, as well as of the devices used to facilitate its consumption, are at the heart of the unavoidable parts of these lags. Environmental concerns, land use conflicts, and political decision processes are primary sources of some of the "avoidable" parts of the lags.

For example, it takes 3 years to build a refinery and at least as long to locate a place which will permit it to be built. It takes five years to locate and bring a new off-shore oil field into production, and fully as long to get agreement to allow the area to be drilled. A nuclear power plant requires five or six years for construction and almost an equal time to proceed through the prior approval procedures.

The "avoidable" lags result primarily from sincere efforts by "interested groups" to assure environmental

Chart G·3
GROSS NATIONAL PRODUCT VS ENERGY CONSUMPTION (1970)

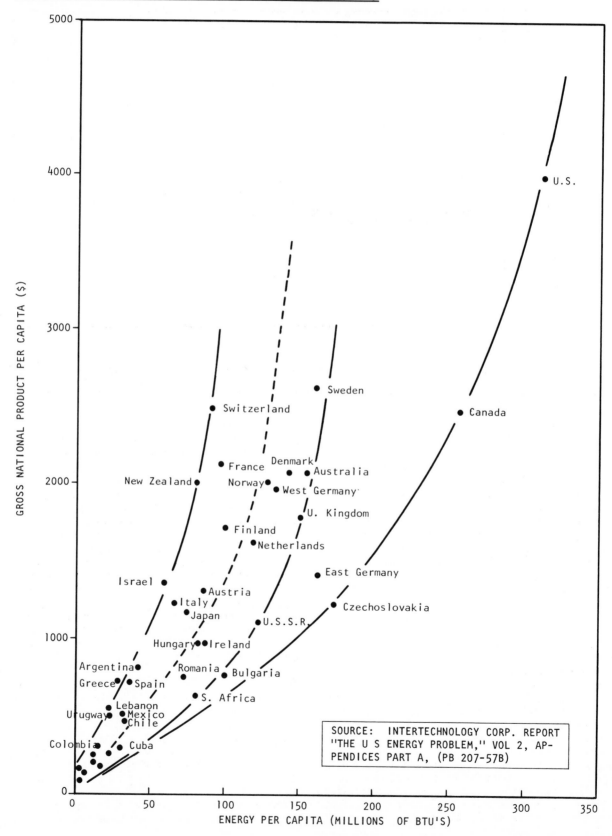

SOURCE: INTERTECHNOLOGY CORP. REPORT
"THE U S ENERGY PROBLEM," VOL 2, AP-
PENDICES PART A, (PB 207-57B)

Chart G•4
RESERVES-RESOURCES VS CURRENT RATES OF CONSUMPTION

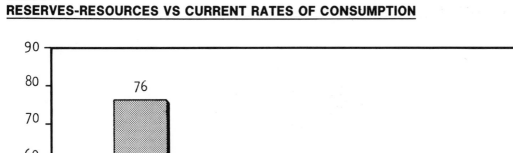

Wide bars show percentages of total United States reserves and resources of currently useful fossil fuels.

Narrow bars show percentages of current total energy consumption obtained from those fossil fuels.

protection and restrict land uses to those they see as desirable. One of the ultimate consequences to the community at large, however, is additional sluggishness in the response of the energy industry to changing conditions.

3. Energy Consumption

On the consumption side of the energy picture, shifts in energy use patterns are similarly slow. The average automobile has a useful life of a decade, a house heating system about 20 years, and the house itself as much as 50 years. Similarly long times are often needed to redesign, test, and place new energy-efficient equipment into production. Examples are industrial machinery, motor vehicles, and electrical generation equipment.

In examining energy consumption, it is conventional to divide the overall market for energy into at least four submarkets: residential, commercial, industrial and transportation. For some purposes it may be necessary to develop more detailed breakdowns. A review of past trends and the current situation as regards consumption by markets is an almost necessary introductory exercise to any forecasting attempt. Therefore, Tables G•1, G•2, and G•3

were used to set the stage for the judgmental forecasts of energy demand which appear in Chapter 6.

There are undoubtedly hundreds of uses for energy, but as Table G•1 shows, in each of the major markets, two or three major end-use categories account for the bulk of that market's total consumption. Table G•2 collects those major and end-uses from each market to show that a mere 12 applications account for all but 3 percent of the nation's total consumption.

A further breakdown of the industrial sector by industries, as on Table G•3, shows that a similar concentration pattern exists here, with 16 industries accounting for some 50 percent of total industrial consumption. Note that the use of energy sources as a raw material; e.g., petrochemical feedstocks and asphalt, is included in the industrial category.

This appendix has provided a concise summary of the current situation regarding energy supply and energy demand in the United States. The summary amplifies the information presented in Chapter 5 and provides a foundation for evaluating the energy forecasts in Chapter 6.

Chart G•5
THE RESERVES-RESOURCES RECTANGLES FOR THE UNITED STATES

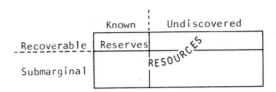

The two small rectangles to the left of the vertical dividing line represent known deposits, and the two to the right represent unknown deposits. The two small rectangles above the horizontal dividing line represent recoverable minerals, and the two below represent submarginal minerals. The "known-recoverable" rectangle represents reserves, and everything else is called resources,

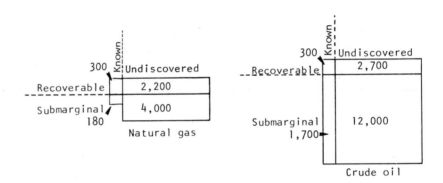

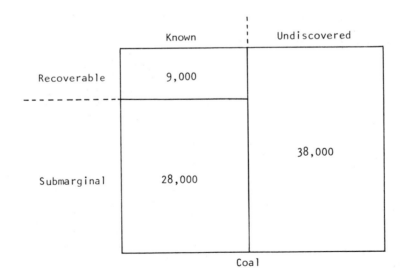

United States reserves and resources of natural gas, crude oil, and coal, in quadrillion Btu. These diagrams are all drawn to the same scale, as are others to follow in this series, to facilitate visual comparison.

Note: Charts G•5, G•6, and G•7 are adapted from material in John C. Fisher, *Energy Crises in Perspective*, John Wiley, New York, 1974.

Chart G·6
RESERVES-RESOURCES RECTANGLES FOR THE UNITED STATES

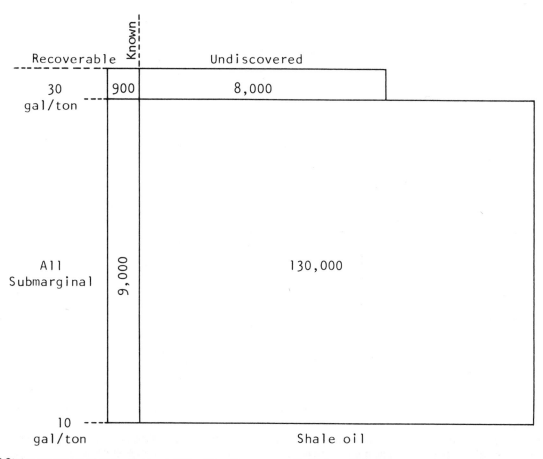

United States resources of shale oil, in quadrillion Btu. Resources estimated to yield in excess of 30 gallons of oil per ton of shale are distinguished from those estimated to yield between 10 and 30 gallons per ton. Resources yielding between 5 and 10 gallons per ton, not shown in the figure, are estimated to provide an additional 800,000 quadrillion Btu.

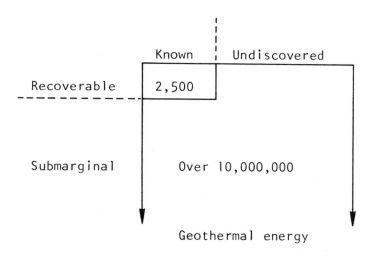

United States geothermal heat reserves and resources in quadrillion Btu.

Chart G•7
RESERVES-RESOURCES RECTANGLES FOR THE UNITED STATES

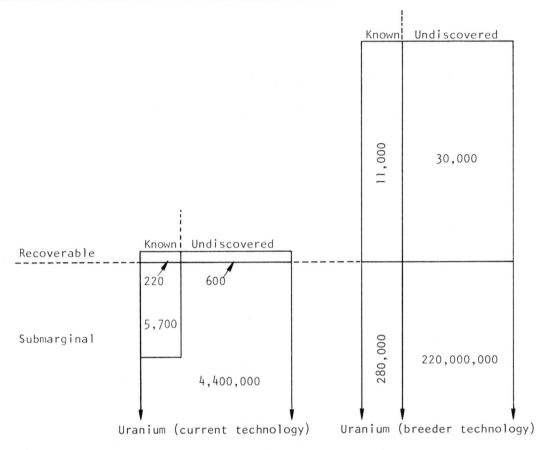

United States reserves and resources of uranium in quadrillion Btu. Although current technology is able to utilize only about 1.5 percent of the potential energy of uranium, breeder reactor technology may be able to utilize 80 percent.

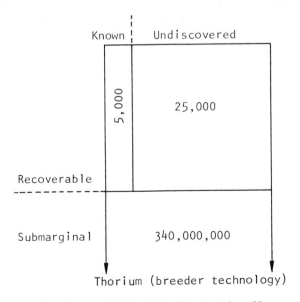

United States reserves and resources of thorium in quadrillion Btu, based on 80 percent conversion of thorium to fissionable nuclear fuels.

Table G.1

ENERGY CONSUMPTION IN THE UNITED STATES BY END USE 1960-1968
(Trillions of Btu and Percent per Year)

Sector and End Use	Consumption		Percent of National Total	
	1960	1968	1960	1968
Residential				
Space heating	4,848	6,675	11.3%	11.0%
Water heating	1,159	1,736	2.7	2.9
Cooking	556	637	1.3	1.1
Clothes drying	93	208	0.2	0.3
Refrigeration	369	692	0.9	1.1
Air conditioning	134	427	0.3	0.7
Other	809	1,241	1.9	2.1
Total	7,968	11,616	18.6	19.2
Commercial				
Space heating	3,111	4,182	7.2	6.9
Water heating	544	653	1.3	1.1
Cooking	98	139	0.2	0.2
Refrigeration	534	670	1.2	1.1
Air conditioning	576	1,113	1.3	1.8
Feedstock	734	984	1.7	1.6
Other	145	1,025	0.3	1.7
Total	5,742	8,766	13.2	14.4
Industrial				
Process steam	7,646	10,132	17.8	16.7
Electric drive	3,170	4,794	7.4	7.9
Electrolytic processes	486	705	1.1	1.2
Direct heat	5,550	6,929	12.9	11.5
Feed stock	1,370	2,202	3.2	3.6
Other	118	198	0.3	0.3
Total	18,340	24,960	42.7	41.2
Transportation				
Fuel	10,873	15,038	25.2	24.9
Raw materials	141	146	0.3	0.3
Total	11,014	15,184	25.5	25.2
National total	43,064	60,526	100.0%	100.0%

Note: Electric utility consumption has been allocated to each end use.

Source: Stanford Research Institute, using Bureau of Mines and other sources.

Table G·2
MAJOR USES OF ENERGY: 1968

	Percent of Total
Transportation (fuel; excludes lubes and greases)	24.9%
Space heating (residential, commercial)	17.9
Process steam (industrial)	16.7
Direct heat (industrial)	11.5
Electric drive (industrial)	7.9
Feedstocks, raw materials (commercial, industrial, transportation)	5.5
Water heating (residential, commercial)	4.0
Air conditioning (residential, commercial)	2.5
Refrigeration (residential, commercial)	2.2
Lighting (residential, commercial)	1.5
Cooking (residential, commercial)	1.3
Electrolytic processes (industrial)	1.2
Total	97.1%

Source: Stanford Research Institute

Table G·3
INDUSTRIAL USES OF ENERGY: 1968

Iron and steel	13.6%
Petroleum refining	11.3
Paper and paper board	5.2
Petrochemical feedstock	4.9
Aluminum	2.8
Cement	2.1
Ammonia	2.0
Ferrous foundries	2.0
Carbon black	0.9
Grain mills	0.8
Copper	0.8
Glass	0.8
Concrete	0.7
Meat products	0.7
Soda ash	0.7
Sugar	0.7

Source: Stanford Research Institute

FOOTNOTES

1. U. S. Government Printing Office, *Historical Statistics of the United States Colonial Times to 1957*. United States Government Printing Office, Washington, D. C.

2. Fremont Felix, *World Markets of Tomorrow,* Harper and Row, New York; 1972.

3. The heavy concentration of energy intensive capital goods production relative to the total output in those and other Communist-world countries may explain their heavy energy consumptions.

APPENDIX H

World Mineral Resources

This appendix summarizes data on the estimated resources of selected metals and minerals on a world-wide basis. The source for all these data is: Brobst, D. and Pratt, W. (Eds) "United States Mineral Resources." Geological Survey Professional Paper 820, United States Dept of the Interior, 1973.

The following units and abbreviations are used:

bt: billion tons
mt: million tons

bmt: billion metric tons
mmt: million metric tons

bst: billion short tons
mst: million short tons

1 metric ton = 1.1 short ton (approx)

The minerals and their resource situations are:

1) *Aluminum*

12-15 bt of bauxite. In addition, vast amounts of other potential sources of aluminum such as alunite, aluminous shale and slate, aluminum phosphate rock, etc.

2) *Copper*

344 mst of identified resources. These include specific identified deposits not all of which may be graded nor may it all be economically recoverable at present. In addition, 400 mst of hypothetical resources which are undiscovered as yet but have been geologically predicted.

3) *Iron*

252,000 mmt of identified reserves from which economical recovery is possible today. 779,000 mmt of identified resources (including the above reserves) not all of which has been evaluated at present, so that economic recovery may not be possible in some cases.

4) *Fluorspar*

190 mst of identified economically recoverable reserves. 573 mst of hypothetical resources which may contain some material of ore grade but much of these resources are exploitable only under more favorable economic conditions.

5) *Manganese*

6500 mt of identified deposits. The economic recovery of these deposits is possible now. 7,700 mt specific, identified deposits not recoverable economically at present. 10,000 mt of undiscovered but geologically predicted deposits.

6) *Nickel*

9.3 bst sufide deposits containing 0.2.to 3.0 percent nickel. 4.8 bst laterite deposits containing 0.5 to 2.5 percent nickel.

7) *Sulfur*

29 bmt identified in the United States of which 200 mmt is economically recoverable now. 245 mmt of identified resources in Canada and 40 mmt in Mexico. Not all of these are recoverable now. About 2 bmt of apparent reserves occur elsewhere in the world.

8) *Zinc*

235 mmt economically recoverable at present. 1,255 mmt identified but sub economic. 3,575 mmt undiscovered but expected.

Note: "Economically recoverable at present," "currently recoverable," etc, mean profitable extraction is possible with current technology and under present economic conditions.

APPENDIX I

Revenues Required to Yield Adequate Returns on Equity

Table I•1 details the calculations of increased revenues needed by the investor-owned electric utility to achieve adequate returns on common equity during the period 1967 through 1973. These figures are discussed in detail in Chapter 9.

Table I•1
INVESTOR OWNED ELECTRIC UTILITY INDUSTRY
Revenue Increases To Achieve Adequate Return on Equity: 1966-1973
(Millions of Dollars or Percent)

	Unit or Calculation	1967	1968	1969	1970	1971	1972	1973
1. Actual Earnings on Common	($)	2,630	2,681	2,823	2,972	3,281	3,721	4,083
2. Average Common Equity......	($)	20,655	21,822	23,209	25,253	28,185	31,681	35,631
3. Actual Return on Common Equity	(%)	12.70	12.30	12.20	11.75	11.63	11.73	11.45
4. Adequate Return on Common Equity	(%)	13.00	13.60	14.00	14.50	14.80	15.00	15.00
5. Actual Revenues	($)	17,386	18,800	20,324	22,276	25,053	28,437	31,848
6. Revenues if Previous Year had Provided Adequate Return on Equity	(16)* × (5)	17,386	18,920	20,954	23,256	26,673	30,537	34,248
7. Incremental Revenue...........	(6) — (5)	—	120	630	980	1,620	2,100	2,400
8. Incremental Earnings...........	(7) × 48%	—	58	302	470	778	1,010	1,150
9. Actual Earnings	$	2,630	2,681	2,823	2,972	3,281	3,721	4,083
10. Earnings if Previous Year had Provided Adequate Return on Equity	(8) + (9)	2,630	2,739	3,125	3,442	4,059	4,731	5,233
11. Earnings for Adequate Return on Equity in Current Year..................................	(4) × (2)	2,683	2,960	3,250	3,662	4,170	4,750	5,350
12. Incremental Earnings...........	(11) — (10)	53	221	125	220	111	19	117
13. Incremental Revenues	(12) × 2.082	111	461	261	460	231	40	244
14. Percent increase (%)	(13) ÷ (6)	0.64	2.42	1.25	1.97	0.87	0.16	0.71
15. Adequate Revenues	(13) + (6)	17,497	19,381	21,215	23,716	26,904	30,577	34,492
16. Factor For Next Year	(15) ÷ (5)	1.0064	1.031	1.044	1.065	1.074	1.075	1.083

* Use Value from Previous Year

APPENDIX J

The Zero Intercept Method

The zero intercept method of classifying and allocating customer related costs, attempts to identify the cost of distribution plant related to a hypothetical zero-load situation, on the premise that there is a demand component present even for the smallest size of each type of distribution equipment. It relates the installed book cost to the current carrying capacity or demand rating of the equipment for each type of distribution equipment. A curve is plotted of cost (on the y-axis of a graph) per unit

(e.g., per foot of wire, or per transformer) versus current carrying capacity or demand rating (on the x-axis of a graph). The curve is then extrapolated back to its y-axis intercept to determine the hypothetical cost of a piece of equipment capable of supplying no load. (See Charts J•1, J•2, and J•3 which follow.) This zero-intercept per unit cost is then multiplied by the number of units in the system to obtain the customer portion expressed in dollars of that type of equipment.

The minimum practical size method uses, for a per-unit customer related cost, the book cost of the minimum size of each type of equipment that has actually been installed in the utility system, on the premise that a certain greater than zero size must be installed in order to have a physical strength capable of withstanding wind and ice loadings, etc.

Chart J•1
SINGLE PHASE OVERHEAD TRANSFORMERS

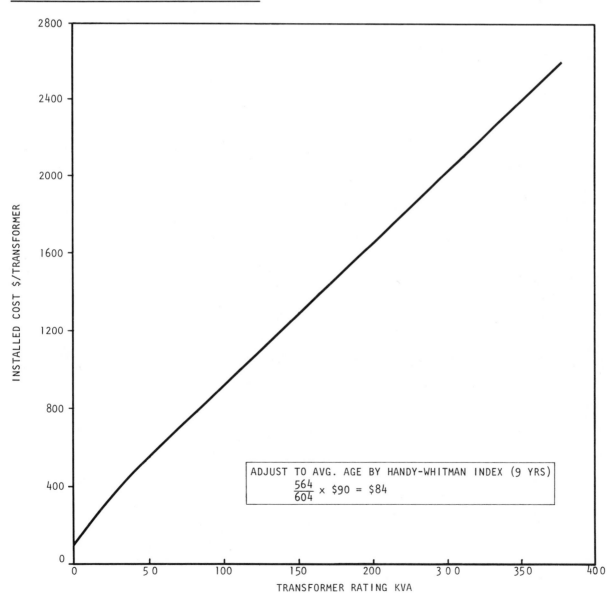

ADJUST TO AVG. AGE BY HANDY-WHITMAN INDEX (9 YRS)
$$\frac{564}{604} \times \$90 = \$84$$

Chart J•2
UNDERGROUND PRIMARY

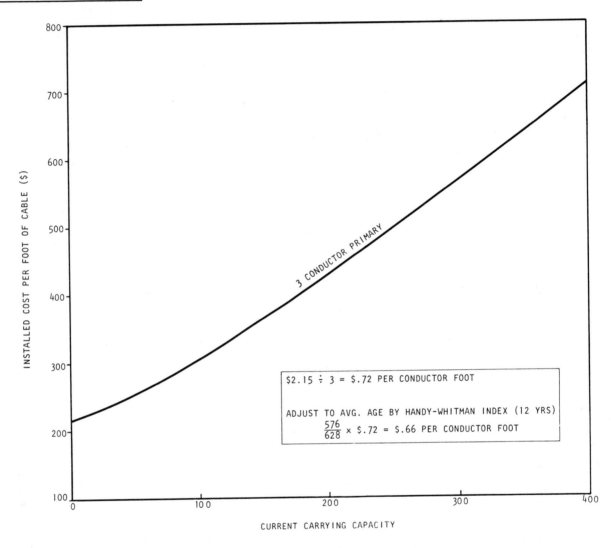

CURRENT CARRYING CAPACITY

$2.15 ÷ 3 = $.72 PER CONDUCTOR FOOT

ADJUST TO AVG. AGE BY HANDY-WHITMAN INDEX (12 YRS)
$$\frac{576}{628} \times \$.72 = \$.66 \text{ PER CONDUCTOR FOOT}$$

Chart J•3
NORMAL SPAN RURAL CONSTRUCTION

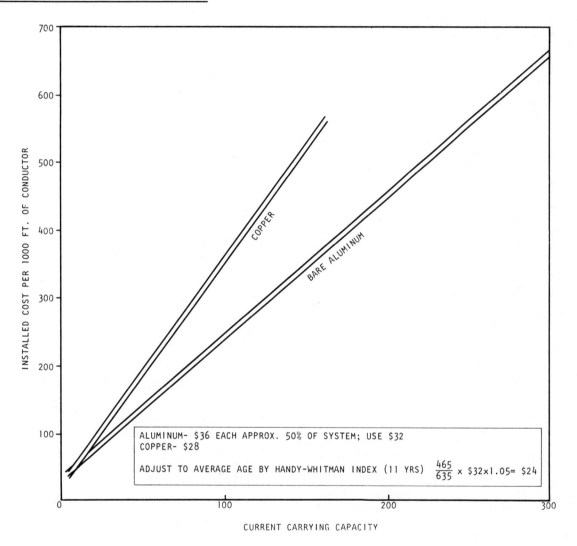

ALUMINUM- $36 EACH APPROX. 50% OF SYSTEM; USE $32
COPPER- $28

ADJUST TO AVERAGE AGE BY HANDY-WHITMAN INDEX (11 YRS) $\frac{465}{635}$ × $32×1.05= $24

APPENDIX K

Summary of EEI Rate Research Committee Study

Adapted from Studies by E. I. Rudd & R. N. Rau titled
THEORETICAL RATE DESIGN
FOR MODEL ELECTRIC COMPANY

Recent studies in the fields of: (a) costs of service and, (b) rate design by the Rate Research Committee of the Edison Electric Institute employed a hypothetical, but typical, Model Electric Company as the vehicle around which the studies were developed. These studies were done in the early 1970's before the recent increases in interest rates and fuel costs; thus, some of the numbers are somewhat outdated. The rate-making principles discussed have *not* been similarly outdated.

Revenues, sales, a system load composite, operating and maintenance expenses, depreciation, taxes, plant in service and depreciation reserve were developed for the Model Electric Company. Some of this information is shown as Tables K•1, K•2 and K•3 and on Chart K•1. The model company served six classes of customers. An illustrative cost allocation was performed on each element of the revenue, expense and rate base, assigning all expenses and plant of the Model Electric Company to the six classes of customers using the non-coincident demand method. However, the demand allocation factors for three other methods (peak responsibility, average kilowatthour load, and average and excess demand) were also developed for comparison purposes. See Table K•4.

Then having the costs so assigned, the next steps to be undertaken in the analysis of the Model Electric Company were: a) the computation of the amount of revenue required of each class to cover its full costs of service and b) the development of rate forms and specific pricings to provide the revenues required. The second step involves starting with the revenue requirement for each class of customers and determining an equitable scheme for apportioning that total requirement among the customers in the class in a manner to give proper consideration to the range in size of customers from smallest to largest users, to the various possible levels of load factor from the lowest to the highest, and to the probable high diversity between some groups of customers and the probable low diversity between others.

In recognition of this need to distinguish between the manners in which costs are incurred, the cost allocation carefully kept all costs segregated into three basic cost components: the demand component, the energy component, and the customer component. Such segregation by components was needed for the rate design aspects of the study.

This cost information is summarized on Table K•5 and

K•6. Table K•5 shows the annual expense assignments to three of the six classes of customers (i.e. large commercial and industrial, small commercial and industrial, and residential). Table K•6 shows the elements of the rate base as allocated to the three classes. On these two exhibits are assembled all the costs of serving the three classes of customers.

The next step is to design specific rates and pricings for each class to properly collect the total costs assigned to each class.

To the allocated costs must be added a full rate of return and the income taxes and revenue taxes related thereto. On Table K•5 this is a matter of adding revenue taxes to the subtotal of expenses as is done on Line 15. On Table

Table K•1
Model Electric Company
ANNUAL REVENUE AND KILOWATTHOURS

OPERATING REVENUE

REVENUE FROM SALES OF ELECTRICITY

Residential sales	$120,000,000
Commercial and industrial sales:	
Small	52,000,000
Large	132,000,000
Public street and highway lighting	5,000,000
Sales to railroads and railways	9,000,000
Sales for resale	2,000,000
Interdepartmental sales	—
Total revenue from sales of electricity	$320,000,000

OTHER OPERATING REVENUES

Forfeited discounts	$ 1,100,000
Miscellaneous service revenues	100,000
Sales of water and water power	600,000
Rent from electric property	2,400,000
Interdepartmental rents	—
Other electric revenues	800,000
Total other operating revenues	$ 5,000,000
TOTAL OPERATING REVENUE	$325,000,000

ANNUAL KILOWATTHOUR SALES

Residential sales	5,230,000,000
Commercial and industrial sales	
Small	2,220,000,000
Large	11,920,000,000
Public street and highway lighting	140,000,000
Sales to railroads and railways	750,000,000
Sales for resale	240,000,000
Interdepartmental sales	—
TOTAL ANNUAL KILOWATTHOUR SALES	20,500,000,000

Table K·2
Model Electric Company
PLANT IN SERVICE

	Average Balance Beginning and End of Year
INTANGIBLE PLANT	
Organization ....$	350,000
Franchises and consents	150,000
Miscellaneous intangible plant	—
Total intangible plant ....$	500,000
STEAM PRODUCTION PLANT	
Land and land rights.........................$	8,000,000
Structures and improvements............	115,000,000
Boiler plant equipment	232,500,000
Engines and engine driven generators.....................................	—
Turbogenerator units.........................	122,500,000
Accessory electric equipment	52,500,000
Misc. power plant equipment	7,000,000
Total steam production plant .... $	537,500,000
NUCLEAR PRODUCTION PLANT	
Land and land rights..........................$	300,000
Structures and improvements............	2,000,000
Reactor plant equipment	6,000,000
Turbogenerator units.........................	1,000,000
Accessory electric equipment	600,000
Misc. power plant equipment	600,000
Total nuclear production plant .... $	10,500,000
HYDRAULIC PRODUCTION PLANT—PUMPED STORAGE	
Land and land rights........................... $	1,550,000
Structures and improvements............	13,000,000
Reservoirs, dams, and waterways	34,150,000
Water wheels, turbines and generators...................................	18,400,000
Accessory electric equipment	4,350,000
Misc. power plant equipment	850,000
Roads, railroads and bridges	200,000
Total hydraulic production plant......... $	72,500,000
OTHER PRODUCTION PLANT	
Land and land rights......................... $	31,000
Structures and improvements............	189,000
Fuel holders, producers and accessories...................................	450,000
Prime movers.....................................	4,150,000
Generators...	10,400,000
Accessory electric equipment	750,000
Misc. power plant equipment	30,000
Total other production plant.............. $	16,000,000
TOTAL PRODUCTION PLANT............ $	636,500,000

Table K·3
Model Electric Company
PLANT IN SERVICE

	Average Balance Beginning and End of Year
TRANSMISSION PLANT	
Land and land rights.......................... $	15,500,000
Structures and improvements............	5,250,000
Station equipment	69,000,000
Towers and fixtures	32,500,000
Poles and fixtures	650,000
Overhead conductors and devices.....	21,500,000
Underground conduit..........................	2,550,000
Underground conductors and devices	21,000,000
Roads and trails................................	550,000
Total tranmission plant .... $	168,500,000
DISTRIBUTION PLANT	
Land and land rights........................... $	13,500,000
Structures and improvements............	17,500,000
Station equipment	130,500,000
Storage battery equipment................	—
Poles, towers and fixtures	62,500,000
Overhead conductors and devices.....	92,500,000
Underground conduit..........................	73,500,000
Underground conductors and devices	87,000,000
Line transformers	55,500,000
Services	23,500,000
Meters...	42,500,000
Installations on customers premises ..	500,000
Leased property on customers premises..	—
Street lighting and signal systems......	10,500,000
Total distribution plant .... $	609,500,000
GENERAL PLANT	
Land and land rights........................... $	395,000
Structures and improvements............	27,000,000
Office furniture and equipment..........	3,750,000
Transportation equipment..................	10,850,000
Stores equipment	750,000
Tools, shop and garage equipment	2,750,000
Laboratory equipment........................	2,250,000
Power operated equipment	1,800,000
Communication equipment	450,000
Miscellaneous equipment	1,450,000
Total general plant............................. $	55,000,000
TOTAL ELECTRIC PLANT IN SERVICE..	$1,470,000,000

Chart K·1
Model Electric Company
SYSTEM LOAD COMPOSITE SUMMER PEAK PERIOD

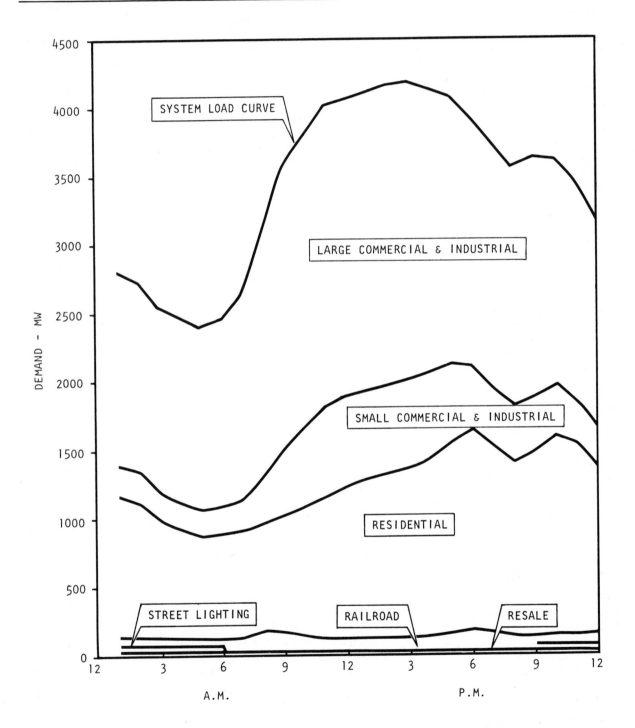

Table K•4
Model Electric Company
DEMAND ALLOCATION FACTORS
(Percentages)

Customer Class	Demand Allocation Method			
	Peak Responsibility	Non-Coincident Demand	Average and Excess Demand	Energy *
Residential	29.06	31.38	30.89	26.68
Small C&I**	15.72	14.48	14.16	11.36
Large C&I**	52.20	48.39	49.23	56.42
Street Lighting	0.00	0.90	0.88	0.73
Railroad	2.07	3.91	3.88	3.67
Resale	0.95	0.94	0.96	1.14
Total	100.00	100.00	100.00	100.00

* Allocation in terms of kilowatthours consumed

** Commercial and Industrial

K•6 it is a matter of computing a full return requirement on the rate base. The return requirement is comprised of the return on the rate base, the state and federal income taxes associated with the equity portion of return and the revenue taxes, computed as follows:

Return		7.5%
Income taxes		
Return	7.5	
Deductions (interest, addl depr)	4.9	
Return less deductions	2.6	
Taxable Income:	5.9	
Income tax 55.9% × 5.9		3.3
Subtotal		10.8%
Revenue Tax (.01943)		0.2
Total		11.0%

This 11.0% applied to the dollars of total rate base in each of the components gives the return component of cost. The sum of the total annual expenses of Table K•5 on Line 16 and the annual return and income taxes on Line 13 of Table K•6, constitute the total annual revenue requirement. For example, in the Large Commercial & Industrial class, this total amounts to some $140,000,000.

Each of the three cost components varies in response to a different parameter. The demand component of cost, being principally plant-related, exists to accommodate the group or diversified maximum demands of customers; therefore the unit divisors for the demand costs are annual

class peak demands. The energy component of costs, principally fuel-related, is a function of number of kilowatthours required by customers; and so is divided by annual kilowatthours. The customer component of cost, principally comprised of local distribution facilities, services, meters, and billings, is essentially independent of maximum demands and hours of use and therefore simply are divided by number of customers. This procedure has been followed on Tables K•5 and K•6 to obtain unit expenses and unit return and income taxes. Note that the KW and KWH divisors are as at the customers' meters so that the unit costs obtained will be expressed in terms of metered quantities.

The next task is to combine these unit costs into a rate form for the Large Commercial & Industrial class of customers. Table K•7 begins that task in the first column, by carrying forward the unit costs developed on Tables K•5 and K•6 and adding them together to develop total annual and total monthly costs on lines 18 to 20 and 23 to 25.

For the Model Electric Company, the monthly customer component of cost for large commercial and industrial customers is $61, the energy cost is $4.20 per megawatthour (or 0.42¢ per KWH) and the demand component cost is $3.47 per KW. Except for consideration of the load factor—coincidence factor relationship, the analysis would be complete, having developed a three-part rate, each part sensitive to one of the three parameters by which the costs were separated. The customer cost is complete as it appears in the first column, and can be used directly as a service charge in the cost-based rate form. The energy cost is also complete in the first column, and can be used directly as a kilowatthour charge in the cost-based rate

Table K-5
Model Electric Company
DEVELOPMENT OF UNIT EXPENSES

	1. COMMERCIAL & INDUSTRIAL—LARGE			2. COMMERCIAL & INDUSTRIAL—SMALL			3. RESIDENTIAL		
	Demand	Energy	Customer	Demand	Energy	Customer	Demand	Energy	Customer
1. *Annual Expenses*(1)									
2. *Oper & Maint*(2)									
3. Production	$14,534,904	42,294,125	—	$4,349,358	8,515,796	—	$9,425,611	20,000,128	—
4. Transmission	2,551,120	—	—	743,080	—	—	1,610,440	—	—
5. Distribution	4,205,000	152,000	350,000	2,359,000	31,000	2,242,000	3,317,000	72,000	9,332,000
6. Cust Acct(2)	—	—	60,300	—	—	1,345,300	—	—	8,586,800
7. Sales	—	—	1,153,700	—	—	1,366,500	—	—	4,744,800
8. Adm & Gen'l(2)	2,599,900	5,183,200	191,000	909,900	1,043,600	604,900	1,752,700	2,451,000	2,767,500
9. Total	23,890,924	47,629,325	1,755,000	8,361,338	9,590,396	5,558,700	16,105,751	22,523,128	25,431,100
10. *Depreciation*	15,158,800	—	514,300	5,675,400	—	1,365,900	10,415,600	—	5,632,000
11. *Taxes*									
12. Property, Etc	1,319,600	—	41,200	485,600	—	109,300	901,700	—	450,900
13. Payroll, Etc	253,000	504,300	18,600	88,500	101,500	58,900	170,500	238,500	269,300
14. *Subtotal*	40,622,324	48,133,625	2,329,100	14,610,838	9,691,896	7,092,800	27,593,551	22,761,628	31,783,300
15. *Revenue Tax* (.01943)	789,292	935,236	45,254	284,044	188,314	137,813	536,143	442,258	617,550
16. *Total Annual Expense* = Cost at 0% *Return*	$41,411,616	49,068,861	2,374,354	$14,902,882	9,880,210	7,230,613	$28,129,694	23,203,886	32,400,850
17. *Units at Meters*(3)	2,083,000 KW	11,920,000 MWH	5,237 Custs	570,000 KW	2,220,000 MWH	136,300 Custs	1,230,000 KW	5,230,000 MWH	1,019,000 Custs
18. *Annual Expense per Unit*	$19.88	$4.12	$453.38	$26.15	$4.45	$53.05	$22.87	$4.44	$31.80

1. As allocated to classes of customers.
2. Abbreviations are:
   Oper & Maint = Operation and Maintenance
   Cust Acct = Customer Accounts
   Adm & Gen'l = Administrative and General
3. From Basic Data of Model Electric Company. Units are class annual peaks at meters (KW), annual megawatthours at meters (MWH), number of customers (Custs) unless otherwise noted.

Table K-6
Model Electric Company
DEVELOPMENT OF UNIT RATE BASE AND ANNUAL RETURN COMPONENT OF COST

	1. COMMERCIAL & INDUSTRIAL—LARGE			2. COMMERCIAL & INDUSTRIAL—SMALL			3. RESIDENTIAL		
	Demand	Energy	Customer	Demand	Energy	Customer	Demand	Energy	Customer
1. Rate Base									
2. Plant in Service									
3. Production	$308,002,350	—	—	$92,165,000	—	—	$199,733,700	—	—
4. Transmission	82,672,570	—	—	24,080,246	—	—	52,184,946	—	—
5. Distribution	142,623,000	—	16,638,000	80,004,000	—	44,194,000	112,492,000	—	182,216,000
6. General	20,924,700	—	652,800	7,700,200	—	1,734,000	14,298,200	—	7,149,500
7. Total	554,222,620	—	17,290,800	203,949,446	—	45,928,000	378,708,846	—	189,365,500
8. Depreciation Reserve	(151,772,898)	—	(4,328,016)	(54,978,883)	—	(11,495,668)	(103,308,001)	—	(47,397,638)
9. Net Plant in Service	402,449,722	—	12,962,784	148,970,563	—	34,432,332	275,400,845	—	141,967,862
10. Working Capital	10,605,504	8,998,969	637,269	4,234,012	1,807,118	1,800,204	7,392,079	4,239,425	8,645,574
11. Contrib Aid Const*	(1,659,417)	—	(193,583)	(702,140)	—	(387,860)	(1,622,635)	—	(2,628,365)
12. Total Rate Base	$411,395,809	8,998,969	13,406,470	$152,502,435	1,807,118	35,844,676	$281,170,289	4,239,425	147,985,071
13. Annual Return & Inc Tax Comp* to Net Rate Base 7.5% = 11.0% ×	$45,253,539	$989,887	$1,474,712	$16,775,268	$198,783	$3,942,914	$30,928,732	$466,337	$16,278,358
14. Units At Meters*	2,083,000 KW	11,920,000 MWH	5,237 Custs	570,000 KW	2,220,000 MWH	136,300 Custs	1,230,000 KW	5,230,000 MWH	1,019,000 Custs
15. Annual Return & Inc Tax per Unit	$21.73	$0.08	$281.59	$29.43	$0.09	$28.93	$25.14	$0.09	$15.98

* Abbreviations are:
Contrib Aid Const = Contributions in Aid of Construction
Inc Tax Comp = Income Tax Computation
KW = Kilowatts
MWH = Megawatthours
Custs = Customers

ECONOMIC GROWTH IN THE FUTURE

Table K·7
Model Electric Company
COORDINATES FOR COST CURVE: COMMERCIAL & INDUSTRIAL—LARGE
(USING INDIVIDUAL CUSTOMER ANNUAL MAXIMUM DEMAND OF 500 KW AND AVERAGE MONTHLY MAXIMUM DEMAND OF 450 KW)

	Unit(1)	Average Monthly Load Factor										
1.		0%	10%	20%	30%	40%	50%	60%	70%	80%	90%	100%
	(1)	(2)	(3)	(4)	(5)	(6)	(7)	(8)	(9)	(10)	(11)	(12)
2. *Characteristics*												
3. KWH Per Year		0	394,200	788,400	1,182,600	1,576,800	1,971,000	2,365,200	2,759,400	3,153,600	3,547,800	3,942,000
4. KWH Per Month		0	32,850	65,700	98,550	131,400	164,250	197,100	229,950	262,800	295,650	328,500
5. Coincidence Factor Percent(2)		0	49	71	80	83	86	88	89	90	93	100
6. Coincident Demand—KW		0	245	355	400	415	430	440	445	450	465	500
7. *Annual Expenses = Cost @ 0% Return*												
8. Customer Comp(3)	$453.38/Cust	$453	$453	$453	$453	$453	$453	$453	$453	$453	$453	$453
9. Energy Comp	$4.12/MWH	0	1,624	3,248	4,872	6,496	8,120	9,744	11,369	12,993	14,617	16,241
10. Demand Comp	$19.88/KW	0	4,871	7,057	7,952	8,250	8,548	8,747	8,847	8,946	9,244	9,940
11. Total		$453	$6,948	$10,758	$13,277	$15,199	$17,121	$18,944	$20,669	$22,392	$24,314	$26,634
12. *Annual Return & Inc Tax Comp(4) to Net 7.5% Return*												
13. Customer Comp(3)	$281.59/Cust	$282	$282	$282	$282	$282	$282	$282	$282	$282	$282	$282
14. Energy Comp	$0.08/MWH	0	32	63	95	126	158	189	221	252	284	315
15. Demand Comp	$21.73/KW	0	5,324	7,714	8,692	9,018	9,344	9,561	9,670	9,779	10,104	10,865
16. Total		$282	$5,638	$8,059	$9,069	$9,426	$9,784	$10,032	$10,173	$10,313	$10,670	$11,462
17. *Total Annual Cost @ 7.5% Return*												
18. Customer Comp(3)	$734.97/Cust	$735	$735	$735	$735	$735	$735	$735	$735	$735	$735	$735
19. Energy Comp	$4.20/MWH	0	1,656	3,311	4,967	6,623	8,278	9,934	11,589	13,245	14,901	16,556
20. Demand Comp	$41.61/KW	0	10,194	14,771	16,644	17,268	17,892	18,308	18,516	18,725	19,349	20,805
21. Total		$735	$12,585	$18,817	$22,346	$24,626	$26,905	$28,977	$30,840	$32,705	$34,985	$38,096
22. *Average Monthly Cost @ 7.5% Return*												
23. Customer Comp(3)	$61.25/Cust	$61	$61	$61	$61	$61	$61	$61	$61	$61	$61	$61
24. Energy Comp	$4.20/MWH	0	138	276	414	552	690	828	966	1,104	1,242	1,380
25. Demand Comp	$3.47/KW	0	850	1,232	1,388	1,440	1,492	1,527	1,544	1,562	1,614	1,735
26. Total		$61	$1,049	$1,569	$1,863	$2,053	$2,243	$2,416	$2,571	$2,727	$2,917	$3,176

1. Data in lines 8-10 and 13-15 are from Table K·5, line 18 and Table K·6, line 15.
2. From Chart K·2 showing load factor-coincidence factor relationship for large commercial and industrial customers.
3. Comp = Component
4. Inc Tax Comp = Income Tax Computation

form. The demand cost, however, requires further attention.

The nature of the load factor—coincidence factor relationship is shown on Chart K·2. In brief, it demonstrates that for groups of customers, an increase in customer load factor is accompanied by a loss of diversity. It is apparent that low load factor customers have considerable diversity among themselves and their diversified or group demand is much less than the sum of their individual demands. For example, for a group of customers with 20 percent monthly load factors, the group demand would be about 70 percent of the sum of the individual customer demands. On the other hand, for a group of customers with 100 percent load factors there is no diversity; the peak loads of such customers being totally coincident with each other.

Because of this fundamental variation of diversity with customer load factor, one KW of individual customer demand of a 20 percent load factor customer should be priced lower than one KW of individual customer demand of a 100 percent load factor customer. Since 20 percent load factor customers impose demands 70 percent as large as 100 percent load factor customers, they should be charged only 70 percent as much demand cost.

Table K·7 gives recognition to this basic relationship by analyzing the characteristics of load factor groups from 0 percent to 100 percent using a customer with a 500 KW annual maximum demand as a vehicle. (Note that the final results will be re-expressed as unit charges.) The coincidence factor corresponding to each of the group load factors is applied to the annual maximum billing demand of 500 KW, to obtain the diversified demand. This demand times the unit cost per KW gives the total cost in the demand component for each of the load factor groups. This result appears on Line 25 of Table K·7 and indicates that the 500 KW customer with a 20 percent load factor must bear a monthly demand cost responsibility of $1,232; while the 500 KW customer with a 60 percent load factor must bear a monthly demand cost responsibility of $1,527.

A plot of demand costs is next made to permit conversion of the demand cost pattern into a unit pricing usable in a rate statement. This is done in Chart K·3, where each of the plotted points is connected by a solid line. The demand costs vary smoothly from 0 percent to 100 percent load factor, with the same characteristic shape as the coincidence factor-load factor curve.

Finally, it is possible to determine graphically several blocks or steps which result in charges approximately the same as those indicated by the curve. For example, the portion of the curve up to 100 hours use is almost a straight line and a rate equivalent to cost can be reasonably established by the straight line running from the origin to a level of about $1,085 per month at 100 hours use of demand. In the first 100 hours use, the demand charges increase from $0 to $1,085; therefore the rate of increase is $10.85 for each hours use of demand. Remembering that $10.85 is a cost-rate specific to a customer with an annual maximum demand of 500 KW and an average monthly maximum demand of 450 KW, the monthly $10.85 per

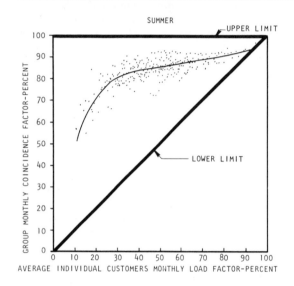

Chart K·2
THE AVERAGE TREND IN RELATION BETWEEN COINCIDENCE FACTOR AND LOAD FACTOR BASED ON DATA FOR ALL THE GROUPS OF CUSTOMERS STUDIED
(4,082 Large Industrial and Commercial Customers)

hour can be reduced to a per KW unit basis by dividing by the 450 KW of average monthly maximum demand. The result is a charge of 2.41¢ per hour per KW or 2.41¢ per KWH.

By setting a charge at this rate, for use from 0 to 100 hours, revenues are obtained which closely approximate the manner in which the costs are incurred for customers with up to 100 hours use of their demand. To follow the demand cost curve beyond 100 hours use, a similar technique is used to approximate the solid curve with a series of straight line segments. Five straight-line segments have been drawn in order to follow the demand cost curve closely while limiting the number of rate blocks. Note that the first block charge is considerably higher than the blocks following. This is in recognition of the rapid loss of diversity with increasing load factor in the low load-factor range. When past the knee of the curve at about 300 hours use, the rate of loss of diversity slackens.

Thus, a customer of given size can add to the hours use of his demand in the region from 300 to 600 hours use, with a much less than proportional increase in demands and demand costs. This characteristic primarily results from large commercial and industrial customers using the same equipment for longer hours, perhaps by adding a second work shift, or by working 6 days a week rather than 5 days. Accordingly, the demand increment charge can be low in the region from 300 to 600 hours use and the Model

Electric Company could set its demand charges at only 0.10¢ per KWH.

The demand charges developed for the large commercial and industrial customers are shown on Table K•8, together with the customer charge and the energy charge, both taken from Table K•7. Thus, a three-part rate has been developed. The service charge is $61.25 per month. The energy charge is 0.42¢ per KWH. The demand charges range from 2.41¢ per KWH for the first 100 hours use of demand to 0.21¢ per KWH for the use in excess of 600 hours. In the basic form shown here, the service or customer charge is independent of KWH, size, and coincidence of demand; the energy charge is independent of fixed customer costs, size and coincidence of demand; and the demand charge is independent of fixed customer costs and energy costs while recognizing the probable coincidence of the customers' peak demands.

The development of a basic rate form for the Small Commercial & Industrial class of customers follows essentially the same procedures. The relevant tabulations and graphs are presented as Tables K•9 and K•10 and Charts K•4 and K•5.

The residential class of customers has the same fundamental characteristics working within it as do the large and small commercial and industrial classes. This is

Chart K•3
Model Electric Company
COMMERCIAL & INDUSTRIAL—LARGE: PLOT OF DEMAND COMPONENT OF COST AND GRAPHICAL DETERMINATION OF APPROPRIATE CHARGES

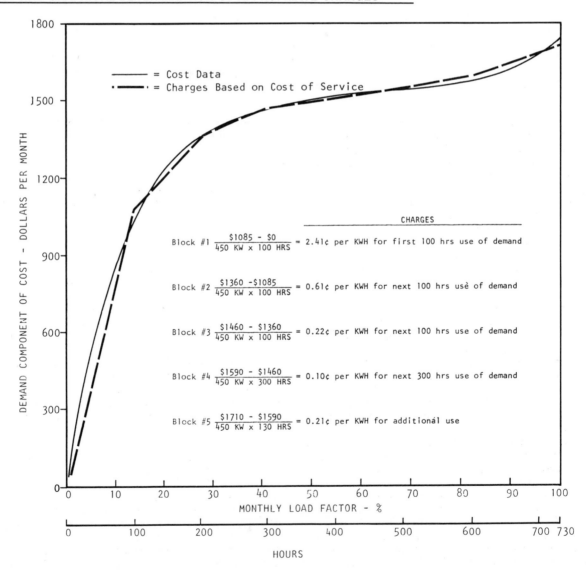

Table K•8
Model Electric Company
MONTHLY BILLING RATE BASED ON COST OF SERVICE:
COMMERCIAL & INDUSTRIAL—LARGE

Basic Form

Service Charge[1]	$61.25 per month
Energy Charge[1]	0.42¢ per kwhr

Demand Charges[2]

2.41¢ per kwhr for the first 100 hours' use of monthly demand
0.61¢ per kwhr for the next 100 hours' use of monthly demand
0.22¢ per kwhr for the next 100 hours' use of monthly demand
0.10¢ per kwhr for the next 300 hours' use of montly demand
0.21¢ per kwhr for the additional use.

1. From Table K•7
2. From Chart K•3

true even though the customers of the residential class tend to be more homogeneous in their patterns of use. Consequently, it is possible to use the same techniques to develop a three-part rate for residential customers. Three-part residential rates are not typical, however, and the normal residential rate form is usually developed somewhat as follows. The first step is to determine the characteristics of the customer to be studied. This can be for a hypothetical customer using lights and minor appliances, to which is added in sequence major-use appliances. However, another approach is to choose typical customers of the Model Electric Company whose uses increase from zero to 600 KWH in the average month. The diversified maximum demand for the average week day during the summer-peak period for each use selected, must be obtained from load data developed from customer surveys.

From this load data for the residential class, it is possible to plot the annual average use and maximum demand for twelve different customer groups as shown on Chart K•6. Also drawn on this chart is a line which expresses the average for the points plotted. Table K•11 employs six points from the average line of Chart K•6 and develops average annual and monthly total costs-to-serve for each, using unit values from Tables K•5 and K•6. The unit rate base values are obtained from Table K•6 by dividing line 12 by line 14.

Chart K•7 shows the relation of the costs and energy use, as derived from lines 15 and 19 on Table K•11. To show the relation between costs and rate revenue, a typical rate line has been added. It will be observed that the rate line crosses the cost-to-serve at 0 percent return at about 80 KWH per month. This means that all customers using less than 80 KWH per month are served below the bare cost. Perhaps 10 to 15 percent of the customers may be included in this group.

The typical rate structure associated with this dashed line is given at the top of Table K•12. Below it is an

alternate rate structure which would match more closely the cost-to-serve at a 7-½ percent rate of return. The alternate rate is shown as the dotted line on Chart K•7. The alternate rate form requires fewer blocks and matches rates more closely to costs to serve, but it has the disadvantage of charging the small user higher rates than at present.

Chart K•4
SMALL GENERAL SERVICE CUSTOMER
LOAD STUDY COINCIDENCE FACTOR
—LOAD FACTOR RELATIONSHIP
WINTER 1959-1960 AND SUMMER 1960

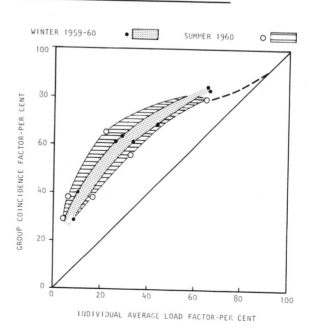

403

Table K-9
Model Electric Company
COORDINATES FOR COST CURVE COMMERCIAL & INDUSTRIAL—SMALL
(USING INDIVIDUAL CUSTOMER ANNUAL MAXIMUM DEMAND OF 10 KW AND AVERAGE MONTHLY MAXIMUM DEMAND OF 8.5 KW)

						Average Monthly Load Factor						
	Unit(1)	0%	10%	20%	30%	40%	50%	60%	70%	80%	90%	100%
	(1)	(2)	(3)	(4)	(5)	(6)	(7)	(8)	(9)	(10)	(11)	(12)
1.												
2. *Characteristics*												
3. KWH Per Year		0	7,446	14,892	22,338	29,784	37,230	44,676	52,122	59,568	67,014	74,460
4. KWH Per Month		0	620	1,241	1,862	2,482	3,102	3,723	4,344	4,964	5,585	6,205
5. Coincidence Factor—Percent(2)		0	38	53	64	70	75	78	81	85	91	100
6. Coincident Demand—KW		0	3.8	5.3	6.4	7.0	7.5	7.8	8.1	8.5	9.1	10.0
7. *Annual Expenses = Cost @ 0% Return*												
8. Customer Comp(3)	$53.05/Cust	$53	$53	$53	$53	$53	$53	$53	$53	$53	$53	$53
9. Energy Comp	$4.45/MWH	0	33	66	99	133	166	199	232	265	298	331
10. Demand Comp	$26.15/KW	0	99	139	167	183	196	204	212	222	238	262
11. Total		$53	$185	$258	$319	$369	$415	$456	$497	$540	$589	$646
12. *Annual Return & Inc Tax Comp(4) to Net 7.5% Return*												
13. Customer Comp(3)	$28.93/Cust	$29	$29	$29	$29	$29	$29	$29	$29	$29	$29	$29
14. Energy Comp	$0.09/MWH	0	1	1	2	3	3	4	4	4	5	6
15. Demand Comp	$29.43/KW	0	112	156	188	206	221	230	238	250	268	294
16. Total		$29	$142	$186	$219	$238	$253	$263	$271	$283	$302	$329
17. *Total Annual Cost @ 7.5% Return*												
18. Customer Comp(3)	$81.98/Cust	$82	$82	$82	$82	$82	$82	$82	$82	$82	$82	$82
19. Energy Comp	$4.54/MWH	0	34	67	101	136	169	203	236	269	303	337
20. Demand Comp	$55.58/KW	0	211	295	355	389	417	434	450	472	506	556
21. Total		$82	$327	$444	$538	$607	$668	$719	$768	$823	$891	$975
22. *Average Monthly Cost @ 7.5% Return*												
23. Customer Comp(3)	$6.83/Cust	$6.83	$6.83	$6.83	$6.83	$6.83	$6.83	$6.83	$6.83	$6.83	$6.83	$6.83
24. Energy Comp	$4.54/MWH	0.00	2.81	5.63	8.45	11.27	14.08	16.90	19.72	22.54	25.36	28.17
25. Demand Comp	$4.63/KW	0.00	17.59	24.54	29.63	32.41	34.73	36.11	37.50	39.36	42.13	46.30
26. Total		$6.83	$27.23	$37.00	$44.91	$50.51	$55.64	$59.84	$64.05	$68.73	$74.32	$81.30

1. Data in lines 8-10 and 13-15 are from Table K•5 line 18 and Table K•6, line 15.
2. From Chart K•4 showing load factor-coincidence factor relationship for small commercial and industrial customers.
3. Comp. = Component
4. Inc Tax Comp = Income Tax Computation

Table K•10
Model Electric Company
MONTHLY BILLING RATE BASED ON COST OF SERVICE:
COMMERCIAL & INDUSTRIAL—SMALL

Basic Form

Service Charge[1] $6.83 per month

Energy Charge[1]   0.45¢ per kwhr

Demand Charges[2]

2.71¢ per kwhr for the first 100 hours' use of monthly demand
0.66¢ per kwhr for the next 100 hours' use of monthly demand
0.45¢ per kwhr for the next 100 hours' use of monthly demand
0.30¢ per kwhr for the next 300 hours' use of monthly demand
0.50¢ per kwhr for the additional use.

1. From Table K•9
2. From Chart K•5

Chart K•5
Model Electric Company
COMMERCIAL & INDUSTRIAL—SMALL: PLOT OF DEMAND COMPONENT OF
COST AND GRAPHICAL DETERMINATION OF APPROPRIATE CHARGES

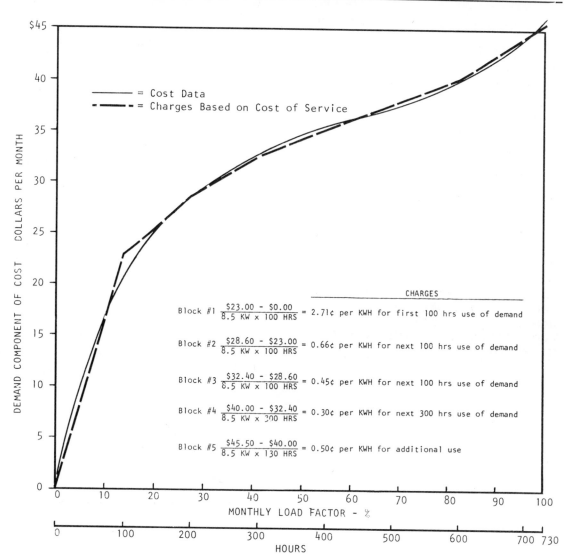

= Cost Data
= Charges Based on Cost of Service

CHARGES

Block #1 $\frac{\$23.00 - \$0.00}{8.5 \text{ KW} \times 100 \text{ HRS}}$ = 2.71¢ per KWH for first 100 hrs use of demand

Block #2 $\frac{\$28.60 - \$23.00}{8.5 \text{ KW} \times 100 \text{ HRS}}$ = 0.66¢ per KWH for next 100 hrs use of demand

Block #3 $\frac{\$32.40 - \$28.60}{8.5 \text{ KW} \times 100 \text{ HRS}}$ = 0.45¢ per KWH for next 100 hrs use of demand

Block #4 $\frac{\$40.00 - \$32.40}{8.5 \text{ KW} \times 300 \text{ HRS}}$ = 0.30¢ per KWH for next 300 hrs use of demand

Block #5 $\frac{\$45.50 - \$40.00}{8.5 \text{ KW} \times 130 \text{ HRS}}$ = 0.50¢ per KWH for additional use

DEMAND COMPONENT OF COST · DOLLARS PER MONTH

MONTHLY LOAD FACTOR - %

HOURS

405

Table K·11
COORDINATES FOR RESIDENTIAL COST CURVE

	Unit (1)	(2)	(3)	(4)	(5)	(6)	(7)
1. *Characteristics:*							
2. KWH for Year		0	600	1,200	2,400	4,800	7,200
3. KWH per Month..................		0	50	100	200	400	600
4. Coincident Demand-Watts.		0	170	380	820	1,470	2,020
5. *Rate Base*							
6. Customer Comp*	$145.23	145.23	145.23	145.23	145.23	145.23	145.23
7. Demand Comp.	228.59/KW*	0	38.86	86.86	187.44	336.03	451.73
8. Energy Comp.	0.81/MWH	0	0.49	0.97	1.94	3.89	5.83
9. Total.................................		145.23	184.58	233.06	334.61	485.15	612.81
10. *Annual Expense @ 0% Return*							
11. Customer Comp................	$31.80	31.80	31.80	31.80	31.80	31.80	31.80
12. Demand Comp.	22.87/KW	0	3.89	8.69	18.75	33.62	45.20
13. Energy Comp.	4.44/MWH	0	2.66	5.33	10.66	21.31	31.97
14. Total per Year		31.80	38.35	45.82	61.21	86.73	109.97
15. Average per Month........		2.65	3.20	3.82	5.10	7.23	9.16
16. *Annual Return Comp. to Net 7.5% = 11%*		15.98	20.30	25.64	36.81	53.37	67.41
17. *Total Cost-to-Serve @ 7.5% Return on Rate Base*							
18. Total per Year....................		47.78	58.65	71.46	98.02	140.10	177.33
19. Average per Month		3.98	4.89	5.96	8.17	11.68	14.78

* Abbreviations as listed on preceding tables

Chart K·6
Model Electric Company
RELATIONSHIP OF AVERAGE WEEKDAY MAXIMUM DEMAND (MW) TO ANNUAL USE (MWH) BASED ON ANNUAL KWH GROUPS SUMMER 5-6 P.M. RESIDENTIAL

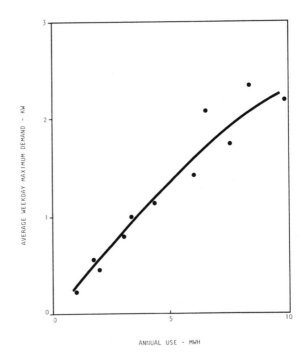

Chart K•7
COST CURVE: RESIDENTIAL

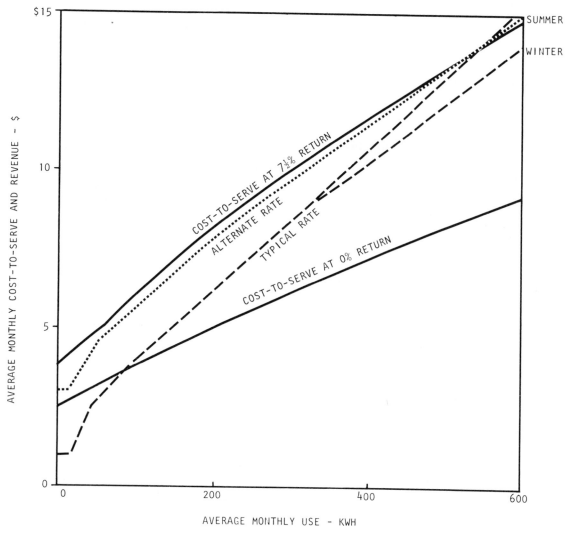

Table K•12
TYPICAL RESIDENTIAL RATE

Minimum $1.00—includes 15 kwhr

Next   35 kwhr at 4¼ cents per kwhr

Next   50 kwhr at 3   cents per kwhr

Next 200 kwhr at 2¼ cents per kwhr

Next 300 kwhr at (2¼ cents per kwhr (summer)
                (1¾ cents per kwhr (winter)

All additional kwhr at 1¾ cents per kwhr

ALTERNATE RESIDENTIAL RATE

Minimum $3.00—includes 15 kwhr

Next   35 kwhr at 4¼ cents per kwhr

Next 150 kwhr at 2¼ cents per kwhr

All additional
        kwhr at 1¾ cents per kwhr

APPENDIX L

Load Factor— Capacity Factor Relationships

Load factor, capacity factor, and reserve margin are interrelated concepts. The generally accepted definitions of the terms, as given in the Edison Electric Institute *Glossary of Electric Utility Terms,* are as follows:

(a) *Load factor* (L) is the ratio of the average load in kilowatts supplied during a designated pepriod to the

407

peak or maximum load in kilowatts occurring in that period. It may be derived by dividing the kilowatt-hour output (O) in the period by the product of the maximum or peak demand (P) in kilowatts and the number of hours in the period.

(b) *Capacity factor* (C) is the ratio of the average load on a machine or equipment for the period of time considered to the capacity rating of the machine or equipment (usually at the time of peak load).

(c) *Reserve margin* (R) or capability margin is the difference between net system capability (usually at the time of system peak load) and system maximum load requirements (peak load). On a national basis it is the difference between aggregate net system capability of the various systems in the nation and the sum of the system maximum loads, without allowance for time diversity between the loads of the various systems.

Chart L•1
RESERVE MARGIN, LOAD FACTOR, AND CAPACITY FACTOR
TOTAL ELECTRIC UTILITY INDUSTRY

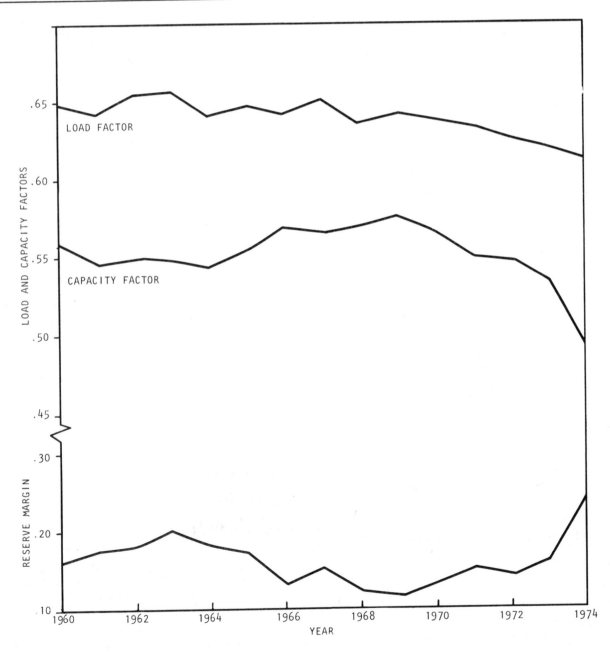

For purposes of this analysis, these definitions can be expressed in symbolic terms as follows:

$$L = \frac{O}{P(K)}$$

$$C = \frac{O}{I(K)}$$

$$R = \frac{I - P}{P} = \frac{I}{P} - 1$$

where: C = capacity factor
I = net capability (kilowatts)
K = constant = hours per year
L = load factor
O = output (kilowatthours)
P = peak demand
R = reserve margin expressed as a ratio.

Substitution of the first two of the above equations into the third yields the relationship:

$$1 + R = \frac{L}{C}$$

Estimates of installed capacity on a nameplate basis, as well as O and P, can be obtained for past years from the Edison Electric Institute publications, *Historical Statistics* and *Statistical Yearbook,* for both the total electric utility industry and the investor owned segment of that industry. The nameplate capacity figures can be reduced by 5 percent to obtain an approximate measure of the net capability, I. The successive I figures (which are given as of December 31 each year) can be averaged to obtain an approximation to the average capability each year. Finally, these average I values can be combined with the O and P estimates to yield load factors, capacity factors, and reserve margins. The results of such calculations appear on Chart L•1 for the period from 1960 through 1974.

The financial forecasting model used in this study assumed that, in the future, nationwide average capacity factors would change approximately as shown in Table L•1. If these figures are combined with assumed national load factor trends and estimates of the desired reserve margins, the required capacity additions can be determined.

The study assumes that the load factor deterioration which has been experienced over the last decade can be stopped at about the .60 level and reversed so that by the end of the forecast period it has returned to the .65 region. Under such circumstances, the capacity figures shown in Chapter 6 will result in the following changes in reserve margin: a decrease during the remainder of the 1970's and early 1980's; a leveling during the middle 1980's; and a slow decrease during the 1990's, staying generally within the boundaries of 15 and 25 percent over the years from now to 2000. On a name plate basis, of course, the calculated reserve margins would be accordingly higher.

If the load factor improvement cannot be achieved, however, the assumed capacity factors are too high and the installed capacities too low to permit reasonable reserves to be maintained. A load factor which remained unchanged at .60 through the forecast period would combine with the assumed capacity figures to yield a seriously deteriorating reserve margin; e.g. 11 percent by 1990 and 3 percent by 2000. Thus a constant, rather than a gradually improving, load factor would require construction of additional new capacity over and above the figures estimated in the study.

Some of the potential sources for improved load factor are: (1) a near-saturation of air conditioning installations coupled with continued rapid growth of electric space heating, and (2) various peak load pricing techniques (including summer-winter differentials and interruptible rates) which may effect a gradual change in the use habits of significant numbers of customers.

Table L•1
CAPACITY FACTOR*:
TOTAL ELECTRIC UTILITY INDUSTRY

	1975	1980	1985	2000
Coal	.48	.50	.46	.42
Oil & Gas	.44	.43	.40	.40
Nuclear	.58	.65	.68	.73
Hydro & Other	.54	.50	.50	.50
Total	.48	.50	.52	.58

*Capacity Factor =

$$\frac{Output}{.95 \ (Nameplate \ Capacity) \ (Hours \ per \ year)}$$

APPENDIX M

Normalizing versus Flow-Through Accounting

Normalizing and flow-through are terms used to describe two accounting techniques used in the utility industry to relate financial (or book) accounting to tax accounting, particularly with regard to the treatment of depreciation charges and investment tax credits. An extended discussion of this subject is provided in the book *Public Utility Accounting: Theory and Application,* by James E. Suelflow, published by Michigan State University Public Utilities Studies in 1973. This Appendix provides a simplified and summarized discussion of the subject.

Depreciation expenses recognize the gradual extinguishing of the useful life of an electric utility's plant and equipment assets in the process of providing utility services to customers. Accounting for depreciation expense considers that: (a) the net cost of each such asset (i.e. the original cost less the salvage value) is the amount to be allocated systematically as depreciation over the useful life of that asset, and (b) no more and no less than the net cost of the asset is properly depreciable.

For financial reporting purposes, depreciation of utility plant assets is most commonly charged to operating expenses on a straight-line basis; i.e. the annual depreciation charge for a given unit of plant equals its net cost divided by the number of years of its useful life. Almost without exception, state regulatory commissions as well as the FPC have the authority to prescribe the book depreciation method and the depreciation rates to be used by utilities under their jurisdiction. Suelflow summarized the policies of each of these regulatory bodies at the time of publication of his book on Table 9, pages 88, 89.

For income tax purposes, the Internal Revenue Service allows the use of several accelerated methods of depreciation. These methods assume higher depreciation charges in the earlier years of an asset's life than the straight-line method. The reverse is true in the later years of life. Therefore, when assets are newer, the depreciation expense is greater, the associated taxable income is lower, and the income tax is less than under straight-line depreciation methods. As the assets age and depreciation expenses decline, taxable income increases until, at some point, income taxes are higher than if straight-line methods were used.

So long as the growth of the dollar value of a company's plant assets continues to be vigorous, the effect of high depreciation charges on newer assets outweighs the low depreciation charges on old assets, and income taxes are lower than under straight-line depreciation methods. Inflation reinforces this effect since new assets are more costly than similar assets were in past years. If growth and inflation slow sufficiently, the day will be reached when income taxes under accelerated depreciation will be higher than under straight-line depreciation. Under current conditions in most of the electric utility industry the use of accelerated depreciation for tax purposes has the effect of reducing current tax expenses.

Flow-through accounting allows the benefits of these lower current tax expenses to "flow through" to the current customers of the utility company in the form of lower prices for service. No current provisions are made to protect future customers who may be forced to pay higher prices to cover the higher taxes in that future period when aging assets, slowing growth, and lower inflation may combine to produce *higher* taxes under accelerated depreciation.

If normalization accounting is used, however, the company must include a deferred tax expense as well as a current tax expense in its income statement. The deferred tax must be sufficiently large so that when it is combined with the current tax expense, the total of the two is equal to that which the company would have had to pay if it had chosen to use straight line depreciation for tax purposes.

The deferred taxes are not paid out immediately but rather are accumulated in a deferred tax account during the early years of each asset's life. This accumulation is designed to provide for the time when the tax expense will be greater in the later years of the asset's life. During that future time, the accumulations in the deferred tax account will gradually be decreased. Over the entire life of the assets, taxes will be "normal"; i.e. they will be the same as if the company had used straight line depreciation for both book and tax purposes.

Similar accounting provisions have been used to alter the impact of the investment tax credit provisions in the internal revenue code. These provisions were first incorporated into the Revenue Act of 1962. They were designed to encourage investment in production facilities by providing for a tax credit equal to a certain percentage of the cost of such facilities. This tax credit was applied as a reduction of the company's income tax liabilities in the year in which the qualifying facilities went into service. The provisions of the original act required that the cost basis for the facilities be reduced by the amount of the tax credit when calculating depreciation expenses.

The provisions of subsequent revenue acts which govern the use of the investment tax credit have changed significantly from those of the 1962 act. It is neither feasible nor necessary to discuss the changes in detail in this Appendix.

However, flow-through accounting principles as applied to the investment tax credit would "flow through" the entire income tax benefit of the credit in the year when the credit was "earned"; e.g., the 1962 act established this as the year in which the qualifying facilities went into service. On the other hand, normalizing principles would require that these credits be accumulated in a Deferred Investment Tax Credits account and that the tax savings from each qualifying facility be spread over the useful life of that facility.

Bibliography

"Aluminum," *Metals Week,* June 5, 1971.

American Assembly. *Overcoming World Hunger.* Englewood Cliffs, N. J.: Prentice-Hall, 1969.

American Enterprise Institute for Public Policy Research. *The Phenomenon of Worldwide Inflation.* Washington, D. C.: American Enterprise Institute for Public Policy Research, 1974.

Archer, A. A. "Progress and Prospects of Marine Mining." *Mining Magazine,* March 1974, pp. 150-63.

Atomic Energy Commission. *Reactor Safety Study.* Washington, D. C.: Atomic Energy Commission, August, 1974.

Atomic Energy Commission, Office of Planning and Analysis. *Nuclear Power Growth 1974-2000.* WASH 1139 (74). Washington, D. C.: Atomic Energy Commission, 1974.

Ayres, R. U. and Kneese, A. V. "Economic and Ecological Effects of a Stationary Economy." *Annual Review of Ecology and Systematics* (1971).

Baran, Paul A. *The Political Economy of Growth.* New York: Modern Reader Paperbacks, 1957.

Barnett, Harold and Morse, Chandler. *Scarcity and Growth.* Baltimore: The Johns Hopkins Press, 1963.

Barry, R. Steven. "Reflections on the Limits to Growth." *Bulletin of the Atomic Scientists,* November, 1972, pp. 25-27.

Bary, Constantine W. *Operational Economics of Electric Utilities.* New York: Columbia University Press, 1963.

Bauchau, Christian. "Essai de typologie quantitative des gisements de plomb et de zinc avec la repartition de l'argent." Bur. Recherches *Geol. et Minieres Bull.,* 1971, Sec. 2, No. 3, pp. 1-72; No. 4, pp. 1-47.

Becker, Gary. "An Economic Analysis of Fertility." *Demographic and Economic Change in Developed Countries.* National Bureau of Economic Research. New Jersey: Princeton University Press, 1970.

Beckerman, Wilfred. "Economic Development and the Environment: A False Dilemma." *International Conciliation* January, 1972.

Beckerman, Wilfred. *Two Cheers for the Affluent Society.* New York: St. Martin's Press, 1974.

Behan, R. W. "The Litany of Scarcity Versus the Challenge of Abundance." *Journal of Soil and Water Conservation,* Vol. 28, March-April, 1973, pp. 50-51.

Bell, D. *The Coming of Post-Industrial Society.* New York: Basic Books, 1973.

Berelson, B. *World Population: Status Report 1974.* New York: Population Council, 1974.

Bermanke, Ben, and Jorgenson, Dale W. *The Integration of Energy Policy Models.* Discussion Paper No. 428. Cambridge, Mass.: Harvard Institute of Economic Research, 1975.

Bischoff, J. L., and Manheim, F. T. "Economic Potential of the Red Sea Heavy Metal Deposits." In *Hot Brines and Recent Heavy Metal Deposits in the Red Sea,* edited by E. T. Degens and D. A. Ross, pp. 535-49. New York: Springer-Verlag, 1969.

Blaugh, Mark. *Economic Theory in Perspective.* Homewood, Ill.: Richard D. Irwin, 1968.

Blechman, B. M.; Gramlich, E. W.; and Hartman, R. W. *Setting National Priorities: The 1975 Budget.* Washington, D. C.: Brookings Institution, 1974.

"A Blueprint for Survival." *The Ecologist,* Vol. 2, No. 2, January, 1972, pp. 1-44.

Bonbright, James C. *Principles of Public Utility Rates.* New York: Columbia University Press, 1961.

Bosselman, Fred; Callies, David; and Banta, John. *The Taking Issue* (A Study of the Constitutional Limits of Governmental Authority to Regulate the Use of Privately-Owned Land Without Paying Compensation to the Owners). Washington, D. C.: U. S. Government Printing Office, 1973.

Bostom, Kurt, and Peterson, M. N. A. "Precipitates from Hydrothermal Exhalations on the East Pacific Rise." *Economic Geology,* Vol. 61, 1966, pp. 1258-65.

Bosworth, Barry; Duesenberry, James S.; and Carron, Andrew S. *Capital Needs in the Seventies.* Washington, D. C.: Brookings Institution, 1975.

Boulding, Kenneth. *Beyond Economics.* Ann Arbor: University of Michigan Press, 1968.

————. *Economics as a Science.* New York: McGraw-Hill, 1970.

————. "The Economics of the Coming Spaceship Earth." In *Environmental Quality in a Growing Economy,* edited by Henry Jarrett, pp. 3-14. Baltimore: Johns Hopkins University Press, 1966.

————. "Valuation as a Process." In *Transportation and Community Values,* Report of a Conference Held in Warrenton, Virginia, March, 1969, Part III, pp. 31-38. Washington, D. C.: Highway Research Board, 1969.

————. "The Wolf of Rome." *Business and Society Review,* No. 2, Summer, 1972, pp. 106-9.

Brinck, J. W. *Note on the Distribution and Predictability of Mineral Resources.* EUR 3461.3. Brussels: European Atomic Energy Community—Euratom, 1967.

Brooks, David B. *Low-Grade and Nonconventional Sources of Manganese.* Resources for the Future. Baltimore: Johns Hopkins University Press, 1966.

Brooks, Harvey. "The Technology of Zero Growth." *Daedalus,* Fall, 1973, pp. 139-52.

Bureau of the Census. *Population Report Series P-25,*

Number 470. Washington, D. C.: Department of Commerce, 1974.

————. *Projections of the United States Population by Age and Sex, 1972 to 2020.* Washington, D. C.: Department of Commerce, 1972.

————. *Statistical Abstract, 1974.* Washington, D. C.: Department of Commerce, 1975.

Bureau of the Census, and Bureau of Mines. *Historical Statistics of the U. S. Colonial Times to 1957.* Washington, D. C.: U. S. Government Printing Office, 1960.

————. *Raw Materials in the United States Economy, 1900-1966.* Bureau of the Census Working Paper 30, edited by Vivian Eberle Spencer. Washington, D. C.: Department of Commerce, 1969.

Bureau of Mines. *Commodity Data Summaries* Appendix I to Mining and Minerals Policy. Washington, D. C.: U. S. Government Printing Office, 1974.

————. *Mineral Facts and Problems.* Bulletin 650. Washington, D. C.: U. S. Government Printing Office, 1970.

Caywood, Russell E. *Electric Utility Rate Economics.* New York: McGraw-Hill, 1972.

Chamberlain, Neil. *Beyond Malthus, Population and Power.* New York: Basic Books, Inc. 1970.

Chapman, L. D.; Tyrell, T. J.; and Mount, T. D. *Electricity Demand in the U. S.: An Econometric Analysis.* Oak Ridge National Laboratory Report ORNL-EP-49. Discussed in "Electricity Demand Growth and the Energy Crisis," *Science,* Vol. 178, No. 4062, November 17, 1972.

Chase, S. "The Club of Rome and Its Computer." *Bulletin of the Atomic Scientists,* March, 1973, pp. 36-39.

Chen, Kan; Lagler, Karl F.; and Berg, Mark R.; Buskirk, E. Drannon, Jr.; Gray, Donald H.; Herpolsheimer, Karl; Jones, T. Jeffrey; Kral, George; Mathes, J. C.; McGuire, John; Michael, Donald N.; Pollock, Stephen M.; Rehfus, Ruth. *Growth Policy: Population, Environment, and Beyond.* Ann Arbor: University of Michigan Press, 1974.

Chenery, Hollis. "Growth and Structure." *Finance and Development,* Vol. 8, No. 3, September, 1971, pp. 16-27.

Christensen, L. R., Jorgenson, D. W., & Lau, L. J., "Transcendental Logarithmic Production Frontiers," *Review of Economics and Statistics,* February, 1973.

Christensen, L. R., and Jorgenson, D. W. "U. S. Real Product and Real Factor Input, 1929-1967." *Review of Income and Wealth,* March, 1970.

Clement, R. C. "Conservation: A Positive Position." *I.E.E.E. Spectrum,* August, 1973, pp. 44-47.

Cloud, Preston E., Jr. "Mineral Resources from the Sea." In *Resources and Man,* edited by Preston E. Cloud, Jr. San Francisco: W. H. Freeman and Co., 1969.

Cole, H. S. D.; Freeman, Christopher; Jahoda Marie; and Pavitt, K. L. R., eds. *Models of Doom: A Critique of the Limits to Growth.* New York: Universe Books, 1973.

Coulomb, R., "Contribution a la Giochimie de l'uranium dans les Granites Intrusifs," Rapport C.E.A., No. 1173, 1959.

Commerce Technical Advisory Board. *Recommendations for a National Energy Program.* Washington, D. C.: Department of Commerce, 1974.

Commission on Marine Sciences, Engineering, and Resources. *Our Nation and the Sea.* Washington, D. C.: U. S. Government Printing Office, January, 1969.

Committee for Economic Development. *Achieving Energy Independence.* New York: Committee for Economic Development, 1974.

————. *International Economic Consequences of High Priced Energy.* New York: Committee for Economic Development, 1975.

————. *Social Responsibilities of Business Corporations.* New York: Committee for Economic Development, 1971.

Commoner, Barry. *The Closing Circle: Nature, Man, and Technology.* New York: Alfred A. Knopf, 1971.

Commoner, Barry; Boksenbaum, Howard; and Corr, Michael, eds. *Energy and Human Welfare: A Critical Analysis.* New York: Macmillan, 1975.

Conference Board. *Energy Consumption in Manufacturing* (A Report to the Energy Policy Project of the Ford Foundation). Cambridge, Mass.: Ballinger Publishing Co., 1974.

Congressional Research Service, Library of Congress. *Toward a National Growth and Development Policy: Legislative and Executive Actions in 1970 and 1971.* 92nd Congress, 2nd Session. Washington, D. C.: U. S. Government Printing Office, 1972.

Cost Allocation Committee of Engineering Committee of National Association of Railroad & Utilities Commissions, "Comparison of Methods of Allocating Demand Costs, *Electric Utilities,*" June, 1955.

Council on Environmental Quality. *Environmental Quality* (The Third Annual Report of the Council on Environmental Quality). Washington, D. C.: U. S. Government Printing Office, August, 1972.

————. *Environmental Quality* (The Fourth Annual Report of the Council on Environmental Quality). Washington, D. C.: U. S. Government Printing Office, September, 1973.

Council on Trends and Perspective. *Economic Growth: New Views and Issues, Enterprise in a New Economic Era.* Washington, D. C.: Chamber of Commerce of the United States, 1975.

Cox, D. P.; Schmidt, R. G.; Vine, J. D.; Kirkemo, H.; Tourtelot, E. B.; and Fleischer, M. "Copper." In *United States Mineral Resources,* Professional Paper 820, U. S. Geological Survey. Washington, D. C.: U. S. Government Printing Office, 1973.

Daly, Herman E., ed. *Toward a Steady-State Economy.* San Francisco: W. H. Freeman and Co., 1973.

Darmstadter, Joel. *Energy in the World Economy: A Statistical Review of Trends in Output, Trade, and Consumption.* Resources for the Future. Baltimore: Johns Hopkins University Press, 1971.

Darney, Arsen, and Franklin, William E. *Salvage Markets for Materials in Solid Wastes.* Washington, D. C.:

Environmental Protection Agency, 1972.

Davidson, Ralph K. *Price Discrimination in Selling Gas and Electricity.* Baltimore: Johns Hopkins University Press, 1955.

de Chardin, Teilhard. *The Future of Man.* New York: Harper & Row, 1964.

———. *The Phenomenon of Man.* New York: Harper & Row, 1959.

Denison, E. F. *Accounting for United States Economic Growth, 1929-1969.* Washington, D. C.: Brookings Institution, 1974.

Denison, Edward F. *Why Growth Rates Differ.* Washington, D.C.: Brookings Institution, 1967.

Department of Commerce. *Input-Output Structure of the U. S. Economy: 1963.* Washington, D. C. Office of Business Economics, 1969.

———. "The Measurement of Productivity." *Survey of Current Business, Part II,* by E. F. Denison, D. W. Jorgenson, and Z. Griliches. Washington, D. C.: U. S. Govt. Printing Office, 1972.

Department of Interior, "A Drill Hole Every 20 Miles Urged by Penn State Scientist to Uncover U. S. Mineral Wealth," News Release, Washington, D. C., September 16, 1974.

——— *U. S. Energy Through the Year 2000.* Washington, D. C.: U. S. Government Printing Office, 1972.

Department of Labor, Bureau of Labor Statistics, *Monthly Labor Review,* various issues.

DeVries, Egbert, ed. *Essays on Unbalanced Growth: A Century of Disparity and Convergence.* New York: Humanities Press, 1962.

Domar, Evsey D. *Essays in the Theory of Economic Growth.* New York: Oxford University Press, 1957.

Domestic Council Committee on National Growth. *Report on National Growth 1972* (First Biennial Report on National Growth as Required by Section 703[a] of the Housing and Urban Development Act of 1970). Washington, D. C.: U. S. Government Prinitng Office, February, 1972.

Doran, John J., et al. *Electric Utility Cost Allocation Manual.* Washington, D. C.: National Association of Regulatory Utility Commissioners, 1973.

Dror, Yehezkel. *Public Policymaking Reexamined.* San Francisco: Chandler Publishing Co., 1968.

Dubos, René. "Promises and Hazards of Man's Adaptability." In *Environmental Quality in a Growing Economy,* edited by Henry Jarrett, pp. 23-39. Baltimore: Johns Hopkins University Press, 1966.

Edison Electric Institute, *Glossary of Electric Utility Terms.* New York: Edison Electric Institute, 1970.

Edison Electric Institute. *Pocket Handbook of Industry Statistics.* New York: Edison Electric Institute, 1973(a).

———. *Statistical Yearbook.* New York: Edison Electric Institute, 1973(b).

Ehrlich, Paul, and Holdren, John. "Human Population and the Global Environment." United Nations Symposium on Population, Resources and Environment, Stockholm, 1973.

Ellul, Jacques, *The Technological Society.* New York: Alfred Knopf, 1964.

Ellis, J.; Harris, D. P.; Van Wie, N. *A Subjective Probability Appraisal of the Uranium Resources of New Mexico.* Grand Junction, Colo.: U. S. Atomic Energy Commission, unpublished manuscript.

Engineering & Mining Journal, March, 1974.

Environmental Protection Agency. *Alternative Futures and Environmental Quality.* Office of Research and Development, Washington Environmental Research Center, Environmental Studies Division. Washington, D. C.: Environmental Protection Agency, 1973.

———. *The Cost of Clean Air* (Annual Report of the Administrator of the EPA to the Congress of the United States). Washington, D. C.: U. S. Government Printing Office, 1973.

———. *The Economics of Clean Water* (Annual Report of the Administrator of the EPA to the Congress of the United States). Washington, D. C.: U. S. Government Printing Office, 1973.

Erickson, Ralph. "Crustal Abundance of Elements, and Mineral Reserves and Resources." In *United States Mineral Resources,* Professional Paper 820, U. S. Geological Survey, pp. 21-26. Washington, D. C.: U. S. Government Printing Office, 1973.

Executive Office of the President. *A Look at Business in 1990.* White House Conference on the Industrial World Ahead: A Look at Business in 1990. Washington, D. C.: U. S. Government Printing Office, November, 1972.

Faucett, J., and Associates, *Data Development for the I-O Energy Model,* Final Report to the Ford Foundation Energy Policy Project, Washington, D. C., May, 1973.

Federal Energy Administration. *Project Independence Report* and subsidiary documents. Washington, D. C.: U. S. Government Printing Office, 1974.

Federal Power Commission. *1970 National Power Survey.* Washington. D. C.: Federal Power Commission, 1971.

———. *Statistics of Privately Owned Electric Utilities in the United States.* Washington, D. C.: Federal Power Commission, 1973.

Federal Power Commission, National Power Survey, Technical Advisory Committee on Finance Report. *The Financial Outlook for the Electric Power Industry.* Washington, D. C.: Federal Power Commission, December, 1974.

Felix, Fremont. *World Markets of Tomorrow.* New York: Harper & Row, 1972.

Ferguson, C. E. "The Simple Analytics of Neoclassical Growth Theory." *Quarterly Review of Economics and Business,* Spring, 1968, pp. 69-83.

Fisher, F. M., and Kaysen, K. *The Demand for Electricity in the United States.* Amsterdam: North Holland Publishing Co., 1962.

Fisher, John C. *Energy Crises in Perspective.* New York: John Wiley & Sons, 1974.

413

Fisher, Joseph L., and Potter, Neal. *World Prospects for Natural Resources.* Resources for the Future. Baltimore: Johns Hopkins University Press, 1964.

Ford, Andrew. *A Dynamic Model of the United States Electric Utility Industry, 1950-2010.* Hanover, N. H.: Dartmouth College, 1975.

Ford Foundation Energy Policy Project. *A Time to Choose* and related publications. Cambridge, Mass.: Ballinger Publishing Co., 1974-75.

Forrester, Jay W. *Principles of Systems.* Cambridge, Mass.: Wright-Allen Press, 1968.

———. *World Dynamics.* Cambridge, Mass.: Wright-Allen Press, 1971.

Gabor, Dennis. *Thoughts on the Future.* MR-179, A Speech Delivered on October 20, 1972, at the Institute of Government and Public Affairs, University of California at Los Angeles.

Galbraith, John Kenneth. *The Affluent Society.* Boston: Houghton Mifflin Co., 1958.

———. *Economics and the Public Purpose.* Boston: Houghton Mifflin Co., 1973.

Garfield, Paul J., and Lovejoy, Wallace F. *Public Utility Economics.* Englewood Cliffs, N. J.: Prentice-Hall, 1964.

Georgescu-Roegen, Nicholas. *The Entropy Law and the Economic Process.* Cambridge, Mass.: Harvard University Press, 1971.

Goldberg, E. D. "The Oceans as a Chemical System." In *The Sea,* edited by M. N. Hill, Vol. 2, pp. 3-25. New York: John Wiley & Sons, 1963.

Goldberg, E. D., and Arrhenius, G. "Chemistry of Pacific Pelagic Sediments." *Geochimica et Cosmochimica,* Octa 13, 1958, pp. 153-212.

Goldschmidt, V. M. *Geochemistry.* New York: Oxford University Press, 1954.

Gordon, Myron J. *The Cost of Capital to a Public Utility.* East Lansing: Michigan State University Press, 1973.

Gordon, Richard L. *Economic Analysis of Coal Supply: An Assessment of Existing Studies.* University Park, Penna.: Pennsylvania State University Press, 1975.

Gordon, T. J., and Ament, R. H. *Forecasts of Some Technological and Scientific Developments and Their Societal Consequences.* Report R-6., Palo Alto, California: Institute for the Future, September, 1969.

Gorman, J. A. "Non-financial Corporations: New Measures of Output and Input." *Survey of Current Business,* March, 1972.

Gramm, W. Philip. "Inflation: Its Cause and Cure." *Review,* Federal Reserve Bank of St. Louis, February, 1975.

Gray, John E. *Financing Free World Energy Supply and Use.* Washington, D. C.: Atlantic Council of the United States, 1975.

Green, G., "Geochemical Table of the Elements for 1959,"

Bulletin of the Geological Society of America, vol. 70, 1959.

Gross, Bertram M., Ed. "Social Goals and Indicators for American Society." *The Annals of the American Academy of Political and Social Science,* May and September, 1967.

Gutmanis, Ivars. *The Generation and Cost of Controlling Air, Water and Solid Waste Pollution: 1970-2000.* Washington, D. C.: Brookings Institution, 1972.

Halvorsen, R. "Sierra Club Conference on Power and Public Policy." Burlington, Vt.: Public Resources, 1969.

Hamberg, Daniel. *Models of Economic Growth.* New York: Harper & Row, 1971.

Hansen, Alvin. *Full Recovery or Stagnation.* New York: W. W. Norton and Co., 1938.

Hardin, Garrett. "The Tragedy of the Commons." *Science* 162, December 13, 1968, pp. 1243-48.

Harrod, Roy. *Towards a Dynamic Economics.* New York: Macmillan, 1948.

Hass, Jerome E.; Mitchell, Edward J.; and Stone, Bernell K. *Financing the Energy Industry.* Cambridge, Mass.: Ballinger Publishing Co., 1974.

Hayami, T. and Ruttan, V. *Agricultural Development.* Baltimore: The John Hopkins Press, 1971.

Heilbroner, R. L., and Allentuck, J. "Ecological 'Balance' and the 'Stationary' State." *Land Economics,* Vol. 48, No. 3, August, 1972, pp. 205-11.

Helbling, Hans H., and Turley, James E. "A Primer on Inflation: Its Conception, Its Costs, Its Consequences." *Review,* Federal Reserve Bank of St. Louis, January, 1975.

Henderson, James M. and Quandt, Richard E. *Microeconomic Theory.* New York: McGraw-Hill Book Company, 1971.

Herfendahl, Orris C., and Knuse, Allen V. *Economic Theory of Natural Resources.* Columbus, Ohio: Charles E. Merrill Publishing Co., 1974.

Hewett, D. F. "Cycles in Metal Production." American Institute of Mining, Metallurgical, and Petroleum Engineers, *Technical Publication* 183, Trans., 1929.

Higgins, Benjamin. *Economic Development: Problems, Principles, and Policies.* Rev. Ed. New York: W. W. Norton and Co., 1968.

Horgan, J. D. "Technology and Human Values: The 'Circle of Action.'" *Mechanical Engineering,* August, 1973, pp. 19-22.

Hoselitz, Bert F., ed. *Theories of Economic Growth.* New York: Free Press, 1960.

Hubbert, M. King. "Energy Resources." In *Resources and Man,* edited by Preston E. Cloud, Jr. San Francisco: W. H. Freeman and Co., 1969.

Hudson, Edward A., and Jorgenson, Dale W. *Tax Policy and Energy Conservation.* Discussion Paper No. 395. Cambridge Mass.: Harvard Institute of Economic Research, 1975.

Ingersoll, Robert, "A Mixed View of Seabed Mining," *Interocean 73, 1974.*

Institute for Contemporary Studies. *No Time to Confuse: A Critique of the Final Report of the Energy Policy Project of the Ford Foundation.* San Francisco: Institute for Contemporary Studies, 1975.

International Monetary Fund. *International Financial Statistics.* Washington, D.C.: International Monetary Fund, 1971.

Johnston, J. *Econometric Methods.* New York: McGraw-Hill, 1963.

Jorgenson, Dale W. *Consumer Demand for Energy.* Discussion Paper No. 386. Cambridge, Mass.: Harvard Institute of Economic Research, 1975.

Joskow, Paul L. "Public Utility Rate Structures in a World of Rapid Inflation and Environment Concern." M.I.T. Energy Conference, February, 1973.

Julien, Claude. *America's Empire.* New York: Pantheon Books, 1972.

Kahn, Alfred E. *The Economics of Regulation.* New York: John Wiley & Sons, 1970.

Kahn, H., and Wiener, A. J. *The Year 2000.* New York: Macmillan, 1967.

Kaufman, R., and Rothstein, A. J. "The Oceans: Future Source of Minerals." *Proceedings of Council of Economics,* American Institute of Mining, Metallurgical, and Petroleum Engineers, 1971, pp. 67-74.

Kaysen, Karl. "The Computer That Printed Out Wolf." *Foreign Affairs,* July, 1972, pp. 660-68.

Kendrick, J. W. *Postwar Productivity Trends in the United States, 1948-1969.* New York: Columbia University Press, 1973.

Keniston, Kenneth. "A Second Look at the Uncommitted." *Social Policy,* Vol. 2, No. 2, July-August, 1971, pp. 6-19.

Keynes, J. M. "Economic Possibilities for our Grandchildren," *Essays in Persuasion.* New York: Norton, 1963 (originally published in 1931).

Keynes, John Maynard. *The General Theory of Employment, Interest and Money.* New York: Harcourt, Brace, and World, 1964.

Klein, L. *Econometrics.* Evanston, Ill.: Row, Peterson & Co., 1953.

————. *Economic Fluctuations in the U. S.* New York: John Wiley & Sons, 1950.

Klein, L. R. *An Essay on the Theory of Economic Prediction.* Chicago: Markham Publishing Co., 1971.

Klein, Rudolph. "Growth and Its Enemies." *Commentary,* June, 1972, pp. 37-44.

Krige, D. G. "A Statistical Analysis of Some of the Borehole Values in the Orange Tree Goldfield." *Journal of Chem., Met., and Mining Soc. of South Africa,* Vol. 53, No. 2, 1952.

Kunkel, John H. *Society and Economic Growth: A Behavioral Perspective of Social Change.* New York: Oxford University Press, 1970.

Kuznets, Simon. *Modern Economic Growth Rate Structure and Spread.* New Haven: Yale University Press, 1966.

Kuznets, S. *National Income and Its Composition, 1919-1938.* New York: National Bureau of Economic Research, 1941.

Landsberg, H. H. et al. *Energy and the Social Sciences.* Washington, D. C.: Resources for the Future, 1974.

Lasky, S. G. "How Tonnage and Grade Relations Help Predict Ore Reserves." *Engineering and Mining Journal,* April, 1950, pp. 81-85.

Leontieff, W. *Input-Output Economics.* London: Oxford University Press, 1966.

————. "The Structure of the U. S. Economy." *Scientific American,* April, 1965, pp. 25-35.

Lindblom, Charles Edward. *The Intelligence of Democracy.* New York: Free Press, 1965.

Linden, H. R. *Review of World Energy Supplies.* London: International Gas Union, 1973.

Linder, Stafan, *The Harried Leisure Class.* New York: Columbia University Press, 1970.

Lipsey, R. G., and Lancaster, Kelvin. "The General Theory of Second Best." *Review of Economic Studies,* Vol. XXIV, 1956, pp. 11-32.

"A Little More Time," *The Economist,* June 29, 1974.

Liviatan, N. "A Diagrammatic Exposition of Optimal Growth." *American Economic Review,* June, 1970, pp. 302-9.

Lovering, T. S. "Mineral Resources from the Land." In *Resources and Man,* edited by Preston E. Cloud, Jr. San Francisco: W. H. Freeman and Co., 1969.

Lovins, Amory B., "World Energy Strategies," *Bulletin of the Atomic Scientists,* May, 1974, pp. 14-32.

Malenbaum, W., et al. *Material Requirements in the United States and Abroad in the Year 2000.* Research Project at the University of Pennsylvania for the National Commission on Materials Policy, 1973.

Malthus, Thomas Robert. *An Essay on the Principle of Population.* Ann Arbor: University of Michigan Press, 1959.

Marchetti, C. *Energy Needs of the World.* Laxenburg, Austria: International Institute for Applied Systems Analysis, 1975.

Martindale, Don. *The Nature and Types of Sociological Theory.* Boston: Houghton Mifflin Co., 1960.

Matheron, G. *The Theory of Regionalized Variables and Its Applications.* Les Cahiers de Morphologie Mathematique de Fontainebleau, 1971.

Matthews, William and Wilson, Carroll L. (eds.). *Man's Impact on the Global Environment.* Cambridge: The M.I.T. Press, 1970.

McDevitt, James. *Minerals and Men.* Resources for the

Future. Baltimore: Johns Hopkins University Press, 1965.

McHale, John. *World Facts and Trends.* New York: Collier Books, 1972.

McKelvy, V. E. "Mineral Resources Estimates and Public Policy." In *United States Mineral Resources,* Professional Paper 820, U. S. Geological Survey, pp. 9-19. Washington, D. C.: U. S. Government Printing Office, 1973.

Meadows, Dennis L., et al. *Dynamics of Growth in a Finite World.* Cambridge, Mass.: Wright-Allen Press, 1974.

Meadows, Donella H., and Meadows, Dennis L. *A Summary of Limits to Growth—Its Critics and Its Challenge.* Mimeographed Paper Presented at Yale University, September, 1972.

Meadows, Donella H.; Meadows, Dennis L.; Randers, Jorgen; and Behrens, William W., III. *The Limits to Growth.* New York: Universe Books, 1972.

Mero, John L. "The Outlook for Mining in the Ocean." *Proceedings of Council of Economics,* American Institute of Mining, Metallurgical, and Petroleum Engineers, February 19-23, 1967.

Mesarovic, M. D. *Theory of Multi-Level Hierarchical Systems.* New York: Academic Press, 1970.

Miller, A. R.; Densmore, C. D.; Degens, E. T.; Hathaway, Hathaway, J. C.; Mannheim, F. T.; McFarlin, P. F.; Pocklington, R.; and Jokela, A. "Hot Brines and Recent Iron Deposits in Deeps of the Red Sea." *Geochimica et Cosmochimica,* Acta 30, 1966, pp. 341-59.

Miller, M., and Modigliani, F. "Some Estimates of the Cost of Capital to the Electric Utility Industry: 1954-57." *American Economic Review,* Vol. 56, No. 3, June, 1966, pp. 333-91.

Mishan, Ezra. *The Costs of Economic Growth.* Baltimore: Penguin, 1967.

Mishan, E. J., "Growth and Antigrowth, What are the Issues?" *Challenge,* May-June, 1973, p. 30.

Mishan, E. J. *Technology and Growth.* New York: Praeger Publishers, 1970.

Moynihan, Daniel P. "Counsellor's Statement." In *Toward Balanced Growth: Quantity with Quality.* National Goals Research Staff. Washington, D. C.: United States Government Printing Office, 1970, p. 12.

Moody's Public Utility Manual. New York: Moody's Investors Service, 1973.

Morgenstern, Oskar. "The Compressibility of Economic Systems and the Problem of Economic Constraints." *Zeitschrift fur Nationalokonomie,* Vienna, 1966.

Morris, H. T.; Heyl, Allen V.; and Hall, Robert B. Lead Chapter in *United States Mineral Resources,* Professional Paper 820, U. S. Geological Survey. Washington, D. C.: U. S. Government Printing Office, 1973.

Morse, P. M., and Kimball, G. E. *Methods of Operations Research.* New York: John Wiley & Sons, 1951.

Mumford, Lewis, *Technics and Human Development: The Myth of the Machine.* New York: Harcourt Brace Jovanovich, Inc., 1971, p. 276.

Musgrove, P. A. "The Distribution of Metal Resources (Tests and Implications of the Exponential Grade-Size Relations)." *Proceedings of Council of Economics,* American Institute of Mining, Metallurgical, and Petroleum Engineers, 1971.

Myers, M. G. "Equilibrium Growth and Capital Movements Between Open Economies." *American Economic Review,* May, 1970, pp. 404-5.

Myers, Stewart C. "The Application of Finance Theory to Public Utility Rate Cases." *The Bell Journal of Economics and Management Science,* Vol. 3, No. 1, Spring, 1972, pp. 58-97.

National Academy of Engineering, Task Force on Energy. *U. S. Energy Prospects: An Engineering Viewpoint.* Washington, D. C.: National Academy of Engineering, 1974.

National Association of Railroad & Utilities Commissions, Engineering Committee, Cost Allocation Committee. "Comparison of Methods of Allocating Demand Costs." *Electric Utilities,* June, 1955.

National Commission on Materials Policy (NCMP). *Material Needs and the Environment Today and Tomorrow.* Washington, D. C.: U. S. Government Printing Office, June, 1973.

National Economic Research Associates. *The Studies of Residential Demand for Electricity: A Critique.* New York, N. Y.: National Economic Research Associates, August, 1973.

National Goals Research Staff. *Toward Balanced Growth: Quantity with Quality.* Washington, D. C.: U. S. Government Printing Office, 1970.

National Petroleum Council. *U. S. Energy Outlook, Energy Demand, 1972* and related documents. Washington, D. C.: National Petroleum Council, 1972.

New York Stock Exchange. *The Capital Needs and Savings Potential of the U. S. Economy: Projections Through 1985.* New York: New York Stock Exchange, September, 1974.

Nichols, Donald. "Land and Economic Growth." *American Economic Review,* June, 1970, pp. 332-40.

Nordhaus, William. *The Allocation of Energy Resources.* Washington, D.C.: Brookings Institution, 1973.

Nordhaus, William D., "Resources as a Constraint on Growth," *The American Economic Review,* May, 1974, pp. 22-26.

Nordhaus, William. "World Dynamics: Measurement Without Data." *The Economic Journal,* Vol. 83 #332, Dec. 1973, pp. 1156-1183.

Nordhaus, William, and Tobin, James. "Is Growth Obsolete?" In *Economic Growth,* National Bureau of Economic Research. New York: Columbia University Press, 1972.

Oak Ridge National Laboratory. "Energy Expenditures Associated with the Production & Recycle of Metals." CRNL-MIT-132. 1971.

Odum, Howard, T., *Environment, Power, and Society,* New York: John Wiley & Sons, 1971.

Oerlemans, T. W. et al. "World Dynamics." *Nature* (August, 1972), p. 251.

Office of Management and Budget. *Social Indicators 1973.* Executive Office of the President. Washington, D. C.: U. S. Government Printing Office, 1973.

Olson, Charles E. *Cost Considerations for Efficient Electricity Supply.* East Lansing: Michigan State University Press, 1970.

Opler, M. E. "Themes as Dynamic Forces in Culture." *American Journal of Sociology,* Vol. 51, November, 1945, pp. 198-206.

Oshima, Harry. "The International Comparison of Size Distribution of Family Incomes with Specific Reference to Asia." *Review of Economics and Statistics* (November, 1962).

Passell, Peter, and Ross, Leonard. *The Retreat from Riches—Affluence and Its Enemies.* New York: Viking Press, 1973.

Patterson, Sam H., and Dyni, John R. "Aluminum and Bauxite." In *United States Mineral Resources,* Professional Paper 820, U. S. Geological Survey. Washington, D. C.: U. S. Government Printing Office, 1973.

Pearl, A. "An Ecological Rationale for a Humane Service Society." *Social Policy,* September-October, 1971, pp. 40-41.

Phelps, George E. *A Research Report on the Subject of Rate of Return on Common Equity.* Fountain Valley, Calif.: Phelps Utility Advisory Service, 1972.

Phillips, Charles F., Jr. *The Economics of Regulation.* Homewood, Ill.: Richard D. Irwin, 1969.

Potter, Neal, and Christy, Francis T., Jr. *Trends in Natural Resource Commodities.* Resources for the Future. Baltimore: Johns Hopkins University Press, 1962.

Preston, Ross S. *The Wharton Annual and Industry Forecasting Model.* Studies in Quantitative Economics, No. 7, Wharton School. Philadelphia: University of Pennsylvania Press, 1972.

Rand Corp. *Some Implications of Policies to Slow the Growth of Electricity Demand.* R990-NSF/CSA, June, 1972.

Reich, Charles. *The Greening of America.* New York: Random House, 1971.

Reichle, L.F.C. *From the Energy Gap to the Nuclear-Electric Economy.* New York: Ebasco Services, 1975.

Reilly, William K., ed. *The Use of Land: A Citizens' Policy Guide to Urban Growth.* New York: Thomas Y. Crowell Co., 1973.

Reno, Horace T. *Iron: A Materials Survey.* U. S. Bureau of Mines I. C. 8574. Washington, D. C.: U. S. Government Printing Office, 1973.

Revelle, Roger. "Will the Earth's Land and Water Resources Be Sufficient for Future Populations?" United Nations Symposium on Population, Resources and Environment, Stockholm, 1973.

Revelle, Roger, ed. *Rapid Population Growth.* Baltimore: Johns Hopkins University Press, 1971.

Richter-Bernburg, Gerhard. Geologische Geselzmässigkeiten en der Metallführung des Kupferschiefers: Lagerstättinforschung (Reichstelle fur Bodenforschung) N. F., No. 73, 1941.

Rieber, Michael, and Halcrow, Ronald. *U. S. Energy and Fuel Demand to 1985: A Composite Projection by User Within PAD Districts.* Center for Advanced Computation. Urbana: University of Illinois Press, May, 1974.

Rigg, John B. "Minerals from the Sea." *Ocean Industry,* April, 1974, p. 213.

Ross, P. N. *Development of the Nuclear Electric Energy Economy.* Pittsburgh: Westinghouse Electric Corp., 1973.

Ryder, Norman B. "Two Cheers for ZPG." *Daedalus,* Fall, 1973, pp. 45-62.

Samuels, W. J., and Trebing, H. M. *A Critique of Administrative Regulation of Public Utilities.* East Lansing: Michigan State University Press, 1972.

Schlipp, P. A. (ed.), *Albert Einstein: Philosopher-Scientist.* New York: Harper & Row, 1959.

Schultze, Charles et al. *Setting National Priorities, the 1973 Budget.* Washington, D.C.: Brookings Institution, 1972.

Schumacher, E. F. *Small Is Beautiful: Economics as if People Mattered.* New York: Harper Torchbooks, 1973.

Seaborg, Glenn T. "The Erehwon Machine: Possibilities for Reconciling Goals by Way of New Technology." In *Energy, Economic Growth and the Environment,* edited by S. Schurr. Washington, D. C.: Resources for the Future, 1972.

Shell, Karl, ed. *Essays on the Theory of Optimal Economic Growth.* Cambridge, Mass.: M.I.T. Press, 1967.

Singer, D. A.; Cox, D. P.; and Drew, L. J. *Grade and Tonnage Relationships Among Copper Deposits.* U. S. Geological Survey. Washington, D. C.: U. S. Government Printing Office, forthcoming.

Slichter, Sumner H. *Economic Growth in the United States: Its History, Problems, and Prospects.* Baton Rouge: Louisiana State University Press, 1961.

Smith, Adam. *An Inquiry into the Nature and Causes of the Wealth of Nations.* London: W. Strahan and T. Cadell, 1776.

Sommers, Albert T. *Answers to Inflation and Recession: Economic Policies for a Modern Society.* New York: Conference Board, 1975.

Sommers, Paul M., and Suits, Daniel B. "A Cross-Section Model of Economic Growth." *The Review of Economics and Statistics,* May, 1971, pp. 121-28.

Spann, Robert M. "Federal Regulation of Electric Utilities via Taxation and Litigation: An Analysis of Changes." Conference on Regulatory Reform, American Enterprise Institute for Public Policy Research, 1975.

Squires, A. M. "Clean Fuels from Coal Gassification." *Science,* April 19, 1974, p. 340.

Stanford Research Institute. *Meeting California's Energy Requirements 1975-2000.* SRI Project No. ECC-2355. Stanford: Stanford Research Institute, May, 1973.

Stiglitz, J., (ed.), *The Collected Scientific Papers of Paul A. Samuelson,* vol 1, pp 513-536, MIT Press, Cambridge, Massachusetts, 1966.

Steele, Henry. Research for the Ford Foundation Energy Policy Project. Washington, D. C.: Resources for the Future, 1974.

Straus, Simon. "Does the Pattern of Oil Prices Set a Precedent for Metals?" *Mining Congress Journal,* Vol. 60, No. 14, 1974, pp. 43-52.

Suelflow, James E. *Public Utility Accounting: Theory and Application.* East Lansing: Michigan State University Public Utilities Studies, 1973.

Swamy, Dalip S. "Statistical Evidence of Balanced and Unbalanced Growth." *The Review of Economics and Statistics,* August, 1969, pp. 288-303.

Taussig, R. T. *Bibliography and Digest of U. S. Electric and Total Energy Forecasts: 1975-2050.* New York, N. Y.: Columbia University, 1974.

Taussig, R. T., and Apte, P. G. *U. S. Energy Forecasts: A Critical Review of Forecasting Methods.* New York, N. Y.: Columbia University, 1974.

Taylor, Lester D. "The Demand for Electricity: A Survey." *The Bell Journal of Economics,* Spring, 1975, p. 74.

"A Little More Time," *The London Economist,* June 29, 1974.

Tinbergen, J. *Statistical Testing of Business Cycle Theories: Business Cycles in the U.S.A., 1919-1932.* Geneva: League of Nations, 1939.

Trebing, H. M. *Essays on Public Utility Pricing and Regulation.* East Lansing: Michigan State University Press, 1971.

———— *Performance Under Regulation.* East Lansing: Michigan State University Press, 1972.

Trebing, H. M., and Howard, R. H. *Rate of Return Under Regulation: New Dimensions and Perspectives.* East Lansing: Michigan State University Press, 1969.

Turner, Carolyn, ed. *Managed Growth.* Chicago: Urban Research Corp., 1973.

United Nations Department of Économic and Social Affairs. *Electricity Costs and Tariffs: A General Study.* St/ECA/156. New York: United Nations, 1972.

U. S. Congress, House. *Growth and Its Implications for the Future, Part 1* (Hearing with Appendix Before the Subcommittee on Fisheries and Wildlife Conservation and the Environment of the Committee on Merchant Marine and Fisheries), 93rd Congress, 1st Session. Washington, D. C.: U. S. Government Printing Office, May, 1973.

————. "Solar Energy Research." Staff Report of the Committee on Science and Astronautics. Washington, D. C.: U. S. Government Printing Office, 1973.

U. S. Geological Survey. *United States Mineral Resources.* Professional Paper 820, U. S. Geological Survey. Washington, D. C.: U. S. Government Printing Office, 1973.

U. S. Government Printing Office, *Historical Statistics of the United States Colonial Times to 1957.* United States Government Printing Office, Washington, D. C.

Vennard, Édwin. *The Electric Power Business.* New York: McGraw-Hill, 1970.

Wagar, J. Allen. "Growth vs. the Quality of Life." *Science,* June 5, 1970, pp. 1179-84.

Wallich, Henry. "Eco-Doom: The Limits to Credulity." *Business and Society Review,* No. 2, Summer, 1972, pp. 103-5.

————. "How to Live with Economic Growth." *Fortune,* October, 1972, pp. 114-22.

Wan, Henry Y., Jr. *Economic Growth.* New York: Harcourt Brace Jovanovich, 1971.

Weidenbaum, Murray L. *Financing the Electric Utility Industry.* New York: Edison Electric Institute, 1974.

Weinberg, Alvin M., "Global Effects of Man's Production of Energy," *Science,* October 18, 1974, p. 205.

Weintraub, Andrew; Schwartz, Eli; and Aronson, J. Richard. eds. *The Economic Growth Controversy.* White Plains, N. Y.: International Arts and Sciences Press, 1973.

Wiener, Norbert. *The Human Use of Human Beings.* 1950. Reprint. New York: Avon Books, 1967.

Wilkinson, Richard G. *Poverty and Progress: An Ecological Perspective on Economic Development.* New York: Praeger Publishers, 1973.

Wilson, J. W. *Residential and Industrial Demand for Electricity: An Empirical Analysis.* Ann Arbor: University Microfilms, 1969.

Wolfgang, Marvin E., ed. "The Future Society: Aspects of America in the Year 2000." *The Annals of the American Academy of Political and Social Science,* Vol. 408, July, 1973.

List of
Charts and Tables

* *The following charts through Chart 7·8 summarize different food and population scenarios for South East Asia.*

Index